WORLD

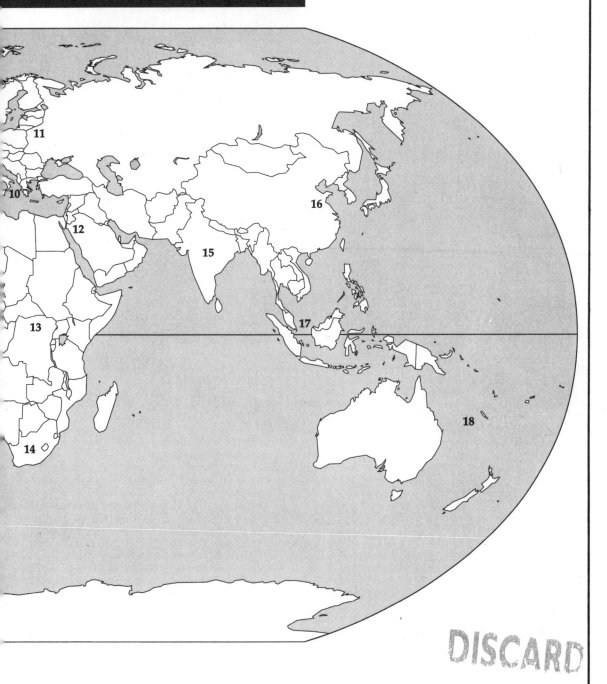

10. Southern Europe

11. Eastern Europe and
    the Soviet Union

12. Middle East and North Africa

13. Sub-Saharan Africa

14. South Africa

15. Southern and Central Asia

16. East Asia

17. Southeast Asia

18. Australia, New Zealand,
    and the Pacific

OUR FAMILY, OUR FRIENDS, OUR WORLD

OUR FAMILY
OUR FRIENDS
OUR WORLD™

An Annotated Guide to
Significant Multicultural Books for
Children and Teenagers

LYN MILLER-LACHMANN

R. R. BOWKER
New Providence, New Jersey

Published by R. R. Bowker, a division of Reed Publishing (U.S.A.) Inc.
Copyright © 1992 by Reed Publishing (U.S.A.) Inc.
All rights reserved
Printed and bound in the United States of America

Computer composition by Vance Weaver Composition, Inc.

Library of Congress Cataloging-in-Publication Data

Miller-Lachmann, Lyn, 1956–
        Our family, our friends, our world : an annotated guide to
significant multicultural books for children and teenagers / Lyn
Miller-Lachmann.
                p.   cm.
        Includes indexes.
        ISBN 0-8352-3025-2
        1. Children's literature—Bibliography. 2. Young adult
literature—Bibliography. 3. Pluralism (Social sciences) in
literature—Bibliography. 4. Ethnic groups in literature—
Bibliography. 5. Minorities in literature—Bibliography.
I. Title.
Z1037.M654 1992
[PN1009.A1]
011.62—dc20   92-24549
                                                                     CIP

Cover: UNITED NATIONS PHOTO (133139)
          By Y. Nagata

Maps were created using Adobe Illustrator 3.0
and MicroMaps Program MapArt on the Macintosh.

ISBN 0 - 8352 - 3025 - 2

9   780835   230254

To my children, Derrick and Madeleine

CONTENTS

LIST OF CONTRIBUTORS

Michael Afolayan is a Ph.D. student and lecturer at the University of Wisconsin, on leave from a teaching position in African literature at Obafemi Awolowo University in Nigeria. [Chapter 13. Sub-Saharan Africa]

Christine Behrmann is the supervising children's materials specialist for the New York Public Library. [Chapter 11. Eastern Europe and the Soviet Union]

Annette Blank is the retired head of the Children's Department of the Enoch Pratt Free Library, Baltimore, Maryland. [Chapter 9. Western Europe]

Heather Caines is a children's librarian for the New York Public Library. [Chapter 6. Mexico and the Carribbean]

Ellin Chu is the young adult consultant for the Rochester (N.Y.) Public Library. [Chapter 2. United States: Asian Americans]

Judy Fink is the assistant director of children's services for the Urbana Free Library, Urbana, Illinois. [Chapter 10. Southern Europe]

Oralia Garza de Cortes is a children's librarian at the Austin Public Library, Austin, Texas. [Chapter 3. United States: Hispanic Americans; Chapter 6. Mexico and the Caribbean]

Elaine Goley is an elementary school library media specialist in the Houston Independent School District, Houston, Texas. [Chapter 4. United States: Native Americans; Chapter 8. Great Britain and Ireland]

Melinda Greenblatt is a field librarian for the Library Power Project of the American Reading Council, New York, New York. [Chapter 15. Southern and Central Asia; Chapter 18. Australia, New Zealand, and the Pacific]

April Hoffman is the library media specialist at Randall Elementary School in Madison, Wisconsin. [Chapter 1. United States: African Americans]

Patricia Kuntz is the African Studies Outreach Director at the University of Wisconsin, Madison, Wisconsin. [Chapter 13. Sub-Saharan Africa; Chapter 14. South Africa]

Ginny Lee is an elementary school library media specialist in Hayward, California. [Chapter 16. East Asia; Chapter 17. Southeast Asia]

Suzanne Lo is the head librarian at the Asian Branch of the Oakland (Calif.) Public Library. [Chapter 16. East Asia; Chapter 17. Southeast Asia]

Susan Ma is the head librarian at the Rosegarden Branch of the San Jose (Calif.) Public Library. [Chapter 16. East Asia; Chapter 17. Southeast Asia]

Joan McGrath is an educational consultant with Lakeview Educational Services, Toronto, Ontario. [Chapter 5. Canada]

Elsa Marston is a freelance author who has written extensively on the Middle East. [Chapter 12. The Middle East and North Africa]

Lyn Miller-Lachmann is a freelance author and a reference librarian at Siena College, Loudonville, New York. [Chapter 7. Central and South America; Chapter 14. South Africa]

Brenda Naze is an English teacher at Malcolm Shabazz High School in Madison, Wisconsin. [Chapter 13. Sub-Saharan Africa]

Sandra Payne is the Staten Island Borough Coordinator of Young Adult Services for the New York Public Library. [Chapter 1. United States: African Americans]

Reeves Smith is the library media specialist at Lowell Elementary School in Madison, Wisconsin. [Chapter 1. United States: African Americans]

Carolyn Vang Schuler is the children's consultant for the Monroe County Library System, Rochester, New York. [Chapter 2. United States: Asian Americans]

FOREWORD

*O*ur Family, Our Friends, Our World: An Annotated Guide to Significant Multicultural Books for Children and Teenagers admirably fills a long-standing and growing need for a reference work that provides children and their parents, teachers, and librarians with evaluations of the large array of fiction and nonfiction on multicultural themes. Elementary, middle, and high school students are learning and socializing with classmates from increasingly diverse backgrounds. Joining long-established residents of this country with European, African, Hispanic, and Native American backgrounds are the children of the new immigrations from South and Central America, East and South Asia, the Middle East, Eastern Europe, the Caribbean, and elsewhere.

We will enhance opportunities for our children to live and learn together if we can provide them with fair and accurate materials that describe one another's heritage and experiences. This volume assists children and the adults in their lives in that task. Chapters address each of the major ethnic groups represented by present-day school children, presenting the wealth of books on the countries from which their ancestors came and from which children and their parents come today. The best of these works provide children with a sense of their past, a compelling treatment of current dilemmas, and positive models for solving problems, developing identity, and building self-esteem.

As a critical bibliography, *Our Family, Our Friends, Our World* is a unique and important resource. Even many of the best multicultural works have shortcomings and blind spots. The authors of each annotation alert adults to instances when they will need to sensitize young readers to the biases and inaccuracies in the fiction and nonfiction they will be reading. With the help of sensitive adults, young people will learn to read critically and to look behind stereotypes to the richness, diversity, and universal elements within each culture.

Despite the impressive number of recently published multicultural works for children, much more needs to be written, and publishers need to increase their commitment to the development of multicultural works for children of all ages. The contributors to this volume offer exemplary guidance, in the introductions to each chapter and in the editor's general introduction, to the directions authors and publishers must take if they are to provide the range and depth of materials our children now need to become sensitive and mature members of their ever more diverse nation and their ever more interconnected world.

For all the reasons I have noted, *Our Family, Our Friends, Our World* stands as the primary reference guide for multicultural fiction and nonfiction for children. I encourage all the audiences for whom this book is intended to use it. Children will now be able to find the books that speak to their heritages and those of their schoolmates and neighbors. Parents, teachers, and librarians now have before them the critical guidance necessary to allow them to work together in fashioning curricula that take cognizance of the multicultural character of their children's world. Librarians, authors, and publishers can find in the introductory essays and entries of this book agendas for action to create more and better multicultural works.

The editor and authors of this work have provided a most valuable resource for both children and adults. As adults, our task is to make use of this volume ourselves and to make it available to our children and students. We must, and I am confident we will, return to this book again and again as we work to fashion the multicultural education our children need and deserve.

James P. Comer, M.D.
Professor of Child Psychiatry
Yale University Child Study Center

ACKNOWLEDGMENTS

I would like to express my appreciation to those who helped me in the preparation of this book: to the Publisher at Bowker, Marion Sader, who presented me with the idea of a multicultural bibliography and who continued to play a role in turning that idea into reality; to Nancy Bucenec, the Editor who shaped the manuscript into a book; to Ellen LiBretto, whose advice and encouragement were so valuable and so important in the critical early stages of this project; and to Michael Dubiac, who endured the frustration of a nine-inch Macintosh SE/30 screen to assemble the maps preceding each chapter.

I would also like to thank both my husband, Richard Lachmann, for his support all along the way, and my son, Derrick, whose stories about his mother's "chapters" would fill another whole book.

INTRODUCTION

The United States and Canada are diverse societies in an increasingly interdependent world. During the past two decades, books for children and young adults have come to reflect that diversity and interdependence. Many of these works are outstanding examples of fiction and nonfiction that open the world to young people and increase in each one of them their awareness of and pride in their own heritage. Others may be flawed in terms of style or content but are nonetheless useful in presenting aspects of diverse cultures and in sparking discussion and further thought about the presentation itself. Still others, unfortunately, serve to reinforce stereotypes and misconceptions; in extreme cases, these works may prove hurtful to young people whose life and background have been portrayed in an insensitive manner. Librarians, teachers, and others who work with children have called for a means of assessing books that deal with the diverse cultures both in the United States and Canada and all over the world. While groups such as the Council on Interracial Books for Children have published and circulated general guidelines, applying those guidelines is most effective when one examines specific titles as examples.

Our Family, Our Friends, Our World: An Annotated Guide to Significant Multicultural Books for Children and Teenagers contains annotations of approximately 1,000 books published between 1970 and 1990. It is a unique reference source in several ways. First, it is both multicultural and international in focus, with chapters on the four principal minority groups within the United States—African Americans, Asian Americans, Hispanic Americans, and Native Americans—as well as chapters on the countries and regions of the world. The emphasis in the international chapters is on presenting examples of the cultural diversity that exists within each region. Thus, the chapter on Great Britain and Ireland or the one on Western Europe gives special attention to books that reflect the increasingly multicultural nature of those societies, and the chapter on sub-Saharan Africa criticizes those works that present the continent as a standardized whole rather than treating it as a diverse region with many ethnic groups, languages, religions, and ways of life.

Second, *Our Family, Our Friends, Our World* is as inclusive as possible within its limitations of space and scope. It is not a recommended list. While many of the books have been recommended for library purchase and for use in the class-room, the shortcomings of others have been examined. Thus, librarians and teachers can see why a book or a series of books has been judged imperfect, and this purpose is as useful in honing one's own critical capabilities as seeing what has been recommended and why. The drawback of this method is that, despite the large number of books that is included—more than in virtually any other annotated bibliography or review source on multicultural literature—some books have been excluded for seemingly arbitrary reasons. Yet even a recommended list will exclude books that the compilers may have simply overlooked or otherwise not had access to, and the implication under those circumstances is that the book has been found deficient, with no reason given. Furthermore, no print bibliography of this size can keep up with everything published. By applying general criteria to specific titles, this bibliography provides the back-ground information and tools necessary to analyze any book published in the future.

Third, the annotations in *Our Family, Our Friends, Our World* are lengthier than those found in most bibliographies. Ranging from 60 words for works of series nonfiction to 300 words or more for fiction works and complex works of nonfiction, the annotations explain the strengths and weaknesses of the title in question. When a title is seen as flawed, clear reasons are given. In many cases, the reviewer has commented on the audience for the book and how the book can be used most effectively in a library or classroom setting. Some annotations feature comparisons with other annotated works, older "classics" on the subject, or other books by the same author, about the same subject, or in the same series.

Finally, each chapter has been compiled by an expert in that area, often with help from additional consultants. Among the valued contributors are public librarians, school library media specialists, teachers, educational consultants, academicians, and authors of children's books. These contributors have years of experience in the evaluation of children's books and have provided an insider's perspective into the culture or region in question.

THE NEED FOR A MULTICULTURAL BIBLIOGRAPHY

Increased Diversity

The United States and Canada are more diverse societies today than they were a century ago, or even 20 years ago. Whereas immigrants of the past century came principally from Europe, today's immigrants come from a wider area and bring with them a greater variety of languages and cultures. Areas from which the "new immigrants" come include Mexico, Central and South America, Southern and Central Asia, East Asia, Southeast Asia, and the islands of the Pacific Ocean. According to the 1990 U.S. Census, the previous decade wit-nessed an astronomical growth in immigration to the United States from Latin America and Asia. During the 1980s, the Hispanic population of the United States increased by 56 percent. The Asian population more than doubled during the same period, increasing by 107.8 percent.[1]

Although African Americans have been living in the United States and elsewhere in the Americas for centuries—the involuntary immigrants of the slave trade—the civil rights movement and migration from the South to the

North and from the Caribbean to the United States and Canada are factors that have increased their visibility. There is also a growing awareness of the history and contributions of Native Americans, the original settlers of the continent.

The result of 20 or more years of increased immigration, the struggle for civil rights, and the emphasis on returning to one's roots has been a questioning of the "melting pot" ideology of the last century. As Joan McGrath points out in her introduction to the chapter on Canada, that country has never embraced the melting pot but rather has adopted a model of "cultural pluralism," in which the unique culture and heritage of each group are preserved and celebrated. More recently, American educators have come to embrace cultural pluralism as well. With African Americans, Asian Americans, Hispanic Americans, and Native Americans composing the majority of students in large urban public school systems today and estimates that one third of the entire school-age population will be composed of these groups by the end of the century,[2] the need to locate and select good multicultural books takes a new urgency. Many of these young people have become alienated from school and read poorly and reluctantly, if at all. African-American author Walter Dean Myers has observed that, for minority children, positive images in books can enhance self-awareness and self-esteem, contributing to higher achievement in school and a greater appreciation of reading.[3] Although still embraced by traditionalists, the melting pot model has harmed many youngsters in its demands that all conform to a single cultural model in order to attain success. Because of persistent discrimination, many could not achieve that success; others, condemned for who they were and torn between two worlds, found their belief in themselves shattered. The result has been classroom conflict, low self-esteem, low achievement, and high dropout rates. Among the worst consequences of the melting pot model has been the encouragement of the immigrant child's rejection of the parents' culture in the process of assimilation.[4] Today, Dr. James Comer and others have called for more parental involvement in troubled inner-city and minority schools in order to affirm the relationships between parents and children and between families and schools.[5] Multicultural books are a key element in bridging these gaps. The best books in this bibliography link past and present, pointing out the contributions of previous generations. In addition, the recommended books give young readers positive adult role models—parents, relatives, teachers, and others— within the minority community. Through good multicultural literature, children and teenagers come to realize they are not alone.

For students in the other two thirds of the school-age population multicultural books also serve an important purpose. In a diverse society, few can avoid coming into contact with those from a different background and culture. Whether the result is cooperation or conflict or is mutual understanding or mutual distrust depends upon each group's level of awareness of the other. There are plenty of works that present mainstream culture and have a majority perspective. For the relationship to work both ways, other perspectives must be acknowledged and explored as well.[6] These perspectives must not be superficial or stereotyped but must present each culture in all its diversity, complexity, and depth.

Global Interdependence

As our own societies change, so do their relationships with the world as a whole. We live in a global economy and can no longer afford to isolate ourselves. A stock market crash in New York sets off financial spasms in Tokyo, Hong

Kong, Bonn, and London. The explosion in foreign trade both creates jobs for U.S. and Canadian workers and takes them away. War and natural disaster in Central America and elsewhere send tens of thousands of immigrants pouring across our borders. The destruction of tropical rain forests alters the world's climate and food supply, and the destruction of the ozone layer—the result of industrialized nations' overuse of certain chemicals—endangers the people and the environment of less industrialized countries in the Southern Hemisphere as well. On the positive side, our ability to understand and to work with the people of other nations has led to and will continue to lead to scientific and artistic advances, more equitable distribution of resources, and peaceful resolution to conflicts.

For years educators have bemoaned American schoolchildren's ignorance about the world as a whole. It has been alleged that most high school students cannot find on a map the countries in Europe, Asia, South America, and Africa. Ignorance about the world and its people—about our commonalities as well as our differences—has resulted in painful instances of imperialism and exploitation in which all have emerged losers. If our children are to grow up able to make informed decisions in an increasingly interdependent world, they must become aware of that world at an early age.

Curricular Changes

As educators have become aware of the increasingly multicultural nature of our society and of our increasing global interdependence, many have called for far-reaching changes in the academic curriculum. For example, the New York State Department of Education has taken steps toward the development of a "curriculum of inclusion." In pursuit of that goal, a task force undertook its own review of curriculum materials "to see if they are free of bias and if they faithfully represent the pluralistic nature of our society."[7] When the materials were found to be inadequate, the department formulated a plan for including the perspectives of minority groups in the United States and of the people of Africa, Asia, and Latin America. Other individual school districts across the country and state departments of education have moved to more diverse, globally oriented curricula. Although the initial impetus has been for changes in social studies curricula,[8] other disciplines have not been left untouched. Global environmental issues have been introduced into science curricula,[9] and scientists and inventors from around the world, as well as those who are members of minority groups within the United States and Canada, have received recognition in the schools. The new emphasis on multicultural curricula has focused attention on the contributions made by African American and Native American societies to the study of mathematics. The unique and powerful place of language arts in a broader multicultural curriculum has also been stressed.

> In a multicultural curriculum there are few stimuli with greater potential to move people to action than literature. Because it tells the stories of human events and the human condition and not simply the facts, literature does more than change minds; it changes people's hearts. And people with changed hearts are people who can move the world.[10]

Finally, the trend toward interdisciplinary studies has had a profound impact on the use of multicultural materials, as works of literature about the environment, for instance, have been brought into science classes, and novels and short stories set in other countries are read as part of the social studies curriculum. This interdisciplinary approach is closely tied to another major curricular change—the move toward whole language and the use of trade books, as opposed to textbooks and basal readers, in the classroom.

As many school districts confront low motivation and low levels of literacy and critical thinking, there has been an emphasis on using trade books to teach reading, writing, and "active critical thinking."[11] Students are being encouraged to write about what they have read as well as to generate their own stories. As part of this approach, the disciplines of social studies, science, and mathematics are not seen as separate entities but as opportunities to foster reading and writing in additional subject areas.

All of these curricular changes have had a profound impact on school and public libraries. Librarians are being asked to work more closely with classroom teachers to provide trade books, and collections are needed that support a broader and more culturally diverse curriculum. A survey of school and public library collection development policies throughout the United States, conducted in the early 1980s by Patricia Beilke and Elaine Sciara, indicated an "increased awareness of the long-range damaging effects of bias and stereotype on the self-esteem and self-identity of the youth of the minority/migrant group, as well as on the attitudes and social adjustments of the majority-society members"; virtually all the libraries surveyed gave significant attention to the collection of multicultural materials and the use of some established criteria to evaluate those materials.[12] This trend toward increased awareness of multicultural materials in libraries has accelerated since that time, due in part to social changes, in part to changes in the school curriculum, and in part to the explosion in multicultural publishing at the end of the 1980s.

THE PUBLISHING OF MULTICULTURAL BOOKS: AN OVERVIEW

Before the 1960s

The history of U.S. publishing about minorities and about the world as a whole has been one of stereotyping and distortion. Seen through American eyes, minority groups and the rest of the world appeared exotic, inferior, sometimes threatening, and often a source of ridicule. Individual differences were ignored in the course of presenting common characteristics attributed to each group. The stereotypes of Native Americans, blacks, and Asians became popularized in nineteenth-century American literature, including many works now accepted as classics. These books, of which Mark Twain's *Adventures of Huckleberry Finn* is perhaps the most well-known example, reflect the attitudes of their time, the isolation of the United States from the rest of the world, and the dominance of white males within the professions of writing and publishing. (Some have argued for the removal of books such as *Huckleberry Finn* from classrooms and libraries; a healthier response may be their study in the context in which they were written.)

As children's literature emerged as a separate genre in the late nineteenth and early twentieth century, the focus, as with adult books, was on the lives of middle-class white Americans. Characters with other backgrounds generally appeared only in minor roles, complete with the now well-established stereotypes corresponding to those roles. Major characters also conformed to their own stereotypes, as exemplified in Helen Bannerman's 1929 work *The Story of*

Little Black Sambo. During the next decade, approximately a dozen other children's books with African-American protagonists were published. Virtually all focused on plantation life and featured indolent, happy-go-lucky slaves.[13]

Images of those living outside the United States were equally misleading during the early part of the century. Europeans objected to the portrayals of their countries in the Twins series, because the depicted way of life (windmills and wooden shoes for the Dutch twins, lederhosen for their German counterparts) bore little resemblance to the reality. While Chinese Americans continued to be ignored in children's books published in the United States,[14] books on China itself were full of distortions and stereotypes in both their text and illustrations. "Squinty eyes and buck teeth" prevailed (and still do in some works). The well-known and oft-reprinted 1938 picture book *The Five Chinese Brothers,* by Claire Bishop, "pivots on the premise that all Chinese look alike."[15] Leo Politi, whose writing career spanned four decades, from the 1940s to the 1970s, became one of the most famous and prolific writers about ethnic groups and foreign countries. His many works covered exotic holidays and customs, which were presented on a superficial level and, despite characters who came from the groups and countries presented, from an outsider's perspective. These and similar books showed little understanding of the rich and varied lives of the individuals represented. Illustrations of Mexicans in sombreros and huaraches and Chinese with Fu Manchu mustaches and long flowing robes were outdated when Politi's books first appeared; they are even more so today.

The First Wave of Multicultural Publishing: The 1960s and 1970s

Nancy Larrick's study, "The All-White World of Children's Books," published in the April 11, 1965, issue of *Saturday Review,* proved to be a watershed in our level of awareness of the distortions and omissions in children's books about minorities. Larrick surveyed 63 mainstream publishers who had published a combined total of 5,200 children's books between 1962 and 1964. Black characters appeared in only 6.7 percent of those books, either in text or in illustrations. More than half of the stories were set outside the United States or before World War II, and the portrayals of black Americans were filled with bias and stereotypes, according to Jeanne S. Chall and coworkers.[16] Larrick's article, which coincided with the civil rights movement, the rise of black activism in the late 1960s, and the increased availability of funds for schools and libraries, moved publishers to add books about African Americans and other minorities to their list.

As a result, many new African-American authors and illustrators broke into print during the late 1960s and early 1970s; among them were Eloise Greenfield, Virginia Hamilton, Patricia and Fredrick McKissack, Alice Childress, Sharon Bell Mathis, Rosa Guy, Walter Dean Myers, Muriel and Tom Feelings, Jerry Pinkney, and Leo and Diane Dillon. As reported by Jeanne S. Chall, Eugene Rodwin, Valerie W. French, and Cynthia R. Hall, the percentage of mainstream press children's books that featured black characters more than doubled between 1973 and 1975, to 14.4 percent. Virtually every major publisher produced at least one children's book with a black protagonist. Blacks appeared in many different situations and locales, in contemporary as well as historical fiction and in many works of nonfiction as well.[17] This trend continued almost up to the end of the decade, as additional new authors emerged, with their own perspectives on African-American history and contemporary life. With the publication of her *Song of the Trees* (1975) followed by *Roll of Thunder, Hear My Cry* (1976), which won the prestigious Newbery Medal, Mildred D. Taylor directly challenged the stereotypes of black life in the South by throwing a strong light on white racism. Nonetheless, her African-American characters were not portrayed as victims of that racism but as strong, loving family and community members who emerged triumphant, if not unscathed.

Also in the 1970s, Hispanic writers such as Nicholasa Mohr moved into the mainstream for the first time. Mohr's novels *Nilda* (1973), *El Bronx Remembered* (1975), *In Nueva York* (1977), and *Felita* (1979) presented the urban Puerto Rican experience. Other newcomers to publishing success during this decade were Native-American author Jamake Highwater, whose novel *Anpao: An American Indian Odyssey* (1977) was a 1978 Newbery Honor Book, and Asian-American Lawrence Yep, whose *Dragonwings* (1975) and *Child of the Owl* (1977) received awards and distinctions too numerous to list. An interesting trend during this decade was the disproportionately high percentage of books by minority authors that went on to receive prestigious prizes and distinctions, leading one to believe that multicultural books, particularly those written by authors from the group itself, had to be substantially superior in order to be published in the first place.

In 1968 the American Library Association established the Mildred L. Batchelder Award to honor outstanding books published in translation, with the aim of encouraging U.S. publishers to make available to young people authentic voices from abroad. The number of such books has increased since the late 1960s, although most of the Batchelder winners, as well as other translations, have been works from Europe. Although originally published in Germany, a notable exception to this pattern of publishing translations during the 1970s was Latin American author Antonio Skarmeta's *Chileno!* (1979), the story of a Chilean teenager experiencing political repression and exile. In the early 1980s, more translations appeared from elsewhere in the world, among them the 1983 Batchelder winner *Hiroshima No Pika*, from Japan.

Two Steps Back: The 1980s

The early 1980s witnessed a retrenchment in publishing books by and about minorities in the United States. Although his own works continued to appear regularly, Walter Dean Myers observed that new African-American writers could no longer break into the mainstream as easily. Even some established writers suddenly had trouble getting their stories published (there were five- or six-year gaps in the publishing histories of several very well-known African-American and other minority authors), and many award-winning books were allowed to go out of print. Myers cited the decline in political activism, the conservative backlash of the late 1970s and early 1980s, and reductions in government funding as causes for the retrenchment. He added:

> Publishing companies had never tried to develop markets for Third World literature. Instead, they had relied upon purchases made through Great Society government funds, and when these were phased out the publishers began to phase out Third World books.[18]

In the 1985 edition of *CCBC Choices*, a publication of the Cooperative Children's Book Center at the University of Wisconsin, Kathleen T. Horning and Ginny Moore Kruse observed an increase in the number of titles about "topics of international understanding," but they too lamented the lack of books by minority authors.

Only 18 children's books published in the U.S. in 1985 were either written or illustrated by black Americans, and books by and about Hispanics, Native Americans, Asians and other ethnic minorities were even fewer in number during the year. We find such a statistic appalling and hope to see a reversal in 1986.[19]

Horning and Kruse saw virtually no improvement the following year, but by 1987 they did note an upswing in publishing on multicultural topics, with increased participation by minority authors. However, the increase from 18 to 30 African-American authors was not as substantial as one might conclude, because there had been an increase in new titles published overall.[20] Furthermore, during the lean years of the 1980s, some well-known authors and illustrators published more than one book, so the small numbers belied an even more desperate situation for the aspiring minority writer or illustrator. While Horning's and Kruse's statistics cannot be compared directly with those of Larrick or Chall et al.—one set focuses on the number of African-American characters and the other on the number of authors and illustrators—they point out changes in our standards and expectations. In particular, the growth of multicultural publishing in the 1970s established the fact that the profession of writing children's books was no longer the province of the white male (or female, as the latter have come to dominate the field). Authentic treatments required participation by minority authors themselves; social justice demanded it.

The Emergence of the Small Presses

While the mainstream presses were pulling back in the 1980s from their commitment to multicultural literature, alternative presses emerged or expanded to fill the void. Many of the new presses established in the 1970s had folded by the end of the decade, but others, such as Children's Book Press in San Francisco, survived and prospered during the lean years. Children's Book Press thrived by finding a niche—the publication of folktales and original picture book stories in attractive, colorful bilingual editions. Spanish, Korean, Vietnamese, and Hmong were among the languages included, and the books found an appreciative audience among new immigrants and those who worked with them.

In the 1980s Black Butterfly Press and Just Us Books were among the half dozen or so new ventures that published African-American authors frozen out of the mainstream. Arte Público Press, a publisher of books for adults focusing on the various Hispanic-American experiences, branched out into young adult fiction during the 1980s, bringing back into print four of Nicholasa Mohr's books and launching the careers of several other authors. A number of Native American publishers came into existence during this period, bringing to print the works of, among others, the author-storyteller Joseph Bruchac. Other small presses, perhaps more focused on political issues or general multicultural publishing, also filled the void created by the major houses. Several authors who began the decade writing for small presses found their work accepted by large presses at the end; one of the most visible examples is the Chicano author Gary Soto.

The Rebirth of Multicultural Publishing

By the end of the 1980s the field of multicultural publishing had experienced a revitalization that went beyond even the gains of the 1970s. The success of small presses and their authors was one factor, but the main one had to do with major demographic changes during the decade. Audiences had grown; the world had become smaller. A new wave of minority authors emerged on the scene. Many of these authors are being given a chance to grow and develop rather than having to prove perfection with their first manuscript; as a result, works by minorities are not only among the award winners but also in the average. A greater diversity of statements is being made, and readers are learning about the multiplicity of life-styles, communities, and experiences within each minority group.

With the resurgence in publishing about minority groups within the United States and Canada, two parallel trends have continued. One is what Rudine Sims calls the "melting pot" book (not necessarily to be confused with the melting pot theory). This type of book presents minority characters who are essentially indistinguishable from middle-class white ones.[21] Ethnic background or race is displayed only through illustrations or through a few lines of text; at the most, very superficial cultural characteristics (such as what the family eats for dinner) are brought in. Examples of the melting pot book are Ann Cameron's Julian series, featuring an African-American protagonist, and Joanna Hurwitz's *Class President* (1990), one of a series with this particular volume presenting Julio, a Puerto Rican child. Though the books have been criticized for presenting a homogenized middle-class suburban American culture, many teachers and librarians have praised them for showing the commonality of human experience and the possibilities for attaining a truly egalitarian, color-blind society. In such books, images of minorities are positive, though little of their heritage is shown. What these books emphasize, therefore, is not our differences but rather our similarities.

The opposite has also happened. More and more books about African Americans and other minorities focus exclusively on questions related to heritage, conficts and issues within the minority community, and culturally specific developmental issues. For instance, several books published at the end of the 1980s examined class differences within the African-American community and the fact that skin color, body type, and hair may indicate one's social status or lack thereof. Distinctions between new immigrants and those who have resided in the United States or Canada for several generations are dealt with in several recent fiction titles, as are distinctions among those who have come from different countries within a region (such as Cambodia and China) or different ethnic or class groups within a country.

Despite these welcome changes, there still are major gaps. In particular, Hispanic-American and Asian-American authors and characters continue to be underrepresented. In fiction, various large and growing immigrant communities hardly appear at all, among them Dominican Americans, immigrants from Central America, Filipino Americans (between 1970 and 1980 the fastest-growing group of immigrants from Asia), and people from Southern and Central Asia. Many Hispanic writers are gravitating toward alternative presses rather than trying to break into the mainstream, and Asian-American writers have complained about the difficulties of getting their fiction published in English in the United States. One of the principal barriers continues to be the absence of minority editors within mainstream publishing houses. Even when minority authors do not face overt discrimination (and in fact some publishers of juvenile books have initiated competitions to attract minority writers), there is great concern that a manuscript—particularly if it is a hard-hitting inside portrait of another culture, complete with frank language or a somewhat unusual style—will not be understood or else will be "toned down" on its way to publication.

The International Scene

The rapid growth in multicultural publishing has pointed out the need to examine each title for its quality of writing and presentation. This is true not only for books about minority Americans—where more new writers are seeing the light of day, and not all must meet the almost unattainable standard of excellence that faced their predecessors 20 years ago—but perhaps even more so for books set in other countries. With the rise in mergers and acquisitions, which is resulting in large publishers' becoming part of multinational corporations, the number of books imported from other countries has increased astronomically. Not all of these books can be considered multicultural, for whatever cultural content they may have had originally has been excised in the process of world-wide republication.

At the same time, we have seen a significant increase in books by authors from abroad, including those who do not hail from Europe. Novelists from Latin America, the Caribbean, the Middle East, South Africa, China, and Japan have weighed in with authentic portrayals of their country's culture and of political and social conflicts facing their land. Among the most highly recommended works of juvenile fiction have been those of Jamaican James Berry, Colombian-born Lyll Becerra de Jenkins, Syrian-born Rafik Schami (whose novel *A Hand Full of Stars* won the 1991 Batchelder Award), South African exiles Sheila Gordon and Beverley Naidoo, and Yoko Kawashima Watkins, whose autobiographical novel portrays a Japanese child living in Korea during World War II and her family's escape at the end of the war.

In addition to publishing the works of authors from non-European countries, publishers have moved toward better and more authentic works about foreign countries by U.S. and Canadian authors. Many of these authors, including Allen Say, Paul Yee, and Lawrence Yep, trace their heritage to the countries in question. Others—for example, Suzanne Fisher Staples, whose novel set in Pakistan, *Shabanu: Daughter of the Wind* (1989), has been praised for its authenticity—have spent many years living in the place where their book is set.

Another interesting trend in international publishing is the acknowledgment of the existence of cultural diversity in many European countries. Like the United States and Canada, these countries are becoming more multiethnic as well, with immigration from the West Indies, Africa, the Middle East, and Asia. Although few of these works have crossed the Atlantic so far, or perhaps been published in the first place, Sarah Hayes's and Jan Ormerod's picture books about Gemma and her Jamaican family in England; Susan Price's novel of anti-Pakistani prejudice in England, *From Where I Stand* (1984); and Mette Newth's outstanding and memorable tale, *The Abduction* (1989), of an Inuit couple captured and tortured by Norwegian villagers, exemplify a growing multicultural awareness elsewhere.

Nonetheless, problems characteristic of earlier books about foreign countries continue to exist. Despite the process of urbanization that is going on throughout the world, there continues to be an overemphasis on rural life. This is true for virtually all regions of the world, but especially so for Mexico, Great Britain and Ireland, all areas of Africa except South Africa, East Asia, and Australia, New Zealand, and the Pacific. In some areas of the world, there is a dearth of fiction, and what there is focuses on Americans visiting those countries. Among the problem areas in this respect are Southern Europe, the Middle East and North Africa (except Israel), Southern and Central Asia, and Southeast Asia. For other areas, there is little but folktale, itself a statement about what writers and publishers see as representative of the culture of that area. True to some extent for Native Americans, the predominance of folk or traditional literature is quite marked for Mexico and parts of the Caribbean, sub-Saharan Africa, and most of Asia. Virtually nothing of any kind—fiction, nonfiction, or folktales—exists for the Pacific Islands.

In other cases, book publishing follows the news, and much of the fiction published on hot topics abroad is either not fully realized as fiction or else fails to grasp the complexity of the issue. This can happen anywhere, but the large proportion of failed issue-oriented juvenile novels about Central and South America points to the pitfalls of this genre. Finally, some regions of the world continue to attract stereotypes and distortions. Africa in particular is a critical area. There is a tendency to treat the entire continent as if it were one country; to portray Africans in illustrations as exotic, funny looking, and all looking alike; and to overemphasize folklore and rural life. With the exception of adult books suitable for young adults and perhaps a handful of other books, those about sub-Saharan Africa, not including South Africa, have been written by outsiders. While African-American authors and illustrators themselves may have treated the continent and its people with more respect, even many of them still provide a distorted or overly generalized picture.

It is hoped that the chapters in this bibliography will alert writers and publishers, as well as teachers, librarians, parents, and others, to the areas of greatest strength and deficiency in the publication of multicultural books for children and teenagers. Many of the titles included are outstanding examples of how cultures can be portrayed. Through their flaws, others warn of the problems, pitfalls, and dangers involved in the creation of multicultural books. If authors, illustrators, and publishers can address the areas of greatest need by producing authentic, fully dimensional works of fiction and nonfiction for readers at all grade levels, much of this volume's purpose will have been fulfilled.

THE SCOPE OF THE BIBLIOGRAPHY

All of the books included in *Our Family, Our Friends, Our World* have been published in English in the United States or Canada. For a title copublished in both countries, the full bibliographic information for the U.S. edition has been given, and, when possible, the Canadian publisher has also been indicated. Bilingual editions have been included, although books that are exclusively in another language have not. Although most of the books in the bibliography are still in print, some are not, and others might have gone out of print since the bibliography's publication. (Conversely, paperback editions of hardcover titles may have been issued since; those who wish to acquire the books specifically in either hardcover or paperback should check the most recent edition of *Books in Print*.) Contributors have chosen to annotate out-of-print books if they feel the book is superior and should be put back into print or if a widely available out-of-print book illustrates key aspects and themes, whether positive or negative.

In most cases, defining what constitutes a multicultural book for inclusion in the bibliography has been fairly clear-cut. If the principal characters in a work of fiction or the principal personages in a work of nonfiction are members of the targeted minority groups or residents of a foreign country, the book has been considered for inclusion. If the work's setting is a minority community within the United States or Canada or a foreign country, it has also been considered. Finally, if the theme of the book, or a significant part of its content, gives insight into a culture different from that portrayed in mainstream U.S. fiction, the book has been considered.

Questions arise, however, when a book featuring minority characters could have just as easily featured white middle-class characters, or if a story set abroad could have, without any changes, taken place in the United States or Canada. Another issue has to do with minority characters who are not the principal characters but important secondary ones. In the first case, the book has generally been included, as the presentation of minority characters who are indistinguishable from their white counterparts, with the exception of illustrations or a few lines of text, is a major trend in juvenile publishing today. However, the homogenized cultural content of these books has been pointed out by the contributor, and in chapters in which this is a common pattern—such as the already large chapter on African Americans—only a few of these books have been included as examples. In the second case—books set abroad (and often originally published abroad) without any identifying cultural or historical content—the titles have generally not been included in the bibliography. Otherwise, the large number of books published by multinational corporations for a worldwide audience and stripped of all of their original cultural content to maximize their appeal would crowd out the chapters on Great Britain and Ireland, Western Europe, East Asia, and Australia, New Zealand, and the Pacific. As a result, books set in other countries must give readers some insight into their setting. When members of minorities are major secondary characters, the books have generally been excluded, for the principal focus in such books is not on that character's life and culture. Exceptions have been made, however, when a superficial or stereotypical presentation of the secondary character requires reconsideration of a book that has been embraced by many teachers and librarians as "multicultural." Exceptions have also been made when there is little material available on that culture or theme and the treatment of the secondary character is particularly well developed.

In determining if a book is multicultural and qualifies for inclusion in the bibliography, contributors have used other criteria. Special attention has been given to authors who are members of a minority group or from another country, or if the work has been published in translation, provided there is identifiable cultural content. The publishing history of a book has been taken into account, as has the overall significance of the author. Finally, an effort has been made to locate and evaluate books published by small presses that specialize in multicultural publishing.

Although this bibliography is essentially inclusive (to the extent to which that is possible), there has been emphasis on evaluating "significant" works. Thus, when decisions have had to be made, titles that exemplify certain patterns and trends have been included. Well-known and well-regarded books that merit reconsideration or that have been a source of controversy over the years have also been evaluated. Particularly for the upper grades, there has been an attempt to present the work of major authors for adults if any of those authors' works are appropriate for older teenagers. Some noteworthy figures in contemporary world literature whose work appears in this bibliography include Maya

Angelou, Rudolfo Anaya, Louise Erdrich, Jamaica Kincaid, Agatha Christie, Andre Brink, Nadine Gordimer, and Bruce Chatwin.

All of the books included in the bibliography have been published since 1970. In some cases, however, the works are revisions or republications of earlier editions or are recently published children's editions of classics or folktales. The year 1970 has been chosen because earlier works are outdated, unavailable, and often filled with the distortions and stereotypes that characterized publishing about other cultures before that time. Many of the reissues have been revised, and if a work written in the 1940s, 1950s, or 1960s has been republished in the 1980s or 1990s, that means a publisher has judged it to be up-to-date, relevant, and meeting the current standards of cultural sensitivity. Needless to say, our contributors have furnished their own judgment.

In the case of series nonfiction or books on current events, an even later cutoff date has been used. With the exception of biographies about deceased figures, virtually no series book published before 1985 has been evaluated, and contributors have pointed out cases in which even later publications have become dated. In chapters where difficult decisions have had to be made on what to include, some contributors have chosen to select the newest works in that area. This is particularly true for the picture books presenting African Americans and sub-Saharan Africa, about which the contributors have explored recent trends rather than duplicate existing (and often older) bibliographies on those subjects.

In selecting books to be included, contributors have used a priority system, with the highest priority given to contemporary fiction and trade and series nonfiction. The bibliography's emphasis has been on giving youngsters a picture of the current situation of each group or region. In the case of series books, however, only a sampling of each series has been presented, and further comparisons of the various series have been made in the chapter introductions. In the case of historical fiction, priority has been given to titles set in the twentieth century, and in several chapters a number of titles present the Holocaust and World War II. Books treating the Holocaust are each evaluated within the chapter corresponding to the country of their setting, so that such titles appear in several different chapters. Other works of historical fiction have been included if they examine intercultural relationships within the United States and Canada or elsewhere, or if they provide significant insight into the culture. For instance, a highly recommended samurai novel set in nineteenth-century Japan has been included, whereas historical fiction about pharaohs in Egypt has not.

Many of the multicultural works published now and in the past have been folktales; in some areas, virtually everything published is folktale or adaptations of traditional literature. Unfortunately, to explore a country or ethnic group exclusively through its folklore is to receive a distorted picture. Young children cannot distinguish fantasy from reality, and a child who understands that fairy tales from Western culture are purely fantasy may take parallel tales literally when the culture is a distant one. After reading a number of folktales from Africa, for instance, a child may conclude that the entire continent is filled with wild animals, and all the people live among the lions and elephants in remote rural villages. Thus, an attempt has been made here to present folktales and traditional literature only selectively. The principal criterion is that the title be relevant to the group's contemporary situation, providing insight into its members' heritage and present-day concerns, values, and life-styles. Titles that use folklore to describe encounter between two cultures are also included; in this category are Native-American tales from both North and Central America about an indigenous community's first encounter with whites. Revised editions of well-known and heavily used works of traditional literature, such as the Uncle Remus tales, have been evaluated for the quality of their presentation and their cultural sensitivity.

On the whole, contributors have aimed for balance between fiction and nonfiction and for emphasis on present-day life. As many commentators have pointed out, excessive concentration on folktales, customs, festivals, and a group's history leads readers to believe that bygone ways are actually those of the present (one of the principal flaws of Politi's work and other books published at that time). Too, readers are apt to glean from the books only the most exotic aspects of other cultures and what is different from their own way of life. Such focus in the multicultural curriculum does not enable students to see themselves as they live today, to understand people from other cultures, and to explore global concerns.[22]

To facilitate use in the curriculum, chapters have been subdivided according to grade level rather than age level. Placement is according to interest level rather than reading level, although contributors have taken the reading level into account when choosing an interest level and making cross-references from one interest level to another. The four interest levels are P–3 (preschool through third grade), 4–6, 7–9, and 10–12. Most of the picture books and beginning chapter books are in the P–3 section. Middle-grade fiction and nonfiction are annotated in the 4–6 section, as are most of the beginning geography and biography series books. Most young adult fiction and nonfiction titles are in the 7–9 section; the middle or junior high school level is when most students read young adult fiction and write their first research paper. Adult books suitable for young adults, as well as the most sophisticated series books, are annotated in the 10–12 section.

Adult fiction and nonfiction titles have been included in this bibliography if they have a special focus on youth, and if, in the case of novels, they touch upon developmental and moral issues of interest to teenagers. Many autobiographies, particularly those about the author's coming of age, have been included in this section. Novels such as Ben Okri's *Flowers and Shadows*—its 19-year-old author's exposé of generational conflict and corruption in an upper-class Nigerian family—and Nadine Gordimer's acclaimed *My Son's Story*—centered on a teenager's discovery that his political activist father is having an affair—have also been annotated. Other nonfiction for adults has been included if the presentation is of special interest to older teens or if the book is especially useful for reports and term papers.

Each contributor has judged the most appropriate grade level for a book, although the publishers' intentions, as indicated by their catalog listings, have been considered. For series books, a principal age level has been assigned to each series as a whole. When a contributor has felt that a book appeals to more than one grade level, cross-references from the additional level to the principal one have been supplied.

Because of space limitations, annotations for more than one book have at times been combined in a single entry. This is particularly true for books in a publisher's series, when one or two books about a given region have been chosen for annotation (more if there are wide variations in approach and accuracy) and others simply mentioned in the chapter's first entry for that series. When a number of biographies—series or separate titles—have been written about the same person, contributors have in some cases (particularly in the

African-American chapter) annotated the best biography for each grade level and briefly discussed some of the others that are available. Finally, if an author whose title is annotated has written similar books, the contributor has mentioned and perhaps briefly described those other books.

CRITERIA FOR EVALUATION

Reviewers of children's books have generally used literary quality as the standard for evaluating fiction. They take into account characterizations, plot, theme, setting, and writer's style. Currency, accuracy, and balance are primary concerns in the evaluation of nonfiction, along with the clarity and interest of the writing and the author's organization and use of visual and finding aids. The quality and appropriateness of illustrations, along with their relationship to the text, are principal issues in the evaluation of picture books and other highly visual materials. Finally, reviewers often take the audience into account, judging if a particular work is appropriate for its stated audience and how it may be used by teachers, librarians, parents, and children.

Although literary quality has been used to evaluate the materials annotated in this bibliography, it cannot be the only standard. To address the needs of our changing global society, books must have more. As the renowned author Eloise Greenfield so eloquently put it,

> The books that reach children should: authentically depict and interpret their lives and their history, build self-respect and encourage the development of positive values; make children aware of their strength and leave them with a sense of hope and direction; teach them the skills necessary for the maintenance of health and for economic survival; broaden their knowledge of the world, past and present, and offer some insight into the future. These books will not be pap—the total range of human problems, struggles and accomplishments can be told in this context with no sacrifice of literary merit. We are all disappointed when we read a book that has no power, a story that arouses no emotion, passages that lack the excitement that language can inspire. But the skills that are used to produce a well-written racist book can be used as well for one that is antiracist. The crucial factor is that literary merit cannot be the sole criterion. A book that has been chosen as worthy of a child's emotional investment must have been judged on the basis of what it is—not a collection of words arranged in some unintelligible but artistic design, but a statement powerfully made and communicated through the artistic and skillful use of language.[23]

Various individuals and organizations have developed sets of criteria for evaluating children's books that have a multicultural or international focus. Perhaps the most well-known and heavily used of these is the pamphlet *Ten Quick Ways to Analyze Children's Books for Racism and Sexism*, published by the Council on Interracial Books for Children (CIBC). The CIBC suggests examining the illustrations for stereotypes, tokenism, and "minorities in subservient and passive roles."[24] With respect to the text, the CIBC calls for an examination of the story line, the life-styles depicted, the relationships between people, the heroes and why they are considered heroic, the use of language, and the author's perspective. Finally, the council asks teachers, librarians, and parents to consider the book's total effect on a minority child's self-image, to study the author's and illustrator's background and qualifications, and to examine the copyright date in the context of publishing trends.[25]

Most contributors to this bibliography have adapted or expanded upon this list of criteria, applying it as well to international books and nonfiction. Some of the major concerns follow.

1. General Accuracy

Errors and omissions in nonfiction and fiction have been pointed out. In some cases, there have been glaring flaws in an author's scholarship; in others, the errors and omissions are in themselves less serious, but there is a pattern of sloppy research and presentation. The question of accuracy extends beyond the bare facts to the authentic portrayal of thoughts and emotions. For instance, in Bruce Brooks's *The Moves Make the Man*, the narrator, Jerome, hardly reacts to the racial slurs and overt discrimination that he endures. Far more authentic in expressing black children's responses to racism in the South are Mildred D. Taylor's various novels. Of concern as well are cases in which the author has omitted or changed facts to increase a book's appeal or to conform to the expectations of a U.S. readership. Books that provide an artificially happy ending, at odds with what really happened, exemplify this pattern, as do biographies that gloss over the subject's flaws and failures.

2. Stereotypes

When an author assigns general characteristics to a group—particularly if those characteristics have long been attributed to the group—rather than exploring its members' diversity and individuality, it can be said that the author has engaged in stereotyping. Stereotyping may occur in characterization (by assigning physical, social, and behavioral qualities to all members of a group and by allowing that single set of attributes to overshadow the development of a character's unique and full personality), plot development (by making characters play certain roles "typical" of their group or by having all the problems solved by whites or by Americans), theme (by presenting issues and problems as facing only that group and all members of that group), setting (by showing all members of the group living in the same kinds of places, such as ghettos for African Americans and tepees for Native Americans), language (by having all members of a group speak alike, usually in dialect), and illustration (by making all the minority or foreign characters or personages "look alike"). At present, there seems to be more overt stereotyping of foreign nationals than of minorities in the United States and Canada. For instance, while no recently published book portrays African Americans as happy-go-lucky people who live only in the present and have a natural talent for song and dance, that stereotype is at the core of Miriam Cohen's portrayal of Brazilians of African heritage in *Born to Dance Samba*.

3. Language

The language that an author uses should be appropriate to the age group. In her biography of Matthew Henson, Jeri Ferris remarks ironically that "he was the wrong color." Yet the young children at whom this biography is aimed cannot perceive the subtlety and will therefore conclude that Henson, who was black, really was the wrong color.

Those who produce and use multicultural books must make sure the terminology is up-to-date, and that there are no loaded words. As Native American author Michael Dorris has written, "*I* isn't for Indian; it is often for Ignorance."[26] This has been an especially critical problem in works about Africa, in which outdated and pejorative terms such as "Bushmen," "Hottentots," "primitive," "native," "tribe," and "huts" still appear with regularity. In other cases, an older term is still used (such as "Indian"), but the appropriateness of its use depends upon the context. The best way to keep up-to-date is to read the current educational and review literature; some key articles have been cited in the reference section of this bibliography.

Another issue related to language is the use of dialect. Authenticity is important; the words themselves and their expression in print should ring true. Dialect should not be used to ridicule or stereotype or to make characters or personages seem less intelligent. One should be suspicious if all the characters of a given group, and none of the other characters, use dialect.

A related issue is that of racial or ethnic epithets. Here again, the maturity level of the reader and the composition of the class must be taken into account. If individual children will suffer humiliation or pain as a result of reading epithets, or if less tolerant youngsters will seize upon and use those words, one should reevaluate before using the book. Contributors to this bibliography have pointed out where racial and ethnic slurs (as well as profanity in general) are used and have recommended the title for more mature readers.

4. The Author's Perspective

Reviewers and critics have debated whether an author who is not a member of a cultural group can write about that group. Elizabeth Cleaver's *The Enchanted Caribou* and Jan Hudson's *Sweetgrass* are two works, annotated in this bibliography, that have inspired controversy for that reason. Although an author's cultural background, knowledge, and qualifications should certainly be examined, the real issue is one of perspective.

Perspective refers to the author's mind-set and point of view in creating the work. At the time of creation, was the author—regardless of his or her own cultural background—thinking as a member of the group or as an outsider looking in? Like actors who sometimes take on a role so thoroughly that they come to be identified with it (and occasionally act it out in real life), some authors have the capacity to "become," intellectually and emotionally, a member of another culture. Although she is a white South African, Beverley Naidoo writes so convincingly from a young black child's point of view because she is able to take on the perspective of her characters.

When an author looks at a culture from an outsider's perspective, the result is, at best, superficiality and, at worst, stereotyping and judgmentalism. There is also a general sense of inauthenticity, for the author has not fully grasped the characters' or personages' language, emotions, thoughts, concerns, and past experiences. Key events and experiences may have been left out and undue emphasis placed on elements pertaining to the author's culture, but not to the subject's. For example, biographies of African-American abolitionists that suffer from a white (some have used the term "Eurocentric") perspective emphasize the role played by white abolitionists in the Underground Railroad, when most of those who worked for it were black. In contrast, Patricia and Fredrick McKissack point out in their biography of Frederick Douglass that had the British won the American Revolution, the slaves would have been freed in 1833 rather than 1863—not an issue white authors would normally think of, but of enormous significance to the slaves themselves and to succeeding generations. In other cases, the author's value system dominates, with those who conform to it being portrayed positively and those who do not shown as the villains. Books that portray Native Americans as gentle, nature-loving "noble savages" are guilty of this; they are even more so if they present in a negative light those who fought for their land and their rights.

Just as authors from outside a group can write convincingly about that group, being a member of the group is no guarantee that an author's perspective will be with the group. Class and political divisions within the group may carry over into a work of fiction or nonfiction. For instance, Chilean photojournalist Alex Huber has omitted any mention of dictatorship or political conflict in his series volume *We Live in Chile*. Whether this is due to his own political loyalties, to his unwillingness to divulge the negative aspects of his country to North American children, or to constraints imposed by the publisher, the result is the same—an incomplete and distorted picture.

Publishers may impose their own limitations upon an author's perspective as well. Most children's editors are white and female; most publishing company executives are white and male. Changes in language, style, story line, and exposition can occur when the editors working on a book project do not share, or simply do not understand, the author's perspective. This can be a serious problem in series nonfiction, due to the rigid format of those books and the failure of some publishers to use area specialists and consultants.

5. Currency of Facts and Interpretation

It is important to check the copyright date of any work, not only to assess its place in publishing trends (as pointed out earlier, multicultural publishing, like wine, has good years and bad) but also to know how recent the information is. Even so, a recent copyright date is no guarantee of currency. Some books may have been revised in a perfunctory manner, with spotty inclusion of the latest events. More problematical are books that rely upon outdated terminology and interpretations. Though published in 1989, K. C. Tessendorf's *Along the Road to Soweto* is straight out of the 1950s in terms of its language, perspective, and attitudes. Several recently revised books in the Lerner Visual Geography series maintain their earlier prodevelopment perspective, failing to acknowledge today's environmental concerns and the fact that, for most Third World countries, Western-style development has provided little benefit to the majority of the people. The use of area specialists and consultants can help publishers avoid producing books that are dated before they go to press. Keeping up with current events and subject-area literature can help teachers, librarians, and reviewers identify stale information and interpretations.

6. The Concept of Audience

As pointed out earlier, those who use multicultural books should be sensitive to the emotional, intellectual, and developmental level of the children who will read them. Writing about books featuring African Americans, Rae Alexander has argued that a book must be appropriate for an all-black classroom, an all-white classroom, and an integrated classroom.[27] Nevertheless, authors and publishers have their own sense of audience, and subtle differences do occur. The "melting pot" books identified by Rudine Sims are clearly geared to a general audience, while books that explore issues about heritage and cultural values, such as Camille Yarborough's *The Shimmershine Queens*, or concepts of self-image as they relate to physical and cultural characteristics, such as Rita Williams-Garcia's *Blue Tights*, will have special appeal to members of that specific group, although their themes are relevant to other youngsters as well. At the same time, an author writing about a culture from an outsider's perspective will generally be directing the book to his or her own cultural group, but children from the group portrayed in the book may very well notice its inauthenticity.

A challenge for authors who write about minority Americans and young people living abroad is developing the reader's empathy. Even if the author is writing from an insider's perspective, few readers will naturally share that perspective. An effective book will transport the child or teenage reader so deeply into the culture that the young person will identify with the characters or personages and perceive events and issues through those characters' eyes. Youngsters will feel emotions of outrage, sadness, joy, and triumph along with the characters or personages and will be motivated to "do something." That "something" may range from developing more tolerant attitudes to befriending a classmate from another cultural group to joining an environmental or human rights club.

7. Integration of Cultural Information

In order for readers to empathize fully with characters and situations, cultural information must be presented in a manner consistent with the flow of the story. Too often, authors condescend to their readers, halting the story to explain cultural details, as if readers will not get them unless they are spelled out in this way. Furthermore, cultural information should not be presented as exotica but as a normal part—whether major or minor—of an individual's life. Given today's level of assimilation and worldwide urbanization and homogenization, an individual's culture may not be a significant part of his or her life, and that should be acknowledged as well.

8. Balance and Multidimensionality

Much emphasis has been placed on the need for a balanced treatment of issues, especially in nonfiction. In most cases, authors try to present both sides of a controversy, but in the evaluation of these works, certain issues arise.

Though authors seek an "objective" presentation, subtle biases sometimes creep in. Authors may take sides without admitting it, perhaps by giving more attention to one point of view than another or by presenting the other side's perspective in a cursory or inaccurate manner. For example, the Let's Visit Places and Peoples of the World volume on El Salvador contains errors in its presentation of the left-wing opponents of the government and fails to mention the diverse points of view within the opposition. The result is a portrayal of the entire opposition as Marxist guerrillas. Biases may be a result of the author's personal political views, or they may reflect cultural blinders, as when a work of nonfiction on a Third World country adopts the perspective of the U.S., Canadian, or British government rather than presenting questions and controversies from the point of view of the country's citizens themselves, or when a country's history is examined only in its relation to the West.

Whereas some books take sides while claiming to be objective, other books are more open in stating their viewpoints. These books, too, may be considered biased, but they are valuable because they present one cultural perspective and may be read as examples of that perspective. For instance, Margaret Randall's *Sandino's Daughters* openly sympathizes with the Sandinista revolution, yet that book reveals to readers the beliefs, values, and views of a group of Nicaraguan women. Similarly, Mildred D. Taylor does not balance the white racists in *The Friendship* with an equal number of kind and tolerant whites. Her purpose is clear—to show both the harsh reality that southern blacks experienced in the days of Jim Crow and their ability to maintain their dignity under those circumstances. S. T. Tung's middle-grade novel of the Communist revolution in China, *One Small Dog*, is passionately anti-Communist, but the events and perspectives presented give insight into a way of life and provide depth for any discussion of the contributions and faults of the 1949 revolution.

Finally, the attempt to present both sides of a question introduces biases when a reality is unavoidably multifaceted. Just as characters may be one-dimensional, two-dimensional, or multidimensional, so may cultures. A stereotyped, one-dimensional portrayal of an African-American community, for example, may show all its members living in ghettos and using drugs. A two-dimensional portrayal may show some using drugs and others working hard to succeed and to improve their community. A fully multidimensional portrayal, such as that found in Walter Dean Myers's powerful *Motown and Didi*, explores the community in light of many individual dilemmas and perspectives. The people are neither romanticized, nor their problems sensationalized. While the book ends on a positive note, with the two teenagers gaining self-awareness and strength through their relationship with each other and with adult role models in the community, this is no work of propaganda. The problems and obstacles are real, Myers presents them with honesty, and the choices each protagonist makes will force readers to think about all sides of the issues.

9. Illustrations

Both picture books and most juvenile nonfiction rely heavily upon illustrations. The issues in evaluating text material also apply to the evaluation of illustrations. Illustrations must be accurate and up-to-date; they must not stereotype a group by making all its members look similar and engaging them in activities or behaviors traditionally attributed to that group; they must not homogenize other racial and ethnic groups by giving them Caucasian features with darker coloring; they must not ridicule by exaggerating racial or ethnic features. As in the text, members of other groups must be seen in illustrations in a multiplicity of roles and situations. There is a tendency to show members of other cultures in exotic costumes, practicing exotic customs. Rather, illustrations should reflect everyday life as it is today or as it was during the historical period presented in the text. Illustrations should be attractive and appealing to young people. Captions in nonfiction should be as specific as possible as to location and situation, and photos should never be recycled from one volume to another within a country series. Series publishers who use the same photos for various countries in a region are implying that none of the countries has a unique history.

Conclusion

The criteria detailed here are by no means exhaustive. Many of the contributors to this bibliography have discussed other issues and criteria in their chapter introductions. For instance, the three contributors who have compiled the chapter on East Asia explore the role of color photography in acquainting young people with a distant culture. In general, the emphasis has been upon presenting what a work contributes as well as where it falls short; very few books have been considered "not recommended" on all counts. Many contributors have urged classroom presentation of an essentially worthwhile but flawed book as a means of sensitizing children and teenagers to the key issues. Other books provide understanding of one aspect of a subject, or one point of view, but require supplementation for young people to receive the full picture.

THE STRUCTURE OF THE BIBLIOGRAPHY

Chapter Introductions

Each chapter begins with a general introduction, written by the contributor or contributors for that chapter, unless otherwise noted. The introduction gives an overview of trends in publishing about the group or region. Although the introduction is not meant to be a history of the group or region, some basic facts, themes, and concepts are presented in order to put the individual books into context.

Each introduction also details the contributors' criteria for selecting and evaluating books. Outstanding books that touch upon the key themes are listed and briefly described. In some cases, books that have been criticized in the annotations are discussed, principally to illustrate criteria and themes, but the focus is on the positive.

The final part of the chapter introduction (although some contributors have placed this section at the beginning) consists of a comparison of the various series in a given area. The principal features of each are outlined, with the series evaluated in terms of attractiveness, readability, interest, currency, accuracy, and cultural sensitivity. While most of the geography and biography series offer titles for many regions of the world, one cannot conclude that a series that gets a positive evaluation in one chapter will necessarily do so in another. While contributors' criteria and priorities may differ somewhat, the series themselves are often stronger in one area of the world than in another, depending upon the authors' and editors' skill and expertise and the publishers' revision schedule. Even within a region, some volumes are more successful than others.

Entries

Entries vary in length, based on the complexity, originality, and nature of the work. The lengthiest entries are generally for fiction and for the most interesting and/or controversial works of nonfiction. Space may also be devoted to examining major flaws, providing a history of the author or work, or giving background information about the book's content and themes. The longest entries run from 200 to 300 words, although some may be even longer.

Entries of 100 to 200 words are typical of most trade nonfiction titles—competently written books with no major flaws and no distinguishing features in their content and approach. Even shorter entries, from 60 to 100 words, cover individual series volumes.

As stated earlier, entries may include mentions or brief descriptions and evaluations of other books within a series, other biographies of the same subject, and other works by the same author. Only the book in the main entry appears in the indexes, however.

Within each grade level, books are listed alphabetically by author, editor, or compiler. If there is no identifiable author (as in the Visual Geography series and about half a dozen other works), the book is listed by title. There is a special note for bilingual editions, revised editions, and reissues. If the book is a translation, the name of the translator and the original language, if known, are given. Whenever possible, bibliographic information is provided for both library binding or hardcover (with precedence given to library binding) and paperback editions of the work; however, new editions will have been published and older ones taken out of print after this bibliography's publication. The o.p. designation, for "out of print," is used only when all editions have gone out of print. If the library binding and hardcover editions are out of print but the paperback edition is still in print, only the paperback edition will be listed.

In determining interest level, a book's readability and reading level are only two factors out of many. If a book's reading level seems unusually high or low for the interest level, the annotation may contain comments about its suitability for better readers or for reluctant readers. Teachers and librarians may also want to use their discretion in selecting books from a higher or lower interest level in order to reach special readers.

As discussed previously, cross-references are provided when the contributor has felt that the book crosses interest levels. Only the main entries—not the cross-references—are numbered and indexed. Cross-references may also be provided if a book covers more than one cultural group or region, as when a novel about an immigrant youngster takes place partly in the country of origin and partly in the United States. In rare cases, a book is fully annotated in both chapters.

Some of the chapters have been compiled by several contributors, each of whom has annotated a portion of the titles. In these cases, the author of the annotation is indicated by his or her initials, which follow the entry. Occasionally, an entry originally submitted for one chapter has been placed in another; the original author of the annotation is also indicated by initials at the end of the entry.

Appendixes

Each contributor has provided a reference section geared to teachers, librarians, and others who work with children. Contained in the reference section are sources for further reading and information. These sources may be books and periodicals that give an overview of the history and culture of the group or region and provide information on recent developments. The sources may also be other published bibliographies that aided the contributor in compiling the list. Finally, some contributors have provided a list of resources in other media, such as television programs, feature films, and videos.

Following the reference section are the indexes, which provide access through author, title, with both book titles and series titles included, and subject. There is also a master list of the series in a separate appendix, with individual volumes listed and an asterisk next to those that have received annotations.

GENERAL SOURCES

In preparing their chapters, contributors have used a variety of sources to locate multicultural books in their area. One source has been publishers' catalogs and announcements. Numerous publishers have furnished review copies, thus facilitating the inclusion of the book in the bibliography. In a few cases, contributors were unable to obtain the book either in libraries or through publishers, and those titles, unfortunately, had to be left out. The author and contributors to this volume are grateful to those publishers who generously supplied review copies.

General bibliographies such as *A to Zoo* (R. R. Bowker) and *Children's Catalog* (H. W. Wilson) have helped contributors to identify books published in the past three decades that are still in print. Contributors have also consulted "Best Books" lists, including various lists produced by the American Library Association (ALA) and the New York Public Library. Several contributors found the ALA Best Books for Young Adults list especially helpful in suggesting adult books suitable for young adults. Three lists published by the New York Public Library—*The Black Experience in Children's Books, Celebrating the Dream*, and *Books for the Teen Age*—are more focused on multicultural books and have been quite helpful for this reason. *Booklist, School Library Journal, Council on Interracial Books for Children Bulletin*, and other professional periodicals contain specific subject bibliographies from time to time. These, as well as subject bibliographies that have appeared elsewhere and are cited in the reference section, have proved useful to contributors.

Many of the contributors have consulted reviews in a variety of professional periodicals. Often reviewers have disagreed on the quality and value of a given title, and in any case the contributors have made their own independent judgments. However, reviews are an excellent source for finding out both what has been published and some of the issues other professionals in the library and educational field have raised with respect to the title.

As subject specialists, the contributors have applied their own knowledge to the location and evaluation of books in their respective chapters. In some cases, they have helped identify books that appear in other chapters. When there has been more than one contributor to a chapter, the reviewer's initials will appear at the end of the annotated entry. Occasionally the initials L.M-L. will appear at the end of an annotation, indicating that the annotation was written by this book's author, Lyn Miller-Lachmann. Many contributors either are members of the cultural group and/or have lived in the country or region under treatment. In their library and classroom situations they have used many of the books that appear in this bibliography. Therefore, their suggestions for using the books are frequently based on actual experience. As a result, *Our Family, Our Friends, Our World* has been a totally collaborative effort, in which author and contributors have learned from each other and worked together to produce an important resource for young people of all cultures and for those who care about them.

Notes

1. Felicity Barringer: "Census Shows Profound Change in Racial Makeup of the Nation." *New York Times*, March 11, 1991: A-1.
2. Nancy F. Chavkin: "Joining Forces: Education for a Changing Population." *Educational Horizons* 68 (Summer 1990): 190.
3. Walter Dean Myers: "The Reluctant Reader." *Interracial Books for Children Bulletin* 19 (1989), 3–4, 14–15.
4. Patricial Beilke and Frank J. Sciara: *Selecting Materials For and About Hispanic and East Asian Children and Young People.* Hamden, Conn.: Library Professional Publications (1986), 19–20.
5. James P. Comer: *School Power.* New York: The Free Press (1980), 126.
6. Timothy V. Rasinski and Nancy D. Padak: "Multicultural Learning Through Children's Literature." *Language Arts* 67 (October 1990): 576.
7. Thomas Sobol: "Understanding Diversity." *Educational Leadership*, November 1990: 28.

8. Kenneth Cushner: "Adding an International Dimension to the Curriculum." *The Social Studies*, July/August 1990: 167.

9. Ibid., 168–169.

10. Rasinski and Padak: "Multicultural Learning," 580.

11. Virginia Kalb: "Curriculum Connections: Literature." *School Library Media Quarterly*, Spring 1989: 143.

12. Beilke and Sciara: "Selecting Materials," 115–116.

13. Dharathula H. Millender: "Through a Glass Darkly." In *The Black American in Books for Children: Readings in Racism*, 2nd ed. (ed. by Donnarae McCann and Gloria Woodard). Metuchen, N.J.: Scarecrow Press (1985), 115.

14. Ruthanne Lum McCunn: "Chinese Americans: A Personal View." *School Library Journal*, June/July 1988: 50.

15. Ibid., 51.

16. Jeanne S. Chall et al.: "Blacks in the World of Children's Books." In *The Black American in Books for Children*, 213.

17. Ibid., 215–217.

18. Walter Dean Myers: "The Black Experience in Children's Books: One Step Forward, Two Steps Back." In *The Black American in Books for Children*, 224.

19. Kathleen T. Horning and Ginny Moore Kruse: *CCBC Choices 1985*. Madison, Wis.: Cooperative Children's Book Center (1985), 1.

20. Kathleen T. Horning and Ginny Moore Kruse: *CCBC Choices 1987*. Madison, Wis.: Cooperative Children's Book Center (1987), 2.

21. Rudine Sims: *Shadow and Substance: Afro-American Experience in Contemporary Children's Fiction*, 2nd ed. Chicago: NCTE/ALA (1982), 33.

22. James Lynch: *Multicultural Education in a Global Society*. New York: The Falmer Press (1989), 36–37.

23. Eloise Greenfield: "Writing for Children: A Joy and a Responsibility." In *The Black American in Books for Children*. Metuchen, N.J.: Scarecrow Press (1985), 21.

24. Council on Interracial Books for Children: *Ten Quick Ways to Analyze Children's Books for Racism and Sexism*. New York: Council on Interracial Books for Children (n.d.), 1.

25. Ibid., 1–5.

26. Michael Dorris: "*I* is Not for Indian." In *Books Without Bias: Through Indian Eyes* (ed. by Beverly Slapin and Doris Seale). Berkeley, Calif.: Oyate Press (1988), 36.

27. Rae Alexander: "What Is a Racist Book?" In *The Black American in Books for Children*, 53.

1

UNITED STATES:
AFRICAN AMERICANS

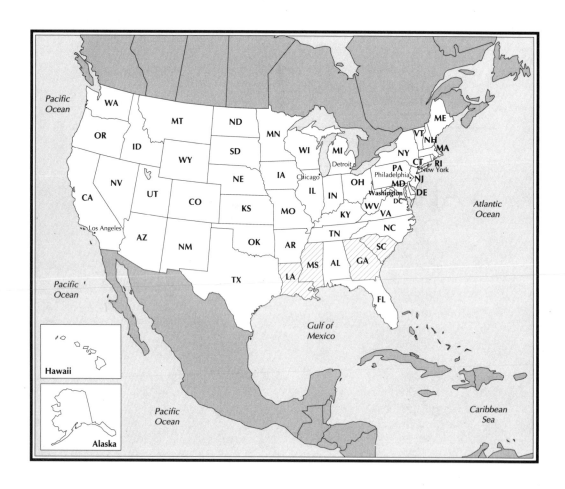

STATES WITH HIGHEST CONCENTRATION OF AFRICAN AMERICANS	CITIES WITH LARGEST AFRICAN - AMERICAN POPULATION
1. Washington, D.C. - 65.6%	1. New York - 2,102,512
2. Mississippi - 35.6%	2. Chicago - 1,087,711
3. Louisiana - 30.8%	3. Detroit - 777,916
4. South Carolina - 29.8%	4. Philadelphia - 631,936
5. Georgia - 27.0%	5. Los Angeles - 487,674

Source: 1990 U.S. Census

1

UNITED STATES: AFRICAN AMERICANS

by April Hoffman, Sandra Payne, and Reeves Smith

After years of neglect, children's and young adult books about African Americans are beginning to appear in larger numbers. This is true for both fiction and nonfiction. Several publishers, including Chelsea House and Silver Burdett, have initiated series that focus exclusively upon black Americans who have made significant contributions to politics and society. Other publishers of biography series have added volumes on African Americans; many of these noteworthy achievers, such as the scientist Benjamin Banneker and the explorer Matthew Henson, were up until now often omitted from textbooks and other sources. Recent histories have dealt with resistance to slavery, the civil rights movement, and the role African Americans have played in the development of our nation's culture and the arts. Children's and young adult fiction have seen the appearance of more black characters, in more books written by black authors, and with some shifts in themes. Particularly noteworthy are a growing number of characters who search for their roots in African culture and in the lives of those of earlier generations who struggled and succeeded in the new land to which they had been forcibly brought.

Because of the recent increase in the number of titles, as well as the continued popularity of earlier works now considered to be "classics," the process of selection for this bibliography has been a difficult one. We have established 1970 as the cutoff year, although many fine titles published before that date are still in print. (Some of these titles have been mentioned in the reference section; others are within annotations.) Mirroring the situation throughout the publishing industry, many of the newest titles have been picture books, and a sampling of recent ones has been included here. The list for the middle grades and young adults combines the latest works with classics that, because of changing circumstances in African-American communities, have taken on new importance. In nonfiction, the books selected for review relate to the elementary or secondary school curriculum, present information heretofore unknown to young people, and fill gaps in the spectrum of the African-American experience. In positive or negative ways, these books exemplify criteria that should be taken into account when choosing and using books about African Americans. Although most of the books are positive examples, in some cases the contributors in this chapter have chosen to reconsider a book that has been generally accepted as significant but may contain stereotypes and other flaws.

Controversy has raged over whether an author who is not African American can write about that group. Whereas noted white authors such as Ann Cameron, William Loren Katz, Milton Meltzer, and Vera B. Williams have produced highly recommended works of history and fiction, and Janet Bode and Pat Costa Viglucci have written sensitively about interracial romances and families, special attention in this list has been given to new and emerging authors of African-American heritage. During the lean years of publishing about African Americans in the early and mid 1980s, most of the handful of books written or illustrated by those of African-American heritage tended to be by the same people. Among the prominent, and prolific, were Virginia Hamilton, Joyce Hansen, Patricia McKissack, Walter Dean Myers, Mildred D. Taylor, and Mildred Pitts Walter, as well as the illustrators Ashley Bryan, Pat Cummings, and Jerry Pinkney. As publishers began to open their doors to lesser-known authors in the latter half of that decade, promising newcomers entered the field. This list recommends first or second works by Candy Dawson Boyd, Kay Brown, Angela Johnson, Emily Moore, Dori Sanders, Rita Williams-Garcia, Johnniece Marshall Wilson, Jacqueline Woodson, and Camille Yarborough—some of the "new voices" whose careers bear watching.

Because of the large number of books and the need to save space, discussions and recommendations of some books are included within annotations of others. If an author of fiction or nonfiction has written similar books (other biographies for that age group, picture books, or longer books about the same characters or with the same themes and approach), those titles are listed at the end of the annotation. Annotations of biographies generally contain listings of and brief comments on additional books, possibly geared to other age groups, about the biographee. Other nonfiction annotations may list or compare various books on the subject. However, when an author writes both fiction and nonfiction, books for different age groups, or books with widely diverse approaches and themes, each has received a separate entry. For example, Virginia Hamilton has works of folklore, biography, fantasy, and fiction for three different age groups on the list. Although principally a writer of fiction, Walter Dean Myers has authored both humorous and serious works for middle graders and young adults, and his 1988 *Fallen Angels*, set far from Harlem in the jungles of Vietnam, represents a departure from everything else he has written.

In examining works of fiction and nonfiction, the contributors have focused on additional elements besides the traditional definitions of literary merit. Some questions we asked are the following:

(1) To what extent are the characters portrayed—through text and illustrations—as African American? Is the only way the reader knows about their race through illustrations? Are those illustrations accurate, neither exaggerating nor minimizing physical features? Do black characters all look alike—the same color and the same features?

(2) How is dialect used? Will teachers who are not African American feel comfortable reading it? Is it used to demean or ridicule people?

(3) To what extent are the conflicts, issues, and specific details unique to African Americans, and to what extent are they universal? To whom is the book addressed—African-American youngsters or a general audience? In a novel addressing the latter, could white middle-class characters have been substituted, with little or no change in the content of the work?

(4) How are customs, dress, religion, and other aspects of African and African-American culture portrayed?

(5) In a work of history, biography, or historical fiction, does the author perpetuate or reinforce stereotypes that were developed to rationalize slavery and/or promote white supremacy? For example, the third sentence of Jeri Ferris's *Go Free or Die: The Story of Harriet Tubman* reads, "But Harriet was different from most slaves—she wondered why such things [slavery] should be." Harriet Tubman was not different from most other slaves in this respect, and the implication is demeaning to "most other" slaves.

(6) To what extent do the characters in a novel have a "history" as African Americans, communicated by family members, other adult role models, and their own discovery of their heritage? Are adults shown as positive role models? How is the past portrayed?

(7) Are personal and family problems in African-American communities treated realistically, or are they either downplayed or sensationalized?

(8) Is the language appropriate to the audience's developmental age? For instance, in Jeri Ferris's *Arctic Explorer: The Story of Matthew Henson*, one sentence reads, "He was the wrong color." This is meant sarcastically but never explained in a book for elementary-age readers. Children of that age believe that what they read is true, especially if it is in a "true fact" book.

(9) Is the treatment appropriate to the age group? This is a crucial issue with books that present racism or urban pathologies in their most brutal manifestations, with the expression of stereotypes, epithets, and racial slurs on the part of whites or else the graphic depiction of violence, sex, and drug use.

(10) Are problems solved by African Americans themselves or by benevolent whites?

(11) Where there is a black protagonist, is that protagonist the principal actor, or merely the observer, narrating a story about white characters?

(12) Are the characters or personages presented as "model victims," or are they allowed to be human beings capable of the full range of human emotions? How realistic is it to portray members of a disenfranchised group as passively accepting mistreatment instead of being angry?

(13) Are there a variety of class backgrounds, settings, and family situations portrayed?

(14) Do other ethnic groups appear, and how are they treated?

(15) In the case of nonfiction, is the story presented from an Afrocentric, rather than a Eurocentric, perspective? For instance, many biographies of Martin Luther King Jr. note only Gandhi's influence on him, ignoring the role of (often little-known) African-American leaders and suggesting that nonblacks had to lead the way. On the other hand, in their biography *Frederick Douglass: The Black Lion*, Patricia and Fredrick McKissack note that Douglass had turned 16 in 1833 and, had the British won the Revolutionary War, he and all the other slaves would have been freed that year.

Some of these questions are more relevant to fiction or nonfiction, picture books or books for older readers. In most cases, the answers to these questions indicate the quality of the treatment, but in others, such as whether universal conflicts or those particular to African Americans are the principal focus, they may merely point to a book's theme or approach and to how the book can best be used with young readers.

Given the publicity about crack cocaine, teenage pregnancy, and crime in the inner city, it is not surprising that much recent fiction deals with inner-city problems. For beginning readers, Vera B. Williams's *Cherries and Cherry Pits* and June Jordan's *Kimako's Story* present resourceful young girls whose dreams, determination, and innocence help them to make the best of life in an otherwise bleak environment.

Books for the middle grades reflect an increasing realism and harshness, as children themselves come to realize that dreaming will not make inner-city problems go away. Perhaps the most pessimistic of these novels is Walter Dean Myers's highly acclaimed *Scorpions*, the story of an overwhelmed 12-year-old whose life spins dangerously out of control when he is given a gun and told to take over his brother's gang. Although about heroin addiction, Alice Childress's *A Hero Ain't Nothin' But a Sandwich* and Sharon Bell Mathis's *Teacup Full of Roses* have gained new significance with the emergence of the crack epidemic, which has destroyed families and entire communities. Yet young adult readers can find teenage characters who confront the difficulties in their lives and search within themselves and each other for strength in Myers's *Motown and Didi*, Childress's *Rainbow Jordan*, and Rita Williams-Garcia's *Blue Tights*. The difficulties of being a newcomer to the city and from a different class background are portrayed in Rosa Guy's *The Friends*, which also contrasts the life and culture of U.S.-born blacks to those of West Indian immigrants. For mature young adults, one of the most complex and thought-provoking works of fiction set in the inner city remains James Baldwin's classic *If Beale Street Could Talk*.

One source of strength for African-American characters confronting problems is the extended family. These problems can range from a fear of thunderstorms (Mary Stolz's *Storm in the Night*) to anxiety about a grandparent's visit (Angela Johnson's *Tell Me a Story, Mama*) to material deprivation (Alan Schroeder's *Ragtime Tumpie*). Besides offering support and examples from their own childhood, older people—parents, grandparents, aunts, and uncles—often carry the message of a noble past, when Africans and African Americans struggled, persisted, and worked together to overcome obstacles. In Mildred Pitts Walter's *Justin and the Best Biscuits in the World*, Justin's grandfather, a Missouri rancher, tells of the black cowboys who helped to settle the West. During the eight-day celebration of the Kwanzaa, an African-American holiday, the entire extended family pitches in to help Chris and his unemployed father in Walter's *Have a Happy*. Ninety-year-old Cousin Seatta in Camille Yarborough's *The Shimmershine Queens* urges young Angie and her often disruptive schoolmates to learn more about their African roots in order to improve their feelings about themselves.

Also emphasizing the importance of heritage is the large number of works of historical fiction on the list as well as more contemporary novels set in the South. Originally published for adults, Olivia Butler's *Kindred* features a young black woman, married to a white writer, who journeys back in time to the antebellum South, where she becomes a slave and is brutalized by a white plantation owner. Other outstanding works about slavery and Reconstruction include Joyce Hansen's *Out from This Place* and Belinda Hurmence's *Tancy*. The fiction of Mildred D. Taylor (*The Friendship; Roll of Thunder, Hear My Cry; Let the Circle Be Unbroken;* and *The Road to Memphis*) portrays a violent, racist, and oppressive South during the 1930s and 1940s; even so, her principal characters, the Logans, survive, maintain their dignity, and even prosper against all odds. With the 1950s came school integration; several novels—Bruce Brooks's *The Moves Make the Man*, Brenda Wilkinson's *Not Separate, Not Equal*, and Ntozake Shange's *Betsey Brown*—show the stresses and conflicts resulting from that experience.

More recently, the South has come to be presented as a place where young African Americans can discover who they are and where they came from, as the unhappy, isolated Sheema does with such poignancy in Virginia Hamilton's *A Little Love.*

Many of the themes raised in fiction are picked up again in recently published nonfiction. Works of history, such as William Loren Katz's *Breaking the Chains,* uncover incidents of slave resistance never discussed in history textbooks. Although most of the histories focus on either slavery and Reconstruction or the civil rights movement, both older and recent works examine the contributions of blacks who settled the West (Charlotte R. Clark's *Black Cowboy,* Ruth Pelz's *Black Heroes of the Wild West,* and William Loren Katz's *The Black West*) and made crucial advances in science and engineering (Portia R. James's *The Real McCoy,* Louis Haber's *Black Pioneers of Science and Invention,* and Robert C. Hayden's *Eight Black American Inventors*). Milton Meltzer's classic, now revised, *The Black Americans* is a collection of primary-source documents from all periods of African-American history.

Biographies of African Americans present both the well-known and the obscure, covering all fields of endeavor. Particularly interesting are collective biographies of women whose lives have been until now unknown to all but the most serious scholars. An early work of this type is Olive Burt's *Black Women of Valor.* Dorothy Sterling's *Black Foremothers* is a more recent addition to this area, and Brian Lanker's *I Dream a World* contains interviews with black women who continue to shape our country's history today. While most of the biographies are either third-person narratives of the biographee's life or personal interviews, *Black Heroes: 7 Plays,* edited by Errol Hill, presents dramatic moments from the lives of seven African-American heroes; the plays themselves have been authored by playwrights of distinction. A highly acclaimed individual biography of Langston Hughes, presented through drama, is Ossie Davis's *Langston: A Play.*

Many of the nonfiction works discuss the role of African Americans in literature and the arts. Among them are works of folklore and the oral tradition: *Jump!* and *The Tales of Uncle Remus,* both adaptations of the Brer Rabbit stories; *The People Could Fly,* Virginia Hamilton's well-rendered and culturally rich anthology of folktales; and *Talk That Talk,* a thorough and somewhat scholarly collection of folktales, tales adapted from the oral tradition, and original stories. Although most biographies of popular entertainers (as well as sports figures whose careers did not involve the breaking of the color barrier) have been left off the list, noteworthy histories and collective biographies in this area include James Haskins's trio—*Black Music in America, Black Theater in America,* and *Black Dance in America;* Charlotte Greig's *Will You Still Love Me Tomorrow?* a history of all-female popular music groups; and Donald Bogle's *Blacks in Film and Television.* The list also contains poet Maya Angelou's autobiographical *I Know Why the Caged Bird Sings* and Alan Schroeder's *Ragtime Tumpie,* a fictional rendering of an incident from the childhood of dancer Josephine Baker.

Most of the nonfiction on current affairs that is included in this list examines the legacy of the civil rights movement; in fact, few books outside this area have been published for children and young adults as opposed to adults. Robert Sam Anson's *Best Intentions: The Education and Killing of Edmund Perry* (New York: Random House, 1988) and Terry Williams's *The Cocaine Kids: The Inside Story of a Teenage Drug Ring* (Reading, MA: Addison-Wesley, 1990) deal with issues facing African-American youths, but they take a more sociological approach and have therefore not been included. However, the lively format and direct approach of Nelson George's *Stop the Violence* make it an ideal work for young adults, who will see their favorite rap stars speaking out against drugs and urban violence. Several advice and self-help books, also authored by popular black entertainers, are on the list, among them Bill Cosby's *Love and Marriage* and Malcolm-Jamal Warner's *Theo and Me*, making personal advice a (fictional) family affair. Interracial dating is the subject of Janet Bode's insightful and upbeat *Different Worlds*; this controversial issue and the related one of interracial families are also the subject of four novels on the list: Pat Costa Viglucci's *Cassandra Robbins, Esq.*, which, too, maintains an upbeat tone; Olivia Butler's *Kindred* and Virginia Hamilton's *A White Romance*, which are more critical of interracial relationships; and Dori Sanders's *Clover*, a sensitive tale of a white woman who pledges, after her black husband's accidental death on their wedding day, to raise his 10-year-old child.

Most of the biographies on the list belong to a publisher's series; however, only a few of those series are dedicated exclusively or even primarily to biographies of African Americans. Lerner's Ethnic Achievers series is geared to the upper-elementary grades and features mainly sports stars and entertainers. Lerner/Carolrhoda's Creative Minds series, for the same age group, focuses on historical and political figures. Unfortunately, some of those titles are marred by poor writing and lack of sensitivity to stereotypes embedded in language. Silver Burdett's series The History of the Civil Rights Movement, directed toward middle schoolers, presents political leaders in visually interesting volumes that contain chronologies, time lines, maps, and copious photos and drawings. In some cases, however, the text tends to be dry and choppy. The best of the series titles in terms of text and visuals is Chelsea House's Black Americans of Achievement, which gives a balanced and sophisticated view of the biographee, putting him or her in context as well as telling a life story. Also praiseworthy are the biographies written by Patricia and Fredrick McKissack for the People of Distinction series published by Childrens Press. The McKissack biographies tend to appeal to an older age range (middle and junior high school) than most of the People of Distinction volumes; they are characterized by unusually lively writing and an African-American perspective that leads the reader toward new information and new ways of looking at issues.

This chapter was assembled by three contributors—April Hoffman, Sandra Payne, and Reeves Smith—with occasional entries by Lyn Miller-Lachmann. The initials of the contributor, or contributors, follow each annotation. Each of the three main contributors provided notes for the introduction, which was written by Lyn Miller-Lachmann. The introduction reflects the collective sentiment of all those involved in putting this chapter together.

PRESCHOOL–GRADE 3

1   Adler, David A. ***Jackie Robinson: He Was the First.*** Illus. by Robert Casilla. SERIES: First Biography. Holiday House 1989, LB $12.95 (0-8234-0734-9). 48pp. Nonfiction.

This is the best of several recently published introductory biographies about Robinson. It is an accurate and informative account about the man and the time in which he lived. It is accessible to second- or third-grade-level readers. The book's design is spacious and attractive, and Casilla's appealing watercolor illustrations are on almost every page. What sets Adler's book apart from others is his sensitivity. He conveys the racism of the time without repeating racial slurs and epithets. This is certainly not the case with Margaret Davidson's *Jackie Robinson, Bravest Man in Baseball* (Dell, 1988). Davidson's use of demeaning names and specific racial insults almost sounds as though she fears that the terms may be lost to this generation unless she repeats them.

Another title, Jim O'Connor's *Jackie Robinson and the Story of All Black Baseball* (Random House, 1989), is easier to read. It is a Step 4 Step into Reading Book. Its strength is that O'Connor mentions some of the Negro Baseball League players, such as Satchel Paige and Cool Papa Bell. There are also black-and-white photos of them. Still, Adler's book is the choice selection. He has also written a First Biography of Martin Luther King Jr.   A.H.

2   Cameron, Ann. *Julian's Glorious Summer.* Illus. by Dora Leder. Random House 1987, LB $5.99 (0-394-99117-6); P $1.95 (0-394-89117-1). 64pp. Fiction.

Although 7-year-old Julian has nothing to do, he tells his friend Gloria he can't ride her bike because he has too many chores. Gloria protests to Julian's strict father, who, when he realizes his son has lied, indeed loads Julian down with chores. Julian begs his mother to intercede; she tells him that sometimes suffering is the beginning of happiness. She insists that he suffer a bit more and also that he tell her what he really thinks about bicycles. Julian admits that he does not like them because he is afraid of falling off. Three weeks later, Julian finishes his chores, and his father rewards him with . . . a bicycle. After initial hesitation, Julian learns to ride, and he and Gloria spend the rest of the summer exploring on their new (and for Julian, hard-earned) bikes.

Only in the illustrations do the characters appear African American. They speak standard English, and there are no descriptions of hair or skin tones. Conflicts are personal, among family and friends, rather than social or racial. Cameron's themes are universal ones—the importance of honesty, the benefits of hard work, and the need to face up to and overcome one's fears. Cameron has written several other books about the lively, likable Julian, his close, loving family, and his friends; they are *The Stories Julian Tells* (Random House, 1981), *More Stories Julian Tells* (Random House, 1986), *Julian, Secret Agent* (Random House, 1988), and *Julian, Dream Doctor* (Random House, 1990).   R.S.

3   Carter, Polly. *Harriet Tubman and Black History Month.* Illus. by Brian Pinkney. SERIES: Let's Celebrate. Silver Burdett 1990, LB $10.98 (0-671-69109-0). 32pp. Nonfiction.

If any Harriet Tubman biography can compete with Ann McGovern's popular and appealing *Wanted Dead or Alive: The Story of Harriet Tubman* (Scholastic, 1977), it is this one. Colorful and attractive, it is written for beginning readers and older youngsters who have difficulty reading. Pinkney's scraffito illustrations appear to be scratched through a black overcoat to reveal vibrant colors underneath. The four chapters are each only a few pages long, with most of each page filled with pictures. The text is simple yet exciting. Dialogue adds to the excitement and is taken from Tubman's actual words. The incidents incorporated into this short biography are accurate and involve feelings that young children can understand.

The book's only weakness is its final chapter, which is abrupt and may give readers the misconception that after the Civil War, African Americans lived "happily ever after." However, the overall strengths of the book far outweigh this flaw.   A.H.

4   Clark, Charlotte R. **Black Cowboy: The Story of Nat Love.** Illus. by Leighton Fossum. E. M. Hale 1970. unp. Nonfiction. o.p.

This picture book biography of Nat Love, alias Deadwood Dick, will make an excellent addition to elementary school and public libraries. Both Clark's exciting text and Fossum's colorful, stylized illustrations portray the West as it was, as opposed to Hollywood's image of it. The cowboys and frontierspeople are white, black, and Hispanic. The only ethnic minority missing is the Asians, who also helped to develop the West.

The account of Nat's encounter with the Indians lacks the degree of sensitivity shown in the rest of the book: at one point Clark refers to them as "redskins." A reissue of this book will require more careful editing. Still, the story and pictures are full of the action small children love, and a new edition is bound to meet with success.   A.H.

5   Gianni, Gary. **John Henry.** Illus. by the author. SERIES: Kipling Press Library of American Folktales. Kipling Pr. 1988, HB $9.95 (0-9437-1818-X). 32pp. Nonfiction.

This title is designed as an oversize picture book with busy and exciting illustrations of watercolor over pen-and-ink drawings. The print is large, the margins are wide, and each page has small black or white stars signifying the series.

This rendition of the folk legend ties it to the westward movement as well as to the American tall-tale tradition. The foreword, written by a professor of folklore and American history, sets it in time and place, and the illustrations place it unmistakably on the western frontier during the industrial revolution.

The strength of this title lies in its illustrations depicting blacks and Asians working to build the railroads; they show that the West was not won by whites alone. However, Gianni has chosen to write the story in black English. The problem with using dialect is that most white Americans do not understand that black English is as valid as standard English, and the book may be misused for that reason.

A classic that has yet to be bettered is Ezra Jack Keats's telling of the same story, *John Henry: An American Legend* (Knopf, 1965), which is still in print.

A.H.

6   Gleiter, Jan, and Kathleen Thompson. **Matthew Henson.** Illus. by Francis Balistreri. SERIES: Raintree Stories. Raintree 1988, LB $15.33 (0-8172-2676-1); P $9.26 (0-8172-2680-X). 32pp. Nonfiction.

Of the recently published biographies of Matthew Henson, this one is the most accessible to grade school children. It is in picture book format, and the illustrations are colorful and exciting. The text focuses more on the expedition than on the man, and children will enjoy reading it for the high adventure and the details of the perilous trip. The racism that robbed Henson of his share of the fame, riches, and dignity he deserved is explained simply and concisely in the last paragraph; the explanation is appropriate for this age group.

The busy watercolor illustrations add to the book's beauty and excitement, so it is unfortunate that one of them is the book's sole flaw. On one of the first pages, when Henson is being introduced, there is a full-color portrait of Robert Peary. Children who read no further or who only leaf through the book will assume that Henson is a blue-eyed, ruddy-faced Caucasian. It is a shame that readers must wait until the very last page to see a close-up portrait of Henson.

Because of the emphasis on both explorers and continents in the elementary school curriculum (and because most of the explorer biographies are about genocidal exploiters such as Columbus), it is important for library collections to have several biographies of Henson, who respected and was respected by the native Inuits of the North Pole.   A.H.

7   Golenbock, Peter. *Teammates.* Illus. by Paul Bacon. Harcourt Brace Jova-
         novich/Gulliver 1990, HB $15.95 (0-15-200603-6). 32pp. Nonfiction.

Integration in major-league baseball was a painful and difficult process. Many heroes emerged, not the least of whom was Jackie Robinson, the first black to play for a major-league team. At the beginning of this biography for the primary grades, Golenbock artfully blends information about how segregation affected black baseball players with biographical information on Robinson himself. In the last few pages, Brooklyn Dodger Pee Wee Reese is introduced. Southerner Reese's public display of solidarity with Robinson in front of a hostile crowd was key in gaining acceptance for integrated ball teams. It is unfortunate, however, that this title ends with that historic event. The last page shows Reese with his arm around Robinson, and the final words are "'I am standing by him,' Pee Wee Reese said to the world. 'This man is my teammate.'" In presenting this as the conclusion, the author diverts the spotlight from Robinson to a white "benefac-tor." For many, this decision mars an otherwise fine book.

The mix of sepia-toned vintage photographs with soft watercolor illustra-tions makes this an unusually handsome title. The picture book format and large print will attract beginning readers, but words such as "audible," "initially," and "savior" might discourage them.   A.H.

8   Greenfield, Eloise. *Grandpa's Face.* Illus. by Floyd Cooper. Putnam/Philomel
         1988, HB $13.95 (0-399-21525-5). 32pp. Fiction.

Tamika is a young black girl who lives in a brownstone with her parents and her grandpa. She has a very close relationship with her grandpa, who is an actor. What fascinates Tamika the most about him is his face. She can tell all about what he is thinking and feeling from observing his facial expressions. Even when he has to reprimand her, Tamika can look at Grandpa's face and know he loves her.

One day, while Grandpa is rehearsing his lines, Tamika enters his room unobserved. She listens to him recite his lines, and then she sees him make a face in the mirror that she has never seen before. It is the sort of face that could never love her or anyone. She begins to misbehave in front of her beloved grandpa, wondering if he will ever show her that mean face again. Finally, she admits her fear to him, and he reassures her that nothing will ever make him stop loving her. She realizes that he puts on his mean face only when he performs a role in a play.

This picture book is excellent in every respect. The illustrations reveal Grandpa's facial expressions and convey the family's racial heritage. Cooper illustrates a scene from the play in which Grandpa performs; it appears to be drawn from a moment in African-American history. The text and illustrations work well together. At one point Tamika refers to her grandpa's brown, sturdy face; it is the sole reference in the text to the family's race. The image communicated through text and illustrations is thoroughly positive. Tamika's intact, multigenerational family is middle class. Grandpa has a full range of interests—actor, confidant, perhaps with a romantic side as well. The text reads aloud well, and the large, colorful pictures make this an ideal choice for story hours. It can also be used to introduce the craft of acting and drama to young children, who, like Tamika, are just beginning to understand the difference between invention and reality.   R.S.

9   Greenfield, Eloise. *Nathaniel Talking.* Illus. by Jan Spivey Gilchrist. Black Butterfly 1989, HB $11.95 (0-86316-200-2). 32pp. Fiction.

Nine-year-old Nathaniel B. Free talks about his life, his feelings, and his thoughts in 18 rap poems. He talks about the recent death of his mother, his relationships with his father and his extended family, making friends, and his hopes and dreams for himself. Some of the poems adopt the meter and the rhythm of the 12-bar blues, for Nathaniel's daddy likes to play the blues on his old guitar. His grandmother dances to the music of the 1940s and plays the "bones"; another poem describes the sound and rhythm of the "bones," an instrument originally brought from Africa.

Read aloud, this book is a unique introduction to several forms of poetry and music, originating in Africa but as contemporary as the now-popular rap. Nathaniel is an intelligent, thoughtful youngster, one inspired by the many children the author has met on her speaking tours at schools and libraries. Nathaniel's feelings and aspirations will strike a chord with children of all races and backgrounds, yet his means of expressing himself is firmly grounded in his own African-American culture. Jan Spivey Gilchrist's black-and-white pencil illustrations reflect the wide range of Nathaniel's feelings—pride, sadness, delight, reflection, appreciation, and, finally, hope. The reader cannot help but be drawn into empathy with Gilchrist's vividly portrayed characters. Published by a small press specializing in African-American fiction for children, this unusual and valuable work should become a part of every multicultural collection, where it can be used to encourage both reading aloud and dramatic performance.

L.M-L./R.S.

10   Greenfield, Eloise. *Paul Robeson.* Illus. by George Ford. HarperCollins 1975, LB $14.89 (0-690-00660-8). 32pp. Nonfiction.

This picture biography is an example of the outstanding titles on black Americans published by Crowell (now part of HarperCollins) in the 1970s. Luckily, this book is still in print. Winner of the 1976 Jane Addams Book Award for promoting the cause of peace, social justice, and world community, it is written in a direct and engaging style that takes into account the developmental level of its intended audience. For example, on the death of Paul's mother when he was 6, Greenfield writes, "At first Paul could not believe that his mother was really dead. But he knew it was true because he missed her so much." Greenfield tells of Paul's position as the youngest in a loving family that was part of a caring black community. She conveys the influence of his militantly proud older brother and his wise and respected father. Children will be interested in reading about how he handled the racism and brutality of his college football teammates.

Greenfield tells simply and honestly how Robeson became disillusioned with America's racism and how his political activities caused the end of his career and the beginning of his persecution by the U.S. government. Her reporting of the mob violence and police brutality at Peekskill is frank, yet understated. George Ford's strong, bold brown brush strokes express Robeson's strength and determination. This fine biography should be made available to all elementary-age children. Greenfield has written two other biographies of black Americans for the youngest biography lovers: *Rosa Parks* (HarperCollins, 1973) and *Mary McLeod Bethune* (HarperCollins, 1977).   A.H.

Hamilton, Virginia. *The People Could Fly: American Black Folktales.*
See entry 31, Grades 4–6.

11   Harris, Joel Chandler. *Jump! The Adventures of Brer Rabbit.* Adapted by Van Dyke Parks and Malcolm Jones. Illus. by Barry Moser. Harcourt Brace Jovanovich 1986, LB $14.95 (0-15-241350-2). 40pp. Nonfiction.

This is a relatively recent adaptation of the Uncle Remus folktales that Joel Chandler Harris collected. Only five stories are featured in this slim, oversize book, but there are two sequels—*Jump Again!* and *Jump On Over!* and there may be more forthcoming. The appearance of this attractive picture book is enhanced by Moser's sunny watercolor washes, which occasionally sweep across a full two-page spread. It is interesting to contrast Moser's visual interpretations with Jerry Pinkney's, in the Julius Lester adaptation *Tales of Uncle Remus.* Pinkney presents the animals as countrified folk; Moser portrays them as southern gentlemen, dandies even. Both styles contribute to their stories.

Parks's text attests to his musician's ear. Repetition of phrases such as "he lay low" (he hid) will delight children, and there are many wonderful instances of onomatopoeia, such as the sound "blippety-blip." The last page presents the music and lyrics for "Hominy Grove," the song Parks and Martin F. Kibbees wrote for the cassette of *Jump!* produced by Warner Brothers.

As with Lester's adaptation, this title has won many accolades. Librarians would be wise to purchase both versions of the Uncle Remus tales.   A.H.

12   Howard, Elizabeth Fitzgerald. *Aunt Flossie's Hats (and Crab Cakes Later).* Illus. by James Ransome. Clarion 1991, HB $12.95 (0-395-54682-6). 32pp. Fiction.

Since her first book, *The Train to Lulu's* (Bradbury, 1988), Howard has grown substantially as a writer. Like the earlier work, this one is drawn from her experiences of growing up in Baltimore. Here, two young sisters' visit to Aunt Flossie's house and their customary rummaging through Flossie's hatboxes become an opportunity to retell the family stories. One hat smells smoky, a result of the big fire in Baltimore. Another was worn at the parade to celebrate the victorious soldiers' return from World War I. All of the returning soldiers are black, highlighting the (often disproportionate) contributions African Americans have made to their country's war efforts. But the final story, which the sisters help to tell, is the climax of the book. Flossie's best hat has fallen into the water. Daddy gets muddy enough but fails to retrieve it. Mommy almost falls in trying to snag it with a stick. Finally, a young boy passing by sends his dog in to fetch the hat, and the boy and his dog save the day.

The text and illustrations express a sense of humor. Rituals are a source of closeness in this family, and the book can be used in the classroom to help young children identify their own family stories and rituals. Ransome's rich oil-on-canvas paintings convey the author's nostalgia for her childhood and her mental picture of the earlier time described by her great-aunt. Illustrations reflect the passage of time. Flossie is a young woman at the time of the fire and the parade, and both girls are clearly smaller on the day the hat falls into the water. On the whole, tight writing and attention to detail have combined to make this a successful picture book.

L.M-L.

13   Howard, Elizabeth Fitzgerald. *The Train to Lulu's.* Illus. by Robert Casilla. Bradbury 1988, LB $13.95 (0-02-744620-4). 32pp. Fiction.

Sometime during the 1930s two small black girls, Babs and Beppy, are sent by their parents alone on a train from Boston to Baltimore to visit Lulu. The older sister, Beppy, must devise ways to keep her sister amused as well as to keep her from eating her lunch too early on the nine-hour trip. When they arrive in Baltimore, aunts and uncles greet them, and a representative from Travelers' Aid supervises them until Lulu arrives.

An added note places the book in context as a fictionalized childhood memoir. Yet it is not very successful at conveying the wonder and excitement that any child traveling alone for the first time would experience. It also does a poor job of showing what train travel was like during its heyday prior to World War II. Because the text and drawings lack the flavor and ambience of the historical period, the audience begins to experience the same boredom that little Babs is feeling. After leafing through a few pages, one, too, is tempted to ask, "How much farther is there left to go?" The banality of the story is paralleled by the blandness of the artwork. While the two main characters are shown fully, other objects are fuzzy or merely geometric shapes. New York's skyscrapers look like a collection of shoeboxes. The reader longs for the scenic beauty that made riding the rails such a unique form of transportation.

This "memoir" seems quite idealized, with no treatment of the racial climate during that period. Of course, the youngsters do not cross the Mason-Dixon line and are thus not subjected to the indignities of Jim Crow. (At Baltimore, continuing passengers were forced to switch to "colored-only" cars.) Yet the black conductor featured here would not have existed; the best job on a train that blacks during the Great Depression could have aspired to was porter. Because the many racial and historical aspects of the story seem to have been omitted, it is especially hard to recommend this book to young readers of African-American heritage.

R.S.

Hudson, Wade, and Valerie Wilson Wesley. *Afro-Bets Book of Black Heroes from A to Z: An Introduction to Important Black Achievers for Young Readers.* See entry 36, Grades 4–6.

14 Johnson, Angela. *Tell Me a Story, Mama.* Illus. by David Soman. Orchard 1989, LB $13.99 (0-531-08394-2). 32pp. Fiction.

As a mother puts her daughter to bed, the little girl hears stories from her mother's childhood. The mother describes in detail a story about her own mother, Aunt Jessie, and the mean old neighbor lady. Grandmother is coming to visit, and the girl asks how long she will stay, an exchange that leads to another of her mother's stories. The little girl also hears of the time her mother and aunt were sent to live with relatives because their parents had to work, and of the day her mother finally moved away.

This is a childhood memoir of a mother as told by her little girl. The child has heard the stories so many times she can recite them almost verbatim. These stories place her at the center of a multigenerational family. The virtues of this book lie in its portrayal of a black family that is loving, caring, hardworking, and ongoing. Nurturing values learned in one era are passed along to each succeeding generation. Aid in times of need comes not only from one's immediate family but also from grandparents, aunts, and uncles. The interdependence of this extended African-American family makes this an ideal picture book for showing that culture to children in the primary grades. The illustrations communicate the warmth and happiness in the faces of the characters as they experience and recall events in the family's history.

Johnson is the author of two other excellent picture books that explore family relationships—*Do Like Kyla* (Orchard, 1990) and *When I Am Old with You* (Orchard, 1990).   R.S.

15 Jordan, June. *Kimako's Story.* Illus. by Kay Burford. Houghton Mifflin 1981, LB $6.95 (0-395-31604-9). 48pp. Fiction.

Seven-year-old Kimako lives with her mother and baby brother in an inner-city neighborhood in New York. When her mother goes back to work at the beginning of the summer, Kimako is left alone to take care of her brother. Staying indoors and watching television all day bores her, so she asks her cousin, who attends City College, to bring her books. One of the books contains verse, and this inspires Kimako to write and draw a series of puzzle poems.

Kimako has befriended Bobby, a Puerto Rican teenager who lives in the neighborhood. When he visits Puerto Rico for a week, Kimako takes care of his dog and, for the first time, feels safe from the bullies and drunks on her street. With the dog to protect her, she begins to spend more time outside. She visits the park and draws a map of her neighborhood. After Bobby comes back, she plans to ask her mother for her own puppy.

This is a culturally conscious book that portrays urban life in realistic detail, though always from a child's point of view. The language is very simple, yet it evokes the sights, sounds, and dangers that occur in an urban area. The apartment building stoop is Kimako's safe haven. One gets a sense of the warmth she feels while her mother painstakingly fixes her hair. The unexplained family situation that forces her single mother to find a job deprives the 7-year-old of her urban nest of wonders and makes her a lonely prisoner in her own apartment. Kimako's acceptance of herself, adaptability, and resourcefulness—as evidenced by her reliance upon reading rather than TV to fill the emptiness in her life, her creation of the puzzle poems, and her use of Bobby's dog—are key to her own survival and an inspiration to young children of all races. From the text and the childlike stick-figure drawings, one can see that the street where she lives is a melting pot of America. Blacks, Hispanics, and whites live and work side by side. Every moment Kimako gets to spend out of the apartment is special, as is, in so many ways, this story of her summer. R.S.

16 Langstaff, John M., ed. ***What a Morning! The Christmas Story in Black Spirituals.*** Arrangements for voice and piano by John Andrew Ross. Illus. by Ashley Bryan. Macmillan 1987, HB $12.95 (0-689-50422-5). 32pp. Nonfiction.

Ashley Bryan is peerless in his rendition of people of African descent, and his golden, glowing illustrations in this book make it seem as appropriate for a library's art section as the music one. Here he has given us a visual rendition of Negro spirituals selected to tell the Christmas story. The idea of a children's book featuring a black holy family is a unique idea and a welcome one, but it is Bryan's pictures that star in this volume. They show a rich variety of skin colors and features, and the final illustration of the black Christ child is the most engaging of all.

Langstaff has selected five spirituals, and the arrangements for voice and piano by John Andrew Ross follow Bryan's stunning two-page spreads. Opposite the music is also a one-page picture. Each song is introduced by a corresponding biblical verse. Whether or not this holiday book is appropriate in public school collections is open to debate, but public libraries should purchase several copies to meet the seasonal demand. A.H.

17 Lowery, Linda. ***Martin Luther King Day.*** Illus. by Hetty Mitchell. SERIES: On My Own Books. Lerner/Carolrhoda 1987, LB $9.95 (0-87614-299-4); Lerner 1989, P $4.95 (0-87614-468-7). 64pp. Nonfiction.

Although the format is similar to other publishers' beginning readers series, some of the vocabulary and concepts in this title might prove difficult for young children. To help youngsters, the book begins with an author's note, in which terms such as "civil rights" and "unjust laws" are explained. The author touches on the highlights of King's life and the civil rights era in order to explain the holiday. Mitchell's watercolor and black-and-white illustrations enhance the text.

This is a well-presented first biography of King, but primary students will be best served if a teacher reads it aloud and leads a discussion on the ideas expressed. A weakness is that only Gandhi is mentioned as influential in King's political development. This is a common flaw in King biographies. Omitting mention of African Americans such as Frederick Douglass as influencing King helps to perpetuate the misconception that earlier African-American leaders did not exist, and more recent generations have had to rely upon outside leadership. A.H.

18 McKissack, Patricia. ***Mirandy and Brother Wind.*** Illus. by Jerry Pinkney. Knopf 1988, LB $13.99 (0-394-98765-9). 32pp. Fiction.

Mirandy's Ma Dear says that whoever catches Brother Wind "can make him do their bidding." Mirandy dreams of catching him and making him be her partner for the cakewalk, because she knows she will win the cake for sure. Grandmama Beasley tries to discourage her: "Can't nobody put shackles on Brother Wind, chile. He be special. He be free." Ezel, the clumsy neighbor boy, hangs around, hoping Mirandy will give up and dance with him. But she is too busy chasing Brother Wind. After several misses, she catches him in the barn. Then at the cakewalk she hears the other girls laughing at her friend Ezel because of his clumsiness. So she lets the wind go, after demanding that Ezel, whom she chooses for her partner, be given the gift of dancing like the wind.

The story takes place in an all-black community in the rural South at the turn of the century. It is based upon McKissack's own grandparents, who, as teenagers, had won the cakewalk, a dancing competition introduced in the United States by slaves. Written in dialect, the text is intended to be read aloud, or imagined as read aloud, in the tradition of African-American storytellers relating their family's lore. Like many family stories, this one has a supernatural element, drawn from the comparison of the winning dancer to the wind. The theme of freedom figures heavily here, as the wind is free, and the winning dancers perform with the spirit and abandon of the wind. A lively, moving tale of one determined child, this story can also help youngsters probe more deeply into the roots of African-American culture and society. Jerry Pinkney's vivid, vibrant watercolors capture the essence of the text and give the reader a clear sense of time and place.

L.M-L.

19   Mattox, Cheryl Warren, ed. *Shake It to the One That You Love the Best: Play Songs and Lullabies from Black Musical Traditions.* Illus. with reproductions of artwork by Brenda Joysmith and Varnette P. Honeywood. Warren-Mattox Productions 1990, P $7.95 (0-9623381-0-9). 56pp. Nonfiction.

Librarians lucky enough to have seen this unusual book are incredulous that it is both the author's first book and the first title by a new small press. It is a collection of African and African-American children's songs. Game songs and lullabies are included. Each song is accompanied by either a short explanation or direction for a children's game. Everything about this title speaks quality—the text, the design, the artwork, and most of all the concept of combining different art forms in one children's book. The pages are bordered by photos of colorful African weavings, and every few pages there is a reproduction of artwork by contemporary African-American artists Varnette P. Honeywood and Brenda Joysmith. Honeywood's art is either acrylic or stylized collage; Joysmith works in pastels.

Among the songs included, with music provided, are "Mary Mack," "Hambone," and "There's a Brown Girl in the Ring." The well-known "Short'ning Bread" is presented as a lullaby. Although the title can be purchased singly as a paperback, it can also be ordered with an accompanying audiocassette. Folkways Records has recorded and distributed ten-inch records with many of these songs. This beautiful book—and its joyful presentation of a variety of African-American art forms—is in itself a cause for celebration.

A.H.

20   Mendez, Phil. *The Black Snowman.* Illus. by Carole Byard. Scholastic 1989, HB $13.95 (0-590-40552-7). 48pp. Fiction.

Young Jacob Miller resents his family's poverty and the fact that there will be no presents for Christmas. He blames his family's plight on the fact that they are black, and he wishes he were born white. His brother suggests they go outside and build a snowman. Soot and grime have turned the snow black, and the boys wrap the finished black snowman in a colorful cloth, which brings it to life in the form of a West African storyteller. The snowman visits Jacob in his dreams and later saves him and his brother from a fire.

The book admirably tries to build a connection between today's alienated youth and their long-lost, proud traditions. However, the vehicle used—that of a magical device, the West African Kente cloth that covers the snowman—is not all that credible. The Kente cloth has more powers than those under the cape of Superman, for it can restore the boy's damaged self-esteem. Yet if the cloth is so powerful that it can summon the strength of an ancient civilization, bring inanimate objects to life, and teach self-respect, why didn't one of its former owners use its powers to escape capture and slavery? Children, especially those who, like Jacob, have recognized the gap between their lives and those of mainstream America will raise questions like this and thus reject the book's premise. The story line and beautiful illustrations might make this a successful read-aloud for younger, less sophisticated children, but on the whole it is a clumsy, convoluted attempt to approach a serious subject in a novel way.   R.S.

21   Ringgold, Faith. *Tar Beach.* Illus. by the author. Crown 1991, HB $14.95 (0-517-58030-6). unp. Fiction.

It is 1939 in Harlem, and eight-year-old Cassie Louise Lightfoot lies on the roof of her building—her "tar beach"—and dreams of flying. She dreams of flying over the George Washington Bridge and owning it. Her father worked on the bridge, and it opened the day she was born. She also dreams of owning the union building that her father is helping to build. That way, "it won't matter" that her father can't join the union because he is "colored or a half-breed Indian, like they say." Finally, she stops by the ice cream factory and owns it, just to make sure that when they're all rich, they'll have ice cream every night.

Tar Beach is drawn from Ringgold's story quilt of the same name (reproduced on the dust jacket), which is part of a five-quilt series entitled "Woman on a Bridge." The quilts are part of the collection at the Guggenheim Museum. The illustrations inside the book are full-color paintings, bordered by sections from the quilt. The overall design of this book is outstanding, and it shows youngsters the different media that are available for self-expression. Ringgold's semi-auto-biographical story is charming and magical. The theme of flying is drawn from African-American folklore, in which flight became a symbol of freedom. The poverty, discrimination, and insecurity faced by Cassie's mixed-race family is transformed through imagination into a child's vision of a better world. All the details are from a child's perspective, from the labelling of the buildings as simply "the union building" and "the ice cream factory" to Cassie's decision to take her little brother along so he won't tell her parents. This fine book will be savored and appreciated by young children but should also be made available to older children and teenagers who are studying art and contemporary artists. Ringgold's biography is included in Leslie Sills's book, *Inspirations: Stories about Woman Artists* (Whitman, 1990).   L.M-L.

22   Schroeder, Alan. *Ragtime Tumpie.* Illus. by Bernie Fuchs. Little, Brown/Joy Street Books 1989, HB $14.95 (0-316-77497-9). 32pp. Fiction.

This engaging picture book is a fictionalized biography of the famed African-American dancer Josephine Baker. Set in St. Louis, Missouri, in 1915, the text and pictures portray events that were key to young Josephine's decision to leave her hometown for Harlem in pursuit of her dream. At the beginning of the story she is sitting in the city's big produce market, trying to catch whatever falls to the ground to help feed her impoverished family. Later, she goes to the railroad station to pick up stray pieces of coal that have fallen off the hopper car. She thinks of her father, Eddie, a jazz drummer, but when she returns home, her stepfather, Arthur, scolds her for dancing and dawdling on the way. When winter comes, Josephine and her mother dance in their apartment to keep warm. Then in spring, a traveling medicine man calls an impromptu dance contest, and little Josephine is the star.

The text and the paintings evoke perfectly the mood and setting of the story. Music is everywhere, and the people revel in ragtime jazz, an African-American art form. The paintings deserve special praise. Some of the drawings give the aura of a golden era gone by; in others, the characters come alive in hot pinks and sunburst yellows.

Tumpie is full of ambition, courage, and determination to use the gifts given to her by her musician father. Through faith in herself, she moves from terrible poverty to a life of fame. All of the dramatically reconstructed events actually took place. The fact that the characters are African American is never discussed directly in the text, but the illustrations say quite specifically that black is beautiful. As this book shows, African Americans have a renowned cultural heritage. Among their gifts to the world were a new music and dance that traced their roots to Africa but were forged right here in the American Middle West.

R.S.

23   Stolz, Mary. *Storm in the Night.* Illus. by Pat Cummings. HarperCollins 1988, LB $12.89 (0-06-025913-2). 32pp. Fiction.

Thomas and his grandfather are sitting in the dark because a storm has knocked out the electricity. Grandpa cannot read, Thomas cannot watch TV, and it is too early for bed. The only thing left to do is for Grandpa to tell a story about his childhood. Grandpa tells about his dog that was so scared of storms that he would hide under the bed, and Grandpa would have to go with him. Thomas tells his grandpa that he is not afraid of storms, or of anything else. So Grandpa tells Thomas of the time he was so scared during a storm that he dove under the bed himself and left his frightened dog stranded outside. Since his parents were not home, he had to summon his courage to go outside, where he saw a man holding his dog. The man scolded Grandpa for not taking better care of his dog, and Grandpa learned that by caring for others he could overcome his own fears.

As with many picture books, this one features black characters in the illustrations, but the story does not concentrate on that culture. Set in a rural or suburban area, it reflects a homogenous American society, with the universal theme of an older adult providing safety, reassurance, and continuity for his grandchild. The book presents its theme effectively, however, and the evocative illustrations deserve special kudos. Text and illustrations provide an ambience of sound and fury for Grandpa to tell of his experiences. As the storm worsens, Thomas and the reader both hope Grandpa can pull something out of his past to help deal with this ever-threatening situation. The loss of electricity forces the characters to return to an earlier era, when electronic gadgets did not exist and people actually had to speak to each other; this gives Grandpa the opportunity to become the family's oral historian.

Thomas and his grandfather appear again in *Go Fish* (HarperCollins, 1991), which is written for middle-grade readers. Centered on the theme of fish and fishing, this novel offers an African folktale, told by Grandpa, and a stronger connection to Thomas's African-American heritage.   R.S.

24   Williams, Vera B. *Cherries and Cherry Pits.* Illus. by the author. Greenwillow 1986, LB $13.88 (0-688-05146-4). 32pp. Fiction.

An unseen narrator tells of Bidemmi, the young black girl who lives on the floor above. Bidemmi loves to draw with magic markers. Whenever the narrator gets a marker with a color she thinks Bidemmi does not have, she brings it upstairs. Bidemmi always starts her drawings with a single dot. From there, a picture and story evolve. The four most recent drawings concern cherries and cherry pits. The figures in the first three pictures all eat their cherries and spit out the pits. In the fourth drawing, Bidemmi shows herself eating the bagful of cherries and carefully planting the pits. Soon a cherry tree blossoms, and people come from all over to eat the cherries. From their pits, a whole orchard blooms in her once-squalid urban neighborhood.

Similar in approach and theme to *Kimako's Story*, this book presents a small child's view of the city. The picture stories are a fable for contemporary urban America; while others are content to eat the fruit and toss away the by-products, Bidemmi uses the pits to transform an entire neighborhood. She demonstrates that using one's talents and resources can have an impact far beyond one's wildest dreams. For African-American children who may feel like prisoners in an urban detention center, this story presents some ideas for changing the landscape and may be used as a starting point for class discussions and action. The simplicity of the text makes it a credible and valuable source of hope for young children. The message is universal, easy for children of all backgrounds and colors to grasp and appreciate. The illustrations are like the text—childlike yet straightforward, evocative of what Bidemmi is trying to show us.   R.S.

GRADES 4–6

25   Adoff, Arnold. *Malcolm X.* Illus. by John Wilson. HarperCollins 1970, P $4.95 (0-06-446015-0). 40pp. Nonfiction.

This is a great choice for reluctant readers at the older elementary level. The print, margins, and frequent illustrations make it accessible; the seriousness of the subject matter and its treatment keep it from being too babyish.

Adoff begins with the KKK's terrorization of young Malcolm's family, his father's fatal "accident," and his hurt when he realized whites considered him inferior. His descent into crime and his prison experiences are presented objectively. The ending may confuse readers because of the lack of resolution of his assassination. Adoff does clarify why Malcolm Little became Malcolm X and, finally, Malcom Shabazz.

Another fine biography of Malcolm X at this reading level is Florence M. White's *Malcolm X: Black and Proud* (Dell Yearling, 1975). Better readers may prefer the Chelsea House (1990) biography of Malcolm X by Jack Rummell. High school students should be steered toward Malcolm X's autobiography and any of his treatises.   A.H.

26 Boyd, Candy Dawson. ***Charlie Pippin.*** Macmillan 1987, HB $12.95 (0-02-726350-9). 182pp. Fiction.

Spunky sixth grader Chartreuse (Charlie) Pippin sells pencils and other items before school. Her enterprise has come to the attention of the principal at her Berkeley, California, elementary school, and he calls her parents. Her father, a successful businessman himself and a veteran of the Vietnam War, blows up at her, leaving her confused and bewildered. The only way she can understand her father's anger, she reasons, is to join the war and peace committee for her class project and to research the Vietnam War. Her questions lead her to Uncle Ben, also an embittered war veteran. She learns more about the peace movement and enters a district-wide speech contest, in which she develops stage fright and loses miserably. Frustrated in her attempts to understand her father, she sneaks off to Washington with Uncle Ben to see the Vietnam War Memorial. There are consequences at home and school when she returns, but Charlie's determination and concern encourage her father to open up just a little bit.

Boyd's strong-willed female protagonist and her use of humor keep this serious work from becoming preachy. She portrays with much complexity and sensitivity a close-knit middle-class black family in a multiethnic community. The fact that a disproportionate number of the soldiers who risked and lost their lives in the Vietnam War were black receives a great deal of treatment, but Boyd avoids stereotyping the Vietnam veterans. Uncle Ben and Oscar, Charlie's father, are able to go on with their lives, but they remain scarred by the experience, and the understanding of family members often goes a long way toward healing those wounds. This is an intelligent book, one that will appeal to thoughtful elementary-age readers of all backgrounds.   L.M-L.

Brooks, Bruce. ***The Moves Make the Man.***
See entry 56, Grades 7–9.

Burt, Olive. ***Black Women of Valor.***
See entry 58, Grades 7–9.

27 Coil, Suzanne M. ***George Washington Carver.*** Illus. with photos. SERIES: First Books. Franklin Watts 1990, LB $11.90 (0-531-10864-3). 65pp. Nonfiction.

There have been several recently published biographies of George Washington Carver for elementary school children. This is one of the best. Archival photographs of Carver at Tuskegee appear every few pages, and the text is historically accurate, informative, and interesting. When an unfamiliar word is presented, its meaning immediately follows in parentheses. The book's design, with its large print and plenty of white space, will appeal to young readers and those for whom reading is a struggle. In short, this is a fine addition to the biography shelf. The last few pages offer five ideas for activities and experiments, such as making peanut butter and growing a sweet potato vine. An index and a bibliography of four other good biographies for young people are included.

Better readers may enjoy *George Washington Carver, Botanist,* by Gene Adair, which is a title in the excellent Chelsea House series Black Americans of Achievement. For elementary school collections, there is an accessible biography by Barbara Mitchell entitled *A Pocketful of Goobers: A Story About George Washington Carver.* This is one of the better titles in the Lerner/Carolrhoda Creative Minds Biographies series.   A.H.

28   Ferris, Jeri. *Arctic Explorer: The Story of Matthew Henson.* Illus. with photos. SERIES: Trailblazers. Lerner/Carolrhoda 1989, LB $11.95 (0-87614-370-2); 1990, P $5.95 (0-87614-507-1). 80pp. Nonfiction.

This handsome book has been thoroughly researched and beautifully designed. The print is large yet there is plenty of margin. Both the book's subject and its cover will attract readers. Black and white photos of the Arctic expedition appear throughout.

The author does a fine job of presenting expedition leader Peary, Henson, and the actual expedition to the North Pole. Her writing conveys both the beauty and the terror of the trip. She does not shirk from reporting unpleasant details, such as the explorers' killing and eating their sled dogs to avoid starvation. Peary accurately comes across as self-serving, humorless, and insecure; Henson as intelligent, courageous, and easygoing. Another of the book's strengths is its sensitive portrayal of the Inuits.

Ferris also communicates the injustice of Peary's receiving all of the fame and financial reward when it was Henson's abilities that ensured their survival. Unfortunately, her handling of the race issue mars an otherwise outstanding book. She presumes too much sophistication on the part of her young readers. Children believe what they read, especially when it is in a "true fact" book. Two sentences, meant to be ironic, are not clarified and sound blatantly racist if taken literally. They are "He was the wrong color," and "As usual, Matt ate with the crew, not with the other expedition members." Examples such as these point to the need for extra sensitivity in writing and editing books on black Americans for elementary-age readers.

The bibliography features nine primary and eight secondary sources, and there is a thorough index.   A.H.

29   Ferris, Jeri. *Go Free or Die: A Story about Harriet Tubman.* Illus. by Karen Ritz. SERIES: Creative Minds Biographies. Lerner/Carolrhoda 1988, LB $9.95 (0-87614-317-6); 1989, P $4.95 (0-87614-504-7). 64pp. Nonfiction.

Like others in its series, this is an attractive, slim volume with full-page black-and-white illustrations interspersed throughout. It is accessible to third graders and, were it to be a stronger work, a good choice for older students who read below grade level. The four chapters cover Tubman's life until her first escape. An epilogue summarizes her remaining years. Although no sources are noted for the conversations that appear in the story and there is no bibliography, Ferris's history is generally accurate. The fast-paced action will involve youngsters immediately and keep them reading.

However, this book must be used with great caution. Two of the illustrations show slave children in clothes that appear too fine and too contemporary. Like many authors who write about the Underground Railroad, Ferris chooses to portray only whites helping Tubman escape. In reality, runaway slaves were most often helped by other blacks. Finally, the author's carelessness leads to colossal insensitivity. The third sentence in the foreword reads, "But Harriet was different from most slaves—she wondered why such things [slavery] should be." Harriet Tubman was *not* different from "most slaves" in this respect, and to state that she was implies that the others were too content or too stupid to question their wretched place in society.

The publisher promises to change this sentence for the next printing. In the meantime it is imperative that librarians and teachers point out the subtle racism inherent there; otherwise, children may accept it as fact. This can provide an opportunity to discuss critical reading with students. In any case, the best Tubman biography for this age group remains Ann McGovern's *Wanted Dead or Alive: The Story of Harriet Tubman* (Scholastic, 1977). A.H.

30   Ferris, Jeri. *What Are You Figuring Now? A Story about Benjamin Banneker.* Illus. SERIES: Creative Minds Biographies. Lerner/Carolrhoda 1988, LB $9.95 (0-87614-331-1). 64pp. Nonfiction.

This short, accessible biography will appeal to third graders and up. Ferris has written an accurate account of Banneker's many achievements, yet readers will be left with the feeling that his life was, in reality, quite bleak. Children will be intrigued to learn that Banneker's grandmother was banished from England as a young girl for spilling a bucket of milk and sent to the colonies to work as an indentured servant. (Oddly, Ferris does not mention the commonly accepted notion that Banneker's grandfather was an African prince.) What comes through most vividly is the solitary quality of Banneker's life. The occasional full-page watercolor washes are in black and white, adding to the desolate feeling. At the end of the book is an appendix with four facts unrelated to the text, including a math problem for students to decipher.

For older and more sophisticated readers, Kevin Conley has written *Benjamin Banneker: Scientist and Mathematician* (Chelsea House, 1990). It is a shame that the most gripping Banneker biography for upper elementary students is out of print. This is Claude Lewis's *Benjamin Banneker: The Man Who Saved Washington* (McGraw-Hill, 1970). Nonetheless, because the revolutionary era and inventors are part of the elementary school curriculum, library media centers should make an effort to include materials on Banneker. A.H.

Greenfield, Eloise. *Nathaniel Talking.*
See entry 9, Grades PS–3.

31   Hamilton, Virginia. *The People Could Fly: American Black Folktales.* Also available as a cassette tape, narrated by James Earl Jones and Virginia Hamilton. Illus. by Leo and Diane Dillon. Knopf 1985, LB $15.99 (0-394-96925-1). 192pp. Nonfiction.

Many fine adaptations of African-American folktales have been published recently. Even so, this is one of the finest. Award-winning author Hamilton has adapted these stories in a brisk style that makes them especially accessible to young readers. In fact, her use of short, simple sentences should spark the interest of children who have trouble "getting into" a book. Written in a clear, modified English, with an emphasis upon representing speech patterns (without excessive reliance upon dialect) and onomatopoeic sounds, this collection is also an excellent choice for reading aloud. Teachers can read selections exactly as they are written and avoid the dilemma of whether to use dialect.

The book is divided into sections on animal stories, supernatural stories (a favorite of kids, who enjoy scary stories), and other categories. A story from the section on slave tales of freedom gives the book its title. The story tells of some slaves' magical disappearance from the cotton fields of a cruel plantation owner; it can be interpreted on many levels. After each story, Hamilton notes the source, the context in the slave psyche, the social context, and other relevant information.

Leo and Diane Dillon's black-and-white illustrations are bold, yet fanciful. They appear every few pages. Wide margins add to the text's accessibility to young readers. A cassette tape of the stories, read by the inimitable James Earl Jones, is available, and slower readers would be well served to listen to the tape as they read the book. A.H.

32   Hancock, Sibyl. *Famous Firsts of Black Americans.* Illus. by Shelton Miles. Pelican 1983, HB $10.95 (0-88289-240-1). 128pp. Nonfiction.

This small, slender volume includes one- to two-page biographies of 20 black Americans who are well-known to students of black history. Unfortunately, only a few of them will be familiar to the general public. Hancock has selected people from a variety of careers and arranged them in chronological order. Her first entry is the explorer Estevanico Dorantez; her last is Jackie Robinson. It is interesting that she did not include more recent black achievers and included only two women—Phillis Whitney and Marian Anderson.

The biographies are concise, objective, and written in short, simple sentences. They are accessible to fourth-grade readers, although the small print may prove intimidating. Because the language is so straightforward, this would be a better source than a children's encyclopedia for first reports. A.H.

33   Hansen, Joyce. *The Gift Giver.* Clarion 1980, HB $13.95 (0-395-29433-9); 1989, P $3.95 (0-89919-852-X). 128pp. Fiction.

The story concerns a close-knit group of fifth graders living in the Bronx, as told by one of their members, Doris. Through the strength of his personality, Sherman is the natural leader of the group. None of the children is particularly interested in school; their lives revolve around the playground and the apartment building stoop. The dynamics of the group change when Amir, the new kid on the block, quietly joins the gathering.

Soon afterward, Sherman runs away. The social services department has removed Sherman and his siblings from the care of their aged grandmother. Refusing to go to a foster home, Sherman hides in an abandoned basement. Amir and Doris help him; Amir reveals to them that he too is living with foster parents and has been separated from his siblings. Doris becomes closer to Amir, begins to do better in school, and helps to keep her own family together when her father loses his job. Unfortunately, Amir must leave at the end, but he has given Doris and the others the confidence to continue without him.

Hansen's novel speaks directly to the African-American community about its history, needs, and aspirations. Characters are not involved in winning the approval of white people but rather stick together in times of crisis, helping each other to survive and to grow. There are numerous descriptions of African-

American hairstyles. The kids "signify," and the neighborhood playground is the center of their lives. Most of the children live in extended-family homes, and their teachers make an effort to provide the students with a sense of their heritage and history. The wise Amir is a positive role model for the other youngsters, encouraging them to achieve more and take pride in themselves, their families, their community, and their race.   R.S.

34   Hansen, Joyce. *Yellow Bird and Me.* Clarion 1986, HB $12.95 (0-89919-335-8). 180pp. Fiction.

In this sequel to *The Gift Giver*, Amir has just left Doris for a group home, and she grieves for her best friend. She is not the only one who misses Amir. James, known as Yellow Bird, has been tutored by Amir, and now Yellow Bird wants Doris to tutor him. The class clown, Yellow Bird tries out for a drama club, but the teacher prohibits him from joining because of his behavior. He runs away from school and is punished.

Urged by Amir, with whom she corresponds, Doris agrees to tutor Yellow Bird. He tries hard and takes his studies seriously with her, but a learning disability makes it hard for him to read or write. His teacher accuses him of cheating, and when he escapes from school again, she sends him to a class for the developmentally disabled. There, he is unhappy and out of control. The drama teacher sees him and offers him a major part in the play; with Doris's help, he is the star.

Although the setting for the novel is an urban area and the characters are African American, the story is a universal one, and therefore the book should be enjoyed by most older elementary-age youngsters. It portrays learning-disabled children sympathetically and will help both teachers and students replace ignorance and prejudice with understanding. Many African Americans believe they are disproportionately victimized by misdiagnoses and are tracked into developmentally disabled classes rather than receiving help for specific learning disabilities.

The book also provides an insightful slice of life of the black community. The barber shop and the beauty parlor (where Doris works despite her parents' prohibition) are central to neighborhood cohesiveness, recreation, and information. Hairstyling is a bone of contention and an issue of concern within the black community.   R.S.

Harris, Joel Chandler. *Jump! The Adventures of Brer Rabbit.*
See entry 11, Grades PS–3.

35   Haskins, James, and Kathleen Benson. *Space Challenger: The Story of Guion Bluford.* Illus. with photos. SERIES: Trailblazers. Lerner/Carolrhoda 1984, HB $9.95 (0-87614-259-5). 64pp. Nonfiction.

This biography is important for its subject area, but it is a solid work also. The book is slender, with a 12-page center section of color photos. The print is large and the margins wide, but the vocabulary and sentence structure make it difficult for some elementary-age readers. To assist the age group that is this book's principal audience, the authors have provided a 29-word glossary.

Children will find here both African-American and space flight history, as well as Bluford's life story. Another plus is that the authors mention women pilots and astronauts. Those too young to decipher the text will enjoy the colorful photos of the astronauts floating and working in the space shuttle. An index is included.   R.H.

36   Hudson, Wade, and Valerie Wilson Wesley. *Afro-Bets Book of Black Heroes from A to Z: An Introduction to Important Black Achievers for Young Readers.* Just Us Books 1988, P $7.95 (0-940975-02-5). 53pp. Nonfiction.

This oversize paperback lists 50 black, but not necessarily black-American, heroes in alphabetical order. Each is accompanied by a black-and-white photograph or picture and an upbeat biography of approximately 200 words. For readers familiar with some of these biographees' lives, the breezy tone of the text may be disconcerting. The book does exactly as the subtitle states—it introduces role models. For a more complete presentation, students must look elsewhere.

The Afro-Americans chosen for inclusion are a surprising mix of famous persons such as King, and less famous—with a few total surprises, such as Leslie Uggams. It is as though the authors picked their own personal favorites, with little regard for historical importance. This is a refreshing approach, but readers will be relieved to know that the publisher promises more volumes.

This new and small press is an important one for librarians to know. From the few books they have published it is clear that their mission is to enhance Afro-American children's self-esteem by building racial pride and an appreciation for their African heritage.

Afro-Bets are cartoon drawings of black children whose bodies form letters and numbers. In this title they are used to spell out each biographee's name. All books published by this press are worthy of purchase.   A.H.

37   Lester, Julius. *The Tales of Uncle Remus: The Adventures of Brer Rabbit.* Illus. by Jerry Pinkney. Dutton/Dial 1987, LB $16.89 (0-8037-0272-8). 176pp. Nonfiction.

This book and its sequel, *More Tales of Uncle Remus: Further Adventures of Brer Rabbit, His Friends, Enemies, and Others*, are two of several new adaptations of the folktales originally collected by Joel Chandler Harris. Harris's invention of the "contented slave," Uncle Remus, who told stories to a white plantation child, and his attempt to duplicate black speech exactly as he heard it make the original collection not only difficult to read but also offensive. Thus, Lester's adaptation is a welcome addition to African-American literature.

Lester mixes standard English and southern black English in a pleasing combination. He also purposefully switches tenses and makes occasional references to such contemporary phenomena as shopping malls and television. All of these devices bring the stories interestingly up to date while making them sound authentic. Above all, they are fun to read aloud, and their presentation encourages readers to "talk" them and ad lib instead of reading them exactly as they are written. And Lester is right. What better way is there to understand and teach about the oral tradition in African-American culture than to be a part of it?

Jerry Pinkney's colorful watercolor illustrations are as lively and humorous as the stories they enhance. This book and its companion have won too many honors and accolades to list. They are a necessary part of any library collection serving children.   A.H.

38   Levine, Ellen. *If You Traveled on the Underground Railroad.* Illus. by Richard Williams. Scholastic 1988, P $2.95 (0-590-40556-X). 64pp. Nonfiction.

This inexpensive paperback offers a wealth of historically accurate information. Levine uses a question-and-answer format, with one question per single page or double-page spread. She packs a great deal of information in simply written answers. There are approximately 30 questions about what the Underground Railroad was, how it worked, and what life was like under slavery. Levine credits both blacks and whites with helping on the railroad; too many books credit only benevolent whites, which is untrue and patronizing. The illustrations appear to be brown pencil sketches. Located in the margins of every page, the sketches enhance the text and, along with the wide margins, create a visually welcoming read for third grade and up.   A.H.

Lowery, Linda. *Martin Luther King Day.*
See entry 17, Grades PS–3.

Mattox, Cheryl Warren, ed. *Shake It to the One That You Love the Best: Play Songs and Lullabies from Black Musical Traditions.*
See entry 19, Grades PS–3.

39   Meltzer, Milton. *Mary McLeod Bethune: Voice of Black Hope.* Illus. by Stephen Marchesi. SERIES: Women of Our Time. Viking 1987, LB $10.95 (0-670-80744-3); Penguin/Puffin 1988, P $3.95 (0-14-032219-1). 64pp. Nonfiction.

Meltzer has presented a concise, accurate biography of one of the nation's great educators. It touches upon the highlights of her life, though more anecdotes and quotes from Bethune herself would have given it a warmer, more personal quality. The author does include one fine remembrance of Bethune by poet Langston Hughes, who, during the Depression, received room and board in exchange for reading his poems to the students at Bethune-Cookman College.

There are several other biographies of Bethune available. The easiest to read is Eloise Greenfield's *Mary McLeod Bethune* (HarperCollins, 1977), which is published in picture book format. Patricia McKissack's *Mary McLeod Bethune: A Great American Educator* (Childrens Press, 1985) is more appropriate for middle school readers.   A.H.

40   Miles, Betty. *Sink or Swim.* Knopf 1986, LB $11.99 (0-394-95515-3); Avon 1987, P $2.75 (0-380-69913-3). 198pp. Fiction.

Eleven-year-old B.J. Baxter is waiting with his mother and several other black families for the bus that will take the children from New York City to rural New Hampshire as part of a two-week Fresh Air program. Understandably, B.J. is nervous. When he arrives in New Hampshire, he meets the Robertses, the white family that is his host. He has to get used to an entirely new way of life, but he fits in easily with the help of the Roberts children and their many animals. As time passes, B.J. learns to swim, makes raspberry jam, takes care of the animals, builds a rabbit hutch, picks corn, and goes camping. The members of the all-white community give him a warm welcome wherever he goes.

This is a story about a kinder, gentler, charming America that is seldom dealt with in books about black characters. It will appeal to a general audience, as the focus is on how white people in rural New Hampshire work and play, as seen through the eyes of an inner-city visitor. The book stresses that, although people may have different ways of speaking, skin colors, and socioeconomic status, it is how we treat each other that really counts. Respect for differences and awareness of our underlying humanity are crucial to building bridges and living together in a racially and culturally diverse society.   R.S.

41   Moore, Emily. *Whose Side Are You On?* Farrar, Straus & Giroux 1988, HB $11.95 (0-374-38409-6). 128pp. Fiction.

Sixth grader Barbra has just failed math, and her teacher has assigned classmate T.J. Brodie to be her tutor. For years, T.J. has pestered her, and she considers being grounded from her best friend's birthday party just to avoid working with him. Yet under T.J.'s tutelage she finally begins not only to understand math but also to like the rebellious youngster who lives alone with his frail grandfather. Then T.J. disappears, and Barbra learns he is in a juvenile home. She blames the grandfather and mounts a protest, but when she learns the truth—that T.J. has run away—she is ashamed of herself. Nonetheless, her experience of standing up for T.J. and for another classmate—the overweight, unpopular Kim—teaches her much about herself and about the value of friendship.

Moore develops her story well, so that Barbra's quick rush to activism and her subsequent disillusionment are credible. She does not give up acting on her convictions, but she has learned to do so in a constructive way. Positive adult role models abound in this novel, from Barbra's high-powered professional mother to Ms. Stone, the strict teacher who provides her students with the cultural information and social and academic skills important for building self-esteem. The novel is set in a middle-class neighborhood of Harlem, and the author makes it clear that not all of that area is a drug-infested slum. In fact, her Harlem is rich in cultural resources, from the playground where the children gather to the library that is named for the noted African-American poet Countee Cullen.   L.M-L.

42   Myers, Walter Dean. *Me, Mop, and the Moondance Kid.* Delacorte 1988, HB $13.95 (0-440-50065-6). 128pp. Fiction.

Moondance and his older brother T.J. have just been adopted, so they have been separated from their best friend, Mop, a little girl who is still living in the Dominican Academy, an orphanage and school in a city somewhere in New Jersey.

Jim and Marla Kennedy have visited the orphanage several times, and Mop thinks they are looking her over. The Kennedys are the coaches of the Elks, the Little League team that Moodance and T.J. have just joined. Mop believes that if she shows the Kennedys what a good ball player she is, her adoption will be ensured. The academy's imminent closing increases the pressure on her.

Mop gets assistance from some unlikely sources—Peaches, a wino who says he played baseball during the time of Ty Cobb, and Sister Carmelita, a former star pitcher in Little League. The Elks must confront their rivals, the Eagles, known for their poor sportsmanship. In the meantime, Peaches helps foil an attempted robbery of Sister Carmelita. The team wins, Peaches gets a regular job, and the Kennedys adopt Mop.

The ethnic backgrounds of the characters are never mentioned in the mostly humorous, lighthearted text. The illustrations dispersed throughout indicate which characters are black or white; black characters also use modified black speech or dialect. The neighborhood in which the story takes place is a mainstream, middle-class, peacefully integrated area. The homeless alcoholic gets a janitor's job and is quickly rehabilitated. Relationships are interracial and harmonious. Rather, friction occurs between boys and girls, skilled and nonskilled athletes, and high-achieving adults and children. Women are given great prominence and serve as positive role models. Mop is a star catcher, T.J.'s and Moondance's adoptive mother works outside the home, the coach of the Elks is a woman, and Sister Carmelita was once a champion pitcher.   R.S.

43   Myers, Walter Dean. ***Scorpions.*** HarperCollins 1988, LB $12.89 (0-06-024365-1); 1990 P $2.95 (0-06-447066-0). 216pp. Fiction.

Twelve-year-old Jamal Hicks's life changes forever when he takes over leadership of his older brother's gang, the Scorpions, and obtains a gun. Failing in school and burdened with home responsibilities, the well-meaning but overwhelmed youngster has been asked by his imprisoned brother, Randy, to lead the gang so that its profits from drug dealing can be used to finance Randy's appeal. Jamal's best friend, Tito, discourages him from joining, but on seeing that Jamal is leaning toward the gang, Tito joins, too, in order to protect his friend. The gun has powers beyond Jamal's wildest dreams. He uses it to intimidate a bully at school, and the gang members at first obey, but Jamal is clearly in over his head. Rivals in the gang threaten him, and Randy is almost killed in prison. Tito saves his desperate friend, but he is almost destroyed in the process, and the two must separate forever.

In what is in many ways his bleakest novel, Myers portrays with great poignancy a youngster whose life is out of control. There is much irony in Jamal's situation. For instance, school officials force him to take psychoactive drugs without his full knowledge or understanding in order to control his occasionally disruptive classroom behavior. Yet Jamal is not a passive victim; in fact, he struggles against his fate. Trying to avoid the gang, he takes a job, but one of the gang members causes him to be fired. Dramatic action, tight plotting, and sharp, believable dialogue will attract readers at all ability levels. Myers's portrayal of the urban environment is realistic—he neither sensationalizes his characters' world to attract readers nor softens the reality to make it palatable. With more and more inner-city teenagers carrying guns, this powerful novel shows how reliance upon violent, seemingly easy solutions leads to far bigger problems.   L.M-L.

44   Palcovar, Jane. ***Harriet Tubman.*** Illus. by Alex Bloch. SERIES: What Was It Like? Childrens Pr. 1988, LB $8.95 (0-516-09554-4). 48pp. Nonfiction.

Considering how shoddy this small book appears, one is surprised to find that the biographical facts are accurate. The text begins on the verso of the title page, and 1/4-inch margins make each page appear quite crowded. Occasionally, the text is swallowed in the binding. Infrequent black-and-white illustrations, clumsily executed and not always in concert with the text, add to the book's cheap look.

Still, the book has a gimmick that just might lure fiction lovers into reading biographies: it is written as a first-person narrative. Reluctant readers love the ease with which they can devour these intimately written tales. The drawback, of course, is that the personality that comes through may be nothing like that of the real Harriet Tubman. Nevertheless, this is a short, fast-paced, accurate account of her life. There is no index, bibliography, or table of contents, and the book seems designed to be read in one marathon reading, as there are no chapters. A chronology is included. This series also contains a biography of Jackie Robinson.   A.H.

45   Patrick, Deane. *Martin Luther King, Jr.* Illus. with photos. SERIES: First Books. Franklin Watts 1990, LB $10.90 (0-531-10892-9). 64pp. Nonfiction.

This sturdy, attractively designed volume is a choice King biography for elementary school students who need a clear and sequential reporting about his life. The format of short chapters, each divided into several sections, helps children find specific information and understand what they are reading. These minisections are separated by a space, and each is preceded by bold print summarizing in two or three words what the sparse text will discuss.

The print is large and strong, the margins ample. It is a visually pleasing book and one that children will feel confident using. Photographs, both in color and in black and white, are placed throughout but never give the book a cluttered appearance. The text is both to the point and interesting. It does an excellent job of presenting King in a human way, in words young students will understand, and, because of this, it will be far more useful for school reports than a children's encyclopedia. Highlights of King's life and the civil rights movement are included. An index, also appropriate for beginning researchers, concludes the book.   A.H.

46   Pelz, Ruth. *Black Heroes of the Wild West.* Illus. by Leandro Della Piano. Open Hand 1990, HB $9.95 (0-940880-25-3); P $5.95 (0-940880-26-1). 54pp. Nonfiction.

This small book, written for fourth grade and up, is composed of nine short stories about both men and women. Better known among them are explorers Estevan and Jean-Baptiste Point DuSable, frontiersman James Beckwourth, and cowboy Bill Pickett. The inclusion of Estevan and DuSable may be useful to educators intent on counterbalancing the emphasis upon Columbus's "discovery" of the New World.

Pelz's stories are not riveting, but the title fills a need. As of 1990, there were no other recently published works of nonfiction on the black West for this reading level. The black-and-white watercolor-wash illustrations have a naive quality that, for the most part, gives them dignity and beauty. Librarians who want to present their patrons with books that reflect our pluralistic society will be happy to learn about this small publishing house.   A.H.

47   Tate, Eleanora E. *The Secret of Gumbo Grove.* Franklin Watts 1987, HB $11.95 (0-531-10298-X); Bantam 1988, P $2.95 (0-553-27226-8). 266pp. Fiction.

Gumbo Grove is a beach town in South Carolina, where blacks, regardless of their abilities, work at menial jobs serving the white tourists. Eleven-year-old Raisin has learned in school that blacks never did anything "worth talking about." But when Raisin volunteers to help elderly Miss Effie clean up the cemetery behind the old New Africa No. 1 Missionary Baptist Church, she discovers some secrets, not the least of which is that the town's founder was a black man who is now buried in that weed-choked cemetery. Her efforts attract the ire of Miz Aussie Skipper, another town elder who has accepted favors from whites to keep fellow blacks in line. Other community members do not want to be reminded of their ancestors, whether they be slaves, criminals, or successful landowners who were forced off their property by the whites after Reconstruction.

As a mystery, the novel is somewhat slow moving, with the ending fairly obvious by the middle of the book. However, it provides an intimate and well-drawn portrait of a small southern town, with all the conflicts, intrigues, and general gossip coming to the surface. Raisin is a multidimensional character; she can be shrill and headstrong as well as generous, determined, and resourceful. Other characters—particularly her parents, her sister Hattie, and the neighborhood loser, Big Boy—are equally fleshed out. Tate sends black readers a clear message about the importance of uncovering one's history, but she does so through characters who are realistic and appealing. This book is most appropriate for better readers in the upper elementary grades.   L.M-L.

48   Taylor, Mildred D. *The Friendship.* Illus. by Max Ginsburg. Dutton/Dial 1987, LB $11.89 (0-8037-0418-6); Bantam (published along with *The Gold Cadillac*) 1989, P $2.75 (0-553-15765-5). 56pp. Fiction.

This novel presents a single incident experienced by the four Logan children, whose story has been told in several novels for young adult and middle-grade readers. In this novel, the four children are sent to buy aspirin at Wallace's general store, where 6-year-old Little Man is insulted by the Wallace sons. As they are leaving, a retired sharecropper, Mr. Tom Bee, enters the store and is also insulted by the sons, who refuse to extend him credit. He asks to see their father, whom he calls by his first name. John Wallace appears, sells Mr. Tom Bee what he wants, then admonishes him to stop seeking him out and speaking to him without using the formal term Mister.

Mr. Tom Bee refuses. As he tells the children, he had once saved the young John Wallace from drowning; the orphaned Wallace even lived with him for a while. The boy assured Bee they would always be friends and he could always call him John. But now Wallace has betrayed the friendship, and when Mr. Tom Bee returns to the store for tobacco, Wallace shoots him in the leg. Still, Mr. Tom Bee will not quit calling him John.

The plot is absolutely spellbinding, and at only 53 pages the story could be used as a read-aloud. Yet it should be used with caution. Although the children are of grade school age, the author's portrayal of crushing racial oppression and intolerance may make this more appropriate for older readers. True to the state of affairs at the time, the book is full of savage racial slurs and stereotypes expressed by the white characters. The atmosphere of the rural South is hot and suffocating, with tension building from the first page. Older elementary students need to be prepared with information about the state of race relations in the South before the civil rights movement. Furthermore, relating the story of Mr. Tom Bee's singular stance against betrayal and oppression to the struggle of blacks against the South African government can place the events in a context that today's youngsters can more readily understand. The novel may also be used to show how peer group expectations often reinforce racism and violence against innocent people.

Another book about the Logan children for this age group is *Song of the Trees* (1975).

R.S.

49   Taylor, Mildred D. ***The Gold Cadillac.*** Illus. by Michael Hays. Dutton/Dial 1987, LB $11.89 (0-8037-0343-0); Bantam (published along with *The Friendship*) 1989, P $2.75 (0-553-15765-6). 48pp. Fiction.

In Ohio, Wilma's and 'lois's upwardly mobile black family is almost torn apart when their father buys a gold Cadillac. Whereas their father is pleased with his symbol of success, their mother refuses even to ride in the car. She wants to save money for a larger house in a nicer neighborhood. Failing to gain his wife's adulation, Father decides to visit his parents in Mississippi. Since a black man driving alone in the South with such a fancy car risks all sorts of harassment, his family and relatives offer to accompany him. Their festive caravan begins to lose steam once they enter the South, a fearsome place where blacks cannot eat in restaurants, sleep in hotels, or speak their mind to a white person. The Cadillac gets separated from the other cars in the caravan during a traffic jam, and shortly thereafter Father is arrested. The family is too frightened to continue the trip in the Cadillac, so they backtrack to Memphis and borrow a less ostentatious car from relatives there. Upon their return to Ohio, Father sells the Cadillac and applies the money to a new house.

During World War II, thousands of African Americans left the South to find employment in northern factories. Although discrimination existed, their opportunities for upward mobility were still many times better than in the South. The Cadillac became a symbol of newfound success, more visible than the new home on which the mother in this novel has set her hopes. The differences in their perceptions lead to the family's frightening journey. That plot device also allows readers to experience the brutal, humiliating, and monolithic system of legal segregation in the era of Jim Crow. This was nothing less than an American version of apartheid, and the novel portrays it so powerfully that readers will not forget one of the darker moments of their country's history. Finally, the story has a lot to say about family values. Black success is more truly symbolized by the family's achievements and level of contentment than by the outward trappings of the well-to-do.

R.S.

50   Turner, Glennette Tilley. ***Take a Walk in Their Shoes.*** Illus. by Elton C. Fox. Dutton/Cobblehill 1989, HB $14.95 (0-525-65006-7). 174pp. Nonfiction.

This collective biography is valuable because it includes African Americans seldom presented for young readers yet whose achievements would interest them. Notable among these are inventor of the automatic traffic light and gas mask Garrett Morgan, pitcher Leroy "Satchel" Paige, and tireless human rights crusader Ida B. Wells. Altogether there are 14 entries, and only 4 of these are of better-known African-American heroes. Each entry is less than ten pages long and will be accessible to most older elementary and middle school readers. Each biography is followed by a short play about the biographee. These skits involve 2 to 15 students and may be used for classroom performance without the author's permission.

Unfortunately, the skits, coupled with occasional pencil illustrations, detract from this title. Both are of amateurish quality and raise the price of the book. The plays lack interest and pizzazz and add no information about the biographee.

For schools and libraries looking for plays about African Americans, three very good ones have been written, though only one is still in print. It is *Langston: A Play* (Delacorte, 1982), written by actor Ossie Davis about the poet Langston Hughes. Davis is also the author of the exciting *Escape to Freedom: A Play About Young Frederick Douglass* (Viking, 1976, o.p.). Alice Childress has authored *When the Rattlesnake Sounds* (Coward, McCann, 1975, o.p.), a short play about Harriet Tubman, to be performed by three women. This latter title would be a good choice for fifth grade through high school, although the religious references may make it more appropriate for churches and religious schools than for public schools.   A.H.

51   Walter, Mildred Pitts. *Have a Happy.* Illus. by Carole Byard. Lothrop, Lee & Shepard 1989, HB $10.95 (0-688-06923-1). 106pp. Fiction.

In the life of a child, the second most anticipated day of the year is the birthday. Unfortunately for Chris, his birthday falls on the most anticipated day—Christmas. Chris, an 11-year-old black youth, feels doubly cheated this year because his father has been out of work for 18 months. Chris would like a bicycle for a present, for then he can get a paper route and contribute to the family finances.

After Christmas, Chris's family dresses in traditional African garb and gathers at an uncle's house for the celebration of the African-American holiday known as Kwanzaa. Each day of the Kwanzaa is represented by a different principle. On the fourth day, celebrating the "Ujama," the principle of cooperative economics, Chris gets his bike, which the entire family has chipped in to buy. When Chris applies for the paper route, he discovers serendipitously that the district manager's position is vacant too. However, his dad would need $300 to secure a bond in order to get the position. Chris offers to sell his bicycle, but, on the last day of the Kwanzaa, representing "faith," his father lands the job and does not have to post the bond.

The story succeeds in presenting its theme—that the keys for a black child's growth are family ties and a connection to one's rich African heritage. Being able to rely on an extended network of relatives and African forebears can bring a child through any crisis, emotional or financial. The desperation of underemployment that so many black males experience and the possibility of family dissolution are well illustrated here. Even so, the father does not abandon his family. The Kwanzaa and its principles symbolize and celebrate the means by which African-American families survived in the face of four hundred years of obstacles. African traditions, food, clothing, and language are explored, and the treatment of various celebrations, all occurring at the same time, show how African-American culture draws upon the traditions of many different places where black people have lived.   R.S.

52   Walter, Mildred Pitts. *Justin and the Best Biscuits in the World.* Illus. by Catherine Stock. Lothrop, Lee & Shepard 1986, HB $11.95 (0-688-06645-3); Knopf 1990, P $3.25 (0-679-80346-7). 128pp. Fiction.

Ten-year-old Justin Ward lives with his widowed mother and two bossy sisters. His unwillingness to clean his room results in his being grounded; his attempts at cooking end in disaster. When his grandfather visits and sees him sitting amidst the rubble in his room, the older man invites Justin to stay with him for the summer on his ranch in Missouri. Justin learns more about the ranch and about the history of black cowboys after the Civil War. Moreover, he learns to make his bed, fold his clothes, and cook. He finally attends a rodeo, where Grandpa Ward wins a prize for his biscuits, and Justin himself wins a handful of ribbons and a cowboy hat.

This is a fine example of a story that can be enjoyed by all ethnic groups while providing African-American youngsters with a sense of history, pride, and empowerment. Grandpa Ward expresses this best when he tells Justin why their ancestors moved to Missouri: "You must know where you've come from in order to find the way to where you want to go." Facing odds as great or greater than anything encountered today, the ancestors of contemporary African Americans worked hard and prospered.

On the surface, this is a coming-of-age tale. A young, fatherless boy is taken under the wing of a surrogate father, who helps him overcome obstacles and mature into manhood. What makes this book unique is that the boy does not overcome a bully or score a touchdown; his maturation is in the form of domestic accomplishments. It is manly to be self-sufficient on the homefront; washing, cleaning, and cooking are not gender-based activities. By giving Justin a racial and family foundation for meeting challenges and achieving an objective, Grandpa Ward provides a role model for young readers as well.   R.S.

Webb, Sheyann, and Rachel West Nelson. ***Selma, Lord, Selma: Girlhood Memories of the Civil Rights Days.***
See entry 127, Grades 10–12.

53   Wilson, Johnniece Marshall. ***Robin on His Own.*** Scholastic 1990, HB $12.95 (0-590-41813-0). 154pp. Fiction.

Robin's mother has just died after a long illness, and it seems his whole world is coming apart. Aunt Belle, who stayed with him during his mother's final illness and is still taking care of him, has announced that she is getting married and moving from their home near Pittsburgh to Wheeling, West Virginia. Robin's father, a jazz musician, is playing more and more gigs out of town and is now talking about selling their house. Even though Robin has his pets—Watusi the cat and Pollymae the parakeet—and his friends, he is bored, lonely, sad, and scared. At the end of a long summer, as his father is packing to move out, Robin tries to run away, but, unwilling to leave his animals behind, he doesn't get very far and almost loses his life in the process.

Wilson's story rings true. Robin's grief is believable and compelling, as is his attachment to the animals who seem to be the only friends who understand and are always there. Wilson also skillfully portrays the adults who are so caught up in their grief and their own lives that they fail to notice Robin's increasing sadness. She captures the boredom of a summer with nothing to do almost too well; parts of the story move slowly and appear more to provide background information than to move the plot along. Nonetheless, this is a good book for children who are experiencing major upheavals in their lives and who, like Robin, may have no one but their pets to trust. The audience for this novel is universal. Besides Aunt Belle's role in the extended family, the wedding at the St. James AME church, and some turns of speech, there is little here that is uniquely African American. Wilson is also the author of *Oh, Brother* (Scholastic,

1988), which is a lighthearted treatment of sibling rivalry for middle grade readers. L.M-L.

54   Yarborough, Camille. *The Shimmershine Queens.* Putnam 1989, HB $13.95 (0-399-21465-8). 142pp. Fiction.

Fifth grader Angie's father has just moved out, and her 90-year-old cousin Seatta is visiting from Alabama. The young girl is enthralled by her cousin's stories of slavery and resistance. According to Cousin Seatta, slaves survived by dreaming about education and a better life; when they failed to dream and instead accepted white stereotypes of themselves, then family dissolution, violence, and crime ensued. Seatta urges Angie to dream (the "get-up gift") and to strive for the realization of her dreams (the "shimmershine").

All around her, Angie sees the results of negativism and hopelessness. Her building is filthy and dangerous. Her depressed mother sleeps all the time. Bullies regularly disrupt her class in school. Angie convinces her friend, Michelle, to use the get-up gift to shine in school, but their rowdy classmates taunt them. The balance changes when Ms. Collier, an African-American performing artist, arrives to teach a dance and drama workshop. She refuses to be driven out by misbehavior, and she organizes the children to put on a play set in West Africa and dealing with the slave trade. Angie is selected as the narrator, but deteriorating conditions at home threaten her participation. She loses self-esteem and is caught shoplifting. Finally, her mother steps in, convincing Angie to honor her commitment and perform in the play.

What separates this book from others set in the inner city is the author's placement of urban pathologies in the context of slavery's legacy. Seatta's first-chapter speech sets the tone, emphasizing the importance of African and African-American history to the self-esteem of African-American youngsters. Aimed at a black audience primarily, this book reproduces black speech and contains references to skin color, grades of hair, and other racially based physical characteristics, issues of which black readers are more cognizant. Many readers will identify with life in the housing project and in inner-city schools, but the author ultimately offers hope and guidance to her young audience.   R.S.

GRADES 7–9

55   Altman, Susan. *Extraordinary Black Americans: From Colonial to Contemporary Times.* Illus. with photos. Childrens Pr. 1989, LB $30.60 (0-516-00581-2). 240pp. Nonfiction.

This title includes one- to two-page profiles of 85 African Americans well-known enough to be assigned as school reports but not necessarily found in encyclopedias. Included are inventors, rights activists, scientists, educators, explorers, musicians, writers, and colonial and revolutionary era heroes. No contemporary entertainers and only four professional athletes are included. The biographies are in chronological order. An index allows readers to quickly locate specific entries. Occasionally there is an entry on a group of people or an event important in Afro-American history, such as the Little Rock Nine, the Emancipation Proclamation, or King's "I Have a Dream" speech. These entries increase the book's value as a resource.

Besides the index there are footnotes and a selected bibliography. The bibliography serves to identify the author's sources, and librarians should note that most of the books are too difficult for children.

The writing is direct and interesting. Although the biographies appear to be historically accurate, their brevity does not allow for in-depth or well-balanced accounts of the subjects' lives. Black-and-white photographs or portraits accompany most entries, and a gray, African-motif border design enhances the book's overall appearance.

As with any collective biography, there are entries one wishes were included but were not—a good reason to purchase several titles of this type. Because this book will be most heavily used during Black History Month (February), librarians may want to purchase two so that one is available for reference use during that time. To assign a collection's only copy to the reference shelf would limit its availability, and children need ample opportunity to meet these African Americans.

A.H.

Bode, Janet. *Different Worlds: Interracial and Cross Cultural Dating.*
See entry 103, Grades 10–12.

56   Brooks, Bruce. *The Moves Make the Man.* HarperCollins 1984, LB $13.89 (0-06-020698-5); P $2.95 (0-06-447022-9). 280pp. Fiction.

Thirteen-year-old Jerome excels at both his studies and basketball. His life changes when the courts order the Wilmington, North Carolina, schools to desegregate, and he is the only black child eligible to enter the all-white middle school. Soon afterward, his mother is injured in a freak accident (his father had been killed in an accident years earlier), and Jerome enrolls in a cooking class so he can help his two older brothers at home. There he meets Bix, a troubled white youngster who is the only other boy in the class. A racist basketball coach refuses to let Jerome join the team, so he practices his "moves" on a court in the forest. He sees Bix on the court one evening and tries to teach him the game, but Bix refuses, for seemingly irrational reasons, to learn the all-important fakes. Later, Jerome learns some reasons for Bix's odd behavior—his mother is in a mental institution, and his stepfather is cold and unsupportive. Ultimately, Jerome accompanies Bix to see his mother in the hospital. After enduring racist insults at a lunch counter along the way, Jerome watches in horror as Bix runs away after his mother fails to recognize him.

Anyone who loves baseball or basketball will enjoy the intricate descriptions of these sports. Jerome is a strong and likable youngster, and his grasp and account of the events in his life are rendered with a sophistication beyond his years. His voice lacks bitterness despite the harshness of his life; he views adults, especially white adults, as well-meaning but bumbling incompetents. However, the book is full of demeaning racist slurs, almost all of them directed at the black characters. Most are used by one black character against another, in situations that are often inappropriate. Events such as being left off the team and being insulted at the diner seem to occur in a vacuum, without having much impact upon Jerome. His single-parent home has an idyllic setting; the difficulties of raising three teenagers alone are never explored. Rather, Bix's situation and the pathology of his family receive the most treatment. Whereas black culture is described in terms of athletic prowess and inconsistent use of black speech, white culture is delved into in much greater detail. Ultimately, Jerome serves as the narrator and observer of the white boy, Bix, who is the focus of the story.

57 Brown, Kay. ***Willy's Summer Dream.*** Harcourt Brace Jovanovich/Gulliver 1990, HB $13.95 (0-15-200645-1). 132pp. Fiction.

The posters of Dr. J. and Muhammad Ali tacked to the wall of Willy's bedroom reflect the heroes of this 14-year-old Brooklyn youth. Willy, the only child of a now-single parent, is learning disabled. He has been teased unmercifully by neighborhood homeboys in his clumsy attempts to play basketball. The summer moves slowly and is painfully uneventful until the arrival of Kathleen, the beloved niece of his neighbor, Mr. Bowers. It is love at first sight for Willy, but beautiful Kathleen is several years older and maternal. She expresses her kindness and natural affection for Willy by means of a series of tutoring sessions in which his reading and comprehension skills grow. When Kathleen returns home, Willy is able to use his newfound confidence and skills to help a young boy in dire need.

This is a reflective and inspirational novel by visual artist Brown. Descriptions are vivid and tangible. Although Willy's heroes and the books Kathleen gives him reflect their African-American heritage, the themes are universal. Any youngster who has had to confront extraordinary obstacles and disappointment will find solace in Willy's plight and take courage in his triumph. This quiet love story set in the 1980s would be most appealing to junior high students.   S.P.

58 Burt, Olive. ***Black Women of Valor.*** Illus. by Paul Frame. Julian Messner 1974. 96pp. Nonfiction. o.p.

Burt presents four "less famous crusaders" in interesting biographies of approximately 20 pages each. The subjects are Juliette Derricotte, a young woman who dedicated her short life to increasing interracial understanding; Maggie Mitchell Walker, who struggled to improve women's chances of employment in traditionally male professions; Ida Wells Barnett, whose investigative reporting and activism helped to end the common and heinous practice of lynching; and Septima Poinsette Clark, an innovative educator. Occasional pencil drawings accompany each biography.

The writing style appeals to children. Though the book is ideal for middle school students, teachers and librarians will need to push it, as children often hesitate to try biographies of people with whom they are not familiar. At the end of the book Burt lists 62 other "black women of valor" and points out that "new crusaders are appearing every day among us." There is an index but no bibliography.   A.H.

59 Childress, Alice. ***A Hero Ain't Nothin' But a Sandwich.*** Avon 1973, P $2.50 (0-380-00132-2). 128pp. Fiction.

Thirteen-year-old Benjie is nodding out daily in school. He truly believes that he is not yet a heroin addict. Benjie's story, seen through the eyes of his family, friends, drug dealer, and teachers, is told in alternating chapters. The love and despair of his family weigh equally as heavily as do the disdain and indifference of his drug dealer. Nearly 20 years following publication, this young adult novel remains as fresh as it was when first published, with its distinctive cadences for each voice. Still here, 20 years later, are drugs. Crack cocaine is being mixed with heroin, Benjie's "drug of choice." Childress also tackles here the content of contemporary classroom textbooks, still a thorny issue in some school districts. Though the main character is 13, this book has attained the status of a classic young adult novel, crossing over to appeal to both junior and senior high readers. S.P.

60 Childress, Alice. ***Rainbow Jordan.*** Avon 1982, P $2.95 (0-380-58974-5). 128pp. Fiction.

Rainbow's mother, Kathy, was a teenage mother at 15. Now 29, with a 14-year-old daughter, Rainbow, she still hasn't come to terms with what it truly means to be a responsible parent. Consequently, Rainbow has been placed in the interim care of foster parents—Miss Josephine and Mr. Harold—a childless couple. The alternating chapters are the voices of Rainbow, Miss Josephine, and Kathy, three generations of women living life and struggling through love lost and diminished hope. Ultimately two generations triumph as Rainbow and Miss Josephine offer one another mutual support and respect. This story of strong women and the strength of individuals living in a foster care environment is a multidimensional portrait of many different kinds of African-American women, from the central characters to the supporting teachers and clients within Rainbow's orbit. For junior and senior high readers. S.P.

61 Darby, Jean. ***Martin Luther King, Jr.*** Illus. with photos. Lerner 1990, LB $14.95 (0-8225-4902-6). 112pp. Nonfiction.

This attractively designed biography, written for middle and high school students, has many strengths. The author credits by name some of the African-American leaders who influenced King, and readers will learn of two civil rights martyrs seldom mentioned in children's books—Emmett Till and James Meredith. Also, King's efforts to end the discrimination oppressing northern blacks is covered, and his opposition to the Vietnam War is touched upon, although no reference to it is listed in the index. Finally, of all the recently published books on this era, this title's photographs most accurately reveal the feelings of those who lived then.

Each of the ten chapters begins with the years to be covered and an appropriate quote from those years. The presentation is informative, interesting, and easy to follow. In many respects, Darby's work seems to be a model for what a book on King and the civil rights era should be. There is one problem, however. In writing about the younger black Americans who were impatient for social change and critical of King's nonviolent tactics, Darby slips into black English when she quotes their slogans. No other black figure is quoted in black English. Given the fact that the vast majority of white Americans have not yet accepted black English as a valid language, her choice may be interpreted as a means of caricaturing, and, hence, dismissing, the militants and their positions. The book concludes with an epilogue and contains a glossary and an index. A.H.

62 George, Nelson, ed. *Stop the Violence: Overcoming Self-Destruction.* Pantheon 1990, P $7.95 (0-679-72782-5). 79pp. Nonfiction.

Plaguing a number of rap music concerts in the past were incidents of violence, as spillovers of activities in local communities. Popular rap stars and the National Urban League came together to create a movement among rap music's fans to work toward positive alternatives for stemming violence at concerts and in local communities. This book is but one of the projects, which include a recording and a music video. Speaking most directly to black teenagers, this book includes lyrics and essays by rap stars; statistics; interviews; and statements from rap fans commenting upon crime, drug abuse, education, and aspirations. The message here is that youth action can make a positive impact upon local neighborhoods. Accompanying the text are copious photographs that will enhance this book's appeal.   S.P.

63 Gilman, Michael. *Matthew Henson.* Illus. with photos. SERIES: Black Americans of Achievement. Chelsea House 1988, LB $17.95 (1-55546-590-0); P $9.95 (0-7910-0207-1). 110pp. Nonfiction.

Of the recent works on Matthew Henson, this is by far the most thorough; it is an outstanding resource for middle and high school reports and projects. The book is rich in details about both Henson and the Arctic expeditions. Gilman's lively writing style will involve readers in the trips' triumphs and disasters. He effectively conveys the racism that robbed Henson of the fame and attention he so richly deserved. By using quotes and historical facts, he presents both Henson's perseverance in trying to gain recognition for his achievements and his ability to put his disappointments in perspective and get on with his life. It is ironic that for all his sensitivity to this kind of racism, the author portrays the Inuit in a patronizing manner.

All of the biographies in this series provide a chronology, a bibliography, and an index.   A.H.

64 Greenfield, Eloise, and Alesia Revis. *Alesia.* Illus. by George Ford. Putnam/Philomel 1981, HB $9.95 (0-399-20831-3). 80pp. Nonfiction.

Alesia is a real person who was partially paralyzed in a car accident when she was 9. This book is composed of her diary entries during the next eight years. Although Alesia wears a leg brace and is often confined to a wheelchair, her outlook remains optimistic. This young woman's emotional maturity is impressive.

Readers will meet an African-American teenager who, except for her inability to walk independently, is like other 17-year-olds, black and white. Her loving family and friends return her affection and accept her as she is—serene yet spunky.

Pencil drawings highlight most of the pages, and there is a center section of black-and-white photographs. The diary format and the liberal use of dialogue will appeal to young readers. While it shows what life is like for a teenager with a disability, this unusual work also helps youngsters to see the similarity of Alesia's hopes and dreams to their own.   A.H.

65   Guy, Rosa. ***The Disappearance.*** Dell 1979, P $3.25 (0-440-92064-7). 246pp. Fiction.

With his trademark toothpick dangling from the corner of his mouth, Imamu Jones looks to the world like a youthful and hardened criminal. He has just been acquitted of involvement in a robbery that ended in the murder of a local shopkeeper. Imamu's innocence has been accepted by a caring woman, Ann Aimsley, who is willing to bring him into her middle-class Brooklyn home, miles away from his neglectful alcoholic mother in Harlem. Amidst this comfortable environment with a strong father, two spoiled daughters (Gail and Perk), an eccentric tenant, and a beautiful doting godmother, Imamu begins to put down some roots. When Perk, the younger daughter, disappears, fingers point at Imamu, who, with the assistance of Gail, searches to find Perk before it is too late. This mystery sings with the rhythms of Caribbean expressions and dialect and is a page turner that will hold junior and senior high school students until the very end. This is the first in a series of Imamu Jones mysteries. *The Disappearance* is followed by *New Guys on the Block* and *And I Heard a Bird Sing.*   S.P.

66   Guy, Rosa. ***The Friends.*** Bantam 1974, P $2.95 (0-553-20595-1). 185pp. Fiction.

Fourteen-year-old Phyllisia is easy prey for Beulah and her attendant classroom buddies. She is new to the city, recently arrived from the West Indies. However, she is fortunate to have as her protector a brash though small-statured, superior, gum-popping girl, Edith Jackson. Reluctantly, Phyllisia accepts a friendship with this girl so opposite in appearance, motive, and manner from her. The Cathy family is dominated by Phyllisia's and her sister Ruby's strong-willed, proud, overbearing, and overprotective father, whose power and strength are as apparent as the beauty and fragility of the girls' dying mother. Not only is there a test of wills between the girls and their father in the new country, but there is also between the sisters a sibling rivalry and a love that are realistic and sometimes tragic.

As the circumstances of death, abandonment, poverty, riots, and an indifferent educational and social system work to separate Phyllisia and her friend Edith, the bond of friendship between these girls remains. *The Friends* is a classic story of an immigrant family striving to make the United States its home while holding fast against the perceived destructiveness of urban America. This is Guy's first book of a trilogy set in the 1960s. Unfortunately, the companion novels, *Edith Jackson* and *Ruby*, are currently out of print. A more recent work of Guy's, though one flawed by didacticism and a less-than-sympathetic protagonist, is *The Ups and Downs of Carl Davis III* (Delacorte, 1989).   S.P.

67   Haber, Louis. ***Black Pioneers of Science and Invention.*** Illus. with photos. Harcourt Brace Jovanovich 1970, HB $15.95 (0-15-208565-3). 192pp. Nonfiction.

This collective biography will be useful to teachers as well as to students. Featured are 14 scientists and inventors whose careers have been fairly well documented. Each is featured in a 10- to 20-page chapter that discusses inventions in addition to the discrimination and other obstacles each inventor encountered. Haber's research appears scrupulous. Footnotes appear at the bottom of the page, and there is a separate bibliography for each biographee. Photocopies of correspondence, inventions, designs, and patents accompany many entries.

Besides George Washington Carver and Benjamin Banneker, inventors include Garrett Morgan (traffic light and gas mask), Percy Julian (synthetic cortisone), Lewis Latimer (electric light), Charles Drew (blood bank), and Daniel Hale Williams (open heart surgery). As with any black history, this information will undoubtedly be eye-opening to most readers. An index is included.

A.H.

68   Hamilton, Virginia. ***Anthony Burns: The Defeat and Triumph of a Fugitive Slave.*** Knopf 1988, LB $12.99 (0-394-98185-5). 192pp. Nonfiction.

Burns was a runaway slave who was caught and jailed in Boston in 1854. Thousands of abolitionists, both black and white, rushed to his aid, making this a *cause célèbre* of the decade. Despite free legal defense, Burns lost his case under the Fugitive Slave Act of 1850 and was returned to the South, where he was continually brutalized. After northerners purchased his freedom, Burns attended Oberlin College and became a minister, only to die at the age of 28.

Author Hamilton has won many accolades for her ability to write a factual historical account in such a creative, evocative way. Her eloquence portrays better than any other book the horror faced by slave families and their children's total bewilderment. She also conveys the various ways slaves coped with that "peculiar institution" and how they retained many aspects of their African heritage. Ironically, her enormous literary ability will cost this book readers. Shifts from past to present tense (as Burns's own thoughts in prison are recounted) and other creative twists will confuse those who are not able readers. Foreseeing this, Hamilton has included a five-page list of personages and an epilogue, as well as selections from the Fugitive Slave Act. There are a bibliography and an index. A.H.

69   Hamilton, Virginia. ***A Little Love.*** Putnam/Philomel 1984, HB $12.95 (0-399-21046-6). 207pp. Fiction.

Bombs are ticking away inside Sheema's head. Slow in school, overweight, frequently withdrawn and depressed, the vocational high school student has only her friend Forrest to lean on. Her guardian grandparents, Granmom and Granpop, are both elderly and now showing the beginning stages of senility. Sheema finds herself thinking more and more of her father, whom she has never seen. It is apparent that Sheema, who takes pride in her accomplishments in cooking and presentation in her food service classes, has inherited these creative skills from her father, who was known as an accomplished sign painter. In a rare moment of clarity, Granmom gives Sheema an album containing photographs and drawings created by her father. With this package, she and Forrest set out on a journey across the southern United States to look for a father who will perhaps offer his daughter a little love. Hamilton successfully creates a story of young people searching to fill the blank spaces of their personal history through a quest for love. Sheema and Forrest are ordinary working-class teenagers who attain a certain dignity and even heroism through their concern for and support of each other. The setting, in a grimy industrial city in the Midwest, is exceptionally well drawn, reinforcing the sense of bleakness and depression that permeates Sheema's life. S.P.

70   Hamilton, Virginia. *Sweet Whispers, Brother Rush.* Putnam/Philomel 1982, HB
     $12.95 (0-399-20894-1). 215pp. Fiction.

At the very moment Teresa saw the tall, handsome young man standing alone
on the streetcorner, she fell in love. He was a man like no other—elegantly
dressed, aloof, hand cupped to his ear, listening to, perhaps, a distant sound.
Shortly thereafter, Teresa realizes that this man, Brother Rush, is a ghost, visible
only to her; her brother, Dabney; and the housekeeper, Miss Pricherd. Brother
has come "home" to assist his family through a very difficult period. The
youngest brother of Teresa's mother, he had actually died years before in an
automobile accident. At the moment, the household has no center. M'Vy, Teresa's mother, lives at home only on the weekends. She is a single parent
working as a private-duty practical nurse. Dabney, Teresa's older brother, is
developmentally disabled, with the mind of a child. Teresa is weary of her
parental role, though she dearly loves Dabney. What no one realizes is that a rare
congenital disease that has taken the lives of many of the males in the family has
come to take Dabney. Through a series of trips to her unremembered childhood,
Teresa discovers her family heritage, pure love, and the power of forgiveness.
This beautifully crafted young adult novel works on many levels—as a ghost
story, a mystery, a family story, and a tale of coming of age.   S.P.

Hamilton, Virginia. *A White Romance.*
See entry 110, Grades 10–12.

71   Hansen, Joyce. *Out from This Place.* SERIES: Walker's American History Series for
     Young People. Walker 1988. Fiction. o.p.

After Easter and Obi escaped enslavement, they were both captured by Confederate soldiers. Again Obi has escaped, this time leaving behind a lonely 14-year-
old Easter. Easter is determined that she, Obi, and a younger boy, Jason, will be
reunited. Jason has been sold as a wedding gift to Missy Holmes. Easter escapes
the Confederate soldier camp where she has disguised herself as a boy in order
to find Jason and other slaves with whom she is acquainted. Jason is now a
pampered house slave, reluctant to run away with Easter. Nevertheless, she is
hidden in the slave quarters, where she stays until a group of slaves have
determined that they would do well to escape to a free island just off the coast of
South Carolina, now held by Yankee soldiers. Hansen's historical novel continues through four years to the end of the Civil War, years in which the newly
freed slaves lived under the principles of democracy and free enterprise before
being crushed again by a seemingly unjust presidential order. Fast moving and
historically accurate, with compelling, believable characters, this search for a
fated love and family is the sequel to *Which Way Freedom?*   S.P.

72   Haskins, James. *Black Dance in America: A History Through Its People.*
     HarperCollins 1990, LB $14.89 (0-690-04659-6). 224pp. Nonfiction.

Opening with an account of slaves made to exercise on board ship for the
amusement and profit of the slave traders, this history of American dance comes
alive on the very first page. The development of American dance theater and
social dance would look very different were it not for the dancers and choreogra-
phers whose careers are traced in this accessible introduction for junior high and

senior high students. Readers will be introduced to the well-known contemporary talents such as Alvin Ailey, Gregory Hines, Bill T. Jones, and Arthur Mitchell, as well as to talents perhaps lesser known to teenagers such as Talley Beatty, Katherine Dunham, the Nicholas Brothers, and Pearl Primus. It becomes apparent that the tradition of sharing dances and keeping them alive as dance history is passed from dance teacher to choreographer to dancer. These 300 years of dance history end just at the beginnings of the 1980s. There are a selected bibliography and an index.   S.P.

73   Haskins, James. *Black Music in America: A History Through Its People.* Illus. with photos. HarperCollins 1987, LB $12.89 (0-690-04462-3). 224pp. Nonfiction.

Haskins traces the effects of black music on America and America's effect on black music. He divides the book into sections representing periods in black musical history. Within each chapter he focuses on three or four of each era's major contributors. Haskins tells how drums and, when they were forbidden, feet communicated messages that the slaves dared not verbalize. He then examines minstrelsy, popular ballads, ragtime, blues, the development of jazz, the impact of the Harlem Renaissance on black music, the beginnings of modern jazz, soul music, the burgeoning popularity of gospel, and, finally, music from the 1970s to the present.

The book imparts a great deal of information both on the development of distinct American musical forms influenced by African traditions and on race relations in America. Not everyone who has contributed to black American music could be included. Why Tina Turner rates one and a half pages while Roland Hayes and Jimi Hendrix don't even appear in the index could spark exciting discussions in middle and high school classrooms and stimulate hard-to-reach students to read some of the short biographies contained in this volume. There is a selected bibliography of books and articles as well as an index.

A.H.

74   Haskins, James. *The Life and Death of Martin Luther King, Jr.* Illus. with photos. Lothrop, Lee & Shepard 1977, LB $13.88 (0-688-51802-8). 176pp. Nonfiction.

This 1977 biography remains one of the best on King for several reasons. One is Haskins's familiarity with and understanding of African-American history. Most biographies credit only King's father and Mahatma Gandhi as his major influences, but Haskins lists the black American leaders who were King's role models. When he does mention Gandhi, he explains that it was Gandhi's experiences in South Africa that forged his political philosophy.

This title is also unusual because it traces King's moral development. King began his career as a crusader for black American civil rights; by the time of his assassination, his understanding had extended to issues of poverty, class structure, and the Vietnam War. Finally, Haskins does not avoid the FBI's allegations that King was involved in extramarital affairs. A large part of the book's later chapters deals with James Earl Ray's life. Haskins presents the facts and allows readers to formulate their own opinions about whether Ray was hired to assassinate King as well as about other controversies surrounding King's life and death. Haskins includes a selected bibliography and an index as well as black-and-white photos.

A.H.

75 Hayden, Robert C. *Eight Black American Inventors.* Illus. with photos and diagrams. Addison-Wesley 1972. 142pp. Nonfiction. o.p.

This title will be helpful to schools developing a multicultural unit on inventors and inventions. The inventors that Hayden features are Frederick McKinley Jones, Lewis H. Latimer, Jan E. Matzeliger, Elijah McCoy, Garrett Morgan, Norbert Rillieux, Lewis Temple, and Granville T. Woods, all of whose contributions were made in the previous century or in the early twentieth century. In a text that will be discernible to most middle schoolers, Hayden presents information about each inventor's personal life as well as his inventions. Occasional black-and-white photos and diagrams are included. Hayden conveys the grit and perseverance that the eight displayed in combating the racism they faced.

The acknowledgments illustrate how carefully researched the text is. An index is included. Hayden has written another book, *Seven Black American Scientists*, which was unavailable for review. Librarians should check their holdings to see if they own it, as it is out of print.

Inventor or invention units are a good place to begin focusing desperately needed attention on African Americans' societal contributions as good materials are available. Besides many titles on George Washington Carver and the collective biographies of inventors reviewed in this chapter, there are at least two other children's books available. Both of these were written by Barbara Mitchell for Lerner/Carolrhoda. They are *Raggin': A Story About Scott Joplin* (1987) and *Shoes for Everyone: A Story About Jan Matzeliger* (1986). Surely there will soon be a children's title on Garrett Morgan, whose invention of the automatic traffic light children encounter daily. Other sources on this topic are Empak Publishing Company (520 North Michigan Avenue, Suite 1004, Chicago, IL 60611), which publishes sets of classroom booklets at both the elementary and intermediate levels, and Chandler White Publishers (30 East Huron Street, Suite 4402, Chicago, IL 60611), which produces six Black Science Activity Books. These books include product information and classroom activities on black Americans' inventions. They are in comic book format and sell for $1.00 each.   A.H.

76 Humphrey, Kathryn Long. *Satchel Paige.* Illus. with photos. SERIES: Impact Biographies. Franklin Watts 1988, LB $12.90 (0-531-10513-X). 128pp. Nonfiction.

Prior to Jackie Robinson crossing the "color barrier" in baseball, black players played on the segregated teams of the Negro Baseball League. Not surprisingly, many far surpassed major leaguers in ability. One of the better players was Leroy "Satchel" Paige, famous for his amazing pitching ability and his longevity as a pitcher.

This is one of the first of a growing number of books on the Negro Baseball League, an important part of American history about which young people deserve to know. Humphrey is to be congratulated for undertaking the Paige biography and writing it so well. She resists the temptation to present this incredibly gifted athlete as one-dimensional; in fact, a hallmark of the book is its presentation of Paige's strengths and faults as a man. There is also much information about how racism manifested itself during this era.

This book will be equally appropriate in elementary, middle, and high schools. Younger children will enjoy reading about Paige's athletic prowess. Middle and high school students can read it on a deeper level, learning about the man and the society in which he lived. Humphrey uses many quotes throughout the book; carefully researched, these help readers identify with the people portrayed.

The text is followed by statistics, an index, and a bibliography for young readers. The bibliography is disappointing, simply because of the lack of books for young people on the Negro Baseball League or its players at the time of this book's publication.   A.H.

Hurmence, Belinda. *Tancy.*
See entry 113, Grades 10–12.

77   Jakoubek, Robert. *Adam Clayton Powell, Jr.* Illus. with photos. SERIES: Black Americans of Achievement. Chelsea House 1990, P $9.95 (0-7910-0213-6). 112pp. Nonfiction.

This is an important title for middle and high school students because Powell is a perfect example of how successful black American leaders are often delegitimized. In this clearly written, historically accurate, and well-balanced account, readers will meet this brilliant legislator whose race and naïveté were used to destroy his advocacy.

As with all the titles in this outstanding series, the wealth of captioned photos alone tells a great deal about black history. Readers gain an understanding of both the biographees and the systems in which they functioned. All of the series' exemplary titles include a chronology, an index, and a section for further reading.

Perhaps after enough time has elapsed, Powell will be remembered not as a playboy but as an activist who successfully sponsored 49 pieces of legislation, much of it benefiting inner cities, and as a proud black American whose refusal to "shuffle" caused his political and personal downfall. Books such as this one will hasten that process.   A.H.

78   Katz, William Loren. *Breaking the Chains: African-American Slave Resistance.* Illus. with prints and photos. Atheneum 1990, HB $14.95 (0-689-31493-0). 208pp. Nonfiction.

In a world of children's books that perpetuate the lie that most slaves accepted servitude, this book tells the truth and documents it. For this reason, it is a valuable addition to children's and young adult collections. Along with Julius Lester's *To Be a Slave* (Dial, 1968) and Milton Meltzer's *The Black Americans: A History in Their Own Words* (HarperCollins, 1984), it should be part of any core collection on the African-American experience.

Katz divides the book into 13 chapters that follow the history of African Americans in the United States. A few chapters are on such topics as the importance of the slave family and how communication was incorporated into Christian spirituals. By themselves, these topics are riveting, but Katz's writing style and extensive use of quotes, statistics, and specific incidents make the book even more engrossing. Facts new to most adults as well as children fill the pages. Readers learn, for instance, that by 1701 there were 150 recorded incidents of slave ship rebellions and that there were a host of ways in which slaves resisted or escaped. Because most accounts written for children center on escaping via the Underground Railroad, on abolitionists such as Frederick Douglass and Sojourner Truth, or on insurrectionists such as John Brown and Nat Turner, this book makes a unique contribution to the literature. Above all, it focuses on the slaves whose lives were not recorded in the history books but who resisted their fate nonetheless.

Reproductions of archival prints appear throughout the book, which concludes with an extensive bibliography and an index. Two other titles relating to this subject and recommended for elementary readers are Florence B. Freedman's *Two Tickets to Freedom: The Story of Ellen and William Craft* (Bedrick, 1971), which is now available in paperback, and Judith Berry Griffin's *Nat Turner* (Coward, McCann, 1970). Unfortunately, the latter title is no longer in print, and it is hoped that the book will soon be reissued. A.H.

79   Kosof, Anna. *The Civil Rights Movement and Its Legacy.* Illus. with photos. Franklin Watts 1989, LB $12.90 (0-531-10791-4). 112pp. Nonfiction.

Kosof draws from the documentary "Eyes on the Prize," her own personal experiences during the civil rights era, and "hundreds of hours" of interviews in writing this excellent overview. The majority of the book is a clearly written account of the civil rights movement. The author begins with the 1954 Supreme Court school desegregation decision and then covers Emmett Till's murder, the Montgomery bus boycott, the Little Rock school desegregation battle, sit-in strikes to desegregate public places, the Freedom Rides, the Birmingham Sunday School bombing, the Selma march, and, finally, the passage of the 1965 Voting Rights Act.

Kosof assumes that her audience has no prior knowledge of these events, and she presents them in an interesting and informative text. She discusses how the fight for justice and equality inspired others, such as activists for women's rights and gay liberation. The book's last chapters tell how the Reagan Administration hindered race and class struggles for justice and abetted the creation of a permanent, often black, underclass. Source notes, a bibliography of recommended reading, and an index are included in this highly recommended work. A.H.

Larsen, Rebecca. *Paul Robeson: Hero Before His Time.*
See entry 117, Grades 10–12.

80   Lester, Julius. *This Strange New Feeling.* Dutton/Dial 1982, HB $14.95 (0-8037-8491-0); Scholastic 1985, P $2.50 (0-590-41061-X). 160pp. Fiction.

Ras escapes to freedom only to be returned to slavery by the greed of the very man who has inspired his escape route. But the next time Ras is to leave, he takes along his beloved Sally. Following the death of her abusive mistress (the protagonist of another story), Maria is sold by the master to a free-born black man, Forrest. Forrest assures Maria that, though they cannot legally marry in Virginia, his will provides for her freedom following his death. A twist of fate, however, keeps her in bondage. Married on a plantation, William and Ellen Craft leave the state of Georgia disguised as a white master and slave on a perilous four-day journey to Philadelphia via land and sea. As two of the most visible escaped slaves in the North, the Crafts were among the first threatened by legal bounty hunters under the Fugitive Slave Act. These three love stories, which are based on actual slave narratives, reflect a wide range of emotions, from the first stirrings of innocent love to the everlasting bonding of mature affection. Lester's retelling dramatizes the personal narratives of ordinary individuals facing extraordinary pressures as they struggle for love and, above all, for freedom.

S.P.

81 McKissack, Patricia. *Jesse Jackson: A Biography.* Illus. with photos. Scholastic 1989, HB $11.95 (0-590-43181-1). 112pp. Nonfiction.

McKissack's engaging biography will interest readers immediately. She describes Jackson's childhood experiences, feelings, and reactions so vividly and poignantly that readers will empathize with him and remember specific incidents long after the book is finished. She does not ignore what some would describe as Jackson's character flaws. Instead, she presents both his detractors' and his admirers' viewpoints and allows readers to form their own opinions. It is particularly to McKissack's credit as a biographer that this is a well-balanced account, for it is obvious from the tone of the work that she is an ardent Jackson fan.

The book would fit most comfortably in a middle school library, but because of the intimate writing style and the fact that nearly every other page carries a photo, it would be a good choice for high school students with poor reading skills. The bibliography includes magazine articles as well as books, and the books are under the headings "for children" and "for adults." The index is thorough.

A second new Jackson biography is Dorothy Chaplik's *Up with Hope: A Biography of Jesse Jackson* (Dillon Press, 1990). This title presents a factual, less personal view of Jackson but will be helpful for students writing reports about him.

A.H.

82 McKissack, Patricia, and Fredrick McKissack. *Frederick Douglass: The Black Lion.* Illus. SERIES: People of Distinction. Childrens Press 1987, LB $11.95 (0-516-03221-6). 136pp. Nonfiction.

Patricia McKissack's People of Distinction biographies are exceptionally good. On this one she has collaborated with her husband, and the result is as strong as her books on Martin Luther King Jr., Mary McLeod Bethune, and Paul Laurence Dunbar. The accuracy of the facts presented and the consideration of the biographees' strengths and weaknesses are two reasons for the books' excellence, but there is more. This title is written from an African-American perspective, which startles the reader with new insights and information. Examples of this are when northern white abolitionists are shown as less than perfect and when the authors state that had the British won the Revolutionary War, Douglass and all the other slaves would have been freed as early as 1833.

Each chapter begins with an appropriate Douglass quote and ends with a "hook," a sentence that motivates the reader to keep reading. Douglass's intelligence, political shrewdness, majestic demeanor, and unflinching determination to end injustices toward black Americans are conveyed here. The only criticism of this title is that some of the vocabulary and sentence structures are more sophisticated than the book's physical appearance suggests. Fourth and fifth graders, who might be able to read other biographies in this series with ease, will struggle with the material here.

There are archival photos and illustrations in a center section, and a chronology and index are included. Another equally fine Douglass biography for middle school and older students is Sherman Apt Russell's *Frederick Douglass* (Chelsea House, 1988), one of the titles in the series Black Americans of Distinction. Younger children can be guided to Louis Santrey's *Young Frederick Douglass: Fight for Freedom* (Troll, 1983). High school students should be encouraged to read Douglass's autobiographies.   A.H.

83   McKissack, Patricia, and Fredrick McKissack. ***A Long Hard Journey: The Story of the Pullman Porter.*** Illus. with photos. Walker 1989, LB $18.85 (0-8027-6885-7). 160pp. Nonfiction.

Winner of the 1990 Coretta Scott King Award, this impressive title introduces young adults to both an important African-American civil rights activist they might not otherwise meet, Asa Philip Randolph, and an era important in black American history. After the Emancipation Proclamation, many former slaves were employed as porters on the newly built Pullman sleeping coaches. Although at first such positions represented desirable employment, porters soon tired of being underpaid and continually subjected to humiliations by both management and passengers. A. Philip Randolph headed the arduous, lengthy struggle to unionize these workers. The Brotherhood of Sleeping Car Porters became the first black union to win concessions from a hostile corporation headed at one time by Robert T. Lincoln, the cruelly racist son of President Lincoln.

This volume will be one of the most handsome in a nonfiction collection, albeit one with several printing errors due to careless production. Yet the design is exemplary; even the table of contents is visually pleasing. A poem precedes both the entire work and each individual chapter.

Although the text is presented clearly, and interesting facts are interspersed throughout, the subject will be too difficult for most students, unless they have special background or advance preparation. For those who are interested in labor struggles or history in general or who are politically sophisticated, this is an outstanding choice. Because of the importance of this era in African-American history, the book should be included in all collections that serve young adults. An epilogue, bibliography, and index are included.   A.H.

84   Mathis, Sharon Bell. ***Teacup Full of Roses.*** Penguin/Puffin 1972, P $3.95 (0-14-032328-7). 125pp. Fiction.

Mattie's obsessive love for her first-born son, Paul, has turned self-destructive. Twenty-four-year-old Paul is an aspiring artist who has succumbed to heroin. This easy-to-read young adult novel opens on the eve of the graduation of younger brother Joe, which coincides with Paul's release from a rehabilitation center. As the entire family's attention is focused on the self-destructive Paul, Joe is determined to escape. He plans to join the navy, marry his sweetheart, Ellie, and send money home to support his younger brother, David, and his parents. Joe also wants to deliver a final message to Paul's drug dealer. This is a dramatic, hard-hitting story of a family plagued by an outside force tearing at what was once a healthy, intact unit. Originally published in 1972, this story of codependency and tragedy remains current with the rise of today's crack epidemic, which, like the heroin epidemic of the 1960s and 1970s, has devastated families and communities. Currently marketed for ages 10–14, this novel is appropriate for and has much to say to both junior and senior high school students.

71

S.P.

GRADES 7-9

Meltzer, Milton, ed. *The Black Americans: A History in Their Own Words, 1619–1983.*
See entry 118, Grades 10–12.

85   Miller, Marilyn. *The Bridge at Selma.* Illus. with photos. SERIES: Turning Points in American History. Silver Burdett 1985, LB $12.79 (0-382-06826-2); P $5.96 (0-382-06973-0). 64pp. Nonfiction.

This is a rather dry and occasionally confusing account of the 1965 march from Selma, Alabama, to the state capital to secure voting rights for Selma's black citizens. There are many clear black-and-white photographs depicting the events that occurred on this historic occasion, but young readers must struggle to understand some new, complicated information. To make matters worse, every few pages there are double-page spreads of a different color, which address topics unrelated to the preceding pages.

In spite of these drawbacks this is an important addition to children's collections for several reasons: It introduces youngsters to important events and people and explains why the movement needed national media attention to succeed. It also broadens their knowledge of the era, so that they understand there was more to the issues than the Montgomery bus boycott and King's "I Have a Dream" speech. Most important, it shows—in photo after photo—that the leaders of this movement were black.   A.H.

86   Moore, Yvette. *Freedom Songs.* Orchard 1991, HB $14.95 (0-531-05812-3). 168pp. Fiction.

Every Easter Sheryl and her family travel from their all-black neighborhood in Brooklyn to North Carolina to visit her mother's family. But in 1963, when she is fourteen, conflict is in the air. Sheryl feels it when she goes to Hodges's store, where the black customers are waited on last and the owner washes the water fountain out with ammonia after her brother drinks from it. She also witnesses her nineteen-year-old uncle, Pete, who is a Freedom Rider, checking the farm buildings and vehicles for bombs. Upon returning to Brooklyn, Sheryl persuades her friends to hold a benefit concert to raise money for the Freedom Riders. The process of planning the concert leads to some squabbles with friends and a romance with classmate Darin, but Sheryl's efforts take on a new meaning when Pete is killed by a bomb and the family defiantly returns South for the funeral.

This novel shows how ordinary teenagers grow and are changed by political struggle. Sheryl and her Southern cousins have the usual concerns—clothes, makeup, boys—but we also see them at the lunch counter being carried away by the police. While the youngsters act in heroic ways, they are also presented as full human beings, with all their flaws. Moore conveys the sense of being part of a struggle yet distant from it, as the Brooklyn teens are; they are safe but also very aware of their connection to those who aren't. This first novel is quite well written. Though she doesn't use dialect, Moore conveys through language a sense of the era. She communicates important themes and ideas without being preachy. While this book is clearly rooted in a place and time, the issues it presents are very much alive today. A discussion of solidarity work during the

Civil Rights movement might touch upon such efforts against apartheid in South Africa.

L.M-L.

87 Myers, Walter Dean. ***Fallen Angels.*** Scholastic 1988, HB $12.95 (0-590-40942-5); 1989, P $3.50 (0-590-40943-3). 309pp. Fiction.

Following his 1967 graduation from high school, Richie Perry has no desire to drift through the next few years waiting to accumulate enough funds to attend college. He enlists in the army, hoping to gain direction and purpose. It is the Vietnam War era, and although everyone hears rumors that peace may be at hand, Richie is sent to the front lines to serve a tour of duty with other equally young soldiers. On the jungle battlefields, black and white men and women find themselves dependent upon each other for survival, and close friendships are made, only to be tragically cut short. Here, too, Richie kills his first Vietcong soldier, only to realize his victim was no older than he.

This harrowing, yet heroic, young adult novel marks a break from much of Myers's previous work, with the family as the center and humor as a kind of glue holding the story together. This is a gripping coming-of-age story of teenagers finding themselves in the middle of a war, the goals of which were never fully understood by either the soldiers or their folks back home. The language is restrained, making this an appropriate work for both junior and senior high students, yet Myers effectively communicates the horror of war; nothing about the experience of battle has been romanticized.

S.P.

88 Myers, Walter Dean. ***Hoops.*** Based upon an original screenplay by John Ballard, with additional material by Dennis Watlington. Dell 1983, P $3.25 (0-440-93884-8). 192pp. Fiction.

Playing basketball is a refuge for 17-year-old Lonnie. He plays pickup games in his Harlem neighborhood with a group of regular teammates who have their eye on competing in the upcoming citywide Tournament of Champions. Their coach, now a recovering alcoholic who used to be the neighborhood wino, was known in better days as Cal "Spider" Jones. Seeing something of himself in Lonnie, Cal is determined not to let the influence of gambling steal away Lonnie's chance for achieving a winning game at the tournament and an opportunity for an athletic scholarship. Sports fans will appreciate Myers's play-by-play action supported by winning characters that even non–sports fans can relate to. Myers's sequel, *The Outside Shot*, follows Lonnie to a college in Indiana, where he utilizes the training instilled in him in New York. This easy-to-read novel will appeal to both junior and senior high school students. A more recent work, *The Mouse Rap* (HarperCollins, 1990), also uses a basketball theme and a fast-paced, lighthearted approach in presenting inner-city life.

S.P.

89 Myers, Walter Dean. ***Motown and Didi: A Love Story.*** Viking 1984, HB $12.95 (0-670-49062-8); Dell 1987, P $2.95 (0-440-95762-1). 264pp. Fiction.

Motown has been a fairly self-reliant Harlem teen. After running away from a foster home, he has been living on his own in an abandoned building for four years. He dreams of a steady job and a real apartment. Didi dreams of attending college and escaping Harlem, her alcoholic mother, and her drug-addicted brother. Motown and Didi meet when Didi is attacked by minions of her brother's vicious drug supplier, Touchy; Motown comes to her rescue. As Motown and Didi's friendship grows into love, they discover they have more in common than just loneliness.

This is an urban, contemporary story of love flourishing against the odds. Typical of Myers's characters are the supportive adults who give sage advice and act as strong role models. Myers explores fully the complex dilemmas facing the young couple. Through their relationship and the encouragement of an adult mentor, the two teenagers discover their heritage as African Americans. They confront the thorny choice between either remaining in their troubled, dangerous community and trying to improve it or leaving it and loved ones in order to attain success in the white world outside. Myers's 1986 novel *Crystal*, also published by Viking, illustrates the same conflict of family and community versus the trappings of success in the white world as experienced by a beautiful, aspiring fashion model. Although *Crystal* is less complex and compelling than *Motown and Didi*, it is also recommended for young adult readers.   S.P.

Myers, Walter Dean. *Scorpions.*
See entry 43, Grades 4–6.

90   Rummell, Jack. *Langston Hughes.* Illus. with photos. SERIES: Black Americans of Achievement. Chelsea House 1988, LB $17.95 (1-55546-595-1); 1989 (P $9.95). 111pp. Nonfiction.

The best recently published young people's biography of Langston Hughes is, not surprisingly, a Chelsea House title that will appeal to adults as well. This publisher cannot be praised enough for its biography series; the only drawback is a binding that doesn't stand up to the use these books receive. Junior high and high school students will appreciate Hughes's determination to leave home and pursue his desire to become a poet, as well as his attempts to be "discovered" while working as a busboy. (Among other things, he left a poem he'd written on writer Vachel Lindsay's dinner plate. It worked.) As with other books in this series, this one is accurate and contains a wealth of African-American history in both the text and the many black-and-white photos that appear throughout. It also presents a well-balanced view of Hughes, not a sugarcoated one, and Hughes fans may cringe at learning about situations in which the poet himself was painfully insensitive. The book ends with a chronology and an index.

Not all of Chelsea House's biographies of black Americans are found in this series. Some appear in the series American Women of Achievement and World Leaders—Past and Present. All of these are most economical if purchased in paperback. Least expensive of all are the titles that are being issued as rack-size paperbacks. They will appeal more to the middle and high school set, although the photographs are not as clearly reproduced.   A.H.

Rust, Edna, and Art Rust, Jr. *Art Rust's Illustrated History of the Black Athlete.*
See entry 122, Grades 10–12.

91   Sebestyen, Ouida. ***Words by Heart.*** Little, Brown/Joy Street Books 1979, HB $13.95 (0-316-77931-8); Bantam 1983, P $2.95 (0-553-27179-2). 135pp. Fiction.

Lena knows, by heart, enough Bible verses to win a heated competition in recitations at a local church in the West at the turn of the century. By heart, Lena also knows that her relationship with her father is, ultimately, the most special one of her life. Her father had hoped to escape the racism of the South by relocating to an area where neighbors are expected to be fair and justice is purportedly evenhanded. Early on, these hopes are dashed, and Lena watches fearfully as her brave and fearless father faces tyranny straight on. The feel of this novel for junior high students is cinematic, with sympathetic characters even among those who violate the basic human rights of Lena's family. The novel is historically accurate and challenges the misconception that the extremes of racism in the United States existed only in the South. As new information surfaces about the black frontierspeople and cowboys who helped to settle the West, one's understanding and admiration of these courageous pioneers—who battled race hatred along with the elements—are only further deepened by reading this novel.

S.P.

Sills, Leslie. ***Inspirations: Stories About Women Artists.***
See entry 427, Grades 7–9.

92   Smead, Howard. ***The Afro-Americans.*** Illus. with photos. SERIES: The Peoples of North America. Chelsea House 1989, LB $17.95 (0-87754-854-4); P $9.95 (0-7910-0256-X). 127pp. Nonfiction.

This terse account of the past four centuries touches upon the major events in African-American history. The material is accurate and is presented from an Afrocentric perspective. The black-and-white photos are interspersed throughout and enhance the text. The concepts presented and their level of presentation make this volume suited to junior high and high school.

The narrative begins chronologically with the slave trade. Smead does not gloss over the atrocities committed in the name of capitalism. The chapter on slavery succinctly recounts the number and variety of slave rebellions. This is important because so many children's books perpetuate the misconception that attempts at freedom were few and that most abolitionists were white. The following two chapters, on the Civil War and Reconstruction and on segregation and Jim Crow, cover the manipulation of those in power to maintain the oppression of the freed slaves. Successive chapters cover the migration north (including the development of the urban ghetto and the Harlem Renaissance), the civil rights movement, and black nationalism.

A rather disconcerting addition to the title is a center section of color photos featuring blacks in the performing arts. Nowhere in the text are the pictures explained, and the choice of artists seems bizarre. (They run the gamut from Alvin Ailey to the Fat Boys.) The corresponding higher price makes this book more practical if purchased in paperback, although the binding is not adequately reinforced. The volume features a bibliography and an index.

A.H.

Taylor, Mildred D. ***The Friendship.***
See entry 48, Grades 4–6.

93   Taylor, Mildred D. *The Road to Memphis.* Dutton/Dial 1990, HB $14.95 (0-8037-0340-6). 290pp. Fiction.

Cassie Logan is now 17. It is the beginning of her senior year. In order to ensure that her education would be the finest available to a black Mississippi high school student, her parents have elected that she attend school in Jackson. Her return, however, has been delayed by a bout of early fall pneumonia and near tragedy. The characters of *Let the Circle Be Unbroken* and *Roll of Thunder, Hear My Cry* have now aged and, in some cases, matured. The year is 1941, just prior to the bombing of Pearl Harbor. The rumors of war and the injustices of Hitler seem far away to Cassie, who continues to witness the horrors of racism, injustice, and humiliation right at home in Mississippi even as her childhood friend Harris speaks of being a soldier-patriot. Using the automobile as a metaphor for change and deliverance, Taylor creates scene after scene, building upon an afternoon in an automobile repair shop in which Cassie and her friends are taunted, humiliated, and threatened with assault. The ever-gentle Moe explodes with anger as he proceeds to lash out against the racist tormentors, beating them with a tire iron. It is with the help of the misunderstood, misjudged Jeremy, relative of the tormentors, that Moe is able to escape. Jeremy makes possible the group's harrowing escape by truck and car north to Memphis. The group's journey to Memphis and back in an era of practiced inequality compresses the experience of true fear and unequal services along the nation's highways. However, through this curtain of darkness appears a kind, reassuring, handsome journalist, Solomon Bradley, who sees in Cassie the promise of love and greatness as well as the workings of a mind that never stops questioning. At no moment does the quest of these young people for a new kind of freedom ring false. This is an extraordinary story, a page turner, distilling what will be for today's readers a historic period.   S.P.

94   Taylor, Mildred D. *Roll of Thunder, Hear My Cry.* Dutton/Dial 1976, HB $14.95 (0-8037-7473-7); Bantam 1984, $3.95 (0-553-25450-2). 210pp. Fiction.

One of four children of Mississippi land-owning blacks, Cassie Logan has not wanted for much in her short life. Among the sharecroppers of the area, the Logans are proud and respected. However, in order to keep his land, Cassie's father must work away from home for extended periods of time with the railroad. There is a closeness and warmth in this family in times of impending danger, but the children live with the reality of lynchings, burnings, tar and featherings, and a host of other inhumane actions and malevolent racist threats. Through Cassie's fourth-grade eyes, the reader experiences an episodic year that tears away at the cocoon of innocence provided by a protective, nurturing family. Though the narrator is not a teenager, teen readers will discover a remarkable family story, told in Cassie's voice, which is followed by Taylor's equally remarkable 1981 novel *Let the Circle Be Unbroken*.   S.P.

95   Taylor-Boyd, Susan. *Sojourner Truth.* Illus. SERIES: People Who Have Helped the World. Gareth Stevens 1990, LB $11.95 (0-8368-0101-6). 68pp. Nonfiction.

This accurate and informative biography will be especially useful in middle school library media centers, although some elementary and high school students may find it appropriate. It is a slender, sturdy volume that is punctuated throughout with illustrations, both in black and white and in color, of archival materials. One third of each page is vertical border, and many of the illustrations and their captions appear here. Within this wide margin are also many quotes by Truth and her contemporaries. These quotes attest to Truth's determination and saucy wit. Boldface headings on almost every page break the monotony and help students pick out the main point of that section of text. Because the book has neither chapter headings nor a table of contents, these headings are particularly useful.

This biography presents Truth as an advocate for women's rights as well as a champion of slaves and, later, of freed slaves. The final section, on Truth's legacy, emphasizes that both of these struggles continue today. An appendix provides addresses of organizations that advocate the rights of women and African Americans. There are also an unusually thorough bibliography, a glossary, a chronology, and an index.

An equally fine Truth biography for this age group is Peter Krass's *Sojourner Truth: Anti-Slavery Activist* (Chelsea House, 1988). Another, geared more to reluctant readers, is Edward Beecher Claflin's *Sojourner Truth and the Struggle for Freedom* (Childrens Press, 1987), which is the most engagingly written of all of them. A biography written for younger children is Jeri Ferris's *Road to Freedom: A Story About Sojourner Truth* (Lerner/Carolrhoda, 1988). Unfortunately, this title cannot be recommended. Twice Ferris implies that Truth's daughters "preferred" or "chose" to remain slaves, perpetuating a misconception that has been used throughout history to justify slavery.   A.H.

96   Thomas, Joyce Carol. *Marked by Fire.* Avon 1982, P $2.75 (0-380-79327-X). 172pp. Fiction.

Named Patience and Strong, Abby's parents were destined to have her as their one and only special child. Born in 1951 in an Oklahoma cotton field in the aftermath of a tornado, Abby was birthmarked on her cheek with a scar resembling a cotton bloom. The women surrounding her mother in that cotton field have determined that Abby is more than special: She is destined in a way unlike other children. She is the favored child of the community. Her gifts of intellect and musicality are recognized early on. But it is her gifts of patience and perceived prophecy that Mother Barker, the community's spiritual-root doctor, is eager to build upon. Mother Barker has agreed to pass on her knowledge to Abby. In a voice echoing the call and response patterns of the black ministry, Thomas follows Abby past her high school days. Tragedy, jealousy, and insanity engulf the residents of this Oklahoma community. Abby plans to continue her education at a university in a premedicine program and to utilize the heritage passed down from generations of folk medicine healers. Though some incidents appear contrived and sensationalized, there are the beginnings of many rich characters in this first novel in a series followed by Thomas's *Bright Shadow* and *Water Girl*. Similarity to the works of other black writers—Toni Morrison and Alice Walker in particular—is apparent here; even so, *Marked by Fire* and its sequels offer a promise somewhat unfulfilled.   S.P.

97   Viglucci, Pat Costa. *Cassandra Robbins, Esq.* Square One 1987, P $4.95 (0-938961-01-2). 176pp. Fiction.

Biracial Cassandra was adopted as an infant by a loving, white family as its second adopted child. Now 17, Cassandra has been told that if she wore a little bit of makeup she would be beautiful instead of merely pretty. She has even more of an incentive to look beautiful. Josh, an O.J. Simpson look-alike room-mate of her college student brother Todd, will be staying with her family during the summer vacation. Though Cassandra and Josh are immediately drawn to one another, there is tension in the beginning as they vie for the same summer position as a lab technician. Both Josh and Cassandra continually find them-selves treated negatively as minority people in an area of the country where the population of black people is small. Here is a love story beginning and ending in affection with appealing central characters in a contemporary suburban setting. The psyche of the young woman is revealed in her search to reaffirm the unique qualities of her biracial African-American identity.   S.P.

Warner, Malcolm-Jamal, and Daniel Paisner. ***Theo and Me.***
See entry 126, Grades 10–12.

98   Wilkinson, Branda. ***Not Separate, Not Equal.*** HarperCollins 1987, LB $12.89 (0-06-026482-9). 152pp. Fiction.

Seventeen-year-old Malene is one of six students who integrate a Georgia high school in 1965. She has to put up with hostility from white students and the community, and she wonders whether integration is worth it. In fact, a well-liked first grade teacher at the all-black school is dismissed as soon as white students appear, simply because she lacks course credits. After being dismissed early one afternoon because of a bomb threat, the six confront racist Wiley Parker while walking home and are imprisoned for hours in his garage. Under crisis, the teenagers cry, argue, and eventually gain an understanding of them-selves and each other.

In contrast to most of the "social conscience" books written during the 1960s, this is an African-American perspective of school integration. Wilkinson shows that integration was a mixed blessing, as greater educational opportunities for a few were accompanied by continuing discrimination and inequality. The six "guinea pigs" in this novel do not benefit from the experience. Malene, who has recently suffered the loss of her parents and is trying to adjust to a different (and on the surface, more comfortable) life-style after her adoption by the wealthy Freemans, has a particularly difficult time. Wilkinson also explores class differ-ences within the African-American community in a small Georgia town, a dimension missing from the earlier generation of books about this subject. Although the narrative suffers from jarring shifts in the point of view and some awkwardness in the conveying of background information, it has much to say about race relations and people's intentions—good, bad, and neutral—in a time of social change.   L.M-L.

99   Williams-Garcia, Rita. ***Blue Tights.*** Dutton/Lodestar 1988, HB $12.95 (0-525-67234-6); Bantam 1989, P $2.95 (0-553-28293-X). 138pp. Fiction.

It is not enough that at 15 Joyce has the body of a fully grown woman; her teacher has just informed her that her body is too abundant for the ballet stage. Behind her back, Joyce is called Big Butt. She has attracted the wrong kinds of masculine attention from both teenage and middle-aged men. Still loving dance despite repeated rejection, she enrolls in a tough, disciplined African dance class for which the drummer, J'had, a young Black Muslim, plays. For Joyce, it is love at first sight. For J'had, who is streetwise yet conservative, young love is something to be kept at arm's length; he is terrified of such youthful passion.

Joyce is a memorable young woman brought to life via dance and romance. The shifting point of view illustrates the painful gap between Joyce's desire to be "cool" and accepted and the disrespect with which she is treated by others; only when she begins to take pride in herself as a young black woman do her true gifts show through. Williams-Garcia handles well the divisions within the black student community that are based on skin color, body type, and social class. Her knowledge of dance, both classical and African, is extensive. For these reasons, her first novel will find an audience among both junior and senior high school students but will have special appeal to African-American teenagers.

Williams-Garcia is also the author of *Fast Talk on a Slow Track* (Dutton/Lodestar, 1991). This novel, which is recommended for a slightly older young adult audience, explores a bright but arrogant middle-class black teenager's first encounter with failure as he flunks his summer college-preparatory classes, reconsiders his decision to attend an Ivy League school, and instead takes a job as a door-to-door salesman.   S.P.

100   Woodson, Jacqueline. *The Dear One.* Delacorte 1991, HB $14.00 (0-385-30416-1). 145pp. Fiction.

Twelve-year-old Feni considers her birthday and her life ruined when her mother announces that Rebecca, the daughter of a college friend, will be staying at their comfortable suburban home for several months. Rebecca, who is fifteen and pregnant, lives in Harlem, and her ailing mother is unable to care for her. Feni remembers Rebecca as bossy and snobbish, and conflict erupts even before Rebecca arrives. Feni resents her parents' divorce, her mother's alcoholism and process of recovery, the fact that her mother, a public relations executive, is never at home, and her grandmother's death in a freak accident several years earlier. Feni also dislikes the social life of her upper middle class black community, and even her one friend is drawing away from her. Yet street-hardened Rebecca and Feni begin to grow close as they recognize shared bonds of disappointments, sorrow, and strength. Before giving her up for adoption (in an open adoption), Rebecca names her baby girl after Feni, and the two part as each other's best, and perhaps only true, friend.

As in her middle grade novel, *Last Summer with Maizon* (Delacorte, 1990), Woodson explores the theme of friendship. This memorable, poignant young adult novel is filled with three-dimensional child and adult characters. Woodson allows her characters to be cruel, snobbish, and resentful, but also honorable and generous, in believable ways. Virtually all the characters are African-American females, and, in addition to being a source of strength for each other, they present a range of choices and lifestyles. Feni is upper middle class. She attends an exclusive private school, and her world of large homes, social clubs, and plans for college is all-black. One of her mother's friends is a lesbian who lives with her lover. Rebecca's mother is downwardly mobile; a single mother with four children, she lives in a Harlem tenement. Woodson's insights into various African-American experiences are also universal insights, as she concludes this beautiful and wise story with Feni musing upon the connections among generations and the stories women tell as they wait for their daughters to grow up.

L.M-L.

Altman, Susan. *Extraordinary Black Americans: From Colonial to Contemporary Times.*
See entry 55, Grades 7-9.

101   Angelou, Maya. *I Know Why the Caged Bird Sings.* Bantam 1970, P $4.50 (0-553-27937-8). 256pp. Nonfiction.

In this, the first of a lyrical multivolume autobiography, we meet a young Marguerite, who, with her older beloved brother Bailey, lives with their shop-keeper grandmother and uncle in Stamps, Arkansas. With vivid memory, Angelou recalls their subsequent move to St. Louis during her eighth year, when she was raped by her mother's boyfriend. Her World War II adolescent years show a teen full of ambition. Through determination and with the support of her remarkable mother, she secures, at age 15, a position as the first black woman trolley car conductor in San Francisco. This volume closes with the birth of her son when she is 16 years old. Teen readers will find here a full lifetime of living in Angelou's short 16 years. Her inspiring, heart-wrenching story continues in *Gather Together in My Name, Singin' and Swingin' and Gettin' Merry Like Christmas,* and *The Heart of a Woman,* all published in paperback by Bantam. Older teenagers should be encouraged to read Angelou's poetry as well.   S.P.

102   Baldwin, James. *If Beale Street Could Talk.* Dell 1974, P $4.95 (0-440-34060-8). 213pp. Fiction.

Tish and Fonny (Alfonso) were destined as Harlem playmates to spend their lives together. Now 19-year-old Tish is pregnant, and Fonny, an aspiring artist, is in jail, mistakenly identified as a rapist. Through Tish's voice, the reader comes to know the dreams and frustrations facing the young and quickly maturing lovers as both Tish and Fonny's family work desperately to free Fonny from jail. Baldwin's characters are complex and confrontational, yet nurturing as they face issues ranging from religious skepticism and creative processes to racism and police brutality. The language of this powerful love story is frank, and it is thus recommended for mature high school readers.   S.P.

103   Bode, Janet. *Different Worlds: Interracial and Cross Cultural Dating.* Franklin Watts 1989, LB $12.90 (0-531-10663-2). 120pp. Nonfiction.

Convinced that "romance is definitely not going out of style," Bode has written a handbook specifically for teenagers involved in relationships with members of other races or cultural groups. Opening with a discussion of the roots of prejudice, the author presents a clear explanation of how attitudes have shifted or in some cases remained inflexible. That inflexibility, according to the author, is particularly embodied in parents of dating teens. Most enlightening for readers are the interviews with couples and in some cases their parents. The range of American cultures is reflected in the pairings: biracial/white, Mexican American/Scottish American, Chinese American/white, Indian American/Hispanic, and Filipino American/white. The evolution of these relationships is traced through interviews with the young people, who speak candidly of the ups and downs of their particular relationship. The statements by social workers and family therapists are insighful and reassuring, thereby providing a means for coping with parental and societal pressures to discontinue dating. Also presented are the positive values of flourishing in the open, allowing young people to experience a normal dating pattern without the negative stresses attached to those who date outside their racial or cultural group. Ultimately upbeat, this handbook is useful not only for dating teens but also for teen readers seeking ways of living in harmony within our increasingly multicultural communities. Included are a list of organizations concerned with interracial and cross-cultural matters and a bibliography of useful print and nonprint materials. Another worthy title on this subject is *Coping with Cross-Cultural and Interracial Relationships* by Sandra L. Smith (Rosen Press, 1990).   S.P.

104   Bogle, Donald. ***Blacks in American Films and Television: An Illustrated Encyclopedia.*** Simon & Schuster 1989, HB $22.95 (0-671-67538-9). 700pp. Nonfiction.

Bogle is the foremost scholar on African Americans working in film and television. The author of *Brown Sugar: Eighty Years of America's Black Super Stars*, and *Toms, Coons, Mulattoes, Mammies, and Blacks* has gathered for this large-format encyclopedia 90 years of achievements by black filmmakers, actors, producers, comedians, dancers, and musicians working in the cinema industry. This very accessible and unique encyclopedia is divided by sections focusing on Films, Television, TV Movies, Mini Series, and Specials, and there are individual profiles that are short biographies of filmmakers and actors. This book currently stands alone in its subject area and appeal to young adult audiences. Many libraries may purchase it for reference collections, but its price makes it cost-effective for a number of collections that circulate materials to young people.
                    S.P.

105   Butler, Octavia E. ***Kindred.*** 2nd ed. Beacon 1979, P $8.95 (0-8070-8305-4). 264pp. Fiction.

Dana is a young, struggling writer who has recently married Kevin, a white writer also near the beginning of his career. As they are unpacking belongings in their new home, Dana feels an overwhelming dizziness and nausea. In the next instant she travels from her comfortable suburban Los Angeles home in the year 1976 to the early-nineteenth-century South. There she finds herself in the middle of a river rescuing Rufus, a small white boy, from drowning. But Rufus's father is on the riverbank with a shotgun, waiting to kill her. She miraculously vanishes and reappears in her twentieth-century home. This is to be the first of many journeys to the plantation. Rufus grows into a spoiled, self-destructive youth. Heir to his vicious slaveholder father's plantation, he brutalizes Dana; thus begins the lineage of her family.

This complex and compelling story of love, hatred, slavery, and intertwined families is one that older readers will find difficult to abandon. It raises questions concerning interracial relationships and puts them in a historical perspective. Dana's journey in time and place is a means of finding out about herself and her past. *Kindred* is an excellent introduction for older readers to the work of one of this country's premier science fiction writers.   S.P.

Childress, Alice. ***A Hero Ain't Nothin' But a Sandwich.***
See entry 59, Grades 7–9.

Childress, Alice. *Rainbow Jordan.*
See entry 60, Grades 7–9.

106 Cosby, Bill. *Love and Marriage.* Doubleday 1989, HB $21.95 (0-385-24664-1). 283pp. Nonfiction.

Looking back upon the years of childhood, comedian Bill Cosby tells the reader of his first observation of a teenage kiss. From that point, young love evolves toward lifelong marriage. This is Cosby's most accessible and appealing book for the teen audience. Here is the portrait of an intact black family sustained by love and humor. As one of prime-time television's most visible fathers, Cosby's brand of humor is familiar to many teenagers. Though this is not the typical advice book, it does act as a kind of universal prescription for living in harmony with loved ones.   S.P.

107 DeCarava, Roy, and Langston Hughes. *The Sweet Flypaper of Life.* Howard Univ. Pr. 1985, HB $26.95 (0-88258-152-X). 112pp. Nonfiction.

Sister Mary Bradley may be elderly, but she is "not prepared to go." She is not ready to meet St. Peter because she has more of an interest in the people of her world, her Harlem. This collaborative book of black-and-white photographs and text originally published by Hill & Wang in 1955 and reissued in 1985, successfully marries the work of two creative artists—photographer Roy DeCarava and writer Langston Hughes. Hughes's fictional grandmother keeps her ever-benevolent and watchful eye on the neighborhood. She is universal as the wise elder, passing on her memories to another generation. This special book begs to be read aloud.   S.P.

George, Nelson, ed. *Stop the Violence: Overcoming Self-Destruction.*
See entry 62, Grades 7–9.

Gilman, Michael. *Matthew Henson.*
See entry 63, Grades 7–9.

108 Greig, Charlotte. *Will You Still Love Me Tomorrow? Girl Groups from the 50s On.* Virago Press/Doubleday 1989, P $14.95 (1-85381-002-9). 224pp. Nonfiction.

For the last half of the twentieth century, contemporary popular music has been enriched by the sound of women singing. The author describes "girl groups" as those having "three or more young women singing pop tunes in vocal harmony together." Taken as a whole, African-American girl groups have been and remain among the most influential of the genre. The book's title is taken from the 1960s hit by the Shirelles. The author traces the history of this music from the 1950s through the late 1980s from a feminist perspective. Most illuminating are the excerpts from candid interviews with singers, songwriters, and producers who speak of the music and the careers—some short and some lifelong. The spectrum of contemporary popular music is here: rock 'n' roll, soul, disco, punk, and rap. Greig explores how the music has changed from the lyrics of longing in the 1950s to the streetwise, take-charge lyrics of the 1980s rappers. Among the groups featured are the Chantels, the Ronettes, the Chiffons, the Jaynettes, the Supremes, the Marvelettes, the Honey Cone, the Three Degrees, Sister Sledge, the Pointer Sisters, the Bluebelles, Klymaxx, and Salt 'n' Peppa. Two major disappointments are that this text lacks an index and a discography. S.P.

109 Gross, Linda, and Marian E. Barnes, eds. *Talk That Talk: An Anthology of African-American Storytelling.* Simon & Schuster 1989, HB $24.95 (0-671-67167-7); P $12.95 (0-671-67168-5). 521pp. Nonfiction.

This scholarly anthology of almost 100 African-American stories told in the oral tradition will be helpful to students of African-American history, as well as to librarians and storytellers. Its format makes it most appropriate for a high school audience, but it will be an entertaining read for capable readers in middle school and the upper elementary grades, where selections can also be read aloud in classes. Following an introduction by the prominent professor of Afro-American studies Henry Louis Gates Jr., the book is divided into sections based on story types. There are animal tales and fables, including *Anansi* and *Brer Rabbit*, and there are ghost tales, humorous tales, and tales of home and family. There are also sections devoted to sermons, to "History Remembered," and to "Raps, Rhythms, and Rhymes." Some of the stories come from West Africa and the Caribbean. Many are adapted or retold; some are original; a few are reminiscences. Sources are cited, and after each section there are one or more commentaries by scholars whose credentials appear, along with other contributors, in the section on Biographical Notes. The storytellers include, among others, Langston Hughes, Zora Neale Hurston, Maya Angelou, Martin Luther King Jr. (as well as his daughter Yolanda, who tells a story about him), Dick Gregory, and Hugh Morgan Hill, alias Brother Blue.

All the selections are short and compelling. Many are lively enough to keep a broad range of age levels amused, but because they relate to the values of African-American culture and various incidents in history, the stories are more than merely entertaining. Preceding the index is a list of stories that will appeal especially to children. There is also a helpful section, "Further Reading," with suggested works listed by type and grade level. This collection is a valuable resource for adults, young adults, and children, and it should be in every public and school library. A.H.

Haber, Louis. *Black Pioneers of Science and Invention.*
See entry 67, Grades 7–9.

Hamilton, Virginia. *Anthony Burns: The Defeat and Triumph of a Fugitive Slave.*
See entry 68, Grades 7–9.

Hamilton, Virginia. *A Little Love.*
See entry 69, Grades 7–9.

Hamilton, Virginia. *Sweet Whispers, Brother Rush.*
See entry 70, Grades 7–9.

110 Hamilton, Virginia. *A White Romance.* Putnam/Philomel 1987, HB $14.95 (0-399-21213-2); Harcourt Brace Jovanovich 1989, P $3.95 (0-15-295888-6). 233pp. Fiction.

Talley's all-black high school has just become integrated as a magnet school. Worried about her safety, her single father insists that she carry a knife and not become friendly with any of the white students. Yet while jogging, she meets Didi, a white girl who is involved in a relationship with a drug addict, another white newcomer to the school. Because Didi's boyfriend Roady lives alone in an apartment in a dangerous part of town, Talley offers to meet Didi there and walk her home. At Roady's apartment Talley meets David, the high school drug dealer. She falls in love with David, who is also white and who owns property in the area. David cruelly exploits Talley, whose reputation suffers by being associated with him. He takes her to a heavy-metal concert, but when she panics and becomes ill, he shows no concern, only resentment that she has inconvenienced him. The two drift apart; although Talley still loves David, she begins to take an interest in a more wholesome black classmate.

Even though the protagonist is black, the main focus is on a group of self-destructive white youths. Talley travels great distances to provide for the physical and emotional well-being of her white friends. Her own community is portrayed no less darkly: Most people are either out of work or underemployed. The neighborhood is dangerous, with the chance of violent confrontation just below the surface. Even so, several of the black characters make better friends for Talley than the aimless, addicted, and promiscuous whites who ultimately take her virginity and self-esteem. This novel is meant as a cautionary tale. Talley's apparent intelligence does not keep her from getting herself into a bad situation, for she, like many adolescent girls, is blinded by her longing for an identity and her fascination with a different way of life. R.S./S.P.

Haskins, James. *Black Dance in America: A History Through Its People.* See entry 72, Grades 7–9.

Haskins, James. *Black Music in America: A History Through Its People.* See entry 73, Grades 7–9.

Haskins, James. *The Life and Death of Martin Luther King, Jr.* See entry 74, Grades 7–9.

111 Hill, Errol, ed. *Black Heroes: 7 Plays.* Applause Theater Book Publishers 1989, P $12.95 (1-55783-027-4). 426pp. Nonfiction.

Dramatic moments in the lives of seven men and women have provided inspiration for seven plays spanning the years 1935–1988. These are productions suitable for performance by senior high school students covering black achievement in the Americas during the nineteenth and twentieth centuries. A short biography of the playwright and the hero introduces each play. The plays are as follows: *Emperor of Haiti* (Jean-Jacques Dessalines), by Langston Hughes; *Nat Turner*, by Randolph Edwards; *Harriet Tubman*, by May Miller; *In Splendid Error* (Frederick Douglass), by William Branch; *I, Marcus Garvey*, by Edgar White; *Paul Robeson*, by Phillip Hayes Dean; and *Roads of the Mountaintop* (Martin Luther King Jr.), by Ron Milner. Inspirational and nonsimplistic, this collection of plays could easily be read as companion pieces to biographies and historical accounts. S.P.

112   Hurmence, Belinda, ed. *Before Freedom, When I Just Can Remember: Twenty-seven Oral Histories of Former South Carolina Slaves.* John F. Blair 1989, P $8.95 (0-89587-069-X). 135pp. Nonfiction.

In preparation for a future project, Hurmence discovered oral narratives about slavery and the Reconstruction era in North and South Carolina. *Before Freedom* contains 27 interviews, edited for clarity by Hurmence, of men and women who were in their 80s, 90s, and 100s when they were interviewed during the Great Depression era. Their lives were remembered as children and young adults, and most of the memories are quite vivid. These brief passages are moving and poignant, giving a sense of everyday life as experienced by black people from the time of the Civil War through Reconstruction. This is the companion volume to the 1984 *My Folks Don't Want Me to Talk about Slavery*, which contains 21 oral histories of North Carolina men and women of the same era. This work is useful for both junior high and senior high students.   S.P.

113   Hurmence, Belinda. *Tancy.* Clarion 1984, HB $12.95 (0-89919-228-9). 203pp. Fiction.

Like his father before him, who had taken sexual liberties with one of the slave women, so attempted Billy Gaither with Tancy. Now Tancy has come to know that she and Billy are half-siblings. Following Billy's death and emancipation, Tancy leaves the Gaither plantation and the now old and lonely Mrs. Gaither behind to begin a long search for her mother, Lulu. During these first days of emancipation, Tancy has an advantage as a slave kept as a housemaid; she can read and write. Working for the Freedmen's Bureau, in a clerical position and as a teacher, she is able to continue her search for Lulu. When they meet, it is not necessarily the joyous homecoming that Tancy has hoped. This historical novel creates a believable portrait of a young woman searching for identity among people experiencing complex shifts and social change. Highly recommended for junior and senior high school readers, it shows how relationships created under a system of slavery—between blacks and whites and among blacks themselves —were altered for better and for worse, and that freedom itself brought pain and struggle as well as joy.   S.P.

Jakoubek, Robert. *Adam Clayton Powell, Jr.*
See entry 77, Grades 7–9.

114   James, Portia P. *The Real McCoy: African-American Invention and Innovation, 1619–1930.* Illus. Smithsonian Institution Pr. 1989, P $17.50 (0-87474-557-8). 110pp. Nonfiction.

The origin of the expression "the real McCoy" has been lost to many. Young people may be surprised to know that, yes, there was a real McCoy—Elijah. Among his more than 50 inventions, the patented device for lubricating railroad engines was one that industry experts found to be of incomparable quality. McCoy is but one of a number of African Americans who passed along scientific knowledge by invention or innovation. Inoculation against smallpox was suggested by Onesimus, a slave held by Cotton Mather. Norbert Rilleaux patented a system for production that revolutionized the sugar industry. Garrett Morgan and Lewis Latimer were both early pioneers in electrical engineering. This book was written as a catalog to accompany an exhibition sponsored by the Anacostia Museum in Washington, D.C. Illustrated with black-and-white photographs and patent drawings, it serves as a fine introduction to the contributions made by African Americans to science and industry.   S.P.

115   Katz, William Loren. *The Black West.* 3rd ed., rev. and expanded. Illus. with photos. Open Hand 1987, HB $29.95 (0-940880-17-2); P $15.95 (0-940880-18-0). 348pp. Nonfiction.

Katz's exhaustive and fascinating documentary of black Americans in the West is another example of scrupulous research in presenting the truth about American history. His writings on the African-American experience are first-rate. This title, first published by Doubleday in 1971, covers black explorers, cowboys, fur traders, homesteaders, infantry and cavalry, and frontier women; these six topics comprise only half of this monumental work. Filled throughout with archival photos that enhance the text, *The Black West* appears to be primarily for young adults, but it is, in fact, a valuable resource for teachers in elementary schools. The book covers many subjects addressed in the curriculum and in research assignments—cowboys, the Pony Express, and the Gold Rush, to name a few. With the emphasis on Columbus's "discovery," teachers will appreciate this counterbalancing information on black explorers. Includes an appendix, a chapter-by-chapter bibliography, and an index.   A.H.

Katz, William Loren. *Breaking the Chains: African-American Slave Resistance.* See entry 78, Grades 7–9.

Kosof, Anna. *The Civil Rights Movement and Its Legacy.* See entry 79, Grades 7–9.

116   Lanker, Brian, and Barbara Summers, eds. *I Dream a World: Portraits of Black Women Who Changed America.* Illus. Stewart, Tabori & Chang 1989, HB $40.00 (1-55670-063-6). 168pp. Nonfiction.

Seventy-five notable African-American women were photographed and interviewed by photographer Brian Lanker over a two-year period. Accompanying the stunning, large-format, full-page black-and-white portraits are excerpts from extended interviews. The collective portraits speak to the range of African-American experience, touching upon the themes of racism, family strength, educational goals, spiritual values, career achievements, and dreams for the future. After a foreword by Maya Angelou, the book opens with an interview and portrait of civil rights activist Rosa Parks. Also included are Toni Morrison, Leontyne Price, Althea Gibson, Angela Davis, Coretta Scott King, Shirley Chisholm, Oprah Winfrey, Katherine Dunham, and Barbara Jordan. Young adults will also be introduced to women perhaps less familiar, but equally inspiring and powerful.   S.P.

117   Larsen, Rebecca. *Paul Robeson: Hero Before His Time.* Illus. with photos. Franklin Watts 1989, LB $13.90 (0-531-10779-5). 160pp. Nonfiction.

Larsen has written a carefully researched biography. Her liberal use of quotes from primary sources helps readers to know Robeson, a Renaissance man who was an all-American football star, a Phi Beta Kappa scholar, a lawyer, an actor, a singer, a political activist, and a martyr. His fascinating life, coupled with Larsen's smooth writing style, will keep middle and high school students turning the pages; this is a biography that can be read straight through. The author presents her subject as a tireless crusader who paid dearly for his outspoken militancy on behalf of oppressed people.

Teenagers may find Robeson more worthy of their interest if told that his name was banished from all of the various reference books and encyclopedias that had lauded him prior to the McCarthy era and that entries for him later reappeared in these same "scholarly" and "objective" tomes.

This biography contains a center section of photos, a bibliography, an index, and copious notes. Though a worthy title, it should not replace Virginia Hamilton's award-winning *Paul Robeson: The Life and Times of a Free Black Man* (HarperCollins, 1974) or Susan Robeson's *The Whole World in His Hands: A Pictorial Biography of Paul Robeson* (Citadel Press, 1981). The latter title is by Robeson's granddaughter and has several hundred photographs, including a section showing the police brutality and mob violence at the 1949 Peekskill concert.   A.H.

Lester, Julius. *This Strange New Feeling.*
See entry 80, Grades 7–9.

McKissack, Patricia, and Fredrick McKissack. *A Long Hard Journey: The Story of the Pullman Porter.*
See entry 83, Grades 7–9.

Mathis, Sharon Bell. *Teacup Full of Roses.*
See entry 84, Grades 7–9.

118   Meltzer, Milton, ed. *The Black Americans: A History in Their Own Words, 1619–1983.* Illus. HarperCollins 1984, LB $14.89 (0-690-04418-6); 1987, P $5.95 (0-06-446055-X). 320pp. Nonfiction.

This outstanding book presents an overview of black American history told by those who lived it. Meltzer has selected from such diverse sources as speeches, autobiographies, interviews, diaries, letters, and court and legislative testimony to ensure that readers hear from a variety of people, both educated and illiterate, men and women, enslaved and free, famous and forgotten. The entries tell in firsthand accounts what it was like to be black during the eras of slavery, the emancipation, Reconstruction and its tragic overthrow, the mass migration of southern rural blacks to northern and western cities, the Harlem Renaissance, the Great Depression, the New Deal, and the civil rights movement, as well as during the bitterly disappointing decades that have ensued.

Selections are arranged chronologically. Meltzer briefly introduces each one to help the reader understand the historical context. His choices, coupled with these introductions, often deliver great emotional impact. Entries will help readers see how historical events influence individual lives and how the refusal of African Americans to accept oppression passively has shaped history. As a whole, the entries illustrate how difficult the struggle for equality and justice has been and continues to be.

Inevitably, some voices have been omitted. Meltzer makes no reference to Malcolm X, yet one entry is by Marcus Garvey, whose ideas helped to forge Malcolm X's political beliefs. Meltzer's decision adds to the book because students seldom hear about Garvey; more are familiar with Malcolm X, whose own autobiography is available and accessible. But whatever the reasons for Meltzer's choices, his sensitivity toward, interest in, and knowledge of African-American history make this a strong and credible collection, one that has appeared on numerous recommended lists.

Ideal for older high school students, this will be a difficult book for most young teenagers to read, partly because of archaic language but mostly because of their universal lack of deep knowledge of American history. Nevertheless, it must be considered a primary purchase for a collection serving both middle and high school students. Teachers of American history may want to read pertinent selections; the testimonies illustrate that not all Americans view historical events and figures the way that mainstream textbooks present them. This volume should replace Meltzer's earlier *In Their Own Words: A History of the American Negro, 1619–1865*. Includes a note on sources and an index.   A.H.

119   Morrison, Toni. ***The Bluest Eye.*** Simon & Schuster/Washington Square Pr. 1970, P $3.95 (0-671-53146-8). 160pp. Fiction.

Through the now mature eyes of Claudia, we look back to the 1940 summer during which she and her sister Frieda are growing up in Lorain, Ohio. Into their lives enters an 11-year-old foster child, Pecola. That summer the unloved and unlovely Pecola is sexually assaulted and impregnated by her father, Cholly Breedlove. She retreats to a world imagined more beautiful through the blue eyes for which she longs and fantasizes. The voices and histories of the adult characters are multidimensional, complex, and fully fleshed. This is a mature novel and, as Morrison's first, serves as a sophisticated teen reader's entry point to the subsequent works of this dynamic and influential American writer.

S.P.

Myers, Walter Dean. ***Fallen Angels.***
See entry 87, Grades 7–9.

Myers, Walter Dean. ***Hoops.***
See entry 88, Grades 7–9.

Myers, Walter Dean. ***Motown and Didi: A Love Story.***
See entry 89, Grades 7–9.

120   Patterson, Lillie. ***Martin Luther King, Jr. and the Freedom Movement.*** Illus. with photos. SERIES: Makers of America. Facts on File 1989, HB $16.95 (0-8160-1605-4). 192pp. Nonfiction.

More serious high school students, or those able to understand sophisticated vocabulary and political concepts, will find this an informative history. Patterson chronicles the key events of the period in a way that will be especially interesting to young adults. Her coverage of the Little Rock desegregation and her quotes from Sheyann Webb and Rachel West Nelson's *Selma, Lord, Selma* (Univ. of Alabama Pr., 1980) illustrate poignantly how the movement involved even young children. By mentioning the contributions of Bayard Rustin, James Baldwin, Harry Belafonte, and others, she shows that, although the focus was on helping southern blacks, many of the nation's black leaders aggressively supported the movement. Politically oriented students will be intrigued by the sequence of steps in Gandhi's *satyagraha* campaign, upon which King drew for his methodology. Another unusual feature is Patterson's inclusion of lyrics and music for several of the freedom movement's songs, which were so important to keeping up the momentum and courage of the movement's participants. More than other books on the subject, this title places the movement in a global context. After finishing the book, readers will have gained insight into how so many people were willing to make the "titanic sacrifice," putting their safety and their lives on the line for civil rights.

At the book's conclusion is a chronology listing significant events in Dr. King's life; a section for further reading, which discusses in paragraph form other relevant materials; and an index.

A.H.

121   Reynolds, Barbara A. *And Still We Rise: Interviews with 50 Black Role Models.*
USA Today Books 1988, P $14.95 (0-944347-02-9). 221pp. Nonfiction.

Subtitled *Interviews with 50 Black Role Models*, this is a collection of pieces that originally appeared in similar formats for the inquiry or opinion pages of the national news daily *USA Today*. Among the interviewees selected are Bill Cosby, Malcolm-Jamal Warner, Oprah Winfrey, Nikki Giovanni, and Coretta Scott King. Perhaps lesser-known to teenagers are the accomplishments and philosophies of Marian Wright Edelman, Randall Robinson, John Johnson, Niara Sudarkasa, and Tony Brown. The interviews, which average three pages per subject, are positive in tone, inspirational, and forward looking. There are a variety of professionals in the collection: activists, congressional representatives, communications executives, elected officials, an astronaut, clergy, athletes, writers, musicians, educators, entertainers, anthropologists, and lobbyists. This is an appealing collection suitable for both junior and senior high school students, one which gives a sense of various professions, what it took for African Americans to attain success in them, and the directions in which these achievers are headed in the future.

S.P.

Rummell, Jack. *Langston Hughes.*
See entry 90, Grades 7–9.

122   Rust, Edna, and Art Rust, Jr. *Art Rust's Illustrated History of the Black Athlete.*
Doubleday 1985, P $15.95 (0-385-15140-3). 448pp. Nonfiction.

The careers and achievements of contemporary athletes are of perennial interest to sports fans. A number of the athletes, particularly in the fields of horse racing and golf, may be little known to young adults. Here their achievements are seen as part of the struggle against racism in America. The sports areas represented are baseball, boxing, football, basketball, track, horse racing, golf, ice hockey, and tennis. This illustrated encyclopedia, originally published in 1985, remains useful for its entries that portray skilled, inspirational, and pioneering teams, athletes, and coaches. It is highly recommended for use with junior high and senior high students, to whom it will have great appeal.

S.P.

123   Sanders, Dori. ***Clover.*** Algonquin Books of Chapel Hill 1990, HB $13.95 (0-945575-26-2). 196pp. Fiction.

Hours after his wedding to Sara Kate—a white woman—Gaten Hill, a black South Carolina principal, is killed in an auto accident. He leaves behind a 10-year-old child, Clover, who has lost her mother years earlier. Aunt Ruby Helen wants Clover to live with her in Maryland, but Sara Kate had promised Gaten she will take care of the now-orphaned child. She settles into Gaten's house and raises Clover, all the while braving the disapproval of Clover's aunt and uncle, who run the family peach orchard. Told in Clover's first-person voice is the story of how she and Sara Kate adjust to Gaten's death and to each other and how the white stepmother gains the eventual acceptance of her stepdaughter's black relatives. Along the way are descriptions of cultural differences in food, hairstyle, and clothing, as well as in the expression of grief and love.

The strength of this novel lies in its portrayal of an interracial family's adjustment to the death of a loved one. Gaten has brought a diverse group of people together, and, once he is gone, they must find ways of getting along without him. Clover's own reactions to the death of her father are believable and moving, and her observations of Sara Kate's grief reflect the self-centered perspective of a child on the verge of adolescence. There is much complexity in Sanders's presentation of the South today, a place where feelings of tension and mistrust are shared by all sides, even though crude, monolithic oppression no longer exists. If the novel has one weakness, it is the too-adult tone of Clover's narrative, the price the author perhaps has to pay to achieve this level of insight and literary elegance.   L.M-L.

124   Shange, Ntozake. ***Betsey Brown.*** St. Martin's 1985, HB $12.95 (0-312-07727-0); 1986, P $8.95 (0-312-07728-9). 208pp. Fiction.

Thirteen-year-old Betsey Brown of St. Louis is one self-confident girl. After all, one would have to be if one aspires to sing backup for Tina Turner. It is 1959, and the comfortable childhood that Betsey has known is about to change with the onset of school integration. For Betsey this means not only the destruction of friendships, but fear of the unknown white world. With humor and sass, the world of this middle-class girl comes alive in Shange's semiautobiographical novel about a family of several generations under one roof, living in an environment with poetry, music, song, dance, familial love, and black pride. Written as an adult novel, its appeal spans the junior high and senior high levels.   S.P.

Smead, Howard. ***The Afro-Americans.***
See entry 92, Grades 7–9.

125   Sterling, Dorothy. ***Black Foremothers: Three Lives.*** 3rd ed. Feminist Pr. 1988, P $9.95 (0-935312-89-7). 174pp. Nonfiction.

The three lives featured are those of runaway slave Ellen Craft and political activists Ida Wells-Barnett and Mary Church Terrell. After the foreword by African-American author Margaret Walker, there is a lengthy introduction summarizing the contributions of these three women and the important historical events of their lifetimes. The introduction sets the tone for this scholarly yet engrossing volume.

One would assume that because of Craft's ingenious and dangerous adventure, her biography would be the most exciting of the three. Strangely, this is not so. Perhaps this is because she was unable to leave letters, journals, or diaries—slaves were prohibited by law from learning to read and write—and so readers cannot truly "meet" her. This is certainly not the case with the other two biographees. Their personalities and viewpoints come across vividly, enthralling and motivating readers. This work is best suited to high school students, but elementary and middle schoolers can be guided to Florence B. Freedman's *Two Tickets to Freedom* (Bedrick, 1971), which is an account of Ellen and William Craft's escape, and to Olive Burt's *Black Women of Valor* (Julian Messner, 1974), which includes a chapter on Ida Wells-Barnett.   A.H.

Taylor, Mildred D. **The Road to Memphis.**
See entry 93, Grades 7–9.

Taylor, Mildred D. **Roll of Thunder, Hear My Cry.**
See entry 94, Grades 7–9.

Thomas, Joyce Carol. **Marked by Fire.**
See entry 96, Grades 7–9.

Viglucci, Pat Costa. **Cassandra Robbins, Esq.**
See entry 97, Grades 7–9.

126   Warner, Malcolm-Jamal, and Daniel Paisner. **Theo and Me.** Dutton 1988, HB $14.95 (0-525-24694-0). 160pp. Nonfiction.

Celebrities frequently receive many letters from fans seeking advice. Malcolm-Jamal Warner of television's "The Cosby Show" is no exception. Gathered here are excerpts from fan letters to his character, Theo. Though stating that he is not an expert in the helping profession, Warner gives useful and sound advice. The chapters touch upon some of today's most pressing issues that concern youth: race relations, teenage pregnancy, drug abuse, sexuality, suicide, depression, friendship, family relationships, high school, and life after high school. It is not often that television spawns an African-American youngster whose appeal is truly universal. Malcolm-Jamal Warner takes on that responsibility in this advice book whose appeal is also universal. Included are resources for further assistance for both teenagers and parents.   S.P.

127   Webb, Sheyann, and Rachel West Nelson. **Selma, Lord, Selma: Girlhood Memories of the Civil Rights Days.** As told to Frank Sikora. Illus. with photos. Univ. of Alabama Pr. 1980, HB $12.95 (0-8173-0031-7). Nonfiction.

More than any other book on the civil rights movement, this one enables readers to experience what it must have felt like for the participants. It comprises the recollections of two young women who were 8 years old in 1965 and 18 years old when they recorded their impressions, and therefore it speaks as effectively to children and young adults as it does to adults. Journalist Frank Sikora did the newspaper-style interviews, without a tape recorder, of Sheyann and Rachel approximately ten years after their active involvement in the turbulent "Selma winter." Sikora focused primarily on the girls' feelings about the events themselves, and these are presented simply and eloquently, in the girls' own words.

By using the technique of direct narrative, Sikora captures the fears, bewilderment, and pride of these two spunky children. It is disconcerting to read of children's efforts to understand the murders of close friends or the "logic" of white supremacists willing to club and gas even the most defenseless members of the march. It is also painful to hear them relate their gratefulness for the orange "jungle juice" and bologna sandwiches the civil rights workers passed out to them so they wouldn't go hungry that day. Yet one also reads of Sheyann and Rachel's glee at being held on Dr. King's lap while adults looked on with envy. Although the book was published for adults and would definitely appeal to young adults as well, it would also make an excellent read-aloud for an elementary school class, because it illustrates, in a child's language, the role children can have in social and historical events.   A.H.

128   Williams, Juan. *Eyes on the Prize: America's Civil Rights Years, 1954–1965.* Illus. with photos. Viking 1987, P $10.95 (0-14-009653-1). 305pp. Nonfiction.

Originally broadcast in 1987, the PBS television series "Eyes on the Prize" recreated for viewers the era of intense civil rights activity spanning the years 1954–1965. Through the oral histories gathered, this story of freedom, which opens with the dismantling of school segregation, brings alive for students a period of American history not so long ago. Throughout the text are a number of black-and-white photographs used in the television series. Perhaps more formidable to some teen readers would be the companion volume, *Voices of Freedom,* which continues to trace the movement from the 1950s to the 1980s.   S.P.

2

UNITED STATES:
ASIAN AMERICANS

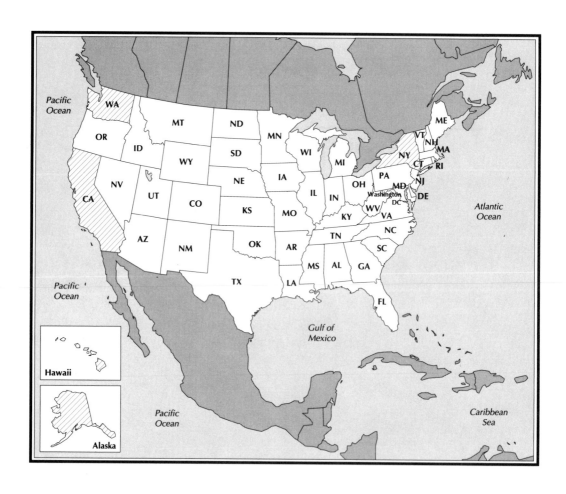

STATES WITH HIGHEST
CONCENTRATION OF
ASIAN AMERICANS

1. Hawaii - 61.8%
2. California - 9.6%
3. Washington - 4.3%
4. New York - 3.9%
5. Alaska - 3.6%

Source: 1990 U.S. Census

PLACES OF ORIGIN
OF ASIAN AMERICANS
BY PERCENTAGE

1. China - 22.6%
2. Philippines - 19.3%
3. Japan - 11.7%
4. India - 11.2%
5. Korea - 11.0%
6. Vietnam - 8.4%
7. Hawaii - 2.9%
8. Samoa - 0.9%
9. Guam - 0.7%

2

UNITED STATES:
ASIAN AMERICANS

by Ellin Chu and Carolyn Vang Schuler

Asian Americans are the fastest-growing and most diverse minority group in the United States. According to "A New Look at Asian Americans" in the journal *American Demographics*, October 1990, page 26, "The number of Asian Americans grew from 3.8 million in 1980, to an estimated 6.9 million in 1989. This 80 percent increase was spurred by 2.4 million Asian immigrants who arrived in the United States during the 1980s." Among the leading countries of origin are the Philippines, Vietnam, China, Korea, Taiwan, Cambodia, India, Laos, and Japan. The statement is made in the May 1990 issue of *American Demographics* that "by the year 2010, as many as 38 percent of Americans under the age of 18 will belong to minority groups." It is incumbent upon us and our children to learn more about the cultures of these newest Americans. In fact, many Americans do wish to become better acquainted with the arts, foods, literature, history, and contributions of their Asian-American neighbors. However, they need guidance in how to go about it.

It is important to keep in mind that just as there is a tendency to lump all those between the ages of 12 and 18 together under the rubric "young adult" no matter how different the individuals, so are "Asian Americans" undifferentiated. In considering the available materials, keep in mind that within the Asian-American category are peoples from totally differing cultures—often cultures that have been in mortal conflict with each other at various times over thousands of years. In addition, the term "Asian American" encompasses people who have been in the United States and Canada for three or more generations as well as those who literally "came over on the last boat."

In researching the literature for appropriate materials, the authors found it necessary to become acquainted with what it is that determines stereotypical treatment of the Asian-American population. Two excellent resources clearly define the criteria for analyzing books on Asian Americans. "Criteria for Selecting Books about Various Ethnic Groups" are outlined in Appendix A of *Literature for Children about Asians and Asian Americans* by Esther C. Jenkins and Mary C. Austin (Greenwood Press, 1987). Additional excellent and specific evaluation questions for analyzing Asian-American literature for youth are compiled in the special double issue of the Council on Interracial Books for Children Bulletin

(Vol. 7, Nos. 2 and 3, 1976), "Asian Americans in Children's Books." In addition, numerous conversations with a variety of Asian Americans over the years were helpful.

Literature for children has developed beautifully since the early 1970s, when most books on Asian cultures were "racist, sexist, and elitist, and . . . the image[s] of Asian Americans [that they presented were] grossly misleading." [1] While there is still a dearth of materials on the most recent immigrants (e.g., Filipinos, Vietnamese, and Laotians), particularly at the picture book level, the entry of Asian Americans into the literature has occurred in a very comfortable and natural manner. Criticism of the most recent books indicates that Asian-American protagonists reveal little, if anything, about their homeland and ancient customs. Furthermore, these newer books tend to be about every issue except the immigration experience. The only element to which Asian-American readers can relate is the fact that the person in the book is of the same heritage. In some cases, such as Kline's *Horrible Harry's Secret* (Viking, 1990), the text does not even indicate any enlightening information about the child's background. For some people, access to the various cultures may be difficult because subject headings prominently feature the real issues of the text and ignore the fact that there is an Asian-American character present. This may limit access to such noteworthy treatments as Helen Coutant's *First Snow*, in which a Vietnamese-American girl faces her grandmother's impending death. Perhaps omitting references to racial heritage can be construed in a positive way—that all Americans, no matter their heritage, are Americans first. In the meantime, however, even with immigration increasing, there is still a need to highlight these particular cultures. Until recently, the authors have not deemed it important to define how long the immigrants have been in the country or how many generations have passed since their arrival. In spite of these omissions, Asian-American readers can relate to the characters at the simplest level.

We have previously mentioned that there are distinctions among Asian cultures. One must keep them in mind, but one must also be aware of three characteristics by which writers tend to measure Asian-American assimilation. A book written about Americans with an Asian cultural background is not successful if one measures its success by the extent to which Asian Americans in it have assimilated the values, the attitudes, and the mannerisms of white middle-class Americans.

Illustrations in picture books have vastly improved since the early 1970s. The Fu Manchu mustaches, short straight cereal-bowl haircuts, buck teeth, myopic vision, and clothing that were cruelly and offensively indicative of ancient ways are not seen as often. Children and young adults now wear sneakers and faddish tops, decorate their rooms with the newest "hot items," live in contemporary homes with modern conveniences, and sport the latest in hairstyles. Regardless of perspective, artists interpreting for the authors are more aware of these cultures and illustrate the texts more accurately. It is obvious that they are using Asian-American models and have kept in tune with the newest "look" in areas such as Chinatown. In addition, there seems to have been an increase in the number of books about Asian Americans written by Asian Americans themselves.

1. "Asian Americans in Children's Books," Interracial Books for Children Bulletin, Vol. 7, Nos. 2 and 3, 1976, p. 3.

Another positive trend in current books is that the stereotypes that often surface in the form of teasing and insensitivity by one character are now corrected by another character. Many more erroneous attitudes remain to be conquered, but at least an attempt is now being made to educate the uninformed or the misinformed.

One excellent way to overcome our preconceived ideas and educate ourselves is to "Read more about it." Unfortunately, many library collections still house some pre-1975 titles that perpetuate stereotypes, especially among their children's book collections. The following helpful resources give fair and positive treatment of Asian Americans from different countries and in different stages of acculturation. Most have been published since 1980. We have tried to indicate those books that are inaccurate or written in any way that is demeaning.

The young adult books included in this chapter are as varied as the needs they meet, from formula romances to works of considerable literary merit and from standard "assignment" books to unique personal portraits. What all this material does have in common is that it is all "true" and does not debase either the cultural integrity or the common humanity of the people who are the subjects.

Currently, the most glaring gaps in the literature include young adult novels with an American setting and an Asian-Indian or Pakistani immigrant protagonist. Fiction told from a male Asian-American teenager's point of view is almost nonexistent as well. Finally, biographies of famous "achievers" with an Asian heritage are scarce.

As the next decade passes, we look forward to the field becoming inundated with books about Asian-American children and young adults for whom there is now no relevant literature. These books will increasingly feature those people who are just now, in the beginning of the 1990s, coming from Asia to America. As this population increases, so will the quantity and quality of the literature in this field.

PRESCHOOL–GRADE 3

129 Battles, Edith. ***What Does the Rooster Say, Yoshio?*** Illus. by Toni Hormann. Albert Whitman 1978. 32pp. Fiction. o.p.

While visiting the play farm with their mothers, a Japanese boy and an American girl meet and discover that their linguistic differences extend even to the way each makes animal sounds. When Yoshio sees ducks, he says, "Ga, ga!" and not "Quack, quack!" as Lynn does. And so it goes with each animal, with the children's frustration giving way to laughter as they try one another's language. To their delight they finally hear a cow say "moo" and make identical sounds. The Japanese and English words for each animal are provided in the illustrations. Unfortunately, this is a good idea rather unsuccessfully executed. The text is so brief that sometimes it is confusing. The primary-grade audience who would appreciate the idea of communicating in various ways may be put off by the preschool format, outdated illustrations, and old style. Also, the illustrations are of greeting-card caliber and add little. An updated version would be more helpful. C.V.S.

Brown, Tricia. *Chinese New Year.*
See entry 146, Grades 4–6.

130   Bunting, Eve. *The Happy Funeral.* Illus. by Vo-Dinh Mai. HarperCollins 1982. 40pp. Fiction. o.p.

This is the account of how a young girl, Laura, feels when her grandfather dies and what transpires around her between the time of his death and the funeral. Since Laura and her family are Chinese American, the beliefs, traditions, and customs surrounding the death generate a very specific societal experience. The text is sensitive, quiet, and loving, and the portrayal of grief realistic. The illustrations fit the text well by the very elements that they reveal. There are hints of Chinese culture in the food and its preparation, the incense sticks, and the art (as shown in the picture of the kite). Even the picture of Chinatown is accurate, unlike Leo Politi's *Moy Moy* (Scribner, 1960), which features an American Chinatown with everyone looking very much as if he or she is still in China. The descriptions of activities also enrich the reader's knowledge of this particular culture in counterpoint to the fact that the emotions that are experienced by the survivors of any death anywhere are the same no matter what their nationality. This is beautifully summed up in the last sentence, "She never said it was happy for us to have him go." Here we learn about the acts of mourning that make this funeral specifically Chinese American: the service at the Chinese Gospel Church, the candy that is passed out to "sweeten your sorrow," the jazz band that plays hymns "all jazzed up," and the burning of the cardboard house. This is a worthy book for all ages, but it will speak especially to a Chinese-American child who experiences the loss of a loved one. It is also a valuable resource for Chinese-American children not living in a Chinese community who seek to know a little of their own civilization.   C.V.S.

131   Coerr, Eleanor. *Chang's Paper Pony.* Illus. by Deborah Kogan Ray. SERIES: I Can Read Books. HarperCollins 1988, LB $10.89 (0-06-021329-9). 64pp. Fiction.

Thousands of Chinese came to this country between 1850 and 1864 to seek their fortunes in gold. Though they were industrious and contributed much to the growth of the West, few of them made the fortune that they sought. It is during this time that we meet Chang, the son of Chinese immigrants, who is lonely in his new home in California in spite of the thousands of people who settled there during the Gold Rush. More than anything else, he wants a pony of his own. Grandpa Li says that the only pony they can afford is the one in the picture on the wall. Chang tries his hand panning for gold but finds that hard work and honesty are more rewarding. Chang's name and costume are Chinese, and his Oriental ways are mocked by insensitive miners. His experiences are those of a Chinese immigrant, but his loneliness in a new home and his dream of a pony are universal feelings, making him a character with whom any young reader can identify. The adults are not portrayed particularly well, but all in all this succeeds as easy-reading historical fiction written about an interesting period of American history. The illustrations capture beautifully the rough-and-ready nature of the frontiersmen as well as the simplicity and orderliness of the Chinese Americans. Useful for units on cultures and the American West.   C.V.S.

132   Coutant, Helen. *First Snow.* Illus. by Vo-Dinh Mai. Knopf 1974, LB $6.99 (0-394-92831-8). 36pp. Fiction.

Lien, a little Vietnamese girl, hears that her grandmother is dying. Not understanding the word, she thinks at first that it has something to do with the long-anticipated first snow, the kind of weather she has never seen. Finally, after no explanation from others, she gathers enough nerve to ask her grandmother what dying means. Grandmother tells her to go outside when the snow starts to fall in order to learn what dying is. Lien discovers that dying means her grandmother will change form but still live on in some way. Unlike Tomie dePaola's *Nana Upstairs, Nana Downstairs* (Putnam, 1973), the grandmother does not actually die in the story. It is not important that she does or does not. Lien has learned that Grandmother will always be alive in spirit. The text is simple, complemented by gentle black-and-white illustrations that extend the storyline and reveal Asian characters. The narrative is basically an attempt to explain death to any child. Although the book has been criticized for providing little information on Vietnamese life, it indeed has everything to do with Vietnamese life. There is a mixture of cultures (Vietnamese incense-burning rituals and the novelty of snow in America) and a marvelous demonstration of the Buddhist belief that life and death are but two parts of the same reality.   C.V.S.

133   Friedman, Ina R. *How My Parents Learned to Eat.* Illus. by Allen Say. Houghton Mifflin 1984, LB $13.95 (0-395-35379-3). 32pp. Fiction.

In a Japanese-American kitchen, a small girl tells the story of her parents and how it happens that she is equally at home using chopsticks or a knife and fork. Uneasy because of cultural dining differences, John, an American sailor, had never asked his Japanese date, Aiko, to dinner. With his time in Yokohama running out, he secretly went to a Japanese restaurant and learned to use chopsticks. At the same time, Aiko took lessons from her great uncle. But, to her surprise, when she and John went to dinner, she discovered that her great uncle had taught her to eat European style, not as Americans do. Soft, full-color drawings mirror the gentle humor of the story and also point out the meshing of the Japanese and American cultures. This would be useful in introducing a unit on foods of the world, manners and customs, and, of course, the Japanese American.   C.V.S.

134   Girard, Linda Walvoord. *We Adopted You, Benjamin Koo.* Illus. by Linda Shute. Albert Whitman 1989, LB $12.95 (0-8075-8694-3). 32pp. Nonfiction.

This is a first-person narrative, written mainly to help adopted children understand and come to terms with their circumstances. Benjamin relates the story of how he is brought to the United States. His true story gives the reader insight into his development as a Korean American. When Benjamin realizes he does not look like his parents, we learn of his difficulties in adjusting to the news of his adoption. This difficulty is beautifully balanced by a positive portrayal of his athletic ability. Benjamin is a nonstereotypical Asian-American child, but through him we experience the pain of his adoption discovery, hear the answers to unanswerable questions, and are made aware of the insensitivities of his peers. Overall, the book uses both humor and compassion to teach readers about parenting and the Asian-American experience. It asks questions all adoptees ask, touches briefly on the insensitivity of strangers who would rudely inquire about his background, and allows Benjamin the opportunity to participate in the adoption of yet another child of similar circumstances. The author wisely avoids the larger issues of adoption and presents a simple, serviceable book for use at all levels.

C.V.S.

135   Kline, Suzy. *Horrible Harry's Secret.* Illus. by Frank Remkiewicz. Viking 1990, LB $10.95 (0-670-82470-4). 52pp. Fiction.

Korean-American children will appreciate the fact that Song Lee is someone of their ethnic background. However, she could be "anychild, anywhere," who has ever been the object of a classmate's crush. The only reference to Song Lee's Asian ancestry surfaces through a note she writes to Harry in which she mentions her grandfather's death in the Korean War. The rest of the activities in this reader, are, basically, light second-grade fare, including a child who loses a tooth, a boy who is more affected by his parents' divorce than he would like to let on, and the throes of first love. Still, the unexaggerated illustrations that portray Song Lee as Asian will attract a child of like heritage. That is where the similarity ends, however. Song Lee dresses like all of the other children. Moreover, she serves as a positive role model for girls as she shares her water frog with the class, much to the delight of Harry, who instantly falls in love. The brief mention of the war may serve as a catalyst to introduce the subject to this grade. Also, the last sentence summarizes the book's message for every child: "Sometimes when we share the horrible truth, we become closer friends."

C.V.S.

136   Levine, Ellen. *I Hate English!* Illus. by Steve Bjorkman. Scholastic 1989, LB $12.95 (0-590-42305-3). 32pp. Fiction.

Recent immigrant Mei Mei and her family move from Hong Kong to New York City, where they encounter a strange new language and way of life. They settle comfortably into Chinatown, where the sights and sounds are familiar. Mei Mei resists learning English and because of her obstinacy is sent to a resource room to study the language in isolation. There she meets a clever teacher, Nancy, who subtly influences Mei Mei to converse in English and discover the benefits of using both languages. The illustrations for this picture book very definitely display Asian children, although some may object to the exaggerated almond-shaped eyes of the people. In particular, the poses of the people that show crossed, almond-shaped eyes are clearly stereotypical and inappropriate for this title. The biggest objection to the story, however, is the unrealistic resistance of Mei Mei to change. New languages, sights, and sounds are the delicacies of children. It is more likely that parents and grandparents, more than children, would want to hang on to the culture and language of their people. They are truly the ones who get upset that children become so Americanized that they do not remember the ways of the old country or their heritage. Despite its flaws, teachers and parents may use this title to think about how it feels to be in a strange place. It is also a good discussion piece to introduce the need for change and the concept that the world is made up of all different kinds of people.

C.V.S.

MacMillan, Dianne, and Dorothy Freeman. *My Best Friend Duc Tran: Meeting a Vietnamese American Family.*
See entry 152, Grades 4–6.

137   Paek, Min. *Aekyung's Dream.* Bilingual ed., rev. ed. Trans. into Korean by the author. Illus. by the author. Children's Book Pr. 1988, LB $12.95 (0-89239-042-5). 22pp. Fiction.

In a bilingual book originally published in 1978, Aekyung, a young Korean girl, must come to terms with her new home in America. She must also deal with teasing and taunting classmates who are insensitive to her feelings and her inability to speak English. With help and encouragement from her supportive family, she is successful. A unique aspect of this story is that the plot centers on a Korean family instead of the more commonly featured Chinese or Japanese experience. The flavor of Korea is shared with the reader in highly stylized pictures and in the unusual vocabulary. This picture book may be shelved either in the preschool/elementary area of libraries or in their language development collection. The English translation into Korean by the author pegs this as an excellent resource for new immigrants who are caught in transition from the old ways to the new. It is also a simple lesson for those students who are being introduced to Korean as their second language. Paek writes from firsthand experience as a newcomer to this land and produced this book to encourage children, Korean as well as others, to persevere in their efforts to adjust to an unfamiliar and sometimes cruel new society.   C.V.S.

138   Sobol, Harriet Langsam. *We Don't Look Like Our Mom and Dad.* Illus. with photos by Patricia Agre. Coward, McCann 1984, LB $9.95 (0-698-20608-8). 32pp. Nonfiction.

This black-and-white photo-essay reveals the life of the Levin family, American parents with two Korean-born adopted sons. In many ways it parallels *We Adopted You, Benjamin Koo* (Albert Whitman, 1989) by Linda Girard. However, this interpretation captures a real family as a whole. Each boy, 10-year-old Eric and 11-year-old Joshua, "has a different biological mother, but in the Levin family, they are brothers." All of the excellent photos reflect two very typical boys in very normal dress, activities, and states of emotion. The photos seem to capture the questions, the anger, the hurts, and the curiosities related to being adopted. This is an outstanding study of the power of family love. It also relates information about Korean-American children who have adjusted beautifully to a new culture. The other aspect that adds to the strength of this book is the fact that the two adopted boys exist in a world with other Asian-American children, but whose parents are Asian. This will be very useful in collections for years to come as more and more immigrants and Asian-born adoptees come to the United States and Canada.   C.V.S.

139   Stock, Catherine. *Emma's Dragon Hunt.* Illus. by the author. Lothrop, Lee & Shepard 1984, LB $9.55 (0-688-02698-2). 32pp. Fiction.

The author explores Chinese mythology through a contemporary story about a little girl and her grandfather. Grandfather Wong arrives from China and introduces dragon lore to his granddaughter, Emma. Frightened at first, Emma is intimidated into lying awake one night contemplating the notion of dragons dancing on her roof. The next day she and her grandfather set out to discover what dragons are all about. Grandfather skillfully introduces Emma to the concept of dragons in nature as the cause of earthquakes, heat waves, solar eclipses, and thunderstorms. The number of natural phenomena that occur within a few days, while contrived and unbelievable, are used by the author to lend some mystery to the Chinese myths. The interesting theme, with the exception of the first page ("Emma was excited," but she looks as if she has just lost her best friend), is supplemented by attractive and whimsical illustrations. The illustrations help depict the American way of dress, eating, and living, as well as Chinese culture and art. For example, the family is shown one evening eating with knives and forks and another evening with chopsticks. Despite its occasional contrivances, this is certainly a gentle introduction to Chinese folklore, a discussion of natural events, and a tender intergenerational and intercultural story.

C.V.S.

140   Surat, Michele Maria. *Angel Child, Dragon Child.* Illus. by Vo-Dinh Mai. Raintree 1983, HB $14.65 (0-940742-12-8). 35pp. Fiction.

New immigrants from any country face a period of homesickness, uncertainty, and adjustment to their new life, all of which is embodied in this touching tale of a young Vietnamese girl, Ut. Her two older sisters seem confident and happy, but Ut misses her mother, who is still in Vietnam and who would tell Ut to be an Angel Child and be happy in her new school. But the other children tease Ut and her sisters for their "odd" clothing and their "funny" words. Ut is angry, but she copes as bravely as she can, like a dragon.

One day when she is caught fighting with Raymond, a red-headed boy, the wise and perceptive principal, like an understanding angel, puts the two in a room together with the injunction that Raymond write Ut's story because Raymond needs to learn to listen and Ut needs to learn to talk. Overcoming both fear and judgment, they learn. The whole school is moved as the principal reads Ut's story, as written by Raymond. The school mounts a fair to raise money to send for Ut's mother. By the time her mother arrives, Ut has made it through a whole year of school. She and her sisters have traded their Ao Dai (Vietnamese dresses) for jeans and T-shirts. They speak English. They are becoming American. But a part of them will always be homesick for Vietnam. The final scene of the story is the arrival of "Mother!"

The illustrations in colored pencil by the versatile and now well-known Vietnamese artist Vo-Dinh Mai evoke sympathy for the plight of the young innocent in an uncomfortable if not terrifyingly new and unwelcoming situation. In addition, they offer flashes of Vietnamese culture and an idea of how life even in America might be different for a Vietnamese child than what it would be for a child who had never been anyplace else but America.

G.L./S.L./S.M.

141   Turner, Ann. *Through Moon and Stars and Night Skies.* Illus. by James Graham Hale. HarperCollins 1990, LB $12.89 (0-06-026190-0). 32pp. Fiction.

This is a generic, easy-to-read Asian-American tale that serves well as an introduction to the concept of foreign adoption. It is only through the illustrations that the reader can determine the suggested nationality of the narrator. From the depicted countryside of the child's homeland, the appearance of the people, and the activities, it appears to be Vietnam. Other than that, it is just the story of a boy who "went on a plane and flew for a day and a night through . . . ." He has feelings of fear of the unknown to tackle before accepting the love of a loving family. For foreign-born, adopted children, that is a major battle, and having a particular book to relate to in this sense will be of tremendous benefit to them.

The boy's adoptive parents spent a great deal of thought in paving the way for their new child. Before his arrival, they sent pictures that showed the quilt he will have for a blanket each night. It is this slight grasp at familiarity to which the child will also relate. The activity itself is a good suggestion for other parents in the process of adopting a foreign child. Therefore, this book would serve well in a parenting collection as well as in one geared to children. The story is simple, but it is an excellent introduction and one that can be read by beginning readers.

C.V.S.

142 Uchida, Yoshiko. ***The Birthday Visitor.*** Illus. by Charles Robinson. Scribner 1975. 32pp. Fiction. o.p.

An awful thing has happened to spoil Emi's seventh birthday. A horrid man, a minister from Japan, is arriving right on the day of her planned birthday celebration. Emi doesn't want Reverend Okura to come, because ministers from Japan are very proper, dull, and absolutely no fun. When November 14 arrives, she receives a few surprises. For gifts she is given a pink wool dress and a heart-shaped locket. Mr. and Mrs. Wada come for dinner, and the unwelcome Reverend Okura arrives to immediately preside over the burial of a dead sparrow that another child has found. An unhappy 7-year-old unexpectedly has a happy birthday anyway and discovers a very interesting Reverend Okura along the way. Emi's feelings of frustration at not being able to have what she wants are discussed in a way children can understand. However, the book endorses the stereotype that Asian people are cool, collected, and unemotional. The Asian-American connection? The blue-and-orange illustrations evoke the feelings of a charming family from Japan. The illustrations do not prepare us for a life other than in Japan. The Japanese women are also portrayed as bowing incorrectly. This book is really dated, like some other picture books by Uchida that have long outlived their usefulness in collections. Weed this one immediately unless yours is a last-copy center or a historical collection.

C.V.S.

143 Uchida, Yoshiko. ***The Rooster Who Understood Japanese.*** Illus. by Charles Robinson. Scribner 1976. 32pp. Fiction. o.p.

Whether the rooster Mr. Lincoln actually understood Japanese or not, he did understand that the function of a rooster was to crow at the crack of dawn. Unfortunately, the crotchety next-door neighbor objects to the rooster reveille and demands that Mr. Lincoln be relocated at once. Mrs. Kitamura, the rooster's owner, is very upset over the situation until Miyo, the little girl next door, finds him a good home by placing an ad in her school paper. The storyline is very low-key, and the ending, in which Mrs. Kitamura invites the neighbor to a celebration party and befriends him, is a little too predictable and unrealistic. On the plus side, the book's main assets are an attractive representation of a dual Japanese-American life-style, the depiction of a resourceful little girl, and a mother who is also a doctor. Even the usually stereotyped stern grandmother figure is independent and a good role model for children. The book was not an essential first purchase at the time of publication, but it serves well today for the reasons stated above. Again, it is a trend toward the Asian-American book that concentrates on the issue and just happens to have an Asian-American protagonist, rather than a book specifically about a Japanese-American child.

C.V.S.

144   Waters, Kate, and Madeline Slovenz-Low. *Lion Dancer: Ernie Wan's Chinese New Year.* Illus. with photos by Martha Cooper. Scholastic 1990, LB $12.95 (0-590-43046-7). 32pp. Nonfiction.

It is the Chinese New Year, and Ernie Wan, the eldest son of a Kung Fu master, will soon perform his first Lion Dance on the streets of Chinatown in New York City. Through text and brilliant color photos, we observe firsthand the preparations for this very important dance. Juxtaposed among those activities are moments of family involvement that present the reader with a glimpse into the life of contemporary Chinese Americans. All of the children and adults are dressed in very modern clothes, except when donning the dance costumes. Readers also observe the family eating a Chinese festival feast prepared in a modern kitchen, performing the Buddhist ritual of offering food and incense at the altar, and even videotaping the ceremony for posterity. This picture book carefully and accurately portrays the life of a Chinese-American family in the 1980s. It also provides a sterling example of the ancient customs that are important for them to preserve, yet at the same time allow them to function in a modern world. Interestingly enough, it is not a celebration unlike any other New Year's gala. In many ways, for Chinese Americans *Lion Dancer* is the most important title on this entire list. It totally succeeds in capturing the life-style that exists in Chinatown today. Teachers will welcome the intimate and unique introduction to this culture. This *is* Chinatown and this *is* the Chinese New Year celebration. An added bonus is the inclusion of the Chinese horoscope, which names each year after an animal.

C.V.S.

GRADES 4–6

145   Andrews, Jean F. *The Secret in the Dorm Attic.* SERIES: Flying Fingers Club. Gallaudet Univ. Pr. 1990, P $3.95 (0-930323-66-1). 100pp. Fiction.

When his hearing friend Donald from back home visits Matt at his dorm at the school for the deaf, the boys start to investigate some strange happenings in the attic. In a subplot, Donald also learns firsthand what it is like to be left out when Matt and his friends sign and fingerspell too much for him to participate. This entry in the Flying Fingers Club fiction series also introduces Saleem, a deaf boy from Pakistan who is new at the school. Since protagonists of Pakistani nationality are practically nonexistent in literature for young readers, this will be one character to whom Pakistani Americans can relate. The story itself is typical bulk literature fare. However, the many faces of prejudice—against both the deaf *and* hearing, as well as against Asians—surface as Donald, Matt, Saleem, and, later, Donald's sister Susan explore unusual circumstances. Because Saleem is seen talking to a suspect, he too comes under close surveillance. His descriptions of Pakistani ways, however, help explain situations with the suspect as well as inform the reader about his native land. As with many of the more current book illustrations, Asian-American Saleem, too, sports a very American look with his sweats, sneakers, and hairstyle, replete with cowlick.

C.V.S.

Brown, Dee Alexander, and Linda Proctor. *Lonesome Whistle: The Story of the First Transcontinental Railroad.*
See entry 165, Grades 7–9.

146   Brown, Tricia. *Chinese New Year.* Illus. with photos by Fran Ortiz. Henry Holt 1987, LB $12.95 (0-8050-0497-1). 48pp. Nonfiction.

"Gung Hay Fat Choy!" "Wishing you good fortune for happiness." As Chinese Americans in San Francisco prepare for Chinese New Year, the author and the photographer chronicle their preparations in both words and pictures. The text, which is informative and well organized, is unfortunately accompanied by black-and-white photos that are often dark. Thus, it lacks the vibrant character of *Lion Dancer* by Kate Waters (Scholastic, 1990), whose rich and bold color photos are full of the same action. Not every collection will need this for its holiday books, since seldom does a child have to report on Chinese New Year. However, for large collections, it will be useful to supplement books on Chinese Americans.   C.V.S.

147   Christopher, Matt. *Shortstop from Tokyo.* Illus. by Harvey Kidder. Little, Brown 1988, P $3.95 (0-316-13992-0). 121pp. Fiction.

When Sam Suzuki joined the team as shortstop, Stogie resented having his favorite position taken from him, even temporarily. But Sam was an excellent player and was liked by all of the boys. He was very proud of his glove, which had been autographed by a famous Japanese ball player. One night Stogie found Sam's glove on the ground and elected not to take it inside for safekeeping. The glove was ruined by the gnawing of porcupines. Stogie had to prove his innocence to Sam, who accused him of willfully damaging it in retaliation for bumping him out of the shortstop slot. There is plenty of exciting game action, with play-by-play descriptions that will appeal to sports readers today as much as they did in the 1970s, when the book was originally published. There is no mention of Japan at all, except for the glove anecdote, yet, in the reading of this book, Japanese-American children will have someone to whom they can relate.   C.V.S.

148   Estes, Eleanor. *The Lost Umbrella of Kim Chu.* Illus. by Jacqueline Ayer. Atheneum 1978. 86pp. Fiction. o.p.

Without permission, Kim Chu borrows her father's prize-winning umbrella with the secret scroll. Through events that take place while she is trying to retrieve the umbrella after it gets stolen, we learn a little of the ways of the Chinese in Chinatown in the early 1970s, a Chinatown that has faded from the picture. There are no real contemporary sites and sounds, the grandmother is an unsettling and somewhat abusive character, the parents work in a Chinese restaurant, and even Kim herself is not a particularly modern child. Furthermore, the illustrations give no hints or distinguishing marks to indicate that it is New York's Chinatown. Still, there is that omnipresent emotion of losing something that did not belong to you in the first place. Asian-American children may find Kim very brave. However, an updated text with more modern artwork is what this book needs if it is to be a viable resource for Asian-American children.   C.V.S.

149   Howard, Ellen. *Her Own Song.* Atheneum 1988, LB $12.95 (0-689-31444-2). 160pp. Fiction.

A combination of straight narrative and flashbacks (in italics) helps to tell this story of 11-year-old Mellie, who, because of serendipitous events, discovers the real details surrounding the events of her birth and first four years of life. The strange twists of events seem implausible but in reality are based on a factual incident. (The historical novel was inspired by an article that the author saw in a newsletter about a girl whose first adoptive parents were Chinese.) What is strongly gleaned from this narrative is the climate of racism and oppression that was prevalent on the West Coast at the turn of the century. From the flashbacks the reader learns of Mellie's mother's plight, of her stepmother's death, and of the horrible practice of selling American babies to Chinese couples during this period in American history. When Aunt Estie decides to spend a month at the beach, Mellie is left to care for the home with her father. One day her father is injured at work and hospitalized. When Geem-Wah, the owner of a Chinese laundry and the man who holds the key to events surrounding Mellie's birth, insists on driving her to the hospital in search of her father, Mellie's introduction to the Chinese community and her relationship to it begins. The story is engrossing and reads quickly. It is an eye-opener, not only to learn of the strange baby-selling practice and prejudice against the Chinese but also to understand the vehement resistance expressed when a Caucasian ventured into the sacred and protected world of the Chinese in America.   C.V.S.

150   Lord, Bette Bao. *In the Year of the Boar and Jackie Robinson.* Illus. by Marc Simont. HarperCollins 1984, LB $12.95 (0-06-024004-0). 176pp. Fiction.

It is 1947 in Brooklyn, New York, and Bandit, now called Shirley Temple Wong, must adjust to a new way of life. At first she is welcomed by her classmates. However, as each day passes she finds it increasingly difficult to release the Chinese customs so ingrained in her. She feels, too, that she has failed to represent the Chinese well in this strange new world. Shirley's happiness returns when she is befriended by the toughest girl in the class, who introduces her to stickball, the Brooklyn Dodgers baseball team, and the team's hero, Jackie Robinson. Throughout this upper elementary novel, the reader learns about the Chinese way of life and becomes sensitive to the adjustment that one must make after moving to new territory, whether it be around the corner or across the world. Any child who has been displaced by a move will find this to be a globally appealing story. Those looking for positive, forward thinking, nonstereotypical sex role models will appreciate the female protagonist's love for baseball. This book is an excellent read aloud, and teachers and parents will find many areas that generate discussion.   C.V.S.

151   McDonald, Joyce. *Mail-Order Kid.* Putnam 1988, LB $12.95 (0-399-21513-1). 125pp. Fiction.

Flip Doty, without parental permission, has ordered a fox by mail. Naturally, there ensues a battle between parent and child over the issue of keeping it. Temporary conditions are established for keeping the fox, but, in spite of all attempts, Flip is unable to maintain his end of the bargain. His greatest argument for keeping his pet is a comparison between his 6-year-old adopted Korean brother and his fox. He argues that since they were both selected for the family by a mail-order procedure, both are equally worthy of adoption. In the end, Flip learns to accept his brother and to understand his difficulties in adjusting to a new environment, and he concedes that a fox needs to live in its own environment because of choice. There are a few problems with the book. The legal aspects of ordering a fox and keeping a wild animal as a pet (illegal in most states) is one. Another problem is the overly simplistic way that conflicts are resolved. Also, it is pretty standard formula literature. However, adopted Korean-American children may relate well to the circumstances and identify with both the displaced fox and Todd, Flip's brother. There is a very touching episode in which Todd momentarily desires to see his "real" mother and must be comforted in the best way possible. This is a genuine universal emotion to which children will relate.

C.V.S.

152 MacMillan, Dianne, and Dorothy Freeman. *My Best Friend Duc Tran: Meeting a Vietnamese American Family.* Illus. by Mary Jane Begin. SERIES: My Best Friend. Julian Messner 1987. 38pp. Fiction. o.p.

Best friend Duc Huu Tran introduces Eddie Johnson to Vietnamese customs, foods, holidays, family celebrations, and value systems in a very educational and informative way. Part of the My Best Friend series, this title is probably the better of the two books published so far that deal with Asian Americans. The juxtaposition of both boys' lives and the circumstances in which they are both involved are more realistic than in *My Best Friend Mee-Yung Kim* (Julian Messner, 1989), by the same authors. The illustrations show that Duc and his family dress, eat, work, and play just as millions of other Americans do. They also manage to keep part of their heritage alive by responding to contemporary situations by using some of the ancient approaches. The family extols family unity and values, and, in the demonstration of these, the reader discovers what is valued by the Vietnamese. The titles in this series are excellent resources to introduce younger students to the thousands of years of Asian ways of life and how Asian peoples maintain their traditions and customs while fitting into a more demanding society. Both books include a brief bibliography, but only *My Best Friend Mee-Yung Kim* contains a glossary of terms used. The books in this series will also serve adoptive families well by teaching them, in a nutshell, about the passions, values, and heritage of the children who will soon be part of their family unit.

C.V.S.

153 Martin, Ann M. *Yours Turly, Shirley.* Holiday House 1988, LB $12.95 (0-8234-0719-5). 133pp. Fiction.

What makes this book so appealing, in spite of major flaws, is that there is a "universal hurt." Any child who has been the brunt of name calling of any order will understand Jackie's hurt. Shirley, Jackie's American sister, is a dyslexic fourth grader with a terrible self-image. She constantly compares herself to her gifted older brother and her newly adopted and intellectually quick Vietnamese sister. Thus the real dilemma: sibling rivalry. Jackie is a child from everywhere. The book gives very little information about Vietnam itself or the culture from which Jackie comes. There are only minor references to explain the circumstances that ensued before her adoption. This story is not particularly well written, and the adult characters, with the exception of the teacher, Mr. Bradley, are weak, sometimes moronic, and occasionally insensitive. Also, in the writing there are a few too many "r's" substituted for "l's" when Jackie speaks, which smacks a little of "cultural jokism." In addition, many of the sentences are exaggerations, perpetuated stereotypes, or samples of overkill (e.g., "taken her to a million doctors" and "difficult as learning Chinese"). Nevertheless, we are not beaten over the head with cultural information either. The text is more involved with the theme of sibling rivalry. It just so happens that one of the main characters is Vietnamese, reflecting the trend of concentrating on the issue and not the nationality of a child.

C.V.S.

154   Mayberry, Jodine. *Filipinos.* Illus. with photos. SERIES: Recent American Immigrants. Franklin Watts 1990, LB $12.40 (0-531-10978-X). 64pp. Nonfiction.

Focusing on immigrants to America, this series examines the reasons for emigration, the life-styles—old and new—and the contributions of various Asian people to American culture. Part of the Recent American Immigrants series, this title provides an excellent resource for students studying the assorted cultures. Demographics of population are beautifully displayed, giving the young researcher a quick summary of the movement of people to the United States. There are excellent charts, well-produced black-and-white and color photos, simple, uncluttered maps, an introductory contents page with a clear outline of the book's text, open and spacious page layout with plenty of white space, and a quick, ready-reference readable text. Also included in full-page sidebar format and photos are capsule-sized biographies of distinguished Asian Americans for each culture presented in the series. Equally strong works are Mayberry's *Chinese* and *Asian Indians*, by Susan Gordon. Overall, this series is a valuable and recent resource. There is no glossary, but there are both a brief bibliography and an index.

C.V.S.

155   Paterson, Katherine. *Park's Quest.* Dutton/Lodestar 1988, HB $12.95 (0-525-67258-3); Penguin/Puffin 1989, P $3.95 (0-14-034262-1). 148pp. Fiction.

In the course of the American presence in Vietnam, a multitude of children issued from lonely GI fathers and alluring Vietnamese mothers. What happens to these children, especially if the father is killed and the child is sent to the father's family in the United States? *Park's Quest* offers us one possibility.

Park is an 11-year-old boy, an Arthurian devotee, on a quest to find out more about his father, who was killed in Vietnam and about whom no one wants to talk. The intertwining of excerpts from Arthurian tales with the present story is intriguing and provides a reason to introduce a quest.

Needing a father at this age and needing that his mother stop grieving after ten years, Park goes to visit his dead father's side of the family: "Generals and colonels and gentleman Virginia farmers . . ." On the Virginia farm he meets relatives, including his father's younger brother, who works the farm for an invalid grandfather. However, these people do not measure up to Park's lyrical notions of knights and ladies or of gentlemen and generals, and certainly not to his idealized image of his father. Not the least of his shattered images is a 10-year-old girl who looks "Chinese or Vietnamese." Who is she and what is she doing on his father's farm? She is impudent, sassy, and feisty, and through this Vietnamese half-sister Park learns the truth about his family and the value of acceptance and understanding. This sensitive story provides young readers with a set of memorable, fully realized characters and insight into a painful chapter of both America's and Vietnam's past.

G.L./S.L./S.M.

156 Scarboro, Elizabeth. *The Secret Language of the SB.* Viking 1990, LB $11.95 (0-670-83087-9). 129pp. Fiction.

Sometimes we are so intent on studying and understanding the treatment of Asian-American adoptees and their adjustment in this country that we neglect the reactions of the American child who has had his or her daily routine altered, particularly if the adoptee's brother or sister has been an only child. Such is the case in this story. We are given snippets of information from Susan, the Taiwanese foster child who temporarily usurps Adam's attention and special-ness within his family while she awaits her adoptive family. However, the main thrust of this story, told from Adam's perspective, is how *he* adjusts to Susan. It is simply a story of different cultures and a special friendship that develops when both characters "give in" a little to help one another. Susan's performance anxiety about reading aloud in class is a universal trauma for children. Its inclusion in this story makes it a modest bibliotherapeutic read. As with many recent books, acceptance of an Asian-American child into an American family is pretty normal, allowing the author to drive home a message that would appeal to many, regardless of cultural heritage. C.V.S.

> Surat, Michele Maria. *Angel Child, Dragon Child.*
> See entry 140, Grades PS–3.

157 Uchida, Yoshiko. *A Jar of Dreams.* Atheneum 1981, LB $11.95 (0-689-50210-9). 131pp. Fiction.

Prejudice, malice, violence, hatred. All of these feelings of whites toward the Japanese surface in the form of Wilbur Starr in this story set in California during the depression. Rinko, 11, desperately wants a life like all Americans. Instead, she is chastised and made to feel unworthy because she is Japanese. It is through the help of her Aunt Waka, visiting from Japan, that she learns to be proud of her heritage. The reader gets a glimpse of this culture from conversational descrip-tions of food and dress, as well as discussions of family unity. There is also mention about the conditions of the boats that carry immigrants from Japan to the West Coast—the horrible wait in order to be processed at Angel Island's Immigration Station and the blatant signs of anti-Japanese whites. Running through the story are many parallel themes that can be compared with happen-ings in today's world. Read in this way, the book is an excellent bit of current history as well as historical fiction, with relevance to the boat people, "white man's territory," disabilities, self-esteem, high unemployment rates, and the generosity of true friends. Readers may also enjoy more of Rinko's adventures in *The Best Bad Thing* (Atheneum, 1983) and *The Happiest Ending* (Atheneum, 1985). C.V.S.

158 Uchida, Yoshiko. *Journey Home.* Illus. by Charles Robinson. Atheneum 1978, LB $12.95 (0-689-50126-9). 131pp. Fiction.

A sequel to *Journey to Topaz*, this is the compassionate story of a Japanese-American girl, Yuki, and her family's adjustment after they are released from

Topaz, the concentration camp to which they were confined during World War II. At first restricted to Salt Lake City and later to a shared, cramped apartment over a jointly owned store in California, Yuki learns that, even now that the war is over, being Japanese is no easier than it was before the war. When brother Ken, now a soldier, finally returns from duty—wounded and bitter—Yuki and her parents struggle to help him face the reality of prejudice and hatred toward the Japanese in America. The cruelty and hurt this family endures help them to appreciate each other. This realistic depiction of postwar attitudes is a fine conclusion to the earlier book.

C.V.S.

159   Uchida, Yoshiko. *Journey to Topaz.* Illus. by Donald Carrick. Scribner 1971. 149pp. Fiction. o.p.

When the Japanese bombed Pearl Harbor, 11-year-old Yuki Sakane, her college student brother, Ken, and her parents were living in San Francisco. Ken and Yuki, who were born in the United States, were, of course, citizens. However, their parents, kept by law from becoming citizens, were declared enemy aliens. Father, as a community leader, was immediately arrested and sent to a prison camp. The other Japanese on the West Coast were sent to camps to live behind barbed wire. First, the Sakanes lived in a horse stall at a converted racetrack. Then the camp was moved to a barren desert in Utah. Mother and Yuki adjust to the harsh conditions, make new friends, and keep in touch with their former American neighbors, accepting the fact that "fear sometimes makes people do terrible things." Ken feels bitter, but after Father is released on parole and rejoins the family, the young people volunteer for the all-Nisei combat team. The Sakanes are fictitious, but most of their experiences happened in real life to the author and her family. Some have criticized this book for showing the incarcerated Japanese as too passive in accepting their fate. However, all of the happenings were thought to be temporary, and probably fear of the unknown within the known is what drove the people to accept their fate. The story is reminiscent of the same journey that befell Esther Hautzig and her family as described in *The Endless Steppe* (Harper & Row, 1968). While the treatment was perhaps not so harsh in Uchida's work, the comparisons are real: the dust storms, the forced move from a secure and comfortable home, the separation of the father from the family, the squalid conditions. It is a powerful reminder of a part of our history that, without vigilance, could easily happen again. A good lesson to share.

C.V.S.

160   Yep, Laurence. *Child of the Owl.* HarperCollins 1977, LB $12.89 (0-06-026743-7). 217pp. Fiction.

Twelve-year-old Casey was tough, independent, and accustomed to moving around. She and Barney, her father, never stayed anywhere very long, moving on when Barney's gambling debts demanded it. Now Barney was hospitalized, the result of a mugging, and Casey is sent to San Francisco to stay with her maternal grandmother, Paw-Paw, in Chinatown. Barney never talked about their being Chinese, and Casey suddenly realizes she knew little about herself or her heritage. She feels out of place in Chinatown. Gradually through Paw-Paw's wisdom and understanding, Casey finds comfort and begins to learn of her background. All of this knowledge gives her a sense of belonging and a strength that helps her come to terms with her father's gambling and find her own place

in life. This is an excellent story. The reader is introduced to all aspects of
Chinese culture—its music and art, its legends and fairy tales, the mystical and
mythical properties of jade, and the very history of the Chinese in North
America. Casey does not speak Chinese, and her grandmother speaks very little
English, which provides an interesting conflict within the novel. Yep has painted
quite a realistic picture of Chinatown that includes the wealth, the poverty, and
the diversity within the community itself, as well as the pride in racial origin that
the older generation strives to maintain and the younger generation seeks to
remember. C.V.S.

Yep, Laurence. *The Rainbow People.*
See entry 177, Grades 7–9.

161 Yep, Laurence. *Sea Glass.* HarperCollins 1979. 213pp. Fiction. o.p.

Yep's fourth novel shares a number of themes with its immediate predecessor,
Child of the Owl—ethnic identity, generational conflicts, people's expectations.
It's not as good, but it is still fine reading. Thirteen-year-old Craig Chin has
problems. He is not accepted by the kids in Concepcion (the town to which he
has moved from San Francisco's Chinatown) as "Western" enough, and yet he is
too Western for the elder Chinese. He doesn't understand his slick, athletic
cousins' total rejection of their Chinese heritage. He is heavy and clumsy and,
somehow, cannot meet his father's expectations that he be an outstanding
basketball player. It is not until he meets semirecluse Uncle Quail that Craig
begins to find a way of being himself and of being accepted for what he is rather
than what others want him to be. The cast of characters is strong, from Craig's
mother, father, and uncle to Kenyon, a fast-talking, smart-mouthed girl whose
cultivated indifference masks her hurt over her parents' coldness toward her; she
and Craig become close friends. Craig at times seems to be too understanding,
but it doesn't seriously flaw the story. Yep has produced another good ethnic
story with wide appeal. C.V.S.

GRADES 7-9

162 Ashabranner, Brent, and Melissa Ashabranner. *Into a Strange Land: Unaccompanied Refugee Youth in America.* Illus. with photos. Putnam 1987, HB $14.95 (0-
399-21709-6). 160pp. Nonfiction.

These are the true experiences of many young Southeast Asian refugees coming
alone to America. The focus of this title is on the unaccompanied refugee minors
program and on placement in temporary, small-group homes and foster families. The adjustments these teenagers must make and the difficulties they face in
learning to live in a new and alien culture are movingly described. The culmina-
tion and success of the program are illustrated by the stories of youngsters who
have begun to live independently—without government support or supervision. The book was created especially for teenagers by a noted writer for youth
and his anthropologist daughter. E.C.

163 Betancourt, Jeanne. *More Than Meets the Eye.* Bantam 1990, HB $14.95 (0-553-05871-1). 166pp. Fiction.

This very contemporary young adult novel effectively paints a portrait of a variety of Asian-American experiences and problems.

Elizabeth, who is second in academic rank in the sophomore class, wants to date Ben Lee, who is first (which her parents attribute to teacher preference for Asian Americans). Ben likes Elizabeth, too, but hesitates to go against his family's pressure to date only Chinese girls. When Elizabeth begins to help a new Cambodian girl learn English, more prejudices are expressed, including Ben's, against the new immigrant. When a Korean family buys a local store, the hostility at school engulfs the whole community. All is too happily and quickly resolved at the end to be really believable, but the book has much merit in that such a variety of assumptions and misunderstandings are exposed in an entertaining format. The attractive cover adds to the appeal to teens.   E.C.

164 Bode, Janet. *New Kids on the Block: Oral Histories of Immigrant Teens.* Franklin Watts 1989, HB $12.90 (0-531-10794-9). 126pp. Nonfiction.

Eleven teenagers relate their experiences in regard to leaving their homelands and adjusting to a new life in America. These are varied, vivid accounts by adolescents from eleven different countries and cultures, including Afghanistan, China, India, the Philippines, South Korea, and Vietnam. Their experiences in America are equally diverse, although they all encountered difficulties. Some of the teens have lived in America for more than half their life; others are newcomers. Some live alone; others stay with their family.

Each chapter begins with a paragraph or two about objective background, the country of origin, and the teenage narrator's personal history. Then each teen describes his or her current daily life in the United States, hopes and plans for the future, and reflections on the initial cultural shock and adjustment. Some offer advice on meeting the challenge of adapting to foreign ways. All are thankful for the opportunities available to them in America. This is fascinating reading for American-born teenagers and comfortingly familiar for other immigrant teens. It is also one of the few books that present the experiences of immigrant youngsters from Southern and Central Asia.

165 Brown, Dee Alexander, and Linda Proctor. *Lonesome Whistle: The Story of the First Transcontinental Railroad.* Illus. with photos. Holt, Rinehart & Winston 1980. 144pp. Nonfiction. o.p.

In this book, adapted for young readers from his *Hear That Lonesome Whistle Blow* (Holt, Rinehart & Winston, 1977), Brown provides an excellent resource describing the creation of the first transcontinental railroad and the men who built it. The account richly demonstrates how the Chinese, slotted into degrading stereotypes, were selected for their work. The narrative relates how they were treated—first as laborers who toiled under adverse conditions for meager pay, and later as immigrants who attempted to use the railroad. It is an excellent work to use in a social studies unit about the settling of America, particularly the American West. Unlike most books about this grand undertaking, the author takes us one step beyond in order to experience the events of the first travelers and also to tell us the fate of the men who built this great land bridge, ironically, between the east and west. Teachers and other educators can also use this to draw parallels between the treatment of the Chinese and the Native Americans during the same time frame and their treatment today.   C.V.S.

166   Brownstone, David M. ***The Chinese-American Heritage.*** SERIES: America's Ethnic Heritage. Facts on File 1988, HB $16.95 (0-8160-1627-5). 132pp. Nonfiction.

This is a clearly written volume covering the history of the Chinese in the United States. It has a limited number of photographs and is pleasantly laid out. Although part of a series written for young adults, it is the series' only volume that covers an Asian-American group. Unfortunately, the material on recent history already seems quite dated. The suggestions for further reading, while extensive, also contain considerable material written in the 1970s. The cover is exceptionally unexciting and unappealing.   E.C.

167   Cebulash, Mel. ***Carly and Co.*** Ballantine 1989, P $2.95 (0-449-14555-7). 201pp. Fiction.

This lightweight teenage detective novel includes a Vietnamese-American boy, Sandy (Soon Tek Ahn), as the heroine Carly's best friend. He does appear prominently on the cover, which is quite well designed and will appeal to teens. An attempt is also made to incorporate expatriate Vietnamese culture into the story. For instance, Sandy's father is overprotective and strict, not wanting his son to become too American. Overall, though, the book is shallow, rather preachy, and superficial in its presentation of Sandy's heritage, with an unrealistic plot line as well.   E.C.

168   Crew, Linda. ***Children of the River.*** Delacorte 1989, HB $14.95 (0-440-50122-9). 213pp. Fiction.

After fleeing the Khmer Rouge with her uncle's family, 17-year-old Sundara in Oregon still feels guilt over the death of the young cousin she could not save. She is haunted by fears for the fate of her own family as well. She struggles to fit into her new American life while putting up with the different kinds of rules her Cambodian aunt and uncle set. As her friendship with Jonathan McKinnon develops into romance, Sundara is forced to confront her worst fears and to resolve them. Through this situation she finds that she can adapt to American life while honoring her Cambodian heritage.

This first novel vividly evokes in great depth the painful emotions and experiences that many recent refugee Asian Americans still carry with them. Details of Sundara and her family life are authentically and honestly rendered. Crew has created a strong, spirited heroine who will appeal to all American teens. This beautifully written novel received Honorable Mention in the Delacorte Press Competition for Outstanding First Young Adult Novel. It was deservedly chosen for American Library Association Best Books for Young Adults as well.   E.C.

169   Gregory, Diana. ***One Boy at a Time.*** SERIES: Sweet Dreams. Bantam 1987, P $2.50 (0-553-26671-3). 150pp. Fiction.

Set in San Francisco, this teenage romance is narrated in the first person by Wendy Fong. Wendy is third-generation American on one side and fifth generation on the other. Her father owns an Asian import business, and her mother is an aerobics teacher. She and her family are comfortably Americanized while maintaining their Chinese heritage. The plot line concerns Wendy's trying to decide which of two boys (both Caucasian) she really, really wants for a boy-friend. In the course of the book, Wendy's family celebrates Chinese New Year. Many traditions and their meaning are accurately described in detail. The family's interactions are comfortable and affectionate. The cover photograph of Wendy is outstanding. This is the one book in the Sweet Dreams series that has an Asian-American protagonist.   E.C.

170   Irwin, Hadley. *Kim/Kimi.* Atheneum 1987, HB $12.95 (0-689-50428-4); Puffin 1988, P $3.95 (0-14-032593-X). 200pp. Fiction.

Before Kimi Yagushi was born, her father died, disowned by his family for marrying a Caucasian. When Kimi's mother remarried, baby Kimi became Kim Andrews, who grows into adolescence as part of a close, loving suburban household in Iowa. As a teenager, she is self-conscious because she "looks different" from everyone else in town. At 16, Kim suddenly flies out to California to contact her Japanese father's family. She stays with a Japanese-American family (the first she has ever met), whose members enlighten her (and presumably the reader) about such exotic Japanese-American customs as sleeping on a futon and using chopsticks. They introduce her to foods that she says "looked odd and smelled even stranger." More important, Kim (and the reader) learn about recent Japanese-American history, especially the existence of the humiliating relocation camps during World War II. By the end of the novel, Kim/Kimi finally does meet her paternal aunt and grandmother.

Unfortunately, none of the characters except Kim/Kimi is completely drawn. That Kim/Kimi could grow up in total ignorance of the most commonplace Asian-American customs is unbelievable. Also, there are a number of incidents in which stereotypes are perpetuated. In one example, an Asian child on an airplane thinks Kim/Kimi is her cousin just because her name is Kimi and she looks Asian. Do the authors really think all Asians look alike? All in all, there are better written and more credible books now available about the Asian-American experience.

171   Miklowitz, Gloria D. *The War Between the Classes.* Delacorte 1985, HB $13.95 (0-385-29375-5); Dell 1986, P $2.95 (0-440-99406-3). 158pp. Fiction.

Utilizing an actual classroom experiment in this contemporary young adult novel, Gloria Miklowitz explores some of the barriers that social class and prejudice present for American teenagers today. In a class experiment, Japanese American Emiko (Amy) Sumoto is assigned to a much higher social class than her wealthy boyfriend Adam. Meanwhile the couple struggle with the disapproval of Amy's traditionalist family as well as the social snobbery of Adam's mother. By the book's end all the conflicts are resolved and everyone accepts everyone else. An attractive cover and Miklowitz's readable style make this an easily read novel with appeal for young adults.   E.C.

Noda, Gloria. *The Asian Face: A Styling Guide.*
See entry 186, Grades 10–12.

172   Okimoto, Jean Davies. *Molly by Any Other Name.* Scholastic 1990, HB $13.95 (0-590-42993-0). 257pp. Fiction.

Molly is biologically Asian; however, she was adopted as an infant by a loving Caucasian family in Washington State. At 17, Molly is torn between her desire to seek out her birth heritage and loyalty to her parents.

In the course of the novel, much information is conveyed on the adoptee search process. The Japanese-Canadian birth mother's point of view is presented sympathetically, as are the conflicting emotions of Molly's parents. A happy resolution is achieved when Molly's search is successful, and Molly's parents participate in a reunion with her birth mother. Unlike Hadley Irwin's *Kim/Kimi* (Macmillan, 1987), this book focuses primarily on the feelings of all of the family members rather than the bitter experiences of the Japanese in North America. The subplot about Molly's friendship and eventual romance with Japanese-American Raymond enhances this book's appeal for series-oriented teens.

E.C.

173   Pascal, Francine. *Out of Reach.* SERIES: Sweet Valley High. Bantam 1988, P $2.95 (0-553-27596-8). 151pp. Fiction.

Yes, this is a series romance, with all that that implies—soap opera style, somewhat shallow plot, neat resolution at the end—but this is a series book with a positive difference. In fact, it is the only Sweet Valley High title in which an Asian-American girl is the heroine. American-born Jade Wu is a newcomer to Sweet Valley from the sheltered Chinese environment of San Francisco's Chinatown. Although she has had many years of ballet training, her father forbids her to dance in public. She is, of course, chosen to be the star dancer in a school production. She also secretly dates a Caucasian boy. In her anxiety about suburban acceptance, Jade also tries to keep secret her grandparents' ownership of the local laundry, which she feels displays "all the stereotypes about Chinese people rolled into one." Jade's various attempts at deception do catch up with her, however. In the end, her father, mother, and grandparents do attend her outstanding performance. Her father meets and approves of her Caucasian boyfriend. Ultimately Jade herself refuses to accept a prized internship for which she would have been constrained to deny her heritage by changing her last name from Wu to Warren. Many issues are raised in this series book that an Asian-American suburban teenage girl can identify with.

E.C.

Paterson, Katherine. *Park's Quest.*
See entry 155, Grades 4–6.

174   Stern, Jennifer. *The Filipino Americans.* SERIES: The Peoples of North America. Chelsea House 1989, HB $17.95 (0-87754-877-3); P $9.95 (0-7910-0290-X). 110pp. Nonfiction.

Each of the volumes in this series provides an in-depth account of a specific immigrant community. Outstanding people of achievement are profiled. Well written and attractively illustrated with black-and-white and color photos, this excellent series is singularly appropriate for junior and senior high school students. This particular volume chronicles the immigration of Filipinos to the United States from the beginning of the century to the present, with references to the Philippines' history as both a Spanish and American colony and finally an independent nation. Conditions in both places are explored. Includes a bibliography and index. Other books in the series present Chinese Americans, Indo-Americans, Indo-Chinese Americans, Korean Americans, Japanese Americans, and Pacific Islanders.   E.C.

Uchida, Yoshiko. ***Desert Exile: The Uprooting of a Japanese American Family.***
See entry 190, Grades 10–12.

175   Winter, Frank H. ***The Filipinos in America.*** Illus. with photos. SERIES: In America. Lerner 1988, LB $9.95 (0-8225-0237-2). 71pp. Nonfiction.

One of the Lerner series on immigration entitled In America, this book provides a readable and balanced, though somewhat superficial, introduction to the fastest-growing Asian immigrant group in the United States. The author provides a background history of the Philippines and discusses changes in attitudes toward those who came to the United States. There is little treatment of the reasons for the immigration or the socio-economic background of the immigrants, and Winter's assertion that Filipino-Americans are the fastest-growing Asian-American group today is ten years out of date. Much of the focus seems to be on distinguished individuals rather than on the experiences and conditions of most Filipino Americans, and, in this respect, this volume and series take a different approach from that taken by Chelsea House's Peoples of North America. Includes index. Other volumes in this series present Americans from China, the East Indies and Pakistan (one volume), Japan, Korea, Lebanon, and Vietnam.   E.C./L.M-L.

Yep, Laurence. ***Child of the Owl.***
See entry 160, Grades 4–6.

176   Yep, Laurence. ***Dragonwings.*** HarperCollins 1975. 248pp. Fiction. o.p.

This is the kind of book that wins awards. The descriptions are haunting and beautiful. A whole world is created in which honor, following a dream, and being true to oneself are tied in with San Francisco's Chinatown in the early 1900s. Moon Shadow is 9 years old, 8 by demon reckoning, when he comes to the Land of the Golden Mountain in order to see his father for the first time. He learns of his father's former life as a dragon and of his dream to fly again. Moon Shadow supports this dream because he knows it is important. They leave the company, the group of Tang men who live and work together, in order to live in the demon world so that they can pursue their dream. The two dreamers endure the great earthquake and have to start over, but eventually they do fly, only to realize that other things are important too. Moon Shadow is 15 when they finally fly, but most of the story takes place when he is younger. This is a skillful blend of fact and fiction. The descriptions are so superior that illustrations are not needed. The story is long and difficult at times, but young adults and a very special upper elementary age reader will be enchanted. The blend of fantasy and reality that forms through the vehicle of an Asian-American father and son will evoke feelings for the homeland among first-generation Chinese Americans.

C.V.S.

Yep, Laurence. ***The Rainbow People.*** Illus. by David Wiesner. HarperCollins 1989, LB $13.89 (0-06-026761-5). 190pp. Nonfiction.

Unlike most folklore collections, this focuses on the folklore of a very specific audience—the Chinese Americans who came over from China starting in the 1840s to work in the orchards of northern California. These men, who had to leave their families behind, passed their evenings by telling stories. Twenty of the 69 stories collected during a 1930s WPA project have been selected for inclusion here. Yep conveys a down-to-earth humor and a simple lyricism in all of the tales; the tone seems to reflect what might have originally been heard in the original telling. There are five sections of stories, each with an introduction that explains why Chinese Americans related the stories, why they were a source of energy and remembrance, and how they evolved from their own experiences in a brand-new world. Yep's style is liquid, and the stories make excellent read-alouds and a high-quality resource for the storyteller.   C.V.S.

Yep, Laurence. ***Sea Glass.***
See entry 161, Grades 4–6.

GRADES 10–12

Ashabranner, Brent, and Melissa Ashabranner. ***Into a Strange Land: Unaccompanied Refugee Youth in America.***
See entry 162, Grades 7–9.

Crew, Linda. ***Children of the River.***
See entry 168, Grades 7–9.

178   Houston, Jeanne Wakatsuki, and James D. Houston. ***Farewell to Manzanar.***
Bantam 1983, P $3.50 (0-553-27258-6). 177pp. Nonfiction.

This personal recollection by Jeanne Wakatsuki Houston of growing up in Manzanar, a Japanese-American internment camp, during World War II has now become a "classic." It is similar in some ways to Esther Hautzig's *The Endless Steppe.* The tragedies, the constant fear, the injustice of it, and yet the human dignity, courage, warmth, and sense of survival in spite of reasons to despair make this a very special book for high school students as well as for adults.   E.C.

179   Kadohata, Cynthia. ***The Floating World.*** Viking 1989, HB $17.95 (0-670-82680-4). 196pp. Fiction.

This Japanese-American coming-of-age novel takes place in the 1950s in the "floating world" of transience—"the motel towns floating in the middle of fields and mountains." Always moving, teenage Olivia and her family live a life on the road. Post–World War II anti-Japanese prejudice is dealt with only indirectly. Although told from the point of view of an adolescent, the book is rather slow moving and complex and would appeal more to adults.   E.C.

180   Kitano, Harry H. L., and Roger Daniels. *Asian Americans: Emerging Minorities.*
Prentice Hall 1988, P $22.14 (0-13-049164-0). 214pp. Nonfiction.

This excellent workmanlike volume imparts extensive information on the history and current status of Asian groups in the United States. One of its greatest virtues is the conciseness with which the information is imparted. It is the only volume that includes Pacific Islanders as a distinct group. Respect is shown both for the individuality of each group's experiences in the United States and for the commonality of Asian-American experiences.

In addition to bibliographic notes at the end of each chapter, there are suggestions for further reading on each topic covered. Census data from 1980 for each Asian group are included as an appendix. Although there are no illustrations, high school students will appreciate the amount of information conveyed without extraneous verbiage.

181   Kwong, Peter. *The New Chinatown.* SERIES: American Century Series. Hill & Wang
1987, HB $18.95 (0-8090-7255-6); Farrar, Straus & Giroux/Noonday Pr. 1988, P
$7.95 (0-374-52121-2). 198pp. Nonfiction.

Devoted exclusively to New York's Chinatown—more particularly its economic history—this scholarly yet readable history would prove extremely useful to senior high school students who wish to delve more deeply into the history of this famous Asian-American community and to perceive the impact that the new immigration has made on it. The focus is upon the community as it exists today, rather than in past decades, and readers will learn about many of the current problems facing the residents, including sweatshop labor and gangs. The index is particularly useful, allowing the high school researcher to concentrate on specific topics of interest.   E.C.

182   Lee, Mary Paik. *Quiet Odyssey: A Pioneer Korean Woman in America.* Univ. of
Washington Pr. 1990, HB $20.00 (0-295-96946-6); P $10.95 (0-295-96969-5).
201pp. Nonfiction.

The author of this autobiography is one of the fewer than 100 Koreans to first arrive in the United States. Mary Paik Lee left Korea with her political refugee parents in 1905 at the age of 5. After her father labored on sugar plantations in Hawaii for a year and a half, the family moved to California, where Mrs. Lee still lives. Though from the educated elite in Korea, her family labored in poverty in the United States following emigration.

Sucheng Chan, modestly cited as editor, has by her background research and verification created a scholarly document in addition to the autobiography itself. While the detailed documentation and comprehensive bibliography are more than high school students will want to wade through, the autobiography itself makes fascinating reading. The gifted high school student may also be interested in Dr. Chan's illuminating essay on the historiographer's role. The lengthy introductory essay supplies much helpful information for putting the work into context. Most of the more than 700,000 people in the United States who are of Korean ancestry have arrived over the past 20 years. Little has been written about early Korean history here, and this is a spellbinding and unique account of that earlier time.   E.C.

183   Lo, Steven C. *The Incorporation of Eric Chung.* Algonquin Books of Chapel Hill 1989, HB $14.95 (0-945575-18-1). 199pp. Fiction.

The hero of this sly and clever novel describes the experiences of a new immigrant in minute, fascinating, and hilarious detail. Librarians and pages will particularly enjoy Eric Chung's experiences as a Stack Control Assistant at the Texas Tech University library. Eventually, Eric becomes involved in a disastrous "fast-track" business venture that allows the author to satirize modern American corporate business practices. Eric's culture shock and gradual enlightenment provide the sophisticated high school reader with a fresh way of considering some common modern American life-styles.   E.C.

184   McCunn, Ruthanne Lum. *Chinese American Portraits: Personal Histories 1828–1988.* Chronicle Books 1988, HB $29.95 (0-87701-580-5); 1989, P $16.95 (0-87701-491-4). 176pp. Nonfiction.

Ruthanne Lum McCunn has called upon her skills as a research librarian to dig out information, upon her experience as a teacher to educate us, and upon her talent as a writer to relate the true life stories of some remarkable people, all of which combine to evoke a fascinating history of Chinese people in America. Family histories as well as individuals are featured in photographs and words, as is author Eleanor Wong Telemaque. Each biographical sketch is dramatic and illustrates a discrimination or a hardship experienced.   E.C.

Miklowitz, Gloria D. *The War Between the Classes.*
See entry 171, Grades 7–9.

185   Moore, David L. *Dark Sky, Dark Land: Stories of the Hmong Boy Scouts of Troop 100.* Tessera Publishing 1989, P $14.95 (0-9623029-0-2). 191pp. Nonfiction.

David Moore, a remarkable teacher at Edison High School in Minneapolis, organized a Hmong Boy Scout troop in 1981. It was composed primarily of Hmong teens who, originally from Laos, had made their way to refugee camps in Thailand and from there to the United States. In the process, each surmounted a variety of life-threatening episodes. The experiences of these teens were so harrowing and their struggles so compelling that Moore conceived the idea of setting down their individual stories of courage and survival. This is a unique book in many ways—in the formation of the Boy Scout troop itself, as well as in the telling of the escapes and the resettlement of the teenagers. Each of the fifteen accounts is greatly enhanced by a portrait drawing of the young protagonist. These enthralling stories of bravery and endurance can make textbook accounts of this recent history come alive for students, particularly teenage boys. A brief chronology of Hmong history is given at the end of the book. An extremely limited bibliography is included. Almost any segment of any of the individual accounts would make a spellbinding booktalk. Although the author's style is somewhat amateurish, the book is highly recommended.   E.C.

186   Noda, Gloria. *The Asian Face: A Styling Guide.* Illus. Kodansha International 1986, P $14.95 (0-87011-731-9). 120pp. Nonfiction.

Suitable for adults as well as teens, this unique title for women with Asian features offers basic practical information on skin care, makeup, and hairstyling.

During early adolescence, when some Asian-American girls become intensely involved with appearance and begin to experiment with makeup, they may adapt "tips" and styles intended for Caucasian faces and hair. Sometimes the results are not what they expected. This book deals with the many facial and hair characteristics common to Asians. It offers useful and expert advice, particularly on skin sensitivities, hair care, and makeup tricks to flatter eye, nose, and cheek contours. The profiles at the end of the book feature a variety of real Asian and Eurasian women who offer the reader the benefit of their own experiences. *The Asian Face* is especially helpful for Caucasian parents of Asian girls.

Stern, Jennifer. **The Filipino Americans.**
See entry 174, Grades 7–9.

187 Sung, Betty Lee. **Chinese American Intermarriage.** Center for Migration Studies 1990, HB $19.50 (0-934733-47-3); P $14.50 (0-934733-48-1). 140pp. Nonfiction.

Many Asian-American young adult novels involve interracial dating. Here is a new scholarly study that will also be of interest to teens, particularly Chinese and other Asian-American teens. The statistical and research material is presented plainly enough for high school students, but of greater interest for them will be the considerable anecdotal "case histories" of the 50 interracial couples who were interviewed in some detail. Dr. Sung does focus rather more on immigrant Chinese Americans than on second- and third-generation Americans. For the most part, the Chinese families here are more distant and disapproving, far less welcoming and benevolent, than my own experiences would indicate. In addition, the thoroughly integrated Chinese-American population that existed prior to 1965 is almost overlooked. This somewhat limits the long-term overview.   E.C.

188 Tan, Amy. **The Joy Luck Club.** Putnam 1989, HB $18.95 (0-399-13420-4); Ballantine 1990, P $5.95 (0-8041-0630-4). 288pp. Fiction.

Mature adolescents as well as adults can probably learn more about Chinese-American culture from this outstanding best-selling novel than from most nonfiction accounts. When one reads this book, one practically becomes both first- and second-generation Chinese American and learns the culture from within. It is interesting to note that this novel is written entirely in the first person singular (although from a number of points of view), whereas the older, autobiographical *Fifth Chinese Daughter* by Jade Snow Wong (Harper, 1945) is in the traditional Chinese literary form of the third person singular.   E.C.

189 Telemaque, Eleanor Wong. **It's Crazy to Stay Chinese in Minnesota.** Thomas Nelson 1978. 118pp. Fiction. o.p.

Based on the author's own memories of her Middle Western girlhood, this unique book touches on many facets of growing up both Chinese and mainstream American at the same time. The plot concerns American-born Ching's efforts to save her family's restaurant business and her summer romance with a Chinese-born student. In the process we are introduced to everyday facts of life for many Chinese Americans. This was the first young adult novel to present a realistic picture of Chinese-American life in the heartland of the United States. It demystified and helped to erase the myth of the alien "inscrutable Oriental." It is still one of the best, most accurate portraits of a first- and second-generation Asian-American family. The Grant Wood–style Chinese-American cover photograph is especially witty. Unfortunately this book has been out of print for some time. E.C.

190   Uchida, Yoshiko. ***Desert Exile: The Uprooting of a Japanese American Family.***
       Univ. of Washington Pr. 1982 (0-295-95898-7); P $10.95 (0-295-96190-2). 154pp.
       Nonfiction.

American-born Yoshiko Uchida had grown up in Berkeley and was already attending the University of California when Pearl Harbor was attacked. Her Japanese-born father was abruptly seized and held incommunicado by the FBI. She, her mother, and her sister were soon uprooted from their home and interned in horse stalls in a stable at a nearby racetrack. They were then sent on to Topaz, a bleak "camp" in the Utah desert, where her father eventually joined them. The grace and spirit of the camp inhabitants, in an attempt to maintain a sense of community and go on with life behind the barbed wire, are communicated vividly. Uchida's experiences, documented here, form the basis of two of her novels—*Journey to Topaz* and *Journey Home*; reading both novels and this autobiography provides insight into the creative process and the origins of fiction in a writer's own life. E.C.

191   Uchida, Yoshiko. ***Picture Bride.*** Northland Pr. 1987, HB $14.95 (0-87358-429-5);
       Simon & Schuster 1988, P $6.95 (0-671-66874-9). 216pp. Fiction.

As the book begins, Hana Omiya is arriving in San Francisco in 1917 as a young "picture bride" to marry a man she has never met. As the book ends, she has been imprisoned for some time in Topaz, the concentration camp for Japanese Americans during World War II. In between is the story of her life while becoming American. It includes her marriage, motherhood, love, and friendships. This outstanding novel skillfully expresses the fullness of life in this Japanese-American family. The thoughtful older teen will be drawn not only to the sensitive writing but also to the beautiful layout of the book. E.C.

192   Wong, Jade Snow. ***Fifth Chinese Daughter.*** Originally published by Harper, 1945.
       Univ. of Washington Pr. 1989, P $10.95 (0-295-96826-5). 246pp. Nonfiction.

This coming-of-age autobiography was originally published in 1945. At that time, this record of the author's adolescence and the conflicting cultural expectations of those around her became an unexpected best-seller not only in the United States but abroad as well. After having been out of print for some time, it was reissued in 1989 with a new introduction by the author. It still provides a readable, detailed account of growing up Chinese American in San Francisco during the 1920s and 1930s. It would be particularly interesting for students to compare with more recent material such as Maxine Hong Kingston's *Woman Warrior* (Random, 1976) or with such modern novels as Amy Tan's *The Joy Luck Club* (Putnam, 1989).

193   Yung, Judy. *Chinese Women of America: A Pictorial History.* Univ. of Washington Pr. 1986, P $12.95 (0-295-96358-1). 128pp. Nonfiction.

From the cover photograph of a Chinese pioneer woman to the Chinese-American policewoman near the end, this book of annotated photographs documents the history of Chinese women in America far better than words alone would do. *Chinese Women of America* is an outgrowth and extension of a massive research project. It resulted in a traveling exhibit and then in this book. More than 1,000 images of Chinese-American women were collected, and 135 of them are included here. In addition to collecting documents and photographs, the researchers interviewed 274 Chinese-American women of diverse backgrounds in order to compile this history. The majority of Chinese-American women in earlier times were not very literate, nor were they encouraged to express themselves, and so no substantial written record of their experiences has existed until now. The appendixes contain statistical charts that would enhance the use of this excellent and readable book for term papers.   E.C.

3

UNITED STATES:
HISPANIC AMERICANS

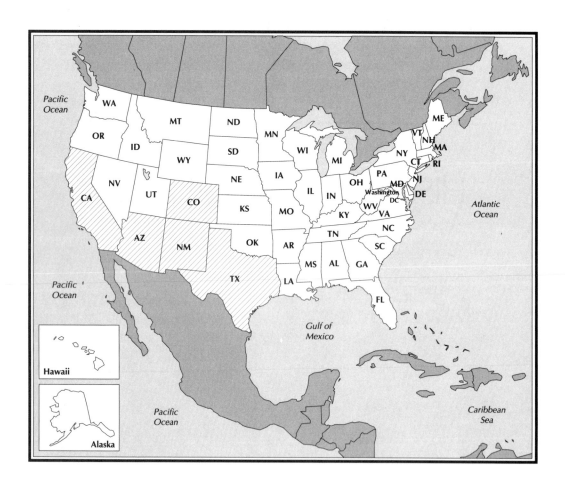

STATES WITH HIGHEST
CONCENTRATION OF
HISPANIC AMERICANS

1. New Mexico - 38.2%
2. California - 25.8%
3. Texas - 25.5%
4. Arizona - 18.8%
5. Colorado - 12.9%

PLACES OF ORIGIN
OF HISPANIC AMERICANS
BY PERCENTAGE

1. Mexico - 60.4%
2. Puerto Rico - 12.2%
3. Cuba - 4.7%
4. Other - 22.7%

Source: 1990 U.S. Census

3

UNITED STATES: HISPANIC AMERICANS

by Oralia Garza de Cortes

The term "Hispanic Americans" is a relatively new one within the library profession, one that offers the most precise classification of the literature about a group whose ethnic roots stem from the cultural heritages of Mexico, Puerto Rico, Cuba and the Caribbean, and Central and South America, but whose home and dual cultural context is the United States of America. In the past, finding books about these various ethnic heritages was difficult simply because either mainstream publishers did not know that these groups in America existed, or they simply chose to ignore them as subjects worthy of characterization. Many who did choose to include them in children's literature also chose to portray them in a context that offered a pastoral view of how a "Mexican" (and, by implication, other "Spanish") was supposed to look and act. In many cases a demeaning or derogatory quality or characterization perpetuated the stereotype that served to distort the image further. The setting and the characters in such well-known works as Leo Politi's *Pedro, The Angel on Olvera Street* (Scribner, 1946) are obsolete. Today's Mexican Americans no longer wear *huaraches* (sandals) or the traditional *zarape* (wool-draped cloth), nor did they when books such as this one were first published. Rather, this was an outsider's and a tourist's perception and nostalgic view of what a typical Mexican should look like.

In the 1960s and 1970s, the few works about Hispanic Americans that were published by major houses featured protagonists who conformed to the prevailing view that speaking Spanish was unacceptable and, further, that assimilating into mainstream American culture was the only redeemable quality to be had.[1] Marie Hall Etts's *Bad Boy, Good Boy* (Crowell, 1967) is a notable example.

During the 1970s, many publications for children were published by small presses, which developed as a result of the need to produce curriculum materials for bilingual children. Federal dollars became available for the development of many of the curricular materials then. However, as the federal education dollar for publication and purchase of books and other published materials dried up, so too did many of these overnight publishing houses. While much of the publishing was in Spanish, many noteworthy titles appeared in English or in a bilingual

---

1. Opal Moore and Donnarae MacCann, "Paternalism and Assimilation in Books about Hispanics." *Children's Literature Association Quarterly* 12 (Summer 1987), 2–3.

format.[2] Among the survivors is Children's Book Press, a nonprofit publisher in San Francisco, California, which has contributed more to the body of literature of children's books about Hispanic culture than any other publisher.

Unlike many of the small presses, however, Children's Book Press was successful in convincing private funders of the need to publish multicultural books for children long before the concept came into vogue. Among the outstanding bilingual titles is *How We Came to the Fifth World/Como vinimos al quinto mundo*, a vibrantly illustrated creation myth from Mexico. The recently published *Family Pictures/Cuadros de familia* is significant for several reasons. Apart from highlighting the cultural customs and family practices of Mexican Americans who have long lived in the United States, the outstanding naive-style illustrations introduce children to the contemporary art of one of the most outstanding Chicana artists in the United States, Carmen Lomas Garza. The appeal of *Family Pictures* will be far-reaching, however, as it becomes introduced to parents involved in intergenerational literacy and writing programs. It may be utilized to stimulate discussion of possible writing topics of these family practices and how these practices have changed, how they are being continued, or whether they are now being lost. *Family Pictures* serves as a landmark in the development of a Mexican-American children's literary history. Rudolfo Anaya's *The Farolitos of Christmas: A New Mexico Christmas Story* and *Rosita's Christmas Wish* by Mary Ann Bruni are two other distinctive titles that also highlight the customs and practices unique to Hispanic cultures, especially at Christmastime.

The immigrant experience is another theme that is reflected in the current works about Hispanic Americans. *Lupita Mañana* and *The Maldonado Miracle* convey the difficulties experienced by children who cross the Mexican border without their parents. In *I Speak English for My Mom*, a young child struggles daily to interpret a new way of life to her mother, who does not yet understand the language. Nicolasa Mohr's "The Conch Shell" in Sylvia Pena's *Tun-Ta-Ca-Tun: More Stories and Poems in English and Spanish for Children* is the touching story of a Puerto Rican immigrant child's longing for the sound of the ocean amidst a world of concrete and cement.

The new Raintree Hispanic Stories series is noteworthy in its attempt to bring to light the important historical figures who have been omitted from most state-approved textbooks. *Vilma Martínez* documents the discrimination experienced by Mexican Americans in Texas during the same period that African Americans were living under segregation in the South. *Carlos Finlay* is the story of the Cuban scientist and physician who developed the research that resulted in a cure for yellow fever. The new Chelsea House biography series on Hispanic-American figures throughout history, Hispanics of Achievement, is certain to fill that gap for young adult readers. In the meantime, the Chelsea House volumes in The Peoples of North America series, as *The Mexican Americans*, *The Cuban Americans*, *The Central Americans*, and *The Dominican Americans*, are excellent in covering the cultural and historical background of the many subgroups that compose today's U.S. Hispanic population. Another useful series in this area is Lerner's series In America Books.

This chapter includes works for children that are finally beginning to be included in the general reference sources. A case in point is the third edition of *A*

2. Gerald Resendez, "Chicano Children's Literature." In *Chicano Literature*, ed. by Julio A. Martinez and Francisco Lomeli. Westport, Conn.: Greenwood Press, 1985, pp. 107–121.

to Zoo: Subject Access to Children's Picture Books (R. R. Bowker, 1989). Although it includes Mexican Americans and Puerto Rican Americans under "Ethnic Groups in the U.S.," it still lags behind in identifying more updated and most certainly more relevant titles than are currently listed.

The dearth of young adult books, however, remains a serious matter that must be addressed by publishers and librarians alike. The classic literary works by Chicano writers such as Rudolfo Anaya, Ernesto Galarza, and Tomás Rivera have been either ignored or disregarded, or both. With the exception of Nicolasa Mohr, Puerto Rican writers have fared no better. Chicano writer Gary Soto has finally emerged into the mainstream with *Baseball in April and Other Stories* after years of publication with small presses. Most teachers and many librarians have thus had to fend for themselves in searching and finding relevant materials for their students and for their collections. An entire generation of Hispanic youth has been denied its rightful heritage because of gross neglect in this area of publishing. This bibliography, though far from all-inclusive, includes some of the most notable authors and writings in this area of Hispanic young adult literature.

Many of the fiction titles listed in this chapter are from small publishing houses. While several are not listed under the author or title guide to *Children's Books in Print*, for the most part they can be found under this major reference source. Most, however, are not included in the subject index of *Children's Books in Print, 1990–1991*.

Although this chapter includes many more fiction titles than are easily identifiable through the normal searching methods, the reality is that nonfiction subjects are much easier to write about and yet less likely to be the target of criticism by librarians and scholars eager to attack the work on the basis of stereotyped images or lack of diacritics. Too, authors from outside the culture have generally been more successful in writing nonfiction, which relies upon factual research and the quality of its presentation, than in depicting the subtle aspects of language, experience, and emotion necessary for a compelling work of fiction. Thus, the majority of the annotations are works of nonfiction.

In an era in which the school dropout rate among Hispanics is already alarmingly high and increasing, we must pay heed to Walter Dean Myers's thoughtful essay "The Reluctant Reader" if we wish to empower children with a sense of positive self-identity and self-esteem about who they are. Through reading the literature that reflects their own cultural experiences, through learning of their history, and through seeing themselves in the literature for children, then perhaps minority youngsters too can begin to see a future for themselves in a society that every day continues to demand more intellectual output than they are currently prepared for.[3]

The titles in this chapter have come from countless years of serendipity, searching among professional journals, scholarly sources, and reference sources, as well as in libraries and bookstores throughout the Southwest and throughout the nation. This chapter represents an attempt to consolidate these titles into a basic source where all teachers, librarians, and parents can find them, enjoy them, and promote them. Through cultural understanding, this world may become a place where mutual respect and coexistence can result in peace.

---

3. Walter Dean Myers, "The Reluctant Reader." *Interracial Books for Children Bulletin* 19 (1989), 3–4; 14–15.

194   Anaya, Rudolfo A. *The Farolitos of Christmas.* Illus. by Richard C. Sandoval. New Mexico Magazine 1987, P $7.50 (0-937206-06-7). 32pp. Fiction.

Three days before Christmas, fourth-grader Luz worries that her family will not be able to celebrate Christmas in the traditional spirit this season. Her grandfather has caught a cold and has been ordered to bed. Without her *abuelito*'s (grandfather's) help in lighting the bonfires for the shepherds, she fears that the shepherds will choose another place in which to perform the traditional shepherds' play. Determined to find a way to lure them to her home, she invents an ingenious modern-day method, using the votive candles her mother has purchased for the Christmas Vigil, placing them in paper bags filled with sand.

The folkloric ritual of lighting the *luminarias* or *farolitos* on Christmas Eve is popularized in this story by a noted northern New Mexican author. The nicely illustrated full-color picture book for children transforms an ancient custom, which, embellished by Anaya's imagination, offers us a possible origin of the modern-day practice of using paper bags, votive candles, and sand to light the way for the Holy Family's search for an inn.

However, the author or editors should have included more background information about the origin of the now-popular tradition. One possible explanation for the practice of lighting a bonfire on Christmas Eve is that Spanish New Mexicans wanted to ensure the Christ Child would not abandon them the way they feared the Spanish Crown had. The lights thus served as a beacon of hope to the settlers. Another possible explanation, from the Texas region, connects the practice to that of welcoming visitors to one's home to view the *Niño Dios* (Christ Child).

195   Atkinson, Mary. *María Teresa.* Illus. by Christina Engle Eber. Lollipop Power 1979, P $5.95 (0-914996-21-5). 39pp. Fiction.

Maria Teresa's mother is enrolled as a student at Ohio Western University, and Maria Teresa finds herself also a new student, a recent transplant from New Mexico. Her first day at school, however, begins on a sour note: the teacher and the students have a hard time pronouncing her name, the school rules are dramatically different from those at her previous school, the local grocery store does not carry the essentials for home-style cooking, and the local library lacks the familiar Spanish books she likes to read. In her attempt to cope with the problems of adjusting to an alien environment, Mari Tere, as she is known, confides in her puppet friend Monteja la Oveja (Monteja the Lamb), who speaks only Spanish. Monteja is outraged to learn that the children laugh at Mari Tere. For Show-and-Tell time, Mari Tere decides to take her puppet lamb to school. The children are fascinated by the lamb and discover that they must learn Spanish in order to be able to communicate with the mysterious object. Excellent for its treatment of children's feelings about being different, this book also has an effective resolution, one that shows the value of trying to comprehend and accept cultural differences. Educational attainment is emphasized, as both Mari Tere and her mother attend school. The protagonist's resourcefulness will appeal to young readers, as will the device of the puppet who can talk and express feelings.

196   Brown, Tricia. *Hello Amigos.* Illus. with photos by Fran Ortiz. Henry Holt 1986, LB
$12.95 (0-8050-0090-9). 48pp. Nonfiction.

Young Frankie is a Mexican American from San Francisco's Mission district who,
on the occasion of his birthday, shares with his readers the excitement and
anticipation of that important day. In a first-person narrative, Frankie introduces
us to his large family, consisting of his parents and seven brothers and sisters.
Frankie also shares with readers a day in his fun-filled school and home environment, where he is nurtured by loving teachers and caring adults. When school is
out, Frankie anxiously awaits the family celebration, which finally takes place
when all gather together to feast upon his mother's delicious homemade Mexican dinner. The family and Frankie's friends are also treated to a serenade of
songs performed by a local *mariachi* group, one of whose members is a friend of
Frankie's father. Finally, the breaking of the *piñata* takes place. Here, the unique
style of the breaking inside the family's living room is a testament to innovative
ways that families find in an effort to keep alive a favorite cultural tradition.
Sharp black-and-white photos capture the ambience of a happy child nurtured
by the warmth of a caring family and other deeply concerned adults, such as his
teacher and boys' club supervisor.

197   Bruni, Mary Ann Smothers. *Rosita's Christmas Wish.* Illus. by Thom Ricks. TexArt
1985, HB $14.95; (0-935857-00-1). 48pp. Fiction.

Every year during the Advent season, Los Pastores of San Antonio, a group of
amateur actors from San Antonio, Texas, reenact a centuries-old medieval tradition that was carried over to the Americas with the arrival of the Franciscans, the
Spanish order of religious men. After the *conquistadores*, the Franciscans came to
the New World to convert those in the region to Christianity. A popular method
for conversion at the time was the use of drama, specifically the morality play as
an instrument of faith. The *pastorela*, or shepherds' play, tells the story of the
shepherds' search for the Infant Child. The play is replete with devils and seven
major characters, each symbolic of the seven cardinal sins that Man must
overcome in order to be saved. *Rosita's Christmas Wish* is a story set against that
background.

Nine-year-old Rosita eagerly awaits the beginning of the Christmas season,
when she will enjoy the traditional presentation of the *pastorelas*. Her favorite
character is Gilda, the young shepherdess who accompanies the shepherds on
their journey to Bethlehem. Rosita's best friend, Debbie, will be playing the part
of Gilda this year, and Rosita will be Debbie's *madrina*, or sponsor, for this year's
event. Still, she looks forward to the day when she can play the role of Gilda.

On the evening of the performance, Mr. Elizondo, the play's director (in the
story and in real life), discovers that Rosita indeed knows Gilda's lines, and he
asks her to join Debbie in the role at the final procession.

Ricks's lovely watercolor illustrations depict a lively cast of devils, angels,
and shepherds, set against vibrant barrio scenes, authentically portrayed. The
book includes musical arrangements for the songs, as well as a vocabulary list of
the Spanish words used in the text. It is an excellent introduction to a popular
Christmas tradition in the Southwest and will appeal to youngsters of diverse
backgrounds, who can compare Rosita's Christmas activities to their own.

Codye, Corinn. *Vilma Martínez.*
See entry 212, Grades 4–6.

198   Cruz, Manuel, and Ruth Cruz. *A Chicano Christmas Story./Un cuento navideño chicano.* Bilingual ed. Illus. by Manuel Cruz. Bilingual Educational Services 1980, P $3.95 (0-86624-000-4). 48pp. Fiction.

Diego's and Elenita's father loses his job at the ranch of "los Nopales," and so they must move. On their journey in search for shelter, they meet an old woman selling chocolate, who tells them about a house for rent that belongs to a toymaker. They rent the small home, and the children's father soon finds employment at a shoemaker's shop, but before long he again becomes unemployed. It is the Christmas season, and the townspeople are busy preparing for the celebration.

Diego discovers through his friend Carmela that in the United States a certain benefactor named Santa Claus brings the children their Christmas toys. Diego goes to the toymaker and asks why Santa has never been to his home at Christmastime. Although the toymaker makes all sorts of excuses for Santa, he promises to carve a Chicano Santa Claus, which he places on the display window.

As a group of carolers approaches Diego's and Elenita's house, they recognize the family's poverty and resolve to bring one gift, which they take to the toymaker.

Through the generous toymaker, Diego learns that as long as people are willing to give to and help one another, there will always be a Santa Claus. This is a tender story of a young Mexican boy's discovery of different Christmas celebrations and of the meaning and significance of giving. Illustrations are simplistic, two-tone drawings.

199   García, María. *The Adventures of Connie and Diego./Las aventuras de Connie y Diego.* Rev. ed.; bilingual ed. Trans. by Alma Flor Ada. Illus. by Malaquias Montoya. Children's Book Pr. 1987, HB $12.95 (0-89239-028-X). 24pp. Fiction.

Connie and Diego, a twin sister and brother born in the Land of Plenty, are laughed at and ridiculed because of their different skin coloring. Tired of the cruel teasing, they decide to run away into the forest, hoping to find a place where they will feel at home. There they encounter several animals: a bear, a whale, an eagle, and a tiger. Wishing to emulate these creatures, they ask each to join them in the forest, and each animal declines their request. But it is the patient tiger who points to the positive attributes of their differentness and helps them to accept themselves for who they are.

The story is valuable in demonstrating the uniqueness of each individual and useful in helping children to see the importance of accepting one another as well as themselves, regardless of nationality, color, or race. Bold color illustrations by a noted California Chicano muralist complement this modern fairy tale.

200   García, Richard. ***My Aunt Otilia's Spirits./Los espíritus de mi Tía Otilia.*** Rev.
ed.; bilingual ed. Trans. by Jesús Guerrero Rea. Illus. by Robin Cherin and Roger I.
Reyes. Children's Book Pr. 1987, HB $12.95 (0-89239-029-8). 24pp. Fiction.

Aunt Otilia comes from Puerto Rico each year to visit her kinfolk who live in San
Francisco. Because the home is modest and room is scarce, the guest must share
overnight quarters with her nephew. Each evening, when Aunt Otilia goes to
bed, the young boy hears a knocking on the door and feels the rattling of the bed.
When he asks his aunt about these strange noises, her response is always the
same: "It's just my Spirits." One evening, *Demonio* (little devil, an endearing
term used by the aunt in jest) stays up long enough to "witness" the separation
of the bones from his aunt's body. In his hysteria, he attempts to leave the bed,
only to discover that he has mislaid his aunt's body pieces.

Attractive, bold color illustrations complement a delightfully humorous
ghost story. The tale is derived from the author's earliest childhood recollections
of life in a cultural environment where magic and spirits were a daily part of life.
The book is an excellent read-aloud and may be used for storytelling for all ages.

201   Garza, Carmen Lomas, and Harriet Rohmer. ***Family Pictures./Cuadros de
familia.*** Bilingual ed. Trans. into Spanish by Rosalma Zubizarreta. Illus. by Carmen
Lomas Garza. Children's Book Pr. 1990, LB $12.95 (0-89239-050-6). 32pp. Nonfic-
tion.

Lomas Garza's fond memories of her childhood in rural Mexican-American
South Texas form the basis for her wonderfully sketched paintings that portray
the warmth and cohesiveness of daily family life. Included among the fourteen
scenes are religious occasions such as *posadas*, visits to the shrine of the Virgin of
San Juan, good old-fashioned family outings such as a day at the beach, or
playing the cakewalk at the *feria* (fair) in nearby Reynosa, Mexico. Other everyday family pastimes that Garza has painted and described include watermelon
eating on the porch on a hot summer's evening and the involvement of her entire
family in the preparation of tamales. A logical choice for classroom use, this book
is also an excellent parent-child read-aloud, sure to provoke discussion about
cultures and customs, both past and present. In addition, this is an art book,
introducing young readers to the work of one of this country's finest artists of
Mexican-American heritage.

202   Janda, J. ***The Legend of the Holy Child of Atocha.*** Illus. by William Hart McNich-
ols. Paulist Pr. 1986, P $2.95 (0-8091-6559-7). unp. Nonfiction.

A popular statue of the Christ Child, found in many Catholic Hispanic homes
throughout the Southwest, is the subject of this miracle-legend that stems from
the small town of Atocha, in Spain. Legend has it that when the Moors first
invaded Spain, all of the men in Atocha were taken prisoner and forbidden food
and drink. When the prisoners were finally released, one of them told how a
small child wearing sandals and carrying a basket of food and a gourd of water
had visited the prisoners and fed them and quenched their thirst. Suspecting that
it may have been the work of the Infant Child, a couple who heard the story
visited the local church and discovered that, indeed, the Child's sandals were
worn out, thus verifying their hunch about the local miracle. Tender two-tone
illustrations augment a story told in verse.

MacMillan, Dianne, and Dorothy Freeman. *My Best Friend, Martha Rodríguez.* See entry 216, Grades 4–6.

203　Martel, Cruz. *Yaqua Days.* Illus. by Jerry Pinkney. Dutton/Dial 1976, HB $11.89 (0-8037-9766-4); 1987, P $3.95 (0-8037-0457-7). 40pp. Fiction.

Adán is a young boy in a Puerto Rican family that resides in the Lower East Side of New York. His family owns a bodega, or grocery store, and Adán helps his parents in the small business. On this particular day, he is upset about the rain, which has prevented him from playing in his favorite spot, the East River Park. On his daily route through the neighborhood, Jorge, the mailman, notices Adán's somber mood and inquires. Then Jorge asks Adán about yagua days and is surprised to find the boy has no idea what they are. Jorge does not tell him in detail what they are; he says only that they are fun days when it rains in Puerto Rico.

One morning, Jorge delivers a letter addressed to Adán's parents. The letter came from Corral Viejo, a village in the mountains of Puerto Rico, where Adán's father and Jorge both grew up. Adán visits the island for the first time and is embraced by the many warm and loving relatives that he never even knew he had. His days are filled with the exciting experiences of life in the mountainous village, and he sees the fruits of the family's bodega actually growing on the trees. When it does finally rain during his visit, he discovers for himself the sheer joy of a yagua day.

When Adán returns to New York, he shares with Jorge the common adventure of belly flopping on the edge of the river on a banana leaf on rainy days in Puerto Rico. The black-and-white line drawings are tender illustrations that vividly depict the warm relationships among and between the many family members.

204　Maury, Inez. *My Mother and I Are Growing Strong./Mi mama y yo nos hacemos fuertes.* Bilingual ed. Trans. by Anna Muñoz. Illus. by Sandy Speidel. New Seed Pr. 1979, P $6.95 (0-938678-06-X). 28pp. Fiction.

Emilita and her mother, Lupe, have taken a new job in Ms. Stubbelbine's flower garden. Once a job belonging to Emilita's father, they are replacing him while he is in prison serving time. In addition to the gardening work, Emilita's mom must also learn about trucks and tools and other machinery.

Emilita's joyful spirit and her mom's resolute strength during trying times are the overriding themes of this picture book that focuses on women's issues. Faced with the absence of her husband, Lupe discovers that she must take on chores normally ascribed to men. As she carries out her new role, she discovers unknown inner strengths, as she is forced, for example, to ward off a thief who threatens them in the night.

The treatment of children's fears as they visit their loved ones in prison is realistic yet tender. Everyday social injustices are also delicate issues handled accurately, as Emilita's mother explains to her how her daddy landed in prison in the first place. In all of her actions, Lupe is a teacher and a role model for her child, trying to instill in her daughter a sense of justice, fairness, and the importance of defending oneself from such injustices. As Lupe grows, so does Emilita. And so will Emilita's father, who will soon have to contend with two extra gardeners in a previously male-only job.

This book is unique in its portrayal of the changes that take place in family life when the father is away in prison. It highlights the increased responsibilities and capabilities of women, whose contributions to the family's survival cut across all income and ethnic groups.

Our Hispanic Heritage.
See entry 220, Grades 4–6.

Pena, Sylvia, ed. *Tun-Ta-Ca-Tun: More Stories and Poems in English and Spanish for Children.*
See entry 221, Grades 4–6.

Roberts, Naurice. *Cesar Chávez and La Causa.*
See entry 222, Grades 4–6.

Roberts, Naurice. *Henry Cisneros: Mexican American Mayor.*
See entry 223, Grades 4–6.

205 Rohmer, Harriet, and Cruz Gómez, adapts. *Mr. Sugar Came to Town./La visita del Señor Azúcar.* Bilingual ed. Trans. from Spanish by Rosalma Zubizarreta. Illus. by Enrique Chagoya. Children's Book Pr. 1989, HB $12.95 (0-89239-045-X). 32pp. Fiction.

Alicia and Alfredo enjoy eating their favorite meal cooked by their Grandma Lupe, the delicious and tasty tamales (meat or beans wrapped in corn husks). One evening, as they are gathered around the dinner table, they hear an unusual sound coming from a truck driven by a Mr. Sugar. Mr. Sugar distributes the richest and most delicious desserts. The children stuff themselves with sweets, and every day from that day on, they impatiently await the truck with all its sweet enticements.

Shortly thereafter, the children's habits begin to change dramatically. They become enormously fat and lose their appetite for food. Their energy level is totally depleted, causing them to fall asleep in class. Grandma Lupe, meanwhile, suspecting that Mr. Sugar is a fraud, sets out to find him. She removes his mask and unveils his true identity to her grandchildren. No sooner does Mr. Sugar disappear, than the children begin to regain their healthy eating habits and return to normal.

Chagoya's satirical illustrations flavor this allegorical story of the evil that Mr. Sugar represents. Mr. Sugar can also be seen to represent the perils of alcohol abuse, drug pushers, or any other dangers that children should be made aware of. The story is adapted from a puppet play by Gómez and others; this traditional form of entertainment in Mexico was used by a health clinic's community program in the United States to teach migrant families about proper nutrition.

206 Stanek, Muriel. *I Speak English for My Mom.* Illus. by Judith Friedman. Albert Whitman 1989, LB $10.50 (0-8075-3659-8). 32pp. Fiction.

Growing up in America Lupe is a young girl with many responsibilities, typical of many children her age who are the first in their family to learn English. The daughter of a recently widowed Mexican immigrant, Lupe serves as her mother's translator at the many places they frequent, such as the medical clinic and the local public school. At home, Lupe is the one who answers the phone and interprets the mail. There are times, however, when the responsibility becomes a chore for such a young girl, especially when a dental appointment or an emergency interferes with her already limited playtime.

Black-and-white illustrations tenderly portray the loving mother-daughter relationship. This relationship grows even stronger when Lupe encourages her mother to learn English and become more self-sufficient. The Aztec motif that borders each illustration links the cultural past to modern reality. Stanek's narrative highlights the barriers that immigrants encounter as they struggle in their daily effort to communicate in a foreign-sounding world. It also offers a glimpse into the family life of children in single-parent homes headed by women.

207   Verheyden-Hillard, Mary Ellen. *Scientist from Puerto Rico, Maria Cordero Hardy.* Illus. by Scarlet Biro. SERIES: American Women in Science Biography. The Equity Institute 1985, P $4.50 (0-932469-02-7). 31pp. Nonfiction.

This is the somewhat fictionalized biography of a Puerto Rican scientist who, in addition to her teaching duties at Louisiana State University, also headed the university's Department of Medical Technology. The biography pays special attention to the scientist's impoverished childhood, focusing on the critical choices that Cordero Hardy made as a young girl and that helped her to accomplish her goal of becoming a scientist. Two incidents are highlighted to demonstrate Maria's steadfast determination to succeed. In the first example, at her job, she was demoted from cashier to gift wrapper because of her inability to speak English well enough. After that, she resolved to learn the language. Years later, a professor advised her not to become a scientist, because, as a woman, she was more than likely to marry and abandon her career and profession. She proved him wrong. With black-and-white illustrations. Another book in this series designed to present the contributions of women to the sciences is *Scientist with Determination, Elma Gonzalez*, a biography of the Mexican-American cell biologist.

208   Verheyden-Hillard, Mary Ellen. *Scientist with Determination, Elma Gonzalez.* Illus. by Marian Menzel. SERIES: American Women in Science Biography. The Equity Institute 1985, P $4.50 (0-932469-01-9). 31pp. Nonfiction.

This is a fictionalized biography of a young girl whose inquisitiveness and yearning for education led her to become a research scientist. The facts about Ms. Gonzalez's life story are revealed in very simple terms. The child of migrant workers who emigrated from Mexico when she was 6, she too had to work in the fields, leaving school early each spring to follow the migrant crop with her family. Always, though, Elma was curious, wanting answers to her many questions. Her parents were determined to see her through college and borrowed money to enable her to attend, an unheard-of practice at the time. Today Ms. Gonzalez teaches in addition to her responsibilities as research scientist at a laboratory at the University of California, Los Angeles. Her biography in this series is an inspirational story, simply illustrated.

Anaya, Rudolfo A. *The Farolitos of Christmas.*
See entry 194, Grades PS–3.

209   Anderson, Joan. *Spanish Pioneers of the Southwest.* Illus. with photos by George Ancona. Dutton/Lodestar 1989, HB $14.95 (0-525-67264-8). unp. Nonfiction.

Using professional actors, the writer-photographer team reenacts life on the Spanish hacienda (ranch) of El Rancho de Las Golondrinas in New Mexico during the mid 1700s. Miguel Baca, one of the Baca family's four children, retells a lively fictionalized story of what life was like back in the days when the hacienda also doubled as a hotel and a fort. Ancona's striking black-and-white photographs bring to life daily scenes of ranching and sheep grazing, as well as religious rituals such as children's baptisms and the blessing of the animals. Making history come alive through live performance is a modern, innovative approach in museum studies that succeeds in its objective of bringing children closer to the events of the past. Anderson's and Ancona's effort is an attempt to document that live history. The limitations of the approach, however, lie in its one-dimensional view of the history and heritage of the Southwest, as only one family and one perspective have been presented. The book contains a useful glossary to help readers better understand the many Spanish terms used.

210   Beatty, Patricia. *Lupita Mañana.* William Morrow 1981, LB $12.88 (0-688-00359-1). 192pp. Fiction.

Lupita, aged 13, and her older brother Salvador hail from a small fishing village in Ensenada, Mexico, near the California border. They have recently lost their father in a drowning accident. Their mother, a maid in a hotel, cannot earn enough to maintain their family, and she pleads with her two eldest children to seek employment in the United States in order that they may contribute to the family income. They will succeed with the help of their rich aunt, their mother tells them, her sister who has lived in Indio, California, for several years. Lupita and Salvador undergo harrowing experiences in their attempt to cross the border at Tijuana. They have a hard time making enough to live on and to still be able to send money home. Always the fear of deportation looms.

They arrive in Indio, only to discover a poverty-stricken aunt and her family whose claims of wealth in her letters home were untrue. Lupita then must come to grips with the painful but grim reality of having to watch the assimilation process that her brother undergoes in his attempt to make it in America. In the end, Salvador is deported, not because he is an "illegal," but because he does not know sufficient English to bluff the immigration authorities. After this, Lupita's hope becomes learning sufficient English so that she will not be deported and will be able to earn enough money to return home.

Readers should be aware that the book was written in the early 1980s, when undocumented children were not allowed the benefits of equal educational opportunities in the United States. Federal laws challenged by Mexican-American civil rights organizations helped to change that inequity. Nonetheless, this is a vivid and engrossing portrait of the immigration experience, one that shows the dangers and temptations of life in the United States as well as the necessity of assimilating in order to survive. Lupita's goal of returning home—widely held among immigrants from Mexico—indirectly points to the bleak future facing newcomers who lack an education.

211 Bragg, Bea. *The Very First Thanksgiving: Pioneers on the Rio Grande.* Illus. by Antonio Castro. Harbinger House 1989, P $7.95 (0-943173-22-1). 57pp. Fiction.

Manuel and Fernando are two orphaned brothers, aged 14 and 12, respectively, who live in the mining town of Santa Barbara in New Spain. The year is 1597, and the two youngsters, like many of the town's residents, eagerly await news about the formation of a new expedition to be headed by the governor of Zacatecas, Juan de Oñate. Hoping to avoid work in the dreaded silver mines that claimed their father's life, the boys convince Señor Zaldívar, Don Oñate's nephew, that their skills are invaluable in such an important expedition. They succeed by means of their trained goat, Captain General Martínez.

Once on the expedition, however, they encounter the dangers common to exploration parties of the day. A search for food and water becomes increasingly more difficult amid the dangers of rattlesnakes and coyotes. Captain General Martínez proves to be more useful than as mere entertainment. Once the expedition reaches its destination, Oñate orders that a thanksgiving feast be prepared in celebration of their arrival. Among the invited guests are the Native Americans who guided them through the territory in search of the Rio Grande.

Bragg's is a historical novel that captures the excitement and adventure of a piece of southwestern history, one that precedes the Pilgrims' thanksgiving story by some 24 years. The novel treats Native Americans with respect. Events are portrayed accurately, but the lively adventure story is never bogged down in historical trivia. The spunky boys, Manuel and Fernando, will appeal to modern-day readers, who will appreciate their humor and resourcefulness.

Bruni, Mary Ann Smothers. *Rosita's Christmas Wish.*
See entry 197, Grades PS–3.

212 Codye, Corinn. *Vilma Martínez.* Bilingual ed.; trans. into Spanish by Alma Flor Ada. Illus. by Susi Kilgore. SERIES: Hispanic Stories. Raintree 1990, LB $11.50 (0-8172-3382-2). 32pp. Nonfiction.

As a child growing up in San Antonio, Texas, Vilma Martínez remembers not being allowed to swim in a city park pool in the neighboring town of New Braunfels. In the 1940s and 1950s, Mexican Americans, like black Americans, were victims of discrimination and segregation because of their skin color. As a student, Ms. Martínez constantly had to prove to others, such as her high school counselor and her father, that she would indeed go on to the best college and succeed.

An important remnant of Mexican-American history is featured by this small but inspirational volume that highlights the life of a petite brown woman who first learned to read and write in her native Spanish. Vilma Martínez grew up to become a lawyer, challenging before the highest courts in the land the laws that discriminated against Mexican-American people.

Muted color illustrations accompany the text, which is provided in both English and Spanish. Other Hispanic Americans included in this series are Luis Alvarez, David Farragut, and Carlos Finlay. Biographies of early explorers and missionaries in what is now the United States present Hernando de Soto, Bernardo de Gálvez, Pedro Menéndez de Aviles, and Father Junípero Serra.

Garza, Carmen Lomas, and Harriet Rohmer. *Family Pictures.*
See entry 201, Grades PS–3.

Gillies, John. *Señor Alcalde: A Biography of Henry Cisneros.*
See entry 236, Grades 7–9.

213   Hewett, Joan. *Getting Elected: The Diary of a Campaign.* Illus. with photos by
      Richard Hewett. Dutton/Lodestar 1989, HB $13.95 (0-525-67259-1). 47pp. Non-
      fiction.

Featuring Gloria Molina, the first Chicana elected to the California Assembly,
this photo-essay highlights her candidacy for the Los Angeles City Council. All
of the important aspects of the campaign of an elected public official are discussed: debates, interviews with the press, mailings, and phone calls. However,
specific focus is given to the comprehensive grass roots campaign that includes
door-to-door registration drives, vote-by-mail drives, public forums, and pre-
cinct walking by the candidate. Biographic information on Molina's childhood
traces her remarkable growth and development from nonassertive Spanish-
speaking aspirant to outspoken and eloquent public speaker and women's rights
activist.

The sharp black-and-white photos reveal an energetic, enthusiastic,
hardworking campaign that covers all the ground necessary in the effort to win a
major election.

214   Hewett, Joan. *Hector Lives in the United States Now: The Story of a Mexican-
      American Child.* Illus. with photos by Richard Hewett. HarperCollins 1990, LB
      $13.89 (0-397-32278-X). 44pp. Nonfiction.

Eagle Rock, a residential area of Los Angeles, is home to 10-year-old Hector
Almaraz and his family. The son of Mexican immigrants and himself an immigrant, he has resided in the United States for most of his young life. The photo-
essay reveals Hector's typically normal life-style as he goes to school, plays with
his friends and his brothers, and rides his bike through the neighborhood. It is
also a portrait of the family's decision to apply for amnesty under the new
immigration laws. Through this law, thousands of immigrant families took
advantage of the opportunity to become legal residents and eventually to apply
for U.S. citizenship.

The Hewetts also capture special family rituals, such as when Hector's mom
reads to the children stories from the Bible in Spanish just before bedtime. A very
important occasion in Hector's life is his first Holy Communion. All angles are
covered in capturing the preparatory process leading up to the big day, including
the required church meetings with the *padrinos* (godparents).

The Hewetts place Hector's story within the overall context of the American
immigrant experience. Teachers should find particularly useful the student oral
history project in which Hector and all of his classmates participate, a project
that highlights the immigrant heritage of most Americans. Hector's story is
especially valuable in pointing out the historic moment in U.S. immigration
history when Mexican immigrants in particular no longer needed to hide from
authorities and live in fear of deportation. This book is an excellent source for
research or discussion as well as for expository writing on life in the United
States both before and after the passage of the amnesty law.

215   Hurwitz, Johanna. *Class President.* Illus. by Sheila Hamanaka. William Morrow 1990, LB $12.95 (0-688-09114-8). 85pp. Fiction.

When Mr. Flores, the new teacher, suggests that the fifth graders elect their class officers, Julio knows that his friend Lucas will make the perfect candidate. Although another student, Cricket, is also interested in the position, several events before the nominations demonstrate Julio's capacity as a leader. When a classmate breaks his glasses playing soccer, Julio organizes a bake sale to pay for a new pair. After the principal suspends soccer playing in the playground, Julio takes over from the tongue-tied candidates to become the student spokesperson.

Julio, of Puerto Rican heritage, is portrayed as lacking the self-assurance needed to stand up to his peers. He also does not understand his own leadership potential until Lucas decides to nominate him for class president.

The portrayal of the Hispanic teacher is exemplary. He demonstrates for his students the role of process in consensus-building as well as the essential qualities of a leader. He acknowledges Julio's cultural background, but, although he draws upon Julio's birthplace as a topic for further discussion, that theme is never fully developed in the story. Mr. Flores attempts to discuss Julio's name with him and stresses the importance of cultural pride, but Julio seems unaware until it is pointed out to him. Hurwitz alludes to Julio's cultural background in portraying his family situation. He was born in Puerto Rico. His mother is the head chambermaid at a local hotel, his grandmother cannot read English and speaks only Spanish, and his large family consists of four brothers. There is no father in the story. Still, Julio exemplifies the assimilated Hispanic child who typically comes from a middle-class upbringing and who attends an all-white school, even though he is far from middle class. On the whole, this is a light, charming story that presents some cultural information while exploring universal themes of importance to middle-grade readers.

216   MacMillan, Dianne, and Dorothy Freeman. *My Best Friend, Martha Rodríguez: Meeting a Mexican-American Family.* Illus. by Warren Fricke. SERIES: My Best Friend. Julian Messner 1986, LB $9.98 (0-671-61973-X). 48pp. Fiction.

Kathy is an Anglo-American child who goes to the same school as her good friend Martha. She also lives in the same neighborhood. Every day after school, Kathy visits Martha's home. Always she learns something new and interesting about Martha and her Mexican-American family and the many rituals, customs, and traditions that surround their lives. She learns, for example, to play the fun game called *lotería* (lottery). Martha also teaches her Spanish-language nursery rhymes and games from Mexico. Special rituals such as *quinceaneras* (a girl's special fifteenth birthday celebration) and piñata parties especially fascinate Kathy.

Posadas and the Feast of Our Lady of Guadalupe are two special religious events that Martha invites Kathy to participate in. The cooking of tamales is a major family production that Kathy is also included in. Most of all, however, Kathy is fascinated by the large family unit and close family bonds that tie the Rodríguezes to other members of their extended family. From Martha, Kathy also learns of the importance of the role of the grandmother and the grandfather, as well as of the necessity to support other extended family members who are recently arrived Mexican immigrants.

This chapter book is an excellent source for the teaching of customs and traditions in Mexican-American culture. It should help readers to understand better those unique customs and traditions. It is particularly useful for recent immigrant children as a way to encourage their participation as discussion leaders on a subject with which they may be intimately connected.

The book features tender black-and-white illustrations, a glossary of the many Spanish words used in the text, and a brief bibliography designed to interest young readers in further readings on Mexico.

217   Mohr, Nicholasa. *Felita.* Illus. by Ray Cruz. Dutton/Dial 1979, LB $12.89 (0-8037-3144-2); Bantam 1989, P $2.75 (0-553-15792-2). 112pp. Fiction.

Felita's father decides to move the family from the barrio in order for the children to have a better education and future. Felita and her three brothers do not understand the logic behind the decision, which means they are being asked to give up their friends and their familiar environment for reasons unknown to them. In addition, in the new neighborhood, the children quickly learn that they are not wanted. "Why don't you stay with your own kind?" Felita is asked. The Anglo kids mock her language and her skin color. The problems continue to escalate when her brother is beaten and called a "spick," and the neighborhood kids play pranks on Mami. Her parents come to the grim realization that they must move out before someone gets hurt badly. In an effort to understand her experiences, however, Felita finds solace in the kind words of encouragement and in the wisdom of her aging grandmother, who listens to Felita, allows her to talk out her feelings, and is a source of consolation. During that spring, though, Felita's grandmother dies. Felita's love for and memory of her grandmother live on and are reflected in her love of nature and especially of the flowers she plans to see when she makes a journey to Puerto Rico—the land about which her grandmother has told her so much.

The pain of discrimination as seen and experienced through the eyes of an 8-year-old accurately reflects the overt prejudice against Puerto Rican Americans that existed in the New York of the author's upbringing. The strong bonds between the young and the old that are nourished in childhood in Puerto Rican families form another powerful theme of Mohr's work. This novel provides eloquent testimony of the love and admiration that Felita feels for her grandmother. Either of these themes makes an excellent starting point for classroom discussions and essay topics, allowing children to express their sentiments and their views about Felita's experiences as well as their own.

218   Mohr, Nicholasa. *Going Home.* Dutton/Dial 1986, HB $11.95 (0-8037-0269-8); Bantam 1989, P $2.50 (0-553-15699-3). 192pp. Fiction.

One day, Felita's parents call the family together to announce that the family's lifelong dream of all going together to Puerto Rico for two weeks during the summer will become a reality. But the really good news is that, of the three children, 12-year-old Felita has been selected by her parents to spend her entire summer vacation there, with the many relatives she has always heard about but never met.

Tío Jorge, who has lived with Felita's family ever since Felita can remember, plans to retire to Puerto Rico and is spending the summer there overseeing the construction of his home. Relieved that she will not have to spend her summer either under her mother's watchful eye or with her father, who lately seems to impose stricter rules on her simply because she is a girl, Felita is elated. However, no sooner do they arrive on the island than Felita begins to feel the tension as the cousins call her brothers "gringos" and "Nuyoricans" and tease them for their inability to speak Spanish fluently. Felita ends up in the home of her overbearing, devoutly religious aunt and uncle, whom she finds quite boring. Even the new friends she has made in the church youth program on the island resent her because she seems to have much more freedom back home than they do. Felita is miserable, consumed by the demands her new friends have made on her. Her distraction begins to take its toll on her relationship with her favorite uncle, whom she now finds uninteresting too.

Going Home is this noted Puerto Rican author's sequel to *Felita*. Mohr's sensitivity to the deep bonds of *familia* are especially noteworthy. She excels in her ability to continue the story and character development of the growing Felita in all her moods, emotions, and feelings, and especially in Felita's special relationship with her grandmother, who has instilled in her a love for the island and for all her family members.

This highly recommended novel touches on the desire of all children to become independent and to begin to shape their own sense of identity in light of the conflicts inherent in their culture.

---

219   Munson, Sammye. *Our Tejano Heroes: Outstanding Mexican-Americans in Texas.* Illus. with photos. Eakin 1989, HB $9.95 (0-89015-691-3). 86pp. Nonfiction.

Biographies of individuals, husband-and-wife teams, and families are among the 21 entries that compose this collection of minibiographical stories about Texans of Mexican descent whose leadership abilities have contributed to the state's growth. Among those covered are seven women, including Andrea Castanón Ramírez Candelaria, a nurse who cared for the wounded at the Battle of the Alamo; Lydia Mendoza, a Texas treasure who was the first Texan to be honored by the National Endowment for the Arts with a National Heritage Award; and Emma Tenayuca, a courageous woman who led a massive strike of over 10,000 pecan shellers in San Antonio during the 1930s.

Although the layout of the book is rather unattractive, the stories themselves, though brief, are factual and inspirational. They give students information about notable people generally ignored by history texts. The bibliography with each entry will guide students in further research assignments. There are numerous black-and-white photos of the biographees.

---

220   *Our Hispanic Heritage.* Illus. Raintree 1989. 32pp. Nonfiction. o.p.

A documentary of the national Hispanic Heritage Art Contest sponsored by McDonald's Corporation, this book includes photographs of the winning entries, accompanied by a photo of the participant and a brief statement of the significance of cultural heritage as highlighted in the painting. Unfortunately, the book is quite uneven, as not all the contestants' photos or statements are included. The introduction is by actor Edward James Olmos. Despite its flaws, this is a useful tool that highlights what children consider culturally meaningful. It is particualry valuable for introducing and encouraging participation in competitive cultural arts events.

221 Pena, Sylvia, ed. *Tun-Ta-Ca-Tun: More Stories and Poems in English and Spanish for Children.* Bilingual ed. Illus. by Narciso Pena. Arte Público Pr. 1986, P $8.50 (0-934770-43-3). 191pp. Nonfiction.

Seven poets and nine prose writers of primarily Hispanic heritage contribute to this anthology of 15 poems and 8 short stories unique to Hispanic culture and traditions. Included among the authors are Nicolasa Mohr, whose "The Conch Shell" is the touching story of a Puerto Rican boy's first experiences in New York surroundings. Frank Varela's title story "Tun-Ta-Ca-Tun" is an excellent poetic retelling of the legend of the origins of the island of Puerto Rico. Other noteworthy stories are Pat Mora's and Charles Ramírez Berg's modern retelling of the legend of the poinsettia flower and Alberto and Patricia De La Fuente's fairy story "Sunkissed: An Indian Legend."

The bilingual edition is unique in that it demonstrates the versatility of the poet contributors in their command of both languages, especially Sylvia Novo Pena's and Elsa Zambosco's delightful poetry, which is composed in the two distinct languages. The collection features black-and-white pencil and pen-and-ink illustrations. *Kikiriki: Stories and Poems in English and Spanish for Children* (Arte Público Pr., second printing, 1987) is an earlier volume, originally published in 1981.

222 Roberts, Naurice. *Cesar Chávez and La Causa.* Illus. with photos. SERIES: Picture-Story Biographies. Childrens Pr. 1986, LB $8.95 (0-516-03484-7). 32pp. Nonfiction.

Cesar Chávez made history when the national boycott that he launched in the mid 1960s was declared a success almost a decade later. Chávez urged all American consumers to boycott grapes because of the low wages paid to and other injustices committed against the workers who picked the grapes.

This simply told biography is the story of the life of Cesar Chávez. Because Chávez has dedicated his life to the movement to help farm workers gain their just due and respect, this biography also comprises the story of that movement.

The abundance of black-and-white and brown-tone photographs of family gatherings and important scenes that depict the struggle of the United Farm Workers of America adds a historical dimension that enhances this simplified biography. Other titles that present Hispanic Americans as part of this series are *Everett Alvarez Jr.: A Hero for Our Times, Evelyn Cisneros: Prima Ballerina,* and *Henry Cisneros: Mexican American Mayor.*

223 Roberts, Naurice. *Henry Cisneros: Mexican American Mayor.* Illus. with photos. SERIES: Picture-Story Biographies. Childrens Pr. 1986, LB $8.95 (0-516-03485-5). 32pp. Nonfiction.

This biography of the first Hispanic ever to be elected mayor of a major U.S. city highlights Cisneros's educational accomplishments that presage the subsequent growth and development of his public persona. Roberts attributes his deep sense of pride in his cultural heritage as well as his love of learning to a family tradition handed down through generations. Abundant black-and-white family photos and photos of important political milestones complement the story of a popular American hero. A time line marking the significant accomplishments in Cisneros's life is included.

224 Romano, Branko E. ***Chicken Toons.*** Illus. by the author. Tonatiuh-Quinto Sol 1982, P $2.50 (0-89229-010-2). 95pp. Nonfiction.

This book is a compilation of a series of cartoons drawn by the preteenage author during his involvement in a class project that entailed hatching baby chicks. The result is a highly imaginative, entertaining book that showcases the endless combinations that are possible when word and illustration are combined by a child. The 80 caricatures feature images of everyday life that reflect mass culture. A mostly humorous tone is expressed throughout, principally through the use of satire on mass media images and puns. One in particular, entitled "Asian Toons," is rather stereotyped in its portrayal of the chickens in costume; this, unfortunately, reflects the dominant images presented to children through the media and in schoolbooks.

Branko Romano is the son of the founder and director of this small press, which has built a reputation for publishing significant works of Chicano litera- ture. Given an unusual opportunity to have his work published, the young author-illustrator will inspire older elementary and middle school students in their own creative expressions of personality and provide food for classroom discussions about images in mass culture.

225 Soto, Gary. ***The Cat's Meow.*** Illus. Strawberry Hill Pr. 1987, P $4.95 (0-89407- 087-8). 64pp. Fiction.

Eight-year-old Nicole discovers that her cat has the unique ability to speak in a foreign language—Spanish. But the cat refuses to speak in public, and Nicole is made to feel that she has invented a thoroughly outrageous idea in order to impress her parents, who are oblivious to her concerns and questions.

One evening, as Nicole is feeding her cat, Pip begins her tale. It all began, according to Pip, when Pip ran away from home during the time that Nicole and her family went on their vacation and left her in the hands of the young student who did not feed her because she could never find the cat food. Pip stumbled onto a Mr. Langer, an eccentric linguist who had set a goal for himself to read 10,000 books.

Nicole begs Pip to introduce her to Mr. Langer, but when she finally does meet him, neither Pip nor Mr. Langer acknowledge Pip's new means of commu- nication. Meanwhile, she again desperately tries to tell her parents, to no avail.

A local neighborhood snoop reveals to the police the strange happenings at Mr. Langer's house. His privacy invaded, Mr. Langer flees the neighborhood. Through the experience, Nicole discovers the pain incurred when one meddles in the private affairs of others. But she also discovers the joy that is felt when secrets are respected between friends, and she becomes self-assured in that discovery, as well as in her friendship with her most trusted friend, her cat.

Soto skillfully employs Spanish-language phrases, which adds to the in- trigue of an already strange story that can help elementary-age readers to discuss and explore the nature of communication. Translations of the phrases are de- noted in asterisks and serve as footnotes at the bottom of the page on which the foreign phrase appears. This is the first book for children written by a noted Chicano poet and novelist, whose highly acclaimed short story collection for young adults, *Baseball in April,* is also annotated in this chapter.

226   Sumption, Christine, and Kathleen Thompson. ***Carlos Finlay.*** Bilingual ed.; Spanish trans. by Alma Flor Ada. Illus. by Les Didier. SERIES: Hispanic Stories. Raintree 1990, LB $16.67 (0-8172-3378-4). 32pp. Nonfiction.

The cure for yellow fever, a deadly tropical disease, is normally attributed to Dr. Walter Reed. Although Reed tested the theory that yellow fever was transmitted through the mosquito, it was the Cuban-born scientist Carlos Finlay, a medical doctor, who developed the theory and presented it to Walter Reed's commission. Thirty-six years later, Dr. Finlay's work was finally acknowledged by the International Congress of Medical History. Readers will learn about these omissions in American history through this series, which is intended to educate young Americans about the many important contributions of Cubans such as Finlay and other Hispanic Americans. Critical study of encyclopedia articles, such as those found in *Encyclopedia International* (Lexicon Publications, Vol. 19), confirm the authors' point about existing omissions and demonstrate the accuracy of this series volume.

227   Taylor, Theodore. ***The Maldonado Miracle.*** Avon 1986, P $2.50 (0-380-70023-9). 121pp. Fiction.

José Maldonado is a 12-year-old Mexican youth whose mother has died of cancer and whose father has gone north to the United States in search of a better life. He has lived alone for four months with his dog, Sánchez, waiting for his father to send the money for the border crossing. When his father finally arranges for José to join him, he finds himself in the hands of Gutiérrez, the *Coyote*, whose job is crossing Mexican aliens into the United States. José and Sánchez cross the border at Tecate in the trunk of an old car and head north on the Santa Ana Freeway, to freedom.

Gutiérrez delivers José to his final destination, at a labor camp, only to discover that José's father has gone to do the picking for another crop at a labor camp some 250 miles away. Because Gutiérrez has no intention of waiting for José's father to arrive, José is instantly initiated into the work force. Now that he is "legally" able to work, he discovers and experiences firsthand the cruelty and hardships of farm work and labor camp living.

Due to unforeseen circumstances, José must abandon the labor camp. Fearful that he may be turned in to immigration officials, yet wanting to stay near the labor camp in order to join his father, he finds shelter in a nearby town.

It is at this point in the novel that the story develops its strong mysterious and humorous element, as a religious phenomenon turns a dying old town into a source of curiosity, thanks to José. Taylor's excellent writing of an engaging novel is sure to involve its readers in the curious phenomenon of the story while at the same time it offers a multicultural perspective. Characters are presented in depth, and readers from all backgrounds will empathize with José and follow along eagerly as he uses his considerable intelligence to solve problems.

Verheyden-Hillard, Mary Ellen. ***Scientist with Determination, Elma Gonzalez.***
See entry 208, Grades PS–3.

228   Ashabranner, Brent. *The Vanishing Border: A Photographic Journey Along Our Frontier with Mexico.* Illus. with photos by Paul Conklin. Putnam 1987, HB $14.95 (0-396-08900-3). 175pp. Nonfiction.

The Texas-Mexico border is explored through Conklin's striking photographs, which offer a visual picture of the people of the area commonly referred to as "the border." Ashabranner's and Conklin's travels led them to the major cities along the 2,000-mile stretch, as well as to obscure border towns in the four states of Texas, California, New Mexico, and Arizona.

The narrative includes interviews that Ashabranner conducted with local citizens, both ordinary and prominent. Their stories provide a personal, in-depth exploration of the many issues that affect the people of these communities: immigration, illegal crossings, the economy, culture, unemployment, drug smuggling, a deep-rooted tie to the land, and, most important, the evolution of border culture—the blending of both Mexican and American ways.

Ashabranner's inclusion of the Kikapoo Indians of El Paso and the Tohono O'odham Indians of Arizona is a tribute to his noteworthy effort to present all aspects of life in this region.

229   Ashabranner, Brent, and Melissa Ashabranner. *Into a Strange Land: Unaccompanied Refugee Youth in America.* Illus. with photos. Putnam 1987, HB $14.95 (0-399-21709-6). 160pp. Nonfiction.

The stirring stories, full of the human trauma of war, tell of youngsters sent to America by their parents in order to obtain the best education and be freed from the persecution of communism. Portrayed by Ashabranner's equally stirring photographs are primarily Asian and Cuban youths who were welcomed with open arms and who received moral and economic assistance from the federal government.

Ashabranner focuses mainly on Asian youths, whose immigrant experience is far different from most Latino immigrants of this age. When he does choose to highlight a Latino youth, he slips at one point into a negative stereotype referring to the youth, Mario, as macho. Other Latino youngsters receive sympathetic treatment, yet it is clear that the author feels more emotional ties to the Asians than to the Latinos. Moreover, the book neglects to point out the inequities in U.S. immigration laws that benefited Cuban and Asian communities yet denied the same benefits to Latino populations from Mexico, Guatemala, and El Salvador. No distinction is made between the terms "refugees" and "illegals," key concept terms that to this date determine immigration policy.

230   Bachelis, Faren. *The Central Americans.* Illus. with photos. SERIES: The Peoples of North America. Chelsea House 1990, LB $17.95 (0-87754-868-4); P $9.95 (0-7910-0284-5). 111pp. Nonfiction.

An insightful document on one of America's most recent immigrant groups, this series book offers a lucid analysis of the many factors that have affected this population group, including a long history of oppression in their native countries, persecution, alienation, and, finally, suffering and the devastating effects of war. Immigration and its related side issues—sanctuary and political asylum—are also deftly examined. Particularly revealing is the stark symbiotic relationship that links the two hemispheres of the Americas.

Unlike other books in this series, which recognize the notable achievements of well-known personalities, this volume portrays the Central Americans as a people whose heroes and heroines are still in the making. The author neglects to mention the outstanding literary figures throughout history, such as Ruben Dario, Nicaragua's best known poet, and Miguel Angel Asturias, Nobel Prize winner in literature from Guatemala. A more recent novelist, Arturo Arias from Guatemala, resides in the United States, and Manlio Argueta, the Salvadoran writer currently exiled in Costa Rica, has had works translated into English and published by major U.S. publishing houses.

Beatty, Patricia. *Lupita Mañana.*
See entry 210, Grades 4–6.

231   Beltrán Hernández, Irene. *Across the Great River.* Arte Público Pr. 1989, P $8.50 (0-934770-96-4). 136pp. Fiction.

Kata listens as her anguished mother pleads with her father to let the family stay in Mexico. But economic hardships leave the family with no alternative but to cross the border at the Rio Grande in search of a better life. At the crossing, however, Kata's father becomes separated from the family, and Kata, her mother, and two younger siblings must venture alone into a new land. The "*coyotes*" (smugglers) take the family to the home of Doña Anita, a grumpy old woman who at first grudgingly cares for the family. Kata fears Doña Anita but quickly becomes intrigued by her abilities to perform motions and actions related to faith healing.

Much of the focus of this novel is on the struggle that the family members endure (including the beating and rape of Kata's mother) at the hands of unknown violent persons. The mystery in the story is solved when the gold nugget, the object of the attacker's search, is found. With their newfound money, the family returns to Mexico, where they are reunited with their father, who proceeds to explain his detention and subsequent deportation back to Mexico.

This novel for both young adults and adults is a harrowing portrayal from a young girl's perspective of the dangers that immigrant families face daily in their journey across the Rio Grande. In its positive resolution, though, Beltrán Hernández demonstrates the hopes and joys of many immigrant families whose wish is to return to their native land.

232   Betancourt, T. Ernesto. *The Me Inside of Me.* Lerner 1985, HB $10.95 (0-8225-0728-5). 156pp. Fiction.

Seventeen-year-old Alfredo Flores becomes an orphan overnight when the Mexico City–bound plane carrying his family crashes. While trying to cope with tremendous grief over the sudden loss of his entire family, he must also learn to deal with a new reality—that he is no longer poor, being the beneficiary of an accident insurance policy his parents purchased shortly before takeoff.

An old friend of his grandfather's, Callen, becomes Alfredo's legal guardian and arranges for Alfredo to enter an exclusive West Los Angeles prep school in order to prepare for admission to Stanford in the fall. But not even the wealth that it takes to attend such a school can overcome his previous academic unpreparedness or his uneasiness in an alien environment. At the school, he is drawn to Lenny, the school's outcast.

Alfredo's experience shows the pain and discomfort that arise when facing cultural conflicts and the disrespect of those who cannot accept differences. Yet there is much humor in this insightful story. A particularly noteworthy example occurs when Alfredo is finally able to purchase his dream car. He gets his chance to "pay back" the car salesman—who had assumed he was just another poor Mexican kid—when he makes the salesman deliver the car to his door and then walk back to the dealership. Readers will sense the feeling of victory and the empowerment that come with finally winning after experiencing no-win situations.

233   Bode, Janet. *New Kids on the Block: Oral Histories of Immigrant Teens.* Franklin Watts 1989, HB $12.90 (0-531-10794-9). 128pp. Nonfiction.

The testimonies of 11 teenagers, all recent immigrants to the United States, are featured in this book. Four of the teenagers are from countries in Latin America —El Salvador, Cuba, Mexico, and the Dominican Republic. The teens from El Salvador and Mexico describe the problems in crossing the border illegally and living in fear of deportation; the youngster from Cuba recounts repression in that country. Fourteen-year-old Tito, from Mexico, expresses profound respect for his country's mythology and history. The teens have other problems in common, most notably the adjustment to a more permissive and crime-ridden society. Dominican teen Martha chafes against the restrictions placed by her mother, and Francia, from El Salvador, observes that in some ways there are more safety and freedom in the country she left behind. All combine school with long hours at a job.

While the interviews do not explore issues in great depth, the teens and their stories will appeal to junior-high-school-age youngsters. By allowing her interviewees to speak for themselves and to express their strong opinions on political and personal issues, Bode gives readers a perspective that complements other nonfiction treatments of the immigrant experience. A bibliography is included.

L.M-L.

234   Cullison, Alan. *The South Americans.* Illus. with photos. SERIES: The Peoples of North America. Chelsea House 1991, LB $17.95 (0-87754-863-3); P $9.95 (0-7910-0305-1). 112pp. Nonfiction.

South Americans make up only a small fraction of Latinos living in the United States and Canada, but recent economic and political problems have driven increasing numbers northward. Cullison effectively distinguishes these from other immigrants from Latin America, pointing out their often middle-class status in their home country and their continuing ties to home, as exemplified by their reading their native country's newspapers and voting in its elections. Though few in numbers, South Americans have distinguished themselves in the fields of architecture and social work. Cullison challenges the stereotype of Colombian Americans involved in drug dealing, and his writing is, on the whole, concise and accurate, with individual stories breaking up the narrative. An eight-page color photo spread is well reproduced and appealing; other photos also illustrate the variety of backgrounds and immigration experiences. The book includes an index and a bibliography geared mainly to adults.   L.M-L.

235 Dwyer, Christopher. *The Dominican Americans.* Illus. with photos. SERIES: The Peoples of North America. Chelsea House 1991, LB $17.95 (0-87754-872-2); P $9.95 (0-7910-0287-8). 112pp. Nonfiction.

This series volume provides an in-depth look at a distinct subgroup of Hispanic Americans that has previously been overlooked in the literature for children and young adults. Dwyer traces the history of the people of the island of Hispaniola, beginning with the "discovery" of the island by Christopher Columbus and the subsequent brutal fate of the Indians at the hands of the Spanish. That history is told without the fanfare and romanticism that have tended to characterize descriptions of Columbus's journey. The well-written text combines firsthand personal interviews and keen observation to fill in gaps in current documentation. The immigration issue is thoroughly explored, and its presentation helps to shed light on the injustices of current immigration laws that penalize individuals who strive to keep the family unit intact. Particularly moving is the chapter that discusses the dangers, perils, and tragedy that occur when people take extraordinary risks in search of a new life. One chapter is devoted to the success of several dozen Dominican baseball players and the fashion designer Oscar de la Renta. On the whole, this is a welcome addition to offset the dearth of published works in this area.

236 Gillies, John. *Señor Alcalde: A Biography of Henry Cisneros.* Illus. with photos. SERIES: People in Focus. Dillon 1988, LB $11.95 (0-87518-374-3). 127pp. Nonfiction.

This is a full-length biography for children that documents the life of a notable national Hispanic figure. Cisneros's personal milestones, beginning with his self-motivated leadership drive as a youth, are told within the context of the cohesive, nurturing family that cultivated his leadership potential. His political accomplishements, from his modest beginnings as a city councilman representing the Mexican-American community to his election and subsequent reelection as San Antonio's first Mexican-American mayor, are a tribute to his determination. The proliferation of black-and-white photos of his family enhance the former mayor's popular image. An essay that outlines his rules for personal decision making is included, as are a time line of his life and a brief history of Texas and Mexico that should help to place Cisneros's family within its proper historical context. This Cisneros biography is an inspirational one, serving to introduce youngsters of elementary and middle school age to the calling and the highest ideals of public service.

237 Harlan, Judith. *Hispanic Voters: A Voice in American Politics.* Illus. with photos. Franklin Watts 1988, HB $12.80 (0-531-10586-5). 112pp. Nonfiction.

This book provides excellent documentation of the key issues that are at the heart of the Hispanic vote throughout the United States. The author specifies the four subgroups of Hispanics in the United States—Mexican Americans, Puerto Ricans, Cubans, and Central and South Americans—and focuses on the issues important to each of them, namely, education (including bilingual education), immigration, the Voting Rights Act, and single-member district representation.

Highlighted are the works of notable figures such as the late Willie Velásquez in the area of voter registration, specifically his Southwest Voter Registration and Education Project, and the work of the civil rights litigation group MALDEF, the Mexican American Legal Defense and Education Fund. Notably missing, however, is the work of Ernesto Cortés and the Industrial Areas Foundation, whose grass roots organizing efforts in Texas, California, and the Northeast have done much to train ordinary people in holding politicians accountable for their actions and in becoming more knowledgeable in the art of public discourse. Nonetheless, this is an ideal work for government and civics classes and an important addition to any library collection serving young adults.

Hewett, Joan. *Getting Elected: The Diary of a Campaign.*
See entry 213, Grades 4–6.

238   Larsen, Ronald J. *The Puerto Ricans in America.* Rev. ed. Illus. with photos. SERIES: In America. Lerner 1989, LB $9.95 (0-8225-0238-0). 79pp. Nonfiction.

This is an introductory look at the sub-group of Hispanic Americans whose cultural ties are in the Caribbean island of Puerto Rico. Larsen begins by giving a brief history of the island. Included here is the evolution of its political history, from its earlier status as a colony of Spain to its current commonwealth status. A chapter on migration illuminates for the reader the history of Puerto Rican migration to the United States. Stated succinctly are the many, primarily economic, reasons for the migration. Other chapters discuss the problem of discrimination and the work that various community and educational organizations are doing in order to improve the overall quality of life. The final chapter highlights the accomplishments of well-known figures in the fields of government, business, arts and literature, entertainment and sports. Missing from this last group, however, are noted literary figures and scholars such as Nicholasa Mohr and Nicolás Kanellos, who have much to offer young readers by virtue of their work in the fields of writing, teaching, and publishing. This series also contains a volume entitled *The Mexicans in America.*

239   Meltzer, Milton. *The Hispanic Americans.* Illus. with photos by Morrie Camphi and Catherine Noren. HarperCollins 1982, LB $13.89 (0-690-04111-X). 149pp. Nonfiction.

This book provides an overview of the Hispanic population group, told from both a historical and a sociological perspective. Meltzer carefully differentiates between the three major cultural groups that compose Hispanic Americans. Much attention is paid to Mexican Americans, primarily because they are the largest subgroup of Hispanics in the United States. Meltzer is succinct in defining the major issues at the heart of Hispanic politics—education, immigration, jobs and employment, and, finally, discrimination. Included is a four-page bibliography of sources cited in this work. While the book could certainly use revision, principally to bring the numbers and issues up to date and to examine the more recent arrival of Central Americans, it nonetheless serves as an excellent guide toward an understanding of contemporary Hispanic America.

240   *The Mexican Texans.* 2nd rev. ed. Illus. with photos. SERIES: The Texians and the Texans. Univ. of Texas Institute of Texan Cultures at San Antonio 1986, P $3.95 (0-86701-030-4). 23pp. Nonfiction.

Brief historical essays trace the development of the Mexican American, beginning with the Aztec capital of Mexico, Tenochtitlán. Other major periods presented include that of the Spanish Conquest through the formation of Texas in 1836 up to the 1970s. Short sketches intended to outline the contributions of noted persons follow. Other than reductions or enlargements of the photographs, as well as changes in the layout and design of this publication, there is no information provided that differs significantly from the original edition. Thus, the second edition is sorely in need of updating, having no further information on events and individuals since the early 1970s. Another major omission is the contribution of notable Texan-Mexican women, in both the past and the present. Women who should have appeared include Jovita Idar, who, along with her family, published a Spanish-language newspaper detailing injustices against Mexican Americans, and Emma Tenayuca, the noted San Antonio union activist of the 1930s. Numerous contemporary women with significant accomplishments are also omitted.

241   Mills, Claudia. *Luisa's American Dream.* Four Winds 1981, HB $11.95 (0-02-767040-6). 155pp. Fiction.

Luisa Ruiz is a typical 14-year-old girl. She loves boys and makeup and talking on the phone with her best friend. One afternoon, while Luisa is running an errand for her mother to the local grocery store, she is almost run over by a speedster with a blue Mustang. Travis, the handsome blue-eyed blond, becomes the object of Luisa's crush. The young man, however, is not from the Eastside, where Luisa and her Cuban-American family live. So begins Luisa's quest to hide her background and her nationality from Travis, for fear that she may be rejected if her newfound acquaintance discovers the truth.

Mills's novel is excellent in its treatment of the social pressures that young teenagers feel, especially if they come from a lower socioeconomic background much like Luisa's. The pressures are further exacerbated if the teenager's background also includes a language difference. Luisa's feelings of shame and humiliation about her parents and the other members of her family are not atypical and are treated fairly and realistically. However, in the portrayal of a typical Cuban-American family there are some needless stereotypes, such as the depiction of Luisa's mother as fat and overly emotional and the characterization of one of Luisa's uncles as a gambler and a thief.

Mills makes a worthwhile attempt to include the necessary historical information that should help readers to understand the origins of the Cuban exile experience in the United States. In addition, she provides Luisa with the support system (by way of her best friend, Beth, and her brother's best friend, Tom) that is sometimes needed in order to come to terms with oneself and one's problems.

242   Mohr, Nicholasa. *El Bronx Remembered: A Novella and Stories.* Arte Público Pr. 1986, P $9.50 (0-934770-62-X). 180pp. Fiction.

Mohr's collection of short stories reflects the humor, the sadness, the joy, and the tragedy of life as her memorable characters struggle to find meaning in their world of cultural contradictions. Among Mohr's outstanding stories is "A Special Pet," a powerful tale that portrays children's anger despite their mother's heartfelt effort to give the family a warm and hearty meal. Mrs. Fernandez is faced with a no-win situation when she sacrifices the children's pet hen, Joncrofa (named for their father's favorite Hollywood movie star, Joan Crawford), for a fresh pot of homemade chicken soup for her sick husband. The task is simple enough, because Mrs. Fernandez has learned the art of killing chickens by wringing the neck when she was a young child growing up in Puerto Rico. But when the children discover the fate of their pet, they react with anger. Mrs. Fernandez tries to console them by pretending to revive Joncrofa by giving her a sip of rum, but this time the children accuse their mother of getting Joncrofa drunk.

"Once upon a Time" is a story of children at play, oblivious to the imminent dangers that lie on their doorstep. Several girls are so absorbed in their bouncing ball game that they forget their whereabouts and stumble across a dead man. Unimpressed and undaunted by their discovery, they continue their bouncing game, chanting to the rhythm of a rhyme about a dead baby.

"Shoes for Hector" is a story of a boy's humiliation and embarrassment at having to wear his uncle's borrowed ugly, pointed, narrow orange shoes for his graduation exercises. What money he receives for graduation he uses to buy a pair of shoes to his own liking.

In "Uncle Claudio," two cousins, Jaime and Charlie, discuss the impending departure of their uncle. Uncle Claudio has found life in New York far too different and increasingly difficult. But the last straw comes as he boards the subway train and finds his usual spot. There he runs into two well-dressed youths, one of them the son of a maid he once fired back in Puerto Rico. The frank young man thanks him for having fired his mother, which in turn gave him the opportunity to make a new life for himself in New York. Heartbroken by what he terms a loss of respect and values among youth, Uncle Claudio decides to return to the island. "Uncle Claudio" is a painful story that reminds us of cultural and intergenerational conflicts in immigrant communities. It is also a story of people's inability or unwillingness to accept modern life.

In all these stories, life's irony is eloquently captured by Mohr in her depiction of Puerto Rican life in the Bronx in New York.

Mohr, Nicholasa. **Going Home.**
See entry 218, Grades 4–6.

Mohr, Nicholasa. **In Nueva York.**
See entry 251, Grades 10–12.

243 Morey, Janet, and Wendy Dunn. **Famous Mexican Americans.** Illus. with photos. Dutton/Cobblehill 1989, HB $14.95 (0-525-65012-1). 176pp. Nonfiction.

Nine men and 5 women are among the 14 noted Mexican Americans whose history of accomplishment is recorded in this collective biography. With one or two exceptions, most of those featured are people who have dedicated their lives to social or political causes, working toward the betterment of the Mexican-American community. The stories of the noted individuals contain family as well as personal histories. The authors use many direct quotes and excerpts from interviews conducted with the biographees. Additional information and explanations of use to the reader should have been narrated as extra sentences, rather than given as awkward parenthetical facts. Useful references on each individual should encourage further investigation.

Paulsen, Gary. *The Crossing.*
See entry 253, Grades 10–12.

244 Pinchot, Jane. *The Mexicans in America.* Rev. ed. Illus. with photos. SERIES: In America. Lerner 1989, LB $9.95 (0-8225-0222-4). 94pp. Nonfiction.

A revision of the 1973 original leaves the sections on the origins and history of Mexican Americans relatively unchanged. The first chapter on history briefly presents the origins of Aztec civilization and the Spanish Conquest. Chapter Two presents an excellent history of the Mexican Americans, beginning with the exploration of the Southwest, through the Treaty of Guadalupe Hidalgo (1848), and up to the depression of the 1930s. It is brief but accurate and covers many aspects of the history of discrimination, including the repatriation of many immigrants to Mexico. Brief historical sketches by region are presented.

Issues of importance to the Mexican-American community, namely, education, immigration, and civil rights legislation, are highlighted in this edition. The notable figures included in the final section are drawn from the areas of business, community service, and government. While some celebrated figures representing the arts and literature are included, they are underrepresented in comparison to the figures selected from the high-profile sports and acting professions. On the whole, this book is useful as a classroom tool to supplement the dearth of historical information in textbooks that ignore or dilute the history of the Mexican American. An additional volume in the series, which covers its subject in much the same way and has been revised recently, is Ronald J. Larsen's *The Puerto Ricans in America.*

245 Soto, Gary. *Baseball in April: And Other Stories.* Harcourt Brace Jovanovich 1990, HB $14.95 (0-15-205720-X). 111pp. Fiction.

The everyday life of typical Hispanic youths is the subject of the 11 short stories that compose this collection. Soto focuses on one important aspect of each of his characters' lives. For instance, Gilbert is obsessed with the Karate Kid, whom he sees on video, because he, too, is pursued by a gang of bullies, led by Pete the Heat. After much begging and pleading for his mother to pay for karate lessons, Gilbert realizes his master teacher is, at best, mediocre. His teacher announces that he must close the business, and, although Gilbert's mother encourages him to continue his lessons elsewhere, he has become soured on the experience and abandons his interest altogether.

Manuel, too, idolizes a figure from popular culture—the Richie Valens portrayed in the film *La Bamba*. He signs up to impersonate Valens at a school talent show. Disaster turns to triumph when the scratched record repeats the phrase "para bailar la bamba," and Manuel, desperately playing along, is the hit of the show.

A female protagonist appears in the story "Mother and Daughter." Yollie's single mother cannot afford to buy her daughter a new dress for the school dance, so she dyes an old one. But rain that evening causes the dye to run, and, rather than be embarrassed, Yollie hastens home, angry at her mother and at the fact that they are poor. But when Ernie calls and invites her to go to the movies with him the next evening, Yollie's mother takes out an old cigar box filled with money she has been saving. Together they drive to Macy's to buy a skirt and blouse that won't lose its dye in the rain.

Other young women are featured in tales such as "The Marble Champ," the story of a "brain," Lupe, whose fame lies in spelling bees and not sporting contests. However, with the encouragement of her father, Lupe defeats all the contestants in a marble contest and rewards her hardworking thumbs with a cool splash in her bathroom sink.

Soto uses many idiomatic Spanish expressions that youngsters use in everyday speech. A list of these is included at the end.

The importance of these stories to Hispanic youth lies in their ability to transform simple everyday events steeped in a familiar culture into meaningful, memorable literary works. While the culture is specific, the conflicts and concerns are universal, with broad appeal to teenagers. Nonetheless, Hispanic youngsters will find special significance in Soto's tales and will perhaps be inspired to think about and to write their own stories.

GRADES 10–12

246   Anaya, Rudolfo A. **Bless Me, Ultima: A Novel.** Illus. by Dennis Martinez. TSQ Publications 1972, P $12.95 (0-89229-002-1). 249pp. Fiction.

Seven-year-old Antonio Marez listens as his father and mother deliberate the future of Ultima, the local *curandera* (faith healer) of the *llano* (plains) in Guadalupe, New Mexico. In her old age and with no one to care for her, Ultima has been brought into the Marez home to live out the rest of her life. Antonio reveres Ultima for her holiness and her kindness. Most of all, he is awed by her wisdom and her mystical faith-healing powers, which she uses strictly for the good of the people in the community. But Ultima becomes the subject of a witch-hunt by a local sorcerer who practices black magic and accuses Ultima of exercising her powers to harm his daughters.

Conflict persists as an overall theme of this novel, as Antonio struggles to comprehend the evil forces in the community that have chosen Ultima as their scapegoat. He also struggles to define himself in relation to his family. On the one hand he hears his mother speak about his father's side of the family as a wild, unruly bunch of *vaqueros* (cowboys) while she praises her own family of farmers as more rooted to the earth and thus more settled. Antonio's keen eye also detects his older brothers' unfulfilled potential; he must succeed where his brothers could not. Antonio is a serious young boy who carries the weight of humanity on his shoulders. He seems capable only of serious thought, always reading mystery into everyday life and play.

The events take place in the course of one year in Antonio's life. But in that year, Antonio comes to realize that he has been deeply and personally affected by Ultima's residence with his family. Anaya develops Antonio's character and the psychological depth within through the many dream sequences. His ability to juxtapose the duality of human nature into a novel that works on so many levels is a tribute to his skill as a novelist. This work has received many awards and is considered a classic of Chicano literature.

247   Anaya, Rudolfo A. *Heart of Aztlán.* Editorial Justa 1976, P $7.00 (0-685-78786-9).
209pp. Fiction.

Clemente Chávez is a displaced *llano* (ranch) man from the rural pueblo of
Guadalupe. Forced to move to an impoverished barrio in Albuquerque with his
family, Chávez experiences the slow but steady deterioration of the cohesive
family unit. The conflict between urban and rural living and the persistent
problems of chronic unemployment and job discrimination are issues he must
confront. He is overwhelmed by the harsh realities, but, with the help of Crispín,
the barrio sage whose wisdom he seeks, Chávez's strength is nurtured as he
strives to understand the sources of discrimination, poverty, and inequality that
are at the heart of his people's problems. With encouragement and guidance by
Crispín, he confronts those forces that hold his people helpless, and he is able to
challenge and lead his people to action.

    This is a philosophical novel that parallels the myth of Aztlán (the mytholog-
ical place of the Aztecs, said to be somewhere in what is now the U.S. Southwest) by the development of a Chicano community in New Mexico during the
1940s. By reading this poignant historical novel in light of current realities,
Hispanic-American readers will gain a perspective on their own culture and on a
noble history of resistance. Mature readers from all backgrounds will develop an
understanding of the nature of leadership and the process by which poor and
demoralized communities become mobilized to change their circumstances.

Ashabranner, Brent. *The Vanishing Border: A Photographic Journey Along Our
Frontier with Mexico.*
See entry 228, Grades 7–9.

Ashabranner, Brent, and Melissa Ashabranner. *Into a Strange Land: Unaccompanied Refugee Youth in America.*
See entry 229, Grades 7–9.

Bachelis, Faren. *The Central Americans.*
See entry 230, Grades 7–9.

Beltrán Hernández, Irene. *Across the Great River.*
See entry 231, Grades 7–9.

Betancourt, T. Ernesto. *The Me Inside of Me.*
See entry 232, Grades 7–9.

248   Cisneros, Sandra. *The House on Mango Street.* Random House 1991, $9.00 (0-
679-73477-5). 128pp. Fiction.

There are strong images of the collective cultural experience in this volume of
short stories drawn from the author's childhood as she grew up in the urban
barrios of Chicago. The themes of her stories reflect a childhood marred by
poverty and deprivation. Yet in a highly poetic voice, she expresses anguish and
her deeply felt desire to have a home of her own, which is the focus of this
collection of poems upon which the title is based. Her ability to transform these
moments into exquisite prose is the strength of her writing and the literary mark
of a promising young Chicana author.

Cullison, Alan. *The South Americans.*
See entry 234, Grades 7–9.

Dwyer, Christopher. *The Dominican Americans.*
See entry 235, Grades 7–9.

249 Fernández, Roberta. *Intaglio: A Novel in Six Stories.* Arte Público Pr. 1990, P $8.50 (1-55885-016-3). 160pp. Fiction.

Andrea is the ballerina who left home at an early age and sends back picture postcards of every city in which she has performed, with Nenita collecting these into a family album that becomes the focal point of any discussion about Andrea and her life. Amanda is the seamstress who creates beautiful dresses by day but at night delves into herbs and supernatural encounters. Filomena is the woman from Pascuaro, Michoacán, who comes to Laredo, Texas, to earn her living and ends up staying a lifetime. Leonor is Amanda's sister, who swears by the predictions of her card reading. Esmeralda is Nenita's (the narrator's) friend, the young beauty who sells tickets at the local theater. Zulema is the storyteller who fills Nenita's life with exciting tales of the Mexican revolution.

All six of these women make an indelible mark upon Nenita, the 13-year-old narrator who intricately weaves together the lives of all. Together, their stories form the basis for this novel, the intimate portrayal of daily life in a southwestern town. Fernández has created a novel as intriguing as the format of the genre she has chosen to tell her story. This is a sensitive, sophisticated work, one that will give older teenagers as well as adults a complex portrait of the multidimensional, diverse lives of Mexican-American women growing up and living along the Rio Grande.

250 Galarza, Ernesto. *Barrio Boy.* Univ. of Notre Dame Pr. 1972, P $7.95 (0-268-00441-2). 275pp. Nonfiction.

Barrio Boy is the author's vivid recollections of his childhood growing up in both rural Mexico and Sacramento, California. His keen ability to remember and record the many intricacies of detail makes for a rich portrayal of village life in Jalcocotán in the western mountains of Mexico. Dr. Galarza's is a warm and humorous description of the intimacies of family life and interaction. The autobiography also traces the displacement of the family during the turbulent times of the Mexican revolution, which led to their arrival and subsequent settlement in the barrios of Sacramento.

Unfortunately, only one third of the autobiography covers Galarza's and his family's adjustment to a new life in a different cultural environment. But Galarza speaks with honesty and clarity as he conveys to his readers a life-style replete with family virtues of work and respect for elders—some lasting qualities that permeate his sense of identity as he incorporates these values into the process of his acculturation.

Harlan, Judith. *Hispanic Voters: A Voice in American Politics.*
See entry 237, Grades 7–9.

Meltzer, Milton. *The Hispanic Americans.*
See entry 239, Grades 7–9.

Mohr, Nicholasa. *El Bronx Remembered: A Novella and Stories.*
See entry 242, Grades 7–9.

151

GRADES 10–12

251 Mohr, Nicholasa. *In Nueva York.* Arte Público Pr. 1988, P $8.50 (0-934770-78-6). 192pp. Fiction.

A collection of eight interwoven stories, this book weaves a tapestry about a group of people who serve as the nucleus of a Puerto Rican neighborhood in New York. The first story, "Old Mary," is of an aging woman in her mid to late 50s who, in her usual drunken stupor, relates with excitement and anticipation the homecoming of her 40-year-old son whom she last saw as an infant in Puerto Rico. Mary envisions a warm and happy reunion with William, the handsome, blond, light-skinned son whom she last saw in the cradle of her arms. Instead, she encounters a man who stands not quite four feet tall.

In "The Operation," Mohr effectively uses suspense in focusing on the whereabouts of 7-year-old Jennie Matilda as she drifts about, lost in play. Her mother, meanwhile, is frantic in her efforts to find her. As Jennie jumps over the rooftops in search of a stray cat that has caught her eye, she comes across an old man, a former sea captain. Nate offers her a lollipop and befriends her. He converses with her and proceeds to relate the details of his life story, including his recent operation. He shows Jennie the scars of the operation that he has just undergone while at the hospital. Nate sees to it that Jennie arrives home safely. But Jennie's mother interrogates her, worried that her young daughter might have been molested. Mohr describes well the thought processes of a frightened yet concerned mother, and simultaneously examines the innocence and purity of heart of two strangers who encounter one another in the barrio.

"The Robbery" is a powerful story that presents two sides of a moral and legal dilemma. Two young Puerto Rican boys hold up Rudi's Restaurant. Rudi, the owner, kills one of the boys in self-defense. Mrs. Rodriguez, the mother of the dead Tomás, organizes a peaceful one-woman demonstration in front of Rudi's Restaurant, demanding justice from the man who took her son's life and insisting that Rudi pay for a proper headstone. Rudi, however, considers himself blameless, as he had a legal permit for a gun and claims he acted in self-defense. This is a story of the conflict that occurs when people operate under two sets of laws—the moral and legal codes of law and a mother's sense of justice.

Mohr's writings reflect the universal struggles of the human spirit as expressed by the barrio characters of the Lower East Side. Unlike Mohr's previous writings that feature injustices committed against Puerto Ricans, her collection of short stories looks inward at the Puerto Rican spirit.

Morey, Janet, and Wendy Dunn. *Famous Mexican Americans.*
See entry 243, Grades 7–9.

252 Paredes, Américo. *George Washington Gómez: A Mexicotexan Novel.* Arte Público Pr. 1990, P $8.50 (1-55885-012-0). 302pp. Fiction.

Paredes's historical novel, written in the 1930s but never published until now, traces the development of a Mexican family living along the southern tip of the Rio Grande, along the Texas-Mexico border. The time frame is the mid-nineteenth century, shortly after the Mexican War, when Mexico ceded its large territory to the United States. With the Treaty of Guadalupe Hidalgo (1848), citizens of Mexico overnight became citizens of the United States, and Anglo settlers began to take control of the lands.

The Gómez family must adjust to their new life as American citizens. Wanting to be the best of American citizens, they decide to name their son after that famous hero, George Washington. But the grandmother, unable to enunciate correctly the name of her grandson, calls him Guálinto. Guálinto grows up a keen observer of the daily events that take place as his family struggles to preserve their land, their language and culture, and ultimately their lives in the face of fierce antagonism and hatred. The compelling drama is also the story of the Mexican-American people as they struggle to shape their identity in the face of contrasting cultural values. Excellent, too, is the novel's portrayal of the development of a school system designed to debase a student's culture and self-esteem, thus ensuring the continued failure of its Mexican-American students.

Dr. Paredes's novel was nominated for the American Book Award for 1990. It has been considered a precursor of the Chicano novel, but it is quickly gaining its rightful place as a classic of Chicano literature. It is required reading for all older students and teachers if a true understanding of the historical development of racism against Mexican Americans is ever to be fully understood and ultimately corrected.

253   Paulsen, Gary. *The Crossing.* Orchard Books 1987, LB $11.99 (0-531-08309-8); Dell 1990, P $3.25 (0-440-20582-4). 114pp. Fiction.

Sgt. Robert S. Locke is a soldier in the U.S. Army, assigned to Ft. Bliss, near the Texas-Mexico border. During the day, he performs the duties of his job. In the evening, however, he crosses the border into Juárez, drinking heavily to curb the painful memory of war.

Manny Bustos is a local street boy from Juárez, Mexico, who has learned to survive by being in tune with the language and culture of the streets. His one goal is to cross the border to escape the poverty and misery that he has experienced his entire life.

The two characters are drawn together through several chance encounters as Locke observes Manny and his way of life, and Manny, too, sees the drunken soldier and sets out to rob him in his attempt to find a way to cross the border.

Manny and Sgt. Locke personify the many stereotypes that both groups have about the other. Manny sees the sergeant as one more drunken American; he does not know the pain and trauma of war that Locke suffers. Locke, on the other hand, sees Manny simply as a street boy, with a single goal of stealing money from the Anglos in order to cross into America. Because neither of them speaks the other's language, they are unable to communicate directly with each other.

Paulsen's is a thought-provoking drama, clouded in mystery as the reader is led through Sgt. Locke's oftentimes monotonous soliloquy in his quest to reach a "brain-dead" state. The writing is sharp and vivid. Yet the portrayal of Manny gives the reader the impression that Mexicans and Mexican Americans steal and kill in order to escape poverty. Although Paulsen's aim is to examine the roots of stereotypes, his plotting and his characterization of Manny run the risk of perpetuating them. As a result, this book is best suited for mature, thoughtful readers.

Rivera, Tomás. ***Y no se lo tragó la tierra./And the Earth Did Not Part.***
Bilingual ed. English trans. by Herminio Ríos. Editorial Justa 1971, P $6.00 (0-
915808-09-9). 175pp. Fiction.

In Mexican culture there exists a taboo, based on religious superstition, that if
you curse God's name, the earth will part and you will be swallowed whole.
That belief is the basis of the title of this poignant novel about the life cycle of
Mexican-American migrant farm workers. The unnamed protagonist curses
God's name out of desperation at seeing his family, his friends, and his neigh-
bors endure untold sufferings because of their poverty and destitution.

There are 12 chapters in the novel, each one symbolic of a month in the life
cycle of a migrant's worst nightmares—heat stroke, suicide, humiliation, a
Christmas without gifts for the children. Each is a heartrending story of pain and
suffering. The protagonist begins his story as a young child. In the end, life's
harsh experiences have matured him. Yet he is able to understand life with a
clearer vision, and he is also able to make the connections between the isolated
events he witnesses and describes. He is the symbolic Everyman, who endures
the pain and suffering of mankind.

Rivera's award-winning novel is considered a classic of Chicano literature.
While his is a harsh portrayal of the lives of Mexican migrant farm workers, it is
also a well-drawn metaphor for the suffering of all humanity.

Arte Público Press has published a new translation of Rivera's novel. It, too,
is a bilingual edition, published under the title . . . *Y no se lo tragó la tierra/ . . .
And the Earth Did Not Devour Him* (Arte Público Pr., 1990; ISBN 0-934770-7; P
$8.50), with an English translation by Evangelina Vigil-Piñon.

---

255   Rodriguez, Richard. ***Hunger of Memory: The Education of Richard Rodriguez.***
Bantam 1983, P $4.95 (0-553-27293-4). 195pp. Nonfiction.

This is on one level the autobiography of a Mexican-American boy growing up
in the barrios of Sacramento in the 1950s. Rodriguez, a brilliant scholar, is a keen
observer of life at home and in Catholic parochial schools. At a very young age,
he learns to differentiate between the Spanish-speaking world of his parents and
the English-speaking world of school. He also learns how language works to
distinguish between the private world of his family and the public life of
education and society. Rodriguez's autobiographical writings are extremely controversial because of his public positions on affirmative action and bilingual
education. Opponents of affirmative action have praised Rodriguez's essays
condemning it and bilingual education. Chicano civil rights leaders as well as
literary critics have condemned his positions, as presented in the context of the
autobiography, as well as his eagerness to assimilate into mainstream, English-
speaking America at the expense of his own cultural and family values. In any
case, his arguments are an excellent source for debate and discussion in the
classroom and elsewhere. At the same time, one should keep in mind Rodriguez's excessive reliance upon his personal experience as a source for his political views.

---

256   Santiago, Danny. ***Famous All over Town.*** NAL 1984, P $8.95 (0-452-25511-2).
285pp. Fiction.

Rudy "Chato" Medina is a 14-year-old from the barrios of East Los Angeles. He
has developed the street talk and tough skin of the gang members in his

Shamrock Street neighborhood as a way of coping with the shame and humiliation that a life of poverty and discrimination has wrought. His gang is a "traditional" one: criminal activities consist of joyriding in "borrowed" cars and knife fights with rival gangs.

Rather than focus on a specific plot, the novel portrays aspects of everyday life in the Medina family and family members' interactions, for better or worse. Chato's family is a dysfunctional one. His father is an alcoholic bully, and his mother has decided to end their marriage and return home to Mexico, leaving the older children free to choose their destinations and their ultimate fate. Chato chooses to stay in Los Angeles and live with his older sister, now married, rather than to go with his mother "back home" to Mexico—a foreign country and a place he has never really known. Although liberated from his father's abuse, Chato, at 14 no longer has a family. He narrates the story with humor, but one can detect the sense of loss behind his lighthearted facade.

The author creates an appealing, believable protagonist whose experience represents that of many barrio teenagers. Events and conflicts are presented authentically, without heavy-handedness or sensationalism. When first published, *Famous All over Town* generated much controversy, more about the identity of its author than about the merits of the story itself. Danny Santiago is a pseudonym for the Anglo writer Daniel James. Blacklisted in the 1950s for his political beliefs, James became a social worker in an East Los Angeles barrio, where he gained intimate knowledge of barrio life. At first hailed as a rising young author, Santiago/James was later condemned, even though his critics had nothing but praise for the book itself.

Soto, Gary. ***Baseball in April: And Other Stories.***
See entry 245, Grades 7–9.

257   Soto, Gary. ***Living up the Street: Narrative Recollections.*** Strawberry Hill Pr. 1985, P $7.95 (0-89407-064-9). 159pp. Nonfiction.

Winner of the 1985 American Book Award, this book draws upon Soto's childhood experiences growing up poor and the son of a single female parent farmworker. His episodic stories span the range of adolescent emotions. "Being Mean," for example, is a humorous account of unsupervised children going about their everyday mischievous business—in this case, trying to burn the house down while Mom works long hours at the local cannery. "Fear" is the gripping story of Frankie T., the troublemaker–future criminal, who takes a public beating from the teacher as his classmates look on. Like Frankie, many of them have experienced broken homes and indifference. Soto is an excellent writer endowed with the gift of keen verbal precision. His work will appeal to teens from a variety of backgrounds but will especially engage those Hispanic students who share the same experiences and dilemmas.

4

UNITED STATES:
NATIVE AMERICANS

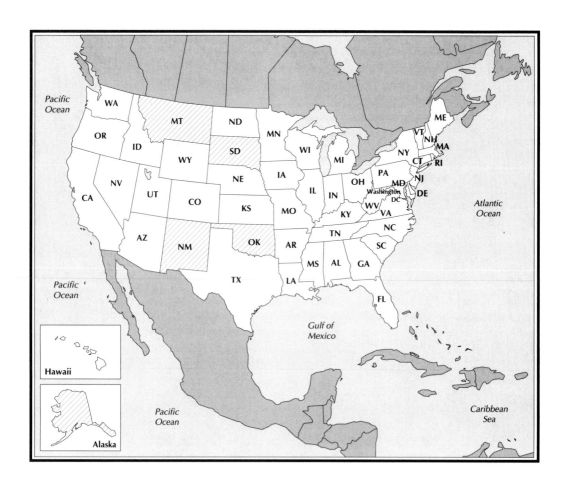

STATES WITH HIGHEST CONCENTRATION OF NATIVE AMERICANS

1. Alaska - 15.6%
2. New Mexico - 8.9%
3. Oklahoma - 8.0%
4. South Dakota - 7.3%
5. Montana - 6.0%

Source: 1990 U.S. Census

LARGEST TRIBES OF NATIVE AMERICANS

1. Cherokee - 232,080
2. Navajo - 158,633
3. Sioux - 78,608
4. Chippewa - 73,602
5. Choctaw - 50,220

Source: 1980 U.S. Census

4

UNITED STATES: NATIVE AMERICANS

by Elaine Goley

As we celebrate in 1992 the quincentennial anniversary of Columbus's "discovery" of the Americas, we should be aware that the New World was inhabited long before Columbus "discovered" it. Anthropologists believe that Native American peoples migrated to the Americas as long as 30,000 to 60,000 years ago, during the ice ages that created the Beringian land bridge from Asia to the Americas.

Very little information is available for young people on the earliest history of Native American peoples. Many of the nonfiction series books on Native Americans that are included in this chapter briefly allude to theories of the migration of these early peoples. The New True Books by Childrens Press includes historical, cultural, and contemporary information on several Native American groups, such as the Apache. This series uses large print, clear and simple language, and appealing color photographs to entice the reader. The books are suitable for younger readers in grades 1 to 4. Though not a series book per se, Simon Ortiz's *The People Shall Continue* is a well-rendered history for very young readers, presented in the style of Native American storytellers.

Other series books for younger readers and middle graders include those published by Rourke Publications in its Original Peoples series. The series includes *Plains Indians of North America* by Robin May, which recounts the history of Native American migration over 30,000 years ago and contains a map giving the distributions of groups in North America. Color graphics and accessible, accurate text make this an attractive, informative series for elementary-age readers. Rourke also publishes a series on major ethnic groups, which is called *Indian Tribes of North America*. This series is also for younger readers. *The Seminole* by Barbara Brooks is an example of one of the titles in this attractive series.

Franklin Watts has also published a fine series of books on Native American groups in its First Books series for the middle grades. *The Shoshoni* by Alden Carter and *The Sioux* by Elaine Landau are examples of this attractive and authoritative series. The Silver Burdett series Alvin Josephy's History of the Native Americans presents the history of various nations from the perspective of their leaders. Robert Cwiklik's biography of Sequoia is a sympathetic and moving treatment of the Cherokee leader whose efforts to make peace were betrayed by the U.S. government.

Other books for older readers and high school students as well as adults who wish to pursue the study of Native American cultures include the series Indians of North America, published by Chelsea House. This excellent series includes *The Kiowa* by John R. Wunder, which is annotated in this chapter. The series accurately portrays the relationship between various ethnic groups and the U.S. government as well as the history and culture of each group covered. The conflicts between the Indians and the white settlers are chronicled in a way that is accessible to older children and high school students. The series covers current Native American/white relations and the recent efforts of Native American groups to maintain their tribal identities as well as their civil rights.

Since so little nonfiction is available for the older reader, we have included material written for adults, but accessible to the older child and adolescent, in order to flesh out the historical context of complex Native American/white relations. Edward S. Curtis's 20-volume series on Native Americans is no longer in print. However, a one-volume book of excerpts from this seminal work, *Selected Writings of Edward S. Curtis*, edited by Barry Gifford, has been included. Other reference works on Native American history and culture, such as the several volumes of the *Native American Handbook*, are available in research collections and libraries. These sources are excellent for the older reader who is interested in pursuing the study of Native American cultures.

Among the adult works for older students included in this chapter are the excellent contemporary novels of Tony Hillerman, which have been made into motion pictures. His novels are detective stories that take place on the contemporary reservation and include realistic portrayals of Native American characters and cultural life. Louise Erdrich's books for adults are also included since her resonant and poetic style in writing about the Native American experience is unique and unequaled in excellence since Faulkner. Jean Craighead George's books as well as examples of Scott O'Dell's and Jamake Highwater's novels are included as models of fine characterization and authenticity of experience in fiction for young people. These books have become known as classics in their own right.

Many of the novels about the Native American experience are works of historical fiction. One of the most well-known examples is Elizabeth George Speare's *The Sign of the Beaver*, set in Colonial America. Donald Worcester's Lone Hunter novels are examples of works that detail Indian life on the Plains before the arrival of white settlers. Conflicts between Indians and whites in the nineteenth century are narrated from the point of view of white characters who have come to realize the injustice of their actions in Kristiana Gregory's *Jenny of the Tetons*, Cynthia DeFelice's *Weasel*, and G. Clifton Wisler's *Winter of the Wolf*. Like many of the novels written by whites in the 1960s about integration and the black experience, these books (as well as Speare's to some extent) say more about majority guilt than about the lives and emotions of Native Americans themselves. On the other hand, Jamake Highwater's acclaimed Ghost Horse trilogy, consisting of the young adult novels *Legend Days, Ceremony of Innocence*, and *I Wear the Morning Star*, chronicles, from a Native American perspective, the epidemic of smallpox and white encroachment that destroy his female protagonist Amana's family and community. With great authenticity and poignancy,

Highwater communicates the pain of nineteenth-century Native American history and its repercussions in the twentieth, as Amana's grandson, abandoned by his mother and in an institution, looks to his grandmother's tales of resistance for strength. Louise Erdrich's trilogy—*Tracks, The Beet Queen,* and *Love Medicine*— follows three generations of Ojibwa women as they adapt to dispossession and life on the reservation.

For the most part, contemporary novels set in the United States focus on individual characterizations and present an optimistic view of Native American life. For many of the characters, the past is, or becomes in times of crisis, a "living heritage." Jean Craighead George's *Julie of the Wolves* and Scott O'Dell's *Black Star, Bright Dawn* feature young Inuit women who use their resources and skills to survive in a harsh environment. His beloved great-grandmother's illness forces a teenage boy to sort out the two worlds in which he has been living in Luke Wallin's *Ceremony of the Panther.* Paul Pitts's *Racing the Sun* and Jean Craighead George's *The Talking Earth* portray assimilated suburban middle-class youngsters who rediscover their traditions. The dual heritage of black Indians—so well-presented in William Loren Katz's nonfiction work *Black Indians: A Hidden Heritage*—is the subject of three fiction titles included here: Faith Ringgold's *Tar Beach,* based on the "story quilt" that she created (see Chapter 1); Virginia Hamilton's *Arilla Sun Down,* which is drawn from her own multiethnic heritage; and Michael Dorris's adult novel *A Yellow Raft in Blue Water,* featuring a contemporary 15-year-old girl with an Indian mother and a black father, struggling to find her place in her family and in the world.

Many of the trade nonfiction books published for children and young adults are surveys of Native American history or collective biographies. However, several works weave into the history a contemporary concern with land use and environmental issues. Russell Freedman's *Buffalo Hunt* assesses the ecological impact of the indiscriminate hunting of the buffalo by white settlers. The near-extinction of an animal species in this case also meant the near-extinction of Indian communities and cultures that depended upon the buffalo in so many ways. *Red Ribbons for Emma,* published by the alternative New Seed Press, chronicles an elderly Navajo woman's fight to preserve her home and her way of life in the face of a coal company's plans to strip-mine on the reservation. Also dealing with these issues in both a historical and a contemporary context is Brent Ashabranner's *Morning Star, Black Sun,* which examines the conflict between the Northern Cheyenne Indians and the government policymakers and corporate interests seeking to gain control of coal-rich reservation lands.

Other interesting and notable works of nonfiction are two books on American Indian art. *Bear's Heart,* edited by Burton Supree, presents the work of a nineteenth-century Cheyenne hunter and artist (in fact, a member of the tribe that is the protagonist of Ashabranner's work) imprisoned by federal authorities and portraying through his art the tragedy of his life. *Many Smokes, Many Moons,* by Jamake Highwater (a cultural anthropologist as well as a noted children's author), is a compilation of various Native American artworks that are used to tell the history of the indigenous people all over the Americas.

Much of the historical literature available consists of adult materials, which are accessible to teens who read well. They include Nabokov's history on Native American population trends and the works of Vine Deloria and others who have chronicled the Native American holocaust of the nineteenth century. A work dealing with more current concerns is Michael Dorris's *The Broken Cord,* a very personal examination of the problems of alcoholism and fetal alcohol syndrome on the modern-day reservation.

Other cultural materials included are some of the vast numbers of books dealing with Native American mythology and folklore. We have included for younger readers a select number of picture book format materials based on Native American folktales. The works of Paul Goble, Tomie de Paola, and Gerald McDermott are some of the best picture books available for young children on this subject. Other works, such as *Doctor Coyote: A Native American Aesop's Fables* by John Bierhorst (annotated in the chapter on Mexico and the Caribbean), introduce middle grade readers to Native American folklore and culture. Bierhorst's research on Native American mythology and his works for older readers on the subject, such as *The Mythology of North America*, are invaluable and accessible sources for the student, educator, and researcher.

In compiling this chapter, we have made an attempt to present materials reflecting the cultural authenticity and diversity of the Native American experience. We have attempted to identify materials representative of the culture and, as far as possible, written and collected by Native Americans. When these are not accessible, we have selected materials with a high degree of cultural validity due to the author's or compiler's acknowledged expertise in this area and containing a high level of scholarship and research reflected therein. To this end, we have sought out scholars of Native American cultures and asked for their help in locating authentic materials. The works of recognized authorities in the field of Native American studies have also been used as authoritative texts as well as sources for other materials evaluated. For this reason, many titles listed in the resources section contain materials of interest to the educator who works with students as well as materials for the student doing research.

We would like to acknowledge the help of Vine Deloria Jr., chairman of the Department of Native American Studies at the University of Arizona, for his help in locating primary source materials. The Native American Broadcasting Company and Chief Harold Tarbell of the Mohawk Nation also deserve thanks for further information on Native American materials and culture. Insofar as possible, we have contacted tribal associations and cultural organizations that publish folklore, mythology, and nonfiction materials concerning aspects of Native American culture. We have also selected materials from regional and ethnic presses that publish Native American materials such as *Baby Rattlesnake* by Children's Book Press of San Francisco.

Since so much cultural information is contained in folklore, an unusually large percentage of the titles included in this chapter reflect this. However, the fiction works to be recommended must also reflect the cultural validity of folklore and traditional Native American life as well as an accurate portrayal of current issues and concerns. Because so much of what has been published on Native Americans is superficial and stereotyped, the emphasis, given limitations of space, is on the most positive contributions to the literature. At the same time, works that embody certain trends—whether positive or negative—or deserve reconsideration in light of emerging concerns or interpretations are included. For instance, works that present Native American youngsters in clearly secondary roles, particularly if the characterization and depictions of cultural heritage are themselves less well developed, are examined critically. The scholarship and cultural validity exhibited in each work have been assessed, with the ideal a marriage of good scholarship and excellent writing skill in presenting the material in a way that will appeal to children and young adults.

It is hoped that the materials in this chapter will introduce the user to authentic materials on Native American life and that this will lead to a continuing journey in search of cultural understanding and appreciation.

PRESCHOOL–GRADE 3

258   Ata, Te. *Baby Rattlesnake.* Adapted by Lynn Moroney. Illus. by Veg Reisberg. Children's Book Pr. 1989, HB $12.95 (0-89239-049-2). 32pp. Nonfiction.

Te Ata is a 92-year-old internationally known Chickasaw storyteller from Oklahoma Territory. She has been telling traditional stories like *Baby Rattlesnake* for 65 years. This is a teaching legend about youth's impetuous nature. It shows what happens when a child attains a skill that he is not mature enough to use properly. It is also the story of a loving family that takes the baby rattlesnake back into the fold and nurtures him even though he has been rash and has committed an offense.

The colorful original illustrations are drawn using paper cuts and gouache. The bright colors of the Southwest and the bold patterns common to Native American art motifs enhance the tale.

Children's Book Press is a small press dedicated to publishing multicultural materials for children, including both traditional and original stories that celebrate minority cultures. These are stories suitable for both minority children and adults as well as children of the majority culture.

259   Baylor, Byrd. *Hawk, I'm Your Brother.* Illus. by Peter Parnall. Scribner 1976, LB $13.95 (0-684-14571-5). 48pp. Fiction.

Parnall's spare, eloquent illustrations underscore the simplicity of Baylor's text. This economy of style contributes to the feeling of folklore this book evokes. It is simply the encounter between a Native American boy and a hawk. The boy envies the hawk's freedom and declares his kinship with the natural world through his relationship with the hawk. The messages are subtle and well presented. They include the Native American reverence for and feeling of unity with the natural world.

In today's world of waste and pollution, the Native American emphasis on conservation and respect for all living things is a crucial one to be shared by everyone. Parnall's exhilarating illustrations along with Baylor's poetic text symbolize the freedom, dignity, and beauty of the natural world and our interdependence with all living things.

260   Cohen, Caron Lee. *The Mud Pony.* Illus. by Shonto Begay. Scholastic 1988, HB $12.95 (0-590-41525-5). 32pp. Nonfiction.

A Pawnee boy goes to the creek to make himself a toy mud pony. Upon returning to his band, he discovers they have left him behind in pursuit of the buffalo. Suddenly, the mud pony comes to life and tells the boy he will find his people and one day become a chief. But the boy must always follow the pony, for she is "part of Mother Earth." The pony's promise is fulfilled; she makes the boy strong in battle against other tribes, and he is made chief, whereupon she returns to the Earth from where she came.

This Pawnee folktale expresses the relationship between humans and nature, as seen by the Native American cultures of the Great Plains. Through words and pictures, the reader gets a sense of Native American life before the encroachment of white settlers. Native American artist Begay has illustrated this work in the earth tones and motifs of southwestern Indian art.

Davis, Deborah. *The Secret of the Seal.*
See entry 272, Grades 4–6.

261   Goble, Paul. *The Great Race of the Birds and Animals.* Illus. by the author. Bradbury 1985, LB $12.95 (0-02-736950-1). 32pp. Fiction.

The Caldecott Award-winning author and illustrator Paul Goble gives us his version of a Cheyenne creation myth in which the Creator organizes a race to decide which animals would rule the world—two-legged or four-legged animals.

   The legend is told in eloquent, simple language evocative of the oral myth tradition. Goble's illustrations are bold, clean, yet detailed and eloquent. He has lived in South Dakota, immersed in Native American history and tradition for years, and his knowledge shows. This is a good introduction for children to the legends and culture of Native Americans.

262   Goble, Paul. *Her Seven Brothers.* Illus. by the author. Bradbury 1988, HB $13.95 (0-02-737960-4). 32pp. Nonfiction.

Caldecott Award winner Goble has lived in the Great Plains and is a scholar who devotes himself to the study of Native American culture and art. He has authenticated his adaptation of this Cheyenne myth by listing sources. He further authenticates the Cheyenne designs that he uses, which date from the nineteenth century and are on view at the Field Museum of Chicago and other museums.

   Goble incorporates the values of several Native American cultures into this story of how the Big Dipper came to be. In nature and cosmology, the stars and planets are Indians who have ascended to the sky. The girl in this legend has no brothers or sisters, but she is never lonely because she can talk to the animals and birds. Goble sets the mood and invokes the style of the oral story-telling tradition by beginning the story around the fire in a teepee at night. Snuggled under buffalo robes, the children wonder how the stars got into the sky.

   Through his clear, crisp, and detailed artwork, Goble gives readers a sense of Native American artistic traditions. His motifs and colors are drawn from nature. The understated text presents the myth in simple, uncluttered language, allowing the artwork to be appreciated for itself. The artist states that he uses animal and bird motifs as well as butterflies and flowers because they echo the Cheyenne idea that flora and fauna share the Earth with us. He sometimes pictures a multitude of flowers, buffalo, or other creatures to remind us of the Creator's generosity—a common theme in Native American folklore and art.

263   Goble, Paul. *Iktomi and the Boulder: A Plains Indian Story.* Illus. by the author. Orchard 1988, LB $14.90 (0-531-08360-8). 32pp. Fiction.

Paul Goble portrays Iktomi as the trickster character in Native American Plains Indian legend. He is clever but foolish, humble but arrogant, both loser and winner. The trickster in Sioux legend is known by other names, such as Coyote. A mischievous liar, he can transform himself magically and usually does so when getting into trouble. In this story, he tries to outwit and best his peers but ends up being crushed by a boulder in his greed and arrogance. We see our own shortcomings in Iktomi's character flaws. He exhibits all of the contradictions and limitations of human nature, and, like a mirror, he is held up to reflect us and warn us against falling victim to these faults. The clean, clear, bold illustrations portray traditional Native American motifs. Other tales of Iktomi, adapted by Goble, include *Iktomi and the Berries* and *Iktomi and the Ducks* (both Orchard, 1990).

264   Joosse, Barbara M. *Mama, Do You Love Me?* Illus. by Barbara Lavallee. Chronicle Books 1991, HB $12.95 (0-87701-759-X). 32pp. Fiction.

The story of this picture book involves an Inuit girl who asks her mother if she loves her, no matter what. She tests the limits of her mother's love. Her mother answers that she loves the child unconditionally. This is an important concept for children, since they must perceive that they are loved unconditionally in order to develop their own self esteem. In this picture book, the unique illustrations in vibrant color depict Inuit life and customs in Alaska on each two-page spread. The glossary presents information about life in the Arctic. The sophisticated illustrations are round and stylized, very reminiscent of the style of R. C. Gorman's works, but more vibrantly colored and more lively in movement. The text and illustration are a perfect match in presenting the style and feeling of a Native American folktale in this original work. The book presents many positive visual and intellectual messages to the young reader, though its theme is clearly universal rather than specific to the Inuit culture.

265   McDermott, Gerald. *Arrow to the Sun: A Pueblo Indian Tale.* Illus. by the author. Viking 1974, HB $14.95 (0-670-13369-8); Penguin/Puffin 1977, P $4.95 (0-14-050211-4). 48pp. Nonfiction.

McDermott won the Caldecott Award for his illustrations of this Pueblo legend. He uses the bold, bright colors of the southwestern desert and sky. Oranges, lavender, greens, blues, and ochre depict the sunsets and blue skies of the desert. The colors are used as a metaphor for nature in this tale, which, like many Native American legends, is intimately connected to the natural world. McDermott's bold geometric shapes, characteristic of southwestern Indian art, blend with the bold natural colors of the Southwest's deserts, rocks, and skies. These geometric shapes tie the legend to the mysteries of Native American ceremony and to a cosmology that depicts the sun and moon as people.

   The artist is well versed in traditional sources for Native American legend and mythology and in the works of John Bierhorst and Joseph Campbell, two of the most respected scholars of Native American mythology. The simple language of this myth, which tells how the spirit of the sun was brought to earth, eloquently represents the religious beliefs of the Pueblo Indians, whose kiva culture vanished a thousand years ago. This book remains one of the most beautiful and important books in the renaissance of Native American folklore published since the early 1970s.

McKissack, Patricia. *The Apache.*
See entry 278, Grades 4–6.

266 Ortiz, Simon. *The People Shall Continue.* Illus. by Sharon Graves. Children's Book Pr. 1988, HB $12.95 (0-89239-041-7). 24pp. Nonfiction.

This is a history of Native American peoples for younger children. The style is that of Native American legends, particularly the epic creation myths. The hand-lettered text and boldly colored illustrations enhance the feel of myth and oral tradition embodied by the text. All aspects of Native American traditional life are explored. This is a teaching story, a role played by many Native American myths, and it has an authentic feel of tribal storytelling. It is meant to instill a responsibility for all life, and in doing so it reflects the Native American spirit.

This title is one of a series of multicultural books published by Children's Book Press. The tone is that of the folktale that teaches a history of the Indian peoples from the creation myths to current traditional life as it is practiced today. The message communicated to children is that Native American culture and values survive in the contemporary Native American.

Ringgold, Faith. *Tar Beach.*
See entry 21, Grades PS–3.

GRADES 4–6

267 Beale, Alex W. *Only the Names Remain: The Cherokee and the Trail of Tears.* Illus. by William S. Bach. Little, Brown 1972. 88pp. Nonfiction. o.p.

Beale describes the Appalachian region of Georgia that served as home to the Cherokee Nation before white men drove the Cherokee into exile. This book is a history of the Cherokee Nation from the time of its first interaction with white settlers, to the codification of the Cherokee alphabet by Sequoyah, who also negotiated with the U.S. government to preserve some of his people's home-land, and finally to President Andrew Jackson's fateful decision to betray this people.

The white men wanted the traditional homeland of the Cherokee for its gold and agricultural potential. The Cherokee lost their rights and were forcibly marched to Arkansas and Oklahoma. This forced march is called the Trail of Tears, because many Cherokee suffered and perished along the way. The story is told in simple but descriptive language that highlights the human story of individuals in addition to presenting facts and dates. The Cherokee experience exemplifies the pattern of white interaction with peaceful groups of Indians. Treaties were broken, trusts betrayed, and brutality and starvation perpetrated on the Cherokee, who, unlike their Plains counterparts, were unarmed and scarcely able to defend themselves.

268 Bernstein, Bonnie. *Native American Crafts Workshop.* Illus. with drawings. Fearon Teacher Aids 1982, P $7.95 (0-8224-9784-0). 92pp. Nonfiction.

The book's introduction includes a map of North America depicting geographic areas and the peoples associated with each specific area. The crafts are described and categorized according to the function associated with each one. Crafts for everyday use include clothing and household implements. Materials and instructions are illustrated with simple black-and-white drawings. Coiled baskets and coiled pots can be used in classroom or library craft programs to introduce students to Native American culture. One of the chapters includes a page on natural dyes used by Native Americans and techniques they employed for dyeing. Ceremonial crafts such as masks, fans, and the ghost shirt compose the next chapter. The ceremonial uses of these items are described. About two pages are devoted to each craft. Musical instruments, Native American games, and Native American cooking take up the last three chapters. Indian traditional designs and colors as well as a list of resources are appended.

The Native American recipes can be used in a unit on Native American culture. The recipes are authentic and easy for children to follow, emphasizing traditional foods and cooking techniques. This book is a cultural resource that replaces the dated Indian craft books of the 50s. The book's strength is that Native American life is described through the step-by-step construction of these crafts within their significance to Native American culture and traditional life.

269 Black, Sheila. *Sitting Bull: And the Battle of Little Big Horn.* Illus. with photos and drawings. SERIES: Alvin Josephy's History of the Native Americans. Silver Burdett 1989, LB $12.98 (0-382-09572-3); P $7.95 (0-382-09761). 130pp. Nonfiction.

The new world was no "undiscovered wilderness" at the time of Columbus. For more than 10,000 years (some scholars say up to 60,000 years) native peoples lived in the Americas. This book helps us to understand that the Indians before Columbus and after were and are people like us, with hopes, dreams, and the desire to protect their families and culture. Sitting Bull was one of these men. He was a great holy man, a religious leader of the Sioux. Black portrays him as a feeling and caring leader. In addition to presenting the man himself, she follows the history of the conflict between whites and Indians. In simple, clear language this series volume communicates the dignity with which these people conducted and defended themselves against the brutality of the white settlers. Other volumes in this series explore the life and heritage of Geronimo, Tecumseh, Sequoia, Hiawatha, and King Philip.

Brown, Dee. *Wounded Knee: An Indian History of the American West.*
See entry 289, Grades 7–9.

Bruchac, Joseph. *Return of the Sun: Native American Tales from the Northeast Woodlands.*
See entry 290, Grades 7–9.

270 Carter, Alden R. *The Shoshoni.* Illus. SERIES: First Books. Franklin Watts 1989, LB $11.90 (0-531-10753-1); 1991, P $4.95 (0-531-15605-2). 64pp.

The Shoshoni people lived in the western third of the United States, in an area known as the Great Basin. Living conditions were harsh in this arid land that could not support big game like the buffalo. This book chronicles the near-demise of the Shoshoni, who now number a mere 16,000. Many of their customs and traditional beliefs have been lost.

Carter begins this series volume with the history of the Shoshoni and their traditional life and customs. He then focuses on the modern descendants of this culture. The color photos of historical interest and contemporary Shoshoni life lend an immediacy to the simple, clear text. The series is useful and attractive. The large print and simple language make the books especially appealing to younger readers as well as to older, reluctant readers. Other volumes present the Apache and Navajo, the Iroquois, the Seminoles, and the Sioux.

271 Cwiklik, Robert. *Sequoia.* SERIES: Alvin Josephy's History of the Native Americans. Silver Burdett 1989, LB $12.98 (0-382-09570-7); P $7.95 (0-382-09759-9). 129pp. Nonfiction.

In the eighteenth century, white European colonists were living on the East Coast of the United States. They increased in numbers and moved further west to find more land, water, and gold. In order to avoid obliteration and to live in peace, the Cherokee Nation had to surrender its lands and traditional culture to make room for the white man. Sequoia, a lame Cherokee, devised a way for his people to live among the whites and still maintain their culture. He developed a unique alphabet for the Cherokee language so that it could be written and preserved. The Cherokee people were not saved from death and hardship. The soldiers of the U.S. government abrogated the treaties, rounded the Indians up, and force-marched them west without adequate food, shelter, or water. This was one of the most famous acts of cruelty and genocide against Native American peoples, the Trail of Tears.

This title is part of a biography series on Native Americans published by Silver Burdett. Other books in the series include *Geronimo*, *Hiawatha*, *King Philip*, *Sitting Bull*, and *Tecumseh*.

This series of Native American biographies is excellent in its historical accuracy, attractiveness, and readability. The authors' sympathies with the Native American leaders are evident. These biographies enable us to know and understand Native American culture and philosophy through a few brave, wise, and cultured leaders. We come to empathize with the Native Americans' history and to see events from their perspective through the lives of these real human beings, who are admirable in their courage by any cultural standard.

272 Davis, Deborah. *The Secret of the Seal.* Illus. by Jody Labrasca. Crown 1989, HB $13.95 (0-517-56725-3). 57pp. Fiction.

Kyo, a young Inuit boy, lives with his family in a small Eskimo settlement. Kyo hopes to harpoon a seal, but once face-to-face with the seal, he realizes that he cannot kill this animal with the trusting eyes. "Tookey" becomes Kyo's friend, whom he visits often. When his uncle comes to visit, Kyo faces the dilemma of being expected to help his uncle hunt for a seal to take back to the zoo in the city. Kyo tries to protect Tookey from being hunted, but by befriending Tookey and habituating her to human companionship, he has compromised her freedom, even her life. Kyo can't bear the thought of Tookey in captivity.

The surprising resolution to the story will satisfy nature lovers while retaining the realism of life in the Alaskan wilderness. The book simply and eloquently illustrates the dilemma of the self-sufficient Native hunter who must feed his family but still respect and conserve nature. Aspects of everyday Inuit life, from Kyo's seal watching to seeing his mother bake bread, as well as the use of authentic Inuit words and names, create a convincing view of the isolated way of life still pursued by some Inuit who wish to retain their traditional life-style. The Inuit customs are shown to be compatible with modern inventions such as the snowmobile, just as the traditional culture makes it possible to utilize nature judiciously, respecting wildlife. This story imparts a somewhat romanticized view of traditional Inuit life today, but it is a sensitive tale that has much to offer to young readers nonetheless.

273 DeFelice, Cynthia. *Weasel.* Macmillan 1990, HB $12.95 (0-02-726457-2). 119pp. Fiction.

Although no Native-American characters appear directly in this novel, it presents an episode in American history that has heretofore received little attention. In the early nineteenth century, the U.S. government hired "Indian fighters," many of them psychopathic killers, to eliminate the tribes in areas coveted by settlers. Many of these mercenaries subsequently turned on the settlers themselves. In this novel, an Indian fighter gone amok, Weasel, wounds the 12-year-old protagonist's father and later kidnaps the boy, who, upon his escape, must deal with his own vengeful impulses.

This is one of the few novels that present to older elementary readers the seamy side of government-Indian relations. It is a well-researched and well-written book that supplements nonfiction treatments and provides a starting point for classroom discussions.

274 Freedman, Russell. *Buffalo Hunt.* Illus. with color reproductions. Holiday House 1988, LB $16.95 (0-8234-0702-0). 52pp. Nonfiction.

The demise of American buffalo herds on the Great Plains meant the end of a traditional way of life and culture for the majority of Native Americans. It also nearly caused the obliteration of Native American peoples. The original buffalo had migrated over the Beringian land bridge, as did the tribal groups that became Native Americans, 30,000 years ago.

The buffalo were integral to the lives and survival of the Indian peoples. These people ate buffalo meat, used buffalo skins for shelter and clothing, and made buffalo bones and sinews into tools, implements, and toys. The buffalo were even central to the religious life of the Indians. Before each buffalo hunt, the hunters would praise the buffalo spirits for their generosity and give thanks to them for sustenance.

This book chronicles the near-destruction of the buffalo herds at the hands of the white hunters hired to feed the railroad crews who opened the American West to settlement by the white population. The buffalo population dwindled from 70 million (National Geographic Society historians estimate over 100 million) to a few hundred in 20 or 30 years. Mountains of buffalo hides and tails were shipped East for souvenirs while the carcasses of the slaughtered buffalo rotted on the Plains.

Freedman's research and historical accuracy are impeccable. The use of color illustrations reproducing historical paintings creates an authenticity rarely found in books for younger readers. Freedman does not condescend to young people. He incorporates all of the style, depth, and content that one would expect in a book written for adults. This is a useful companion to Freedman's book *Indian Chiefs*, which is also annotated in this chapter.

Freedman, Russell. *Indian Chiefs.*
See entry 293, Grades 7–9.

275   George, Jean Craighead. *The Talking Earth.* HarperCollins 1983, LB $12.89 (0-06-021976-9); 1987, P $3.50 (0-06-440212-6). 160pp. Fiction.

Billie Wind attends the Kennedy Space Center School; she understands that the earth is becoming polluted. She does not subscribe to the traditions of her ancestors, the Seminole Indians. Because of her fascination with the scientific, it is difficult for her to believe in talking animals and people who live underground. When she finds herself alone in the Everglades—a punishment for her cynical attitude—she realizes that she must rely on the animals and the earth for survival.

Billie adopts an otter, a baby panther, and a turtle. She hears the message of these animals—that the earth is being destroyed by pollution but that it is possible to save it. George creates a strong, believable, and multifaceted female protagonist with questions about her identity and about the survival of all living things. The book has a purpose—to communicate the Native American reverence for life and concern for the environment—but its award-winning author has crafted a realistic story that gets its message across through good characterizations and a style that will engage the young reader.

276   Gonzales, Catherine Troy. *Quanah Parker: Great Chief of the Comanches.* Illus. by Mark Mitchell. Eakin Pr. 1987, HB $9.95 (0-89015-600-X). 44pp. Nonfiction.

This biography is one of a number of books about Texas and Texans published by Eakin Press. Told in the first person for younger readers, this biography of one of the greatest Comanche leaders tells of Quanah's dedication to his people.

Born of a white mother and Indian father, Quanah lost his family as a child. As a free Comanche, he traveled in both the Indian and white worlds. He practiced Comanche customs but taught the Indians to live in peace and harmony with the white man. Although his life is romanticized to a certain degree, the book achieves historical accuracy. The style is simple, uncomplicated, and accessible to middle grade readers. The fictional dialogue seems natural, promoting an immediacy and the sense that these historical characters were real people.

Gregory, Kristiana. *Jenny of the Tetons.*
See entry 295, Grades 7–9.

277   Landau, Elaine. *The Sioux.* Illus. SERIES: First Books. Franklin Watts 1989, LB $11.90 (0-531-10754-X); 1991, P $4.95 (0-531-15606-0). 64pp. Nonfiction.

Another example of Franklin Watts's attractive and authoritative volumes on Native American nations for the First Books series, this one differs from Alden Carter's *The Shoshoni* in that the contemporary culture of the Sioux receives more treatment, whereas Carter focuses on the extent to which the Shoshoni and their traditions have been wiped out. This book describes the importance of the buffalo to the traditional life of the Sioux and other Plains Indian groups. The culture and mythology of the Sioux are detailed in chapters on games, music, art, and religion. In examining the Sioux struggle for survival against the white settlers of the Plains, Landau discusses the ways in which the culture has survived as well as some of the problems facing modern-day Sioux—unemployment, alcoholism, and continuing pressures to assimilate.

278   McKissack, Patricia. ***The Apache.*** Illus. SERIES: New True Books. Childrens Pr. 1984, LB $9.95 (0-516-01925-2). 48pp. Nonfiction.

This is an attractive, accessible nonfiction series for younger readers and reluctant readers who are intimidated by longer, harder-to-read books. Clear, large print makes this series appropriate for young readers, though some of the concepts presented are quite sophisticated. The series covers nonfiction topics in a variety of subject areas from sciences to several titles on Native American tribal groups. This particular volume is clearly and interestingly written, with tidbits of information that will appeal to youngsters.

279   May, Robin. ***Plains Indians of North America.*** SERIES: Original People. Rourke Publications 1987, LB $15.33 (0-86625-258-4). 48pp. Nonfiction.

This is one of a series of books published by Rourke on indigenous peoples of various cultures. Two of the series titles, this book and one on the Inuit, deal with Indians of North America. The author details everyday life in an Indian camp before the introduction of horses. These were called the "dog days." Women farmed the land while the men hunted on foot. The religious beliefs and cosmology of the Plains people are described. The importance of the spiritual healer, or medicine man, is discussed.

The author describes the buffalo hunt and the way it became transformed into a fast-moving event with the introduction of horses from Europe in the eighteenth century. In the 1870s, there were nearly 100 million buffalo on the Great Plains. The whites hunted the herds to provide meat for the railroad workers and to starve the Indians into submission. By 1889 there were only about 500 buffalo left on the Plains. The importance of the buffalo hunt to traditional Native American life and culture is central to the book. May emphasizes the reality of the hunt as being in harmony with the Native American reverence for life. By killing only as many animals as could be completely utilized by using every part of the animal, Native Americans conserved the animal population. The ecological lesson is clear. If we live in harmony with nature, allowing plant and animal life to replenish themselves, we can ensure our own survival. But when we overhunt and use natural resources wantonly, we endanger our own existence. The text is accurate, and the illustrations from historical sources give an authentic portrait of this period. An index makes the book useful for reports.

280   New Mexico People and Energy Collective. ***Red Ribbons for Emma.*** Illus. with photos. New Seed Pr. 1981, P $12.00 (0-938678-07-8). 48pp. Nonfiction.

This is a photo-documentary relating the contemporary heroism of a Navajo woman living on the reservation. The book depicts the low standard of living and the appalling lack of primary services such as sewers, running water, and electricity in the arid land of the reservation. Emma Yazzi is a grass roots heroine who stands up to the company that has been allowed to mine coal on reservation land. She is a grandmother who is very human, but very self-sufficient. The book describes her fight and passive resistance against both the mining company and the power company operating on reservation land. Her life in the stone and mud hogan, herding sheep among the heavy earth-moving machines operated by the mining company, will interest young readers and help them see the contrast between the traditional way of life that respects the land and the technology that has proven more destructive than helpful. In simple, direct language, the book takes Emma's side and presents her case in an effective, moving way and in her own words. It will serve as a good starter for class discussions. Emma's courage serves as an example to readers that integrity begins with the individual.

281   Pitts, Paul. *Racing the Sun.* Avon 1988, P $2.50 (0-380-75496-7). 160pp. Fiction.

Twelve-year-old Brandon Rogers—called "Cochise" by his friend "Ham" Burger—is a middle-class suburban youngster who is ashamed of his Native American heritage. His father left the reservation to become a university professor and wants as little as possible to do with his past. However, when Brandon's elderly grandfather leaves his reservation home and comes to live with the Rogerses, everything changes. Brandon must share his room with his grandfather and get used to his grandfather's chanting himself to sleep, as well as other strange customs. Under his grandfather's tutelage, Brandon eventually learns to appreciate his Navajo heritage. One of the rituals he begins to observe is a dawn race with the sun. As he adopts aspects of traditional Navajo life as part of his roots and his identity, he must confront his father's assimilationist views, sparking an intergenerational conflict that is common in many cultures as members of the third generation, growing up in mainstream middle-class American society, begin to explore their background and cultural traditions.

Pitts has spent 13 years as a teacher on a Navajo reservation. His familiarity with the culture is evident, as is his understanding of the conflicts surrounding the assimilation process. While this book, geared to older elementary-age youngsters, does not have the complexity and depth of works by Jamake Highwater, Jean Craighead George, and others, it does have universal appeal and may strike a chord with readers from other backgrounds who face similar issues.

282   Speare, Elizabeth George. *The Sign of the Beaver.* Houghton Mifflin 1983, HB $12.95 (0-395-33890-5); Dell 1984, P $3.50 (0-440-47900-2). 135pp. Fiction.

Thirteen-year-old Matt must guard his family's homestead cabin in the wilderness of eighteenth-century Maine. He is left alone for the winter even though he expected his father and mother to return before the first snowfall. His rifle is stolen by a drifter, and hope for survival is dim without the protection of the rifle for defense and for hunting game. His supplies are raided by a hungry bear, and his spirits decline until he meets a young Indian. The boy and his grandfather save Matt from drowning after a bee attack. The Indians of the Beaver Clan nurse Matt back to health, and the Indian boy teaches him to survive in the wilderness. Attean, the young brave of Matt's age, agrees to show Matt how to hunt and track if Matt teaches him to read the white man's writing.

The author illustrates the wisdom of Indian survival, which accepts responsibility for leaving the natural habitat as one has found it. Matt's first-person narrative gives the book an immediacy that draws the reader into the story. The characterizations are believable and sensitively portrayed. Some critics of the book suggest that the author is not Native American and that consequently she simplifies the cultural elements presented about the Indians. On one hand, the Indians appear to conform to the dehumanizing image whites have of the "noble savage" in the wilderness. The fact that Matt, the white youth, is really the main character reinforces this impression. Yet Matt's experiences give him a new respect for the Indians, who are much more adaptable and resilient than he realized. The well-researched details of Indian methods of hunting and survival are fascinating to young readers. Speare creates a wilderness and characters that are believable and fairly authentic. In the classroom presentation of Native American culture, however, it is imperative to utilize materials written by Native Americans, historical sources, and nonfiction as well as fiction.

Supree, Burton, ed. ***Bear's Heart: Scenes from the Life of a Cheyenne Artist of One Hundred Years Ago.***
See entry 306, Grades 7–9.

283   Tannenbaum, Beulah, and Howard E. Tannenbaum. ***Science of the Early American Indians.*** Franklin Watts 1988, LB $10.40 (0-531-10488-5). 90pp. Nonfiction.

The author describes how, historically, Native Americans have used their knowledge of nature and science to survive. Their familiarity with seasonality, astronomy, agriculture, and animal habitats existed long before Columbus brought European science to the Americas. Early Amerinds were deeply religious. It is difficult to separate their scientific achievements from their mythology and religious faith. The Indians of North, Central, and South America made use of their scientific knowledge to adapt their lives to their environment. Their housing, cooking, agriculture, hunting, and medicine were all practiced in harmony with the natural world. European scientific philosophy and practice, on the other hand, depended on subduing nature and conquering the elements. This book draws the contrast between the two cultures and recounts various scientific principles and practices we have learned from Native American peoples. Geared to upper elementary and middle school students, this work will provide a welcome balance to the Eurocentric perspective on the science and social studies curricula.

284   Wolfson, Evelyn. ***American Indian Tools and Ornaments: How to Make Implements and Jewelry with Bone and Shell.*** Illus. with photos, drawings, and diagrams. Random House/David McKay 1981, HB $8.95 (0-679-20509-8). 111pp. Nonfiction.

The author describes traditional methods for making Native American tools and jewelry from shell and bone. Native craftsmen are pictured fashioning these items with traditional tools and in traditional ways. The emphasis is on craftsmanship, but the book also focuses on the importance of conservation and stewardship of the environment. Readers learn of the traditional Native American practice of taking from the earth only what is necessary and not wasting any part of an animal killed for food. Bone, sinews, shell, and every part of the slain animal have been used for something practical or ceremonial.

Instructions are given for finding bones and shells and for crafting traditional items from them. The instructions are clear and simple, and the projects would appeal to children of upper elementary and middle school age, many of whom will want to wear their creations.

285 Worcester, Donald. *Lone Hunter's Gray Pony.* Originally published by Oxford University Pr., 1956. Illus. by Paige Pauley. Texas Christian Univ. Pr. 1985, HB $10.95 (0-87565-001-5). 78pp. Fiction.

This is one of a series of four books about Lone Hunter. This book describes a young Sioux warrior who receives a pony that he will train to hunt buffalo. His bravery and the dangerous training he must master in order to hunt with the men are shown in detail.

The language used in the novel is clear and plain, evocative of both the style of folklore and the tradition of oral storytelling. The warriors are presented as real people with emotions and feelings. Lone Hunter realizes, after a close brush with death, that buffalo hunting is dangerous and requires great skill. When the gray pony saves his life, Lone Hunter realizes their union will be a special and close one. Lone Hunter's relationships with other young warriors in the tribe are presented in depth, as is his relationship with his father. This book gives young people a glimpse of what everyday life was like in the tribe a century ago. But central to the story are Lone Hunter's rites of passage from childhood to manhood. The central character and his peers are portrayed believably and with great compassion and respect for the traditional life of the Sioux.

TCU Press has republished another book about Lone Hunter, *Lone Hunter and the Cheyennes* (1985). The other two in the series remain out of print.

286 Wosmek, Frances. *A Brown Bird Singing.* Illus. by Ted Lewin. Lothrop, Lee & Shepard 1986, HB $10.25 (0-688-06251-2). 120pp. Fiction.

This historical novel features a young Chippewa Indian, Anego, who has been living with a white family ever since her mother's death. Anego dreams that her father, Hamigeesek, will one day return for her. But the Veselkas have been good to her, and despite enduring occasional expressions of prejudice, she has the opportunity for an education and a better life. Thus, she is ambivalent about her father's return, because in many ways she prefers the life she has. Hamigeesek does return, having spent his years away training to be a teacher on the reservation. He accepts Anego's attachment to the Veselkas and agrees to have her remain there to continue her education.

Set in the early years of the twentieth century, Wosmek's novel evokes a time when many Native Americans had to adjust to life on the reservation. Many youngsters were taken in by white families and integrated into white society, thereby losing their Native American identity. Anego, too, rejects much of her heritage. However, Wosmek's lack of familiarity with the Chippewa culture makes her characterization of Anego somewhat superficial and stereotyped, basically consisting of the fact that the child has a "way" with living things. Although the story is told from Anego's point of view, it does not represent a Native American perspective. This is a sweet tale, but readers seeking more substance would be better served by Jamake Highwater's Ghost Horse trilogy.

Wunder, John R. *The Kiowa.*
See entry 309, Grades 7-9.

287   Ashabranner, Brent. *Morning Star, Black Sun: The Northern Cheyenne Indians and America's Energy Crisis.* Illus. with photos by Paul Conklin. Putnam 1982, HB $11.95 (0-396-08045-6). 154pp. Nonfiction.

The Native American reverence for the land and for nature is a common theme in the literature. The reality, however, is more complex, as Ashabranner reveals in this compelling work of nonfiction. In the nineteenth century, the Northern Cheyenne Indians prospered as hunters and warriors on the Great Plains, but as the tribal leader Sweet Medicine had prophesied, disaster would come. Forcibly relocated, most of the tribe perished; the rest escaped to rebuild a community on harsh but beautiful reservation lands administered by the federal government. Government land-use policies proved disastrous, and when, in the late 1960s corporations requested leases to explore for coal, the tribal leaders initially accepted. Soon the impact of this decision became known—the land would be scarred, the air would be fouled, white workers would outnumber Indians 10 to 1 on the reservation. Considering themselves deceived once again, tribal leaders took on the Bureau of Indian Affairs and the coal companies—and won. Even so, the victory cost the reservation millions of dollars in corporate royalties, and the problems of poverty, dependency, and the extinction of language and culture remain.

Ashabranner tells this story from the perspective of the Cheyennes, building his narrative with primary source testimonies and interviews with Indians involved in more recent campaigns. Even George Armstrong Custer is referred to by the name the Indians gave him—Long Hair. In general, issues of land use and energy policy are discussed in a way that is understandable to the average junior high school student, though some background information or explanations may be necessary. Questions for further thought and discussion include the competing interests of urban and rural residents, the balancing of environmental quality with the need for jobs and economic development, and the costs to the Indians of becoming too dependent upon federal agencies or entitlement programs. Dramatic, visually appealing black-and-white photos enhance the text. There are a short bibliography on coal mining in the West and an index.

288   Ashabranner, Brent. *To Live in Two Worlds: American Indian Youth Today.* Illus. with photos by Paul Conklin. Dodd, Mead 1984. 149pp. Nonfiction. o.p.

Ashabranner presents the contemporary lives and dilemmas of Native Americans through a number of teenagers, young adults, and adults. For the most part, his subjects speak in their own words, and they do not minimize the problems facing their communities, problems resulting from a legacy of defeat, oppression, government manipulation, poverty, and a lack of opportunities. However, the stories of triumph—of learning to live in mainstream America with one's sense of heritage intact—stand out. Lynn, a young Navajo, tells of how she conquered low self-esteem to attend a demanding preparatory school far from her family and reservation; today she works with youngsters who are facing the same issues she confronted. Seminole lawyer Jim Shore talks about the accident that blinded him and changed his life; originally destined to be a cattle rancher like his father, he instead took advantage of various special programs to put himself through law school and now works as an attorney for the tribe. Ashabranner examines the lives of Indians who live away from the reservation, in urban areas, and how middle-class and poor "urbies" alike preserve their culture.

Despite the problems raised, the reader senses an underlying pride in Native American culture, which has survived in twentieth-century America despite all obstacles. Ashabranner's subjects are admirable, often heroic, individuals from whom readers can learn a great deal, regardless of their cultural background. Conklin's black-and-white photos reveal much about their subjects—both Ashabranner's interviewees and others encountered in the course of doing research. At a time when many assimilated Native Americans are beginning to recognize and claim their heritage, this book explains why. Includes index.

Beale, Alex W. *Only the Names Remain: The Cherokee and the Trail of Tears.*
See entry 267, Grades 4–6.

Bernstein, Bonnie. *Native American Crafts Workshop.*
See entry 268, Grades 4–6.

Bierhorst, John. *The Mythology of North America.*
See entry 310, Grades 10–12.

Black, Sheila. *Sitting Bull: And the Battle of Little Big Horn.*
See entry 269, Grades 4–6.

289   Brown, Dee. *Wounded Knee: An Indian History of the American West.* Adapted for young readers by Amy Ehrlich from Dee Brown's *Bury My Heart at Wounded Knee.* Illus. with photos. Dell 1975, P $1.50 (0-440-95768-0). 202pp. Nonfiction.

This is an adaptation of Dee Brown's *Bury My Heart at Wounded Knee*, the compelling history of the United States written from the Native American perspective. The Amy Ehrlich adaptation is accessible to the young reader, although less eloquent than Brown's well-crafted prose, which corrects the white expansionist view of U.S. history reinforced by the Hollywood stereotype of the Native American.

This adaptation preserves the spirit, if not the entire historical and emotional content, of Brown's work. It chronicles the genocide of a people and their culture during the nineteenth century. This destruction peaked with the massacre at Wounded Knee combined with the seizure of Indian lands in South Dakota and other parts of the country. Afterward, Native Americans were moved from arid lands to even more arid lands as the white government sought minerals and water. Finally, their source of food, buffalo, and their very culture were taken from them, and they began to live in poverty on reservations, in neither the Indian nor the white world.

Today, living conditions on government reservations are not much better than they were in the nineteenth century. As the author points out, average income on the reservation is a fraction of the average income in the rest of the country. Medical services, educational opportunities, and living conditions are poor; unemployment is rampant. These people pay a high price for their attempt to preserve a traditional culture that has been obliterated by design.

Black-and-white photos, maps, and illustrations are useful and attractive in expanding the text. They aid in recounting and humanizing the trail of broken treaties and broken dreams that characterize Native American life then and now. Includes bibliography and index.

290 Bruchac, Joseph. ***Return of the Sun: Native American Tales from the Northeast Woodlands.*** Illus. by Gary Carpenter. Crossing Pr. 1989, HB $18.95 (0-89594-344-1); P $8.95 (0-89594-343-3). 200pp. Nonfiction.

Bruchac tells us that "stories are the life of a people. They affirm and . . . sustain the values of a culture." Bruchac is a Native American scholar and himself part Abenaki Indian. He is a poet, and this is evident in his retelling of these traditional tales. In Bruchac's fourth collection of Native American folktales he eloquently relates the stories of the Indians of the Northeast Woodlands. All but one of the stories in this collection have ancient roots. They answer the questions of creation and other mysteries of life that Native Americans have told around the winter campfires in their lodges for centuries. These tales touch upon many themes, most notably the sanctity of nature and traditional ways of life that are in harmony with nature and with other peoples.

291 Cannon, A. E. ***The Shadow Brothers.*** Delacorte 1990, HB $14.95 (0-385-29982-6). 180pp. Fiction.

Henry Yazzie has lived with Marcus Jenkins and his family ever since Henry's father sent him, at age 7, to Utah to attend school. Now that they are in high school, Henry and Marcus have begun to draw apart, due in part to Henry's romantic attachment to the wealthy Celia Cunningham and in part to his desire to explore his Navaho heritage.

Though narrated by the Anglo teen, Marcus, the story is as much Henry's as Marcus's. Henry's interest in his heritage is touched off by a letter from his grandfather and an encounter with an angry, unassimilated Hopi youth, Frank. Cannon portrays Henry as a "super-Indian"—intelligent, hardworking, handsome, popular, a sports star—and Marcus is struggling to keep up. Through Frank, the author also shows that not all Native Americans share the same culture, and there have been historic rivalries between tribes, yet each Native-American youngster must confront the dilemma of living in two worlds. Marcus's voice is authentic, with appeal for young adult readers, and, although the issues facing Henry are not explored in much depth, the treatment is inoffensive and may give readers a sense of the conflicts that accompany assimilation.

292 Carter, Forrest. ***The Education of Little Tree.*** Originally published by Delacorte, 1976. Univ. of New Mexico Pr. 1976, HB $16.95 (0-8263-1233-0); P $10.95 (0-8263-0879-1). 227pp. Fiction.

In the years since its initial publication; this book has become a classic and appears frequently on recommended reading lists for middle, junior high, and high school readers. Critics have praised its simple and eloquent first-person narrative and its loving presentation of the ways of life of the Cherokee grandparents who raised Little Tree. The book is written in mountain dialect and describes in detail the traditional wisdom and survival skills of the Cherokee people. However, in the fall of 1991 historian Dan Carter (no relation) uncovered evidence that Forrest Carter (Little Tree), who has also authored historical novels for adults about the Native-American experience, is a pseudonym for Asa Earl Carter, a former Ku Klux Klansman who became an environmentalist and novelist in the last decade of his life. After searching genealogies and other records, Dan Carter could find no evidence that Little Tree or his grandparents ever existed.

New information about this book's origins do not diminish the literary quality or narrative power of the work. Nor has Dan Carter challenged the accuracy of the presentation. Yet it is not autobiography but rather a carefully crafted work of fiction from a man who appears to have rewritten his own life as well.

L.M-L.

Cwiklik, Robert. *Sequoia.*
See entry 271, Grades 4–6.

293 Freedman, Russell. *Indian Chiefs.* Illus. with photos. Holiday House 1987, HB $16.95 (0-8234-0625-3). 160pp. Nonfiction.

Freedman's Newbery Award-winning book chronicles the conflict between the white settlers and Native American tribal groups from the 1840s on. His introductory chapter discusses the dilemma native peoples faced in the nineteenth century: should they fight for their land and traditional way of life or live in peace with the whites who took their land and treated them as less than human? Whether they chose war or peace, the results were the same—Indians died or lost their land and culture.

The main chapters present the stories of six chiefs of Western tribes who led their people during these historic conflicts. Featured are Chief Red Cloud of the Oglala Sioux, Chief Satanta of the Kiowa, Chief Quanah Parker of the Comanche, Chief Washahie of the Shoshone, Chief Joseph of the Nez Percé, and Chief Sitting Bull of the Hunkpapa Sioux. Freedman's subjects are sympathetically but realistically portrayed. They appear as honorable, responsible, dignified leaders who were forced to resolve as best as they could the inevitable conflicts ensuing from the encroachment of another culture. They fought to protect not only their peoples' lives but also a way of life that was thousands of years old.

The human story of the suffering endured by individuals with aspirations, hopes, and dreams not unlike anyone else's is presented by Freedman. These events occur in the context of human loss and suffering, not as sterile historic facts. We see the faces of these people and feel their suffering and anguish for themselves and for future generations. Includes maps and an index.

294 George, Jean Craighead. *Julie of the Wolves.* Illus. by John Schoenherr. HarperCollins 1972, LB $12.89 (0-06-021944-0); P $2.95 (0-06-440058-1). 180pp. Fiction.

Restless and isolated, Miyax (Julie), a 13-year-old Eskimo girl, runs away from her small Alaska village to San Francisco to visit her pen pal and to see the wider world. On the way, she becomes lost. She is on the North Slope of Alaska without a compass or food. The view in every direction is the same. She is alone except for the company of a pack of Arctic wolves. The wolves come to accept her as she comes to love them and to depend upon them. In this story of survival and self-discovery, Miyax learns that she can sustain herself only by listening to the earth and to her traditional culture, which she had previously rejected.

Miyax is between childhood and maturity, between her Eskimo heritage and the white culture. She is trying to find herself, her identity, and her hopes, fears, and beliefs. Through the ordeal of being lost without food or shelter, she realizes that she can be strong. Her survival is her own doing. She uses the traditional wisdom of her culture and her knowledge of the earth and nature to keep herself alive, as we must all do to keep ourselves alive on this planet.

George's language is wonderfully subtle, and she weaves into the story a wealth of scientific and cultural information in a completely natural, unobtrusive way. Through her descriptions, characterizations, and plotting, she shows the wisdom of nature and of Native American ways of life. This now-classic story—winner of the 1973 Newbery Medal—will have special appeal to middle-school-age readers from all backgrounds; through their empathy with Miyax and fascination with the challenges that she faces, readers may identify their own strengths and capabilities and in the process discover a new sense of self and self-esteem.

George, Jean Craighead. *The Talking Earth.*
See entry 275, Grades 4–6.

295   Gregory, Kristiana. *Jenny of the Tetons.* Harcourt Brace Jovanovich 1989, HB $13.95 (0-15-200480-7). 119pp. Fiction.

Eleven-year-old Carrie Hill has been left orphaned and wounded in an Indian raid; her two younger brothers have been kidnapped by the raiders. The head of the wagon train arranges for her to stay behind in Idaho to help the British-born trapper Beaver Dick and his Shoshone wife, Jenny, with their five children. Carrie is angry at the Indians who wiped out her family, and she takes her rage out on Jenny. Jenny understands Carrie's sorrow; her own family was killed by white settlers. Under Jenny's loving hands, Carrie heals and becomes a part of Beaver Dick's family. She learns of the customs of the Shoshone and of their reverence for nature; for instance, they do not hold land as private property, nor do they name places in nature for people, as do the white settlers. As Carrie begins a new life, eventually marrying Dick's trader friend Miles Alexander, tragedy strikes Jenny and her family. An outbreak of smallpox claims Jenny, her newborn child, and all of the other five of her and Beaver Dick's children.

This moving and well-researched work of historical fiction is based on the diaries of Beaver Dick Leigh, excerpts of which appear at the beginning of each chapter. Although Carrie is fictitious, Jenny, Beaver Dick, and their doomed family actually existed as they are presented here. Gregory develops convincingly the relationship between two women from different ethnic groups who have suffered at the hands of the other, and her presentation has much to say to young people today about cross-cultural conflict, the good and evil within each cultural group, and the importance of forgiveness. Although Carrie's voice occasionally slips into that of a modern-day teenager, this is a minor flaw in an otherwise strong work of historical fiction.

296   Hamilton, Virginia. *Arilla Sun Down.* Greenwillow 1976, LB $12.88 (0-688-84058-2). 248pp. Fiction.

Twelve-year-old Arilla Adams is part Native American and part African American. She lives with her parents and her older brother, Jack Sun Run Adams, in a small Ohio town, but her earliest dreams and memories are scenes from a place called Cliffville, where her family lived among the Native Americans. Like other girls her age, Arilla constantly bickers with her brother, whom she both dislikes and admires. Jack Sun Run is militant in his affirmation of his Native American identity. Popular among the girls (especially the Haitian American Angela Diavolad) and skilled at horseback riding and roping, he is seen by many, including Arilla, as hostile and arrogant. Yet Arilla sneaks out at night with Jack and Angela to go roller skating, a forbidden pastime that she loves. In secret, she is writing her autobiography as a means of discovering who she is. When she receives an unwanted birthday present of a horse and reluctantly goes riding with her brother during an ice storm, the chain of events that takes place proves to be crucial in Arilla's understanding of her past and of her own unique gifts.

Hamilton has written a novel of an interracial family that is as complex as the family's own heritage. Dream sequences, with barely comprehended snatches from the past, are interspersed with Arilla's realistic first-person narrative. The effect is authentic and impressive. Characters are multidimensional and memorable. Hamilton contrasts Arilla's endless questioning with her older brother's absolute decision in favor of his Native American side. Native American mythology and contemporary issues permeate this skillfully written tale for good readers of middle school age.

297   Highwater, Jamake. ***Anpao: An American Indian Odyssey.*** Illus. by Fritz Scholder. HarperCollins 1977, HB $13.95 (0-397-31750-6); 1980, P $8.95 (0-06-131986-4). 253pp. Fiction.

Highwater, an award-winning author of fiction and nonfiction, is himself of Blackfoot and Crow heritage. He holds degrees in cultural anthropology, literature, and music. This book is a tapestry of legends from the cultures of the Southwest and the Plains. Like Homer's *Odyssey*, not only is it a story of a journey that one man, Anpao, makes in achieving maturity, but it is also the story of a cultural journey. Anpao wanders in a time and place that are a metaphor for self-discovery.

The legend describes the history of Native American peoples, their relationships to the buffalo and to their environment as well as to their creator. Highwater creates this unique story in the same way that storytellers have passed on traditional stories from generation to generation. He explores the meaning of existence and the interrelationship of all things from a Native American perspective. This book is for the special reader and for young adults who can appreciate the lyric prose style of this exceptional author. Highwater's scholarship as an anthropologist combines with his genius for interpretation and storytelling to make a unique work that is a classic and a genre of its own.

298   Highwater, Jamake. ***The Ceremony of Innocence.*** HarperCollins 1985, LB $12.89 (0-06-022302-2). 186pp. Fiction.

This novel, the second in the Ghost Horse trilogy, follows Amana from the time she becomes an adult, after the death of her husband, to old age, when she struggles with her daughter, Jemina, over the future of Jemina's two sons. Amana's magical powers, detailed in *Legend Days*, have made her an outcast; in addition, her family and most of her tribe have died from disease and starvation. Struggling to survive on her own, Amana befriends the French Cree prostitute Amalia. She reencounters Jean-Pierre Bonneville, the handsome and enigmatic French Canadian, at the trading post; he fathers her child and then abandons her before Jemina's birth. Through Amana's eyes, Highwater details the forced relocation of the defeated and decimated Indians to barren reservations, life among whites who feel nothing but contempt for Indians, and the estrangement of children who have adopted the values and attitudes of the majority society.

Socialized in the ways of whites and filled with hatred for her own heritage, Jemina falls for the debonair circus stuntman Jamie Ghost Horse, who promises her the glamorous life she has read about in magazines. But Jamie loses his job and sinks into despair and alcoholism, leaving Amana to help raise Jemina's two sons, Reno and Sitko.

Highwater sustains the poetic style of *Legend Days* in this work as he gives young readers a personal account of a culture in transition. Details—for instance, Jemina's telephone call to Amana to announce Reno's birth—make tangible the changes that have occurred since Amana's childhood; equally vivid are the painful encounters between Indians and whites and among members of Amana's own family. Although the focus is largely on adult characters, the book will appeal both to young adult readers who have already encountered Amana and to those who have not, but who will be drawn into the moving and realistically portrayed family dynamic. Highwater's saga continues with *I Wear the Morning Star* (HarperCollins, 1986), which details Jemina's younger son, Sitko's, efforts to reclaim his heritage after his mother abandons him in a boarding school, where he is cruelly treated.

299   Highwater, Jamake. ***Legend Days.*** HarperCollins 1984, LB $12.89 (0-06-022304-9). 160pp. Fiction.

This first volume in the Ghost Horse trilogy begins when Amana is 11 years old. She spies an owl, an evil omen. Soon afterward, a smallpox epidemic wipes out her family and her community. Orphaned, she escapes into the woods and is taken in by Grandfather Fox, who changes her orientation into a man's. He gives her the magical weapons of a warrior, but she is not to reveal them or to use them unless her survival and that of her people are at stake. Eventually she finds her way to another tribe; she is taken in and reunited with her now horribly disfigured sister, SoodaWa, and SoodaWa's husband, Far Away Son. At the age of 12, she is obliged to marry Far Away Son who is old enough to be her grandfather. She chafes against the restrictions imposed upon her as a woman, for she believes herself a man, and she resents being forced to marry and care for her sister and husband, for she is in many ways just a child. Against the will of her husband and the tribe, she trades with the whites and goes hunting in times of great starvation, when the buffalo have become scarce. Gradually, she and Far Away Son grow to love each other, but while she is successfully hunting, her husband is killed in a buffalo stampede. As she discovers, her special powers are linked to great personal sorrow.

Highwater creates a legend—a woman whose powers and character make her a heroic figure and a metaphor for the tragedy, courage, and survival of Native Americans. His lyrical prose is at once realistic and magical, and his depth of knowledge of Native American folklore and traditions is evident. Historical events—the smallpox epidemic, conflicts among bands of Indians and with white soldiers, and the starvation brought about by the while settlers' irresponsible killing of buffalo—take on a personal dimension. Through Amana's experiences, young readers will be moved to think about the roles of men and women and about the difficult transition from childhood to adulthood. Though clearly steeped in Native American culture, this gripping, masterfully written novel offers many universal ideas.

300 Highwater, Jamake. *Many Smokes, Many Moons: A Chronology of American Indian History Through Indian Art.* Illus. HarperCollins 1978, HB $15.95 (0-397-31781-6). 128pp. Nonfiction.

This is a chronology of American Indians and their history, art, and culture as well as major events of significance to their development. It is a selective overview of events from the period before the coming of white culture. Highwater begins in 35,000 B.C., with the arrival of the Paleo-Indians from Siberia to Alaska over the Beringian land bridge that formed during a period of glaciation. These were the first Americans, the people who truly discovered America. Highwater includes maps, drawings, and photos of artifacts. Some of the entries are brief but concise, and the overall coverage gives some perspective on the events that shaped the Native American peoples of North, Central, and South America.

301 Hirschfelder, Arlene. *Happily May I Walk: American Indians and Alaska Natives Today.* Illus. with photos. Scribner 1986, HB $13.95 (0-684-18624-1). 160pp. Nonfiction.

Written in short sentences and clear, flowing prose, this is a readable introduction to the contemporary situation of Native Americans and Alaskan Natives. Hirschfelder emphasizes culture, politics (including tribal governance), education, sports, and the arts. Her approach is quite general, and the tone is positive and sympathetic throughout. Alaska Natives receive relatively short shrift in a work that tries to cover all groups equally. The map on each of the endpapers indicates reservations and communities and is quite useful. Also useful is a bibliography, geared to the junior high school student, that is organized by region. An index is included.

302 Hobbs, Will. *Bearstone.* Atheneum 1989, HB $12.95 (0-689-31496-5). 160pp. Fiction.

Part Navajo, part Ute, Cloyd Attcity has been running away from trouble most of his life. His persistent truancy and lack of supervision at home have led the tribal council on his reservation to send him to a group home. Cloyd escapes to find his father, only to discover that his father is in a hospital, in an irreversible coma. When he returns to the group home, he is sent to work for Walter, an elderly white rancher. He runs into the mountains, discovers a bearstone, and gives himself the name Lone Bear. His relationship with Walter is stormy; coming to trust the old man a little, his faith is dashed when Walter brings to the ranch a group of white men who hunt bears "Indian style," with bows and arrows, for sport. He vandalizes Walter's prize peach trees and returns to his grandmother on the reservation, but he feels compelled to resolve his conflict with Walter. When they go to the mountains together to mine gold, Cloyd fails to save a rare grizzly bear from the hunters, but he does succeed in saving Walter, who is injured in the collapse of the mine.

Hobbs has given junior high school age readers a sympathetic and sensitive portrait of a contemporary Native American youth struggling to find his identity. Cloyd feels alone in the world until he befriends Walter, another loner, but closeness brings pain as well as happiness. Cloyd's Native American heritage is evident in the lore of his grandmother, in his belief in the spirit of all living things, and in his disgust with the men who kill animals for fun. The tribe is presented as having authority and taking responsibility for one of its troubled members. Although Hobbs's knowledge of Native American life and culture is superficial in comparison to that of Jamake Highwater, he makes a laudable effort, one that explores the universal themes of identity, cross-cultural relationships, and respect for the environment.

303   Katz, William Loren. ***Black Indians: A Hidden Heritage.*** Illus. with photos. Atheneum 1986, HB $15.95 (0-689-31196-6). 198pp. Nonfiction.

Often minority cultures and their stories are left out of white versions of history. This is true of Native Americans and blacks in American history. History books have been written and rewritten to include Native Americans and blacks separately, but we rarely read about the coalition and intermarriage of blacks and Native Americans.

The Seminoles of Florida accepted numbers of runaway slaves in the eighteenth and nineteenth centuries. Because Native American cultures were largely color-blind, meaning not prejudiced against other races, they accepted blacks and whites and adopted them as full members of their tribes. The stories of these adoptions and intermarriages began with the voyages of Columbus and extend over North and South America and the islands of the Caribbean.

This is the only nonfiction book written for children on black Indians. The author includes an excellent bibliography. The stories of individuals such as Ben Pickett, born to a black Cherokee family in Oklahoma, are told here. The myth of frontier life dominated by white culture is dispelled in this book as Katz tells in eloquent prose the story of two dark races in the American West who frequently united as allies.

Nabokov, Peter, ed. ***Native American Testimony: An Anthology of Indian and White Relations.***
See entry 320, Grades 10–12.

304   O'Dell, Scott. ***Black Star, Bright Dawn.*** Houghton Mifflin 1988, HB $14.95 (0-395-47778-6); Fawcett 1989, P $3.50 (0-449-70340-1). 134pp. Fiction.

Newbery Award winner for *Island of the Blue Dolphins* and winner of the Hans Christian Andersen Award for the body of his work, Scott O'Dell has written another moving and realistic novel about an Inuit girl who enters the 1,100-mile-long Iditarod dog sled race in Alaska. The course runs through the barren winter landscape of Alaska from Nome, along the Yukon River, then southeast to Anchorage. The girl, Bright Dawn, takes over when her father is injured, and she becomes the only female to run in the race. She battles cold, loneliness, hunger, animal predators, and fatigue only to become lost in a blizzard. Bright Dawn gains new respect for her Native American heritage when all of the traditional survival techniques her father has taught her combine to enable her to win the race.

Despite the happy ending, the story is not so far from reality. The Iditarod has been won several times in recent years by a woman. Doubtless, the Inuit spirit and respect for the wilderness and animal life have allowed the Iditarod participants to finish the 1,100-mile course. Young readers can relate to Bright Dawn, a lone child poised on the brink of adulthood, facing enormous odds against her survival. She has harnessed the skills, endurance, and respect for all living things that her people have taught her in order to survive and to triumph, enabling her to gain the respect of her entire community. O'Dell's ability to maintain the tension, suspense, and excitement of the dangerous Iditarod race gives this book appeal to both male and female adolescents.

305 Sneve, Virginia Driving Hawk, ed. ***Dancing Teepees: Poems of American Indian Youth.*** Illus. by Stephen Gammell. Holiday House 1989, HB $14.95 (0-8234-0724-1). 32pp. Poetry.

Virginia Driving Hawk Sneve's book of poems comes out of the storytelling and oral traditions of Native American cultures. Before any of the Native American peoples had a written language, their history and cultural traditions were passed on from one generation to the next orally, through storytelling.

The poems chosen by Sneve are written by young Native Americans. They are simple and eloquent in their language and imagery. Stephen Gammell's drawings reflect the spirit and mystery of the traditional stories, songs, and poems they illustrate. The themes include traditional aspects of Native American culture, such as reverence for life and the cosmology and religion of Native Americans. The conflicts between traditional and modern life are examined as well. It is evident that Native American culture is alive and well through the art of these teenage poets. The kinship with nature and the hopes and fears of a cultural group as well as a nation are voiced in these evocative works, which will appeal to a wide age range of youngsters and perhaps encourage them to write poetry about their own heritage, traditions, and life.

Speare, Elizabeth George. ***The Sign of the Beaver.***
See entry 282, Grades 4–6.

306 Supree, Burton, ed. ***Bear's Heart: Scenes from the Life of a Cheyenne Artist of One Hundred Years Ago.*** Illus. with drawings by Bear's Heart. HarperCollins 1977. 63pp. Nonfiction. o.p.

Bear's Heart was born in 1851 when the Cheyenne still hunted the plentiful buffalo on the Plains. Within his lifetime, Bear's Heart's tribe was confined to reservations with no means of feeding and clothing its members. In the harsh winter of 1874–75, the Indians of the Great Plains left the reservations in order to pursue their traditional way of survival—hunting the buffalo. The U.S. government hunted down these Indians and sent them to prison in Florida and elsewhere.

The illustrations, which Bear's Heart drew in prison, chronicle his traditional life of hunting buffalo on the Plains and his subsequent capture and imprisonment. These illustrations represent a unique form of Indian art called ledger art. The unique story this art tells is one of a dying culture. It is an important art form, Jamake Highwater tells us in the afterword, because little is known about Native American life before the European conquest. This art is also important because it tells a personal story as well as a tribal story of cultural genocide.

The eloquent text explicates Bear's Heart's drawings in a simple and uncluttered way, showing through style as well as content how these people wished to retain the dignity of their traditional way of life. The book presents the history of a personal and communal tragedy in unsequential, unsentimental, unadorned prose and illustration, in a way that is real to young people. The events portrayed speak for themselves of the brutality perpetrated on Native American peoples and their cultural heritage.

Tannenbaum, Beulah, and Howard E. Tannenbaum. *Science of the Early American Indians.*
See entry 283, Grades 4–6.

307   Wallin, Luke. *Ceremony of the Panther.* Bradbury 1987, HB $11.95 (0-02-792310-X). 124pp. Fiction.

Sixteen-year-old John Raincrow, a Miccosukee Indian living in the Everglades, likes to get high with his 20-year-old friend Max. John's father, however, has had enough of his son's antics and sends him to the reservation to live with his elderly great-grandmother, Grandmother Mary. Bored at first, John comes to care deeply for Grandmother Mary, who has the "deer sickness," and when his father comes to get him several months later, John joins his father in searching for the traditional cure—the claws of a panther. As they hunt together, John gains a new respect for his father. He also begins to recognize the irresponsibility and destructiveness of Max's behavior; in addition to drinking and taking drugs, Max kills deer for the fun of it and sells the skins in Miami, a clear violation of tribal custom. The father's and son's search for the panther brings them into conflict with Crane, a white government official entrusted with the preservation of this endangered species. When two panthers die—one at the hands of Crane and the other at the hands of John's father—John must reevaluate for himself his relationship to his father, his heritage, and his natural environment.

Wallin tells a compelling story of an Indian teenager's search for his identity between two worlds. Especially strong is the development of John's relationship to his father from one of conflict to approval-seeking and finally to mature individuation. Although the characters are Miccosukee Indians, and the setting and cultural details are presented convincingly, John's story is a universal one. The one major disappointment is that one does not see the full dimensions of his life—his relationships with other characters besides his father, his school and sports activities, or his plans for the future. Nevertheless, this easy-to-read, action-packed novel, filled with scenes and descriptions of the Florida Everglades, will appeal to young teens and is an especially good choice for reluctant readers.

Wallin is also the author of *In the Shadow of the Wind* (Bradbury, 1984), a novel about the conflict between Indians and whites in the early nineteenth century, told from the point of view of a white youth who defies his community to befriend the Indians.

308   Wisler, G. Clifton. *The Raid.* Dutton/Lodestar 1985, HB $11.95 (0-525-67169-2). 122pp. Fiction.

The western genre has not been kind to Native Americans. Although this young adult western gives a nod to liberal sentiments, it is flawed by stereotypical characters, plot contrivances, and inaccuracies that demean Native Americans. Living on the Texas frontier around the time of the Civil War, 14-year-old Lige Andrews watches in terror as his younger brother is kidnapped by Indians who kill or kidnap as well the entire family of his friend, the freed slave Zeke Jackson. Disguising himself as an Indian, Lige accompanies Jackson on a daring rescue mission. At one point he saves the former slave from capture by bigoted whites, and eventually they free all of the kidnap victims, who are being brutally tortured by the Indians.

Distortions and inaccuracies abound. Although Jackson counsels understanding, observing that the Indians steal settlers' cattle because they do not have enough to eat on the reservation or that the Indian boys may find it as difficult to kill a person as Lige does, the Indians clearly are the enemy. Jackson parallels their capture of the settlers to the African slave trade. The Indians' encampment has a dump, where animal carcasses are left to rot; in reality, white settlers were far more likely to kill surplus animals and leave them to decompose. Wisler does not give the reader an Indian character who is humanized or developed in any way. The African-American Zeke Jackson is also presented in a stereotypical manner. He is always shown as the understanding one, and in several places he, the adult, must also be rescued by the white child, Lige. Wisler is also the author of several other westerns that portray the conflict between Indians and white settlers; they are *Buffalo Moon* (o.p.) and *Winter of the Wolf* (Dutton/Lodestar, 1980).

Wolfson, Evelyn. *American Indian Tools and Ornaments: How to Make Implements and Jewelry with Bone and Shell.*
See entry 284, Grades 4–6.

309 Wunder, John R. *The Kiowa.* Illus. with photos and drawings. SERIES: Indians of North America. Chelsea House 1989, LB $17.95 (1-55546-710-5). 111pp. Nonfiction.

This is part of a series of books on Native American tribes published by Chelsea House. They are well researched and beautifully illustrated with maps, period illustrations, paintings and photographs. The information contained is much more extensive than in most books written for younger readers. However, the text is clear and accessible to fifth grade and up. The content and production quality are far superior to most series books on Native Americans.

A bibliography, fact page, glossary, index, and picture credits are appended. A two-page, boxed story of the picture history of the Kiowa Nation is included in the text; it adds to the book's clarity, accessibility, and appeal. Photos of clothing, shelter, and other artifacts enhance the treatment as well. Several pages of color plates depicting Kiowa art are also included.

GRADES 10–12

Ashabranner, Brent. *Morning Star, Black Sun: The Northern Cheyenne Indians and America's Energy Crisis.*
See entry 287, Grades 7–9.

310 Bierhorst, John. *The Mythology of North America.* Illus. Morrow 1985, HB $13.00 (0-688-04145-0). 259pp. Nonfiction.

Bierhorst, the foremost scholar of Native American mythology and folklore, has written a well-researched book that is accessible to the student and layman. As Bierhorst points out, the indigenous folklore and mythology of a continent are not cultivated like a crop, but handed down through the oral tradition from generation to generation. Bierhorst takes us on a journey that is a metaphor for self-discovery.

Since much of the oral tradition has been lost through cultural extinction, it is imperative that scholars such as Bierhorst research and collect these stories of a people or peoples in danger of extinction. This comprehensive, clearly written study will help high school students and high-level middle schoolers to understand Native American culture and to appreciate its validity. It will also help them to recognize the link between a culture's mythology and the values of its people.

311   Deloria, Vine, Jr. ***Custer Died for Your Sins: An Indian Manifesto.***; Univ. of Oklahoma Pr. 1988 (0-8061-2129-7). 296pp. Nonfiction.

Deloria's brilliant treatise on Indian-white relations in North America is hardhitting and devastatingly truthful. He speaks of white guilt from four centuries of crimes committed against Native Americans. This guilt takes many forms, one of which is a fascination with Indian ancestors, real or imagined. What is the fascination with Indian descent? Do whites need the myth of Indian ancestry to make them feel truly American? Perhaps, says Deloria, but there are more complex reasons for this mythical ancestry. Many whites assuage the guilt they feel from centuries of white abuse of Indians by claiming to be one of them.

Deloria describes the persecution of Native Americans from the time of the Pilgrims to the present day. In the early days of bitter Indian-white conflict, whites gave Indians blankets infected with smallpox in an effort to eradicate them. Deloria covers the history of this conflict from the earliest laws and treaties through the disastrous twentieth-century policies of extermination. Anthropologists, missionaries, and other self-serving whites are given no quarter in Deloria's condemnation. The duplicity of former government agencies who dealt with the Indians and the problems of Indian leadership in today's world are also covered in this thorough and well-documented history, a significant work for high school age readers as well as for adults.

312   Dorris, Michael. ***The Broken Cord: A Family's Ongoing Struggle with Fetal Alcohol Syndrome.*** HarperCollins 1989, HB $18.95 (0-06-016071-3); 1990, P $8.95 (0-06-091682-6). 300pp. Nonfiction.

In 1971, Dorris, then an assistant professor of anthropology, became one of the first single men to adopt a child. The boy he adopted, Adam, was a 3-year-old Native American whose mother had died of acute alcohol poisoning. Over the next few years, Adam fell further behind his peers developmentally and suffered his first epileptic seizures, but Dorris refused to acknowledge anything was wrong; he attributed the teachers' observations to prejudice against Native Americans. Only gradually did he realize the extent of Adam's disabilities and their connection to his biological mother's abuse of alcohol during pregnancy.

After reading the growing body of research on fetal alcohol syndrome (FAS), Dorris embarked upon an investigation of the problem on Indian reservations. Its prevalence appalled him. With their judgment and intellectual capacity impaired, Native American adolescents were repeating the cycle of excessive drinking and promiscuity, with the result of nothing less than the potential decimation of the Native American people.

Dorris draws a compelling portrait of Adam, a developmentally disabled youngster who will never understand the depth of his father's love for him. Teenage readers will come to understand that alcohol abuse is not a "victimless crime." In his frustration and anger, Dorris raises many provocative questions. Should pregnant women be incarcerated to protect their fetus? Should FAS victims—perhaps themselves alcoholics or drug abusers already—be forcibly sterilized to prevent more suffering? Although alcoholism and FAS are not exclusive to Indian reservations, Dorris traces the origins of the problem as it concerns the tragic history of the Native American people. Although he does not hold out a great deal of hope, he does explore sources of strength—the naming ceremony for him and Adam on the Lakota reservation, where a close friend grew up; his marriage to another Native American author, Louise Erdrich; and the efforts of countless Native Americans to preserve their traditions and build a brighter future for new generations. This personal, eloquent, and thought-provoking work has much to say to teenagers of all backgrounds and will be long remembered by those who read it.   L.M-L.

313   Dorris, Michael. *A Yellow Raft in Blue Water.* Henry Holt 1987, HB $16.95 (0-8050-0045-3); Warner Books 1988, P $8.95 (0-446-38787-8). 343pp. Fiction.

A mother's and daughter's flight from Seattle to the Montana reservation where the mother grew up is told from the point of view of 15-year-old part-Indian, part-black Rayona; her mother, Christine; and Christine's "mother," who calls herself Aunt Ida and harbors a family secret. Christine's and Rayona's search for their roots is a painful process that involves confrontation with their past and with the people they have hurt. Unable to accept a situation she cannot control, Rayona runs away. Though she gains skills and self-confidence on her own, she returns to her family and eventually finds her place in the community. Christine, suffering from an alcoholism-related illness, gets a last chance at love with the best friend of her beloved younger brother, Lee, who was killed in Vietnam. Through her daughter and granddaughter, the disillusioned Aunt Ida has her family and her future returned to her, though she must first deal with the family's anger and rejection.

The obstacles facing Dorris's women characters are real and daunting, but their strength, love, and heritage help them to triumph in a way that is believable and moving. The novel is rich in the symbols of Native American tradition—the elements of nature and the three strands of braiding that join past, present, and future. While most of the novel is told from the adult point of view, Rayona's spunk and her complex heritage and family situation will appeal to young adult readers as well. Dorris is honest in presenting the problems of contemporary Native Americans, such as alcoholism, the loss of the ancient traditions, and the difficulties of living in two worlds. Yet there is much room for hope in this female-centered world where one can move ahead only by looking squarely at a painful past.

314   Erdoes, Richard, and Alfonso Ortiz, eds. *American Indian Myths and Legends.* Pantheon 1985, P $12.95 (0-394-74018-1). 527pp. Nonfiction.

One hundred sixty-six legends are included in this volume. According to Erdoes, these legends typify the Native American concept of "the communal nature of the universe." The book includes creation myths, legends about the end of the world, and everything in the human experience between the two.

These legends are told for children and adults. They are often links in a chain of stories delving into a tribe's history and mythology. The latter are divided by theme and reveal common elements of stories from geographically diverse tribes.

The appendix describes each tribe whose folklore is represented in this volume. The folklore included is about one third collected and retold by the editors over the past 25 years. One third are classic myths told here in their original form, and one third from nineteenth-century sources but retold by the authors. This volume steeps the reader in the Indian concepts of power in nature and the interdependence and continuity of life. Older high school students will find this volume most useful for supplemental reading and research projects, but teachers of younger students may adapt parts of it for storytelling or background information.

315   Erdrich, Louise. *Tracks.* Henry Holt 1988, HB $18.95 (0-8050-0895-0); HarperCollins 1989, P $8.95 (0-06-097245-9). 226pp. Fiction.

The author is herself of Ojibwa Indian origin and grew up in North Dakota. This book is the first, chronologically (though most recently published), of three books that include *Love Medicine* (Henry Holt, 1984) and *The Beet Queen* (Henry Holt, 1986). Erdrich's saga of modern life on the reservation and in the city begins with the intergenerational story of Native American women. The scene is set in the book *Tracks*, when a great plague wipes out many Native American groups at the end of the nineteenth century. Indian women are brutalized by their circumstances and by their proximity to white culture that sets them apart and treats them as less than human; nonetheless, their self-sufficiency and resiliency ennoble these women and make them a metaphor for Native American and human survival. Mature teenagers will appreciate this elegantly written and powerful trilogy by one of the foremost authors in the United States.

316   Gifford, Barry, ed. *Selected Writings of Edward S. Curtis.* 3rd ed. Illus. with photographs by Edward S. Curtis. Creative Arts 1976, P $6.95 (0-916870-00-6). 192pp. Nonfiction.

This volume consists of excerpts from Curtis's voluminous records of Native American culture and mythology. The first section contains ten myths collected and transcribed during Curtis's 30 years of extensive fieldwork among the Native American tribes. Curtis's research for his 20-volume work contained information on 80 tribes and included 40,000 photographs. Fifteen hundred of these prints were included in his original work. This massive undertaking was necessary, because, by 1930, when the project ended, Native American culture had been virtually wiped out. This collection of excerpts includes a commentary on the origins of each myth.

Section Two includes detailed descriptions of two ceremonies—the Navaho Night Chant and the Arikara Sun Dance—and their significance in Native American culture. Other sections describe the rites of Native American religious sects, the arts, warfare, and social customs, as well as offer historical information and biographical sketches of various individuals.

Appendixes include notes on Indian music, the vocabulary of the western Algonquin language, and a tribal summary. The book's illustrations are photographs taken by Curtis in the field. They are sepia toned and reveal a great sense of artistic composition. Individual and tribal characteristics are revealed in these portraits of Native Americans and Native American life. Although Curtis was not a trained anthropologist, his love for Native American cultures and his diligence in presenting an accurate portrait of these cultures are apparent in these excerpts from his original works, which are now housed in museum collections. Gifford captures the essence, if not the entirety, of Curtis's work, which is a loving portrait of cultures that have become extinct.

317   Hillerman, Tony. *Coyote Waits.* HarperCollins 1990, HB $19.95 (0-06-016370-4). 292pp. Fiction.

Jim Chee, Navajo and detective for the local constabulary, uses his survival skills and knowledge of Native American culture to solve the mystery of the murder of an alcoholic loner on the reservation. The middle-aged detective employs local lore and Navajo traditional beliefs and superstitions in solving the crime.

Tony Hillerman's best-selling mysteries featuring detective Jim Chee are set in the heart of Navajo country—the New Mexico reservation. He weaves the colors and textures of Native American life in its natural terrain. His characters are a blend of traditional Navajo and modern cop, detective, waitress, and drifter.

Hillerman captures the spirit of the Southwest, evoking place and nature in every chapter. The traditions and perspectives of the Navajo culture permeate every action, every thought of each character. Yet, the characters are remarkably familiar to us. Their traditional concerns of clan affiliation and loyalty blend with the universal concerns of every contemporary individual's desire to comprehend the social and cultural environment. Some of Hillerman's novels are scheduled to appear as major motion pictures.

Katz, William Loren. *Black Indians: A Hidden Heritage.*
See entry 303, Grades 7–9.

318   Kroeber, Theodora. *Ishi in Two Worlds: A Biography of the Last Wild Indian in North America.* Illus. with photos. Univ. of California Pr. 1976, HB $25.00 (0-520-03152-0); P $11.95 (0-520-03153-9). 242pp. Nonfiction.

Kroeber's husband, anthropologist Alfred Kroeber, "discovered" Ishi after he emerged from the wilderness in California in 1911. He was taken to San Francisco by another anthropologist, T. T. Waterman, where he lived at the University of California's Museum of Anthropology. A simplified version of this book written by Kroeber was published under the title, *Ishi, Last of His Tribe* by Parnassus Press in 1964. That version, which is suitable for older elementary and middle school readers, has been re-released in a Dell paperback edition.

The tragic story of the demise of California's Native American population is told through Ishi's personal story of survival after his family was killed by whites. Only seven Yahi Indians survived the attack; one by one the others perished while hiding in the moutains. The photos of Ishi reenacting the traditional skills of his people for anthropologists are fascinating. They reveal a scene that is at once touching—the last years of a culture and the last effort of an individual to pass on his culture—and also ennobling. They show a courageous individual who endured the loss of his people and of his family, and finally his culture and life, but a man who maintained his independence and dignity during his lonely ordeal, which lasted some forty years.

The story is told with objectivity; Kroeber resists the temptation toward sentimentality. The photos are stunning and unequaled for their revelations. The book stands as a classic in popularizing the cultural anthropology of the Native Americans. Its message of cultural extinction is prophetic but must be tempered with the many contemporary accounts of the preservation and resurgence of Native American cultures.

319   Merton, Thom. *Ishi Means Man: Essays on Native Americans.* Illus. by Rita Corbin. Unicorn Pr. 1976, HB $17.50 (0-87775-100-5); P $6.95 (0-87775-074-2). 71pp. Nonfiction.

This is a collection of essays written by Thomas Merton, Trappist monk and scholar. Part One of the book deals with the history of white interaction with the Indians of North America. The essay documents sources describing the history of Native American mistreatment at the hands of the U.S. government. Merton presents his position on the morality of attitudes that other cultures are inferior. He asks us to examine the facts—the genocide of Native American groups at the hands of white political policy and military actions taken against Native Americans in the nineteenth century. He argues that myths of largesse toward Native Americans are self-serving and self-deceptive.

Merton examines the white collective conscience and actions as well as the Native American reaction to the encroachment of white rule and culture. He puts each group's motives and actions in perspective. The image we have of Native Americans is largely a white invention, beginning in the European imagination as the image of the noble savage.

This book can be used in the classroom with young adults to examine attitudes about other cultures, as well as the prejudices we all have but do not often acknowledge. In addition, Merton can be discussed in the context of religious and moral beliefs as they relate to cultural tolerance.

320   Nabokov, Peter, ed. *Native American Testimony: An Anthology of Indian and White Relations.* Illus. with photos. HarperCollins 1979, P $7.95 (0-06-131993-7). 242pp. Nonfiction.

This well-researched work supplies a dimension hitherto missing in the American history one learns in school. The conflict between traditional peoples and white culture is presented here through the type of primary sources that are so often absent from the history that students are taught. These sources represent history from the minority or losing point of view, and they provide an authenticity that only primary-source documents can claim.

The documents composing this volume are first-person accounts of those who witnessed and took part in political, military, and personal conflicts between Native Americans and the U.S. government. The impact made on individuals and cultures as a whole is often dramatic and powerful, as are these accounts by Native Americans from a variety of backgrounds and perspectives. In human terms, the conflict between Native Americans and whites has been devastating not only to the traditional culture but also to the individuals within it. These personal accounts and testimonies by Native Americans make readers aware of the suffering involved when a race and a culture are driven nearly to extinction. The pain of separation from one's family, the forced march hundreds of miles to a new reservation far from all that is sacred and familiar in the culture, and the horror of watching relatives and friends drop due to starvation and exposure along the way personalize the Cherokee experience known as the Trail of Tears. Other moments in history are represented with equal power and poignance in a work that is indispensable to the high school American history curriculum.

321   Thornton, Russell. *American Indian Holocaust and Survival: A Population History Since 1492.* Illus. with photos and maps. Univ. of Oklahoma Pr. 1987, HB $29.95 (0-8061-2074-6). 352pp. Nonfiction.

Russell Thornton is a sociologist who has studied Native American population decline and growth. The first part of this book deals with the origins of Native American peoples, who migrated across the Beringian land bridge between Asia and North America. The author also discusses the reasons for the decline of native populations—disease, alcoholism, wars, and other causes. After the population studies, the most interesting portion of the book contains Thornton's accounts of various Native American ceremonies, their content, and their function in Native American culture. Among these ceremonies is the Ghost Dance. The use of dance and song as well as the function of these religious ceremonies is described.

The uniqueness of Thornton's book lies in his description of the resurgence of Native American populations in the twentieth century. Why and how did these cultural groups survive when every aspect of society worked against the continuation of traditional Indian life? This book will appeal to teenagers because of its detail, theories, and discussions that help to unravel the mystery of Native American cultural survival. Includes index and bibliography.

5

CANADA

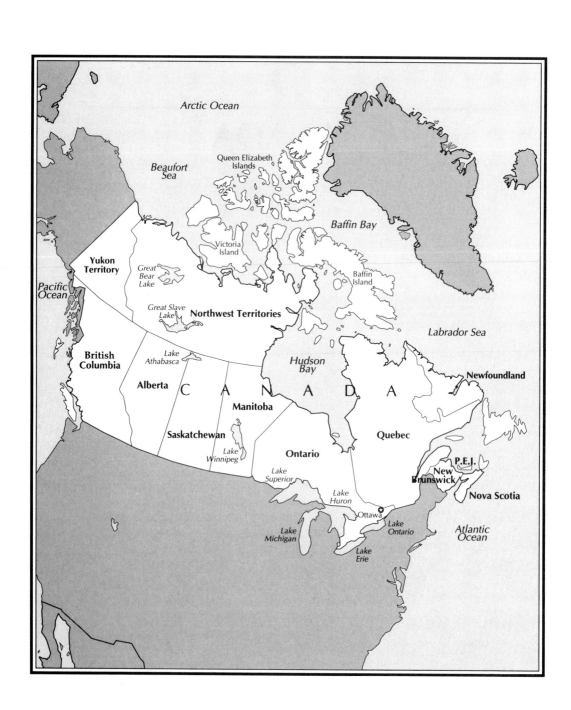

5

CANADA

by Joan McGrath

In order to understand the complexity of the Canadian mosaic, of which Canadian children's literature is but a tiny, though integral, part, some background is required.

More so even than in the United States, which is the nearest and most culturally influential of Canada's neighbors, in Canada, the ethnic and cultural differences among people are consciously maintained rather than amalgamated as in the renowned American "melting pot."

This is not to say that there is no consciousness of a distinctive "Canadian" identity, even though in the troubled 1990s such an identity may best be symbolized by a giant question mark. That identity, whatever it may be, tends to remain hyphenated, as in Italian-Canadian, Ukrainian-Canadian, or, in the case of indigenous peoples, the double-barreled Native Canadian.

The oral tradition of storytelling by Native Canadians, of recent years often captured in print to prevent its being lost or completely distorted, is the oldest "literature" of the continent. Currently the retelling of Native Canadian legendry is a source of much unhappiness and discord, as a rising tide of Native Canadian opinion contends that only those persons within a culture should write of that culture and that all other usage amounts to a form of theft. This is a thorny question that will arise to confront storytellers, anthologists, and collectors in the years to come, in the case not only of Native Canadian stories but also of writings dealing with any ethnic or cultural group of which the writer is not a member.

In this connection, the titles selected here exemplify both the fine quality of work available and the controversial aspects of even the very best of such literature.

For example, Jan Hudson's *Sweetgrass*, an award-winning and much acclaimed novel that imaginatively re-creates the social and personal turmoil of the contact era from the perspective of a young Blood woman, was written by a non–Native Canadian of enormous talent and has been criticized in some reviews for that reason. *The Enchanted Caribou*, a legend retold, was illustrated by Elizabeth Cleaver, herself a legend in Canadian illustration. Both of these

189

works were received with the highest of praise. Only the ancestry of the author and the illustrator has since been held, by some protesters, to be at issue.

Increasingly, Native Canadian writers, illustrators, and storytellers are emerging as very strong talents, and titles such as *April Raintree* by Beatrice Culleton and *Baseball Bats for Christmas* by Michael Arvaarluk Kusugak, as well as the artistry of Roy Henry Vickers in *The Elders Are Watching*, to name only a few, give evidence of the strong and distinctive styles that are now finding their place in both print and the oral tradition.

Certainly the last word has yet to be said in an argument that attempts to establish some form of ownership of Native Canadian and other stories and of the hard-to-define line that divides creative liberty from license.

Canada has often been called, even by its own citizens, "the unknown country." Vast, and to a large extent barren and uninhabitable, Canada stretches from the Atlantic Ocean to the Pacific and from the great undefended border with the United States in the south to the empty north, and few people have ever visited, far less come to understand, more than a tiny fraction of this enormous country.

The pattern of settlement in Canada resembles that of its mighty neighbor to the south, with the great difference that a hostile climate given to extremes of temperature proved less inviting to colonization, which did not proceed as rapidly as in the thirteen colonies.

The first peoples had already been living in Canada from time immemorial. To those native peoples, the interloping "explorers" and "discoverers" were an inexplicable phenomenon. How can that which is in full use be "discovered"? But the tide was flowing and could not be turned back. First in a trickle, then in torrents, the newcomers arrived. Shadowy visitors from Scandinavia, and the Viking settlers of lost Vineland, left little trace of their passing; but then came the French, to create Acadia and New France, and the burly adventurers from the British Isles and other European nations. The first newcomers were traders and prospectors, rootless men without women of their own races, looking for vast, fast profit, and not for new homes. Such men, inevitably, formed liaisons and then intermarried with the indigenous population, and the new Métis nation, the Burnt Wood people of mixed ancestry, was born, often with the birth pangs so movingly described in Brenda Bellingham's *Storm Child*.

The United Empire Loyalists, an influx of English-speaking colonists from the south, were men and women who could not pledge allegiance to the new United States. Leaving their homes and property in New York, New England, and other well-loved homesites, they flooded into Upper Canada, altering forever the English-French balance of the developing, divided country. As described in Robert Sutherland's novel *Son of the Hounds*, Canadians of British and Scottish ancestry fought against the United States in the War of 1812.

Ukrainian and Russian immigrants settled the great prairies, as is so evocatively described by William Kurelek in his *They Sought a New World*; Chinese laborers came by the thousands to build the railways that would in time bring about a united nation; and escaped slaves, fugitives from the cruel plantations of the American South, made their way via the Underground Railroad to freedom under the sign of the Drinking Gourd, the North Star. The young heroines of *Underground to Canada*, by Barbara Smucker, exemplify their courage and determination, and the youngster of today who models her life on that of Harriet Tubman, her heroine, in *Harriet's Daughter* by Marlene Nourbese Philip, demonstrates the lasting influence of these brave pioneers.

The great gold rushes of the Klondike brought yet another generation of get-rich-quickers, some of whom stayed to get rich, or not, including some, like the Chinese of *Tales from Gold Mountain*, who very seldom found the treasure they sought. The floodtide of European immigration at the turn of the century, spurred by upheavals and pogroms in Eastern Europe, brought hopeful, brave, and resolute newcomers to begin new lives, like the gallant child and elderly grandmother portrayed in Constance Horne's *Nykola and Granny*.

The most recent waves of immigration have emanated from Hong Kong, from the Caribbean Islands, from the Indian subcontinent, from Africa, and from South America. These people come as immigrants have always come—to make a better life for themselves and to provide a future for their children. It is not always easy, and such works as Nazneen Sadiq's *Camels Can Make You Homesick* and Jim Henegan's *Promises to Come* bear witness.

In those early days there was little time, or indeed incentive, to sit with quill in hand in a rough-hewn log cabin. Some few precious diaries were kept, a few books and letters written, but a great part of the population in early days was illiterate, and education was minimal. As in any more-or-less preliterate country, stories passed orally from one generation to the next, preserving the riches of ethnic and cultural tradition. These stories have been updated, with modern themes added, in *A Promise Is a Promise, The Enchanted Caribou*, and *The Elders Are Watching*.

The telling of stories continues to this day, but storytellers, literate now, address a vast and far-flung audience unimaginable to the storytelling grandparents of old. Each adds his or her contribution to the Canadian mosaic of work created with Canadian (though not *only* Canadian) children in mind.

It has been an uphill battle for Canadian writers, illustrators, and publishers. Canada is sandwiched, figuratively speaking, between two friendly giants—the United States and Great Britain—both of them producing wonderful children's books in vast quantities, from long-established children's publishing houses, in the language of choice of most Canadian book buyers.

In spite of the odds, Canadian publishing houses have flourished in recent years. Specialty houses include both Annick and Kids Can Press, for children's books; Tundra, which consistently publishes magnificent picture books for both children and adults; Women's Press and Second Story, for feminist work and some children's titles; Western Producer Prairie Books, which showcases western writers; Pemmican Publications, for Native Canadian and Métis work; and Lorimer, which has demonstrated a particular concern for providing multicultural titles dealing with the New Canadian experience. Raincoast and Groundwood have produced handsome children's titles, and firms such as the now defunct Lester and Orpen Dennys developed a prestigious children's book list. Many smaller specialty presses are flourishing, and even though their output tends to be limited, it is often of very high quality and offers new talent an entry into the publishing world.

The game has been worth the candle. Canadians do care about their culture and about its enormous, tangled root system, which gives it a flavor and richness unmatchable by any monolithic culture. There is a burgeoning interest and support for Canadian materials for children and young people that is heartening for those who feel that the development and maintenance of a strong national identity are more important the more complex and difficult the tasks become.

Various nonfiction series have dealt with the subject of Canada over the years, without notable success. The vastness of the country and the complexity of the relationships between provinces and peoples and between the provincial and federal governments make blanket, overall statements of any kind suspect and liable to inaccuracy.

In the main, the various series have been graced with sensational photographs attached to mediocre, uninspired text. Some examples of series are the Canadian Rainbow series from Silver Burdett, which is very colorful and attractive in appearance, but superficial and textbookish, tacking broad and rather pointless questions to nearly every illustration. For first to third graders, who may just possibly not mind the condescending tone, *Canada Is My Country*, from Wayland's My Country series, introduces 26 people from different parts of the country and allows them to describe their various lives and careers. There is lots of color photography and minimal narrative to interest second to fourth graders. Wayland's Countries of the World series title *Canada* is rather more senior, for approximately grades 5 through 8. It introduces Canada to non-Canadians, in a bright, colorful, superficial look at a vast country. Not much can be said in the confines of 48 lavishly illustrated pages.

The McGraw-Hill Ryerson The Canada Series, consisting of 12 titles, provides a general overview in one of its volumes. The 11 other titles each deal with one of the provinces or territories. It was very highly regarded in the late 1970s, when it was published, but it has not been revised since. It is still readable, though less colorful than some other series; even the photography has a dated appearance. It is of interest for grades 5–9. The Enchantment of the World series, from Childrens Press (1987), is a valiant attempt to organize and present a massive subject in a relatively brief space, and the result quite naturally tends toward superficiality. It is, however, bright, readable, and crowded with brilliant color photograhy. It is most useful for the upper elementary and junior high levels.

The following list of annotations is idiosyncratic: They were chosen from among many likely titles because they are works that are related to the topic and that have proven popular both in Canada and, in some cases, abroad. They are works of high quality, accurately reflecting some particular facet of a multicultural society and its history, well written, and, in some cases, handsomely illustrated.

These are by no means the only titles that might have been selected, but they are a personal selection of work that has spoken to at least one reader and left an abiding impression. They reflect only one of Canada's two official languages; a list of equally valuable work in French could no doubt be created by someone qualified to do so.

Strength in diversity is a motto to live by. The bibliography of multiculturally thematic titles selected here symbolizes both qualities.

PRESCHOOL–GRADE 3

322   Andrews, Jan. *Very Last First Time.* Originally published in Canada by Groundwood/Douglas & McIntyre, 1985. Illus. by Ian Wallace. Macmillan 1986, HB $12.95 (0-689-50388-1). 32pp. Fiction.

Eva Padlyat lives in a village on Ungava Bay, in the north of Canada. This is a part of the world few outsiders ever visit, and many people think of Inuit country as a land of continual winter—snowy, barren, and empty. To Eva it is home, and she loves it. Her house is much like houses anywhere in North America, with running water, electricity, and all the usual conveniences, but some things are very different here from anywhere else in the world: like walking on the bottom of the sea.

When the ice has frozen into a crust, Eva and her mother climb beneath the protective roof of ice to gather mussels from the bottom of the sea. Today, however, is different. Today, for the very first time, Eva is going alone into the ice hole.

Lighting the candles she has brought with her, she fills her mussel pan; then she explores the dark cave. For a terrible moment, when her candle flickers out, she is lost in the dark undersea cavern. Quickly she finds another candle and makes her way back to safety.

The adventure is over. Eva will go alone to the bottom of the sea many more times in her life, but this has been the very last first time.

The fascination of participating, even vicariously, in an experience wholly unlike any other, and the rich, velvety, predominantly purple plates that portray this so-different world, give this lovely picture story a place in introductory studies of life in the furthest habitable Northlands.

---

323 Blades, Ann. *Mary of Mile 18.* Illus. by the author. Tundra 1971, HB $11.95 (0-88776-015-5); 1984, P $7.95 (0-88776-059-7). 40pp. Fiction.

Mary Fehr, a Mennonite youngster, lives in a tiny settlement, not large enough to be a village, in the north-central part of British Columbia in the mid 1950s. Hers is a life that would seem comfortless to most people. She and her family live in a log cabin without indoor plumbing or electricity, where a small wood stove heats the cramped living quarters, and where buckets and buckets of powdery snow must be laboriously gathered and melted before mother can do the family wash—by hand.

Nothing comes easily to the Fehr family, including outspoken affection, although affection is certainly there in abundance. Mary does not complain about her harsh environment. She takes hard work at an early age for granted, even though her lot will be harder still when soon now her mother will have a new baby to tend, and Mary will have to help even more.

All she asks is that she be allowed to keep as her very own pet the wolf pup she has found in the woods. Stern father says "No!" Any animals on the Fehr homestead must work, as the people do. There is no room in this stripped-bare life for idle mouths that must be fed. The pup must go back to the forest.

Sadly the child obeys. Unwilling even to eat her favorite supper of moose steak, she goes to bed. In the deep of night, there is a terrible uproar just outside the cabin. A coyote has come to raid the chicken house and might have killed all the precious chickens if he had not been frightened off by Mary's beloved wolf pup, which has found its way back to her doorstep.

Stern Mr. Fehr has the excuse he needs in order to relent and to grant Mary her dearest wish. The cub has proven his usefulness and may stay.

Ann Blades's spare storytelling and her glowing, deceptively simple pictures of a way of life she knows very well indeed have made this lovely picture book a true Canadian classic for small children. Better than most stories for the very young, it conveys both vastness and isolation, as well as the family warmth and self-sufficiency of the Fehr family.

324 Cleaver, Elizabeth. *The Enchanted Caribou.* Illus. by the author. Oxford Univ. Pr. 1985, HB $8.95 (0-19-540492-0). 32pp. Nonfiction.

Retold with stark simplicity, the legend of the white caribou is a story of young lovers parted and magically reunited. A wicked shaman transforms Tyya, the lovely heroine, into a white caribou. In a dream, Etosack, the caribou hunter and Tyya's lover, is given a charm that will restore his beloved. Ever since that day, Inuit hunters always spare a white caribou, for perhaps it too may be an enchanted human being.

The black-and-white illustrations, by famed artist Elizabeth Cleaver, provide the book's chief charm. Their cloudy silhouettes suggest much more than they actually depict.

The author/illustrator recognized the story's wonderful potential for shadow play, a universal art form favored by storytellers. In an afterword she provides patterns for the necessary shadow figures, both human and caribou, with instructions for the shadow theater in which they might perform.

Although currently there is some opposition to the interpretation of Native Canadian legendry by persons from outside the culture, the stark simplicity and archetypal theme of this story, as well as the author's adherence to the traditional form, transcend those objections.

Fujiwara, Alan. *Baachan! Geechan! Arigato: A Story of Japanese Canadians.*
See entry 338, Grades 4–6.

Harrison, Ted. *Children of the Yukon.*
See entry 340, Grades 4–6.

325 Hearn, Emily. *Good Morning Franny.* Illus. by Mark Thurman. Women's Pr. 1984. 32pp. Fiction. o.p.

Franny is a bright-eyed, attractive little girl who is so full of energy that she has to be extra careful not to bowl people over when they get in her way. Several pages into the picture story, the reader discovers that spirited little Franny is a wheelchair child.

One day Franny meets a shy but friendly Chinese child who speaks little English, although she can just manage to say "Good morning." But smiling and pointing can accomplish quite a lot in the way of introductions, and Franny learns her new friend is named Ting Kim, and she enjoys a wheelchair ride on Franny's lap.

Once they have become acquainted, the two meet often and greatly enjoy one another's company, with Franny helping Ting to learn English. Soon she can say "Good night Franny" and is very pleased with herself.

When Franny has to go to the hospital for her regular tests, she is not so sure that Ting has understood, so she is particularly eager to see her friend again once the tests are over. What a shock! The Kim family's little shop is empty. They are gone. Franny is disconsolate.

But Ting has not forgotten her friend. Franny discovers a two-sided message from Ting at the entrance to the park where they have so often played together. As she enters, it says "Good Morning Franny"; as she leaves, she sees "Good Night Franny." Friends may be parted, but friendship lasts.

The minimal text conveys a touching story. The quality of both writing and illustration is excellent. Franny is a multidimensional character, and the presentation is as ethnically accurate as it can be in a few lines of text. Since the publication of this book, Franny has appeared as the protagonist in two other stories by Hearn.

326   Kusugak, Michael Arvaarluk. *Baseball Bats for Christmas.* Illus. by Vladyana Krykorka. Annick 1990, P $5.95 (1-55037-144-4). 24pp. Nonfiction.

Baseball Bats for Christmas is a true tale of a boyhood spent in Repulse Bay on the Arctic Circle—*right* on the circle, as a brass plate affixed to a rock attests.

The unfamiliarity of trees this far north led to the central event of this story. One Christmas season in the 1950s, the all-important supply plane brought among other things six unfamiliar objects, which the pilot, who spoke only English, could not explain. There were green and had spindly branches all over. The puzzled children, who had never heard of a Christmas tree, wondered what they were and why they had been sent. One boy had seen a picture of such an object in a book at the church; it was called a "standing-up," he explained.

After the traditional gift giving and celebrations of Christmas, the standing-ups were still lying about, neglected. What to do with them? Then one of the boys was inspired. The youngsters had balls to play with, but in this treeless land there were few bats. The standing-ups, with all their branches lopped off, made splendid bats! The children could hardly wait for next Christmas to bring them more standing-ups to be made into baseball bats without a moment's delay.

This peep into a world so unfamiliar and extraordinary, except to those for whom it is home, is proof positive, if it were needed, that kids are a lot alike the world over. The glowing illustrations as well as the story bring warmth and color to one of the chilliest, but friendliest, places on earth.

327   Moak, Allan. *A Big City ABC.* Illus. by the author. Tundra 1984, HB $14.95 (0-88776-161-5); P $6.95 (0-88776-238-7). 32pp. Nonfiction.

Bold, bright, and beautiful, this action alphabet book introduces one of Canada's great cities, Toronto, Ontario, and the kaleidoscopic nature of its citizenry.

For each letter of the alphabet there is a brilliant, full-color illustration of some familiar Toronto scenes; for example, "c" is for castle, Toronto's fairytale pile built by an eccentric millionaire, and at the other end of the scale, "j" is for junk store. That's right—not antiques—junk.

Many of the scenes are illustrative of the multiethnic nature of Canada's cities: the open market, which used to be mainly Jewish but is now largely Portuguese, with a smattering of West Indian shops; the fireworks that are a particular feature of Chinatown; the New City Hall and its skating rink, designed by a Finnish architect; and the multicolored crowds on the Island Ferry, shopping at the Variety Store or building snow forts in a back lane.

All the places and activities illustrated will be of interest to young children, and all are full of busy little people working hard at having fun, beginning, appropriately enough, in an airport with multilingual direction signs, as an Air Canada flight is just leaving the ground.

This is an attractive introduction both to a child's-eye view of a particular large city and to the letters of the alphabet.

328   Munsch, Robert, and Michael Arvaarluk Kusugak. *A Promise Is a Promise.* Illus. by
Vladyana Krykorka. Annick 1988, HB $12.95 (1-55037-009-X); P $4.95 (1-55037-
008-1). 32pp. Fiction.

Little Allashua is in terrible trouble. Like all Inuit children, she has been warned
time and time again not to go fishing in the ocean. If she does so, her parents
have warned her, the Qallupilluq will surely catch her. Blithely she promises and
promptly forgets all about both the warning and her promise as she goes to fish
in the ocean.

Sure enough, the Qallupilluq do catch her. They are fearsome creatures,
something like trolls, wearing women's parkas made of loon feathers, and they
are certainly to be avoided. Bad little Allashua escapes from them by making yet
another promise. She assures the terrible monsters that she will bring her
brothers and sisters to the sea ice to be captured if only the Qallupilluq will let
her go!

They agree, and naughty Allashua returns home to tell her mother the
terrible thing she has done and the trouble in which she has involved her family.
She knows that Mother will know what to do to set everything right again. And
she does.

Briskly she announces, "A promise is a promise." If Allashua has promised to
bring the children, bring them she must, but clever Mother lures the Qallupilluq
away from the ocean and into a dance just at the crucial moment. If they are not
present to catch Allashua's brothers and sisters—well, that is not her fault. She
has kept her promise. All ends happily—except for the hungry Qallupilluq.

This happy collaboration between famous children's author Munsch and
Inuit storyteller Michael Kusugak has a fresh and exciting flavor. It brings to
southerners the bogeyman surely invented by Inuit parents to keep their ven-
turesome children safely away from the treacherous sea ice of Hudson Bay.

329   Murdock, Patricia. *Deep Thinker and the Stars.* Illus. by Kellie Jobson. Three Trees
Pr. 1987, HB $14.95 (0-88823-127-X); P $5.95 (0-88823-125-3). 24pp. Fiction.

The little girl has two names. She is "Sharon" for everyday and ordinary times,
but she is also Deep Thinker, her "special name" for special occasions, as is the
custom in her family.

Just now Deep Thinker's family is in a mild turmoil, for Mother is preparing
to fly out of the deep woods country to the nearest hospital, in time for the birth
of an expected and longed-for baby.

Grandmother shows Deep Thinker the cradleboard carved for her by Grandfather, which is now being made ready for the new baby. Together they remember that it was Grandfather who gave Sharon her "special name," and now he is
gone. He cannot name the new arrival.

The baby is a boy, a little brother. Deep Thinker lies awake far into the night,
looking up at the stars and remembering Grandfather's wise eyes, as bright and
twinkling as those very stars.

When Mother and the precious new baby are brought home, everyone
bustles about, preparing a great feast of moosemeat stew, bannock, and cakes. It
is a great day. A great day for Deep Thinker too, for, gazing into the baby's bright
eyes, she has thought of a way to make her dear grandfather a part of the
celebration.

The new baby's "special name" will keep Grandfather's memory alive, for,
just like Grandfather, he will be called the Boy with the Stars in His Eyes.

This simple and charming little story for very young readers carries a warm message about the customs that bind families and cultures together over the years. It is an authentic picture and a fine introduction to the customs and culture of Deep Thinker's people today, who are maintaining their traditions while living in modern times.

330   Poulin, Stéphane. **Ah! Belle Cité / A Beautiful City ABC.** Bilingual ed. (French/English). Illus. by the author. Tundra 1985, HB $14.95 (0-88776-175-5). 32pp. Nonfiction.

As the author says, "Nearly all the people of the world are represented here." Montreal is a most cosmopolitan city, yet at the same time, like all great cities, it is a cluster of neighborhoods. Here are the great monuments, but here also are the little shops, the quiet streets, the parks where small children, muffled against the bitter cold, can still pause to admire a patient horse. This is a child's-eye view of the city.

Montreal is a very French city, but there is room in it for a row of Chinese shops, an Italian grocery, and a yeshiva.

As the double title indicates, this is a double-alphabet book, in which the handsome paintings that accompany and illustrate each letter of the alphabet may have two different legends, as in Q q quai, quay, and L l lac, lake—one in French, the other in English. Sometimes the two languages coincide, as in G g garage; H h Halloween; and W w wigwam. Each separate painting in this lovely book is a conversation piece in itself.

331   Wallace, Ian. **Chin Chiang and the Dragon's Dance.** Published in Canada by Douglas & McIntyre, 1984. Illus. by the author. Macmillan 1984, LB $11.95 (0-689-31170-2). 32pp. Fiction.

Chin Chiang, a small boy who lives in Vancouver's Chinatown, has dreamed of the day when he will participate in the exciting Dragon's Dance on the first day of the Year of the Dragon. Now the time has come, and he is so frightened by the responsibility of it all that he wishes he could turn into a rabbit and scamper away. He cannot do the dance! He will surely stumble, fall, disgrace his family, cause ill fortune. Chin Chiang runs off to hide his misery in one of his favorite places of refuge, the public library.

On the library roof, where he has gone to hide, Chin Chiang unexpectedly finds the answer to his problem, in the person of the elderly cleaning lady, Pu Yee. When Chin Chiang confides in her, she heartens him by dancing with him, practicing the necessary steps, and thereby building his confidence.

When at last Chin Chiang takes his place under the dragon framework, he finds to his delight not only that he can do the Dragon's Dance, but also that he loves every minute of it. At last the celebration is over. Lonely old Pu Yee, invited to join the family as their guest, helps them to usher in a prosperous new Year of the Dragon.

The splendid plates for this book vividly convey Chin Chiang's mood, as illustrations of him pass from the subdued colors of gloom and uncertainty to the joyous blues and reds of festivity.

Authenticity of detail in the Dragon's Dance is doubtful; there seems to be some confusion between the true Dragon's Dance, in which many people must support the dragon's body, and the Lion's Dance, which may be performed by only two people, but the infectious spirit of celebration and joy, as well as the evocation of sympathy and friendship across the generations, gives a generous salute to the Chinese-Canadian community.

332   Wallace, Ian, and Angela Wood. **The Sandwich.** Rev. ed. Illus. by the authors. Kids Can Pr. 1975, P $4.95 (0-919964-02-8). 48pp. Fiction.

Small children in grade school find it desperately hard to be in any way "different." They are happiest when they are completely indistinguishable from the herd, as much like their friends as it is humanly possible to be.

Therefore, second grader Vincenzo Ferrante is unhappy. His grandmother, who looks after him, is ill, and he must take his lunch to school and eat with the other children who cannot go home for the noon break. But whereas they all have the "proper" things to eat, that is, peanut butter and jam on tasteless, sliced white bread, Vincenzo has his favorite, mortadella and provolone on fresh Italian bread. When he opens his lunch bag, the other children hold their noses. "Vincenzo eats stinky meat!" rings out through the cafeteria. The other kids do not appreciate good Italian food.

Vincenzo cannot eat a bite, and he takes his shameful, untouched lunch home to his papa, who, fortunately, understands. He will buy peanut butter and jam if that is what Vincenzo really wants, but he reminds his son, "Always remember—you are who you are, and you have nothing to be ashamed of."

Vincenzo takes another "stinky meat" sandwich to school the next day and calmly ignores the rude remarks. Before long, everybody at the cafeteria is trying a bite and discovering that "it's not bad!" Soon there is only one small bite left for Vincenzo, and there will not be any more rude remarks.

This primary title with its admirable message of respect for customs, behavior, and, yes, food that may not be familiar but may indeed taste even better than one's own has proven enduringly popular with the younger set. A serious message is delivered in terms small children can understand, and the usual response has been a demand to try out a delicious "stinky meat" sandwich just like Vincenzo's.

333   Weber-Pillwax, Cora. **Billy's World.** Illus. by Matt Gould. Reidmore Books 1989. 24pp. Fiction. o.p.

A small boy stands on a lonely hill amid the swirling snow, watching the skidoos on the lake where Uncle James is ice fishing with two friends. Everyone else in the family is busy. Dad is working on the new community center; Mom is shopping; his brother and sister are not there to play with him. Billy decides to visit Granny. He has a job to do there, hauling wood for Granny's old wood stove. Her place is not like home, where Mom has an electric range.

On Friday afternoon Billy and Grampa load the skidoo onto the truck and head for the trapline. They pack all the things they will need for the weekend; Granny packs food for them. The two are very contented together, very much at peace. This gentle picture of a young boy's family life, that in its small compass bridges the traditional ways of his grandparents and the modern life-style of his parents, will ring true with children who make similar adjustments with perfect ease and comfort.

334 Wheeler, Bernelda. *Where Did You Get Your Moccasins?* Illus. by Herman Bekkering. Pemmican Publications 1986, P $5.95 (0-919143-15-6). 26pp. Fiction.

Kindergarten children arriving at their school admire Jody's handsome new moccasins. He explains that his kookum made them for him, and this prompts the other children to ask, "Who is your kookum?"

Jody explains that she is his grandmother. The questions and answers continue: How did she make the moccasins? Where does the leather come from? How did Kookum make the leather? What is deer hide? And so on, all the way to the beautiful decorative beadwork. Kookum got the beads . . . from the store.

The story admirably captures the spirit of friendly inquiry within the multiethnic group of small children who people little Jody's school world. They in their turn will no doubt share stories and arts and crafts that are commonplace in their own home, but are as novel and interesting to the other children as Jody's moccasins are to them. The openness and receptivity of small children is one of their chief charms, and this simple tale, illustrated with generous line drawings, does a fine job of capturing that spirit.

GRADES 4-6

335 Bouchard, Dave. *The Elders Are Watching.* Illus. by Roy Henry Vickers. Eagle Dancer/Raincoast Books 1990, P $14.95 (0-9693485-3-3). 56pp. Fiction.

This lovely book is dedicated to revival, culture, heritage, and environment—all those concepts that responsible people agree must be instilled in today's children, who will be faced with repairing and restoring the damaged heritage left by those who have gone before.

The story line of *The Elders Are Watching* is baldly simple: a young boy is sent to spend some time with his "Ya-A" (grandfather) "to listen, to think and to learn."

Ya-A tells him of the Old Ones—the Elders—they who are still with us, unseen—watching, observing, sorrowing. They are there in the seashore, the night sky, and the ravaged forest.

The message of the Elders is one of warning. The land and all its creatures have not been respected by mankind. Even the great waters are poisoned. The Elders are angry that their trust in those who would follow them has been betrayed. Over and over, in blank verse, the warning note is sounded, almost like a chant or incantation.

The text is simple and repetitive, but the 24 full-page illustrations are outstanding. Large and gorgeously colored, they convey both the beauty of the West Coast, past and present, and the dismay of the Elders as they watch beauty destroyed. Themes and motifs of West Coast Indian art prevail, to stunning effect. The message is thus conveyed most effectively through the visual dimension in a work that will appeal to readers of all ages.

336 Brébeuf, Jean de. *The Huron Carol.* English words by J. E. Middleton, 1926. Illus. by Frances Tyrrell. Lester & Orpen Dennys 1990, HB $15.95 (0-88619-280-3). 32pp. Nonfiction.

One of the best loved of all Canadian Christmas carols is also one of the oldest. *The Huron Carol* was written by Father Jean de Brébeuf, who before his martyrdom in an Iroquoian raid in 1649 was for 22 years a missionary to the Huron nation at Fort Ste. Marie (where Midland, Ontario, now stands). He was unusual for his time in his awareness of and respect for Native Canadian beliefs and spirituality, which he amalgamated into his teaching of Christianity.

He composed his lovely story of Christ's nativity in terms the Hurons could understand and with which they could identify: the blessed infant lies in a lodge of broken bark, swaddled in a ragged robe of rabbit skin; the traditional three kings who come bearing gifts are transformed into three great chiefs from far away; and contemporary artist Frances Tyrrell has preserved the authenticity of the Native Canadian setting so valued by Father Brébeuf.

The delicately colored pen-and-ink drawings are intricately detailed, and the most minute-seeming decoration is a part of the grand design. The constellations in the winter sky, for example, are those that would have been visible in December 1648; the three chiefs from far away are clad in the robes appropriate to great men of the Pacific Kootenay, the Sioux of the Plains, and the Shawnee of the Woodlands.

Only a little of the original Huron language version has survived the years, and the two verses of eighteenth-century French are quite unlike the French spoken today. The text of the present version, in English, was written in 1926 by J. E. Middleton and has taken its place among the Christmas classics.

The present exquisite version will enhance any collection of Christmas books and is a reminder of the building of cultural bridges that had already begun more than 300 years ago.

Canadian Childhoods: A Tundra Anthology.
See entry 354, Grades 7–9.

Cleaver, Elizabeth. *The Enchanted Caribou.*
See entry 324, Grades PS–3.

Downie, Mary Alice, and Barabara Robertson, comps. *The New Wind Has Wings: Poems from Canada.*
See entry 356, Grades 7–9.

337 Ellis, Sarah. *Next-Door Neighbors.* Macmillan 1990, LB $11.95 (0-689-50495-0). 154pp. Fiction.

Sixth grader Peggy, the shy one of the family, has difficulty adjusting to her family's move to Vancouver in 1957. She shuns her neighbor George's eager overtures of friendship because she does not want to be associated with a "loser" and suffers the consequences of an uncharacteristic and boasting lie at school. She and George eventually collaborate on producing a winning puppet show with the help of Sing, the mistreated Chinese servant of neighbor Mrs. Manning. Mrs. Manning's disdain for her "houseboy" is galling and smacks of the highest order of prejudice imaginable. Ellis skillfully interweaves themes relevant to interpersonal relationships—lying, shyness, spiteful prejudice, tolerance, and bullying—into her novel for upper elementary and older readers. There is rich material for thought and discussion here, and it is never belabored by the author. The issue of tolerance of other cultures is explored particularly well in the children's relationship with Sing and his tyrannical "owner." The characters are clearly drawn and believable, and the lessons of history gleaned from a reading of this novel may encourage the reader to explore further this unpleasant era in North American history.   C.V.S.

338   Fujiwara, Alan. ***Baachan! Geechan! Arigato: A Story of Japanese Canadians.*** Illus. by Tom McNeely. Momiji 1989. 32pp. Fiction. o.p.

Following the Japanese attack on Pearl Harbor in 1941, and amidst the hysteria of World War II, one of the most dismal events in Canadian history took place. Peaceful Japanese Canadians—men, women, and children alike—were taken from their West Coast homes and placed in internment camps in the British Columbia interior. There they remained for as long as four years—poorly housed, with no amenities, with inadequate educational facilities for the children, and with wives and families separated from husbands and fathers. Meanwhile, their own well-cared-for homes, fishing vessels, and other property were sold off by the government.

Years later, on September 22, 1988, the Japanese Canadian Redress Agreement was signed. Nothing could give back the lost and sorrowful years, but at least an admission of injustice had been made, and a promise given that no future Canadians would be so unjustly treated.

Baachan! Geechan! Arigato (*Grandmother! Grandfather! Thank You*) is a re-creation of those events, telling the story of Masao and Sumiko, who came as high-hearted young immigrants to make a new life in Canada. They and their three Canadian-born children were interned in an abandoned mining town in the interior, which had been hastily made into a detention camp. After the war, they were resettled; they had the choice of moving east of the Rockies or returning to Japan. They were Canadians. They remained in Canada.

Their story is salutary reading for youngsters who take their rights and freedoms for granted. The course of events is factual, told without rancor. Still, it is a bitter tale, though one with a happy ending. Sumiko, the storyteller, is now Baachan, the grandmother; Masao is Geechan, the grandfather. They have been vindicated by the government's public apology, payment of respect, and reparations. Looking at their happy Japanese-Canadian family of today, they conclude that, despite the deprivations, coming to Canada, and remaining after the war, were good decisions.

339   Garrigue, Sheila. ***The Eternal Spring of Mr. Ito.*** Bradbury Pr. 1985, LB $12.95 (0-02-737300-2). 163pp. Fiction.

After 18 months, war-torn England is a blurred memory for evacuee Sara Warren, who is living with her aunt and uncle in 1941 Vancouver. Far more real are the adventures with her fellow evacuees, Maggie and Ernie, and her special relationship with their Japanese-Canadian gardener, Mr. Ito. The devastating news of the Japanese bombing of Pearl Harbor brings the war close to home again. Cousin Mary's fiancé is killed by a Japanese raid on Hong Kong; Maggie and Ernie's mother is killed during an air raid in England; Mr. Ito's entire family is forcibly interned in an isolated Canadian mountain town; and Mr. Ito dies of self-imposed starvation and exposure. Through it all, Sara remains caring and courageous. She is not embittered by Uncle Duncan's anti-Japanese sentiments, but she manages to bring comfort to Mr. Ito's family by smuggling to them Mr. Ito's 200-year-old bonsai tree, a symbol of endurance and hope. This smuggling episode is a bit contrived, but the emotional impact far outweighs the slight weakness in plot. Garrigue truly brings to life the emotional impact of war. She writes with a clear understanding of differing viewpoints and differing cultures in a nonjudgmental way. Her characters suffer and grow, and in so doing they enrich readers' understanding of life. An important part of American and Canadian history has been described in this novel.   C.V.S.

340   Harrison, Ted. *Children of the Yukon.* Illus. by the author. Tundra 1977, P $6.95
        (0-88776-163-1). 24pp. Nonfiction.

After living and working all over the world, Ted Harrison finally settled in the Yukon, because there, he says, he found Shangri-la. Nowhere else had he found the stunning wild beauty and brilliant colors he longed to paint. Since that day in 1968, Harrison has become the acknowledged artist of the Yukon.

He is particularly interested in capturing the traditional ways of the unspoiled North before, as he fears, the future becomes decided not by the children of the Yukon but by people "far away in boardrooms and government offices, who may never even have seen this remarkable land."

The old ways will be preserved in Harrison's vivid paintings, if nowhere else. Here the Athabascan children observe Discovery Day, the anniversary of the discovery of gold in the Yukon in 1896 and the beginning of the gold rush; they pan for stray grains of gold in the washed-out gravel left by the gold rush miners; and they conduct snowshoe and dogsled races and go fishing and trapping with their fathers. They dance and sing to celebrate *Tauk ee tee see go*—the Joyous Summer Day—because people of northern countries value their short, precious summers.

Harrison's paintings are ablaze with all the colors of the northern lights, the sunrise and sunset brighter than anywhere else in the world. The people of the North live in a hard and demanding but beautiful homeland, which they love. It is fitting that its beauty should be shared with others by an artist who has adopted that region as his home.

341   Horne, Constance. *Nykola and Granny.* Illus. by Don Bescoe. Gage JeanPac 1989,
        P $4.95 (0-7715-7019-8). 169pp. Fiction.

Father, Mother, and his two sisters have gone to some strange, unimaginable place called Dauphin, Manitoba, in Canada, and 10-year-old Nykola is left behind with his Aunt Anna in the Ukraine. Father had already purchased the precious dated steamship tickets when Nykola became too ill to travel. No such thing as a refund was possible, and never again would Father have enough money to take his family to the New World. Now Nykola has recovered and longs to join his family, but he is trapped.

Uncle Feodor, husband of Mother's sister Anna, is a grasping, heartless man. He hides the money sent by Nykola's father to pay for the boy's passage. Nykola knows that his greedy uncle plans to keep him as a captive farmhand, but both nephew and uncle have failed to reckon with Feodor's mother-in-law, Nykola's redoubtable granny.

The valiant old woman, wise in the ways of the world, acquires their all-important passports through judicious bribery, then steals—or rather, reclaims—the money Feodor has hidden.

So begins the voyage. They are on their way, never to return, two unlikely adventurers—a young lad and a frail old woman—determined to find Nykola's family. Their difficulties, those of any naive travelers at the mercy of sharks and profiteers, are frightening and threaten their safe arrival, but at last the ocean is crossed. Now they must find their family, somewhere in the wilderness. And of course they do find Nykola's mother and father, who, like other newcomers from Eastern Europe, have begun to bring the riches of an old-country heritage and culture to a raw new land.

An afterword to the story gives a glimpse of Nykola years later, a man grown, filing for a homestead of his own, and of Granny, buried in the graveyard of the church she helped to establish, with the beloved soil of her homeland, carefully included in her sparse luggage, sprinkled upon her coffin. Some of the Ukraine is buried with the ashes of those earliest Ukrainian settlers who came to people the empty Canadian West.

This fast-moving, suspenseful tale of two intrepid voyagers is a useful and well-researched introduction to a major movement in immigration to Canada at the turn of the century.

342 Houston, James. ***The Falcon Bow: An Arctic Legend.*** Published in Canada by McClelland & Stewart, 1986. Illus. by the author. Macmillan 1986, LB $12.95 (0-689-50411-X). 96pp. Fiction.

The Falcon Bow continues the story of a young Inuit hunter, Kungo, who was introduced in *The White Archer* (1976).

In the earlier tale, Kungo had dedicated his life to revenge upon the traditional enemies of his people—the Indians from the Land of the Little Sticks. His parents had died in an Indian raid, and his little sister, Shula, had been carried off. Kungo had intended to make the Indians pay for their crimes until he discovered that the raid had been a tragic mistake and that the kidnapped Shula was living happily with her young husband, Natawa, a Caribou Indian brave. Kungo forswore his revenge and decided to rebuild his life in a more positive direction.

Now, however, new trouble has arisen. Kungo's people are suffering from a terrible famine and have made up their minds that it is the Indians who are to blame for their misery. The angry Inuits believe the Indians have driven off all the caribou for themselves, leaving the Inuit to starve. Kungo alone has had some contact with the Indians, so it is decided that he should visit their strange land once more, to see if the rumors are true, before a vendetta is launched.

He does so, only to discover that the Indians, too, are starving. The famine has been a phenomenon of nature and nobody's fault. War would only add to the general misery of both the hungry peoples. Once again, Kungo acts as the agent of reconciliation rather than of revenge.

The Falcon Bow illuminates the potentially dangerous situation that can so easily arise between neighbors who do not quite understand one another. Houston spent many years in the North with the Inuit, and his detailed explanations of the construction of snow houses, preparing food and clothing, driving dog teams, and so on, are an enlightening feature of his work.

James, Janet Craig. *My Name Is Louis.*
See entry 361, Grades 7–9.

343   Kaplan, Bess. *The Empty Chair.* Originally published as *Corner Store*, 1975.
Western Producer Prairie Books 1986, P $8.95 (0-88833-205-X). 170pp. Fiction.

The empty chair in her bedroom is beginning to overshadow Rebecca Devine's
life. It had been Mama's chair. When Mama died, 10-year-old Rebecca carried
her chair upstairs, lest anyone else should sit in it. No one must ever, ever, take
Mama's place.

But time heals most wounds, however deep. The northern Winnipeg Jewish
community is unanimous in its belief that Papa should marry again. A man
needs a wife, and his children need a mama.

The local matrons introduce various eligible young ladies but never the right
one, until, one fateful day, Miss Cohen, a schoolteacher, comes to tea. This time,
things are different. She is very nice indeed, and Papa is plainly interested in her.
Before long, a marriage is in the works, and Becky and her little brother are made
a part of the wedding. In spite of the children's initial resistance, Sylvia, their
new stepmother, is winning their affection.

That is when Mama's old, empty chair begins to seem haunted. Becky is torn
by ill-understood feelings of disloyalty to her dear mama, and her spirit becomes
an accuser of a faithless daughter who can learn to accept a newcomer in her
mama's place. Becky becomes afraid to put out her light, afraid to go to sleep.

Papa and Sylvia discover the root of the trouble and explain to Becky that
Mama is at rest and no longer cares who sits in her old chair. A visit to the
peaceful cemetery convinces Becky that this is true. And there is good news to
turn Becky's mind toward life rather than death. A new baby is coming. Life
changes, but life goes on. This is a touching story of a preteenager in a close-knit
community, coping with changes and making a giant step toward womanhood.

344   Kasper, Vancy. *Street of Three Directions.* Overlea House 1988, P $3.95 (0-7172-
2481-3). 141pp. Fiction.

Street of Three Directions, set in the Chinatown area of downtown Toronto, has as
its focus a hard-fought school photography contest.

Two young students, Amanda Chong and James Urquart III, natural rivals
for scholastic honors, soon lock horns over the competition. Both are talented;
both are determined to win.

Both of the youngsters—Amanda, who is Chinese, and James, who is black,
come from ethnic minorities that are all too well aware of racial prejudice and its
evil effects, but even this awareness, unfortunately, does not prevent the ugly
apparition of prejudice from appearing within their own families.

Archenemies at first, James and Amanda draw closer together through their
shared interests, and they close ranks against the pain inflicted by a biased
teacher, Mr. Casper. Those students interested in an archaeological dig taking
place on the pioneer site behind the school must work under the supervision of
Mr. Casper, and the loss of a valuable artifact from the dig brings matters to a
head. Most of the students are only too ready to suspect and accuse one another,
especially across racial lines. Amanda and James, in pursuit of their photography
project, have accidentally acquired the evidence that will solve the mystery,

establish the innocence of the student diggers, and fasten the blame where it properly belongs.

The children in this school story with a message are quite believable, likable, and unsaintly. Their feuds and their loyalties ring true to schoolyard practice, as does their innate sense of fair play when the issue of bias emerges. Wiser than their years, indeed wiser than their elders in many respects, the youngsters refuse to be deflected from the important business at hand, that of getting on with their lives. James and Amanda, at least, have broken through the barriers raised by their parents that would have kept them "with our own kind." Good friends, they have discovered, *are* their own kind.

The solution of the mini-mystery is a touch heavily weighted with coincidence. The setting is well rendered, and the dialogue convincing, however; characterization rather than plot makes this a lively, readable title for the older elementary grades.

345   Kogawa, Joy. ***Naomi's Road.*** Illus. by Matt Gould. Oxford Univ. Pr. 1988, P $4.95
       (0-19-540547-1). 82pp. Fiction.

In 1942 the Japanese Canadians of the West Coast were evacuated and relocated to internment camps for the duration of World War II. Author Joy Kogawa was a young child at the time of this great injustice and upheaval. As an adult, she recounted the story of those sad years in an adult novel based upon the events of her own life, *Obasan*.

Years later, Kogawa retold the same tale, but this time not as an adult speaking to other adults. This time, she wrote from the perspective of a small child very much like herself at the time of the relocation.

Naomi Nakane is about 5 years old in 1942, a doll-like child with black hair, lovely Japanese eyes, and a face like a valentine. Hers is a happy home, with Mother, Father, and older brother Stephen. She has no understanding of the adult events that turn her placid and uneventful life upside down when suddenly her mother must leave the family to tend her own ailing mother in Japan, and Father and Stephen are taken from her into internment camps.

Naomi is left in the care of her aunt. Together they endure the privations of life in a primitive camp in the mountains, where the local people, including the children, treat the young Japanese prisoners as enemies and where the schooling so vital to Naomi's future is grudging and inferior.

The one small candlelight of kindness amid the dark surroundings of the camp is a single friendship with a little girl of Naomi's own age: a child whose simple goodness ignores the difference in her and Naomi's circumstances and who sees only a child, like herself, in great need of company.

When at last Naomi and her family are released and reunited, they want only to put this ugly part of the past behind them. Only Naomi carefully preserves one link with the lost war years: her friendship with Mitzi.

346   Lim, Sing. ***West Coast Chinese Boy.*** Illus. by the author. Tundra 1979, HB $14.95
       (0-88776-121-6). 64pp. Nonfiction.

It was no easy matter, being a West Coast Chinese boy in the depression years. Chinese children born in Canada had a double dose of discrimination to overcome. Lacking jobs, the white population of the day deplored the "Yellow Peril" and generally treated the Chinese badly, while the China-born generation looked down upon those born in this new country as "Siwash" or half-breeds.

Being Chinese was of paramount importance. It was forbidden to speak anything but Chinese at home; the language, art, and culture of China were of supreme importance, not to be compared with lesser rivals. Sing Lim describes the difficulty of his life as a child in these circumstances, always caught in the middle: "It was a struggle between being Chinese and Canadian, between the Chinese culture: so important to the parents' generation, and Canadian culture."

Sing Lim combines the two to happy effect in his life and in his art and especially in this wonderful re-creation of a unique and special childhood. The reader observes the day-to-day activities of school, home, and Chinese lessons, as well as the very special events such as "baby's head shave" at one month (at which time the baby became, officially, one year old) and the funeral of a rich man, "the best parade in town."

The book is alive with the author's art. It contains a myriad of clever and amusing pen-and-ink sketches and 22 full-color monotypes, a difficult form of art, in which the painting is done on glass and blotted with paper.

347 Mackay, Claire. *The Minerva Program.* SERIES: Time of Our Lives. Lorimer 1984, HB $16.95 (0-88862-717-3); P $5.95 (0-88862-716-5). 178pp. Fiction.

Minerva Wright is not all that good at most academic subjects, and she feels like a real disaster in phys. ed., but when it comes to math or computers, she is a whiz kid. It is odd that she should be so keen on computers, when they are her mom's nemesis. Computers have recently been installed at the store where Mom is a checker, and she and her co-workers feel spied upon and useless. All their skills and talents are ignored; they just stand all day, moving packages about and feeling somehow belittled.

Minerva is smart enough to show her mom and the other checkers how to outwit the store computer, but then she faces a challenge of her own. Somebody has tinkered with the marking scheme on the school office computer. Unjustly, Minerva is suspected of cheating and is barred from the computer lab as punishment.

However, spunky Minerva does not give in to such treatment. With the help of her (usually) ornery little brother, James, who answers to the name of Spiderman, she makes her way into the lab, solves the crime, and locates the real criminal. Minerva comes out the winner after all, even in phys. ed.! This engaging story about a bright, energetic black grade school student challenges the stereotype of girls who dislike or even fear mathematics and computers. Minerva is a model of the high-potential student in a working-class, multicultural community, and the book is a readable, nonformula children's detective story at its believable best.

348 Parry, Caroline. *Let's Celebrate! Canada's Special Days.* Illus. by Paul Barker et al. Kids Can Pr. 1987, HB $24.95 (0-921103-38-7); P $14.95 (0-921103-40-9). 256pp. Nonfiction.

What better way to get acquainted can there be than to share a celebration? The award-winning *Let's Celebrate!* introduces Canada's special days and the ways in which they are observed, whether by particular groups or by Canadians in general.

After giving readers a few examples of personal observances, such as birthdays and the different ways they are celebrated, the text divides into four headings corresponding to the four seasons.

Under "Winter," for example, are listed special days that are celebrated respectively by Christians, Jews, Hindus, Buddhists, and Baha'is. Some celebrations and festivals that are very old are included; others, such as Black History Month in February and International Women's Day in March, are relatively new.

A brief but readable text outlines the significance of the various events and gives their countries of origin; many of the short entries are accompanied by cheerful cartoons, poems, riddles, activities, and even recipes for special holiday treats such as Chinese New Year fortune cookies and Jewish hamantashen, three-cornered cookies that are part of Purim tradition.

Some special dates originated in Canada rather than in an "old country," including Dominion Day (sometimes called Canada Day). At least one Canadian celebration, Thanksgiving, resembles its American counterpart but is observed in October rather than November.

Most of the special days listed are happy occasions, but a few commemorate painful events that must never be forgotten, such as Tishah-b'Ab, when Jews mourn the destruction of the Temple, and Hiroshima Day, August 6.

Celebrations unite the diverse group of people who are Canada's hope and strength. The cheerful, racially diverse, flag-waving kids on the book's cover illustrate this. Their happy amity is a pictorial expression of the Canadian ideal.

349   Pearson, Kit. *The Sky Is Falling.* Viking Kestrel 1989, HB $16.95 (0-670-82849-1). 248pp. Fiction.

It is summer 1940, the summer of the blitz in embattled Britain. Terrified parents are sending their children away from the bombing to anywhere that can offer safety until the war is over.

Ten-year-old Norah and her little brother, 5-year-old Gavin, are evacuees, sent to wait out the war years in Canada. Gavin is still young enough to enjoy the adventure, but Norah, older and less outgoing, and without Gavin's elfin baby charm, finds the transition dreadfully difficult.

Things are not made easier by the children's placement in Canada. Norah and Gavin are accustomed to fairly humble surroundings at home, but they are assigned to the Ogilvies, two women they are told to call Aunt Florence and Aunt Mary, who live in a very grand house in Toronto's moneyed Rosedale section.

The chilly Ogilvies are quickly won over by little Gavin's lovable babyishness, but awkward Norah remains a lonely outsider, separated now even from her little brother by the differential treatment he enjoys. Things are no better at school, where her classmates mock her accent and scorn her for fleeing her country, as if that had been her own choice. Ironically enough, her only friend is Bernard Gunter, a lad whose German ancestry makes him a target of abuse as well.

Norah resists becoming Canadianized but gradually finds equilibrium in her new surroundings and with her new family. Like others of the "guest children," Norah and Gavin no doubt returned to their own families at the war's end, but the enforced stay in a country so like and yet so unlike their own affected both the children themselves and the country of their wartime sojourn.

350 Sadiq, Nazneen. ***Camels Can Make You Homesick and Other Stories.*** Illus. by Mary Cserepy. SERIES: Time of Our Lives. Lorimer 1985, HB $16.95 (0-88862-913-3); P $6.95 (0-88862-912-5). 89pp. Fiction.

Camels Can Make You Homesick is a collection of five readable, often humorous stories about Canadian young people with ties to India, to Bengal, and to Pakistan. It is a book particularly welcome in Canadian collections, because South Asian immigrants are a rapidly increasing group in the Canadian school scene, but books and other materials reflecting that community's presence are only now beginning to become widely available.

Some of the children in these stories experience difficulty in bridging their two cultures and in explaining unfamiliar aspects of their heritage to their classmates; some must meet and counter downright unfriendliness; and some have troubles with a gap that is both generational and cultural within their own family circle.

In one of the stories, a Westernized youngster, Amit, does not really feel comfortable with his Bengali grandmother, who is on her first visit to Canada. The chilliness persists until the evening he takes her out to dinner. Since Amit is about 10 years old, dining out means a burger at McDonald's, but Grandmother makes the little expedition a real event, dresses in her best, and thanks the flattered teenage cooks for their excellent performance. Everyone enjoys her pleasure; the outing is a most successful event, and the distance between Amit and his dida (grandmother) narrows appreciably.

All the youngsters whose stories are included here are of both Canadian and South Asian ancestry, and all have their own very special challenges to meet. The author has shared those challenges herself and well understands both the difficulties and delights of being a citizen of two worlds.

Smucker, Barbara. ***Amish Adventure.***
See entry 365, Grades 7–9.

Smucker, Barbara. ***Days of Terror.***
See entry 366, Grades 7–9.

Smucker, Barbara. ***Underground to Canada.***
See entry 367, Grades 7–9.

Sutherland, Robert. ***Son of the Hounds.***
See entry 368, Grades 7–9.

351 Takashima, Shizuye. ***A Child in Prison Camp.*** Illus. by the author. Tundra 1971, P $4.95 (0-88776-241-7). 100pp. Nonfiction.

A Child in Prison Camp is an account, only slightly fictionalized, of years spent in internment camp during World War II, as told by Takashima, a renowned artist of today. Hers is a story of a placid family life of hard work and contentment, rudely brought to an end by the evacuation and relocation of all the Japanese-Canadian citizens of the West Coast. Like all the other members of the Japanese community, the little girl (Shichan, as Takashima calls herself in this semiautobiographical story) and her family are wrenched from their comfortable urban setting and dispatched to what is to them a wilderness—New Denver, British Columbia—high in the Rocky Mountains.

Life in the internment camp is primitive: There is no running water or electric light; outdoor sanitation is crude; and a miserable approximation of education is available only as far as grade 8. No higher education is available for Japanese students, not even those like Shichan's elder sister, Yuki, who were well along in high school at the time of relocation.

Shichan's father particularly is bitter over the Canadian government's treatment of Japanese Canadians, who have been taxed but not allowed to vote. Not until many years after the wartime relocations, when Prime Minister Lester Pearson made public apology to the Japanese Canadians for this "black mark against Canada's traditional fairness and devotion to the principles of human rights," is his anger and hurt pride assuaged.

After the war, Shichan's family is given the choice of emigrating to Japan or moving east of the Rocky Mountains. Like many other West Coast Japanese, they decide to relocate in Toronto. In this new life in the East, Takashima, the real Shichan, establishes herself as a talented artist. Eight of her beautiful, award-winning watercolors illustrate the story of surely the most "disgracefully racist episode" in Canada's history.

352 Vineberg, Ethel. *Grandmother Came from Dworitz: A Jewish Love Story.* French ed., *L'aïeule qui venait de Dworitz*, 1969. Illus. by Rita Briansky. Tundra 1969, P $6.95 (0-88776-161-5). 64pp. Nonfiction.

Three generations ago, little Sarah Elca was born in a Russian-Jewish shtetl, or village, named Dworitz, in what is now Poland. Living in a very strict household, hers was a narrow but satisfying life. She was glad when her careful parents found a very promising husband for her, a devoted young scholar named Mordche Zisel Shapiro. Sarah and Mordche married and lived together contentedly.

In time they had a large family. One of their daughters, Nachama, was particularly attached to her father, but difficult times were making it hard to hold Jewish families together. After the assassination of Czar Alexander II, the severe persecutions known as pogroms began. Many Jews emigrated from Russia to either Canada or the United States. Unwillingly, but out of concern for her safety, her parents allowed Nachama to join relatives in America.

The relatives immediately changed Nachama's name to Emma, in honor of Emma Lazarus, whose poem is inscribed on the Statue of Liberty. Emma made a new life and a new home in this New World but lived the same kind of circumscribed family life as she had in the old country. Then her cousins introduced her to a pleasant young man, Jacob. Almost immediately they decided to marry, but Jacob had no money and no prospects.

In search of work, he traveled to Springfield, Nova Scotia, where he became a peddler to miners' families. He could not afford to come for Emma, so she went to him to be married, by a Protestant clergyman, for there was no rabbi to perform the service. Their Jewish friends read a Jewish service for them in order to satisfy religious requirements.

Emma and Jacob proved to be as happy a couple as Sarah Elca and Mordche Zisel. They had a thriving family and moved to New Brunswick to start a business there. One of their children, who vividly remembers that happiness, is the author of their charming double love story of lives lived in traditional ways and of family traditions lovingly preserved. The charcoal illustrations that adorn the text are an additional delight.

353 Bellingham, Brenda. ***Storm Child.*** SERIES: Time of Our Lives. Lorimer 1985, HB $16.95 (0-88862-794-7); P $5.95 (0-88862-793-9). 124pp. Fiction.

In the 1830s, during the fur trading days in the West, the Factor, or manager, who oversaw the workings of the trading post, was an important local figure. The Factors signed renewable contracts for long periods of time, and it was common practice for them to take Native Canadian wives and raise "country-born" families.

Robert Macpherson is such a Factor. He and his wife, Elizabeth, have a daughter, Isobel, 13 years old. Theirs is, apparently, a happy and contented home, but Macpherson is sick at heart for his own country, Scotland, and is well aware that his wife and child would never be accepted there. He makes the same faithless decision others of his kind have made so often before. On his last trading expedition, he deserts the wife and child who trust him, and he returns to his own European world.

Elizabeth is a realist and has always known that this, or something like this, could happen. She makes a new life for herself, marries the incoming Factor as recommended by Macpherson in his farewell letter, and puts the past behind her.

But Isobel cannot do so. Heartbroken at her father's perfidy, she renounces her white heritage. Henceforth she will be Piegan, of her mother's people alone. They have not deserted her. They have kept faith. Isobel takes her Piegan name, Storm Child, and makes her way to the tepee of her grandparents.

To her dismay, Storm Child soon discovers that her friends, people she loves, and a binding web of loyalties of which she had been unconscious still tie her to the old life and the old ways. She cannot be all Piegan, because she is still and forever half-white. Hers is the pain of the divided heart.

Storm Child herself is a fictional creation, but her story is placed in a setting of historical events and personages, and the course of her life parallels that of all too many "country-born" families. Such intermarriage on a large scale marked the beginning of a whole new nation within a nation: the Métis, or Burnt Wood, people, neither white nor Indian, but a separate people of their own. Many of them, like Storm Child, have bitter wounds to be healed. Their history, of which the fictional story of Storm Child is a fair representation, is an important strand in the tapestry of the Canadian West.

354 ***Canadian Childhoods: A Tundra Anthology.*** Illus. Tundra 1989, HB $24.95 (0-88776-208-5). 96pp. Nonfiction.

This handsome anthology is by its very format a powerful evocation of the famous Canadian mosaic. In this stunning selection from the published works of a galaxy of famous "illustrators who were artists and artists who were illustrators" is a distillation of the incredible richness and variety of the Canadian experience, particularly as it relates to the lives of children. The volume's style and content are as diverse as the lives of the artists and writers themselves.

Here is the work of a Native Canadian, of a child of immigrant parents, of a Japanese-Canadian child unjustly interned with her family in one of the detention camps of World War II, of a child of prosperity, and of boys and girls, city children, village children, and children of the wilderness.

Here too are presented different faiths, cultures, and colors. Fifty lovely full-color paintings and 32 in black and white illuminate unusual work by 15 notable artists. Most of the artists have written an accompanying text, though an occasional essay has been contributed by a sympathetic writer of commensurate reputation.

The way in which each of these artists has managed to retain the fresh eye and the eager zest for life of the child over all the years that have brought each of them to artistic maturity is magical. Some, like William Kurelek, Shizuye Takashima, and Guy Bailey, portray their own remembered childhood; others, like Ted Harrison in the Yukon and Warabe Aska in Toronto and Vancouver, capture the vibrant childhood of today's youngsters, who may in some distant future contribute to just such an anthology their own treasured memories.

355   Collura, Mary-Ellen Lang. ***Winners.*** Originally published in Canada by Western Producer Prairie Books, 1984. Dutton/Dial 1986, HB $10.95 (0-8037-0011-3). 136pp. Fiction.

Jordy Threebears has been placed, unhappily, in eleven foster homes in the past eight years. In line with the then-current government policy of placing Indian youngsters in need of care in "situations within the broader Canadian community," these placements have all been in non-Indian families.

Now there is a new development, both in government thinking and in Jordy's troubled life. Joe Speckledhawk, Jordy's maternal grandfather, is about to be released from prison. He has been imprisoned for what he considers to be no crime, but a meting out of justice: the punishment of those who murdered his daughter, Jordy's mother. Now he is returning to his home on the Ash Creek Blackfoot Reserve, embittered but proud. Jordy is to be placed in his custody.

The situation does not at first appear promising. The reserve is a place of poverty and little opportunity. Can it do for the boy what affluence and comfort have failed to do? Joe (who does not want to be called "Grandfather") is wiser than the others, who have been unable to deal with the unhappy 15 year old. Joe gives the lad a wild little mustang from the prairies for his very own. The horse is as difficult to tame as Jordy himself, but a friend offers sage counsel: "Losers don't try. Winners don't quit." By the story's end, Jordy and his nameless little mustang have proved themselves winners, and Jordy has earned the proud title Siksika—Blackfoot.

This exciting novel has a lot to say, indirectly but very effectively, about the troubled relations between the so-called "broader Canadian community" and the Native Canadian peoples. The story features an unsentimental but moving portrait of strong, supportive family relationships, especially that of the troubled boy and his embittered grandfather, who manages to understand him and his needs as no one else had been able to do.

356   Downie, Mary Alice, and Barabara Robertson, comps. ***The New Wind Has Wings: Poems from Canada.*** Previous ed. entitled *The Wind Has Wings*, 1968. Illus. by Elizabeth Cleaver. Oxford Univ. Pr. 1984, HB $17.95 (0-19-540431-9); P $10.95 (0-19-540432-7). 110pp. Nonfiction.

In 1968, *The Wind Has Wings*, an anthology of Canadian poetry for young readers, won instant acclaim, for both its content and its beauty. The inspired collaboration of editors and illustrator produced a volume that became an immediate Canadian classic.

Sixteen years later, in 1984, *The New Wind Has Wings* still included most of the well-loved material of the earlier publication but also incorporated 19 more poems by some of the most celebrated contemporary Canadian poets.

Many of these poems have their roots in other places and other cultures. Some were translated from the original Yiddish, French, or Eskimo; some appeal to the British tradition and legendry; some, like "Sweet Maiden of Passamaquoddy," are pure Canadianisms, with their roots in the Native Canadian names and terminology that so enrich the countryside; some, like the work of Pauline Johnson, are original work of Native Canadian artists.

The collection is a riot of glowing color, adorned throughout by the work of celebrated Canadian artist Elizabeth Cleaver, whose bold black-and-white prints alternate with collages of the utmost brilliance, worthy in every respect of the poems that they accompany.

And such poems! They feature subjects that young readers enjoy and will return to time and again—some funny, some moving, some that tell stories and others that arouse memories and sensations buried in the depths of every mind, at any age. No collection of Canadian writings for children can be considered complete without this important work.

357   Doyle, Brian. *Angel Square.* Groundwood/Douglas & McIntyre 1984. 128pp. Fiction. o.p.

Multiculturalism does not always offer a peaceful and cheerful state of coexistence. Sometimes, and to some people, it can seem an enforced cohabitation.

Angel Square is such a place. It is in Lowertown, Ottawa, and the time is 1945, just after World War II. This is an area—you could not call it a neighborhood—in which racist name-calling and unfriendliness are the established order of things. There are three schools on the square: St. Brigit's School of the Bleeding Thorns, for the Irish Catholics, who are called "Dogans"; York Street School, for the Jewish students, or "Jews"; and the School of Brother Brébeuf, for French Canadians, always known as "Pea Soups." "All over the square, Dogans, Pea Soups and Jews were tearing the sleeves out of one another's coats and trying to rip each other limb from limb."

Such being the case, crossing the square is not to be undertaken lightly, according to storyteller Tommy, who attends York Street School but is "not anything," neither Dogan, Pea Soup, nor Jew. Everybody calls Tommy "Lamont Cranston," for his ambition is to be like his hero, "The Shadow," hero of 1940s radio who knows what evil lurks in the hearts of men. . . .

This is the state of affairs, when the otherwise meaningless and ritualized baiting is interrupted by a real racial incident. Night watchman Mr. Rosenberg, father of Tommy's best friend, Sammy, is severely beaten in an attack by a man wearing a hood. This, then, is the reality of which the stupid name-calling is the pale reflection.

Tommy determines to live up to his namesake and discover the villain. His methods of detection are unusual and hilarious to say the least. The upbeat ending of this unique, very funny, but very meaningful story shows the transformation of Angel Square into a neighborhood—the kind of neighborhood where friends live together. Not bad going for a Shadow.

358   Greenwood, Barbara. *Spy in the Shadows.* Kids Can Pr. 1990, P $4.95 (1-55074-018-0). 224pp. Fiction.

It is the era of the Fenian uprisings that troubled the usually peaceful Canadian-American border in 1866–1867. Thirteen-year-old Liam O'Brien is torn between two loyalties: His late, well-loved father was an Irish rebel who fought the British, and Liam feels it would be shameful in him to make peace with those who were his father's sworn enemies. But he himself now lives in Canada, not in Ireland. Do the old loyalties and causes still apply? He is not sure.

His dying father had apprenticed Liam to Gottlieb Hahn, an Upper Canadian bell founder, who, although he is hot tempered and a stern taskmaster, has been a true friend to the boy. Hahn and his family shared their home with the orphaned Liam when he was otherwise alone in the world, and the boy knows that he owes loyalty to the Hahns and to his new, peaceful country, as well as to Ireland. Indeed, if it comes to the war the Fenians want, young Isaac Hahn, now in the army, who has been like an elder brother to Liam, may very well be killed in this ancient quarrel that has nothing to do with him or his country.

When Liam's Irish cousin Patrick, a dedicated Fenian, reappears in his life to recruit the teenager as a spy for his militant cause, Liam arrives at the moment in which he must decide. He has only one allegiance to give. Shall it be to the old country or to the new?

Spy in the Shadows gives a vivid and sympathetic picture of youth trapped in webs of intrigue that are not of their own making. Young Liam's divided heart and his final brave and painful decision parallel similar dilemmas and decisions faced by young Canadians even today.

Heneghan, Jim. *Promises to Come.*
See entry 372, Grades 10–12.

359   Hewitt, Marsha, and Claire Mackay. *One Proud Summer.* Originally published by Women's Educational Pr., 1981. Penguin 1988, P $4.95 (0-14-032734-7). 159pp. Fiction.

One Proud Summer, the fictionalized account of the Valleyfield Textile Workers Strike of 1946, goes far to explain the deep and painful rift between Anglophone and Francophone Canadians today. Here, in microcosm, are the sources of bitterness and resentment, as well as the proud spirit that can never be conquered.

It is the story of Lucie Laplante, 13 years old and already a mill hand. The tragic accidental death of her father at that very mill has left the family all but destitute, and the incident ended a bright student's chances for an education. Even the tiny salary she can earn is badly needed. While the teenager bravely faces a necessary lifetime of ill-rewarded toil, certain aspects of work in the mill fill her with dismay: the attitudes of the Anglo foreman toward "Frenchies," the overall racism, the casual sexual harassment of helpless young workers that is endured with resignation as one of the hazards of the job.

Lucie has come upon the scene just at that moment when the simmering resentment of years is beginning to boil over. Against terrible odds, the 3,000 Valleyfield workers fight for fair working conditions and decent pay, protection for child workers, and an end to the punitive system of fines. They face the guns and motorcycles of the establishment with bare hands and courage—and they triumph.

This important story, told from the perspective of young Lucie, is a stirring reminder of the strength and power of workers united against injustice. It is as well a fair representation of the perceptions of French Canadians of a generation ago, whose only contact with English Canada was likely to be that of the oppressed facing the oppressor.

In its characterization of a villainous management *One Proud Summer* is the story of a time gone by, but of a time during which seeds were sown that have since come to harvest. The inclusion of actual press photos of the historic events described lend the story vivid credibility, and the book has been widely studied as an example of historical fiction.

Houston, James. *The Falcon Bow: An Arctic Legend.*
See entry 342, Grades 4–6.

Hudson, Jan. *Sweetgrass.*
See entry 373, Grades 10–12.

360   Hughes, Monica. *My Name Is Paula Popowich.* Illus. by Leoun Young. SERIES: Time of Our Lives. Lorimer 1983, HB $16.95 (0-88862-690-8); P $5.95 (0-88862-689-4). 150pp. Fiction.

The search for one's roots can be very compelling. All her life, 12-year-old Paula Herman has believed that her father died shortly after her birth and that her heritage is completely German Canadian. Then she makes an astonishing discovery. She finds a picture of an unknown young man who looks disturbingly like herself, but the inscription calls him Paul Popowich. It has to be her unknown father! But the name is completely unfamiliar to her; it is certainly not a German name. Her father must have been Ukrainian, and she, Paula, must be half Ukrainian!

Since her mother is unwilling to discuss the past, Paula does some detective work of her own, calling all the Popowiches in the Edmonton telephone book to make inquiries. After many disappointments and false leads, Paula at last finds her grandmother. Having feared her son's only child was lost to her forever, the woman welcomes Paula joyfully. Paul Popowich is indeed dead, but only recently. Grandmother Popowich understands the resentment on the part of Paula's mother, deserted by her feckless husband when Paula was an infant, yet she wants and needs to have some claim on the child who is all that is left to her of her lost son.

So Paula begins the exciting discovery of a whole new (to her) culture and a heritage to which she is entitled. Her life is enriched, and her mother is fair-minded enough to understand the importance of this rediscovery for her daughter.

Many families in a culturally mixed nation are faced with the pain of incompatible families and customs. Sometimes divorce separates children from their cultural roots. This well-plotted mystery is solved when Paula uncovers the truth about her heritage. It gives a glimpse of a complex problem in which, sometimes, two halves do not make a neat whole, but also shows that necessary compromises can offer happy results.

361 James, Janet Craig. *My Name Is Louis.* Penumbra Pr. 1988, P $9.95 (0-921254-06-7). 128pp. Fiction.

Louis Robillard, a 15-year-old Native Canadian, is fully prepared to hate the white man who is building a log retirement home on the property next to that of his family. It means change. The tree he used to climb has been cut down, perhaps to build a bridge, all changes he wants to forestall or prevent.

Reluctantly Louis meets the new person, Matt Prescott from the city. Strangely, Prescott, whose presence Louis so resents, is the one among all his acquaintances with whom it seems natural to discuss his art. Louis, though untutored, has a great natural talent, and Prescott, appreciating this fact, would like to help the youngster to develop an important career in the art world. He takes Louis with him to Toronto—Louis's first visit to a city—and to an art gallery. It is a whole new world, and part of him craves the opportunity to belong and to learn.

But Louis cannot bear to leave the quiet lake he loves, with its lapping waves that have lulled him to sleep all his life. Besides, his family needs him at home. He is the mainstay of the family, for his father is dead and his mother ill. She cannot be left alone.

Louis's ultimate decision keeps him in the North he loves, but with a connection to the art world of the city as well. He is one of the lucky ones; he can make a compromise that will work, both for his family and for his art. Realizing that he has hurt only himself by harboring resentment against all whites, he decides that "You can't keep smashing things forever. It doesn't change things."

Certainly relations between whites and Indians are difficult, often bitterly unhappy, but they need not always be so. For Louis, in this one instance, his new white neighbor turned out to be a friend.

Kaplan, Bess. *The Empty Chair.*
See entry 343, Grades 4–6.

362 Kurelek, William, and Margaret S. Engelhart. *They Sought a New World: The Story of European Immigration to North America.* Illus. Tundra 1985, HB $14.95 (0-88776-172-0); 1988, P $6.95 (0-88776-213-1). 48pp. Nonfiction.

There are many reasons for emigration from an old land to a new one: war, revolution, famine, persecution, conscription, poverty, or merely a longing for freedom of speech. Whatever the impetus, it is a powerful one to move people from one continent to another.

William Kurelek, one of Canada's best-known artists, was the child of an immigrant family. He shared the hardships and the satisfactions that are a part of that experience, and throughout his tragically brief career he recorded the lives of immigrants, their work and play, their good times and bad.

They Sought a New World is a posthumous collection of his work and commentary. Many of the paintings had appeared earlier as illustrations for several of his books; some had never before been published.

Together they provide a great, composite picture of a hard, daunting, but rewarding life. This book is not a tribute to any one particular cultural or ethnic group, but to all the European peoples who contributed, willingly or unwillingly, to the creation of a New World. Here are reconstructions of the comfortless, weeks-long misery of the immigrant ships; the first temporary shelter in the woods; the first arrival on the empty plain, with nothing to be seen for miles but the tiny station; and the raw, new little towns in the middle of nowhere. As time goes by and generations pass, prosperous descendants surpass their brave forebears' highest hopes. And always there are the births, the weddings, the deaths, and the funerals. By its illustrations even more than by its text, this colorful history will help young readers appreciate the building of a new nation.

McClintock, Norah. *Sixty-four, Sixty-five.*
See entry 374, Grades 10–12.

Mackay, Claire. *The Minerva Program.*
See entry 347, Grades 4–6.

Major, Kevin. *Blood Red Ochre.*
See entry 375, Grades 10–12.

Parry, Caroline. *Let's Celebrate! Canada's Special Days.*
See entry 348, Grades 4–6.

Pearson, Kit. *The Sky Is Falling.*
See entry 349, Grades 4–6.

363 Philip, Marlene Nourbese. *Harriet's Daughter.* Women's Pr. 1988, P $7.95 (0-88961-134-3). 150pp. Fiction.

Margaret Cruickshank, 14 years old, is in full rebellion against just about everything, but especially against Dad and his continual lectures on "Good West Indian discipline," of which he feels his North Americanized daughter stands in need. He sees no reason to adjust his patriarchal style to the ways of this new country.

Margaret rejects even her own "meaningless" name. She idolizes Harriet Tubman, conductor of the Underground Railroad, who led fugitive slaves to freedom. Margaret emulates her to the extent that she will answer only to the name Harriet.

Harriet/Margaret organizes the child population of her neighborhood into a giant Underground Railroad game, in which some of them play slaves seeking freedom, others the slave hunters trying to prevent them from escaping. (The roles of slave hunter and bloodhound are so unpopular that they must be assigned by lot.) This works the participants into such a fever of excitement that some of them are unable even to sleep, and their parents, deciding that the game is overexciting, forbid the youngsters to play any longer.

Foiled in this endeavor, Harriet decides to free today's equivalent of a slave, her friend Zulma, who pines for her island home and her "gran" in Tobago but is trapped in cold Toronto with her mother and a bossy, tyrannical stepfather she dislikes.

Harriet sets herself the task of learning the Tobagonian speech patterns, and Zulma is proud and pleased to share her own special language, which is not, as some people mistakenly believe, merely an incorrect variant of English, but a language of its own, with its own rules—easily understood by English speakers, but different.

Since Harriet is as stouthearted and determined as her brave role model, there's little doubt of the outcome of her campaign to help Zulma return to

Tobago. This is a lively evocation of two youngsters of West Indian extraction; one who will thrive wherever she goes, and the other who cannot be content away from her beautiful homeland.

364   Roe, Eliane Corbeil. *Circle of Light.* HarperCollins 1989, LB $13.89 (0-06-025079-8). 248pp. Fiction.

Circle of Light is the enchanting story of a young girl's emergence from the shadow of loss and death into a new world illuminated by her own intelligence, an intelligence she finally begins to understand and appreciate.

Lucy Delaroche, a grade 8 student, has recently lost both her father and her elder brother, and the surviving family must struggle to keep afloat. For that reason, Lucy resists the insistent efforts of her teacher, eager Sister Andrew, to induce her to sit for the province-wide examinations for the honor of her family, her school, and all French Canadians. Why should she do all that extra work for something she does not even want? Why should she strive to spend four years away in a convent high school, far from her friends, and especially from Gabriel, the nicest boy in the school, who is just beginning to notice her?

Lucy relents, does the studying, and triumphs in the examinations. Though there is joy, there is sorrow too. Gabriel has not even stayed to see her reap her reward. Has it all been worthwhile? Eventually, Lucy comes to realize how very worthwhile it has been, indeed, and there is still a surprise in store when the vanished Gabriel returns to visit her.

This story reveals a great deal about the special pride and challenge of being French Canadian in the 1940s. Roe's work is a remarkably affecting and evocative first novel, one filled with memorable characters and situations.

Sadiq, Nazneen. *Heartbreak High.*
See entry 376, Grades 10–12.

365   Smucker, Barbara. *Amish Adventure.* Penguin 1984, P $4.95 (0-14-031702-3). 158pp. Fiction.

In Waterloo County, Ontario—Amish country—a Volkswagen careens through the night, driven by a careless man in a hurry, and disaster follows. The car strikes an Amish buggy, killing the horse and severely injuring the driver.

Twelve-year-old Ian McDonald, a passenger in the car, is on his way to Toronto. His father has suddenly been posted to the Beaufort Sea and cannot take his motherless son with him. Ian has been told that he must stay with his stuffy Aunt Clem, and he is very unhappy about it. Without warning, the accident catapults him onto a relationship with a group of people he had never known existed—the Amish, or Plain People, who deliberately turn their backs on the fashions and conveniences of the modern world in order to live simply and plainly according to the tenets of their faith.

Ian is left to stay with an Amish family, the Benders, until his father can be contacted and arrangements made. At first inclined to scoff at their strange clothes and lack of indoor plumbing, telephones, cars, or television, Ian is drawn more and more to the old-fashioned goodness of their way of life. He discovers that he himself, who has always been something of an unhappy misfit in the city, can adapt to their quiet ways and that he can do a little to play a part in the community by taking on as much as he is able of the injured man's workload. He soon decides that he would far rather stay with the Benders than with his aunt in Toronto.

Amish Adventure is a story of the meeting of two very different cultures. Such a meeting is not always a happy one. A few young toughs from the nearby town delight in harassing the pacifist Plain People, sometimes with dire effect, but for Ian, and for young readers who will learn a little about the alternative life-style that wins the heart of a big-city boy, the Amish way of life is a quiet revelation.

366   Smucker, Barbara. ***Days of Terror.*** Penguin 1981. 152pp. Fiction. o.p.

The Russian Mennonite community lived in a state of fearful suspense at the turn of the century, a time of revolutionary upheaval and anarchy.

Their beliefs prevented the Mennonites from bearing arms, but not from having their sons conscripted into the czar's armies; yet even so, the Russians began to suspect the German-speaking Mennonites of being the spies of their enemies. As the czarist regime crumbled, and civil war began to seem inevitable, the Mennonites had cause to fear that they could be caught in the crossfire.

The Neufeld family, about whom the story of *Days of Terror* revolves, are typical of the Mennonite victims of these terrible times. In addition, the eldest Neufeld son, Otto, has joined a defense league in defiance of the teachings of his faith, and he is now a wanted man. His family does not know his whereabouts or if they will see him again.

At last conditions become so dire that the Neufelds decide to leave their beloved home of 112 years and make a new home across the ocean. Through the eyes of 10-year-old Peter, the reader observes the mass exodus of Russian Mennonites on their way to new lives in Canada and the United States. This is a story that is drawn from the family history of the author and, although fictionalized, has the ring of truth and sincerity.

367   Smucker, Barbara. ***Underground to Canada.*** Penguin 1986, P $4.95 (0-14-031122-X). 157pp. Fiction.

Liza and Julilly, 13 years old, are mistreated slaves on a Mississippi cotton plantation. Torn from their families, they have no hope of any relief from their misery. Then one day they are approached by one Alexander Milton Ross, a Canadian abolitionist who travels the South disguised as a bird fancier. He is a conductor on the Underground Railway, the covert system by which intrepid men and women opposed to the evil of slavery assisted fugitives on their way north, following the "Drinking Gourd," the Big Dipper constellation in which the North Star beckoned the way to freedom.

This gripping story details the two girls' decision to flee and their terrifying journey. Beset by slave catchers with bloodhounds, the girls never knew which chance-met stranger might report them for the reward offered. Much of the time they are without food and at the mercy of the elements.

Offsetting the bleak picture of man's inhumanity to man are those brave souls, both Canadians and Americans, who take enormous risks as a matter of conscience to conceal the escaped slaves from their pursuers and to help them along their perilous way.

A little, if only a very little, of the terror suffered by the fugitives, of the pain, the hunger, and the privation of their lives and of their often bloody struggle for freedom appears in this book; the understated presentation makes it an appropriate title for older elementary as well as middle school students. *Underground to Canada* has proved to be one of the most enduringly popular works of historical fiction for youngsters yet written in Canada, where young people are glad and proud to learn that many of the fugitive slaves, like Liza and Julilly, eventually found a haven in their country.

368   Sutherland, Robert. ***Son of the Hounds.*** Scholastic 1988, P $4.50 (0-590-71952-1). 181pp. Fiction.

Through most of their shared history, Canada and the United States have enjoyed a peaceful, undefended border and an enviable record of amicable relations, but it was not always so: The War of 1812, that curious conflict in which both participants claimed a victory, was fierce and bloody while it lasted.

Jimmy Cameron, a Scots Canadian, is too young to join the militia but quite old enough to fight the Yankee invaders in his own way, especially after they capture and imprison him and his father, a veteran recently crippled at the battle of Queenston Heights who is no threat to anyone. Father and son share the hot blood of the Cameron clan, whose fierce battle cry "Son of the hounds come here and get flesh" had struck terror into the heart of many a foe over the years. That warlike spirit animates the young Jimmy, who escapes from his Yankee captors, manages to inform the militia of the enemy's movements, and eventually joins the Band of Bloody Boys who fought through the Niagara peninsula in the crucial war year of 1813.

Son of the Hounds is a complicated tale of attack and counterattack, espionage, and double-dealing at a time when and in a place where it was uncommonly difficult to distinguish between friend and foe. This detailed account of a half-forgotten campaign, and particularly of the decisive battle of Stoney Creek in June 1813, brings a long-ago conflict vividly to life.

369   Yee, Paul. ***The Curses of Third Uncle.*** Illus. by Don Besco. SERIES: Adventures in Canadian History. Lorimer 1986. 152pp. Fiction. o.p.

It is 1909, and the Chinese homeland has been ruled by the Manchu invaders for far too long. The great leader of his people, Sun Yat Sen, has come to Canada to enlist the help of men like Lillian Ho's father to help out in freeing the mother country. Now, Lillian's father has vanished, and with him all the funds collected to restore the pride of the Chinese community. Dark looks are being cast at his unhappy family, and his youngest brother, sinister Third Uncle, talks of sending his nieces back to a life of misery in China.

Breaking with the traditions of her community, Lillian decides upon decisive action. If no one else believes in her father, she does believe. He is an honorable man who would never ever steal. If he has disappeared, it must be because he is in terrible trouble. She, Lillian, will find him and help him. She will restore the family name.

So begins a daring adventure, as young Lillian ventures into the British Columbia interior, tracing her lost father's known movements. She must overcome both the prejudice of whites who take her concerns lightly and the deep-seated feeling of her own people that young girls should be silent and submissive.

The outcome of Lillian's search is not a happy one, for her honorable father, true to his mission, has been murdered while carrying it out, and the precious funds for Sun Yat Sen's rebellion have been purloined. In the meantime, Lillian has also uncovered the evidence that will reveal the true culprits and restore her family's name. Indeed, her exploit has given that name new luster.

Paul Yee brings vividly to life a little-known segment of Canadian history—the Chinese community of British Columbia at the turn of the century. An absorbing mystery, neatly plotted and with a fascinating cast of characters, spotlights a community whose accomplishments are too little recorded elsewhere and are worthy of celebration.

Yee, Paul. *Tales from Gold Mountain: Stories of the Chinese in the New World.* See entry 377, Grades 10–12.

GRADES 10–12

370   Bell, William. *Forbidden City: A Novel of Modern China.* Bantam 1990, HB $14.95 (0-553-07131-9); P $3.50 (0-553-28864-4). 200pp. Fiction.

Seventeen-year-old Alex Jackson feels much older than his years. He has just returned from China, where he had been with his father, a CBC news cameraman.

While staying in Beijing, Alex learned a little Chinese, explored the wonders of China's capital city, and became acquainted with Chinese students his own age. Because of his increasing familiarity with the scene, he assists his father, a voracious newsman, with local color. During this time of massive unrest, Alex disguises himself with a black wig and face stain. He finds himself in Tienanmen Square on the fateful day, June 4, 1989, when the People's own army massacres the crowds of students who have gathered there to protest for democracy.

Wounded, Alex barely escapes from the scene with his life. His friends have been killed before his eyes. Alex has always professed an interest in warfare and weapons, but upon his return to Canada he smashes his treasured collection of lead soldiers. He feels alien in his own country, where so few share his awareness, as did Ulysses, returned from exotic adventures to live among the unenlightened.

This is a powerful story of a dreadful event in contemporary history and the effect such an event can have upon a too-suddenly initiated youngster. Bell contrasts the safety of life in Canada and the insularity and apathy of Alex's Canadian friends with the courage and commitment shown by the Chinese students who must struggle, even die, for the democracy Canadian youngsters take for granted.

371   Culleton, Beatrice. *April Raintree.* Originally published as *In Search of April Raintree*, 1983. Pemmican Publications 1984, P $9.95 (0-919143-03-2). 187pp. Fiction.

The adoption of Métis and Native Canadian children has been a controversial issue for some time. It has been the subject of several very moving reports and novels, but seldom, as in *April Raintree*, described, even fictionally, by an author who has lived through the experience.

April Raintree is the tragic story of two sisters who are Métis: light-skinned April and darker Cheryl. Their parents are urban Métis, rapidly losing control of their lives through alcohol abuse, poverty, and sheer hopelessness.

Eventually the children are taken from their parents' custody by the children's authority and placed in foster homes. April is the storyteller, and with her the reader shares the pain of separation from her hapless but loved parents, and even from Cheryl, her little sister who is placed elsewhere.

April's first "home" is truly a home, where she is made a part of the family, but then her foster mother falls ill, and she is removed, to be placed in a situation of persecution and virtual slavery. She is actually glad that Cheryl is not with her, trapped in this heartless home that is not a home.

At last, with childhood behind them, the two young women try to make their own ways in the world—April through marriage to a prosperous white man, Cheryl through ever more dangerous and depressing means by which she eventually ends up in the streets.

By the time April finds her lost sister and learns of her plight, it is too late. Cheryl has despaired, and like so many young Métis and Native Canadians, she commits suicide, leaving behind a child, Henry Liberty.

April prepares to begin a new life without the sister she could not save but determined to make a future for little Henry. Author Culleton experienced herself the evils she describes and lost two sisters to suicide. Perhaps an understanding of her tragedy expressed through this poignant work may indeed lead to a brighter future for all the "Henry Libertys."

Doyle, Brian. *Angel Square.*
See entry 357, Grades 7-9.

372   Heneghan, Jim. *Promises to Come.* Overlea House 1988, P $3.95 (0-7172-2297-7). 189pp. Fiction.

The Westovers, a comfortable middle-class family, have come to feel that they owe it to the less fortunate people of the world to make a meaningful contribution. They will adopt a homeless child, as a longed-for "baby sister" for their teenage daughter, Becky.

When Nguyen Thi Kim, a Vietnamese refugee, finally appears in Vancouver, the family is flabbergasted. This is not the expected infant; Kim is another teenager. She proves slow to make friends with her bumptious new western sister, who begins to resent the presence of this interloper. There is a reason behind Kim's reticence; she has a dark secret to conceal.

Tiny Kim, who could easily pass as a 12-year-old, is in reality nearly 17 and has lied about her age in order to have a chance of adoption, a chance for survival. She has endured unimaginable horrors as a refugee from her war-torn homeland; she has been imprisoned and raped by pirates, and she has seen her family slain. She suffers terrible unresolved, undeserved guilt over the death of the little brother she could not save, and she fears that anyone she allows herself to love will also die.

This painful story of the meeting of people from two different worlds points out the necessity for patience and understanding with young people who look outwardly like any ordinary teenager, but who may have suffered experiences and scars that are ineradicable. It is a story that is searingly powerful but that offers hope for a better future.

373   Hudson, Jan. **Sweetgrass.** Originally published by Tree Frog Pr., 1984. Putnam/Philomel 1989, HB $13.95 (0-399-21721-5). 160pp. Fiction.

Sweetgrass is a 15-year-old Blackfoot girl of the Blood tribe, quite old enough, in her cultural tradition, to be a wife. She longs to marry her sweetheart, Eagle Sun, a stalwart warrior, but he is poor. Besides, the white interlopers have upset the traditional monogamous Blood system by trading goods for beautiful young Native Canadian women, who are now being treated by all as a form of trade goods. Sweetgrass fears that the temptations of guns, blankets, and gewgaws will lead to her being sold as well and becoming one of the ominously named "slavewives" of a man richer and older than Eagle Sun.

Troubles other than trade goods have arrived with the Europeans: Liquor and disease have come with them to become the twin scourges of the people of the plains. When epidemic strikes and death is all around her, Sweetgrass proves herself to be a true, heroic daughter of a proud people, worthy to choose a husband for herself. This award-winning first novel, by a gifted writer whose life was to prove tragically brief, is an encapsulation of the agonies and compromises of the mismanaged era of first contact between the invading whites from Europe and the Native Canadians, of which the reverberations still trouble a divided nation to this day.

374   McClintock, Norah. **Sixty-four, Sixty-five.** McClelland & Stewart 1989, P $9.95 (0-7710-5446-7). 156pp. Fiction.

Sixty-four, Sixty-five is a school year, in a white Anglo-Saxon Protestant high school in Montreal. Sixteen-year-old Cally Wright fits right in with the favored color scheme; her new friend, one of the first black students to enroll, does not.

Orlando Verdad is subjected to all the petty persecutions and snubs of which a minority member breaking new ground is only too likely to be a victim. Two factors bring the crisis of prejudice versus justice to a head: Orlando's suspension from the basketball team and his growing friendship—which appears to be more than an ordinary friendship—with Cally.

The story solves no problems, comes to no real conclusions. The increasingly critical issue of interracial boy-girl relationships is hinted at but not dealt with directly. Orlando's family moves away from the unfriendly neighborhood, and Cally must reconcile herself with the other students who have resented Orlando's presence and joined together to ostracize him. Yet shy Cally has made the first move toward a mutual tolerance that will become increasingly important as Canada's population becomes more diverse. Despite its unclear resolution, this is an interesting period piece, a reminder of how far a people has progressed in understanding and how far there is yet to travel.

375   Major, Kevin. **Blood Red Ochre.** Delacorte 1989, HB $15.95 (0-385-29794-7). 147pp. Fiction.

Shanawdithit, last of the Beothuk or Red Ochre Indians of Newfoundland, died in 1829. Her people had been deliberately eradicated by European settlers, who stole their land, cut off their food supplies by netting the rivers and overhunting the forests, brought unfamiliar and fatal diseases into the territory, and, worst of all, hunted the Beothuk as if they had been nonhuman, animal pests.

Past and present meet in the concurrent stories of David, a high school student of modern Newfoundland, and Dauoodaset, a young Beothuk warrior struggling to save his starving people in the tribe's last desperate days.

David has become very interested in a mysterious new classmate, Nancy. Both of the young people are engaged in a study project on the history of the Beothuks, but whereas David embarks upon the subject with moderate interest and enthusiasm, Nancy attacks it with real passion.

Plainly, the fate of the Beothuk is very important and distressing to her. When the project culminates in a visit to Red Ochre Island, the traditional burial place of the Beothuk, it appears that there is some kind of supernatural bond between Nancy and Shanawdithit, and between David and Dauoodaset.

The bloody climax of their dual story, like the historical tragedy of the Beothuk, is brought about by a failure to communicate and a lack of understanding between members of two very disparate cultures. Not a history, not quite a romance, *Blood Red Ochre* combines the two in a thought-provoking study of culture clash and tragedy.

376 Sadiq, Nazneen. *Heartbreak High.* Lorimer 1988, HB $14.95 (1-55028-127-5); P $4.95 (1-55028-125-9). 158pp. Fiction.

Teenagers Rachel Steiner and Tariq Khan are both students at Yorklea High, and until this year neither of them has given a serious thought to the opposite sex.

Suddenly they discover one another, and all else—including studies, school friendships, and their families—fades into insignificance. They are in love, and to them, at this moment, that is all that matters.

Both families see this powerful attack of first love as a disaster. Rachel is Jewish; Tariq a Muslim, and both sets of parents are horrified at even the slightest possibility of an attachment outside their respective faiths. The mothers, in particular, busy themselves with efforts to prevent the young people from seeing one another, with the usual result. Two erstwhile good kids resort to lying and sneaking in order to be together.

Family tension runs high, and things are rapidly going from bad to worse when an accident forces all the parties to focus on reality rather than upon emotional bugbears. Though deploring the possibility of a mixed marriage, the two sets of parents begin to treat each other and their children with respect and understanding.

At the story's end, Tariq is on a summer tree-planting expedition in Canada's North, writing to Rachel, who is hard at work on a kibbutz in Israel. The young people have not forgotten their shared affection, but each has discovered a new interest in the culture and community both have taken for granted in the past.

Heartbreak High has a "soft" ending, which never addresses the consequences of this teen romance should it continue beyond high school dating. Nevertheless, it does highlight one of the most sensitive problems of a culturally diverse society: interracial and intercultural relationships and the rude awakening young people are in for when they defy their parents and society's expectations to stick to their own kind in matters of love.

377   Yee, Paul. *Tales from Gold Mountain: Stories of the Chinese in the New World.*
Published in Canada by Groundwood/Douglas & McIntyre, 1989. Illus. by Simon
Ng. Macmillan 1989, HB $14.95 (0-02-793621-X). 64pp. Fiction.

Although Paul Yee, author of the prize-winning *Tales from Gold Mountain*, is
himself a third-generation Chinese Canadian, he tells the story of Canada's
earliest Chinese citizens with all the passion and immediacy of a man who
shared their hardships.

Theirs was a history of terrible adversity bravely borne and of cruel prejudice
that made a thorny road all the harder to climb. Yee conveys all of this in his
brief, elegant short stories.

Hopeful Chinese immigrants gave North America, the land of their wistful
dreams, the name "Gold Mountain." They hoped that there they too might
share in a wealth not to be found in their ancestral land, but very few of them in
fact made their fortunes. For most of the Chinese, life in Gold Mountain was not
very different from what they had tried to leave behind—unremitting toil,
although now in the goldfields or on the railways rather than in the fields they
had forsaken, with little reward and an unmarked grave at the end of the
struggle.

The Chinese newcomers were not welcomed by white settlers, who made
very good use of their tireless work but feared that a huge influx of underpaid,
willing Chinese labor would eventually threaten their own security.
Discriminatory immigration laws, including the punitive head tax, separated
families, often forever. Even though they worked and saved night and day,
many men were unable to send for their wife and children.

Here, in eight masterful short stories—some two or three pages long—Paul
Yee captures the reality of those lives. The stories are both bitter and romantic,
sometimes funny, often tragic. The stern father in "Forbidden Fruit" cannot let
his daughter find happiness with a worthy and deserving young man of another
race. The young miner in "Spirits of the Railway" fears his father has died
somewhere in this vast, alien land and knows that his father's spirit will require
of him a proper ceremonial burial. In "Friends of Kwan Ming," a prosperous
man eats so much that he comes to an unusual and unpleasant end; "The
Revenge of the Iron Chink" features a wickedly effective practical joke planned
by the salmon cannery workers ruthlessly thrown out of work by a new and
efficient machine.

In these stories and the rest, Yee writes with power and above all with deep
feeling, capturing what he describes as the feeling of being "caught between two
worlds," which he has experienced in his own life. The deceptive picture book
appearance of this handsome oversized volume belies its sophistication. Simon
Ng's subtle, gallery-quality paintings enhance the effect of Yee's compelling
storytelling. They are richly colored, evocative, and haunting, like the enigmatic
empty-eyed golden mask that gazes from the arresting cover. This is a book for
thoughtful readers of high school age and older.

6

MEXICO AND THE CARIBBEAN

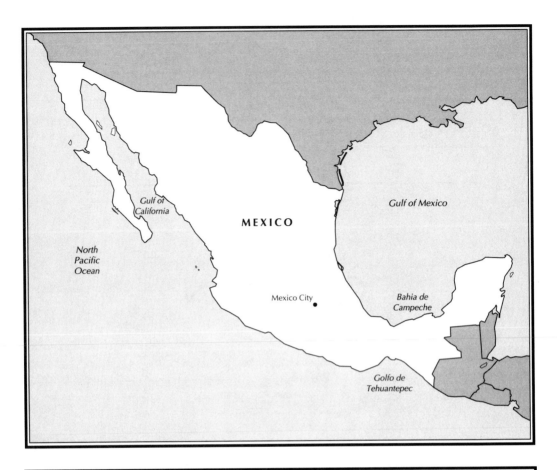

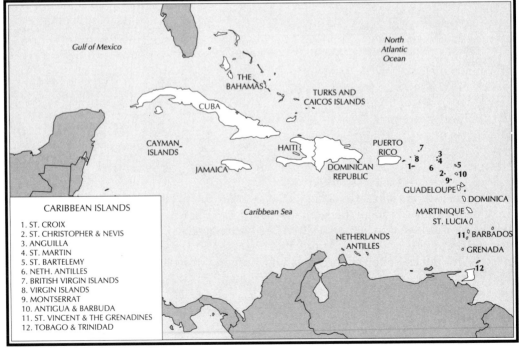

CARIBBEAN ISLANDS

1. ST. CROIX
2. ST. CHRISTOPHER & NEVIS
3. ANGUILLA
4. ST. MARTIN
5. ST. BARTELEMY
6. NETH. ANTILLES
7. BRITISH VIRGIN ISLANDS
8. VIRGIN ISLANDS
9. MONTSERRAT
10. ANTIGUA & BARBUDA
11. ST. VINCENT & THE GRENADINES
12. TOBAGO & TRINIDAD

6

MEXICO AND THE CARIBBEAN

by Heather Caines and Oralia Garza de Cortes

MEXICO

Given Mexico's immense size and proximity to the United States, it is puzzling that the body of literature about such an important "good neighbor" lacks the depth of coverage it deserves. The currently available children's books about Mexico are aimed primarily at providing young readers with the essential, basic information that any good student is expected to know about a country. One need only glance at the 1991 Subject Guide to *Children's Books in Print* to confirm such a listing. With today's learning emphasis on high-order thinking skills and similar methodologies designed to encourage and develop critical thinking, many of these survey books could be found useful for analyzing, comparing, and contrasting. What is lacking, however, are books on Mexico that highlight the distinct cultures and cultural groups unique to specific regions or states within the country. Over 20 years ago M. Evans and Co. published *Viva Morelia*, a book that excels in its effort to provide an anthropological and cultural perspective of the blending of the Indian and Spanish cultures within a specific cultural and geographical area. Lerner's *Focus on Mexico* is a more recent notable effort that closely resembles that approach. Rebecca and Judith Marcus's *Fiesta Time in Mexico* is another worthwhile title that, while presenting the major Mexican celebrations within their religious or historical contexts, also emphasizes the regional uniqueness of the practices.

Another relevant subject area, the Indians of Mexico, reveals an equally long list of books primarily about the Aztecs, the most well known of the ancestors of today's Mexicans. Again, children should be encouraged to compare and contrast the usefulness of the basic information that is to be found in most of these books. With the exception of the Mayan civilization, however, American children's book publishing has neglected the contributions of the other magnificent ancient civilizations within Mexico: the Toltec, the Mixtec, the Zapotec, the Olmec, and the Purepeche or Tarascan cultures, cultures whose civilizations equaled or surpassed those of the Aztec long before the Aztecs rose to prominence. The few books that do mention these civilizations tend to dismiss them as ancestors of the Aztecs.

The recently published scholarly work by John Bierhorst, *The Mythology of Mexico and Central America*, is an invaluable exploration of the complex traditions of the many indigenous groups that have managed to preserve their way of life in rapidly changing times. While this bibliography does not emphasize titles of a folkloric nature, it is difficult to discuss the whole of a country without saying a word about such an important area. Mexican folklore stories reveal much in the way of history and the interaction of cultures. For example, in Anita Brenner's *The Boy Who Could Do Anything and Other Stories* (Addison-Wesley, 1942, 1970), the man-eating giant that goes from village to village demanding sacrifices from the villagers is a fear carried over from the days of the Aztec empire, and thus, young Tepozton, who kills him, is a folk hero. The motif of saving the young baby's life by placing him in a straw basket that floats downstream parallels Moses's story; Tepozton's being eaten whole by the giant and surviving inside the giant's belly is the Jonah story. The motifs are themes carried over through the generations, spanning the three distinct societies that have flourished in Mexico—the pre-Columbian period; the colonial period, when conversion to Christianity was initiated by the Spaniards; and the modern Mexican period, which is represented in the oral tradition of the telling. This is only one example of the richness of culture that can be conveyed by story. Unfortunately, Mexican folklore published in the United States has tended to stereotype the people by the illustration. Dolch's *Stories from Mexico* (Garrard, 1960) is a classic example.

In biography, the Raintree Hispanic Stories series has recently published in attractive bilingual editions *Sor Juana Inéz de la Cruz*, the life of Mexico's greatest mystic poet; *Benito Juárez*, the Zapotec Indian who is today considered the George Washington of his country; and *Miguel Hidalgo y Costilla*, father of the Mexican Revolution. Chelsea's *Zapata* and *Juárez* are both excellent works that not only detail the political lives of Emiliano Zapata, Mexico's finest revolutionary hero, and Benito Juárez but also provide a concise, in-depth analysis of those fascinating periods of modern Mexican history. *Diego Rivera: Mexican Muralist* (Childrens Press, 1990) is an interesting and readable biography of one of Mexico's foremost artists.

Lamentably, little in the way of fiction exposes children to the richness of Mexican culture or the beauty of the land. Several works, however, deserve mention. The naturalist Jean Craighead George's *Shark Beneath the Reefs* introduces readers to the natural beauty of sea life unique to the Sea of Cortez and the Baja California region, interwoven within a modern cultural context. In historical writing, Bea Bragg's *The Very First Thanksgiving: Pioneers on the Rio Grande* explores life on the Chihuahuan desert during the late 1500s and early to mid 1600s in her dramatic story of the Onate expedition. Elizabeth Borton de Trevino's *El Guëro: A True Adventure Story* takes her readers on a journey into the desolate Baja California region during the late 1800s and during the era of the Porfiriato (Porfirio Diaz regime). Américo Paredes's classic novel *George Washington Gómez* for young adults (annotated in the Hispanic Americans chapter and cross-indexed here) is a compelling novel of the Mexicans of the Rio Grande valley region of Texas at the height of anti-Mexican sentiment in the United States. Much more could be written and needs to be written. Mexico was a fascinating place during the early twentieth century, one that inspired such famous writers, artists, and intellectuals as D. H. Lawrence, Ambrose Bierce, John Reed, Leon Trotsky, Ed Weston, and Jean Charlot. It is also the place where today's great writers and artists, such as Gabriel García Marquéz and Luis Buñuel, have chosen to live.

The joint venture of Little, Brown and the Mexican publisher Editorial Novarro in publishing *My Song Is a Piece of Jade: Poems of Ancient Mexico in English and Spanish* in 1984 was a commendable effort to publish authentic works jointly produced in Mexico and the United States. Another area that needs exploring is books in translation. The 1987 Swedish publication of *Rädda Min Djungel* (translated into Spanish as *Salven mi selva*) is a modern-day ecology tale based on the true story of a young boy's effort to save Mexico's tropical rain forest. This book has not yet appeared in English in the United States. In addition, the renaissance in children's book publishing in Mexico offers many opportunities. The magical realism in Gilberto Rendon Ortiz's works for children and other literary works for upper elementary and middle school children are currently being produced by Editorial Amaquemecán in Mexico and are ripe for translation into English.

Librarians, teachers, and children's book publishers can make a significant and worthwhile contribution to the reduction of the dropout problems of Mexican American youths in the United States by legitimizing their dual heritage through books. At the same time, children in the United States will gain a deeper appreciation and a closer understanding of the fascinating neighbor that is Mexico. Many of the books annotated here serve as a starting point, and it is hoped that the gaps in the literature will be filled in the near future.

SPANISH-SPEAKING CARIBBEAN AND HAITI

Of the three regions covered in this chapter—Mexico, the Spanish-speaking Caribbean, and the English-speaking Caribbean—the largest hole in publishing seems to be in the second area of the list. The countries of Cuba, the Dominican Republic, and Haiti as well as the commonwealth of Puerto Rico have attracted little more than series volumes, and in some cases not even that. The multi-layered heritage of these islands' residents—Indian, African, and European—is not reflected in the fiction or trade nonfiction, which tends to focus more on the political problems of the area. Even folklore is lacking; John Bierhorst's comprehensive volume *The Mythology of Mexico and Central America* does not include the traditional myths and tales of the Caribbean.

In the area of fiction, the most prominent theme is the relationship of Puerto Ricans living on the mainland to Puerto Ricans living on the island. Both Cruz Martel's *Yagua Days* and Nicolasa Mohr's *Going Home* (annotated in the Hispanic Americans chapter and cross-referenced here) portray a young "Nuyorican's" journey to Puerto Rico for the first time. Poetry evocative of a Puerto Rican setting comprises two highly recommended works—Arnold Adoff's *Flamboyán* and Charlotte Pomerantz's *The Tamarindo Puppy*. The latter volume combines English and Spanish words in a way that touches upon the dual heritage of Puerto Ricans living on the mainland. Puerto Rico is one of several Spanish-speaking places featured prominently in the bilingual collection of stories and poems edited by Sylvia Pena and published by Arte Público Press, *Tun-Ta-Ca-Tun* and *Kikiriki* (annotated in the Hispanic Americans chapter); in the two collections of songs compiled by Lulu Delacre and published by Scholastic, *Arroz con leche* and *Las Navidades*; and in the collection of short stories from Latin America, *Where Angels Glide at Dawn* (annotated in the chapter on Central and South America). Although its setting is deliberately vague, Eve Bunting's *How Many Days to America?* touches upon economic and political conflicts in Haiti and the Dominican Republic in its depiction of a refugee family taking a rickety boat to safety and freedom.

Unfortunately, virtually no book—fiction or nonfiction—as yet tells us how children actually live in Cuba, the Dominican Republic, and Haiti. Gareth Stevens offers one volume on Cuba in its Children of the World series. Of the general country surveys, Lerner's Visual Geography series offers volumes on all three countries and Puerto Rico. Bright color photos interspersed with impersonal, encyclopedia-like text characterize this series. Because of rapid changes, the volume on Haiti, published in 1988, is already quite dated. The Childrens Press Enchantment of the World series features a volume on Cuba, and Chelsea House presents Cuba, the Dominican Republic, and Haiti in its Let's Visit Places and Peoples of the World series for the junior high level. The focus of the Chelsea House series is primarily on the history and political situation of the country covered. Chelsea House biographies of Fidel Castro, Che Guevara (annotated in the Central and South America chapter), the Duvaliers, and Toussaint L'Ouverture (World Leaders—Past and Present) present historical and political information along with the life of the biographee. Series biographies of political figures (Jose Martí, Luis Muñoz Marín) and scientists (Carlos Finlay) have been published by Raintree for younger readers. Nonetheless, there remains a desperate shortage of fiction and nonfiction on the culture and daily life of the region as a whole and of anything on the Dominican Republic, the original home of some 1 million residents of the United States.

ENGLISH-SPEAKING CARIBBEAN

The richness of the English-speaking Caribbean culture makes it an ideal topic for literary treatment. There is a rich canvas of experiences to capture, a colorful array of local speech patterns and cadences to relate, and vivid scenes of flora, fauna, and landscapes to paint. But it is a fertile field lying fallow. The resultant neglect within this area of literature has produced a paucity of materials, with the shortage most evident in works suitable for children and teenagers. Despite this literary poverty, what exists is very good. Thus the task remains to make readers aware of available materials in order to connect them to this literary gold mine.

The offering in this bibliography is a kaleidoscopic journey through the English-speaking Caribbean. As is widely known, the culture of the Caribbean is a mixture of the mores of the ruling colonial powers, the customs of the African people, and the conventions that are simply indigenous to life in the region itself. It is the strands of this heritage that provide the diverse, yet unified themes that pervade the fiction, nonfiction, biographical, and folkloric genres that compose this bibliography. As a result, recurring motifs in many fiction works are the importance of family and social place, belief in the spirit world and obeah (a type of witchcraft), and the appreciation of nature and exultation in its beauty. Historical works, on the other hand, focus on conflicts between traditional and modern ways of life and between those who seek stability and those who advocate change. Those works chronicle the islands' struggle to attain independence—and then find their place among the more industrialized nations in the face of economic and technological lack.

While there is a sampling of materials on all grade levels, the number of titles for younger and mid-level readers exceeds those for older adolescent readers. This imbalance is demonstrated by the many picture books and the numerous fiction and nonfiction titles for middle readers. Outstanding picture books include *Calypso Alphabet, The Jolly Mon,* and *My Little Island.* Notable books for the mid-level reader include the nonfiction titles *We Live in the Caribbean* and *Caribbean Canvas.* Outstanding nonfiction and fiction for older readers include *The Caribbean: Issues in U.S. Relations* and *Annie John,* respectively, the latter by Jamaica Kincaid, a noted figure in contemporary world literature. However, preeminent among the various books is a collection of stories for older readers entitled *A Thief in the Village and Other Stories* by James Berry, which vividly captures the sights, sounds, smells, and inner workings of contemporary Jamaican life.

In terms of series, those included are quite interesting and well written. Each is unique in its own way, providing a distinctive view of the island or islands covered. While some are photo-essays that focus on children (*A Family in Jamaica*), others are personal vignettes of island life (*We Live in the Caribbean*) or detailed historical, social, and economic surveys (*The West Indies*). Since each is clear and well organized and provides a particular vista of the Caribbean, it is difficult to make a qualitative judgment. However, if forced to choose, readers should be informed that *Jamaica in Pictures* and *The West Indies* are two that stand out for their depth and breadth of coverage.

The introduction for Mexico was written by Oralia Garza de Cortes. She and Lyn Miller-Lachmann co-authored the introduction for the Spanish-speaking Caribbean and Haiti section. Heather Caines wrote the introduction for the English-speaking Caribbean section and contributed the entries for that area.

PRESCHOOL–GRADE 3

378 Adoff, Arnold. *Flamboyán.* Harcourt Brace Jovanovich 1988, HB $14.95 (0-15-228404-4). unp. Fiction.

Culebra Island in Puerto Rico is the setting for this story, written in poetic prose, of the young girl Flamboyán, the girl with hair as red as the flaming red flowers of the flamboyán tree. Each day, and with each passing season, Flamboyán blossoms like the flower. The young girl frolics in the carefree, open air, thriving on the many lovely flowers that abound—periwinkles, bird of paradise, bougainvillea, wild orchids, and flowering lemon trees. While the flora help to strengthen her roots to the island, the fauna help her to be "free as birds in the open sky." But always, it is under the cover of the bright red flamboyán tree that she is able to dream of flying like the many island birds—pelicans, sugar birds, doves, kingfishers, mangrove cuckoos, frigates, and flycatchers.

The panorama of life on the island, with all its charm and beauty, will enchant young children everywhere. The book is excellent for introducing the many types of flowers and animals peculiar to this particular island. Children will also find this small island to be unique in that its inhabitants, like

Flamboyán's family and neighbors, actually live there and earn their living there in diverse ways. For instance, Flamboyán's father is an electrician, and her mother sells fruit and candy. Vibrant watercolor and gouache illustrations mesmerize and invite all children to dream and fly like Flamboyán. O.G. de C.

379   Agard, John. *The Calypso Alphabet.* Illus. by Jennifer Bent. Henry Holt 1989, LB $13.95 (0-8050-1177-3). 28pp. Fiction.

Here is another addition to the perennial genre of alphabet books. This one is unique for its infusion of the lore and mores of the Caribbean. The reader is carried through the alphabet from A to Z, with each page devoted to a single letter. Each lowercase character is followed by an appropriate word or phrase with a descriptive explanation. The essence of each expression (all of which are indigenous to the Caribbean) is depicted in the vibrant pictures, which transport readers to and immerse them in island life. The word "jook," which means to stick or prick, is aptly portrayed by a young boy who, having stuck his foot on a nail, is jumping and writhing in pain.

The paintings, a combination of scratchboard and concentrated watercolor inks, are rustic yet vivid. Although most things described will not be obvious to most preschoolers, the book gives at once an unusual yet informative glimpse of another culture. In one stroke both the alphabet and cultural mores are introduced to young readers.

Includes a word list that provides additional explanation and background for unfamiliar terms. H.C.

Bierhorst, John. *Doctor Coyote: A Native American Aesop's Fables.*
See entry 401, Grades 4–6.

380   Bryan, Ashley. *Turtle Knows Your Name.* Illus. by the author. Macmillan 1989, HB $12.95 (0-689-31578-3). 32pp. Fiction.

Turtle Knows Your Name is the retelling of a story from the West Indies. A young boy who must learn his long name, Upsilimana Tumpalerado, gets some loving assistance from his grandmother. On the day of accomplishment there is great celebration, and he and his granny dance a name dance by the sea.

However, this triumph is not the end of Upsilimana Tumpalerado's problems. His name is so cumbersome that his playmates deride it, calling him Long Name instead, much to his displeasure. Even the animals cannot remember it, or they have no interest in doing so. Upsilimana feels forlorn and dejected, until he meets Turtle, and then his despair turns to delight. For it is Turtle who is cognizant of his name and even more.

This is a warm and touching tale of the love shared between a grandmother and grandson, as well as a telling portrayal of life in the Caribbean. The rich, bold watercolor illustrations at once propel and convey the essence of the story line, which will interest youngsters from preschool through grade 3.

Another tale, based on West Indian folklore, by the same author is *The Dancing Granny* (Macmillan, 1987). H.C.

381 Buffett, Jimmy, and Savannah Jane Buffett. ***The Jolly Mon.*** Illus. by Lambert David. Harcourt Brace Jovanovich 1988, HB $14.95 (0-15-240530-5). 32pp. Fiction.

This is a magical tale of a golden-throated fisherman on the island of Banana-land, in the Caribbean sea, who finds a bejeweled guitar with an inscription upon the back that reads:

I come from the ocean with songs of the sea;
No lesson for learning, just play upon me.
Now go make your music in lands near and far;
Orion protects you wherever you are.

In order to carry out the inscription, the islanders build a boat, enabling the Jolly Mon to travel and share the happiness of this music. He sails from island to island spreading joy, until one day he receives a message. His friend, the ruler of Bananaland, Good King Jones, has died, and the islanders need him to return. Setting out for home, Jolly Mon encounters a band of marauding pirates, who attack him and throw him overboard. However, a dolphin, Albion, saves him and brings him safely to Bananaland. Upon his return the Jolly Mon is crowned the new ruler, and Albion disappears into the sky with the final words: "Rule well, and if you need me, all you have to do is sing."

A superbly crafted story that in text and the full-page color acrylic drawings evokes the charm and idyllic bliss of the islands, if only in the context of a fantasyland. Ideal for extended reading-aloud sessions for preschool through grade 3, this is an inventive and highly successful way to expose young minds to a different culture. H.C.

382 Bunting, Eve. ***How Many Days to America? A Thanksgiving Story.*** Illus. by Beth Peck. Clarion 1988, HB $14.95 (0-89919-521-0). 32pp. Fiction.

A little boy recounts in a delicate, poetic voice the many details of a sudden trip that begins one evening when soldiers unexpectedly visit his family's home. Soon after, the father announces that they must leave. The young family of four joins many other refugees on a dangerous journey in an overcrowded fishing boat that carries them across the waves. The passengers endure hunger, thirst, and the perils of the overburdened boat. In additon, they encounter sea pirates, who are thieves who prey on already powerless victims. When the fishing boat finally reaches land, the men swim ashore and encounter the soldiers who, though offering food and drink, are obligated to turn back the refugees. When they finally land on safe and friendly territory, the refugees are welcomed with open arms. They are fed a Thankgiving dinner, the meal that highlights all that they are indeed grateful for.

This story is a modern-day version of yet another group of pilgrims who, like the pilgrims of old, must leave their homeland due to persecution and build a new life in America. These pilgrims, however, are from the Caribbean, where the turmoil and uncertainty of political events weigh heavily upon the citizens, who then seek refuge and asylum in the United States. Bunting's touching drama expresses the hope that all pilgrims carry with them when traveling on their way to a better life. O.G. de C.

383 Cooper, Susan. *Jethro and the Jumbie.* Illus. by Ashley Bryan. Atheneum 1979. 28pp. Fiction. o.p.

Jethro is furious. He would be 8 next week, and his big brother had promised to take him deep-sea fishing when he reached that age. Now Thomas is saying that Jethro is too small to go! Jethro stomps away up the hill, though he is warned that the trail is supposed to be haunted by spirits of the dead, called "jumbies." Jethro is so angry that he does not care. He is too disgusted to believe in jumbies. But meet one he does, and he finally enlists the creature's aid in changing his brother's mind, with humorous results.

Jethro's adventures with his newly found companion make for an enchanting, warmhearted story. The author has succeeded in capturing the color and rhythm of the local speech patterns (of a locale in the British Virgin Islands) while the artist's line pencil drawings convey the humor and verve of the text. The story is recommended for older picture book readers. H.C.

384 de Gerez, Toni, adaptor. *My Song Is a Piece of Jade: Poems of Ancient Mexico in English and Spanish.* Bilingual ed. Illus. by William Stark. Little, Brown 1984. 48pp. Fiction. o.p.

The sacred Nahuatl poems of the Toltecs, who flourished during the Golden Age of Tula (an ancient Toltec place some 90 miles north of what is now Mexico City), are here adapted for children in this book, which is nicely illustrated with pastel watercolor and wash. The wisdom and beauty of the Toltecs and their love of beauty and nature are evident in these carefully selected texts that also reveal the cult of Quetzalcoatl and his mysterious disappearance. The people's anxiety and their hopes for his return are also recorded in the poems. This bilingual edition, which was simultaneously copublished in Mexico, provides excellent material for the study of Mexico's poems of antiquity, as well as for social studies units that further delve into the roots of ancient Mexican culture and thought. It is also particularly useful for Cinco de Mayo programs and activities. O.G. de C.

385 Delacre, Lulu. *Arroz con leche: Popular Songs and Rhymes from Latin America.* Bilingual ed.; musical arrangements by Ana-Maria Rosado. English lyrics by Elena Paz. Illus. by Lulu Dalacre. Scholastic 1989, HB $12.95 (0-590-41887-4). 32pp. Nonfiction.

The carefree, fun-loving nature of play is lovingly illustrated in this nursey rhyme book with selections of some of the most popular games and rhymes of Mexico, Puerto Rico, and Argentina.

In an era in which high technology and the mass media have dominated children's leisure playtime, this nursery rhyme illustrated in soft pastels will serve both as a useful tool in the restoration of Spanish-language nursery rhyme, game, and song and as an introduction to the culture and language. The English lyrics are not translated literally, thus allowing for free-flowing verses while at the same time capturing the essence of the Spanish verse without changing the context or meaning. Includes musical accompaniments. A more recent work, *Las Navidades: Popular Christmas Songs from Latin America* (Scholastic, 1990), features songs and background information on holiday traditions in Puerto Rico, the Dominican Republic, Venezuela, and elsewhere. O.G. de C.

386   Fisher, Leonard Everett. ***Pyramid of the Sun, Pyramid of the Moon.*** Illus. by the author. Macmillan 1988, HB $13.95 (0-02-735300-1). 32pp. Nonfiction.

There are two structures outside of Mexico City that form a monument to the great Indian civilizations that created them and the subsequent Indian cultures that inherited these structures and used them as sacred temples of worship. These two structures are pre-Hispanic pyramids dedicated to the sun and to the moon. With striking black-and-white illustrations, Fisher has dramatically enhanced the story of a culture that flourished long before the Spanish conquerors came and destroyed these great civilizations. The temples of the sun and the moon are two remaining testaments to that vast and glorious past.

The text, while brief, is at times confusing. It lacks clarity in distinguishing between the distinct cities of Tenochtitlán, capital of the Aztec empire (now Mexico City), and Teotihuacán, capital of the Toltecs and the holy city where the two magnificent pyramids lie. Fisher is explicit in describing the Aztec ritual of human heart sacrifice but without so much as offering an explanation of the philosophy behind the practice. To the Aztecs, the offering of the human heart gave them direct lifeblood from the sun. Without the sun, an Aztec deity, the Aztecs believed all life would perish, and, so, sacrifice was necessary for it to continue.   O.G. de C.

387   Griffiths, John. ***Take a Trip to Puerto Rico.*** Illus. with photos. SERIES: Take a Trip. Franklin Watts 1989, LB $9.40 (0-531-10737-X). 32pp. Nonfiction.

Like its companion books, this introduction to Puerto Rico offers a panorama, via sharp color photography, of the landscape and familiar sights of the island. Prominently featured is the Spanish architecture of the area. The series is intended to introduce its readers to how other people live. This particular series book, unfortunately, falls short of its objective. Griffiths instead offers readers a handy tour book of the island. The lack of chapters makes it difficult to find any logical order to the sequencing of the material.   O.G. de C.

388   Haskins, Jim. ***Count Your Way Through Mexico.*** Illus. by Helen Byers. SERIES: Count Your Way Books. Lerner/Carolrhoda 1989, LB $11.95 (0-87614-349-4); P $4.95 (0-87614-517-9). 24pp. Nonfiction.

The numbers 1 through 10 become a means of showing Mexico's rich history, culture, and ways of life in this series volume. The writing style is simple; with sympathy and understanding, the author presents a wide range of information about the country. The Spanish and Indian words particular to Mexican culture are phonetically stressed and spelled out. Color pencil drawings enhance an aesthetically pleasing way to learn the basic numbers in Spanish. A handy pronunciation guide to the numbers is in back.   O.G. de C.

389   Lattimore, Deborah Nourse. ***The Flame of Peace: A Tale of the Aztecs.*** Illus. by the author. HarperCollins 1987, LB $12.89 (0-06-023709-0). 48pp. Nonfiction.

Two Flint is a young Aztec boy who goes fishing in a nearby lake. He notices that the battle flags are flying on the tower, a sign of imminent danger. His father is sent as ambassador during the Twenty Days of Talking, a neutral period of discussion between tribes. But Two Flint's father is killed in battle. Troubled by his death and puzzled by the fighting, Two Flint questions his mother, who relates to him the story of that brief period when all the tribes were brothers—back in the days when the sacred light of Morning Star burned in the temples. As long as the fires are dying, there can be only war, not peace, he is told.

Two Flint decides to find a solution to the dilemma. As he arrives at a crossroads, he encounters the first evil demon, one who can change the course of the river. Lord River sweeps away Lord Crossroads, only to be blown back by Lord Wind, who in turn is swallowed by Lord Storm's frogs, who hail and rain over Lord Wind. Two Flint continues on his journey, being further challenged by Lord Earthquake, Lord Volcano, Lord Smoking Mirror, and finally Lord and Lady Death. He fights off the seven demons until he reaches the Hill of the Star. As a reward for defeating the demons, Lord Morning Star gives Two Flint the new flame he seeks. Two Flint immediately takes the flame to its proper place on the Aztec temple.

Vibrant colors offer an imaginative look at that era of Aztec history when the various tribes lived in peace and harmony. The inside front and back covers of the book offer a pictorial dictionary of the many symbols used in the story. Lattimore uses her knowledge and expertise to create a beautifully illustrated book, sure to intrigue young children, especially in its meticulously detailed artwork.

O.G. de C.

390   Lattimore, Deborah Nourse. **Why There Is No Arguing in Heaven: A Mayan Myth.** Illus. by the author. HarperCollins 1989, LB $13.89 (0-06-023718-X). 40pp. Nonfiction.

In the beginning, Hunab Ku, the Creator God, ruled in darkness. The other gods —the Sun God, the Maize God, the Moon Goddess, and Lizzard House—sat by his feet, each arguing with the other about who after Hunab Ku was a greater god. After creating the earth, Hunab Ku challenged the gods to create a being who could worship all the gods. The god who could successfully accomplish that task would have the honor of sitting next to Hunab Ku.

Each of the gods attempted to create such a being, but each of them failed. The exception was the Maize God, who took the remains of all the previous attempts at creation and created a being who is part water, part earth, part tree, part land, part sky, part moon, and part sun.

This creation story from ancient Mayan civilization is told with Lattimore's lavish dramatic illustrations that convey the elegant beauty of ancient Mayan mythology.

O.G. de C.

391   Lessac, Frane. **My Little Island.** Illus. by the author. HarperCollins 1984, P $3.95 (0-06-443146-0). 38pp. Fiction.

A young boy takes his friend to visit the little Caribbean island where he was born. He is glad to be home again, and, through all of their activities and adventures, he exults in introducing his friend to the sights, sounds, flora, and fauna of his birthplace. From a visit to the market in the town, and a day spent watching the fishermen perform their craft, his young friend learns much about the social customs and everyday life of a Caribbean island. The two friends also browse in an island shop for presents to take home, enjoy the performance of calypso and reggae music, explore the wild forest, and finally witness and delight in Carnival. Visual artist Lessac has given us a fun-filled vacation that takes the two boys as well as the reader on a jubilant and colorful excursion through daily life on a Caribbean island. Full-page, vivid illustrations transport the reader to this, one of many island paradises. This is a book for parents, teachers, and other adults as well as children to enjoy and appreciate. In classrooms it is particularly useful as a visual introduction to a unit on the Caribbean.

H.C.

392 Lewis, Thomas P. *Hill of Fire.* Illus. by Joan Sandin. SERIES: I Can Read Books. HarperCollins 1971, LB $10.89 (0-06-023804-6); P $3.50 (0-06-444040-0). 64pp. Fiction.

A bored farmer living in a remote village in the state of Michoacán in Mexico is unhappy with his life because "nothing ever happens." His fellow villagers point out that they have everything they need—a market, a school, and a church with a bell that rings on Sunday mornings. One day during planting season, Pablo, the farmer's son, goes to the fields to help his father plow the land. As they are plowing, the plow burrows itself into a little hole. The little hole becomes a greater hole, until soon they hear strange noises coming from underneath the ground. They also observe white smoke creeping out from the ever-growing gap. The farmer and his son witness the birth of a volcano. Although the fictitious farmer and his neighbors were moved from their homes, area people still remember this historic event from the 1940s. At that time, peasant farmers still wore huaraches (sandals), peasant clothes of white broadcloth, and large hats, known as sombreros. Today, the Parícutin volcano is a Mexican landmark. It is still considered an active volcano, though there have been no eruptions in quite a while.

Lewis has narrated an exciting historical novel filled with anticipation and action about a rare eyewitness account; in fact, only two such eyewitness accounts of the Parícutin eruption have ever been documented. The two-tone brown and gray illustrations dramatically re-create a story that comes alive as the excitement builds. Although today Mexican peasants do not dress in the manner of the story's characters, the illustrations are an accurate representation of a historical period.

O.G. de C.

393 Lloyd, Errol. *Nini at Carnival.* First published in the United States in 1979. Illus. by the author. HarperCollins 1979, LB $11.70 (0-690-03892-5). 30pp. Fiction.

The festival of Carnival is the backdrop for the story line and the inspiration for the colorful drawings in this delightful picture book. Everyone is preparing for Carnival except for young Nini. She lacks a costume and is so depressed that she just sits on a box and cries. However, all is not lost. Betti, an older friend, disguised as a fairy godmother, comes to her aid. Betti procurs a costume for Nini, who is eventually crowned Queen of the Carnival, much to her surprise and delight.

The story illustrates the innocence of children's belief in make-believe (evidenced by Nini's acceptance of a fairy godmother) and the beauty of friendship. The short yet potent text is propelled by the luminous illustrations that depict the color and exultation of the celebration. A wonderful story for reading aloud or silently.

H.C.

394 Lye, Keith. ***Take a Trip to Jamaica.*** Illus. with photos. SERIES: Take a Trip. Franklin Watts 1988, LB $9.90 (0-531-10558-X). 32pp. Nonfiction.

Take a Trip to Jamaica is part of a many-volume series highlighting life-styles in many lands. The text provides a cursory overview of the history, geography, currency, postage, economy, education, and culture of the country covered. All of these details are enhanced by colorful photos that capture the flavor of life in the various countries. Because this broad spectrum of information is given in a brief textual commentary, the coverage tends to be sketchy or fragmented, offering only bits of information rather than forming a uniform, continuous thread. Nevertheless, this series is useful for its accessibility to the younger grades.

Includes an index and a facts-in-brief section. For the Caribbean area, the series includes *Take a Trip to the West Indies.*   H.C.

395 Lye, Keith. ***Take a Trip to Mexico.*** Illus. with photos. SERIES: Take a Trip. Franklin Watts 1982, LB $10.90 (0-531-04471-8). 32pp. Nonfiction.

This is a beginning reader with large color photos of places in Mexico and scenes of everyday life. Unfortunately, there are no chapters, so there is no center to the book's arrangement of information. A useful index is included. A section on "Words About Mexico" alphabetically lists the new words used in the text of the book, but no definitions are provided. Additional volumes in this series present Cuba, Haiti, and Puerto Rico.   O.G. de C.

McKissack, Patricia C. ***The Maya.***
See entry 408, Grades 4–6.

Martel, Cruz. ***Yaqua Days.***
See entry 203, Grades PS–3.

396 Moran, Tom. ***A Family in Mexico.*** Illus. with photos. SERIES: Families the World Over. Lerner 1987, LB $9.95 (0-8225-1677-2). 32pp. Nonfiction.

Paula María Fosado, a nine-year-old from a small rural town near Oaxaca, is the focus of this information book that guides the reader through a typical week of daily living, to demonstrate what life in Mexico is like today. The vibrant color photographs showcase many aspects of daily life in Oaxaca, including the cultural significance of the *zocalo* (town square) and Monte Albán, the Zapotec ruins.

While focusing on one child and one family, the author intends to showcase family living in Mexico. Unfortunately, the child is from a wealthy family and thus atypical of most children, whose families work very hard to maintain a middle to working class standard of living or who belong to the urban or rural poor. Because the book centers so much on the regionalism of daily life in Oaxaca, this book is more aptly a look at cultural aspects of that region of Mexico.

Orr, Katherine. ***My Grandpa and the Sea.***
See entry 409, Grades 4–6.

397   Pomerantz, Charlotte. *The Tamarindo Puppy and Other Poems.* Illus. by Byron Barton. Greenwillow 1980. 32pp. Nonfiction. o.p.

This unique poetry book contains 13 poems that use both the English and Spanish languages. The poems reflect the bicultural nature of many Hispanic children, in which use of both languages is a normal part of everyday life. The poems range from the very tender—those that use diminutives quite liberally—to the boisterous. Yet each poem maintains a highly lyrical tone. The content of the poems expresses the beauty of daily life for a child in Puerto Rico. The artwork features a naive style; using primarily orange and yellow tones, the illustrator depicts children and animals in their natural surroundings. The farm, the outdoors, the landscape, and the ocean waters suggest a Puerto Rican island setting.   O.G. de C.

398   Rohmer, Harriet, and Mary Anchondo. *How We Came to the Fifth World: A Creation Story from Ancient Mexico./Como vinimos al quinto mundo.* Rev. ed.; bilingual ed. Illus. by Graciela Carillo and Consuelo Mendez. Children's Book Pr. 1988, LB $12.95 (0-89239-024-7). 24pp. Nonfiction.

According to Aztec mythology, there would be five worlds, each created by a deity and each in turn destroyed by a deity representing one of the four elements of nature: rain, wind, fire, and earth. An adaptation of ancient Aztec mythology, this is the story of life during those ancient epochs. In each epoch, the people become selfish and greedy. As a result, they lose their lives when they anger the gods, which causes the gods in turn to destroy that world. All are destroyed except one couple, who follows the instructions of the god and wins the gods' favor, thus continuing the existence of humans in the newly created world. This story, which resembles in some ways the Judeo-Christian legend of Noah's Ark, features bold color illustrations that enhance the simple, direct text. This book can be used in classes to illustrate and spark discussion about the common threads and themes of various distinct cultures' creation stories.   O.G. de C.

399   Taha, Karen T. *A Gift for Tía Rosa.* Illus. by Dee de Rosa. Dillon 1986. 38pp. Fiction. o.p.

Carmela is a sweet 8-year-old girl who learns the art of knitting from Tía Rosa, her elderly aunt and neighbor. Together, they share many joyful moments designing patterns and coordinating colors. One day, however, Tía Rosa becomes sick and is taken to the hospital. During her two-week hospital stay, Carmela strongly feels her absence. Tía Rosa returns home from the hospital, but Carmela is disappointed to hear that her Tía Rosa is too ill to see her.

Carmela receives a phone call from Tía Rosa. She too has missed Carmela. She invites Carmela to visit, and once more they share in the joys and display of their new creations. During this visit, Tía Rosa surprises Carmela by giving her a silver chain with a small rose, a symbol of her namesake. After a brief period of recovery, Tía Rosa falls ill again and dies in the hospital.

This realistic portrayal of death is handled with honesty and sincerity. Taha's story also captures the strong bonds characteristic of those special relationships found in Hispanic cultures between the young and the old, as shown so poignantly by Carmela's and Tía Rosa's particular affection for each other.

O.G. de C.

400 Tompert, Ann. *The Silver Whistle.* Illus. by Beth Peck. Macmillan 1988, HB $14.95 (0-02-789160-7). 32pp. Fiction.

Miguel's family—he, his baby sister, his mother, and his father—travel the steep mountains of the Oaxaca Valley on Christmas Eve, eager to arrive in time to participate in Midnight Mass and the events surrounding that religious occasion. Miguel has saved his hard-earned money in order to purchase a silver whistle from Diego, the town's silversmith. The whistle is to be Miguel's gift to the Christ Child, to be presented during the evening procession. In the whirl of excitement at the marketplace, Miguel gets distracted by the many family visitors who have filled the stands and begun to sell their crafts and wares. His sympathy for a distraught burro leads him to exchange his money for the burro. Later, he barters away even the burro.

When procession time is at hand, Miguel finds himself with no silver whistle with which to honor the Christ Child. He joins the procession, but instead of giving the new silver whistle he had intended, he offers his own hand-carved wooden whistle.

The story is contemporary, though it resembles the Legend of the Poinsettia and gives that tale a modern twist. Beth Peck's delicate color illustrations portray a Christmas story filled with characteristic bustle and anticipation. However, the illustrations are distorted because they portray only Indians and lead the reader to believe that the entire population of Oaxaca is indigenous; in reality, whites and mestizos (those of mixed blood) inhabit the region as well. In addition, only the jacket flap states that this story took place long ago. The time of the story is omitted from the text itself.   O.G. de C.

GRADES 4–6

401 Bierhorst, John. *Doctor Coyote: A Native American Aesop's Fables.* Illus. by Wendy Watson. Macmillan 1987, HB $14.95 (0-02-709780-3). 48pp. Nonfiction.

The 20 fables retold here were found in a book of fables translated into the Nahuatl language in the Americas some one hundred years after the Spanish Conquest. Wolf and Coyote, eternal enemies, are the two main characters who rely on their own wisdom and wit to guide them in their daily actions.

Watson's illustrations of soft watercolor pastels unfortunately give this book a pop southwestern appearance. Moreover, the illustrations transform the stories into virtual comic strips due to the illustrator's cartoon-style format.

The fables could well have gained their popularity because of the Aztecs' use of *dichos*, the wise sayings that accompany a lesson to be learned. These sayings abound in Mexican figurative speech today.   O.G. de C.

Casagrande, Louis B., and Sylvia A. Johnson. *Focus on Mexico: Modern Life in an Ancient Land.*
See entry 416, Grades 7–9.

de Gerez, Toni, adaptor. *My Song Is a Piece of Jade: Poems of Ancient Mexico in English and Spanish.*
See entry 384, Grades PS–3.

Fisher, Leonard Everett. *Pyramid of the Sun, Pyramid of the Moon.*
See entry 386, Grades PS–3.

402 Gleiter, Jan, and Kathleen Thompson. *José Martí.* Bilingual ed.; Spanish trans. by Alma Flor Ada. Illus. by Les Didier. SERIES: Hispanic Stories. Raintree 1990, LB $11.50 (0-8172-2906-X). 32pp. Nonfiction.

This is an illuminating biography of the life of one of Cuba's most famous heroes. A poet, playwright, and university professor of history and literature, Martí's intellectual development is examined, as is the key leadership role he played in the movement to free Cuba from the Spanish, a role that eventually cost him his life. The book features rich watercolor illustrations and an English and Spanish glossary of new terms used. O.G. de C.

403 Gleiter, Jan, and Kathleen Thompson. *Miguel Hidalgo y Costilla.* Bilingual ed.; trans. from English by Gloria Contreras. Illus. by Rick Karpinski. SERIES: Hispanic Stories. Raintree 1989, HB $11.50 (0-8172-2905-1). 32pp. Nonfiction.

The man considered the father of Mexican independence is the focus of this picture biography that challenges the effectiveness of his leadership in the independence struggle. Unlike the other books in this series that highlight the contributions made by the biographees, this one presents the material in such a way as to cast doubt upon the career of "el Padre Hidalgo." In addition, it omits key issues and actions that are crucial to Father Hidalgo's story. For example, although mention is made that he is of the nobility, the book neglects to tell its readers about his Creole heritage and the role of the Creoles during the colonial period. Moreover, mention of the importance of "Grito de Delores"—the famous speech that Father Hidalgo delivered on the 16th of September—is omitted from the text. The authors also call him the "Father of the Mexican Revolution," a misnomer, as the Mexican revolution is yet another struggle for freedom at a later time in history. In this regard, the Spanish text is more accurate than its English counterpart. Students should be warned of these discrepancies and should be encouraged to use other sources. O.G. de C.

Griffiths, John. *We Live in the Caribbean.*
See entry 420, Grades 7–9.

404 Hubley, John, and Penny Hubley. *A Family in Jamaica.* Rev. ed. of *Jamaican Village,* 1982. Illus. with photos. SERIES: Families the World Over. Lerner 1985, LB $8.95 (0-8225-1657-8). 31pp. Nonfiction.

A Family in Jamaica provides a personal glimpse of the daily events experienced by 10-year-old Dorothy Samuel's family. Readers are given a taste of Jamaican life as they learn about Dorothy's home—a village near Montego Bay—and her family's occupation—farming. Information is also provided about two industries essential to Jamaica's economy—the tourist trade and sugar production. Other topics briefly mentioned include Jamaican history and social customs, examples of which are Columbus's discovery and Britain's colonization, and musical styles (reggae) and island sports (cricket), respectively.

This individualized and detailed account is enhanced by numerous color photographs that faithfully portray life in Jamaica. It is by no means an in-depth study of Jamaican life or its customs or history, but rather a brief introduction suitable for mid-level readers.

A Family in Jamaica is an entry in the series Families the World Over and is representative of the series as a whole. Another volume in the series presents a family in Mexico.

H.C.

405   Joseph, Lynn. *Coconut Kind of Day: Island Poems.* Illus. by Sandra Speidel. Lothrop, Lee & Shepard 1990, LB $13.95 (0-688-09120-2). 28pp. Nonfiction.

Coconut Kind of Day is a delightful collection of poems that relate the events of a day in the life of a young Trinidadian girl. From the crowing of the rooster to the setting of the sun, her day unfolds in sequence. The reader follows her as she arrives late to school, buys ices from the "palet man," helps pull fishing nets from the sea, listens to the "pom-da-de-de-de-dom-pom" of a steel drum, and finally hears the various night sounds outside her window.

In language that sings with the lilt of island dialect, the author describes the sounds, sights, and people of Trinidad. The colorful full-page, double-spread illustrations serve to provide visual enhancement for interpretation of the poetry. So compact and descriptive are the poems that they hang together like the story line of a well-developed picture book. Even though the level of writing carries the work beyond the reach of younger readers, nevertheless the material lends itself to reading-aloud sessions for this age group. This is a wonderful book that provides a glimpse into another child's world. Unfamiliar words and phrases are explained in the author's note at the end of the text.

H.C.

406   Joseph, Lynn. *A Wave in Her Pocket: Stories from Trinidad.* Illus. by Brian Pinkney. Clarion 1991, HB $13.95 (0-395-54432-7). 52pp. Fiction.

This is a collection of six stories from Trinidad, featuring many of the heroes and characters from the island's traditional folklore. The tales are presented in a format that features Tantie, the great-aunt of a small group of young cousins. At appropriate times, or when the cousins request it, Tantie gathers the children together and begins to weave her story-telling magic. Many of the stories originate in West Africa. Others begin right in Trinidad, and still others come from Tantie's own imagination. Some of the traditional folkloric figures encountered here are Ligahoo, Soucouyant, and Papa Bois. In each story, these figures are shown interacting in the daily life of the human protagonists, as Tantie uses them to teach a lesson, to entertain, or to reminisce. For instance, Tantie tells the story "Ligahoo" to warn the children of the dangers of the river during the rainy season. The title story is drawn from Tantie's youth.

While the stories have a certain charm, they are not always fully worked out. Some tales are so short that they are almost anecdotes. Many of them seem to trail off without any real conclusion, "A Soucouyant Dies" being a prime example. Nevertheless, the tales do reveal much about Trinidadian life and customs and are steeped in tradition. The author utilizes the Trinidadian dialect to great effect, giving the stories a touch of island culture that makes them sparkle. Brian Pinkney's scratchboard drawings aptly capture the charm and essence of the life conveyed in these delightful albeit slight tales.

H.C.

407   Lessac, Frane. ***Caribbean Canvas.*** First American ed. Illus. by the author. HarperCollins 1989, HB $14.95 (0-397-32368-9). 20pp. Nonfiction.

The lilt and rhythm of various island dialects capture the imaginations of visitors and linger in their ears long after their departure, while memories of the gentle breezes, blue waters, and golden sunshine warm their thoughts. Here, in characteristic dialect, the flavor of island culture and color are communicated in the short but pithy poems (by various authors) that describe everyday activities, events, places, or people. Each poem is accompanied by an appropriate illustration, usually oil on canvas, but other media are used as well. These include watercolors, gouache, and mixed-media collage. From an author-illustrator who has spent many years on the small island of Montserrat come these telling vignettes from the islands of Antigua, Barbados, Montserrat, St. Kitts, Nevis, and Grenada. A realistic and tangible introduction to Caribbean culture.   H.C.

408   McKissack, Patricia C. ***The Maya.*** Illus. with photos. SERIES: New True Books. Childrens Pr. 1985, LB $9.95 (0-516-01270-3). 48pp. Nonfiction.

In this beginning chapter book on the Mayan Indians, vivid photographs of stone carvings and Mayan ruins provide a visual picture of the past. McKissack offers her readers a composite of life during the Yucatec period, dating back to A.D. 889. She focuses on everyday beliefs and practices such as weddings, customs, religion, art, music, and warfare. One particularly interesting chapter that children will enjoy reading is the one devoted to the customs of child rearing. It discusses certain practices, such as the lengthening and flattening of the forehead and the crossing of the eyes, designed to enhance the beauty of a young child. The inclusion of photographs of today's Maya will help children to see the contemporary aspects of indigenous life. Also included is a one-page vocabulary list of new terms and concepts.   O.G. de C.

409   Orr, Katherine. ***My Grandpa and the Sea.*** Illus. by the author. Lerner/Carolrhoda 1990, LB $12.95 (0-87614-409-1). 32pp. Fiction.

In this retrospective tale, Lila, the narrator, relates a loving memory of her grandfather. While growing up with Grandpa on the small island of St. Lucia, where he was a fisherman, she learned much about the ways of the sea and of the heart. Grandpa's whole life was intertwined with the sea, and his happiest moments were experienced while fishing in his boat, *Fancy Lady*. Deprived of his livelihood when larger, more powerful boats took to the sea, he tried his hand at other jobs, but to no avail. Nothing satisfied him until one day he developed an ingenious idea that allowed him to make a living from what he knew and loved best—the sea. The idea stemmed from his belief that "if we give back something for everything we take, we will always meet with abundance." The idea worked, and Grandpa prospered. This is one of the many lessons that Lila learned from her grandfather and remembers even into adulthood.

Orr's is a charming picture book about an old man's love of the ocean, which he calls "God's World," and his determination, in the face of technological advancement, not to take from nature without giving something back. Vibrant, full-page oil drawings convey the beauty and warmth of the islands as well as of this grandfather and granddaughter relationship.   H.C.

410 Perl, Lila. *Piñatas and Paper Flowers: Holidays of the Americas in English and Spanish./Piñatas y flores de papel: Fiestas de las Américas en inglés y español.* Bilingual ed.; Spanish version by Alma Flor Ada. Illus. by Victoria de Larrea. Clarion 1983, HB $12.95 (0-89919-112-6); P $5.95 (0-89919-155-X). 92pp. Nonfiction.

The most important holidays common to the majority of the Spanish-speaking countries of the Americas are introduced in this sourcebook that presents eight such celebrated commemorations. The narrative relates the differences in the styles of celebration among the various countries. Among the celebrations that are included are *Posadas*, a reenactment of Mary's and Joseph's journey in search of lodgings, and *Día de los Muertos*, the Day of the Dead celebrations that take place at the beginning of November. This is an extremely useful resource book that will also help children understand celebrations pertinent to the United States, such as Columbus Day, in the context of the whole of the Americas. The text is lively with equally lively and appealing two-tone illustrations.

O.G. de C.

Pomerantz, Charlotte. *The Tamarindo Puppy and Other Poems.*
See entry 397, Grades PS–3.

Rohmer, Harriet, and Mary Anchondo. *How We Came to the Fifth World: A Creation Story from Ancient Mexico.*
See entry 398, Grades PS–3.

Somonte, Carlos. *We Live in Mexico.*
See entry 428, Grades 7–9.

Stein, R. Conrad. *Mexico.*
See entry 429, Grades 7–9.

411 Thompson, Kathleen. *Sor Juana Inés de la Cruz.* Bilingual ed.; trans. by Alma Flor Ada. Illus. by Rick Karpinski. Raintree 1990, LB $11.50 (0-8172-3377-6); SERIES: Hispanic Stories. 32pp. Nonfiction.

This is the biography of a remarkably intelligent individual, considered Mexico's finest mystic poet. A learned woman who learned to read at a very young age, she fought the prejudices harbored by society against educated women. She is considered one of the greatest Spanish-language poets.

Thompson cites instances from the biographee's childhood that demonstrate Sor Juana Inés de la Cruz's determination to learn at all costs. For instance, she begged her mother to dress her as a boy so she could attend college. When she did not feel she was excelling, she would cut off her hair as a form of self-punishment.

The great poet grew up surrounded by books and an impressive private library belonging to her grandfather. Her major confrontation, however, was with the then-powerful archbishop over a woman's right to study, write, and participate in the great church debates of the time.

This volume in the Raintree Hispanic Stories series features a bilingual text and attractive full-color pastel illustrations. The text is straightforward but never dull; it highlights a woman's struggle to express her talents despite the rigid constraints of custom and religion. Other Mexicans featured in this series are

Miguel Hidalgo y Costilla and Diego Rivera; the Puerto Rican leader Luis Muñoz Marín and the Cuban poet and patriot José Martí are also included.

O.G. de C.

412   Treviño, Elizabeth Borton de. *El Güero: A True Adventure Story.* Illus. by Leslie W. Bowman. Farrar, Straus & Giroux 1989, HB $12.95 (0-374-31995-2). 112pp. Fiction.

A historical novel set in the late nineteenth century in the Mexico–Baja California region, this account is based on a true story in the author's father-in-law's life. Told in the first person, El Güero (the Blond One) is the son of a wealthy Mexican judge during a time of great political upheaval in Mexico. His father's loyalty to the deposed Mexican president, Lerdo de Tejada, is the cause of the family's being assigned to Ensenada, a desolate Mexican border town in the California region. El Güero, his parents, his sister María—known as Maruca—and their Aunt Victoria are shocked to hear that they must pack up some of their belongings and leave their elegant city home at once. They embark upon a long and arduous journey, braving pirates and high seas, in dangerous and unknown waters.

They arrive at Enseñada to discover that their only shelter is a lone oak tree, and it is there that they begin to rebuild their lives. Setting up a court, El Güero's father attempts to bring law and order to a desolate and lawless region. Aunt Vicky opens a school for the children, and El Güero befriends El Coyote, the son of a local miner who was raised by the Indians, and Brazo Fuerte, a young Indian. The three become dear friends and share in the daily responsibilities of rebuilding. Yet peril looms in the form of Anglo-American settlers, who move into the territory at will and obey no law but their own. They kidnap El Güero's father, but the three youngsters notify the Mexican authorities in time for the judge to be rescued.

This fast-paced historical novel will hold readers' attention and provide another perspective on the settling of the West. It introduces the region of Baja California, a desert area just south of California, where, in the late nineteenth century, the Mexican residents of both Spanish and Native American heritage were threatened by ruthless frontiersmen seeking land, wealth, and power.

O.G. de C.

413   Villacana, Eugenio. *Viva Morelia.* Illus. by Elisa Manríquez. M. Evans 1972, HB $6.95 (0-87131-098-8). 64pp. Nonfiction.

An insider's look at the blending of the Spanish and Tarascan Indian cultures is the focus of this anthropological study of the city of Morelia in the southwestern part of Mexico.

Customs and beliefs, special feasts and celebrations, history and daily life, landscape and landmarks are among the topics discussed in a lively text that employs a first-person narrative to present an authentic view of a unique region of Mexico. Although written 20 years ago, the content continues to be relevant for today's students.   O.G. de C.

414   Anthony, Suzanne. *West Indies.* Illus. with photos. SERIES: Let's Visit Places and
Peoples of the World. Chelsea House 1989, LB $14.95 (1-55546-793-8). 127pp.
Nonfiction.

The Let's Visit Places and Peoples of the World series provides coverage of
numerous countries on the seven continents. Each book furnishes a map of the
area; a facts-at-a-glance section for demographic, geographic, and economic
information; and a history-at-a-glance section, which lists important dates in the
history of the country or area covered.

Following these introductory chapters, the text then addresses such topics as
the region's (or country's) relationship to the rest of the world; geography and
history; people, government, and economy; and culture. Throughout the text,
numerous black-and-white photos and drawings enhance the writing. In addition, a color section, usually in the middle of the volume, depicts scenes of the
country's contemporary life, its geography, and aspects of its culture. This
volume provides an overview of the various island nations of the Caribbean,
while other volumes focus specifically on Barbados, the Bahamas, Bermuda,
Grenada, Jamaica, St. Lucia, and Trinidad and Tobago. A glossary and index are
included.   H.C.

Berry, James. *Spiderman Anancy.*
See entry 433, Grades 10–12.

Berry, James. *A Thief in the Village and Other Stories.*
See entry 434, Grades 10–12.

Bierhorst, John. *The Mythology of Mexico and Central America.*
See entry 435, Grades 10–12.

415   Carroll, Raymond. *The Caribbean: Issues in U.S. Relations.* Franklin Watts 1984,
HB $9.90 (0-531-04852-7). 104pp. Nonfiction.

The Caribbean: Issues in U.S. Relations provides a historical overview of the
Caribbean from the standpoint of the United States. Coverage begins from the
first settlement of the region by native Ciboneys, Arawaks, and Caribs and
moves through the discovery of the area by Columbus, to colonization by the
various European powers, and on to the present day.

Discussion of U.S. involvement in the area begins in the third chapter and
fills the remainder of the text. Much is said about U.S. involvement in the area as
it proceeded from the Monroe Doctrine to U.S. business enterprise and to
political intervention in the Dominican Republic, Haiti, Grenada, and Cuba.

While the book tries to cover the entire Caribbean in a few pages, it does
provide an adequate discussion of this region's development. Events in the
modern history of these islands are presented in the fourth chapter. Here the
author discusses the establishment of Crown Colony government in the British
possessions, the rise of labor, the call for self-governance and federation, and the
eventual establishment of independent states. The final chapters discuss the rise
of Castro and communism in Cuba and their influence in the area, as well as the
importance (to the United States in particular) of the entire Caribbean as a region

and what its future might hold. Teachers will find this a useful introduction to the history of the region. Includes suggestions for further reading and an index.

H.C.

416 Casagrande, Louis B., and Sylvia A. Johnson. *Focus on Mexico: Modern Life in an Ancient Land.* Illus. with photos by Phillips Bourns. Lerner 1986, LB $14.95 (0-8225-0645-9). 96pp. Nonfiction.

The vast cultures of contemporary Mexico are explored through the eyes of four teenagers who represent four distinct areas and ways of life in Mexico. The four include Ana Rosa, a student from Morelia, Michoacán, who is totally absorbed in the plans for her upcoming quinceañera (fifteenth birthday) celebration; Adrian, who comes from Mexico City's urban middle class; Ramiro, also from Mexico City, whose family is among the squatters who live on the edge of the city; and finally, Maruch, a Mayan Indian from a rural village in the Chiapas highlands.

Chapters on various aspects of Mexico's history precede the children's factual story about their individual lives. Illustrated with color and black-and-white photos, drawings, and historical photographs from the distinguished Casasola collection, this is a unique, effective, and appealing way to present a country's history, culture, and current situation. Includes index.

O.G. de C.

417 de la Garza, Phyllis. *Chacho.* Illus. by Fred del Guidice. New Readers Pr. 1990, P $3.75 (0-88336-763-7). 96pp. Fiction.

This work for new and reluctant readers is a western novella set in a modern-day Mexican hacienda. Sixteen-year-old Chacho Rios resents his 24-year-old unmarried sister, Esperanza. Since the death of their father, Esperanza has become the overbearing boss of the family hacienda and runs the ranch with an iron hand. Chacho reveals his feeling about his sister to Don Magdaleno, a neighboring shepherd with a large family, who tends the hacienda's goats. Don Magdaleno is a dreamer who thinks he'll get rich by breeding the herd's does with Chacho's finest ram. This, he feels, can be accomplished only if Esperanza is married off and Chacho takes charge of the family ranch. Together, Chacho and Don Magdaleno concoct a scheme to find Esperanza a suitable match and in this way rid themselves of her manipulation and control

Don Magdaleno and Chacho steal neighbor Don Augustín's horse and pretend the horse has wandered on to their property, so that Don Augustín and Esperanza will have an opportunity to meet. But the plan goes awry as Don Augustín produces witnesses who testify to Chacho's outright theft. Even so, Don Augustín and Esperanza do meet when Esperanza buys the horse to clear the family name. After the goat-breeding scheme fails, Don Magdaleno is exposed as a fraud.

This is a fast-paced and easy-to-read novella, full of adventure, intrigue, and comedy. It also highlights modern dilemmas and issues in Mexico—marriage, divorce, new career options for women, poverty, and the resentment of the rich by the poor. These issues are raised primarily by Doña Eugenia, Don Magdaleno's wife, who, although a secondary character, takes life much more seriously than her husband, whose flawed character limits his accomplishments.

O.G. de C.

418   George, Jean Craighead. ***Shark Beneath the Reef.*** HarperCollins 1989, LB $11.89
(0-06-021993-9). 182pp. Fiction.

Tomás Torres comes from a long line of fishermen. His family lives in a small town in Baja California, by the Sea of Cortez in the Western Pacific coastal area. His two loves are school and fishing. Lately, though, he has become obsessed with his dream of delivering a hammerhead shark before the full view of all the villagers and as a result has neglected his schoolwork.

Because of changes in the local political climate, the village finds itself fighting for its very survival when the political machine enforces new rules designed to push the fishermen out of business. In this way, the government expects to be left free to market the town as yet another tourist attraction. After agonizing over his decision, Tomás realizes that without an education, poverty is inevitable.

George combines her vast knowledge of ocean life with key environmental issues concerning deep-sea fishing. She places her contemporary story within the cultural context of everyday existence in a Mexican village, replete with corrupt politicians in a nonfunctioning bureaucracy and the details of daily life and special events. The result is a novel that is at once wonderfully imaginative, evoking vivid descriptions of deep-ocean sea life, yet at the same time enlightening in its presentation of a modern-day Mexican village. There are, however, some misspellings of Spanish words, as well as a stereotypical scene of Tomás's uncle's taking his siesta under the palm trees, an erroneous portrayal of the sort that promotes among readers a distorted image of Mexican citizens. While the custom in much of rural Latin America is to rest in the middle of the day and to work into the evening, sleeping under the palm tree has unfortunately become in literature a symbol of the "lazy Mexican." Any other location for the uncle's rest would have been far more appropriate.   O.G. de C.

419   Griffiths, John. ***The Caribbean.*** Illus. with photos. SERIES: Countries of the World. Franklin Watts 1989, LB $12.40 (0-531-18274-6). 48pp. Nonfiction.

The Caribbean is an entry in the Countries of the World series, whose scope includes a wide range of nations. The series offers brief yet comprehensive introductions to the area covered, and it highlights those aspects that reveal contemporary life within these countries. Organized in short, one- to two-page chapters or units, the text covers such topics as land and climate, early history, recent history, and ethnic composition. Other subjects include the language, tradition and culture, industry, government, and scenarios of future developments in the area or country. The writing is clear, accurate, and concise. There are numerous maps and color photos scattered throughout the text to provide clarification and enhancement. Includes a glossary, an index, and a listing of books for further reading.   H.C.

420   Griffiths, John. ***We Live in the Caribbean.*** Illus. with photos. SERIES: Living Here. Franklin Watts 1984, LB $10.90 (0-531-03832-7). 60pp. Nonfiction.

Like other books in the Living Here series, *We Live in the Caribbean* is a collection of personal vignettes of various residents of the region. Through the words of the individuals themselves, a colorful and sweeping mosaic is created by the descriptions of their occupations, daily lives, activities, and thoughts about their island homes. Although the work encompasses the entire Caribbean area, the

English-speaking Caribbean is strongly represented. There is sufficient inclusion of the islands of the region—Jamaica, Trinidad, Tobago, Barbados, Antigua, and St. Kitts—to give readers an insight into the islands' cultural, social, educational, and economic life.

Each vignette is accompanied by a photograph of the individual and a brief biographical note. Additional photographs show striking (but at times dated) images of each person's island home. An insightful and true portrait of the English-speaking Caribbean, this text would enhance any teacher's or librarian's introduction of these islands to students. Includes a glossary, an index, and a facts-in-brief section on the social and administrative structure of the islands.

H.C.

421   Hamilton, Virginia. *Junius Over Far.* HarperCollins 1985, HB $11.89 (0-06-022194-1). 274pp. Fiction.

Since the time he was a baby, Junius Rawlings has been cared for, nurtured, and informed about Caribbean life by his loving grandfather, Jackabo Rawlings. The relationship is a warm one, and Junius is so imbued with feeling for his grandfather and the island that had been his grandfather's home that he even adopts the speech patterns of that locale. However, when Junius is not quite 15, Grandfather, tired of the northern winters, returns "over far" to Snake Island, the small Caribbean isle of his birth, to stay at a rundown estate owned by Burtie Rawlings, a distant relative. Deeply affected by his grandfather's departure, Junius feels quite alone, and to fill the aching void by evoking memories of his grandfather, he pores over Jackabo's rambling but colorful letters when they arrive.

Succeeding chapters alternate between Junius's struggle with loneliness and a budding romance, and Jackabo's attempt to cope with his biogoted cousin Burtie Rawlings, at once his companion and foe. These two story lines finally converge, as increasingly incoherent letters arrive from the old man—letters filled with vague references to pirates, kidnapping, and weapons. The tone of these letters leads the family to intercede, as they become concerned about Jackabo's welfare. Longing to see his grandfather and the Caribbean island of which he had so often spoken, Junius implores his father to take him along on the trip to Snake Island. The two journey to the island and arrive in time to both rescue Jackabo from his plight and witness the unraveling of the mystery alluded to in Jackabo's letters.

In a well-written and engrossing novel, Virginia Hamilton captures the enduring bond between a grandfather and grandson, and ultimately the bond of family in general. The characters are well drawn, their various experiences and emotions related with poignance and depth. Equally stunning are Hamilton's descriptions of Snake Island, which impart the essence and beauty of the Caribbean region as a whole.

H.C.

422   Hargrove, Jim. *Diego Rivera: Mexican Muralist.* Illus. with photos. SERIES: People of Distinction. Childrens Pr. 1990, LB $12.95 (0-516-03268-2). 128pp. Nonfiction.

The tumultuous life of Mexico's most famous painter, the muralist Diego Rivera, is told here with honesty, humor, and excitement. While the biography reflects the artist's sense of outrage and the fantastic moods that he acted out frequently in the course of his life, its overemphasis on his extravagant love affairs and marriages unfortunately deemphasizes his importance as one of the world's most sought-after muralists. An eccentric from birth, his eccentricity was indeed expressed even in his early childhood years, and it is shown here with much humor and in vivid detail.

A chronology of Rivera's life, from 1886 through 1957, is included in this somewhat sensationalized, though ultimately informative and entertaining, book.

O.G. de C.

423 Hobbs, Will. *Changes in Latitudes.* Atheneum 1988, HB $13.95 (0-689-31385-3). 162pp. Fiction.

A trip to Mexico forms the backdrop for this novel about an arrogant teenager whose family is in the process of coming apart. Sixteen-year-old Travis, his 15-year-old sister, Jennifer, and their 9-year-old brother, Teddy, join their mother on a budget vacation; their estranged father remains in the States. While Travis and Jennifer pursue members of the opposite sex, the gifted Teddy becomes obsessed with the fate of endangered sea turtles. He and Travis discover a lab run by an unscrupulous Mexican entrepreneur, where the turtles are harvested in the guise of saving them. Teddy sneaks out to save the turtles and dies of a ruptured aneurysm while carrying them to the sea. His death forces Travis to reexamine his own selfish attitudes, and it brings the rest of the family together, at least for the moment.

Narrated by the snide Travis, Mexicans are presented as lazy, stupid, dirty, backward, and corrupt. These are blatant tourist stereotypes and, coming from Travis's perspective, may be seen as part of his "attitude." However, caution should be used, lest stereotypes actually be reinforced; in any case, the sole Mexican who is portrayed in a positive light is a doctor who appears but briefly. The voice is authentic, and many teenagers will identify with Travis, but more thoughtful, sophisticated readers may be turned off by the manipulative and overly sentimental ending. Although this novel does have much to say about the environment and family relationships, it is neither a culturally sensitive work nor an accurate portrayal of Mexico today.

L.M-L.

424 *Jamaica in Pictures.* Rev. ed. Illus. with photos. SERIES: Visual Geography. Lerner 1987, LB $9.95 (0-8225-1814-7). 64pp. Nonfiction.

Lucid descriptions of various countries are provided in the Visual Geography series and include, for the Caribbean, Cuba, the Dominican Republic, Haiti, Jamaica, and Puerto Rico. The topics covered are the land, history and government, culture and daily life, and the economy. Each topic is dealt with in one chapter, with bold headings for the various subtopics, making it easy to locate desired information. The presentation is accurate, thorough, and well developed, considering the brief length of the text. Numerous photos, both color and black and white, and useful maps abound. Includes an index.

H.C.

425 Marrin, Albert. *Aztecs and Spaniards: Cortés and the Conquest of Mexico.* Atheneum 1986, HB $15.95 (0-689-31176-1). 212pp. Nonfiction.

Marrin's work provides a full accounting of the fierce clash that occurred between two opposing civilizations, the Aztec and the Spanish, at the time of the conquest of Mexico by Hernán Cortés.

In his description of Mexico-Tenochtitlán before the conquest, Marrin offers readers a glimpse of Aztec life during this period. He also furnishes much valuable information on Cortés and his dealings in Spain and in Cuba before his legendary feats. Marrin's dislike of the Aztecs, however, is obvious, and he offers no examination of the Aztec religion that centered on the sun as the source of all life. Marrin describes in much detail the strategic military tactics employed by both Cortés and Montezuma in their war efforts. Marrin, however, is partial to the Spanish and portrays Cortés as a hero, going so far as to call him the "father of Mexico," a misnomer that today continues to stir contempt for Cortés. Marrin uses many dated sources, and he does not include any opposing perspective that would question Cortés's mental ability or challenge the messianic story that Cortés forced on his subjects.   O.G. de C.

426   Meador, Nancy, and Betty Harman. *Paco and the Lion of the North: General Pancho Villa Teaches a Boy About Life and Death During the Mexican Revolution.* Illus. Eakin 1987, HB $8.95 (0-89015-598-4). 117pp. Fiction.

The time is the Mexican revolution, and 14-year-old Paco's wealthy hacienda family is the target of attack by Pancho Villa's troops, the revolutionary forces in the northern part of Mexico. Paco is kidnapped by Villa's men and is assigned to be a scout for Villa as well as his horse's attendant. Through direct contact with Villa and his troops, Paco learns firsthand about the revolutionaries' way of life and comes to comprehend the reasons for their struggle. His closeness to the general affords him the privilege of seeing a rare, human side of Villa that few people know. Paco's family's fate remains unclear. The book jacket states they were killed. Paco himself tells another story, and the prologue tells yet another version.

The authors would have done well to provide more descriptive passages so as to present a more complete historical perspective on the Mexican revolution. Readers will not be able to deduce that Villa was part of a broader picture, with Zapata as the general in command of the forces in the south and General Francisco Maderista the commander in chief. All of them opposed Venustiano Carranza and the American interests in Mexico at the time. Moreover, the fighting between *federalistas* and *rurales*, the two opposing forces of the Mexican revolution, is presented quite mildly in comparison to the loss of life and destruction of property that tore the country apart. In addition, the intense hatred between Anglos and Mexicans along the U.S.-Mexican border during this period is not even dealt with.

This unfortunately weak historical novel contains a glossary of Spanish and English terms used and a bibliography for further reference.   O.G. de C.

427   Sills, Leslie. *Inspirations: Stories About Women Artists.* Illus. with photos. Albert Whitman 1989, HB $16.95 (0-8075-3649-0). 56pp. Nonfiction.

One of the four women artists featured in this art biography is Frida Kahlo, the Mexican painter whose intriguing surrealistic artwork has recently captured the attention of art buffs throughout the world. Kahlo's story is one of great strength amid the physical pain she learned to cope with as a result of a bus accident early in her life. Her development as an artist is told in relationship to her ability to endure and depict her pain. Eight color reproductions that demonstrate depth of feeling are included by Sills as examples to teach students about artists' ability to infuse emotion into a painting in order to produce great art. Among the other artists featured in this valuable book is the African-American painter Faith Ringgold, whose *Tar Beach* is annotated elsewhere in this bibliography.

428   Somonte, Carlos. *We Live in Mexico.* Illus. with photos. SERIES: Living Here. Franklin Watts 1985, LB $12.90 (0-531-03820-3). 60pp. Nonfiction.

Twenty-six persons representing a cross section of Mexico's population talk about themselves in relation to their work. Included among the interviewees are the young and the old, villagers and urbanites, and coastal and mountain region citizens. Roughly one fourth of the people featured are female. The first-person narratives prove a useful technique in combination with the three or four color photographs per entry. A one-page fact sheet furnishes essential information on Mexico. Readers should be cautioned about the validity of the listed exchange rate and other statistics. A brief glossary defines Spanish terms as well as other terms used in the text.   O.G. de C.

429   Stein, R. Conrad. *Mexico.* Illus. with photos. SERIES: Enchantment of the World. Childrens Pr. 1984, LB $23.93 (0-516-02772-7). 126pp. Nonfiction.

This is an attractive survey book that emphasizes the many contrasts of Mexico's history and culture. Readers should come away with a clear understanding of the three basic periods of Mexico's history: the pre-Columbian epoch, the colonial era, and modern Mexico. The writing style is interesting, and modern reality is juxtaposed with its pre-Columbian or colonial past to present a more accurate description of the blending of traditions. Both village life and city life are fully depicted, with an accurate balance between them. The major events of Mexican history, however, are too briefly presented. Moreover, the country's economy as well as the problems of migration and pollution are not discussed in any great length. Because much has happened since the publication date, another source should be used to augment this edition.

430   Taylor, Theodore. *The Cay.* Avon 1970, P $3.50 (0-380-01003-8). 144pp. Fiction.

Set on the island of Curaçao during World War II, *The Cay* explores the prejudices and preconceptions about blacks that young Phillip must confront and address when he is shipwrecked and marooned alone with Timothy, an elderly West Indian, after his boat is torpedoed by the Germans.

   After being hit on the head by a plank from the ship, Phillip awakes to find himself on a raft with Timothy, who he describes as a "huge, very old Negro." . . . "He was ugly. His nose was flat and his face was broad; his head was a mass of wiry gray hair." The two of them, along with the captain's cat, Stew Cat, drift for days (during which time Phillip loses his sight as a result of the blow to his head), until they finally reach an island—a cay. They come ashore, and, mostly with Timothy's guidance, build a shelter and wait to be rescued. It is on this cay that, in addition to dealing with the traumatic loss of his sight, Phillip's attitude toward Timothy in particular and blacks in general begins to change. He witnesses Timothy's tenacity, strength, wisdom, and devotion to him and to their survival. The two become close friends, and it is finally Timothy who gives his life during a freak hurricane in order to save Phillip's. Despite the aching void Phillip feels after his friend's death, he is able to persevere because Timothy has trained and prepared him well. Once rescued, he is reunited with his parents, a totally changed young man.

This adventure novel is a moving story of black and white, innocence and wisdom, growing up and surviving. The characters and plot are well drawn and developed, though the book is not without its controversial aspects. Recommended for mature adolescent readers because of the initial raw expressions of bigotry, this is a useful work for the study of the absurdity of racial prejudice and the strength and beauty of acceptance, set against the backdrop of an isolated Caribbean island.   H.C.

Treviño, Elizabeth Borton de. *El Güero: A True Adventure Story.*
See entry 412, Grades 4–6.

431   Vásquez, Ana María B., and Rosa E. Casas. *Cuba.* Illus. with photos. SERIES: Enchantment of the World. Childrens Pr. 1987, HB $23.93 (0-516-02758-1). 128pp. Nonfiction.

This is an overview of Cuba that covers a broad range of topics from geography and topography to history, the arts, sports, and government. Written with an obvious anti-Castro bias, several of the chapters, particularly the ones on the arts and folklore and customs, speak of the grandeur of days gone by. While discussing human rights violations under the Castro government, the writers downplay the major gains achieved since 1959, particularly in the areas of literacy, education, and health. Also omitted is any discussion of the U.S. embargo that prohibits the trade of raw materials between the two countries and that censors the flow of books and other information coming into the United States. Further, the history chapter omits mention of the Bay of Pigs invasion, the Missile Crisis, and the 1980 Mariel boat lifts. It is unfortunate that such bias does not allow for the presentation of all the facts necessary for the development of a critical thinking process. Profusely illustrated with color photographs and other illustrations. A Mini-Facts-at-a-Glance section provides the basic information needed for school reports and includes a chronology of important dates as well as an alphabetical listing of important people in Cuban history.   O.G. de C.

432   Wepman, Dennis. *Benito Juárez.* Illus. with photos. SERIES: World Leaders, Past and Present. Chelsea House 1986, LB $17.95 (0-87754-537-5). 116pp. Nonfiction.

Revered as the father of modern Mexico, ardent constitutional reformist and Mexico's finest statesman Benito Juárez is the subject of this excellent biography that begins with Juárez's decision at a young age to leave his beloved Oaxaca in pursuit of an education. The pure-blooded Zapotec Indian studied law and became a lawyer. He quickly developed a reputation not only for upholding the law but also particularly for defending the poor. In an upbeat and exciting text, Wepman narrates the events that occurred during this period and their effect on Juárez's struggles to enact major reform legislation, both in the state of Oaxaca and nationwide. The focus, however, is always on Juárez's own role. His admiration for the U.S. Constitution is reflected in his persistence in attaining the enactment of a similar constitution in Mexico. His enactment of the *Ley Juarez* formally separated church and state and abolished the absolute power of the Church. It also formally abolished the peonage system. His admiration for

Lincoln and Lincoln's admiration for Juárez are also portrayed. This biography should prove helpful to students who wish to expand their knowledge of American history by comparing it with the history of neighboring lands. Students will also see history from the Mexican perspective, particularly with regard to the U.S. invasion of Mexico during the 1840s and the French invasion of Mexico in the 1860s.

O.G. de C.

GRADES 10–12

Anthony, Suzanne. *West Indies.*
See entry 414, Grades 7–9.

433   Berry, James. *Spiderman Anancy.* Illus. by Joseph Olubo. Henry Holt 1989, HB $13.95 (0-8050-1207-9). 119pp. Fiction.

Spiderman Anancy is a collection of folktales from the Caribbean that centers on the main folk hero of the area, Anancy, who is both man and spider. Although these stories are indigenous to the Caribbean, their real roots stretch back to Africa and its folkloric tradition. The tales were brought to the islands with the slaves and took shape after years of encapsulation within the Caribbean area. The adventures and escapades of Anancy and his friends Bro Tiger, Bro Puss, and Bro Monkey are all related in this collection of 20 stories. Anancy, who has the ability to change his form and nature as the situation demands, is always cunning, and he can outsmart both his friends and opponents.

Although James Berry is an excellent writer, as his *A Thief in the Village and Other Stories* can attest, in *Spiderman Anancy* he seems to have missed the mark. While the stories are somewhat charming, they are not as lucid as they could be. In an attempt to transplant the stories from their African roots and so imbue them with the color, character, and language of the Caribbean, the author loses their inherent focus and humor. The writing becomes fractured and the text almost too involved.

An understanding of the Anancy stories and their history in African culture and then their transference to West Indian culture is needed in order to decipher the stories in *Spiderman Anancy*. Despite these possible drawbacks, the collection is still a viable, if unusual, presentation of the Anancy tales. Therefore, this work is recommended only for advanced young adult readers with the prerequisite knowledge outlined above.

H.C.

434   Berry, James. *A Thief in the Village and Other Stories.* Orchard 1988, HB $12.95 (0-531-05745-3); Penguin/Puffin 1990, P $3.95 (0-14-034357-1). 148pp. Fiction.

A Thief in the Village is a collection of 20 stories portraying contemporary life in Jamaica. The narratives are full of verve, color, humor, and depth. They capture the essence of daily activities and events, cultural mores, and philosophy that occur in Jamaican villages, which are representative of village life in most Caribbean islands.

The devilish pranks by the teenage village boys that are perpetrated on Elias, a crippled boy, and on his unusual pet, Mon-Mon the mongoose, are related in

"Elias and the Mongoose." Who would keep a mongoose as a pet, that dreaded attacker of crops and livestock, is the same question that drives the teenagers to torment Elias. The theme of mischief making and devilment perpetrated on a weaker or ill-matched opponent also appears in "Tukku-Tukku and Samson."

In the title story, "A Thief in the Village," Berry recounts the plantation experiences of a young girl and her brother and their attempts to catch the thief who is stealing livestock and provisions.

Berry's stories are well developed and the characters are true to life. He succeeds in transporting the reader to the tropical isles with his vivid descriptions of place and accurate use of island dialect. The writing is full of the lingo of the Caribbean, as seen in a few lines from "A Thief in the Village":

> He put his arm around Nenna, saying, "Of course you come to mi house. Buddy Willow long-leg chile always welcome to mi house."

Then again in a line from "All Other Days Run into Sunday":

> Usually I think I live in the poorest back-o'wall bush place.

A colorful and charming series of stories set in the Caribbean, this collection is a great addition to any curriculum section on the region.   H.C.

---

435   Bierhorst, John. ***The Mythology of Mexico and Central America.*** Illus. William Morrow 1990, HB $14.95 (0-688-06721-2). 239pp. Nonfiction.

This is an excellent reference source for the myths, or histories, as the local indigenous populations prefer to call them, of the people of the area of Mexico and Central America. Bierhorst first introduces his readers to the storytellers by providing a brief history of the cultures of the people living in five distinct regions. In Part Two, the basic myths are divided into five areas: Beginnings, Destructions and New Beginnings, The Quest for Corn, Sun Myths, and Journeys to the Other World. A brief synopsis accompanies each myth. The myths are grouped into four or five thematic motifs. In Part Three, Bierhorst analyzes the myths he has presented, offering a historical perspective that provides new insights for the viewing of myths not as mere stories that people tell but rather as the stories of a group of people bound together by common belief systems and practices.

Carroll, Raymond. ***The Caribbean: Issues in U.S. Relations.***
See entry 415, Grades 7–9.

de la Garza, Phyllis. ***Chacho.***
See entry 417, Grades 7–9.

---

436   Kincaid, Jamaica. ***Annie John.*** Farrar, Straus & Giroux 1985, HB $11.95 (0-374-10521-9); New American Library 1986, P $6.95 (0-452-26016-7). 148pp. Fiction.

Set in Antigua in the 1940s, this novel chronicles the life of Annie John in vivid, sparkling detail, from her young childhood days to her early adolescent years. Her character, appearance, feelings, friendships, childhood adventures, and escapades are described in such microscopic detail that the reader feels transported to that very time and place. Annie John's triumphs in school are recounted, giving both a sense of her character and intellect, as well as painting a tangible and realistic picture of schooling in the West Indies, with its British influence. Her tender relationship with her mother, whom she admires and adores as a young girl and then grows to despise as she begins to blossom into womanhood, is captured with warmth and truth. While her relationship with her father is affectionate, he seems to dance on the fringes of her life, never really the central focus as her mother is portrayed to be.

This personal portrait is painted against the backdrop of West Indian culture, mores, and society. From the daily activities, and occupations, to belief in obeah (a type of witchcraft), to the relationships in, and structure of, family life, the neighborhood, and society, to the flora and fauna, Jamaica Kincaid captures it all in telling prose. She also portrays effectively both a young girl's coming of age and her venturing into a new world—England, a new educational pursuit, the study of nursing, and eventually a new life. While the growing pains of adolescence and the accompanying experiences are universal, the author roots them in the drama and verve of life in the Caribbean, making those experiences concrete, unique, and personal.   H.C.

437   Kincaid, Jamaica. *At the Bottom of the River.* Farrar, Straus & Giroux 1983, HB $9.95 (0-374-10660-6); Random House/Vintage 1985, P $5.95 (0-394-73683-4). 82pp. Fiction.

Jamaica Kincaid, a native of Antigua, artfully relates her recollections of childhood and adolescence in this short story collection. Although they may be personal, these recollections have a universal cast and could belong to almost any inhabitant of the West Indies. The work is truly an inner dialogue of things remembered from childhood and other past experiences. At times the stories take on the character of rambling entries in a diary, flitting from one thought, experience, or feeling to another. In addition, the abbreviated, staccato sentences evoke a stream-of-consciousness writing style. The reader is taken inside the writer's mind and psyche—able to witness firsthand as the writer thinks and converses with herself. However, others of the stories are more direct and grounded in standard narrative form.

While some stories deal with the relationship between mothers and daughters, others relate the carefree yet confusing experiences of childhood. Additional themes are the social customs, beliefs, and mores of West Indians. Lastly, the dream world of the protagonist and the power and beauty of nature are also motifs. These themes make up the varied tiles of this kaleidoscopic mosaic. The writing is never flat or one-dimensional, but many-faceted, each side catching and reflecting the light in its own way. This treatment is fitting because the collection truly seems to be a journey through the mind. It is a wonderful work recommended, because of its sophistication, for more advanced adolescents. This text would provide an ideal foray into unconventional, personal writing styles for advanced English and literature classes and offers a special view of a rich and varied culture.   H.C.

Marrin, Albert. *Aztecs and Spaniards: Cortés and the Conquest of Mexico.*
See entry 425, Grades 7–9.

Paredes, Américo. *George Washington Gómez: A Mexicotexan Novel.*
See entry 252, Grades 10–12.

Taylor, Theodore. *The Cay.*
See entry 430, Grades 7–9.

Wepman, Dennis. *Benito Juárez.*
See entry 432, Grades 7–9.

438   White, Timothy. *Catch a Fire: The Life of Bob Marley.* Rev. and enlarged. Illus.
        with photos. Henry Holt 1989, P $12.95 (0-8050-1152-8). 464pp. Nonfiction.

Bob Marley, the preeminent figure in reggae music, was an enigmatic individual.
However, through in-depth interviews, research, and skillful writing, White
paints an intimate portrait of the man and his work. Coverage begins with the
events surrounding Marley's birth and moves through to the full flowering of his
manhood and musicianship. His legacy, perpetuated greatly by his son Ziggy, is
also examined. In the first two chapters, the author discusses in depth the milieu
that informed Marley's thinking and music, including Jamaican culture and
belief systems, the influence of Marcus Garvey, Haile Selassie I, and the
cult/religion of Rastafarianism. Interwoven throughout the book is mention of
Jamaica's troubled music business and of reggae politics, providing lucid socioeconomic and political information. All of this material is presented in rich prose,
grounded in White's ability to catch the flavor and essence of the Jamaican
dialect. One comes away with a deep sense of Marley the man as well as a great
deal of information on reggae music.

   Catch a Fire is a riveting and compelling biography. However, the nature of
the topics presented and the complexity of the writing make the book most
suitable for mature young adults. Includes a discography, an extensive bibliography, and an index.   H.C.

7

CENTRAL
AND
SOUTH AMERICA

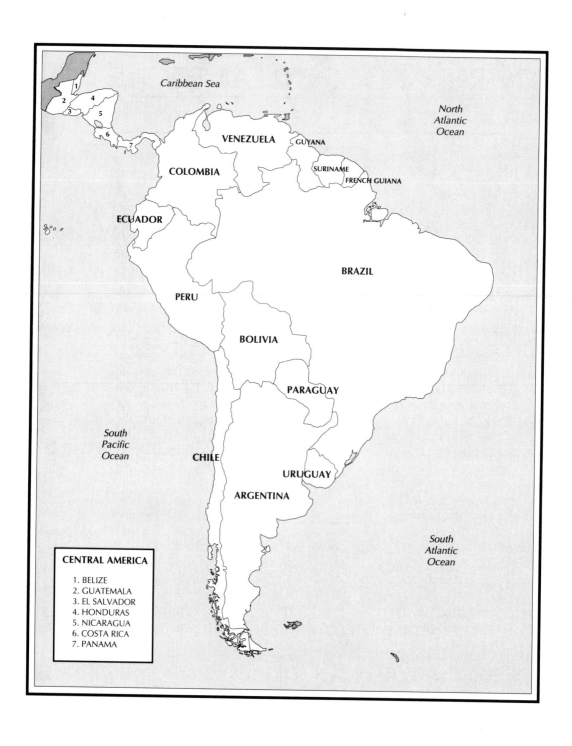

Caribbean Sea

North
Atlantic
Ocean

VENEZUELA

GUYANA

COLOMBIA

SURINAME

FRENCH GUIANA

ECUADOR

BRAZIL

PERU

BOLIVIA

PARAGUAY

South
Pacific
Ocean

CHILE

URUGUAY

ARGENTINA

South
Atlantic
Ocean

CENTRAL AMERICA

1. BELIZE
2. GUATEMALA
3. EL SALVADOR
4. HONDURAS
5. NICARAGUA
6. COSTA RICA
7. PANAMA

7

CENTRAL AND SOUTH AMERICA

by Lyn Miller-Lachmann

The past decade has seen a steady increase in the publication of books set in Central and South America. That increase has paralleled a growing concern with events in the region. In the early 1980s the Sandinista government in Nicaragua and escalating civil wars in El Salvador and Guatemala stirred up controversy in the United States. The Reagan Administration poured massive amounts of military aid into El Salvador and organized and financed a contra army to weaken the Sandinista government; these actions sparked protests throughout the United States and Canada. With the winding down of the Nicaraguan conflict and new rounds of talks in El Salvador at the start of the new decade, new concerns have emerged, foremost among them the environment and the fate of the tropical rain forest along the Amazon River and its tributaries. Several recent titles published for children—both series volumes and individual books—have tended to focus on, or at least to acknowledge, the destruction of the natural environment as an issue in the present and the future.

With the advent of the 1992 observance of the 500th anniversary of Columbus's first voyage to America, publishers have brought out titles documenting encounters between America's earliest inhabitants, the Indians, and the Spanish and Portuguese conquerors. Among them are the outstanding editions of Native American folklore published by Children's Book Press. An example that addresses historical and contemporary conflicts is *The Invisible Hunters*, a cautionary tale from the Miskito Indians of Nicaragua's Atlantic coast. Presented in an English-Spanish bilingual edition, *The Invisible Hunters* describes the disastrous meeting between three indigenous hunters and white men with guns and goods to trade.

Although a relatively large amount of folklore has been published, a conscious decision has been made here to exclude all but those works with direct historical and contemporary significance. Other bibliographies cover the folklore and legends of this area, and John Bierhorst's *The Mythology of South America* and *The Mythology of Mexico and Central America* (the latter annotated in Chapter 6) provide an excellent introduction for older readers.

Several works of history have examined the relationship between the native peoples of America and the European immigrants. Albert Marrin has written a graphic and gripping account of the subjugation of the Inca Empire, *Inca and Spaniard: Pizarro and the Conquest of Peru*. Like *The Invisible Hunters* (though with a very different approach and directed to an older age group), *Inca and Spaniard* alleges that those on both sides contributed to the indigenous community's destruction. The results of European domination are documented in two books focusing on the Mayan Indians of Guatemala. The Mayan Empire had fallen to the Aztecs three decades before the Spanish conquest, and for centuries afterward Mayan communities remained in the highlands, relatively insulated from the fate that befell the Incas, the Aztecs, and other indigenous groups. Even so, traditions and ways of life changed. As Aylette Jenness and Lisa Kroeber point out in their 1975 work, *A Life of Their Own: An Indian Family in Latin America*, years of government discrimination and neglect led to distrust between the highland Maya and the *ladinos* of the city. In the late 1970s, an escalating guerrilla war, fueled by poverty, corruption, and repression, brought the Guatemalan military to the highlands. Tens of thousands of Maya died; many more were driven from their homes. Brent Ashabranner's *Children of the Maya* tells the story of a few of the many thousands who have come to the United States in search of personal safety, freedom, and a better life. For them, exile and the loss of their remaining traditions are the price they pay for their lives.

Latin American culture blends Native American, African, and European traditions, with different combinations in each country that contribute to its unique identity. Over the years, this mix has been influenced by each country's geography and history. Translated works by Latin American authors (as well as one work presenting a type of artisanry found in the region) reflect these influences. *Uncle Nacho's Hat*, a folktale from the Pacific coast of Nicaragua, comments on the tension between stability and change and between tradition and revolution in that country. First published in Venezuela, Kurusa's *The Streets Are Free* is the inspiring true story of a group of Caracas slum children who seek to build a playground in their shantytown. The *arpilleras*—multicolored three-dimensional tapestries made with scraps of cloth, small handmade dolls, and other objects—form the centerpiece of the unusual and attractive *Tonight Is Carnaval*. Originally created in Chile as a means of expressing opposition to a dictatorship, the *arpilleras* are now made throughout the continent and depict scenes of everyday life.

The unique geography of Chile—its proximity to both mountains and ocean and its propensity to earthquakes—is a principal theme of Jacqueline Balcells's collection of literary tales, *The Enchanted Raisin*. *Where Angels Glide at Dawn*, a collection of short stories by various Latin American authors, presents to youngsters the magical realism that has become a hallmark of Latin America's contemporary literary tradition. Some of the region's most well-known authors for adults, including Argentina's Julio Cortazar and Chile's Ariel Dorfman, appear in this collection. One of Latin America's greatest poets, Pablo Neruda, is the subject of another recently published work, Antonio Skarmeta's *Burning Patience*, which invents a friendship between Neruda and his teenage mailman.

Contemporary issues—particularly the environment, human rights, and civil strife—form the themes of much fiction and nonfiction set in the region. Most of those books are written by authors from the United States; however, two outstanding, stylistically unusual young adult novels are the product of Latin American authors.

New works on the environment include *The Great Kapok Tree*, a visually interesting though heavy-handed story set in the Amazon rain forest. More successful in terms of its text is Jean Craighead George's *One Day in the Tropical Rain Forest*, which describes a last-ditch effort to save a small part of the same forest. Author-photographer George Ancona turns his attention to the preservation of the sea turtles on Brazil's northeast coast in *Turtle Watch*.

Many books deal with the issues of human rights and political oppression; among the best are Antonio Skarmeta's *Chileno!*, a credible, compelling portrayal of the pain and dislocation experienced by a family fleeing their country, and Lyll Becerra de Jenkins's *The Honorable Prison*, the story of an entire family forced into internal exile because of the father's political activities. Through precise language, complex, memorable characterizations, and controlled storytelling, the Colombian-born author of the latter work challenges the reader to experience, with all five senses as well as the heart, one of the most extreme examples of human cruelty.

Often taken for granted or not perceived as a basic human right, the ability to read and write is essential for life in a democracy. *And Also Teach Them to Read* presents the Nicaraguan literacy crusade through the eyes of 20 Managua teenagers and their North American leader; this account of young volunteers working with much older people has relevance beyond its setting. For a younger audience, Ann Cameron's *The Most Beautiful Place in the World* is a moving novel of a young Guatemalan boy determined to get an education against all odds.

A number of books examine the conflicts in Central America. *The Forty-Third War*, by Louise Moeri, is a fictionalized account of three peasant boys conscripted into the rebel army; though quite vague in its presentation of the issues, it portrays well the emotions of those caught in the web of violence and the process by which unwilling conscripts eventually become loyal soldiers for the cause. Glenn Alan Cheney's *El Salvador: Country in Crisis* is a more substantive presentation of the civil war in that country. Like most books of this type, it details the positions of all sides and leaves the reader to draw his or her own conclusions.

Several books do take sides, either implicitly or explicitly. Often the problem with biased books is not that they take a position but that the reader does not know that and accepts the information as objective. On the other hand, books in which the author takes sides could provide a valuable approach or perspective that may be missing in more balanced treatments. This is the case with two books that openly oppose U.S. intervention in Nicaragua—Rita Golden Gelman's *Inside Nicaragua* and Margaret Randall's *Sandino's Daughters*. By using the techniques of fiction—first-person "new journalism" in the former work and direct personal narrative in the latter—both authors motivate readers to care about the subject and the people involved, and both allow the voice of the Nicaraguans themselves (rather than merely that of the objective analyst) to come through. Both books demonstrate the potential of nonfiction not only to inform but also to entertain, to inspire, and to persuade.

Numerous nonfiction series have presented the countries of Central and South America. For the youngest readers, the Take a Trip series, published by Franklin Watts, features photographs with a text that consists mainly of captions for the photos. At present, this is the only series geared to first or second graders; in general, it suffers from problems of dullness and the matching of text to photographs. For older elementary students, Silver Burdett's People and Places series offers a lively layout but a choppy text and poor illustrations. Two series—Lerner's Families the World Over and Gareth Stevens's Children of the World—are much more appropriate for this age group. Through text and photos that portray a young person and his or her family, both series provide a sense of daily life and motivate the reader to experience a place through someone else's eyes. Although no one family can be representative of a country as a whole, the better books in each series place each family within a wider context and attempt to compare the child's life with that of other children elsewhere in the same country.

For middle and high school students, the choices in series are far greater. Lerner's Visual Geography series is the most straightforward in terms of conveying information. The slender volumes resemble extended encyclopedia articles in style, organization, and approach. Though ostensibly "objective," the authors' perspectives are mainstream and often quite dated, with a pro-development bias at odds with contemporary environmental concerns. The Enchantment of the World series, published by Childrens Press, also suffers somewhat from dated facts and interpretations, a major problem in such a rapidly changing region. The style varies by author; for instance, Martin Hintz's books feature lively writing, and Marion Morrison's books contain vivid and distinctive photos. The Dillon Press series Discovering Our Heritage presents far more cultural information. There is an extensive discussion of each country's customs, food, and artistic and literary traditions, with folktales and recipes included. The Living Here series published by Franklin Watts takes an unusual approach, presenting each country through interviews with about 25 "representative" people, mostly adults. While these books offer a more varied picture than those on single families, the author's choice of subjects may still distort the picture.

The Chelsea House series, Let's Visit Places and Peoples of the World, focuses on contemporary events and issues in each country. Though not explicitly, some of the books contain a definite point of view. Chelsea House also distributes some of the books of the Let's Visit series that are published in England by Burke Books. Those books, which are quite dated, take a descriptive rather than an analytical approach, with little attention given to the country's history and current problems. The new Portraits of the Nations series, published by HarperCollins, features a rather sophisticated approach and analysis; of all the series, it is the most suitable for older high school students. Geography, history, daily life, and contemporary issues are the chief concerns, though individual volumes vary greatly in the amount of attention devoted to each subject.

PRESCHOOL–GRADE 3

Ancona, George. **Turtle Watch.**
See entry 448, Grades 4–6.

439   Argueta, Manlio. **Magic Dogs of the Volcanoes./Los perros mágicos de los volcanes.** Bilingual ed. Trans. from Spanish by Stacey Ross. Illus. by Elly Simmons. Children's Book Pr. 1990, LB $12.95 (0-89239-064-6). 32pp. Fiction.

A noted author of fiction for adults, Salvadoran Manlio Argueta has written a children's story based upon the *cadejos*, magic dogs that appear in the folklore of his native country. Here, in this original tale, the *cadejos* protect the people of the village. In doing so, they run afoul of Don Tonio and his 13 brothers, landowners who believe the magic dogs are making the people lazy and complacent. Don Tonio and his brothers call in shiny lead soldiers to hunt the *cadejos*, who initially elude the lead figures but cannot resist once their food is taken away. They call upon their great-great-grandparents—volcanoes—and the volcanoes erupt, melting the soldiers' feet and behinds and chasing them away.

In less skilled hands, this tale might have become a pedantic political allegory. Argueta's sense of humor and his attention to a child's perspective make the story work. Children who have collected toy soldiers will appreciate the descriptions of the lead soldiers and certainly smile when the soldiers' bottoms melt on the hot rocks. Elly Simmons's vividly colored illustrations complement the story and add even more excitement. Human faces come alive, yet the dogs are stylized, reflecting their mythical origins. The translation is crisp and readable while maintaining the tone of the original. There are many indirect references to the current situation in El Salvador—for instance, the fact that Don Tonio and his 13 brothers represent the Fourteen Families holding most of the country's wealth and political power—and much food for discussion, but, above all, children from a variety of backgrounds will enjoy this lively and attractive book.

Balcells, Jacqueline. *The Enchanted Raisin.*
See entry 449, Grades 4–6.

440   Cameron, Ann. *The Most Beautiful Place in the World.* Illus. by Thomas B. Allen. Knopf 1988, LB $11.99 (0-394-99463-9). 57pp. Fiction.

Seven-year-old Juan lives with his mother at his grandmother's house in San Pablo, Guatemala. One day his mother falls in love with a man she meets on the street. She goes to live with him and leaves Juan behind in the care of his grandmother.

Juan's grandmother sells *arroz con leche* at the market, and Juan joins her there to shine shoes for a dollar a day. But Juan dreams of going to school, learning to read, and making a better life for himself. He asks some of his customers to teach him to read, but he will not ask his grandmother for permission to go to school. He fears that she, like his mother, does not love him either and only keeps him around to earn money.

Eventually Juan does ask his grandmother, and he is surprised by the depth of her concern for him. Cameron, who was born in Wisconsin but has lived in Guatemala, portrays an appealing and resourceful youngster whose quest for love and a better future has relevance beyond its setting. In simple but vivid language Cameron evokes the feeling of life in another place, and she invites the reader to experience Juan's world with all five senses. Juan's abandonment by his mother is presented matter-of-factly; the event shakes him but does not crush his spirit. This novel will appeal to young readers of both sexes, with a protagonist they will not likely forget.

441   Cherry, Lynne. *The Great Kapok Tree: A Tale of the Amazon Rain Forest.* Illus. by the author. Harcourt Brace Jovanovich 1990, HB $14.95 (0-15-200520-X). 32pp. Fiction.

A woodcutter is told to chop down a kapok tree in the Amazon rain forest. After making a cut, he grows tired and lies down for a nap. During his sleep, the woodcutter is visited by a variety of the species that make their home in the rain forest—birds, snakes, jaguars, and others. Each tells the man how cutting down the tree will destroy its way of life. The final "visitor" is a Yanomano Indian boy, who pleads with the woodcutter to go home and let the tree live. Upon awakening, the woodcutter stares at a deserted forest but imagines all the creatures watching him. He picks up his ax and goes away.

Cherry's exquisitely detailed illustrations increase the reader's awareness of and sympathy for the endangered creatures of the forest. The endpapers feature a guide to the flora and fauna of the forest, from its floor to the trees breaking through the canopy. The author's introduction and the use of the Portuguese word *senhor* to address the woodcutter place the story in Brazil, but, as a map of the world's vanishing tropical rain forests shows, the story could happen in many locations throughout the world.

The text, however, does not measure up to the illustrations and the accompanying material. This is not a story, but a sermon. Each page presents a different animal's plea, leading to a clunky, monotonous repetition. The ending strains credibility and avoids the complex economic issues that led the woodcutter into the forest in the first place. In fact, the woodcutter's motivations are never clear, and it is therefore hard to sympathize with him, even when he does the right thing. The book's strength on a visual level might make it a good choice for a kindergarten or first-grade class, as long as an alternative commentary is supplied, but those who can read it on their own will probably be turned off by its didacticism.

442   Dorros, Arthur. ***Tonight Is Carnaval.*** Spanish ed. available. Illus. with *arpilleras* sewn by the Club de Madres Virgenes of Lima, Peru. Dutton 1991, HB $13.95 (0-525-44641-9). 24pp. Fiction.

Two South American traditions—the *arpilleras* and Carnaval—are the focus of this unusual picture book. Initially created in Chile and dispersed to Peru, Colombia, and other countries, the *arpilleras* are three-dimensional tapestries that feature small dolls sewn into scenes of everyday village and town life. Also used in the *arpilleras* are scraps of wood, plastic, matches, and other objects that enhance its three-dimensional nature. *Arpilleras* sewn in Peru are used to illustrate this story about a boy who will perform on the *quena* (a wooden flute used in the Peruvian highlands) in his father's band at Carnaval for the first time. In the days leading up to Carnaval, the nameless boy practices his songs and helps to harvest the vegetables that will be sold in the village market just before the commencement of the three-day celebration.

The reproduction of the *arpilleras* is excellent; their texture and bright colors come through on the page. Readers can observe the variety of materials and stitches used and the richness of each scene. At the end of the story is a two-page spread that details how the tapestries are made and a glossary that lists the traditional musical instruments of Carnaval in Peru. The text has a musical cadence in keeping with the story, but it does not overpower the illustrations; words and pictures are perfectly matched. Although the protagonist is more a vehicle for narration than a fully developed character, the reader will enjoy following him in the *arpilleras* as he makes his way to Carnaval.

443   Griffiths, John. ***Take a Trip to Panama.*** Illus. with photos. SERIES: Take a Trip.
       Franklin Watts 1989, LB $10.90 (0-531-10736-1). 32pp. Nonfiction.

This volume in the Take a Trip series discusses contemporary problems such as
the destruction of the rain forest and allegations of corruption, assassination, and
drug dealing by former General Noriega. The author also examines *machismo*,
though a poorly chosen accompanying photograph (a group of fierce-looking
dark-skinned men holding liquor bottles) mars the presentation.

444   Kurusa. ***The Streets Are Free.*** Trans. from Spanish by Karen Englander. Illus. by
       Monkia Doppert. Annick 1985, HB $6.95 (0-920303-09-9); P $4.95 (0-920303-
       07-2). 48pp. Fiction.

Many years ago, what is now the *barrio* of San Jose de la Urbina was a single
house on the mountainside. Then people began to pour into Caracas, Venezuela,
from rural areas, and that same mountainside became a slum, with no running
water or sewers, limited electricity, and no playgrounds for the children. After
being almost run down by a truck while playing in the street, three youngsters—
Cheo, Carlitos, and Camila—decide they need a playground. They ask the
librarian for advice and mount a small demonstration outside city hall. They are
almost arrested, but when reporters show up, the mayor promises them their
park. Under the scrutiny of the reporters, the engineer surveys and the mayor
cuts a red ribbon, but as soon as press coverage and the election campaign ends,
nothing more gets done. Finally, the children persuade the adults of the *barrio* to
help; they salvage scrap items and build their own playground.

This tale, based on a true story, provides a realistic, though ultimately
hopeful, view of slum life in one Latin American city. Like many governments in
the region, this one is not openly repressive, but the needs of the poor are rarely
paid heed to. Venezuela is one of the few countries in the region with public
libraries and an active children's book publishing industry, and this is reflected
in the story, as the *barrio* library plays a major role in galvanizing the children to
action. The characters from the *barrio*—both children and adults—are depicted
as streetwise and intelligent; the condescending tone that mars Miriam Cohen's
Born to Dance Samba is fortunately absent here. Black-and-white and color
illustrations show the contrast between the crowded, haphazardly constructed
barrio and the gleaming city below. The characters' facial expressions mirror the
rise and fall of their fortunes, as presented in the text. *Barrio* residents are
multiracial, whereas most of those in power are light skinned, reflecting the
country's ethnic composition and the relationship between ethnicity and social
class. Though the book's small print might intimidate beginning readers, the text
is easy to understand, and the richness of the words and pictures makes this an
excellent choice for a wide range of ages.

445   Lye, Keith. ***Take a Trip to Argentina.*** Illus. with photos. SERIES: Take a Trip. Franklin
       Watts 1986, LB $10.90 (0-531-10194-0). 32pp. Nonfiction.

One of a series on foreign countries and directed at the early elementary grades,
this volume consists of photographs with a text that serves basically as captions
for the photos. Facts about the country are presented briefly, though the author
omits current controversies. All the photos are colorful and clearly reproduced; a
few are interesting in terms of content or composition. Some of the text does not
match the photos. This is particularly true of the historical sections; for instance,

a picture of sheep in a pen is paired with a discussion of the Falklands-Malvinas War. (The author tries to match the text by tacking on the statement that sheepherding is the main industry of the islands.) In general, the writing is choppy and dry, making for a rather uninteresting "trip." Includes index. Other volumes in this series cover Nicaragua, Panama, Peru, Venezuela, and Central America.

446   Rohmer, Harriet. *Uncle Nacho's Hat: A Folktale from Nicaragua./El sombrero del tío Nacho: Un cuento de Nicaragua.* Bilingual ed. Illus. by Veg Reisberg. Children's Book Pr. 1990, LB $12.95 (0-89239-043-3). 32pp. Nonfiction.

Uncle Nacho's hat is tattered and full of holes and of no use to him any longer. But when his niece Ambrosia brings him a new one, he just cannot seem to get rid of the old one. When he throws it into the garbage, Ambrosia's mother returns it to him. He tries to give it away to an old man, but two boys from the village—accustomed to seeing Uncle Nacho in his hat—accuse the old man of stealing the hat, and they return it to Uncle Nacho. Only when Ambrosia tells him to "stop worrying about the old hat . . . [and] think about your new hat instead" does Uncle Nacho feel comfortable leaving his old hat behind and showing off the new one to his many friends and neighbors.

This folktale has been performed by theater groups in revolutionary Nicaragua, where it has become a metaphor for people who think in the same old patterns and have a hard time accepting change. Even though this presentation has a modern flavor, with cars on the road as well as cows and chickens, the colorful illustrations are inspired by traditional Nicaraguan art. The story needs no interpretation to be of interest to young readers. Most will relate to the problem of giving up a favorite toy or article of clothing that has outlived its usefulness, and this story will help them to see why changing whole societies is so difficult. This is a story that works on many levels—personal as well as cultural and political—and it can be used for reading aloud, storytelling, and dramatics, and as a discussion starter in the classroom and elsewhere.

447   Rohmer, Harriet, Octavio Chow, and Morris Viduare. *The Invisible Hunters: A Legend from the Miskito Indians of Nicaragua./Los cazadores invisibles: Una leyenda de los indios miskitos de Nicaragua.* Bilingual ed.; Spanish version by Rosalma Zubizaretta and Alma Flor Ada. Illus. by Joe Sam. Children's Book Pr. 1987, LB $12.95 (0-317-70121-5). 32pp. Nonfiction.

The Miskito Indians of Nicaragua have become victims of the struggle between the Sandinistas and the contras; relocated from and eventually returned to their ancestral lands along the Rio Coco, they are attempting to preserve their culture and their way of life in the midst of war. Since the earliest settlement of the area by the Spaniards, the Miskito have mistrusted outsiders. The quest to maintain their values and life-style against foreign domination is the theme of the folktale *The Invisible Hunters.*

Presented in both English and Spanish with full-color illustrations in traditional style, *The Invisible Hunters* tells the story of three brothers who go hunting along the Rio Coco. They hear a voice, touch a vine, and are made invisible at will. This gives them an enormous advantage in hunting, but they must promise never to sell the meat or to use a gun. Soon white traders arrive and entice the brothers to sell their meat for wine and bright cloth. Later, the brothers buy guns.

They become rich selling the meat to whites, and their fellow villagers starve. Their greed is avenged when Dar, the spirit that made them invisible, refuses to make them visible again, and they must wander the forests calling Dar's name, begging him to make them reappear. The bilingual edition is attractive and readable, and the story has much to say about the situation facing indigenous groups in Central America today.

GRADES 4-6

448   Ancona, George. **Turtle Watch.** Illus. with photos by the author. Macmillan 1987, HB $13.95 (0-02-700910-6). 32pp. Nonfiction.

Scientists watch as a female turtle lays her eggs on a beach in northeastern Brazil. Then they dig up the eggs and take them to the research station, where the eggs will be safe from natural and human predators. The following day, two children find a nest of eggs that the scientists missed. They bring those eggs to the scientists and 53 days later witness the hatchlings make their way out to sea.

Ancona focuses on one effort to save the endangered sea turtles. Previously the children and their father, a fisherman, would have sold the turtle eggs at market and killed the adult turtles for food and materials for crafts. Besides saving endangered species, this conservation effort has raised consciousness about the environment among the residents of the area.

Ancona packs a great deal of information into a short book without sacrificing depth, literary quality, or the appeal of the story line. The text and black-and-white photographs convey a message without preaching, by presenting the story of the eggs, the scientists, and the two children. Ancona's respect for his subjects and his audience is apparent throughout. His writing challenges young readers rather than condescends to them, and he portrays sympathetically—through his sensitive photography as well as through his words—the Brazilian children and their family. This book shows how a well-planned conservation program can address residents' economic needs even as it preserves the environment for generations to come. Includes a bibliography for children and adults.

Argueta, Manlio. **Magic Dogs of the Volcanoes.**
See entry 439, Grades PS-3.

Ashabranner, Brent. **Children of the Maya: A Guatemalan Indian Odyssey.**
See entry 457, Grades 7-9.

449   Balcells, Jacqueline. **The Enchanted Raisin.** Trans. from Spanish by Elizabeth Gamble Miller. Illus. by L. Denise Miller. SERIES: Discoveries. Latin American Literary Review Pr. 1989, P $11.00 (0-935480-38-2). 103pp. Fiction.

The seven stories in this collection from Chile combine realism and fantasy in an imaginative, whimsical whole. The author, whose works are quite popular in her own country, uses the style and devices of traditional folktales, but with a clearly modern orientation. For example, in "The Buried Giant," the king and his subjects are confronted with a restless giant asleep under their country. To stop the constant tremors and earthquakes, the princess and her suitor travel under-ground to the giant's resting place, after making sure they have enough flash-light batteries for the trip. Mountains, volcanoes, and the sea—prominent features of Chile's geography—figure heavily in these stories.

The translation is faithful to the tone of the original Spanish and to Balcells's unique style. In keeping with the literary tradition of her culture, the author uses much hyperbole and metaphor. In the title story an exasperated mother tells her three outrageously unruly sons that their behavior is making her wrinkled and old before her time; her threat becomes reality when she shrivels up and turns into a raisin. The collection is sparsely illustrated, and the children in the primitively styled cover illustration look more European than Chilean. The ingenuous quality of the stories might make them of even greater interest to early-elementary-age youngsters, but the vocabulary level and lack of illustra-tions will frustrate those who are not capable readers. The stories read aloud well, however. A few are significantly weaker than others, but the best ones provide a delightful taste of another land and literary tradition. There is much humor here, as well as fertile material for storytelling and dramatics.

450   Bennett, Olivia. *A Family in Brazil.* Illus. with photos by Liba Taylor. SERIES: Families the World Over. Lerner 1986, LB $8.95 (0-8225-1665-9). 32pp. Nonfiction.

Twelve-year-old Eliane Leonardelli, the daughter of a truck driver in southern Brazil, is the focus of this volume in a series that portrays family life in various countries throughout the world. The book's approach and execution are particu-larly effective. The photography vividly captures Eliane and her large Italian-Brazilian family. The writing is lively, and the author makes an effort to compare Eliane's life to that of other Brazilian youngsters, thereby showing the country's enormous ethnic and cultural diversity. Although Eliane's family is relatively well-off, difficulties are not ignored; for example, even the children have to work to maintain the family's standard of living. Eliane emerges as a likable young-ster, and readers will enjoy this portrayal of her life and her country.

Other books in this series present children and their families in Bolivia, Chile, and Peru.

Cameron, Ann. *The Most Beautiful Place in the World.*
See entry 440, Grades PS–3.

Carlson, Lori M., and Cynthia L. Ventura, eds. *Where Angels Glide at Dawn: New Stories from Latin America.*
See entry 460, Grades 7–9.

Carpenter, Mark. *Brazil: An Awakening Giant.*
See entry 461, Grades 7–9.

451   Cohen, Miriam. *Born to Dance Samba.* Illus. by Gioia Fiammenghi. HarperCollins 1984, HB $10.95 (0-06-021358-2). 149pp. Fiction.

In their slum neighborhood high above Rio de Janeiro's glittering beaches, the people of the Hill of the Cashew Tree prepare for Brazil's annual Carnaval. Maria Antonia dos Santos dreams of being chosen one day as the Queen of the Samba, but this year she has to outdance the pretty newcomer, Teresinha, in order to be picked as the Star of the Kids of the Cashew Tree. In the days before the showdown, Maria Antonia and her boyfriend, Nilton, discover a (modest) stolen treasure, rescue a goat that has stumbled off a cliff, and locate her baby brother, who has been kidnapped by a mentally ill elderly neighbor. These events fail to distract Maria Antonia from her rivalry with Teresinha, but when she emerges the loser, she gains a knowledge of the true meaning of the samba.

Cohen's novel is well written, with vivid descriptions that give the reader a sense of place. Its short chapters and episodic structure will appeal to transitional readers as well as more capable ones. The child narrator is a sympathetic character with an appealing voice.

Cohen's stated intent in writing the novel is to show the "vitality" of Brazil's slum children, as expressed by their love of dance and of Carnaval. The result perpetuates the stereotype of poor people, particularly those of African heritage, as happy-go-lucky, concerned more with enjoying the present than planning for the future. For instance, Maria Antonia skips school to practice her dancing, and her parents do not seem to care. Her older brother Alberto turns down a well-paying job because it will require him to miss Carnaval. While life in Rio's hillside shantytowns may offer joy as well as misery, the story condescends to its subjects and, for the most part, whitewashes the very real difficulties that they face.

452   Cummins, Ronnie. *Guatemala.* Illus. with photos by Rose Welch. SERIES: Children of the World. Gareth Stevens 1990, LB $12.95 (0-8368-0120-2). 64pp. Nonfiction.

Twelve-year-old Maria Reanda is a Mayan Indian in Guatemala. Because her family lives in an area frequented by tourists, her own life is peaceful, but Cummins points out that most Guatemalan Mayas are not as fortunate. This volume in the Children of the World series describes Maria's life, places it in a wider context, and presents additional information in a reference section following the photo-essay. While the appearance and layout are uninspired, the text has balance and depth. The book raises some interesting questions for discussion. For instance, how has tourism changed the Mayan communities that it has protected? An index and bibliography are included. Other volumes present children in Argentina, Belize, Bolivia, Brazil, Costa Rica, El Salvador, Nicaragua, Panama, and Peru.

453   George, Jean Craighead. *One Day in the Tropical Rain Forest.* Illus. by Gary Allen. HarperCollins 1990, LB $11.99 (0-690-04769-X). 56pp. Nonfiction.

The day begins when Tepui, an Indian boy, wakes up and leaves for the science laboratory, where he is helping the scientists explore and protect the forest that is his home. On the way he passes birds, a jaguar, army ants, beetles, termites, butterflies, and other animals who have made the rain forest their home as well. Approaching their forest, however, are 11 bulldozers and 4 trucks, which have orders to cut it down. If Tepui and the scientists can discover a nameless butterfly —one that has not yet been discovered—a wealthy industrialist will buy the forest, preserve it, and name the butterfly after his daughter. Tepui and the scientists have only one day more to find this butterfly.

While Tepui and a scientist search, numerous other activities occur. A mother jaguar tries to protect her two cubs from vicious army ants. Various creatures take up residence in the fur of a three-toed sloth. Woven into the narrative are these descriptions of the rich life of the forest and background information on the world's vanishing tropical rain forests.

This particular forest is saved in the end, but George states that others are not as lucky. The reader gets a sense of the lives—both plant and animal—that are in danger, and her nameless butterfly is symbolic of what we have yet to learn about this complex ecological system. The book combines fiction and nonfiction, conveying information in the context of a gripping, multilayered story that the author has invented. She has done her research, and most of what takes place on that day could have actually happened. (Even the ending may become a possibility, as some Latin American leaders have called for investors to purchase and preserve the forests through a debt-equity swap.) Descriptions are vivid and concise; well-rendered illustrations contribute to the overall elegance of the story. By treating the subject in such a creative fashion, the author not only informs but also motivates readers to care about the tropical rain forest and its fate. The book contains an index and a bibliography geared to young readers.

Huber, Alex. *We Live in Chile.*
See entry 469, Grades 7–9.

Kurusa. *The Streets Are Free.*
See entry 444, Grades PS–3.

Moeri, Louise. *The Forty-Third War.*
See entry 474, Grades 7–9.

454   Morrison, Marion. *Argentina.* Illus. by Ann Savage. SERIES: People and Places. Silver Burdett 1989, LB $11.24 (0-382-09793-9). 48pp. Nonfiction.

A busy and lively layout combining illustrations, photos, captions, and a brief text characterizes this series for the middle elementary grades. Unfortunately, the parts do not add up to the whole, as the illustrations are unsophisticated and the text choppy. Each page focuses on a single subject and contains two or three paragraphs. Though this format may be useful for students writing school reports, little feeling for the country is conveyed. The captions and special boxes are more interesting, because they discuss the "disappeared" and other contemporary topics. Other volumes in this series present Brazil and Central America.

455   Nunes, Lygia Bojunga. *My Friend the Painter.* Trans. from Portuguese by Giovanni Pontiero. Harcourt Brace Jovanovich 1991, HB $13.95 (0-15-256340-7). 80pp. Fiction.

Young Claudio has a special friend, a painter who lives in the apartment above his family's. The painter has taught him about colors—yellows filled with life, mysterious reds, and the strange "color-of-longing." One day Claudio discovers his friend dead, and the neighbors say it was a suicide. But the painter's only other friend, Dona Clarice, denies it. Trying to uncover the truth, Claudio learns that his friend was involved in politics and spent years in prison; only recently, he was once again visited by the police. He also learns that the painter loved Dona Clarice, but she did not want to take third place to painting and politics. Years after their initial romance, he had tried to convince her to leave her family and marry him. Claudio also recalls the painter saying the life had gone out of his work. While Claudio never figures out why his older friend may have killed himself, he accepts the reality with sorrow but with increased appreciation for his own life.

This novel will require some background and discussion to be appreciated fully by a mainstream middle grade audience. Written by one of Brazil's foremost authors for children, it has a foreign feel, particularly in its pacing and its use of language. Claudio's narrative is quite philosophical, filled with musings on the nature of color, art, and life. Still, this is the tale of a young person trying to come to terms with not only the death of a revered older person but also the circumstances of that death. Grownups make choices that seem incomprehensible (and often less than admirable) to children, and Nunes's sparely written story explores that theme with great authenticity and sensitivity. Some of Brazil's history is alluded to here, as is the role of the artist in society, but even more significantly, this novel reflects a literary style characteristic of children's books in Latin America.

Pearce, Jenny. *Colombia: The Drug War.*
See entry 478, Grades 7–9.

GRADES 7–9

456 ***Argentina in Pictures.*** Illus. with photos. SERIES: Visual Geography. Lerner 1988, LB $11.95 (0-8225-1807-4). 64pp. Nonfiction.

This is a general overview of Argentina's geography, history, culture, and economy. The information is well indexed and useful for school reports, although rapid political and economic changes have dated the volume considerably. The perspective is more optimistic and upbeat than current events warrant; however, the "dirty war" receives coverage, and there is some analysis of Peronism and its effect on the country's economy and history. The writing is straightforward and quite dry; the book reads like an extended encyclopedia article. Additional volumes in this series present Bolivia, Brazil, Chile, Colombia, Costa Rica, Ecuador, El Salvador, Guatemala, Guyana, Honduras, Nicaragua, Panama, Paraguay, Peru, Uruguay, and Venezuela.

457 Ashabranner, Brent. ***Children of the Maya: A Guatemalan Indian Odyssey.*** Illus. with photos by Paul Conklin. Putnam/Philomel 1990, HB $14.95 (0-399-21707-X). 97pp. Nonfiction.

In the fall of 1982, migrant farm laborers from Guatemala began to arrive in Florida communities, seeking not only work but also permanent refuge. They were Mayan Indians, descendants of one of the world's great cultures. They spoke no English and very little Spanish, and they were escaping war and repression in their home country.

Ashabranner focuses on the Mayan immigrants of one Florida community, named, not coincidentally, Indiantown (the Indians believed they would be welcome in a place with this name). The author interviews those who have fled and who describe forced relocations from ancestral lands, killings of suspected leftist collaborators by the army, and compulsory military service—reasons why many individuals and families undertook the long, harsh journey through Mexico to the United States. There is not much information on the Mayan culture, which, though threatened, survives today in parts of Mexico and Guatemala. Rather, *Children of the Maya* examines why the Maya left and the life they have made since arriving in the States, where they have struggled to maintain their traditions in the face of an overwhelmingly different and modern culture.

The interviewees tell their stories in their own words, which gives their situation immediacy and allows the reader to empathize with them directly rather than through the mediation of the author. Introductory and concluding chapters place the personal narratives in context and discuss some of the broader issues of U.S. immigration policy. Through text and photos, *Children of the Maya* succeeds in showing the human dimension of the tragedy in Central America and of the promise of a new life in the United States. Includes index and bibliography.

458   Bender, Evelyn. *Brazil.* Illus. with photos. SERIES: Let's Visit Places and Peoples of the World. Chelsea House 1990, LB $14.95 (0-7910-1108-9). 112pp. Nonfiction.

Current issues—including the fate of the Amazon rain forest, hyperinflation and the debt, and the poor quality of education and health care despite Brazil's abundant resources and level of development—receive a great deal of attention in this book. The author emphasizes broad themes and places her facts in context; the book is strong on synthesis and analysis. The visuals are its weakest element. There is one eight-page color spread, and the black-and-white photos are poorly placed in relation to the text. Includes index and glossary. Other books in this series present Argentina, Belize, Bolivia, Chile, Ecuador, El Salvador, Guatemala, Guyana, Paraguay, Suriname, and Venezuela. The Let's Visit series books on Colombia, Costa Rica, Guyana, Honduras, Nicaragua, Panama, Peru, and Uruguay, originally published in England by Burke Books, are also sold by Chelsea House as part of its Let's Visit People and Places of the World series.

Blair, David Nelson. *The Land and People of Bolivia.*
See entry 483, Grades 10–12.

459   *Bolivia in Pictures.* Illus. with photos. SERIES: Visual Geography. Lerner 1987, LB $11.95 (0-8225-1808-2). 64pp. Nonfiction.

This survey of Bolivia's geography, history, culture, and economy is a superior volume in the series. The enormous gap between rich and poor is not downplayed, and the complex issues surrounding the drug trade receive a great deal of attention. Although the more environmentally conscious may question the pro-development bias (exemplified by the suggestion that Bolivia's forests need to be "exploited"), the book seems far less dated than others in the series. Many of the photographs feature the highland Indians and their way of life. The photographs are attractively reproduced and well placed throughout the text.

460   Carlson, Lori M., and Cynthia L. Ventura, eds. *Where Angels Glide at Dawn: New Stories from Latin America.* Intro. by Isabel Allende. Trans. from Spanish by the

eds. Illus. by Jose Ortega. HarperCollins 1990, LB $13.89 (0-397-32425-1). 103pp. Fiction.

Ten short stories by authors from Argentina, Chile, Cuba, El Salvador, Mexico, Panama, Peru, Puerto Rico, and the Puerto Rican *barrios* of New York are included in this volume, which has been selected especially for young people. The stories provide a glimpse into the various cultures and societies of Spanish-speaking Latin America. Some comment directly or indirectly on political issues. In Mario Bencastro's "A Clown's Story," the clown observes the increasing misery and fighting that have put his circus in El Salvador out of business; all he has left is his painted-on smile. Details of the circus will interest young readers, who will discover, among other things, that in many circuses in poor countries, high-wire acrobats perform without safety nets underneath.

Other stories highlight the encounter between two cultures. The protagonist of Barbara Mujica's "Fairy Tale" meets the unexpected when she journeys from her New York *barrio* to visit relatives in Puerto Rico. Her experiences will strike a chord among Hispanic-American youngsters who travel for the first time to their parents' native land. A cultural exchange of another kind occurs in Jorge Ibarguengoitia's "Paleton and the Musical Elephant" when a spoiled Mexico City millionaire calls in some Chicago gangsters to help him steal an unusually talented zoo elephant.

This collection introduces young readers to magical realism. Dreams and the supernatural are elements in most of the stories, and supernatural events often symbolize personal or political milestones. Several of the stories are humorous; the humor is ironic, emerging from the authors' choice of words and expressions. Setting, mood, style, and the authors' unique voices are outstanding features of this volume. There is little explanatory or background material; rather the stories are allowed to speak for themselves. Yet some supplementary information may be necessary to help students appreciate the stories fully.

461   Carpenter, Mark. *Brazil: An Awakening Giant.* Illus. with photos. SERIES: Discovering Our Heritage. Dillon 1987, LB $12.95 (0-87518-366-2). 125pp. Nonfiction.

Attractive photographs and lively writing characterize this book for the middle grades. Part guidebook, part survey, it introduces readers to the many cultures that compose Brazil. Included are several myths and legends from the Amazon Indians and three easy (and tasty) recipes. Although the author emphasizes aspects of daily life of interest to North American children, he does not ignore the problems facing their Brazilian counterparts: poor nutrition, crime, poverty, and the abandonment and homelessness of hundreds of thousands of children. The author has lived much of his life in Brazil, and his familiarity with and feeling for the country is evident. The book includes an extensive glossary, a bibliography, an index, and a listing of the Brazilian consulates in the United States and Canada. Other volumes in the series present Argentina, Chile, El Salvador, and Nicaragua.

462   Castaneda, Omar S. *Among the Volcanoes.* Dutton/Lodestar 1991, HB $14.95 (0-525-67332-6). 192pp. Fiction.

Isabel Pacay dreams of finishing school and becoming a teacher, but the obstacles are daunting. Her mother suffers from a mysterious ailment, and Isabel, the eldest daughter of a Mayan family, must care for her mother and for the rest of the family. She is also in love with handsome Lucas Choy, who does not appreciate her desire to better herself and instead evaluates her attitude toward her family to see if she will be content to take care of him when they are married. Things begin to change, however, when the American researcher Allan Waters comes to the village. No one will speak to Allan except Isabel. The *sanjorín*—the local healer—sees the mother's illness as a sign of bad faith; he can do nothing for her. The crisis comes to a head when Allen arranges for the mother to go to a nearby hospital, and the family journeys by bus and boat for a medical treatment that is alien to their culture.

Descriptive passages reveal Castaneda's intimate knowledge of his material. One gets a sense of the natural beauty of the Guatemalan highlands and of the conflicts faced by Isabel and her family. Many of the characterizations are full and memorable, especially Isabel's and her parents'. Lucas and Isabel's friend Teresa are flatly drawn, however, and one wonders why Isabel and Lucas are attracted to each other in the first place. While the conflict between traditional and Western culture is presented with depth and insight, Castaneda's story-telling sometimes falters. There is a great deal of preachiness; a long section critical of hippie American visitors seems out of place. Scenes involving the Guatemalan military are not well integrated into the larger story and do more to make a point than to further the plot. Descriptive and analytic passages slow up the action and give this book a more specialized than general appeal. On the whole, this book is best suited to better readers and those with an interest in Central American issues or Native American cultures.

463 Cheney, Glenn Alan. *El Salvador: Country in Crisis.* Rev. ed. Illus. with photos. Franklin Watts 1990, LB $12.90 (0-531-10916-X). 127pp. Nonfiction.

Landlessness, overcrowding, poverty, class divisions, despair, and injustice are presented as causes of El Salvador's protracted civil war. This remarkably balanced account does an excellent job of explaining difficult concepts to the reader. The discussion of El Salvador's land reform program is particularly effective; Cheney details the mechanics of the program, evaluates its efficacy, and examines the controversies surrounding it, including the criticisms made by leftist and rightist opponents of the Duarte government that initiated it. In contrast to other works on El Salvador, this one presents the guerrillas with some complexity. Cheney discusses the various ideological positions within the FMLN (Farabundo Marti Liberation Front, the armed guerrilla organization) and the FDR (Democratic Revolutionary Front, the more moderate political organization), as well as life in the guerrilla-controlled zones. The book ends early in 1989 with the election of right-winger Alfredo Cristiani in El Salvador and the inauguration of George Bush in the United States. A bibliography directs readers to periodical sources with more up-to-date information, and this book will certainly give young readers the background to understand that information. An index is also included.

464 *Costa Rica in Pictures.* Illus. with photos. SERIES: Visual Geography. Lerner 1987, LB $11.95 (0-8225-1805-8). 64pp. Nonfiction.

This general overview of the geography, history, government, culture, and economy of Costa Rica avoids the problem of dating by presenting very little information about the country's constructive involvement in surrounding regional conflicts, which culminated in 1987 in the first workable plan for peace in the region. Costa Rica is identified as a democracy with no standing army, but there is no analysis of why the country developed so differently from its neighbors. The country's lack of resources and its level of poverty receive a great deal of attention, as does the structure of its government. Includes index.

Fox, Geoffrey. *The Land and People of Argentina.*
See entry 484, Grades 10–12.

465   French, Michael. *Circle of Revenge.* Bantam 1988, HB $13.95 (0-553-05495-3).
       151pp. Fiction.

Hatreds born of a brutal South American dictatorship erupt in a peaceful Los Angeles suburb when innocent high schooler Robbie Cavanaugh becomes a weapon of revenge as part of a psychology "experiment." Robbie takes the job offered by the cold and mysterious Dr. Salazar because it pays well for very little work. In the lab, however, Robbie is forced to watch graphic scenes of torture while receiving mild electrical shocks. He gradually discovers that the "experiment" involves mind control and that Dr. Salazar wants him to murder Carlos Montano, a school friend of Robbie, as well as the rest of Carlos's family (who changed their surname from Coriz to Montano when they fled to the United States) in retaliation for the betrayal and killing of Dr. Salazar's son back in South America.

The author explores moral questions of justice, violence, and retribution, and his characters and plot are vehicles for that exploration. References to "South America" are misleading, since the continent is treated as if it were a single country. Comparisons between the United States and South America depict the latter as a monolithic region with corrupt, dictatorial regimes, terrorized citizens, and murderous intrigues. Although several chapters are told from Carlos's point of view, his experiences, emotions, and actions fail to ring true. For instance, if he were a junta member's son and Dr. Salazar's son were a government opponent, it is unlikely that the two boys would have been best friends, a relationship that implies a great deal of trust. As an easy-to-read novel with lots of suspense, this may be a popular title for recreational reading, and it might make reluctant readers think as well. Yet it does so at the expense of subtlety in presenting its characters and the political situation in South America.

466   Gelman, Rita Golden. *Inside Nicaragua: Young People's Dreams and Fears.* Illus.
       with photos. Franklin Watts 1988, LB $13.90 (0-531-10538-5). 190pp. Nonfiction.

"Is Nicaragua the one where the good government is fighting the bad guerrillas? Or is it the one where the bad government is fighting the good guerrillas?"
       "Depends who you ask."
Author Gelman asks that question of hundreds of Nicaraguans—young people, their parents, former revolutionaries, soldiers in the mountains, and people she meets on the street. Her interviews give a human history encompassing more than a decade of revolution and war in that Central American country.
       The images are moving: 14-year-old Ramon Rivera's recurrent nightmares of the fighting before Somoza's fall, Evenor Ortega's memories of living in the countryside and teaching poor people there to read during the literacy crusade, a

12-year-old who has joined the army to take revenge against the contras who murdered his parents and little sister, and a government worker who hates the government but calls the contras "thugs." Most of the people Gelman interviews are bewildered by U.S. funding of the contras. They do not understand why they should suffer the loss of their men and the shortages of basic goods that a protracted war causes. Virtually all ask Gelman to tell her government to leave them alone.

In taking the first-person approach that is characteristic of the "new journalism," Gelman does not shy away from expressing her own opinions. Her interviewees include many Sandinista opponents inside the country, but the contras and those who have left Nicaragua for the United States do not appear. For youngsters unaccustomed to hearing harsh criticism of their government's policies, not only from the Nicaraguan youths but also from one of their fellow citizens, reading this book is likely to be a jarring experience. Still, the book is an eloquent presentation of the Nicaraguans' point of view in this conflict, a point of view that has been too often ignored in the United States. Although the book was published before the Sandinistas' electoral defeat, one can see the seeds of that defeat in Nicaraguans' exhaustion after years of war and fairly widespread opposition to aspects of Sandinista rule. Includes index and bibliography.

467   Haynes, Tricia. **Colombia.** Illus. with photos. SERIES: Let's Visit Places and Peoples of the World. Chelsea House 1985, LB $14.95 (0-222-00948-9). 96pp. Nonfiction.

Originally published in England and distributed in the United States and Canada by Chelsea House, this volume differs markedly from Chelsea House's own series. There is much less emphasis on history; geography and daily life are the main subjects covered. Very little attention is paid to current issues, such as the drug war and terrorism, and the general tone is quite upbeat. The author describes major landmarks and tourist attractions in the major cities, making this a more valuable work for young people who will be visiting the country rather than those who are studying its problems and history as part of a social studies class. Includes index but no bibliography.

468   Hintz, Martin. **Chile.** Illus. with photos. SERIES: Enchantment of the World. Childrens Pr. 1985, LB $15.95 (0-516-02755-7). 128pp. Nonfiction.

More than many others, this series book engages readers by presenting interesting tidbits of information, describing individual Chilean youngsters, and posing questions directly to the reader. However, it is in serious need of revision due to recent political changes. The author has chosen to accentuate the positive, giving scarce attention to major human rights violations under the Pinochet dictatorship. Broad generalizations about the "Chilean spirit" and "eagerly hopeful" people obscure deep-seated social, economic, and political conflicts. Includes index but no bibliography or note on sources. Other volumes in this series present Argentina, Bolivia, Brazil, Colombia, Ecuador, El Salvador, and Venezuela.

469   Huber, Alex. *We Live in Chile.* Illus. with photos by the author. SERIES: Living Here. Franklin Watts 1985, LB $12.90 (0-531-18023-9). 64pp. Nonfiction.

Volumes in the Living Here series present the geography, culture, history, and ways of life of a country by means of interviews with some 25 of its citizens. The volume on Chile has been assembled by a Chilean photojournalist who has chosen to focus on the country's great geographical diversity. Among his interviewees are residents of the northern Atacama Desert, where it rains once every two years, and of the remote south and Antarctica. Others are Indians, who have become integrated into Chilean society, farmers, fishermen, miners, large landowners, businessmen, professionals, and others. Like the rest of the volumes in the series, this one presents only one child, a 10-year-old bike racing champion. The author has chosen to accentuate the positive, avoiding any mention of the social and political conflicts that have divided Chile, and for that reason this book is incomplete, although it is an attractive introduction to other aspects of this land. Includes brief facts, glossary, and index. Argentina and Brazil are also covered in the series.

470   Jenkins, Lyll Becerra de. *The Honorable Prison.* Dutton/Lodestar 1988, HB $14.95 (0-525-67238-9); Penguin/Puffin 1989, P $3.95 (0-14-032952-8). 199pp. Fiction.

Colombian-born author Lyll Becerra de Jenkins tells the story of a young woman who must make extraordinary sacrifices due to political events beyond her control. Eighteen-year-old Marta Maldonado's father is a journalist who opposes the ruling general in an unnamed South American country. As punishment for the father's stance in favor of social justice and human rights, the entire family—Marta, her parents, and her younger brother, Ricardo—are forced into internal exile in a remote area of the country. The cold, damp climate is slowly killing Marta's father, who suffers from a chronic lung condition. Food is scarce, and the family is running out of money. Desperate in her isolation, Marta befriends a young man, a local schoolteacher, who ultimately fails her. She and her mother write to high-ranking officials, former allies of her father, but the appeals are ignored.

During her year in internal exile, her "honorable prison," Marta learns to depend on her own resources for survival, and she gains a new understanding of the reasons behind her father's commitment. Jenkins is uncompromisingly honest in her portrayal of the characters' feelings and emotions. For example, Marta and her brother hope at times that their father will die so they will be freed from their lonely exile. Even her minor characters, such as the prison guards and the poor residents of the village, are multidimensional.

Though not instantly accessible, Jenkins's writing has a subtle beauty, and she manages to depict the crushing bleakness and boredom of Marta's life while moving the story along at an acceptable pace. *The Honorable Prison* is not a book for every teenager; many will find it slow going, especially in the early chapters. However, sophisticated young readers will appreciate the graceful writing and the complex, thought-provoking story.

471   Jenkins, Tony. *Nicaragua and the United States: Years of Conflict.* Illus. with photos. Franklin Watts 1989, LB $14.90 (0-531-10795-7). 190pp. Nonfiction.

This book presents the conflicts between the Sandinistas and the Reagan Administration in the context of more than 150 years of U.S. involvement in

Nicaragua's affairs. Jenkins shows how successive U.S. interventions planted the seeds of distrust and how right-wing ideologues within the United States drove the Sandinistas to extreme measures of their own—a predictable outcome, given their leaders' tendency toward socialist dogmatism. The author, a journalist, traveled to Nicaragua in 1986; he compares the reality to the assertions of the Reagan Administration. Though somewhat dry, his account is balanced, well researched, and enlivened by snippets of political humor. While he describes the personalities and background of the various Somozas, one gets very little sense of who the Sandinista leaders are as individuals. That and the fact that the book ends before the Sandinistas' 1990 electoral defeat seem to be the only drawbacks of an otherwise useful survey. Includes time line, glossary, bibliography, and index.

472   Jenness, Aylette, and Lisa W. Kroeber. *A Life of Their Own: An Indian Family in Latin America.* Illus. with photos and drawings. HarperCollins 1975, HB $12.95 (0-690-00572-5). 132pp. Nonfiction.

During the 1980s, successive military regimes destroyed most of the Mayan villages of the Guatemalan highlands and forcibly relocated their inhabitants to "strategic hamlets" under the control of the army. Tens of thousands of Maya died in what has been called genocide by Amnesty International and other human rights organizations.

Published in 1975, this description of one indigenous community gives readers a perspective on a way of life that has all but disappeared in Guatemala. The authors utilize the techniques of anthropology, acting as participant-observers of one relatively prosperous Mayan family. Even so, their host family lives simply, and all members work hard to maintain their standard of living. The authors describe with humor their difficulties in adjusting to certain Mayan customs, and the book focuses on family life, work, education, and the village community. The overall impression is of a society that has adapted gradually to changes in the outside world, incorporating those changes into daily life. The authors present the national government as a remote institution that shows little understanding of or concern for the indigenous communities of the highlands, but there is no foreshadowing of the horrors to come. The writing is clear and straightforward. The authors' closeness to their host family and other village residents makes this more than a dry description of foreign people and customs. An appendix with activities for a variety of interests and age groups also helps to bring the Mayan culture to life. Some of the black-and-white photographs are poorly reproduced, a problem with many books published in the 1970s and earlier. At the same time, this older work documents firsthand a culture that would be virtually impossible to observe directly today. Includes index and glossary of Spanish words; words in the Cakchiquel language are defined in the text.

473   Kellner, Douglas. *Ernesto "Che" Guevara.* Illus. with photos. SERIES: World Leaders, Past and Present. Chelsea House 1989, LB $17.95 (1-55546-835-7). 112pp. Nonfiction.

Kellner's biography of Che Guevara places him in the context of the various Latin American countries where he fought as a revolutionary. Most of the book is about his work in Cuba, from plotting the successful overthrow of Batista to serving in various ministries in Fidel Castro's government to the famous falling-out with Castro that led to his leaving Cuba and dying in a failed guerrilla campaign in Bolivia. Kellner emphasizes that Guevara's brilliance as a guerrilla commander did not carry over into the running of a country. His idealistic theories were disastrous for Cuba's economy, and his hatred of both superpowers angered Castro, who was drawing closer to the Soviet Union. Though this biography contains little information about Guevara as an individual, it does provide a context for his life and an impartial assessment of his role in history; his revolutionary activities are neither glorified nor vilified. Includes bibliography and index, as well as numerous well-captioned photographs. Salvador Allende, Simón Bolívar, Daniel Ortega, and Juan Perón are other Central and South American leaders included in this biography series and presented through a similar approach.

Marrin, Albert. *Inca and Spaniard: Pizarro and the Conquest of Peru.*
See entry 486, Grades 10-12.

474 Moeri, Louise. *The Forty-Third War.* Houghton Mifflin 1989, HB $13.95 (0-395-50215-2). 208pp. Fiction.

Twelve-year-old Uno Ramirez, his best friend, Lolo, and his 15-year-old cousin Nacio are kidnapped from their village and forced to fight in their unnamed Central American country's latest civil war. Their kidnappers are the revolutionaries, but the two sides are seen as essentially indistinguishable in their methods and political positions. In the next eight days, the three boys receive minimal training and are then sent out to fight in a battle in which their side is vastly outnumbered.

Moeri's novel works best as an adventure story. The plot development and pacing are handled quite well. The revolutionary commander emerges as a sympathetic and multidimensional character, and thus it seems convincing when the boys grow loyal to the revolutionary cause, in part out of admiration for their commander and in part out of their need to feel ownership of events beyond their control. The ending leaves much to the reader's imagination and underscores the uncertainty in the boys' lives.

Having set her story in an unnamed country in Central America, Moeri is freed from the need to base her events on real conflicts in, for instance, Guatemala, El Salvador, or Nicaragua. Issues are presented in general terms, from Uno's point of view, and one learns little of the reasons why these countries have been embroiled in decades-long civil wars. Moeri's purpose is clear: She wants to show how war itself is evil and how children throughout the world are forced to fight in wars they do not comprehend. She succeeds in conveying her message in a form that will grip young readers and help them to understand the emotions and experiences of people living in a war zone.

475 Morrison, Marion. *Venezuela.* Illus. with photos. SERIES: Enchantment of the World. Childrens Pr. 1989, LB $15.95 (0-516-02711-5). 128pp. Nonfiction.

The strength of this volume lies in its vivid, well-rendered photography, much of it undertaken by Morrison's husband, a professional photographer. The text is balanced, examining contemporary problems, but the writing is dull and choppy. The author presents a litany of facts, dates, and statistics with very little information specifically directed to young people; rather, the book relies upon the excellent photos and captions to stimulate reader interest. Includes index but no bibiography.

476 Neimark, Anne E. *Che! Latin America's Legendary Guerrilla Leader.* Illus. with maps and photos. HarperCollins 1989, LB $13.89 (0-397-32309-3). 113pp. Nonfiction.

Neimark's biography of Latin America guerrilla leader Ernesto (Che) Guevara focuses on his struggle with severe asthma as the source of his uncompromising support of the poor and dispossessed. He emerges as a sympathetic figure, a defender of the Third World and its common people against domination by both the United States and the Soviet Union. Yet Neimark does not deny Guevara's fanaticism, which led to his embracing a violent solution. She succeeds in showing why he has become such a powerful symbol for rebels throughout the world.

Although the biography is based on Guevara's own writings as well as other primary and secondary sources, Neimark has invented some of the dialogue and a few scenes. She has included a useful bibliography but no index. The chapters are not titled. Maps trace Guevara's two major campaigns, in Cuba and Bolivia, and several photos of Guevara are included. The result, though admittedly "fictionalized," is a lively work, one that many youngsters will want to read straight through.

Nunes, Lygia Bojunga. *My Friend the Painter.*
See entry 455, Grades 4–6.

477 Pascoe, Elaine. *Neighbors at Odds: U.S. Policy in Latin America.* Illus. with photos. Franklin Watts 1990, LB $12.90 (0-531-10903-8). 157pp. Nonfiction.

Focusing on the history of U.S relations with Latin America, Pascoe examines why each developed along different paths politically, economically, and socially and how their interests collided at various points. Her account, while somewhat dry, is clearly organized, easy to follow, and balanced. The treatment is quite general, providing an overview rather than an in-depth analysis. The book concentrates on events before 1920; recent events receive very little attention. Includes bibliography and index.

478 Pearce, Jenny. *Colombia: The Drug War.* Illus. with photos. SERIES: Hotspots. Franklin Watts 1990, LB $11.90 (0-53 i-17237-6). 36pp. Nonfiction.

This book succeeds in presenting a balanced, rather complex picture of the Colombian drug war in very few pages. The author declares the assassination of the leading presidential candidate as the turning point in a war that had been simmering for more than a decade. The roots of the conflict in an unjust and unequal society receive much treatment, and there is some information on the details of how the coca leaf is processed into cocaine that gets shipped to dealers and consumers in developed countries. Pearce, who has written about Latin America for both children and adults, exposes the connection between narcotics traffickers and right-wing death squads, but she also discusses how left-wing guerrillas extorted money from jungle processors. She raises questions about the value of U.S. military aid to Colombia and presents arguments about whether the best strategy is to control cocaine output (the position advocated by U.S. officials) or to reduce demand (the position taken by Latin American leaders, who must deal with the fact that the drug is the most lucrative employment for a large proportion of their citizens). Vividly colored photos, accompanied by excellent captions, enhance the text, which is followed by sections on Colombia's geography and economy, cocaine facts, and statistics as well as a glossary, a chronology, and an index.

479   Sanders, Renfield. *El Salvador.* Illus. with photos. SERIES: Let's Visit Places and Peoples of the World. Chelsea House 1988, LB $14.95 (1-55546-781-4). 104pp. Nonfiction.

This series volume does not shy away from controversy in discussing El Salvador's bloody civil war and the enormous disparities between rich and poor that have led to it. Although he discusses atrocities committed by both sides, Sanders clearly sympathizes with former President Jose Napoleón Duarte, and he accepts the U.S. government's contention that the guerrillas are dangerous Communists funded by Communist neighbors. There is not much detail on the guerrilla movement, however; for example, in identifying the revolutionaries as the FDR (Democratic Revolutionary Front), Sanders does not distinguish the political organization (the FDR) from the more radical armed wing, the FMLN (Farabundo Marti Liberation Front, named for Farabundo Marti, a peasant leader in the 1930s). Because of massive migration from the war-torn countryside, population statistics are out of date, and several other errors involving numbers may be misprints. Includes index but no bibliography.

480   Skarmeta, Antonio. *Chileno!* Trans. from Spanish by Hortense Carpentier. William Morrow 1979. 92pp. Fiction. o.p.

When Chile's elected government is overthrown in a military coup in 1973, Lucho's family flees the country and arrives in Berlin. Depressed over events in his home country, Lucho's father becomes angry, cold, and distant. Lucho is the first in the family to learn German, which gives him increased power and responsibility but exacerbates his conflict with his father. Not quite understanding the ways of the Germans, Lucho gets into a fight with one over a girl and puts his adversary in the hospital. When the injured boy's older brother seeks revenge, Lucho must fight a battle in which he knows he will be crushed. Yet confronting his adversary proves to be an important step in his attainment of manhood, and it establishes his bicultural identity.

Lucho's grit and sense of humor help him to overcome prejudice and to gain the respect of his German peers. The story has a realism and credibility that come from the Chilean author's having witnessed the tragic events of 1973 and experienced the pain of involuntary exile. Characters are portrayed as individuals rather than as stereotypes. One gets a sense of the culture and society that Lucho's family had to leave behind, as well as of the specific aspects (including concerts by exiled New Song bands) of the Chileans' community life abroad. The confusion, loneliness, and homesickness experienced by political exiles are not minimized, yet those aspects do not overwhelm the story, and the novel maintains a positive tone.

Skarmeta's first-person narrative is rambling, with much "telling," no chapter breaks, and, except for the fight scenes, not much action. The style is clearly from another culture. The chattiness, the use of direct, unadorned language (including profanities), and the way in which the author addresses the reader, as if they were friends swapping stories on a streetcorner, might prove jarring, and yet enriching, to readers accustomed to mainstream young adult fiction.

481   Watson, James. ***Talking in Whispers.*** Knopf 1984, HB $10.95 (0-394-86538-3). 143pp. Fiction.

In a fictionalized Chile "between the present and the future," the ruling General Zuckerman cancels an election and orders his army and death squads to assassinate the opposition candidate and all leading opponents of the military regime. Sixteen-year-old Andrés Larreta, the son of a well-known underground folksinger, witnesses his father's capture, then flees into the underbrush to avoid his own arrest. Hitching a ride hours later, Andrés is befriended by the twins Isa and Beto, teenage street puppeteers who oppose the regime that killed their parents. They recognize Andrés as the famous singer's son and take him to their hideout in the ruins of an earlier military bombing. In the week that follows, Andrés witnesses the beating and eventual murder of an American photographer, obtains the photographer's camera and film, which he has developed in a clandestine laboratory, and experiences capture, interrogation, and torture. Although Andrés escapes with his life, he is scarred both physically and emotionally. No longer a child, he and the two puppeteers are on their own in a bleak and frightening world.

On one level, Watson's novel is a fast-paced adventure story, with plenty of action and close escapes. But the British author seeks principally to instruct. The third-person narrator frequently intrudes to pass judgment on characters and events, giving the book a didactic tone. Andrés is, admittedly, a "witness" rather than an active participant, and other characters are one-dimensional. Sensational events are emphasized at the expense of portraying honestly the indignities of daily life under a dictatorship. The British expressions are jarring in the Chilean context, and the narrative seems awkward overall. The author does succeed in capturing certain aspects of Chilean political humor. He has done his research, and despite occasional inaccuracies readers can absorb information on Chile's geography and culture. However, Watson's distance from Chile and his desire to convey a message limit the novel's authenticity and power.

GRADES 10–12

Bender, Evelyn. ***Brazil.***
See entry 458, Grades 7–9.

482   Bierhorst, John. ***The Mythology of South America.*** Illus. Morrow 1988, HB $15.95 (0-688-06722-0). 276pp. Nonfiction.

This is a thorough and clearly presented study of the myths that have flourished among the various native peoples of South America. Dividing the continent into seven regions, Bierhorst examines the types of myths that have characterized each region, including creation myths, trickster stories, and myths about the superiority of men or of women. An introduction defines what is considered myth and discusses the means by which the myths were transmitted and learned; Bierhorst notes that even today new ones are being uncovered. He traces the evolution of myths that crossed regions and were adapted to the particular situation of each native group. Finally, he examines how myths have had political significance throughout history and continue to do so today.

Bierhorst provides both analysis and examples of specific myths. His research is extensive and scrupulous, his account based on both primary and secondary sources. Sketches and photos of masks, pottery, and other crafts complement the narrative and show how myths are transmitted visually as well as orally. Though scholarly in his approach, Bierhorst is never pedantic; his writing is comprehensible to high school students. The format and use of actual myths will appeal to those who might not otherwise pick up this type of book. With its detailed table of contents and excellent index, this is also a useful book for reference in secondary school and public libraries. Published in 1990 is a companion volume, *The Mythology of Mexico and Central America*.

483   Blair, David Nelson. ***The Land and People of Bolivia.*** Illus. with photos. SERIES: Portraits of the Nations. HarperCollins 1990, LB $14.89 (0-397-32383-2). 224pp. Nonfiction.

The Portraits of the Nations series presents countries' geography, history, politics, culture, and economy on a level appropriate for high school students. This study of Bolivia is characteristic of the noteworthy series. Using the *diablada*, or devil's dance, as a metaphor, it discusses the mixture of Native and Hispanic traditions that have contributed to Bolivia's rich culture and yet provided a source of economic and social problems. The country's diverse geography, which includes a piece of the Amazon rain forest as well as highlands and grasslands, receives coverage, as does its often tragic history. Blair examines the dilemmas surrounding the drug trade, which has provided the country with needed income and foreign exchange at the same time as it has led to violence, further concentration of wealth into the hands of an elite, and the expatriation of that wealth. The debt crisis and the conservation of the forest are other issues that receive equally balanced treatment. The excellent bibliography, filmography, and discography are bonuses in this series, which also includes a thorough index. This volume contains dramatic and well-reproduced black-and-white photos as well. Another volume in this series presents Argentina.

Castaneda, Omar S. ***Among the Volcanoes.***
See entry 462, Grades 7–9.

Cheney, Glenn Alan. ***El Salvador: Country in Crisis.***
See entry 463, Grades 7–9.

484   Fox, Geoffrey. ***The Land and People of Argentina.*** Illus. with photos. SERIES: Portraits of the Nations. HarperCollins 1990, LB $14.89 (0-397-32381-6). 238pp. Nonfiction.

This volume in the Portraits of the Nations series concentrates far more on Argentina's history and its recent situations—the legacy of Peronism, the "dirty war," the trials of the generals, and the current economic difficulties—than on geography and culture. Although the latter topics sometimes get short shrift and are sandwiched in between discussions of the current situation, and although special boxes run for pages at a time, interrupting the text, the presentation of Peronism and the dirty war are among the most comprehensive and intelligent seen anywhere, in books either for adults or for children. The bibliography and filmography (the latter covering a highly developed film industry) are annotated in depth and quite useful.

French, Michael. *Circle of Revenge.*
See entry 465, Grades 7–9.

Gelman, Rita Golden. *Inside Nicaragua: Young People's Dreams and Fears.*
See entry 466, Grades 7–9.

485   Hirshon, Sheryl, and Judy Butler. *And Also Teach Them to Read.* Illus. with photos by Larry Boyd. Lawrence Hill 1983, P $9.95 (0-88208-171-3). 224pp. Nonfiction.

In 1980, Sheryl Hirshon, a junior high school teacher from Oregon, left her job and her comfortable life to lead a group of teenage Nicaraguan boys from Managua into the Nicaraguan countryside so they could teach illiterate peasants to read and write. It was a year after the Sandinista revolution, and the revolutionary government had called upon volunteers from all over the world to participate in that country's massive literacy crusade. Hirshon describes the hardships of the rural area where she worked, the daunting task of persuading the peasants to accept the young literacy teachers, and the 15 boys who struggled to adapt, to teach, and to learn under her supervision.

Hirshon's story gives older teenagers a first-person insight into an important historical moment. Her boys emerge as real human beings. They have difficulty adjusting to the rural life, and a few antagonize the people they are supposed to teach. Yet the reader also experiences their sense of triumph when their "students," many old enough to be their parents or grandparents, learn to write their name and read a simple paragraph. Through the slogans of the literacy teachers and the content of what is taught, the reader gains perspective on the culture of a country undergoing revolutionary change. Though Hirshon clearly sympathizes with the Sandinistas (in this book, there is no "enemy" except ignorance), her message is clearly subordinate to the story of her boys and the peasants. The book makes valuable points on the issue of literacy and the contribution that teens can make by volunteering in their own community at home. As presented by Hirshon, the Nicaraguan teenagers are lively and sympathetic, and teenagers in the United States will be able to make observations about the differences and similarities between the Nicaraguan youngsters' lives and their own.

Jenkins, Lyll Becerra de. *The Honorable Prison.*
See entry 470, Grades 7–9.

Jenkins, Tony. *Nicaragua and the United States: Years of Conflict.*
See entry 471, Grades 7–9.

Kellner, Douglas. *Ernesto "Che" Guevara.*
See entry 473, Grades 7–9.

486   Marrin, Albert. *Inca and Spaniard: Pizarro and the Conquest of Peru*. Illus. Atheneum 1989, HB $13.95 (0-689-31481-7). 211pp. Nonfiction.

Before 1500, the Inca Empire, centered in what is now modern-day Peru, was among the most powerful and highly organized in the world. Yet its power was based upon oppression, violence, and the total subordination of the individual for the good of the whole. Eventually, a bloody war between two brothers—heirs to the throne—would divide and weaken the empire.

Enter an equally bloodthirsty group—the Spanish conquistadores, who lusted for individual wealth, fame, and power, and, after defeating the Incas, who turned on each other. Within four years after taking over the Incas' pristine cities, they had polluted the rivers and covered the land with garbage. The Indians were enslaved, humiliated, and brutalized; overwork and disease cut their population in half during the first 30 years after conquest.

Marrin's book reads like a good novel—full of suspense and action. Short, snappy sentences and vivid language convey sophisticated ideas in a way that would appeal even to reluctant readers. The work is based on solid research, including primary sources. Marrin makes his own opinions known as he describes in often excruciating detail torture, executions, and human sacrifice—cornerstones, he argues, of a barbaric era long ago. He shows how both sides made crucial miscalculations and errors. There are valiant men, but no real heroes. To Marrin, women and children are merely victims (albeit at times brave victims), as are, eventually, all the Incas. Exciting and engrossing, this harsh portrayal stands in contrast to accounts that have tended to romanticize one side or another during this period. Includes bibliography and index.

Pascoe, Elaine. *Neighbors at Odds: U.S. Policy in Latin America.*
See entry 477, Grades 7–9.

487   Randall, Margaret. *Sandino's Daughters: Testimonies of Nicaraguan Women in Struggle.* Edited by Lynda Yang. Illus. with photos by the author. Left Bank 1981, P $7.95 (0-919888-33-X). 220pp. Nonfiction.

When the Sandinista front overthrew the Somoza dictatorship in Nicaragua in 1979, a surprising number of the revolutionaries were women. Among them were a high-ranking military commander, an upper-class lawyer who lured a hated secret police chief to her bedroom, where he was assassinated, and several teenage girls who became respected student leaders. During two years of residence in postrevolutionary Nicaragua, the U.S.-born writer-photographer Margaret Randall interviewed dozens of women, young and old, who helped shape their country's history.

Despite occasional political rhetoric, Randall's work captures the spirit of women who risked their lives for change. The direct personal narratives are revealing and fascinating. Randall's subjects represent a wide variety of ages, experiences, and backgrounds. Some of her interviewees are young teenagers who fought in the revolution, among them a teenage mother whose husband was killed soon after their baby's birth. The subjects provide a glimpse into another culture, one in which the place of women has become the source of intense debate. Black-and-white photographs, mostly of the individual women, are attractive and well reproduced. Chapters are titled (some only with the name of the interviewee, however). Because of its political content and frank discussion of sexual matters, this is a book for mature readers, but selected portions can be used with classes as a whole.

Sanders, Renfield. *El Salvador.*
See entry 479, Grades 7–9.

488   Skarmeta, Antonio. ***Burning Patience.*** Trans. from Spanish by Katherine Silver. Pantheon 1987, HB $10.95 (0-394-55576-7); P $7.95 (0-394-75033-0). 118pp. Fiction.

Eighteen-year-old Mario Jiménez is the mailman on the Isla Negra in Chile, where only one resident ever receives mail—the famed Chilean poet Pablo Neruda. Mario invents opportunities to talk with Neruda and later enlists the poet's aid in order to attract and, ultimately, to marry Beatriz Gonzales, the beautiful daughter of the local innkeeper. The night Beatriz loses her virginity is the night Salvador Allende is elected president, the first and only socialist president of Chile. Neruda leaves the Isla Negra to serve as Allende's ambassador to France and returns two years later, dying of cancer. Chile's socialist experiment is dying as well. After the bloody military coup in September 1973, Mario braves soldiers and helicopters to say goodbye to his hero and friend. Several days later, he too disappears, taken away by soldiers, never to be seen again.

The Chilean author Antonio Skarmeta blends fact and fiction, real personages and invented characters, in this lyrical short novel. Political events become milestones in Mario's life, from his seduction of Beatriz to his final disappearance after the coup. Sophisticated readers will appreciate the humor in Mario and Beatriz's courtship as well as the references to Neruda's poetry. Mario's intensely personal understanding of his idol's work may help young people to develop a greater appreciation of poetry and of the natural environment from which much poetic imagery springs. Written in exile, the novel lovingly portrays Skarmeta's homeland and the work and personality of one of its greatest literary figures.

489   Unger, Douglas. ***El Yanqui.*** Ballantine 1988, P $3.95 (0-345-34940-7). 300pp. Fiction.

Despite his mediocre grades, unkempt appearance, and constant state of being stoned on drugs, a lower-middle-class Long Island teenager is accepted by the International Student Exchange program and sent to Argentina. Named James, he is rechristened Diego by his upper-class Argentine family. The year is 1969, and Diego's real brother, Harry, is in Vietnam. His Argentine brothers are secretly attending demonstrations and beginning to dabble in terrorist activities. Diego welcomes the change from his problem-ridden family in the States; he cuts his hair, forsakes drugs (though not alcohol), and willingly wears the suit and tie that comprise the uniform at his exclusive all-boys private academy. Yet his love of adventure and of women draws him into all kinds of trouble, including an automobile accident, an arrest, and a beating by police. Nonetheless, Diego's Argentine family becomes attached to him, making his sudden departure, due to Harry's nervous breakdown in Vietnam, all the more painful.

Unlike many coming-of-age stories involving Americans abroad, this one goes beyond treating Argentina as merely a setting. The Argentine characters, particularly Diego's *mama* and *papa*, are fully realized. As he should be, Diego is a follower, not someone coming in from the North to make things happen. Although Unger admittedly takes some liberties with the history, his picture is less distorted than many others. Ironically, the episodes that take place in the United States ring less true. James's real parents rant and are ineffectual, and scenes of the drug culture are sensationalized. Diego is not the book's most interesting or sympathetic character, but mature teen readers will appreciate the efforts of his Argentine family and friends to help him as he adjusts to a different way of life and tries to leave behind his troubled past.

Watson, James. *Talking in Whispers.*
See entry 481, Grades 7–9.

8

GREAT BRITAIN AND IRELAND

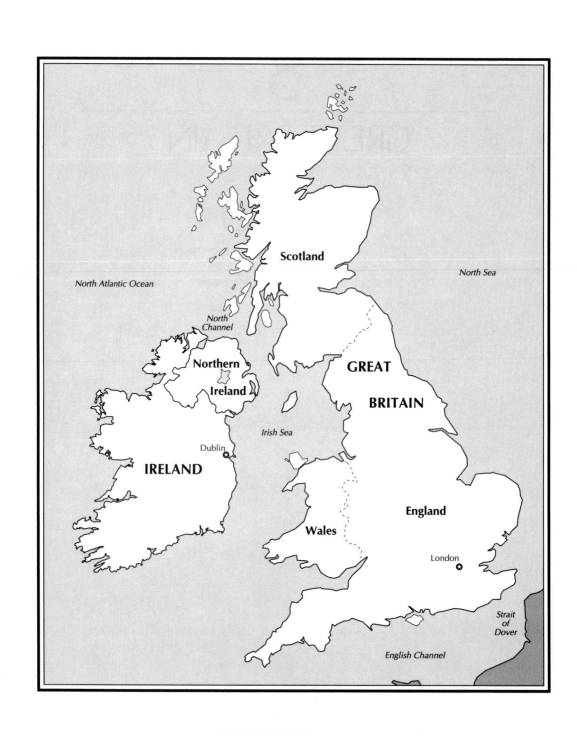

8

GREAT BRITAIN AND IRELAND

by Elaine Goley

The culture of Great Britain and Ireland is familiar to most people in the United States and Canada. Until their independence, both countries were colonies in the British Empire. To a great extent, our forms of government are based on British democracy and common law. Many Americans and Canadians trace their heritage to the English, the Welsh, the Irish, and the Scots-Irish; in fact, the potato famine in Ireland in the 1840s brought almost a million Irish immigrants to the United States. Today, descendants of these and other immigrants from the British Isles return regularly as tourists, keeping the ties alive. Some Irish-Americans have become involved in the deadly religious and political conflict in Northern Ireland, with, as Carolyn Meyer points out in *Voices of Northern Ireland*, the bulk of the sympathy tending toward the Catholic side.

Our ties to Great Britain and Ireland extend beyond the ethnic and political dimension to that of literature. The traditional emphasis on reading "the classics" has exposed adults and children to the great figures of English literature—William Shakespeare, Charles Dickens, Lewis Carroll, Dylan Thomas, James Joyce, and Beatrix Potter, to name just a few. Because many large presses are owned by British entrepreneurs or publish jointly in the United Kingdom, Canada, and the United States, books appear simultaneously on both sides of the Atlantic, their authors requiring no translation. In fact, British cultural elements are more likely to appear in simultaneous publications, whereas works that originate in Japan or Europe tend to be completely homogenized in the export process. As a result, American and Canadian readers are familiar with many contemporary authors whose style may be characterized as peculiarly British. Among those annotated here, with books for children as well as adult books suitable for young adults, are Rumer Godden, James Herriot, Roald Dahl, Nina Bawden, Robert Westall, K. M. Peyton, Aidan Chambers, Gillian Cross, Sue Townsend, Douglas Adams, and Agatha Christie.

The books annotated in this chapter encompass various themes. Several are editions of classic literature. Works from the early twentieth century and earlier are no longer protected by copyright. Thus, publishers can print, adapt, and abridge them freely, and more than one can do so at the same time. A glance at a recent *Books in Print* shows some 20 editions of Dickens's *A Christmas Carol* published especially for children. One, an illustrated version originally produced for adults, has been recommended for young adults because of its accurate reproductions of nineteenth-century scenes, puppets, and sets. Another book, included within the annotation, is criticized because its illustrations and design, while elegant, show little of the story and setting. Many publishers of classics are tempted to produce elegant, and expensive, coffee table books that give little sense of the work itself, and some abridgments geared to children destroy the beauty and meaning of the work in the process of making it "accessible" or (as in the case of some of Shakespeare's plays and other works with potentially controversial content) "acceptable." In addition to *A Christmas Carol*, a version of Dylan Thomas's famous poem *A Child's Christmas in Wales* has been included within the chapter, as have biographies of two other classic authors for children, Lewis Carroll and Beatrix Potter.

Among the books included in this chapter are "modern classics," more recent works of fiction that contain British cultural elements and have already been appreciated by teachers, librarians, and young readers. One of the most well-known authors of modern classics is Roald Dahl. Unfortunately, many of his works contain nasty ethnic and racial stereotypes, but *Matilda*, published shortly before his death in 1990, is recommended here. It, too, relies upon a hyperbolic style that admits a great deal of stereotyping, but the victims are parents. K. M. Peyton's series, represented here by *The Edge of the Clouds*, portrays an upper-class rural family at the turn of the century. Other modern classics have found their way to public and commercial television, widening their audience and giving young readers an opportunity to compare the TV versions with those in print. Among those annotated in this chapter are a volume in Douglas Adams's *Hitchhiker's Guide to the Galaxy*, John Mortimer's *Second Rumpole Omnibus*, and the Agatha Christie mystery *A Pocketful of Rye*. Some of the modern classics, as well as newer works such as James Herriot's *Oscar, Cat About Town* and Berlie Doherty's *White Peak Farm*, emphasize the rural, bucolic life of English villages that have changed little over the centuries. Others, like Mortimer's work and Philip Pullman's series, represented here by *The Tiger in the Well*, are set in a London evocative of the Victorian era. While they provide two perspectives upon the British experience, readers should not be misled into ignoring the rapid economic and cultural changes that the country has experienced since World War II.

The war itself was a critical moment in British history, and one amply dealt with in the literature. Robert Westall is perhaps the most well-known writer about the World War II experience in England. His first novel, *The Machine Gunners*, received substantial attention, and the realistic fantasy, *Blitzcat*, is considered by many to be his most adventurous and significant work. Growing out of his experience with the publication of *The Machine Gunners* was his collection of World War II memoirs and testimonials entitled *Children of the Blitz*. Another personal experience of the war is represented in Michael Foreman's *War Boy: A Country Childhood*, which reveals how rural as well as urban residents endured the terror of nightly bombing. Patrick Raymond's novel *Daniel and Esther* portrays events leading up to the war by means of two young Jewish Britons' growing awareness of the menace posed by Hitler.

While resistance to the blitz during World War II has been characterized as Britain's "finest hour," the country has encountered many difficulties and challenges in the past five decades as well. One of these is the issue of Northern Ireland. When Ireland became independent in 1922, after a protracted struggle,

the northern six counties, with their Protestant rather than Catholic majority,
remained part of Great Britain. The ensuing struggle—economic and political as
well as religious—has been chronicled in several works of nonfiction, among
them James Hewitt's *The Irish Question*, Michael McDonald's *Children of Wrath*,
and Carolyn Meyer's *Voices of Northern Ireland*. Eamon Dunphy also touches
upon the "troubles" in *Unforgettable Fire*, his biography of the superstar Irish
rock band U2.

In addition to the nonfiction, several novels touch upon the problems of
British and Irish youth who face high unemployment and few possibilities for
the future. Gillian Cross's *Chartbreaker* presents a fictional teenager, drifting
away from school and in conflict with her family, who finds both salvation and
additional problems in rock stardom. *Dance on My Grave*, by Aidan Chambers,
portrays two young men from the lower middle class in conflict about their
sexual orientation and confronting a bleak future; the death of one in a motorcycle accident leads the other to contemplate the value of his own life.

The Britain that once controlled a large part of the world is now home to
many people from her former colonies. Chinese, Indians, Pakistanis, Bangladeshis, and blacks from Africa and the Caribbean are among the new immigrants to English cities and towns. Unaccustomed to a great deal of cultural
diversity, the British have not welcomed many of the new immigrants. On the
whole, racial stereotypes in books from England since the 1960s are far more
vicious and overt than those found in their American counterparts. Even well-
meaning works, such as Rumer Godden's *Fu-Dog*, are not without flaws. More of
an issue is the fact that so few multicultural books set in Britain have crossed the
Atlantic, and the process of locating those books and identifying the setting as
England has been a difficult one. For the youngest readers, good choices are
Sarah Hayes's books about Gemma and her family of Jamaican heritage, as
represented by the excellent, though not identifiably British, *Happy Christmas,
Gemma*. A work of nonfiction that also touches upon the experience of blacks
living in England is Obadiah's *I Am a Rastafarian*. *Fu-Dog* is the tale of two part-
Chinese British children who have little cognizance of their Chinese heritage
until one receives a magic toy fu-dog and the two travel to London's Chinatown
to see the gift's giver, their great-uncle. Godden has written other books about
Asian immigrants to England, including *Miss Happiness and Miss Flower*, with
similar themes and plot structures. The only other work of fiction located on this
subject is Susan Price's now out-of-print *From Where I Stand*, a young adult novel
of anti-Pakistani prejudice at a British secondary school. There is a great need for
more works about the diverse peoples now living in Great Britian and for more
sensitivity and awareness on the part of authors from the majority culture.

Ireland and the component parts of Great Britain—England, Scotland, and
Wales—are well represented in the series books, both in country studies and in
biography series. Several of the geography series, most notably those distributed
by Franklin Watts, were actually produced in England. Lerner's Families the
World Over series also originated in England. Though generated in the United
States, *The Land and People of Scotland*, one of the new Portraits of the Nations
series, has a Scottish author. While this is no guarantee of overall quality, the
perspective in all these series books is a British one and should be read accord-
ingly. On the other hand, most of the biography series books originated and
were written in the United States. One consequence is that the subjects—
notably Charles and Diana, Winston Churchill, Margaret Thatcher, rock fund-
raiser Bob Geldof, Boy Scout founder Anthony Baden-Powell, and scientist

Stephen Hawking—are figures whose contributions have had impact on this side of the Atlantic.

Perhaps a British publisher would have chosen differently; perhaps the treatment would be focused more on the subject's place in British history rather than on his or her personal life or universal contribution. The one exception to this pattern seems to be the Chelsea House World Leaders, Past and Present series, which examines each of the biographees within his or her national context and presents a wide variety of British and Irish figures throughout history and in the twentieth century.

PRESCHOOL–GRADE 3

490   Fairclough, Chris. *Take a Trip to England.* Illus. with photos by the author. SERIES: Take a Trip. Franklin Watts 1982, LB $9.40 (0-531-044165). 32pp. Nonfiction.

This is one of Franklin Watts's series on countries of the world for the youngest readers. The large type and color illustrations make this volume accessible to the early grades. An index and glossary of terms add to its usefulness for reports. The book covers topics of interest to students in the early grades, such as sports, home and school life, festivals, and transportation. The clear, simple text and maps aid the reader in understanding the subject. Teachers and librarians have long decried the lack of nonfiction books for younger readers. Watts was one of the first publishers to produce attractive books for this market. This series is the precursor to such popular and useful series as Childrens Press's New True Books. Franklin Watts also offers trips to Wales and Scotland as part of its series.

491   Godden, Rumer. *Fu-Dog.* Illus. by Valerie Littlewood. Viking 1990, HB $14.95 (0-670-82300-7). 64pp. Fiction.

The noted British children's author Rumer Godden creates a realistic fantasy about two children in Britain who are of mixed Chinese and British heritage. They live in Devon, in St. Mary's Green, four hours by train from London's Chinatown, where their Chinese great-uncle owns a restaurant. Young Li-la—one-quarter Chinese in an all-white neighborhood—thinks her appearance odd, with her "slant eyes" and her "dear little face." On her birthday, Li-la receives a tiny toy fu-dog from her great-uncle. She has received many Chinese presents from him before, reminding her of her heritage, but this one is special; it has special powers.

Li-la and her brother Malcolm decide to take the train alone to London to find their great-uncle. Their adventure leads them, miraculously, to the right restaurant and to their uncle and great-uncle. Malcolm sustains a broken arm at a Chinese New Year street festival, but all ends happily when the children and their parents are reunited with their Chinese relatives and culture. This story celebrates the multicultural and multiracial diversity of Britain, a subject rarely attempted in contemporary British publishing. The full-color illustrations create an immediacy to the New Year street procession and to Great-Uncle's Chinese garden in the middle of London. Although the devices of the fu-dog and the children's trip are somewhat contrived and Li-la's self-description rather stereotypical, the book is a relatively sensitive, if naive, portrayal of children who discover their cultural heritage.

A book with a similar theme, but for older elementary readers, is *Miss Happiness and Miss Flower* (Viking, 1987). In that work, Godden, who spent much of her early life in India, presents an Indian girl living in Britain but homesick for her native land; she is helped by two traditional Japanese dolls with miraculous powers.

492   Goodall, John S. *The Story of an English Village.* Illus. by the author. Atheneum 1979, LB $8.95 (0-689-50125-0). 60pp. Fiction.

Goodall's unique, wordless picture books portray everyday rural life in various ages of British history. Other books in this series include *The Story of a Castle* (Atheneum, 1986) and *The Story of a Main Street* (Atheneum, 1987). The full-color illustrations are complemented by half pages that reveal other aspects of everyday life in the village during each major historical period. The story begins in the medieval period, and the reader returns every hundred years thereafter. Goodall's wit and scholarship transcend the traditional picture book audience; all age groups will find this series interesting and informative and will take from it different impressions. Each illustration presents the identical scene a century forward in history, and it is an excellent means of showing how changes come to even the most remote rural areas. This unique and ingenious device, coupled with Goodall's superb watercolor illustrations, makes this book and this series both useful and popular.

493   Hayes, Sarah. *Happy Christmas, Gemma.* Illus. by Jan Ormerod. Lothrop, Lee & Shepard 1986, HB $13.00 (0-688-06508-2). 28pp. Fiction.

Baby Gemma and her older brother are children of Jamaican heritage living in England. The brother tells of their preparations for her first Christmas and their Christmas Day activities. He is old enough to help, but Gemma tears things up, makes a mess, and pulls a star off the Christmas tree. The young narrator doesn't mind the mischief; he is amused by his baby sister's antics. On the big day, she has no idea what is going on and falls asleep long before the fun is over.

This is, above all, a universal story of growing up and sibling relationships as seen through the rosy prism of the Christmas season. That the family, like many others in Britain, is of West Indian origin is mentioned only in their Christmas Day phone call to Jamaica. The extended family is close, with Grandma playing a major role in the celebration. Readers will find the characters' way of celebrating Christmas quite familiar, though some traditions, such as when presents are opened, may differ slightly. The large, colorful pictures feature details of the young children's faces, and the spare text vividly contrasts big brother's new-found capabilities with his sister's babyish escapades. In all respects, this book will appeal to preschoolers and the youngest elementary students, who may also gain an inkling of the great world beyond their own.

Gemma and her brother also appear in Hayes and Ormerod's *Eat Up, Gemma* (1988).

494   Herriot, James. *Oscar, Cat About Town.* Illus. by Ruth Brown. St. Martin's 1990, HB $10.95 (0-312-05137-9). unp. Fiction.

James Herriot has become one of the most loved children's authors. His books for adults and children have endeared us to his tales about being a country veterinarian in the North of England during the 30s and 40s. The large, bright format and color illustrations bring the story of Oscar to life for the reader. The simple text tells Herriot's story of a stray cat who is adopted by an entire village.

Herriot lets us glimpse into rural English village life. His characterizations of villagers and everyday life in England will appeal to young readers and give them a sense of a world both similar and different. Other books Herriot has written for children are *Moses the Kitten, Only One Woof, The Christmas Day Kitten, Bonny's Big Day, Blossom Comes Home,* and *Market Square Dog.*

495   Hughes, Shirley. ***Lucy and Tom's Christmas.*** Illus. by the author. Viking 1986, HB $10.95 (0-670-81255-2); Penguin/Puffin 1987, P $4.95 (0-14-050698-5). 32pp. Fiction.

This picture book illustrates the traditional British Christmas from plum pudding to Christmas crackers. Lucy and her younger brother, Tom, prepare for a traditional Christmas by helping to stir the Christmas pudding. They make their own Christmas cards and paper chains to decorate the hall. All of the shared Christmas traditions of England and the United States are described, including Christmas caroling, letters to Santa, and the Salvation Army Band playing Christmas music.

Additional shared customs include the choosing and trimming of the tree, the children's jubilation at a Christmas Eve snowfall, the opening of the presents in the stockings on Christmas morning, church, and the arrival of all the relatives for a Christmas dinner of turkey and pudding. After dinner Lucy and Tom wear traditional toy paper hats and pull Christmas crackers, which make a popping noise and contain a small prize. Then the bigger presents are exchanged and opened.

Hughes's appealing children and traditional Christmas scenes recall Dylan Thomas's *A Child's Christmas in Wales.* Hughes's characters have wonderfully expressive faces that convey the charm of Christmas in Britain. Young children can compare the traditions depicted here with those in Sarah Hayes's *Happy Christmas, Gemma,* and with their own family's observance.

496   Oakley, Graham. ***The Church Mice at Bay.*** Illus. by the author. Atheneum 1979, HB $12.95 (0-689-30629-6). 32pp. Fiction.

This is one of a series of picture books originally published in England about the raucous and humorous adventures of Sampson, a church cat, and his friends, the church mice of Wortlethorpe. Sampson hopes for a holiday curate who's a nice quiet chap, but the curate is nothing of the sort. He actually dislikes mice so intensely that he considers it Sampson's duty to catch them.

The busy full-color humorous drawings portray English village life in addition to the confusion that Sampson, the church mice, and the curate create. The story will charm beginning readers with a humor that travels well across the Atlantic.

497 Bawden, Nina. *The Finding.* Lothrop, Lee & Shepard 1985, HB $11.95 (0-688-04979-6). 160pp. Fiction.

Eleven-year-old Alex doesn't celebrate his birthday but rather his Finding Day, the day authorities found him, a tiny infant, sleeping in the arms of the Sphinx next to the Embankment of the Thames River. No one came forward to claim him, so he now lives with his adoptive family in a London suburb. When his Gran's neighbor dies and leaves Alex a fortune, a family crisis erupts. His older sister, Laura, who is already jealous of him, tells him she doesn't want him around. His mother and his Gran are arguing over what to do with the money, and Alex's story is in every newspaper. Upset and disoriented, Alex runs away, to be preyed upon by street toughs and taken in by Poll, who shelters a group of troubled youths. Yet Poll's motives seem less than altruistic when one of the youngsters pressures Alex to write a ransom note. Eventually, Alex learns the truth about his mother's fate, and, blindfolded to avoid revealing the location of Poll's house, he is returned on motorcycle to his family.

One of England's foremost novelists for children, Bawden has written several stories about young people in search of family. Besides this one, there is *The Robbers* (Lothrop, 1979; reissued, 1989), about a boy reunited with his father and his stepmother, and *The Outside Child* (Lothrop, 1989), about a girl who discovers her father has an entirely new family that has been kept hidden from her. (Bawden is also the author of *Carrie's War*, a novel set during the Second World War.) *The Finding* is a well-done, suspenseful tale. The pace never lags, and Bawden reveals neither too much nor too little. Laura's and Alex's emotions are believable, as are the reasons for his panicked flight. In concocting his "finding" by Poll and his life at her place, Bawden draws upon Dickens' vision of life with Fagin in *Oliver Twist*. This continuity of setting and circumstance adds depth and interest to this work and makes it an ideal addition to a unit on children's literature from England.

Corfe, Tom. *St. Patrick and Irish Christianity.*
See entry 504, Grades 7–9.

498 Dahl, Roald. *Matilda.* Illus. by Quentin Blake. Viking 1988, HB $14.95 (0-670-82439-9); Penguin/Puffin 1990, P $3.95 (0-14-034294-X). 240pp. Fiction.

Roald Dahl, who died in November 1990, once said that his success in writing fiction for children lay in the fact that he enters into a conspiracy with children against adults. That is precisely what the award-winning author of *Charlie and the Chocolate Factory* (an older book marred, unfortunately, by racial stereotypes) has done with this brilliant story. Matilda is a genius at age 5 in spite of the fact that her parents are idiots. Even though she is forbidden to leave the house during the day when she is left alone, she walks to the library anyway every day, where she teaches herself to read and educates herself.

The adults in this book are typical of most of Dahl's fiction for children. In short, they are stereotypes of the worst sort. Therein lies the attraction of his work for children and the reason it has come under fire from many adults. As reflected here and in his many other works, Dahl's style has been adopted, to a greater or lesser extent, by many British authors for children, who very much take the child's side against the older generation.

499 Foreman, Michael. *War Boy: A Country Childhood.* Illus. by the author. Little, Brown/Arcade 1990, HB $16.95 (1-55970-049-1). 92pp. Nonfiction.

Born in the coastal village of Pakefield, England, in 1938, author/illustrator Foreman was 3 years old when "the bomb came through the roof" of his house. The closest village to the European mainland, the otherwise bucolic Pakefield was a target for German bombers during World War II, in particular for disabled planes that had to dump their loads quickly. Foreman's memories of his early years, experienced during the war, are juxtaposed with discussions, in an adult voice, about wartime equipment, strategies, and events. For instance, he points out that 125 percent of all the homes in Pakefield were either damaged or destroyed, which means that some homes were hit several times. Readers are also treated to drawings of the German aircraft that fascinated Foreman, his brothers, and their friends.

Like those of other British "children of war," Foreman's memories are far from grim. He recalls fondly the many soldiers, from all over the world, who passed through his small village. He describes the games, the wartime propaganda that created a clear sense of good guys and bad guys, the exhilarating defiance of danger. Enhancing the text are bright and expressive watercolor drawings and reproductions of posters. Some of the watercolors communicate powerfully the horrors of war—mothers grabbing their children and escaping in the light of antiaircraft guns, a gray beach surrounded by barbed wire and off limits to children, and shattered houses and trees. Others show strangers and locals from a child's point of view—sometimes amusing, sometimes grotesque. Still others show children playing, seemingly oblivious to the danger on the horizon. Taken as a whole, the text and pictures give the middle-grade reader a rich, complex picture of both war and childhood.

Goodall, John S. *The Story of an English Village.*
See entry 492, Grades PS–3.

McKinley, Robin. *The Outlaws of Sherwood.*
See entry 512, Grades 7–9.

500 Matthews, Rupert O. *Winston Churchill.* Illus. by Doug Post. SERIES: Great Lives. Franklin Watts 1989, LB $11.90 (0-531-18264-9). 32pp. Nonfiction.

This is a series for younger readers who need biographical material on world leaders. Some black-and-white photos are combined with color illustrations to make the material attractive and accessible to the reader. The brevity of the book, the large type, and the attractive format fill a need for easy-to-read biographies for the younger reader.

Additional books in this series present Charles Dickens, Henry VIII, Mary Queen of Scots, Queen Elizabeth I, Queen Victoria, Richard the Lionhearted, and Sir Francis Drake.

501 Moran, Tom. *A Family in Ireland.* Illus. with photos. SERIES: Families the World Over. Lerner 1986, LB $9.95 (0-8225-1668-3). 32pp. Nonfiction.

The approach of this book, presenting the everyday life of an Irish family, personalizes the cultural experience for younger readers. The clear, simple text and numerous color photos hold the reader's interest. An index and Gaelic pronunciation guide and a list of facts about Ireland, followed by a two-page map of the world showing Ireland's location and a picture of the Irish flag, are also included.

The child-oriented approach and the large, easy-to-read text do not condescend to children and may even appeal to reluctant readers and older students who have difficulty reading. Another book in this series features a family in England.

GRADES 7-9

502   Bassett, Lisa. *Very Truly Yours, Charles L. Dodson, Alias Lewis Carroll: A Biography.* Illus. with photos. Lothrop, Lee & Shepard 1987, HB $15.95 (0-688-06091-9). 118pp. Nonfiction.

This biography of one of England's most noted children's authors contains not only his life story but also his correspondence with children. Black-and-white photos of Dodson himself and various child friends of his, often photos taken by himself, will fascinate the reader. Much of Dodson's wit and uncanny charm can be seen in his clever, very often coy and teasing letters to young admirers and friends. To one little boy who complained about having to brush his hair, he suggested that perhaps the child would be better off exchanging his own head for a marble one, since the marble head need not be brushed.

Like Beatrix Potter, Dodson's writing career began with his many correspondences with children. When he wrote *Alice's Adventure in Wonderland* in 1865, the nineteenth-century art of letter writing was in full vogue. Cultivated folk spent hours writing elegant prose to their friends, since it was not yet possible to spend hours on the telephone. Dodson's literary heritage lives on to acquaint each new generation of child readers with the foibles of English life in the Victorian age.

The text and illustrations are accessible to older children. Much of the text is in the form of Dodson's delightful letters to children, which will be enjoyable for the young reader as well.

503   Chambers, Aidan. *Dance on My Grave.* HarperCollins 1982, LB $13.89 (0-06-021254-3). 256pp. Fiction.

Sixteen-year-old Hal Robinson is a loner, uncertain about his future and looking for a "bosom buddy" with a "can of magic beans." After capsizing a boat and losing his pants in the water, he is rescued by 18-year-old Barry Gorman. Hal and Barry become friends instantly, and they discover their relationship goes beyond friendship—both are homosexual and attracted to each other. Barry arranges a job for Hal in the record shop he manages with his widowed mother; they spend every night together as well. For seven weeks, Hal is in bliss, but then he sees Barry with a girl, a Norwegian au pair. He confronts Barry and discovers that his lover's commitment to their relationship is far less than his own. He smashes the office of the record shop and runs out. Barry follows him, only to be killed in a motorcycle accident.

Hal narrates the story as a means of coming to terms with the relationship, Barry's death, and his feelings of guilt, shame, and responsibility. He and Barry had promised to dance on the grave of the one who died first, and Hal has been arrested for dancing on—interpreted as desecrating—Barry's grave. Chambers's sensitive treatment, with its flashes of insight and unexpected bits of humor, builds the reader's empathy for and understanding of the tormented Hal. Descriptions of places and the use of slang establishs the setting in an English town near London. The school system and Hal's uncertainties about the future (specifically, whether to pursue a seemingly useless high school diploma in English literature or to leave school and work alongside his father as a baggage handler at the airport) give teenage readers a glimpse of the life of their working-class British counterparts. This well-written, multilayered story is one of the young adult novels by Chambers, who has also gained distinction as a critic of juvenile literature. Among Chambers's other young adult works are *Breaktime* (HarperCollins, 1978) and *NIK: Now I Know* (HarperCollins, 1988), both of which also portray the growing-up process through a teenage boy's relationships with parents and friends.

504   Corfe, Tom. *St. Patrick and Irish Christianity.* Illus. with photos. SERIES: Cambridge Topic Books. Lerner 1979, LB $8.95 (0-8225-1217-3). 51pp. Nonfiction.

From St. Patrick's birth in A.D. 390 in the West of England to the later years of his life when he wrote an account of how he became a missionary, this book covers his life and influence in Irish culture. The Roman Britain of Patrick's time is described in clear, simple prose, as is his capture by the Irish raiders.

Black-and-white photos and drawings illustrate the venues and way of life in St. Patrick's Britain. Photos of artifacts and historic sites further illustrate life in that age. Photos of Cardiff Castle and the ruins of earlier settlements, encampments, burial mounds, and reinforced walled houses further increase the immediacy of events in St. Patrick's life.

In the year 432 Patrick arrived in Ireland after escaping from his earlier capture, and he set about converting the Irish kings and Druids. The book includes a section on how to convert pagans—not an easy task, even for a saint. The book further illuminates the growth of Irish monasticism in Britain and Ireland after Patrick's death. Legends of St. Patrick's life are also included and explained. The clear, informative text and varied illustrations make this book accessible and attractive to the reader. It is part of the Cambridge Topic Books history series, which is authoritative and attractive.

505   Cross, Gillian. *Chartbreaker.* Holiday House 1987, HB $13.95 (0-8234-0647-4); Dell 1989, P $2.95 (0-440-20312-0). 182pp. Fiction.

Janis Mary Finch is in trouble at home and at school. An indifferent student, she risks failing her examinations and having to look for a job in difficult times. Her depressive mother has taken up with a new boyfriend, whom Janis calls Himmler. After a fight with her mother and Himmler, she runs away and by chance meets the members of Kelp, a third-rate club band. The band leader, Christie Joyce, moves her to London, to live with *his* depressive mother, while he gives Janis a tryout. Her path to stardom, as the tough and wild "Finch," is not without its obstacles, not the least of which is Christie himself. On stage, the two of them begin to abuse each other, to the delight of fans. Offstage, one does not know whether their relationship is one of hatred or love. Having cut herself off from her family in pursuit of stardom and a new identity as Finch, Janis is drawn back as a result of her mother's death, but in an act of betrayal, Christie and his mother notify the media, who turn the funeral into a circus. No longer able to go home again, Janis must examine who she has become and decide whether to continue with Christie and the band.

This finely crafted novel portrays a teenager's search for her identity and a purpose in life. The rock motif will appeal to junior and senior high readers, and it illustrates how various forms of rock—from the Rolling Stones to punk and postpunk—developed in England as an expression of working-class teens' desperation and anger. Cross portrays with great subtlety and skill Janis's physical and emotional transformation, to the point where Janis wonders if Finch is really part of her own character or a media creation. At the same time, within the wild, often cruel, Finch is an insecure, sensitive, and thoughtful young woman who has been denied any other means of expressing her talents. In the end, this memorable protagonist maintains her humanity on her way to the top. Readers, both female and male, will be moved by the circumstances she faces and by her inner struggles.

Dickens, Charles. *A Christmas Carol: In Prose Being a Ghost Story of Christmas.* See entry 527, Grades 10–12.

506   Doherty, Berlie. *White Peak Farm.* Orchard 1990, HB $12.95 (0-531-05867-0). 102pp. Fiction.

Change comes to Jeannie's rural family in Derbyshire. Her Gran sells her house and goes away to die, telling the family she has gone to do missionary work in India. Sister Kathleen sneaks off to nearby Sheffield to marry the son of the neighbor her father detests; she is banned from the farm as a result. Brother Martin, who was supposed to take over the farm, wants to study art in the city. Jeannie herself longs to go to the university. Jeannie's father is bitter and angry. He abuses his wife verbally and considers his daughters useless; he fears the farm will be lost to the family without a man to inherit it. Only when he is injured while mending a wall does he gain an appreciation of the women in his family.

Doherty's story advances through a series of interrelated vignettes. Changes have little to do with the British setting but are among those faced by any rural family in a developed nation, where children have many options, both on and off the farm. Still, cultural and linguistic details surface in this charming novel, which was originally written for BBC Radio Sheffield. Especially strong are the characterizations and the author's subtle use of symbols—such as the father's endless building of walls—to reveal the essence of people and events.

Dunphy, Eamon. *Unforgettable Fire: The Definitive Biography of U2.* See entry 529, Grades 10–12.

507   Garfinkel, Bernard. *Margaret Thatcher.* Illus. with photos. SERIES: World leaders, Past and Present. Chelsea House 1985, LB $17.95 (0-87754-552-9). 112pp. Nonfiction.

This is one of a series of over a hundred biographies of world leaders. These books are attractive, authoritative biographies with copious photos, an index, a chronology, and a bibliography. Such features make them a good source for school reports. The format makes the information accessible, yet attractive, and does not condescend to young readers. This particular volume is a balanced approach to the recent controversial prime minister who was voted out of office by her own Conservative Party in 1991. Garfinkel discusses some of the issues that made her many enemies, but recent events require updating of this book.

Other volumes in this series present Clement Attlee, Winston Churchill, King Arthur, Oliver Cromwell, Eamon de Valera, Benjamin Disraeli, Eleanor of Aquitane, Elizabeth I, William Gladstone, Henry VIII, James I, David Lloyd George, Mary, Queen of Scots, Charles Stewart Parnell, and Queen Victoria, making this the most comprehensive biography series on British and Irish leaders.

508   Greene, Carol. *England.* Illus. with photos. SERIES: Enchantment of the World. Childrens Pr. 1982, LB $17.95 (0-516-02763-8). 127pp. Nonfiction.

This is part of a readable and informative series for middle graders. The book covers England's geography, its prehistory to 1660, 1660 to the present, its industry, and famous Britons. There is a chronology of important dates as well as an index for reports. The photos of contemporary subjects are attractive and engage the reader in England's history and culture. The dour full-page portraits of Queen Victoria and Winston Churchill illuminate the chapter on monarchy and government.

Wales and Scotland are treated in separate volumes as part of this series.

509   Hewitt, James. *The Irish Question.* Rev. ed. Illus. with photos. SERIES: Flashpoints. Rourke 1991, LB $15.93 (0-86592-027-3). 77pp. Nonfiction.

This book, originally published in Britain, discusses the history and current political and social implications of the conflict in Northern Ireland. The copious photographs add interest and depth to the text. Chapters include those on the history of the conflict, the Anglo-Irish accord, and the healing process and possible solutions to the conflict.

The format is appealing and the writing simple and clear, though not exciting. Geared principally to middle and junior high school readers, the book maintains a positive tone and an even-handed presentation, downplaying the conflict's extreme horror and brutality. Nonetheless, it does not romanticize or sensationalize, making it a good source for background reading and reports. There are a chronology of events, a glossary, and an index.

510   Hughes, Libby. *Madam Prime Minister: A Biography of Margaret Thatcher.* Illus. with photos. Dillon 1989, HB $12.95 (0-87518-410-3). 144pp. Nonfiction.

This biography of Thatcher gives a great deal of attention to her lower-middle-class upbringing and her life as Britain's first female prime minister. The daughter of a grocer, she challenged sex-role stereotypes early on, attending Oxford on scholarship and majoring in chemistry. Her main interest, however, was politics, particularly of the conservative kind, and she confronted much traditionalism within her own party on her way to leadership of the Conservative Party and, eventually, to the post of prime minister. In the meantime, she married and had two children; Hughes discusses the challenges of having a successful career and caring for a family (though with the help of nannies).

Hughes focuses mainly on the personal aspects of Thatcher's life and career. Her controversial political positions are discussed in a balanced, though superficial, manner. In citing opposition to some of her more extremist views, such as her stance against immigration, Hughes shows that people within Thatcher's own party opposed her; the opposition did not come only from Laborites. In retrospect, this device is more relevant than one might think; one year after the biography's publication, Thatcher was replaced as leader of her party and as prime minister by the more moderate John Major. On the whole, however, this readable work is most useful by showing the challenges facing a woman on her way to, and at, the top. Dillon Press has also published biographies of Winston Churchill and Stephen Hawking as part of this series, which in general takes a more personal approach to the life of the biographee.

511   Hunter, Mollie. *Cat, Herself.* HarperCollins 1986, LB $12.89 (0-06-022635-8). 280pp. Fiction.

Young Catriona (Cat) McPhie is the daughter of Tinkers, or Travellers, Scots who have rejected a settled existence and steady employment for life on the road. They subsist by harvesting vegetables, doing odd jobs, and selling second-hand goods. Cat has never attended school, but she knows how to beg clothes and food from wealthy townspeople and eventually delivers her mother's baby. Yet Cat is even too much of a free spirit for her community of wanderers. She likes to sneak off with her dog and swim naked in the river. More importantly, she refuses to marry the boy she loves if it means she will have to be subservient to him or to travel with his family and his alcoholic father. As she grapples with questions about her future, Cat must confront the prejudice and violence of her settled neighbors as well as the social changes that threaten the Travellers' way of life.

Hunter's novel features an unusual protagonist trying to fashion a life for herself, on her own terms. The setting is well drawn. In the four years covered in the book, suburbs encroach upon the Travellers' traditional campgrounds, and highways block their view of the sea. Cat's family trades in its horse and wooden cart for a dilapidated car and trailer. The grandmother's stories expose the reader to Scottish lore and another time, when many more people took to the road to escape persecution, poverty, or whatever other troubles faced them. This elegant and poignant tale is an excellent introduction to one of Scotland's foremost authors for children. Among her other young adult novels are two historical works set in Scotland in the early twentieth century—*A Sound of Chariots* (HarperCollins, 1972) and *Hold On to Love* (HarperCollins, 1984)—and one based on the life of Mary, Queen of Scots, *You Never Knew Her as I Did!* (HarperCollins, 1981). She has also written several medieval fantasies for middle grade readers, including *The Haunted Mountain* (HarperCollins, 1972), *A Stranger Came Ashore* (HarperCollins, 1975), *The Wicked One* (HarperCollins, 1977), and *The Mermaid Summer* (HarperCollins, 1988).

512   McKinley, Robin. *The Outlaws of Sherwood.* Greenwillow 1988, HB $11.95 (0-688-07178-3); Ace 1989, P $3.95 (0-441-64451-1). 282pp. Fiction.

In researching for this version of the folk story, McKinley read over two dozen books on Robin Hood, including the classics by Howard Pyle and Alfred Noyes. Her complex style is a curious blend of American English with bits of British spelling and usage thrown in. While not for purist folklore aficionados, the book is a well-crafted novel on a historical theme. While novelization of folkloric themes is not to everyone's taste, this version will appeal to young adults who still find the archaic language of British folklore tedious rather than romantic, as many readers do.

McKinley explains which variants she examined and why she chose the versions she has used here. She examines the issue of historical accuracy as it applies to folklore. She has used the work of scholars such as James C. Holt, professor of medieval studies at Cambridge, in her search for accuracy.

This is a unique example of an American version of British folklore themes. It is a curious blend of original characterization and historical conjecture. Young adults will appreciate this, and it can be used in the curriculum to introduce a period in British history and culture or to explore the nature of folklore and historical fiction.

Meek, James. *The Land and People of Scotland.*
See entry 533, Grades 10–12.

513   Meyer, Carolyn. *Voices of Northern Ireland: Growing Up in a Troubled Land.*
Harcourt Brace Jovanovich 1987, HB $15.95 (0-15-200635-4). 212pp. Nonfiction.

Following her whirlwind journey to South Africa and the publication of *Voices of South Africa*, Carolyn Meyer embarked upon a six-week trip to Northern Ireland. She visited schools, churches, and community centers to explore the area's political and religious conflicts, known as the "troubles," through the eyes of its youth. More successful in making contact with teens than in her earlier work, Meyer gives the reader a balanced picture of Catholics and Protestants, their attitudes toward each other, and their views of the future.

Some interesting information comes out of Meyer's work. Few Catholics want to become part of the Republic of Ireland because of that country's poverty and scanty social benefits. As in both Ireland and England, many young people feel alienated and without hope for the future. Unemployment is high, and working-class youngsters expect to be on welfare, called the "Bru," for much of their lives. In fact, the unresponsiveness and disruption Meyer encountered on many of her school visits (particularly in all-boys' Catholic schools or nonacademic "intermediate schools") possibly reflected the teens' view of school as a dead end. Even sources for hope, such as the Channels of Peace program sponsored by the two denominations, often failed due to the intransigence, conservatism, and lack of positive leadership on the part of the young people involved.

Meyer comes to depressing conclusions, prompted in part, she writes, by the dreary climate, her failure to reach many of the youngsters, their own sense of hopelessness, and her loneliness on the trip. Perhaps her own feelings and worries colored her encounters with her informants. One wishes for a little more life in this work, a little less sameness in the stories. The historical information Meyer presents is quite useful, and it is not always what one would find in survey books written for young adults. To some extent, she resorts to her own stereotyping, particularly in describing Protestants as restrained, reserved, and unemotional; more time with Protestant families might have revealed a more diverse picture. Despite these flaws, this is a valuable work that reveals the history and attitudes behind a seemingly endless conflict. Includes maps, bibliography, and index.

514 Meyer, Kathleen Allan. *Ireland: Land of Mist and Magic.* Illus. with photos. SERIES: Discovering Our Heritage. Dillon 1983. Nonfiction. o.p.

This series for middle-grade readers covers the history, legends, heroes, sports, home life, education, and customs of the country. A list of factual information about Ireland begins the book. An appendix lists Irish consulates in North America, and a glossary defines Gaelic terms used in the book. An index adds to this book's usefulness for school reports. A bibliography, focusing on Irish culture, is also included.

Many of the facts presented are geared especially to an American readership. Among them are tidbits of information about the Irish origins of John F. Kennedy's and Ronald Reagan's families, as well as a longer discussion of immigration and Ireland's many ties to the United States.

515 Peyton, K. M. *The Edge of the Clouds.* Illus. by Victor Ambrus. Penguin/Puffin 1990, P $3.95 (0-14-030905-5). 192pp. Fiction.

This is the second in a trilogy about Christina, whose parents have died. She had been sent to live in the country on a ramshackle English estate with her uncle and two male cousins. The volume begins when Christina and her cousin Will elope. They borrow Uncle Russel's Rolls and drive to Aunt Grace's, where Christina had spent her early childhood.

The rest of the book is the story of Christina's romance with Will and Will's romance with the new occupation of flying airplanes. Will is a pioneer aviator who dedicates his life to flying and Christina, in that order. The book describes English village life in Battersea before World War I. The other two books in the trilogy take place at the family's country estate, Flambards. A good deal of the British horsey set life is presented here; in addition to portraying Will's passion for flying, this novel maintains the emphasis—explored further in the other two Flambards stories—on riding and breeding horses. These two preoccupations will fascinate both male and female adolescent readers, as will the trials and tribulations of Christina's romance and subsequent marriage.

There is something for everyone in these uniquely British romantic novels. Characterization and plot are both strong, and Peyton's literary style is a model for students in middle and high school. The other books in the series are *Flambards* (Penguin/Puffin, 1990) and *Flambards in Summer* (Penguin/Puffin, 1989).

516 Pomeray, J. K. *Ireland.* Illus. with photos. SERIES: Let's Visit Places and Peoples of the World. Chelsea House 1988, LB $14.95 (1-55546-794-6). 128pp. Nonfiction.

This entry in the Let's Visit Places and Peoples of the World series is a general overview of the history, culture, and economy of Ireland. The treatment is clear and simple, ideal for middle schoolers, but the lack of depth will frustrate more sophisticated readers and those looking for information on specific topics. In the first chapter, a photo of a child in Northern Ireland is misleading, for there is almost no information on the six counties that are not part of the Irish Republic. The book includes facts at a glance, a chronology, a glossary, and an index. Other books in the series present England, Scotland, and Wales.

517   Price, Susan. *From Where I Stand.* Faber & Faber 1984. 130pp. Fiction. o.p.

Price draws a picture of racism at a British secondary school. Kamla, a Pakistani girl, is subjected to cruel racial taunts by her classmates. Mary, another student, is subjected to anti-Semitic antagonism. Jonathan, an open-minded friend, and Kamla try to analyze and counteract the hatred at great price to the individuals involved.

The novel shows that although Britain is a nation of immigrants, one that is growing ever more multicultural as new residents arrive from the West Indies, Africa, and southern Asia (from where Kamla's family has come), intolerance has become a major problem. This intolerance is passed on from generation to generation, and conflicts are especially acute in the teenage years, when young-sters are forming their own identities and are especially vulnerable to peer pressure. Price creates believable characters through the plot and dialogue; her situations are quite realistic, as is the language (including slang and profanities) that the teenagers use. The writing style will engage older children and young adults who are exploring issues such as equality and racism in society.

The book can be used to generate discussion of the consequences of racial intolerance, its universality, and the antidotes to it. Although the novel is a portrait of racism in British schools, it does have universal application.

Pullman, Philip. *The Tiger in the Well.*
See entry 535, Grades 10–12.

518   Raymond, Patrick. *Daniel and Esther.* Macmillan 1990, HB $12.95 (0-689-50504-3). 165pp. Fiction.

This novel takes place at Dartington Hall, a progressive school in England. Daniel and Esther are Jewish teenagers dealing with the rise of fascism in Europe. This is a coming-of-age novel concerned with the adolescent search for identity. Daniel and Esther must both deal with their attraction for one another and plan for their future in a world increasingly characterized by violence against their fellow Jews. This violence takes a psychological toll on the observer as well as on the victims.

Daniel's budding career as a musician is encouraged by a refugee professor from Germany, who recognizes the teenager's musical genius. Through him, Daniel becomes aware of the horrors taking place in a not-too-distant land. The contrast between fascism and democracy, terror and relative safety, during the 30s serves as a background for the personal struggles of two adolescents.

The particulars of this novel are British, but the themes are universal to the experience of adolescents. The novel is narrated by Daniel, but the author's complex style and examination of political and psychological issues make this an appropriate work for older, more advanced young adult readers as well.

---

519   Sproule, Anna. *Great Britain: The Land and Its People.* Rev. ed. Illus. with photos. SERIES: Countries. Silver Burdett 1986, LB $15.96 (0-382-09254-6); P $6.95 (0-382-09460-3). 63pp. Nonfiction.

The size and glossiness of this slim volume belie its informational content, which is quite accurate and complete. Older readers will find this series as useful as younger readers find it attractive and accessible. The volume contains sections on Great Britain's geography, government, and economy; a chronology of its history; a list of people in the arts; and a gazetteer and index. The chapter on customs and superstitions is informative and amusing. The bulk of the volume is devoted to the history and culture of England, but Scotland, Wales, and Northern Ireland receive treatment as well. The updated information in this revised edition includes more on Margaret Thatcher's policies and the conflict in Northern Ireland.

---

520   Thomas, Dylan. *A Child's Christmas in Wales.* Illus. by Edward Ardizzone. David R. Godine 1980, HB $13.95 (0-87923-339-7); P $7.95 (0-87923-529-2). 45pp. Fiction.

This classic poem of a childhood Christmas in Wales in the early part of this century is as integral to the literature and folklore of Britain as Shakespeare is. Certainly no adult bibliography of modern British literature would exclude Dylan Thomas's poetry and novels such as *Adventures in the Skin Trade.* The nineteenth-century feel and traditions of Christmas are contained in this poem about customs that have all but vanished in modern life. The real fir tree, the huge family gatherings, and the exchange of gifts no longer exist in many households. Multigenerational families living in the same location are not as common now, but in some reaches of the British Isles the tradition of Christmas paper hats and Christmas crackers still survives. This lyrical poem is enhanced by the addition of elegant pen-and-ink illustrations evocative of earlier times. This edition, with its ample and appealing visuals, will attract younger readers who cannot conjure up images of Christmases past as easily as adults who have been inspired and moved by Thomas's poetry.

---

521   Townsend, Sue. *The Growing Pains of Adrian Mole.* Avon 1987, P $3.50 (0-380-70430-7). 243pp. Fiction.

Another fine example of British social satire is Townsend's irreverent sequel to *The Secret Diary of Adrian Mole, Aged 13³/₄* (Avon, 1984). These books have been compared to Salinger's coming-of-age novel, *The Catcher in the Rye.* This is, like Holden Caulfield's story, a novel of self-discovery that will make teenage and adult readers laugh until they cry. Adrian is self-centered, a hypochondriac, and an adolescent in agony.

Here, Adrian suffers through his father's volunteering his patriotic services in the Faulklands War, acne, and his mother's struggle to find her identity. His mother characterizes Adrian's quest for neatness as "bloody obssessive." Adrian agonizes over every aspect of his life, even his faith. He fears he will have to confess to Grandma that he is no longer a Christian believer. Adrian takes himself and life too seriously, like most of us. He struggles with the realization that he will no longer be an only child, since his mother is pregnant. How humiliating!

The rigidity of the British school system is another source of distress for Adrian, as is the disdain of the Marxist youth club leader, who calls him the epitome of the petite bourgeoisie. These school problems may seem foreign to the American teenager, but they provide insight into a different experience of adolescence in the two countries. As in Roald Dahl's works, parents and other adults are portrayed with a great deal of satire; Townsend's sympathies clearly lie with Adrian, who will grow up in spite of himself and become one of those ridiculous adults.

522   Westall, Robert. **Blitzcat.** Scholastic 1989, P $2.95 (0-590-42771-7). 230pp. Fiction.

We have at last found the animal story (one of the best since Sheila Burnford's *Incredible Journey*). It is British to the core (a cat story) and right up our street (our cup of tea). It is the story of Lord Gort, a black she-cat who trails her owner, a soldier in the British Army during World War II. She travels to their former home in Coventry. Unfortunately, Coventry has been a prime target of Hitler's aerial blitz against England; the famous cathedral and much of the town have been bombed and destroyed.

Lord Gort's heroic journey and her account of the blitz compose this eloquent story. The book compares favorably to Richard Adams's fine work (*The Plague Dogs*) but is more accessible. This unique, well-crafted book provides an unusual perspective on a traumatic event in the history of England and the history of warfare.

Westall is the author of several other young adult novels set in England during World War II. Each one provides a different view of the war experience. Among them are *The Machine Gunners* (Greenwillow, 1976) and *Fathom Five* (1981; Knopf pbk., 1990).

Westall, Robert. **Children of the Blitz: Memories of Wartime Childhood.**
See entry 537, Grades 10–12.

523   Westall, Robert. **The Machine Gunners.** Greenwillow 1975, LB $12.88 (0-088-84055-8); Random House 1990, P $3.50 (0-679-80130-8). 186pp. Fiction.

This is one of Westall's historical novels concerning the home front in Britain during World War II. In this gripping story, a group of boys hides a German machine gun, fallen during an air raid, and puts themselves and their community in danger. The book is drawn from Westall's own experience as a child during the air raids in British cities, and it presents authentically the attitude of adolescent boys who enjoy taking risks. The fear of invasion and the terror of the bombing raids are shown to have complex and powerful effects on the young people involved, as they do on any child of war.

This novel won the Carnegie Medal in 1976 for excellence in children's fiction, and it led to Westall's writing the collection of memoirs published as *Children of the Blitz* (Viking, 1985). Westall has also authored *Echoes of War* (Farrar, Straus & Giroux, 1991), a collection of five short stories about the World War II experience in England and the years immediately following the war. In that work he explores the continuing effects of war on his young characters and their families.

GRADES 10-12

524   Adams, Douglas. *Life, the Universe and Everything.* Published as part of *The Hitchhiker's Trilogy: Omnibus Edition. Crown 1984, HB $15.95 (0-517-55200-0). 227pp./entire volume 512pp.*

This is the third in Adams's *Hitchhiker's Guide to the Galaxy* series, originally written as radio plays in England for BBC radio. The scripts were subsequently turned into a TV series and then into this series of books. The popularity of the series lies with Adams's ability to re-create in his characters what is commonly known as the British eccentric. Arthur Dent, the hapless, clueless human protagonist, discovers that his friend Ford Prefect (a sort of British car) is really an alien travel writer assigned to update a computerized travel book called the *Hitchhiker's Guide to the Galaxy*.

In this book Dent gets stranded when the earth is blown up to make way for a hyperspace bypass. Arthur, it seems, is constantly endangered and insulted by aliens of the galaxy that he never knew existed. He finds himself at an End of the World party in the Restaurant at the End of the Universe. He discovers, as many travelers do, that the more one travels, the more one stays in one place and other bits of inscrutable logic of the universe. Arthur and a bizarre group of aliens try to find the answer to the question "What is the meaning of life, the universe and everything?" only to discover that the answer and the question are mutually exclusive. If the answer were known, the universe would be replaced with something even more bizarre and inexplicable.

Adams's series has proved to be quite popular with older teenagers who appreciate the absurd humor of characterizations, plot, and language as well as Adams's philosophical musings. Young teens who have appreciated the works of D. Manus Pinkwater and Paul Zindel but who are ready to move on to more adult fare will be especially interested, and the peculiarly British elements will give them a wider perspective of this genre of literature.

Bassett, Lisa. *Very Truly Yours, Charles L. Dodson, Alias Lewis Carroll: A Biography.*
See entry 502, Grades 7-9.

525 Bryson, Bill. *The Mother Tongue: English and How It Got That Way.* Morrow 1990, HB $18.95 (0-688-07895-8). 270pp. Nonfiction.

This book covers the history of the English language from its origins 30,000 years ago to the present. Bryson describes the beginnings of human language and its development, culturally and geographically. He tells us that our descended larynx enables us to speak in language rather than in grunts as other primates do. When we see an ape in captivity, we may think, "There but for the grace of my descended larynx go you or I." Of course, there's more to it than that. Apes, as it turns out, do not have the same facial musculature as we do. In addition, their tongues are too long to form words and language.

The author follows the development of English from the Angles and the Saxons to the invasion of the Celts, Normans, Vikings, Germans, and whoever else had a hand in shaping the language we know and love. It turns out that not everyone who contributed to the development of English was a scholar like Dr. Johnson. One of the major contributors to the *Oxford English Dictionary* could not attend the publication party for the work, owing to a prior commitment to an institution for the criminally insane. In fact, the *OED* project was headed by a bank clerk and self-educated philologist, James Augustus Henry Murray, whose 11 children were drafted to help as soon as they learned the alphabet.

But as intricate and confusing as it is, English has become a global language with more students of it than there are native speakers. The book is accessible and authoritative and gives us a good sense of where our language came from. High school students and their teachers will appreciate Bryson's lively writing style and the amusing vignettes that he offers.

Chambers, Aidan. *Dance on My Grave.*
See entry 503, Grades 7–9.

526 Christie, Agatha. *A Pocketful of Rye.* Putnam 1986, HB $16.95 (0-396-08869-4). 176pp. Fiction.

Agatha Christie exemplifies the great British tradition and fascination with murder mysteries; her works have great appeal on this side of the Atlantic among teens as well as among adults. Current imitators such as P. D. James still enjoy worldwide popularity as genre writers on her coattails. More than any others, the Miss Marple mysteries typify Christie's profound appreciation for life in an English village. She always maintained (as does Miss Marple, amateur sleuth) that the English village is a microcosm of life in the world at large, with all of its ugliness, hatred, and malice brewing just below the peaceful surface.

In Christie's view, the country doctor is just as capable of murdering his wife as is the city miscreant. Passions run deep in the village. Miss Marple, as usual, discovers the perpetrator of the murders and the mysteries that the novel unfolds. The elderly, oft-ridiculed amateur detective neatly outsmarts the local constabulary in this perennial favorite. Teenage readers of Stephen King will appreciate seeing what a finely crafted murder mystery really looks like, and an interesting class assignment might be the comparison of Christie's British perspective with King's American one.

Teachers and students should be warned, however, that many of Christie's earlier works, like those of another notable British author, Roald Dahl, contain stereotypes of blacks, Asians, and others. Care should be used in selecting and presenting works by these authors.

Cross, Gillian. *Chartbreaker.*
See entry 505, Grades 7-9.

527   Dickens, Charles. *A Christmas Carol: In Prose Being a Ghost Story of Christmas.* Illus. by Peter Fluck and Oger Law. St. Martin's 1979, HB $9.95 (0-312-13403-7). 79pp. Fiction.

This is perhaps the most famous of English-language Christmas stories. It has captured the hearts and imaginations of adult and child readers for 150 years. This, more than any of Dickens's novels of nineteenth-century London, gives us a glimpse into the Victorian spirit and everyday life. The slave-driving, heartless Scrooge, the 12-hour working day, and 6½-day work week are almost too dreadful for us to imagine today. But Scrooge is once again won over by the ghost of Christmas Future, and Tiny Tim exclaims once more, "God bless us every one."

This edition is designed for a wide range of ages, young adults as well as adults. The illustrations are photographs of finely crafted puppets and sets that recall nineteenth-century London. Unlike other editions of the classic novel, this one has not been abridged for younger readers. The print is small but neatly presented in double columns on the page. The intriguing full-page illustrations make this a good edition to share with junior high and high school students who have a special interest in British history and culture.

A recent abridged version, abridged by Dickens himself and illustrated by Scott Cook, is also available. Published by Random House in 1990, it has the appearance of a coffee table book, but the dark, full-color illustrations reveal little about the story or its setting. The text is appropriate for upper elementary and middle school readers.

528   Du Maurier, Daphne. *Vanishing Cornwall.* Rev. ed. Illus. Doubleday 1981, HB $19.95 (0-385-17832-8). 208pp. Nonfiction.

Cornwall has been the setting for Du Maurier's most famous novels, such as *Rebecca* and *My Cousin Rachel*. Here, she examines Cornish history, its people, customs, superstitions, legends, and folklore. She revisits the settings of her novels, rediscovering the stories and legends of ancient Cornwall. Cornwall has been associated with the legends of King Arthur and Tristan and Iseult, and the author examines these legends as well as the first Norman groups to settle this wild country. The Cornish character and its components are dissected. Color photograhs in this new edition were taken by Du Maurier's son, as were the black-and-white photographs of the landmarks described in the book. This well-written account is valuable for its insight not only into this historic place but also into one author's source of inspiration for her acclaimed fiction.

529   Dunphy, Eamon. *Unforgettable Fire: The Definitive Biography of U2.* Illus. with photos. Warner Books 1988, HB $16.95 (0-446-51459-4); P $9.95 (0-446-38974-9). 313pp. Nonfiction.

Teenagers always enjoy reading about their favorite rock band, and this book goes further than most in providing a social context for the work of the superstar Irish group U2. Dunphy traces the Dublin childhood of the four group members. He examines their influences—new wave, Irish rock music, and American blues. Finally, he describes their rise from one more teenage band in a country considered a rock music backwater to a world-famous group known for its powerful lyrics and its participation in political causes such as Live Aid and Amnesty International.

As an Irish group, U2 has been identified with the cause of Irish nationalism, principally by its American audience. The reality is more complex. Dunphy points out that three of the four band members were raised as Protestants in the predominantly Catholic Republic of Ireland or else were the children of an interreligious marriage. The group has condemned violence on both sides of the conflict in Northern Ireland, and its spokesperson and lead singer, Bono, often criticizes Irish Americans who misinterpret his lyrics and glorify a cause about which they really know very little. While the revised edition of Timothy White's *Catch a Fire: The Life of Bob Marley* (Henry Holt, 1989) is better at combining rock biography with social history, Dunphy's work will appeal to the many fans of U2 and give some insight into their Irish background and persepctive.   L.M-L.

Garfinkel, Bernard. *Margaret Thatcher.*
See entry 507, Grades 7–9.

530   MacDonald, Michael. *Children of Wrath: Political Violence in Northern Ireland.* Basil Blackwell 1986, HB $24.95 (0-7456-0219-3). 194pp. Nonfiction.

Central to the politics of Northern Ireland is the tumultuous struggle between Catholics and Protestants. The struggle is presented by MacDonald not as a religious battle, but one that has a colonial nature. He presents the struggle within its historical, political, and socioeconomic contexts. MacDonald tells us that the Protestants of Northern Ireland accept politically what is considered foreign domination by Catholics, and he explores the pattern of social and economic discrimination against the Catholic population.

MacDonald examines the history of British involvement in Ireland from the twelfth century forward. The Tudors decided to prevent their Catholic enemies in Europe from using Ireland, a Catholic nation, as an ally and strategic staging ground for an attack on England. After three centuries of colonial rule by England, the conflict between colonial rule and nationalism was long established by the time Ireland became independent.

MacDonald discusses the history of Irish resistance from land reform groups and unions to the IRA. MacDonald has presented a clearly written and well-balanced political history based on his own sociological analysis. The history of the conflict is examined up through the conflicts of the 70s. This is an excellent basic work for high school social studies classes, one that will serve as a historical and political introduction for the further study of the conflict in Northern Ireland and of Anglo-Irish relations in general.

531   MacLaverty, Bernard. *Cal.* George Braziller 1983. 170pp. Fiction. o.p.

309
GRADES 10-12

This novel is a character study of 19-year-old Cal, who is entrapped in the struggles of Northern Ireland. Cal is an unwilling participant in an IRA attack that results in the death of a man. When Cal meets the man's 25-year-old widow in the library, he is shocked and overwhelmed with remorse. He finds that he cannot avoid Marcella, and he seeks her out. Their ensuing love affair makes Cal more ambivalent about his role in the "troubles." Will he admit to Marcella his part in her husband's assassination? What will he tell his buddies in the IRA when they contact him for ever more violent acts? Through Cal, MacLaverty displays the human tragedy of violence.

MacLaverty begins the haunting story in an abattoire (a butcher shop), which serves as a metaphor for the violence and suffering on both sides of the struggle in Northern Ireland. Through symbols, characters, and situations, he gives the reader a sense of place and of a war in which everyone is the loser. He shows, quite realistically, how Cal, who is forced to grow up at a young age, is in fact aimless and emotionally stunted. This novel is an excellent one for young adults who are examining the effects of violence and war on society and on the individuals caught up in it.

532   Marwick, Arthur. *Britain in Our Century: Images and Controversies.* Illus. with photos. Thames and Hudson 1985. 224pp. Nonfiction. o.p.

The author covers Britain in this century from the Edwardian age to the present. He includes discussion of the geography, technology, and economics of Britain. The Great War and its consequences as well as the 20s, 30s, World War II, and the postwar era receive extensive coverage. The culture of Britain is explored from Ascot to tea dancing, as well as the political and economic history of the nation. Well-reproduced black-and-white historical photographs enable the reader to see into Britain's past and to experience this history more dramatically.

This century has been a pivotal one in Britain's development. It has marked the dissolution of the most powerful empire since the Roman Empire. The British Empire, created by the age of discovery and the colonial expansion of the following centuries, is much smaller, its influence less pervasive. Yet British culture and political influence still reign in the global community. This book explains why, and it gives high school readers a clear, well-organized overview of the recent politics and history of Britain.

533   Meek, James. *The Land and People of Scotland.* Illus. with photos. SERIES: Portraits of the Nations. HarperCollins 1990, LB $14.89 (0-397-32333-6). 244pp. Nonfiction.

This entry in the Portraits of the Nations series is written by a Scottish journalist, and his familiarity with the region is evident. The work is clearly from a Scottish perspective, though Meek does discuss the magnitude of Scottish emigration and its impact upon the United States and Canada. The presentation is balanced, and stereotypes of the Scottish people and their country held by those in England and abroad receive extensive consideration. The writing is livelier than in most series books; the one flaw in this otherwise solid treatment is the reproduction of the photos, which are often dark and reveal little of Scotland's natural beauty or character. Includes chronology, index, bibliography, discography, and filmography.

Meyer, Carolyn. *Voices of Northern Ireland: Growing Up in a Troubled Land.*
See entry 513, Grades 7–9.

534   Mortimer, John. *The Second Rumpole Omnibus.* Viking 1987, HB $18.95 (0-670-81125-4). 667pp. Fiction.

This volume contains three of John Mortimer's Rumpole novels, which depict the rumpled, bombastic, humbug, pompous but lovable Rumpole of the Bailey featured on PBS television. Mortimer crafted this larger-than-life character from his own experience as a QC, or Queen's Counsel, in the London courts. Mortimer's father was a distinguished trial lawyer at the Old Bailey. Mortimer followed in his father's footsteps, then created the Old Bailey hack, Rumpole. Mortimer has admitted that the witty and sarcastic asides made by Rumpole are often what he would like to say in court. The character was created expressly for the British actor Leo McKern, who is the embodiment of irascibility as Rumpole on the small screen. He is the quintessential London barrister. He crusades for the underdog and the petty criminal in a very irreverent style. He is always tweaking the nose of the rigid and pompous British courts and judges. Rumpole is a skilled defense lawyer whose best advice to his clients is "Never plead guilty."

The perennial crusader, Rumpole fights the British class system and injustice everywhere. His words and actions will introduce Americans to a social order more rigid that that with which they are familiar. Mortimer's witty dialogue and asides will make even the most straitlaced of readers smile. Rumpole must even fight to right injustice at home with his wife, "She Who Must Be Obeyed," and their arguments can be used to spark discussions about power relations in marriage. Rumpole's sarcasm and witty assessment of all he encounters, including people who are "N.O.S." (not our sort), endear him to even the most dedicated of Anglophobes. He is the "True London Eccentric," as our British friends would say.

The novels included in this volume are *Rumpole for the Defense, Rumpole and the Golden Thread,* and *Rumpole's Last Case.* For high school students in English literature and European history classes, Mortimer's Rumpole novels reveal the best and worst of London society in a raucous satire of life in modern Britain.

Peyton, K. M. *The Edge of the Clouds.*
See entry 515, Grades 7–9.

Price, Susan. *From Where I Stand.*
See entry 517, Grades 7–9.

535   Pullman, Philip. *The Tiger in the Well.* Knopf 1990, LB $16.99 (0-679-90214-7). 416pp. Fiction.

This detective story set in Victorian London concludes Pullman's trilogy, which began with *The Ruby in the Smoke* (Knopf, 1987) and continued with *Shadow in the North* (Knopf, 1988). Here, heroine Sally Lockhart is living with her 2-year-old daughter, Harriet. (Harriet's father, to whom Sally had been engaged, was killed at the end of *Shadow in the North*.) Sally receives a mysterious and disturbing legal notice. One Arthur Parrish is suing her for divorce and claiming custody of the child. Although she has never met Parrish, her lawyer seems passive and pessimistic. Records have been forged, and Parrish has connections. Rather than lose Harriet, Sally escapes into London's frightful slums, where she is taken into a settlement house operated by Jewish socialists. She becomes aware of the terrible conditions faced by her country's poor and by the new Jewish immigrants fleeing persecution and pogroms. She also finds out that Parrish is working for the evil Tzaddik, a fat man in a wheelchair who has extorted money from the desperate immigrants and who plans to touch off anti-Semitic violence in England as well. Disguising herself as a servant, she goes to the Tzaddik's underground home, where she discovers he is the half-Chinese former opium dealer Ah Ling, whom she thought she had killed almost ten years earlier (as detailed in *The Ruby in the Smoke*). Revealing herself to the Tzaddik Ah Ling, she survives both attempts to kill her and a building collapse that claims the life of the evil man; she then exposes Parrish and marries the charismatic Jewish socialist journalist Daniel Goldberg.

Pullman's novels, of which this is an example, are fast paced and suspenseful. They immerse the reader in another time and place and are reminiscent of Dickens's works in their vivid detailing of life among the poor in Victorian England. Cultural and historical information, particularly about the conditions in London and the Jewish immigration from Eastern Europe, are seamlessly woven into the story. Fans of this genre will cheer for the good guys—Sally, her old friends, and her new Jewish associates—as they once again triumph over evil by whatever means at hand, using criminal tactics as well as virtue to overcome the enemies that threaten their lives.

Raymond, Patrick. *Daniel and Esther.*
See entry 518, Grades 7–9.

536 Taylor, Judy, Ann Stevenson Hobbs, and Joyce Irene Whalley. *Beatrix Potter 1866–1943: The Artist and Her World.* Illus. with photos and drawings. Frederick Warne; dist. by Penguin 1987, P $19.95 (0-7232-3561-9). 244pp. Nonfiction.

This biography was published in conjunction with the Tate Gallery (London) and Pierpont Morgan Library (New York) exhibition, "Beatrix Potter: Artist and Storyteller." It is a very thorough and authoritative biography of Potter. The contributors are current and former curators of museum collections of Potter's works at the Victoria and Albert Museum (London) and the National Trust Lake District (England), where Potter lived for 30 years.

The book describes Potter's life as an artist and author, beginning with her lonely and Spartan childhood in London. She spent much of her time playing with her pets and drawing alone in her room. She had several careers, first, as a self-taught naturalist artist, then as an author, and finally as a livestock breeder and conservationist in England's Lake District.

The book contains 450 illustrations, many of them reproductions of Potter's work. The book emphasizes her self-taught art techniques as well as her family life and tragic engagement to her editor. Her childhood and life as a young woman were far from idyllic, although she came from a well-to-do middle-class family. The book emphasizes the artist behind the art, with all of her foibles and eccentricities as well as her genius. Although written for adults, the book is beautifully illustrated and crafted, and accessible to older children and young adults.

Taylor has authored an earlier biography of Potter, also published by Frederick Warne (1987). Its title is *Beatrix Potter: Artist, Storyteller, and Countrywoman*.

Townsend, Sue. ***The Growing Pains of Adrian Mole.***
See entry 521, Grades 7–9.

Westall, Robert. ***Blitzcat.***
See entry 522, Grades 7–9.

537 Westall, Robert. ***Children of the Blitz: Memories of Wartime Childhood.*** Illus. with photos. Viking 1985, HB $16.95 (0-670-80134-8). 237pp. Nonfiction.

After the 1975 publication in England of his World War II novel *The Machine Gunners*, Robert Westall began to receive letters from adults who had been children during the Nazi bombing of Britain. In this work, he has assembled testimonies from dozens of witnesses of the Battle of Britain, the time of terror that was also, in Winston Churchill's words, his country's "finest hour." From those who lived in London, in smaller cities and rural areas, and even in Ireland, we receive images of infants in blanket-size gas masks, homemade metal bomb shelters, sleepless nights with the air raid sirens, bombs killing neighbors, friends, family members, and unexploded bombs being played with as though they were exotic toys. Along with the fear, the observers report a sense of adventure and camaraderie; normally reserved people pulled together and became friends for the duration of the blitz, only to pull apart again once the crisis ended. While most of the voices are clearly those of adults looking back on their childhood, many have retained a childlike sense of wonder and adventure.

This is a fine work, one that can be used in its entirety or in parts with young people of a variety of ages. The testimonies are vivid and immediate. Few analyze what the war was about, but they give a perspective on an individual experience. Many of Westall's spirited informants ran away from their country hosts during the evacuation or played in unstable bombed-out buildings; their antics will appeal to today's rebellious teens. Among the revealing photographs are samples of wartime propaganda. Westall's captions comment on those propaganda images and will serve as a useful discussion starter in the classroom, helping young people to learn to "read" graphic images. Read in tandem with Westall's young adult novels of the war, this excellent nonfiction resource allows the reader to explore the relationship between fact and fiction.

Westall, Robert. ***The Machine Gunners.***
See entry 523, Grades 7–9.

9

WESTERN EUROPE

9

WESTERN EUROPE

by Annette C. Blank

Those used to the vast spaces of the United States may find it hard to visualize that some Western European countries are smaller than some of the states.

The rapid political, economic, and social changes that have taken place in Western Europe during the past few years prove the statement that a book can be out-of-date upon its publication. Some such books are included, however, because they contain background information explaining the conditions that led to these changes. In several books on East and West Germany, for instance, the authors stated that there seemed little chance the two countries would work toward unification or that the Berlin Wall would be demolished.

Most of the other books were chosen because they were representative of the types of books used for class assignments, gave a new perspective on a country or region, or else illustrated various methods of presenting information. Most are widely available in libraries, and others should be suggested to libraries.

In many ways, people are becoming homogenized. We have observed the worldwide trend toward buying packaged foods and shopping in hypermarkets as well as, or instead of, shopping in neighborhood fruit and vegetable markets or specialized stores. Each country, though, still retains its own national traditions, holidays, and legends.

Illustrations from translated picture books can offer clues to show differences in countries. Children can study architecture, neighborhoods, food stores and markets, circus scenes and other entertainment, signs, scenery, and other phenomena that are different from those of their own experience. In some picture books translators have changed certain words and phrases to those they thought children would understand. These words and phrases may have changed the spirit of the books. Even though *You Be Me, I'll Be You*, from Belgium, has no set place specified, children can learn that it is fine to be oneself and not have to look the same as everyone else does. A book with few words, *The House from Morning to Night* has several visual clues to show that the setting can be France, from where the book came. In *The Wonder Shoes* from Switzerland, one can see the mountainous scenery and an architecture with unfamiliar chimneys. Both *Erik Has a Squirrel* and *Olson's Meat Pies* are from Sweden. The country is displayed mainly through signs and through the meat pies, which are different from the ones most children would be familiar with. In Astrid Lindgren's book *Lotta's Bike*, Lotta is a determined child. Her village has a fairy-tale appearance with Old World charm. On the light side is *Linnea in Monet's Garden*. This book gives charming glimpses of Paris, Monet's flowers, and his art for a wide range of ages.

Fiction translated into English provides a link to how people live, or have lived, in other countries. Of course, much depends upon how well the translation retains the spirit of the original language. The Mildred L. Batchelder Award honors the most outstanding translated book published for children during the preceding year. The best fiction is able to supply a feeling of place, as well as insight into cultures and the problems of peoples.

Two books by Peter Hartling, originally published in German, bring out how relationships develop between generations. *Crutches* features people displaced right after World War II. In *Old John*, members of a family invite an elderly, and lively, grandfather to their home. *If You Didn't Have Me* is a little boy's story of a summer spent growing into independence. *Buster's World* is about a boy who works his way through escapades and problems with his magic tricks. Each of these children develops methods of coping with problems.

The profusion of books about World War II and the Holocaust makes it difficult to select titles to represent that era. Because the Holocaust was perpetrated throughout extensive areas of Europe, a number of books cover regions larger than Western Europe. These books depict the war years as perceived by people from various cultures and with many viewpoints. They examine how certain populations were treated, sent to be destroyed, or rescued. There are several eyewitness accounts. Dramatic and often graphic books have been written by and about survivors, underground fighters, and others who were young then. Most authors felt an enormous urge to record events of the Holocaust and to teach the future generations about Hitler's regime so that young people may understand it and eventually be in a position to prevent recurrence of the Holocaust.

Books have dealt with the effect of the Holocaust and the war on children, and many are autobiographical. *The Upstairs Room* and its sequel, *The Journey Back*, are about sisters hidden on a farm in Holland. *Touch Wood* is about three sisters, in France, hidden in a Catholic women's residence. Ilsa Koehn survived a different life in Nazi Germany, partly because her parents kept a secret from her. *Anne Frank Remembered* is a compassionate book about events in Amsterdam during the war, written by someone who helped to hide Anne Frank's family.

Both *Night over Day over Night* and *The Abduction* vividly develop the themes of cruelty, brutality, and the devastation wrought when one culture subjugates another. Even though *The Abduction* takes place centuries before the Holocaust, the events and dilemmas facing the characters are strikingly similar. *What Did You Do in the War, Daddy?* is by a non-Jewish woman who describes her feelings of guilt for what was carried out by her parents' generation in Germany during the Nazi era. *We Remember the Holocaust* succeeds in introducing the subject to children older than 9 years of age. While *Rose Blanche* appears to be a picture book, it is actually a devastating book about a child caught in the ruthlessness of war. The title comes from an underground movement (White Rose) in Germany. The movement's history is found in *The Short Life of Sophie Scholl*, a biography of one of its activists, who was executed.

Criminals, Jehovah's Witnesses, Slavs, and Gypsies composed some of the non-Jewish people annihilated under Hitler's plans for a master race. Accounts of these 5 million appear in *The Other Victims*. Outrage over events of the

Holocaust is expressed in many books, and especially in Seymour Rossel's *Holocaust: The Fire That Raged.*

Rescue: The Story of How Gentiles Saved Jews in the Holocaust tells of courageous people who risked their own lives to help save the lives of Jews. Two fictional accounts describe the Danish efforts that helped to save almost all of Denmark's Jewish population. The main characters in *Lisa's War* are several years older than those in *Number the Stars*, but both feature the Danish resistance and present many of the same themes.

Social changes and problems provide recurring themes in series books. Some concerns are about pollution, acid rain, nuclear energy and accidents, unemployment and immigrant labor forces, declining birth rates and payments to families with children, economic changes, prejudice, parental leave, health care, and a variety of other societal issues. Education is of great importance, and in most Western European countries there is virtually no illiteracy.

Each series is geared to the information needs of school assignments. While most series start at the fourth-grade level, some are suitable for reading aloud to young children. Franklin Watts publishes, and distributes, a number of series. The Take a Trip series is mainly photographs, with very brief information to describe each one. These can be read to young children. The Inside books are lengthier and have some of the same information and photographs found in other series. Countries of the World books have two pages to a subject and discuss some problems of each country. The Living Here series covers the occupations and educational requirements of the featured countries. This series and the Food and Drink books are about people's lives, rather than just the facts. Both the Venture and Hotspots series are for junior and senior high school students who need information on topics discussed by the media. All of the books in these groups are useful, but since they overlap in many ways, they should be selected to suit the specific purposes for which they are needed.

Lerner's Count Your Way Books uses the device of the numbers one through ten, together with facing full-page illustrations, as the framework for historical and cultural information. Though the vocabulary is not simple, it can be used with young children. Dillon's Discovering Our Heritage series concentrates on the cultural life of a country, including folktales, legends, and foods with recipes. It also has a chapter on the contributions made to the United States by immigrants of these countries.

There are two different companies' series whose titles begin with "A Family in . . ." Both the Lerner series, Families the World Over, and the Bookwright Press/Franklin Watts series, Families Around the World, have almost the same types of information and almost the same formats. The information is presented on a personal level, through the lives of children and their families.

High school students who need in-depth material have several choices. Often overlooked are U.S. government publications. Country Studies–Area Handbook Program books provide important information about other countries. As with many series, which can be many years in production, publication dates should be noted.

Books in two series are being revised. The Lerner Visual Geography book *Norway in Pictures* is a 1990 revision. This one is bright and appealing, with many color photographs to supplement the information. *The Land and People of Finland* and *The Land and People of France* are two of the new titles in the Portraits of the Nations series, published by HarperCollins; these cover all aspects of a country, from its detailed history to its latest cultural trends.

538   Bernatova, Eva. ***The Wonder Shoes.*** Illus. by Fiona Moodie. Farrar, Straus & Giroux 1990, HB $13.95 (0-374-38476-2). 23pp. Fiction.

In a village lived a little girl named Emma, who was new to the village and lonely because no one would play with her. One day a circus came to town. There was a lovely dancer in red shoes. After the show, Emma talked with the ballerina, who gave Emma the pair of red shoes and taught her how to pirouette. When Emma danced, the children were jealous, and they joked about her shoes. Then Emma had an idea: The children got together to put on a circus, which was a great success. It was especially good because Emma made many new friends.

In this story about an enterprising child and the issue of friendship, the location could be almost any small town. The place is set by the illustrations, which feature a small European village with narrow, winding streets. Each house and chimney have their own individuality. The one-ring circus that comes to town is quite different from the glamorous, three-ring affairs most people know. The mountains and the village could represent a country such as Switzerland, where the author lives. The story was translated into English, but there is no information about the original language.

539   Bour, Daniele. ***The House from Morning to Night.*** Trans. from French. Illus. by the author. Kane/Miller 1985, HB $9.95 (0-916291-01-4). 14pp. Fiction.

Look closely at the many parts of each illustration. All of the people in the house know each other. Watch what happens in each room and outside the house as the hours pass. What parts of the house are the same as yours? What parts are different? What are people buying in the stores? Do you know what the signs say in French? Many people live in a large house. Also, in the building there are stores with special functions. The reader-viewer has to look at every room, for as the hours go by the functions of each room change, and the scenes outside the house change, too.

There is very little text in this unusual book. One has to look carefully at each picture to know what is happening. Children will be able to make up their own stories as they notice how scenes differ from their own home and neighborhood. The book starts on the inside front cover and goes to the inside back cover, presenting a problem for libraries and perhaps making it necessary to prebind the book for circulation.

540   Cohen, Peter. ***Olson's Meat Pies.*** Trans. from Swedish by Richard E. Fisher. Illus. by Olaf Landstrom. R&S Books/Farrar, Straus & Giroux 1989, HB $12.95 (91-29-59180-5). 34pp. Fiction.

Olson's meat pies were famous. They had the best ingredients and a special wrapper. Hugo ran the meat grinder. Strom was in charge of the money. Even Mrs. Olson and the children helped when it was busy. One night Strom ran off with the money. Olson could not pay Hugo. He could not afford to buy the best ingredients. People bought few meat pies since they did not taste good anymore. Olson tried leftovers such as cold porridge and a few fried herrings. Finally, he tossed in almost anything, including pot holders and underwear. People refused to buy his meat pies. Then he put in surprises such as a wristwatch and a real gold earring. People looked for the surprises and tossed the pies. Just when all seemed lost, Strom returned with the money. He had wanted to have a good time for the rest of his life, but he was lonely. He ate a meat pie and realized it was all his fault. Since Strom had spent only seventeen dollars and twenty cents, Olson went out to buy the best ingredients. The pies tasted more delicious than ever. Still, people talked about the strange items that had been in Olson's meat pies.

This is a sad story with a happy ending. Children will giggle over what went into those pies, even as they note Olson's increasing desperation. The book shows children a different type of meat pie, in a different type of wrapper from what they are used to having. There is no location given except for a sign on a store.

541　Haskins, Jim. ***Count Your Way Through Germany.*** Illus. by Helen Byers. SERIES: Count Your Way Books. Lerner/Carolrhoda 1990, LB $11.95 (0-87614-407-5). 22pp. Nonfiction.

This book was published a few months too soon. The first number is about one land divided into two nations, and the hope many have that the country will be united. Three (*drei*) is for Bach, Beethoven, and Brahms. Eight (*acht*) is for the number of lanes of the autobahn in some urban areas. Each number has a facing full-page illustration. The last page is a pronunciation guide to the numbers. The format and some of the illustrations give the work the appearance of a picture book. It actually has bits of nonfiction information and is another way of learning about a country. It should work as a read-aloud for very young children and would be of interest mainly to second through fourth graders.

542　Lindgren, Astrid. ***Lotta's Bike.*** Trans. from Swedish. Illus. by Ilon Wikland. R&S Books/Farrar, Straus & Giroux 1989, HB $13.95 (91-29-59600-9). 32pp. Fiction.

Lotta knows just what she wants, a bicycle of her own. The 5-year-old said she can ride a bike—secretly. Determined to ride a bicycle, she sneaks a ride on a large one that belongs to one of her neighbors, with the usual consequences. She cannot stop it from going down a hill. She even loses a special bracelet. It is a sad birthday for Lotta, but later her father surprises everyone. He has found an old, secondhand bicycle, just the right size for Lotta. Astrid Lindgren's books have been popular for many years. Though she lived in Sweden, her books could take place in many places. The illustrations show a small town with houses that could be a setting for a folktale.

When no Christmas trees are available in her village, the child who could do anything—almost—goes in search of a tree in the sequel, *Lotta's Christmas Surprise*.

543　Lye, Keith. ***Take a Trip to Austria.*** Illus. with photos. SERIES: Take a Trip. Franklin Watts 1987, LB $7.99 (0-531-10365-X). 32pp. Nonfiction.

This is a short book. The format is part of a page of text that describes the color photograph for that page. The usual descriptions are about physical features of the country, some cities and ports, coins and stamps, resources, manufacturing and crafts, education, foods, and other information useful for a report and/or travel. The brief paragraphs may be good to read aloud to nonreaders. The vocabulary is harder than the design of the book would suggest.

Many countries are covered in this series, but some of the volumes are going out of print.

544   Mandelbaum, Piri. **You Be Me, I'll Be You.** (Original title, *Noire comme le café, blanc comme la lune*). Trans. from French. Illus. by the author. Kane/Miller 1990, HB $13.85 (0-916291-27-8). 40pp. Fiction.

Noire comme le café, blanc comme la lune is the title of this book as originally published in Belgium. The French title is closer to the spirit of the book than the English translation. The title could be translated as "black like coffee, white like the moon." Anna, a young child in an interracial family, is unhappy. She decides she is not pretty and wants her father's pale skin and straight hair. He tells her he does not want to be as pale as the moon or to have his straight hair. While they are drinking coffee with milk, Anna notes that her mother is like the coffee, her father is like the milk, and she is like the coffee with milk. They put coffee grounds on his face, and she gives him little braids. Then he puts flour on her face. They also remark that many people are unhappy about how they look, wanting straight hair if they have curly hair, or curly hair if they have straight hair, or tans if they are pale. When they meet Mother, she calls them clowns and tells them to take showers.

Done with touches of humor, the text and illustrations present a loving family relationship. Anna begins to feel positive about herself. It is hard to tell if the mother is upset at what they have done or if she sees some humor in it. Does the father give his skin color a negative connotation? Older children can find questions of their own for discussion. Many will understand that these feelings are universal and that Western European countries, like the United States, have become multiracial, multicultural societies.

545   Peterson, Hans. **Erik Has a Squirrel.** Trans. from Swedish by Christine Hyatt. Illus. by Ilon Wikland. R&S Books/Farrar, Straus & Giroux 1989, HB $12.95 (91-29-59140-6). 28pp. Fiction.

Erik was lonely, as he had no one to play with him. He had a friend, Matt, but Matt had to work. One day Matt came with a large bird cage, which had a baby squirrel in it. He asked Erik to care for the squirrel until it was big enough to care for itself.

Erik's family lived in a small apartment, and Erik's bed was in the crowded kitchen. Erik took care of the baby squirrel, and it went almost everywhere with him. The squirrel was named Jim-Jim and was taken to the market, on a ferry ride, and many other places. Jim-Jim grew big, but Erik wanted to keep him. One day the family came home from shopping and found that the squirrel had pulled down pictures, ripped cushions, and tossed papers. Erik finally realized that Jim-Jim had to be released.

This seems to be a charming story about a boy and his pet. There are problems, though. Should a child be given the care of a wild animal? Should a wild animal be kept captive? Matt takes Erik for a motorcycle ride. Matt wears a helmet, and Erik does not. In one place the text states that Erik is holding his father's hand, but the illustration does not even include his father. Although his parents are mentioned, neither one is pictured. Signs for store names provide some of the few clues to the story's location.

546 Adler, David A. **We Remember the Holocaust.** Illus. with photos. Henry Holt 1989, LB $15.95 (0-8050-0434-3). 147pp. Nonfiction.

This book is based on the testimonies of people who remember pre–Nazi Germany, survivors of concentration camps, and a few children of survivors. There is a discussion of Hitler's ideas and his rise to power, and of the events leading up to the Holocaust. Most people in the book were teenagers when these events occurred. Many found the experiences too painful to remember. The book was written for today's children, who may not know about the Holocaust and who may ask about what happened in it. The first-person accounts and the photographs make the book intense reading. The photographs are from public archives, from survivors, and from others. They add to the pathos of the accounts. We Remember the Holocaust is meant to be an introduction to this painful subject and not the only book on the Holocaust that one should read. It will be a starting point for discussion about this period in history and its effect on those who survived.

547 Björk, Christina. **Linnea in Monet's Garden.** Trans. from Swedish by Joan Sandin. Illus. by Lena Anderson. R&S Books/Farrar, Straus & Giroux 1987, HB $10.95 (91-29-58314-4). 53pp. Fiction.

Linnea's story is the framework for a study of Claude Monet's art and life. Photographs of members of his family provide the personal touch. Linnea, an intelligent, curious child, became interested in Monet's paintings of his garden. Her elderly friend Mr. Bloom took her to Paris and Monet's garden. They were even able to go into Monet's house. They visited several museums, where Linnea learned about Impressionism. This is a lively way to learn about art and flowers and a delightful and original way to meet Paris. Guides for the visitor include a list of museums, places to visit around Paris, and suggested books.

548 Blackwood, Alan, and Brigitte Chosson. **France.** Illus. with photos by Chris Fairclough and illus. by Stefan Chabluck. SERIES: Countries of the World. Franklin Watts 1988, LB $12.40 (0-531-18186-3). 48pp. Nonfiction.

Numerous photographs form a major part of this book. Each double-page spread has a single topic with special photos. Country life, growing up in the city, grape growing, fashions, and religion are a few of the topics covered. Also mentioned, as in many other books in series, is that grocery-shopping habits are changing. While many people still like to shop for food daily in specialty shops and fruit and vegetable markets, the trend is to buy prepared foods in supermarkets or hypermarkets. Some of the photographs in this series are in a few of the other series distributed by Watts. There are a glossary, a list of books to read, and an index. This series has more reading and is slightly more advanced than the Take a Trip series, also by Watts.

Cameron, Fiona, and Preben Kristensen. **We Live in Belgium and Luxembourg.**
See entry 558, Grades 7–9.

Chaikin, Miriam. **A Nightmare in History: The Holocaust 1933–1945.**
See entry 559, Grades 7–9.

Einhorn, Barbara. *West German Food and Drink.*
See entry 560, Grades 7–9.

549   Gallacz, Christophe, and Roberto Innocenti. *Rose Blanche.* Trans. by Martha
Coventry and Richard Graglia. Illus. by Roberto Innocenti. Creative Education
1985, LB $21.35 (0-87191-994-X). 27pp. Fiction.

This tragic book highlights some of the awful emotions and deeds of war
through a story of a young girl. The sparse narrative adds to the tensions
aroused. It is told in the first person and then changes to the third person as it
projects to the climax. Rose Blanche is a child in Germany. After the Nazi
soldiers invade her town, she discovers a group of children behind a fence. She
sneaks food to them regularly. One night she is out in the fog when Russian
soldiers come into the town, and she is killed by soldiers who mistake her for the
enemy.

   The illustrator wanted to portray how a child experiences war without really
understanding it. His efforts succeed. He named her Rose Blanche after the
underground movement in Germany during World War II. This is an illustrated
novel rather than a picture book, and it reveals in poignant detail how devastating war can be and the way that innocent children are drawn in and become its
victims.

550   Härtling, Peter. *Crutches.* Trans. from German by Elizabeth D. Crawford.
Lothrop, Lee & Shepard 1988, HB $12.95 (0-688-07991-1). 163pp. Fiction.

Crutches shows how people will struggle to begin again when all seems lost. Just
at the end of World War II, Thomas and his mother are boarding a train to
Vienna when the crowd separates them. He searches for her on the train but
cannot find her. When he arrives at his aunt's house in Vienna, he finds only
ruins. Later, he learns that his aunt has been killed. As he leaves a shelter, he sees
a man with one leg. The man is walking on crutches, and Thomas decides to
follow him. Reluctantly, Crutches lets Thomas stay with him. Later, when they
move into Bronka's house, they register Thomas with the Red Cross, so that
Thomas and his mother might be able to find each other. Bronka works with an
organization concerned with finding homes for orphaned Jewish children, and
Thomas, who has been indoctrinated with the Nazis' anti-Semitic ideology,
must learn to accept the fact that Bronka is Jewish. Eventually, Thomas and
Crutches move in together and develop a close relationship—like uncle and
nephew—in the year before Thomas is reunited with his mother.

   Crutches is based in part on the author's own experiences. It explores in depth
a special kind of friendship, the kind that develops in times of great social
upheaval. Thomas must learn to confront his own prejudices, to reach out to
others, and to accept help from unexpected sources. This is a moving and
authentic novel of the adventures, emotions, and adjustments of displaced
people searching for a home.

551   Härtling, Peter. *Old John.* Trans. from German by Elizabeth D. Crawford.
Lothrop, Lee & Shepard 1990, HB $11.95 (0-688-08734-5). 120pp. Fiction.

Old John, mother's father, was 75 years old and had many peculiar ways.
Mother, Father, Laura, and Jacob decided to invite Old John to live with them in

Stuttgart, Germany. When he arrived, he proved to be fiercely independent. For instance, he had ideas of his own about what he should do and how he should do it. He expressed himself vehemently. He could upset people and then be lovable. The family had to become used to the idiosyncrasies of his friendships, furnishings, and behavior. As they tried to adjust to each other, a wonderful relationship developed. Then Old John had a stroke. Earlier he had made a new friend, Frau Besemer, who came to help take care of him when he came home from the hospital. At first all went well. Then his body deteriorated while he was trying to prove he was still alert. The family soon realized that he could not be left alone. Jacob and Laura had become fond of their grandfather and his original ways. Old John's death was especially difficult for Jacob.

The author is skillful in portraying affection by and for his characters. As in his earlier novel *Crutches*, he has developed a unique relationship between a child and an adult. Readers soon become as fond of Old John as his grandchildren were. They may have lost an elderly friend and understand Jacob's actions. Children will find a lot of humor in the family's, and Old John's, ways when he comes to live with them, along with the empathy they will feel toward him.

The bits of dialect Old John speaks, references to cities and other places, and Old John's mention of anti-Nazi ideas during Hitler's rule set the scene for this story.

552   Jacobsen, Peter, and Preben Kristensen. *A Family in Iceland.* Illus. with photos. SERIES: Families Around the World. Franklin Watts 1986, LB $11.90 (0-531-180-36-0). 32pp. Nonfiction.

There is a quick tour of Reykjavík before the reader arrives at the Finnsson's farm. The farm has 125 acres of lowland and about 2,500 acres of higher land. Most of the land is used for grazing sheep and a dairy herd. Besides a lot of lamb's meat, the Finnssons sell a lot of wool. Children will be interested to know that each child is given a lamb as a birthday present, which is a natural way of saving. Also, each child receives a horse as soon as he or she is able to ride. Farm life in the far north may mean living in Reykjavík while attending school, helping in the kitchen, and having modern appliances. Children will enjoy comparing their lives with those of the children on this faraway farm. Other books in this series are on France and Holland. Most of the families featured in these books seem fairly well-off, and the focus is on a single family rather than the country as a whole.

553   James, Ian. *The Netherlands.* Illus. with photos. SERIES: Inside. Franklin Watts 1990, LB $11.40 (0-7496-0113-2). 32pp. Nonfiction.

This book has the format to attract those who want to browse through facts and photographs. The information is unencumbered by too many words. It has an oversize format and is similar to the Take a Trip series from the same publisher. Each topic usually has two pages with several photographs. Information covers history, art, foods, and other topics needed for school assignments. There are both a page of facts about the Netherlands and a picture of some of the stamps and coins used there. Also, there are several useful maps. This copy has a typographical error on page 14—part of a sentence is missing. Other volumes in this series present France and West Germany.

554   Lowry, Lois. **Number the Stars.** Houghton Mifflin 1989, HB $12.95 (0-395-51060-0). 248pp. Fiction.

Three years ago the Germans occupied Denmark. The orders had come to close stores owned by Jews, and the Nazis had started to deport some of them. Annamarie Johansen and Ellen Rosen were best friends. Ellen, who was Jewish, came to live with the Johansens after her parents disappeared. When soldiers came to search the Johansens' apartment, Annamarie, just in time, was able to pull off the Star of David necklace that Ellen always wore. Mrs. Johansen took Ellen and Annamarie to visit Uncle Henrik, a fisherman. While in the synagogue on the first night of Rosh Hashanah, the Jewish New Year, the congregation was informed that the Germans planned to round up all of the Jews of Denmark. Other Danish citizens, together with members of the resistance movement, were able to persuade fishermen and other boat owners to take the Jewish population to Sweden. That night many people secretly came to Uncle Henrik's house disguised as mourners behind a coffin; there too came Ellen's parents.

Many underground fighters were killed resisting the Germans, including Annamarie's sister, Lise, and Peter, her boyfriend. Annamarie's many acts of courage, both large and small, marked her own passage from childhood during this dark time. At the war's end she took Ellen's necklace from where she had hidden it and awaited the return of her friend.

An Afterword explains the background of the story. The book is based on real historical events that have been carefully researched. For instance, Annamarie evades food-sniffing dogs by using special chemicals designed to disguise the smell of a food package she smuggles to the fleeing Jews. In fact, citizens who resisted the Nazis developed these chemicals to impair a dog's sense of smell. This 1990 Newbery Medal book has suspense and a lot of action. Characters are believable and yet show the best of what humans are capable (as well as, of course, the worst). Through this book children can be led to feel and understand what it meant to live through those perilous times.

Matas, Carol. **Lisa's War.**
See entry 563, Grades 7–9.

555   Nilsson, Ulf. **If You Didn't Have Me.** Trans. from Swedish by Lone Thygesen Blecher and George Blecher. Illus. by Eva Eriksson. Macmillan 1987, HB $10.95 (0-689-50406-3). 113pp. Fiction.

There is quiet feeling and humor in the story of a small boy's summer. He learns, imagines, grows, and becomes independent. The young boy and his little brother stay with their grandmother, uncle, and aunt on a farm in Sweden, while their parents are building a house in town. The parents are too busy to give the children a lot of attention. Cousin Cilla spends her whole time reading in her room, and she refuses to let the boy in. When he has time, Edwin, the farmhand, talks to the boy about many things, such as how to care for some of the animals. Edwin is the one who finds the boy when he runs away, lonely and scared. The young boy learns to care about his little brother, and he discovers that the rough farm boys can be good friends for sliding down the hay in the barn. On his last day at the farm, he finally is allowed into Cilla's room to see her many books and possessions.

Each chapter is a complete episode, beginning with a report on the progress of the house. This book is made for reading aloud. The translation ably preserves the spirit of the story. Life on a farm in southern Sweden places the location and is part of the action. The publisher was awarded the 1988 Mildred L. Batchelder Award for the most outstanding translated book published for children that year.

Reiss, Johanna. *The Upstairs Room.*
See entry 566, Grades 7–9.

556 Reuter, Bjarne. *Buster's World.* Trans. from Danish by Anthea Bell. Dutton 1989, HB $12.95 (0-525-44475-0). 154pp. Fiction.

Buster lives in Copenhagen, Denmark. His world is a mixture of hardships and fun. His family is poor, and his father has a drinking problem. Buster's magic tricks, some learned from Father, lead him in and out of trouble, whether at school or at a party. Despite his lighthearted attitude, Buster cares deeply about his sister, who has one leg shorter than the other and is constantly teased by the bully, Lars. Buster also cares about the neighbor, Mrs. Larsen, who is very ill and ultimately dies.

Eventually, Buster carries out his plans for revenge against Lars. Then he engineers a scheme against the boys in his class who have gotten him into trouble with their sarcastic, cruel gym teacher. Readers will empathize with Buster as he tries to cope with his world, while they laugh at some of his actions. Several episodes are close to slapstick humor; others are more bittersweet. There is a funny, and touching, encounter between Buster's father and two of Buster's teachers on Parents' Night.

This is the first of several books about Buster, and it has been made into a film. The publisher was awarded the Mildred L. Batchelder Award for 1989, for publishing this outstanding translated book.

Roth-Hano, Renée. *Touch Wood: A Girlhood in Occupied France.*
See entry 569, Grades 7–9.

557 St. John, Jetty. *A Family in Norway.* Illus. with photos. SERIES: Families the World Over. Lerner 1988, LB $8.95 (0-8225-1681-0). 31pp. Nonfiction.

Andrea, 10, lives with her family near a fjord south of Oslo. Her father is an important archaeologist. The book presents the life-style typical of a Norwegian family. Information includes sections on foods, education, shopping habits, recreations, and natural resources. Each page has at least one large photograph. There are also a list of Norwegian words and phrases used in the book and a short list of facts about Norway. The brief books in the Families the World Over Series provide information on a personal level, and the format will attract young readers. Children will be able to contrast their lives with the way the children in this book live. Other books in this series about Western Europe are on France and West Germany.

Schloredt, Valerie. *West Germany: The Land and Its People.*
See entry 570, Grades 7–9.

Schrepfer, Margaret. *Switzerland: The Summit of Europe.*
See entry 571, Grades 7–9.

GRADES 7–9

558   Cameron, Fiona, and Preben Kristensen. *We Live in Belgium and Luxembourg.*
Illus. with photos. SERIES: Living Here. Franklin Watts 1986, LB $12.90 (0-531-
18069-7). 60pp. Nonfiction.

Those studying a country may be interested in more than what is in a usual series
book. These 26 first-person accounts are about occupations and people's lives.
The people tell what they do, the training they have had, and the conditions of
their work. The accounts provide some information about the country's government, arts, manufacturing, and education, as well as other aspects of living there.
The photographs usually show where the person works and the subject at work.
There are a section of facts about the country, a glossary, and an index. Another
book in this series is about the Netherlands.

559   Chaikin, Miriam. *A Nightmare in History: The Holocaust 1933–1945.* Illus. with
photos. Clarion 1987, HB $14.95 (0-89919-461-3). 150pp. Nonfiction.

This well-known work is on almost every list of recommended books about the
Holocaust written for young readers. The book begins by tracing the roots of
anti-Semitism from biblical times through the development of Hitler's ideas.
Also explained are the reasons for his rise to power. There are personal accounts,
poetry, letters, documents, and speeches. These are the records that remained
behind after Hitler almost succeeded in annihilating all the Jews of Europe.
There are chapters on persecutions of non-Jews, on the horrors discovered after
the war, and on how individuals, organizations, and governments reacted after
the war. Most of the photographs were taken surreptitiously by Nazis, ghetto
photographers, and unknown soldiers and civilians. They add an emotionally
powerful visual dimension that enhances the text. There are a lengthy list of
suggested readings and an index in this essential work for those studying the
Holocaust.

560   Einhorn, Barbara. *West German Food and Drink.* Illus. with photos. SERIES: Food
and Drink. Franklin Watts 1989, LB $12.40 (0-531-18232-0). 48pp. Nonfiction.

Those who may not want to learn about another country may be motivated by
cooking and eating its foods. This book covers West Germany's history, geography, and culture through its foods and beverages. There are many recipes with
illustrated directions. A few of the recipes can be prepared in a classroom. Many
photographs present mouth-watering displays of various foods. There is a small
contradiction on page 14, which may confuse readers. The text says that the
corner general stores, colloquially known as "Tante Emma Laden," have been
eliminated by supermarkets. Yet the accompanying photograph is of one these
stores, with the caption stating that this type of store still offers personal service.
Included are a glossary, a list of German words and phrases used, and a short list
of books for further reading. There are several other books in this series, including one on France.

Friedman, Ina R. *The Other Victims: First-Person Stories of Non-Jews Persecuted by the Nazis.*
See entry 574, Grades 10–12.

561 Hargrove, Jim. *Belgium.* Illus. with photos. SERIES: Enchantment of the World. Childrens Pr. 1989, LB $17.95 (0-516-02701-8). 127pp. Nonfiction.

Flanders, in the north of Belgium, is where the Dutch-speaking Flemings live. Wallonia, in the south, has the French-speaking Walloons. The author examines a considerable number of the distinct differences between the two populations, which compose almost separate countries. He also covers the influences on the country that result from its strategic location. Belgium has been a battleground in many wars, as well as the headquarters of many international organizations. There is information of the usual type needed for a report, with a lengthy section on "Mini-Facts at a Glance" for those who want to forgo reading the book. An index is included. This series has books on almost every Western European country.

Harris, Jonathan. *The Land and People of France.*
See entry 576, Grades 10–12.

562 Koehn, Ilse. *Mischling, Second Degree: My Childhood in Nazi Germany.* Greenwillow 1977, LB $12.88 (0-688-80110-2); Penguin 1990, P $4.95 (0-14-034290-7). 240pp. Nonfiction.

Ilsa Koehn could have been "an invisible girl" in her world. A German schoolgirl, she seemed to be the same as every other schoolgirl during the Hitler years. She was even in a Hitler Youth Group, and was sent to an evacuation camp. All might have been the same, except for a secret kept from her until after the war. She knew her father had an important job, enough to be spared a lot of hardships. She also knew that her parents were not Nazi sympathizers. Although her parents loved each other, they were divorced, and Ilsa and her mother went to live with her mother's parents. She saw her father infrequently. When the war ended the Russians came, and she and her mother were hidden from the soldiers who looted the town and raped many of the women. A few weeks later her father returned, and for her the war was over. Eventually she was told the secret that had been kept from her. Her father's mother was Jewish. Ilsa was a "mischling, second degree." That meant according to Hitler's law she was Jewish, though her ancestry was never detected.

This is a first-person account of how a child's life is disrupted by forces she does not understand. Only at the end of the war is she allowed to discover the truth; until then she dutifully follows along with her German peers in showing loyalty to Hitler's regime. Her experience, honestly rendered, gives teenage readers a glimpse into the life of a non-Jewish youngster and provides a counterpoint to the accounts of the Jewish Holocaust victims.

563 Matas, Carol. *Lisa's War.* Scribner 1989, HB $12.95 (0-684-19010-9). 111pp. Fiction.

This book and *Number the Stars*, by Lois Lowry, focus on the same subject, the Nazi takeover of Denmark and the huge effort by Danish citizens that saved almost the whole Jewish population of the country. In contrast to Lowry's novel, this story is told from the viewpoint of a Jewish teenager.

Lisa is 12 the year Hitler triumphs in Denmark. Life has become difficult for the Jews, and everyone wonders what would happen next. Lisa's cousin, Erik, 13, has become a Lutheran, and he is sure he and his parents will be safe. Lisa's father, a renowned physician, treats many underground fighters and hides Jewish patients. He wants to rebel when he has to treat Germans. Lisa's brother, Stefan, is acting strangely, and she discovers he is distributing underground leaflets. She talks him into letting her join him.

On the first night of Rosh Hashanah, the Jewish New Year, Lisa receives a telephone call from her father to come to the hospital and to bring all of her family and friends. The Germans have planned to search every Jewish home, raid the synagogue, and deport all the Jews to concentration camps. Fishermen and other boat owners have been hired to evacuate the Jews to safety in Sweden. Although some refuse to take them, most join in the rescue effort.

This novel is based on a true incident. G. F. Duckwitz, a member of the German embassy staff, risked his life to pass on the warning to the Danes, who alerted the rabbi. Only about 474 Jews were sent to the camps. Some of those were isolated, and some refused to believe anything would happen to them. Matas's book focuses more on the horrors of the era than the Lowry book does, and for this reason it is recommended for more mature readers. It has been followed by a sequel entitled *Code Name Kris* (Scribner, 1990), about the Danish resistance fighters.

Meltzer, Milton. *Rescue: The Story of How Gentiles Saved Jews in the Holocaust.*
See entry 578, Grades 10–12.

564   *Norway in Pictures.* Illus. with photos. SERIES: Visual Geography. Lerner 1990, LB $11.95 (0-8225-1871-6). 64pp. Nonfiction.

This volume is an all-new edition of a book previously published by the Sterling Publishing Company. The large, numerous photographs and the two-column pages provide a readable format. The book covers some history and geography, and the major emphasis is on Norway's development since World War II. Two important chapters are on the economy and on the health care and social welfare services provided by the government. A lot of the services are dependent upon the fluctuating economy. The brief forecast of Norway's future should lead to ideas and questions from readers. Other books in this series present Denmark and Sweden; both have also been revised recently.

565   Ozer, Steve. *The Netherlands.* Illus. with photos. SERIES: Let's Visit Places and Peoples of the World. Chelsea House 1990, HB $14.95 (0-7910-1107-0). 104pp. Nonfiction.

This has most of the information needed about the Netherlands as found in most series books for this grade level. The text covers geography, history, government, the economy, and other aspects of the Dutch way of life. The dense population of the Netherlands and the growth of its industries have created pollution and land-use problems. While the Dutch have drained water to form new land, most of the indigenous animals have disappeared. These and other problems receive a great deal of attention, far more than in other geography series. There are many black-and-white photographs, and in the center is a selection of color ones. Other books on Western Europe in this series present France, Norway, Sweden, and West Germany.

566   Reiss, Johanna. *The Upstairs Room.* HarperCollins 1972, LB $12.89 (0-690-04702-9); 1987, P $2.95 (0-06-447043-1). 196pp. Fiction.

Since 1972, readers of this book have found themselves reliving the story of a child caught in the midst of Hitler's persecution of the Jews. Though reluctant to talk about her experiences because they were too painful, the author did want to record them for her two daughters. *The Upstairs Room* is Anna's story of how she and her sisters, Sini and Rachel, survived the war. Their father wanted to flee to America, but their mother was too ill to leave. Soon it was too late to leave, and their mother died. Their father finally found places for the sisters to be hidden from the Germans.

Anna and Sini were hidden by Dutch farmers, the Oosterveld family, and became part of the family. Anna stayed in bed for almost two years. She had almost no space to move about in the room, and she had to stay away from the window. She rarely glimpsed the outside. For a while, the local Nazi headquarters were housed downstairs. The Germans left March 21, 1945, taking almost everything they could. Anna had stayed in bed for such a long time that she had trouble walking. She did not even desire to go outside to see the arrival of the Canadian soldiers.

The book is honest, graphic, and at times painful to read. It has the immediacy and authenticity of an autobiographical account. When it was first published, there were some objections to the use of profanity by one of the characters. The language is in keeping with the character, but for this and other reasons, the book demands a certain maturity on the part of its readers. *The Upstairs Room* has been followed by a sequel, *The Journey Back* (HarperCollins, 1976), which tells the story of the reunited family after the war. The sequel explores the problems faced by family members in adjusting to a new life together in a war-ravaged land.

567   Roberts, Elizabeth. *Europe 1992: The United States of Europe?* Illus. with photos. SERIES: Hotspots. Franklin Watts 1990, LB $11.90 (0-531-17204-X). 36pp. Nonfiction.

Will there ever be a United States of Europe? The Single European Act, signed in 1986, commits 12 countries to establish by 1992 an area without internal frontiers. This book relates the historical events that led to the founding of the European Community and its sections, how the community was in fact founded, and how the Single European Market will affect the rest of the world. One development has been the economic currency unit, which is the central element of the European Monetary System.

A section of the book is about the functions of the Single European Market. Although written before the monumental changes in Eastern Europe, the work projects into the future and provides a context for examining further, unexpected, changes. Included are a glossary, a detailed chronology, and an index.

The European Community is often in the media, especially in the context of economics. This clearly written treatment should help students understand its implications. It can also be used as a starting point for discussions of the future of U.S. relations with the countries involved.

568 Rossel, Seymour. ***The Holocaust: The Fire That Raged.*** Illus. with photos. SERIES: Venture. Franklin Watts 1989, HB $12.40 (0-531-10674-8). 124pp. Nonfiction.

This is a clearly written book that transmits its anger directly to the reader. Hitler was able to arouse most of the German people to the hatred of a common enemy. His followers were ready to destroy those who were in their way. When the German armies conquered a country, its Jews were separated from others and herded into ghettos. *Judenrate*—councils—were put in charge. When the *Judenrate* looked out for themselves, the Jewish population in the ghetto suffered. In the places where the *Judenrate* pretended to cooperate but really helped Jews, a number of people in the ghettos were able to survive. The author discounts the idea that Jews seldom fought back. Many fought back, resisted, and escaped; even the vilified *Judenrate* sometimes saved many lives. Rossel uses the many incidents of Jewish resistance to show that people must speak up for one another, and if they want to, they can defeat the enemy and survive. He concludes with an analysis of the meaning and repercussions of genocide.

Copious maps and charts illustrate the well-organized text; photos help drive home the impact of the era. There are a detailed chronology of the Holocaust, including events not mentioned in the book; a list of books for further reading and sources consulted; and an index.

569 Roth-Hano, Renée. ***Touch Wood: A Girlhood in Occupied France.*** Four Winds 1988, HB $15.95 (0-02-777340-X); Penguin 1989, P $4.95 (0-14-034085-8). 297pp. Fiction.

''Touch wood'' is what their mother used to say to ward off evil. Using a diary format for this autobiographical novel, the author relates how she and her two younger sisters spent two years of World War II hidden in a Catholic women's residence in Normandy. On October 9, 1940, all Jews had to register with the police. Then came other decrees: All Jews had to wear a Star of David on their jacket or coat. Did celebrating a few Jewish holidays make them Jewish? Renée's family left Alsace for Paris to escape the Germans. Now, life in Paris had become dangerous. Renée, Denise, and Lilly were sent to live with the nuns. At first the experiences were strange to them. They went to their first church service at a Sunday Mass. They learned the catechism, in case they were questioned by the authorities. How could they think of God the Father being at the same time Jesus and the Holy Ghost? Slowly they became used to a new way of living, and eventually they were told they were to be baptized. After the Normany invasion and months of bombings, the sisters came home to their parents, to the same apartment. Renée wondered if she would ever be able to reconcile the two worlds. It would not be possible to return to yesterday, for it was already tomorrow.

Readers really feel the problems the sisters faced while trying to live in two worlds and face the hardships of war. During the war many Jewish children were sheltered by Christians and were therefore forced to reconcile their lives after the war. Readers will learn to understand the trauma these children and their families faced. Many were not able to return to their families, and others faced painful conflicts and adjustments at the war's end.

570 Schloredt, Valerie. ***West Germany: The Land and Its People.*** Illus. with photos. SERIES: Countries. Silver Burdett 1988, LB $14.96 (0-382-09471-9). 45pp. Nonfiction.

Those who use this book should carefully read the captions with each illustration, for much information is crowded into those spaces. Each double-page spread covers a single topic. A lot of the text is on the history of a city and the country. Other topics are social problems such as drug abuse, a high unemployment rate, and immigrant populations. Another section is on the effects of changing demographics in West Berlin, where there is a high percentage of aging people. Events and ideas change quickly. When this was written, the author stated that many Germans hoped there would be one Germany. While this has come to pass, it has radically altered the picture presented here. The book has a reference page of facts, tables, and charts; physical and political maps; and an index. There are many countries covered in this series, including France, the Netherlands, and Belgium and Luxembourg. Users should be warned that the latter two have not been revised recently.

571 Schrepfer, Margaret. ***Switzerland: The Summit of Europe.*** Illus. with photos. SERIES: Discovering Our Heritage. Dillon 1989, LB $14.95 (0-87518-405-7). 142pp. Nonfiction.

This series volume focuses on the historical, geological, and social influences on the Swiss people today. Featured are the variety of Switzerland's land formations, the four main ethnic groups, and the population, which has come from poor countries to work in this country. The chapter on folklore has stories suitable for telling, and a section on foods with two easy recipes to prepare adds a human touch to the otherwise practical, factual information. Students planning to write for information will be helped by the list of the Swiss consulates in the United States. The four-page glossary contains definitions of specialized words used in the text. Some of the other books in this series are on France, Germany, and Sweden. Books in this series were published in several different years, so dates should be checked.

572 Vinke, Hermann. ***The Short Life of Sophie Scholl.*** Trans. from German by Hedwig Pachter. Illus. with photos. HarperCollins 1984, LB $12.89 (0-06-026303-2). 216pp. Nonfiction.

What role did Sophie Scholl's family play in fostering her independent spirit? What ideals and forces led her to action in a nonviolent resistance movement against the Nazi machine? Her brother, Hans, and some of his friends had founded the White Rose movement in Germany as an underground resistance against Hitler's forces. There are many thoughts as to the origin of the name White Rose, but the actual origin is lost in secrecy. Sophie joined the movement shortly after she learned about it. Members were aware that they were risking their lives, and, in the end, Sophie, Hans, and some others were discovered. Sophie and Hans were executed in February of 1943. Through a collage of articles, letters, documents, interviews, personal diaries, and photographs of Sophie and some of her drawings, the author relates the factors that shaped Sophie's life. Most of the material and the main interviews were obtained from one of Sophie's two surviving sisters, Inge Aicher-Scholl. The book ends with a highly political and philosophical interview with the poet Ilse Aichinger. The work has won several awards, including the Jane Addams Award given to children's books promoting peace. Most of all, this excellent biography raises important questions: What are the character traits that leave people powerless and captive of evil leaders? When and how should people resist? What are the forms of nonviolent resistance? How would they work today? All of these are issues for student discussions and debates.

GRADES 10–12

573 Durant, Stephen R., ed. ***East Germany: A Country Study.*** Illus. with photos. SERIES: Area Handbook. U.S. Govt. Printing Office 1988, HB $19.00 (0-16-001696-7). 433pp. Nonfiction.

Students looking for a material for a term paper will find a wealth of information in this thick U.S. government publication on East Germany. The volume is a fairly recent one, though changes have already dated it. It covers almost every aspect of the country's history and life. The chapter "Society and Its Environment" is especially good for background information on the German national character. The photographs, maps, charts, and tables are useful. There are added sections on the Council for Mutual Economic Assistance and the Warsaw Pact. The book should also help students to understand recent changes by providing thorough background information. This series covers over 100 countries, and the books have been published over a period of years. Dates should be checked carefully when reading and using the data. Includes bibliography and index.

574 Friedman, Ina R. ***The Other Victims: First-Person Stories of Non-Jews Persecuted by the Nazis.*** Houghton Mifflin 1990, HB $14.95 (0-395-50212-8). 214pp. Nonfiction.

Jews, Gypsies, blacks, and most Slavs had no place in Hitler's world order. Others, who wanted to be free to live their lives and not serve the master race, were also hunted. They would be eliminated; the mentally and physically handicapped were either sterilized or killed.

The Nazis created experiments to demonstrate, falsely, that Romani, or Gypsy, blood was different from normal blood, and the Gypsies, like the Jews, were exterminated. The book explores the history of prejudice against Gypsies, which existed long before Hitler came to power. Even now, the author points out, the West German government has not acknowledged the Gypsies' suffering.

Approximately 400 black and half-German children were sterilized. In the concentration camps each group had an identifying triangle: Gypsies had brown triangles; Jews wore a yellow Star of David; political prisoners wore red; green was for criminals; Jehovah's Witnesses wore purple; and homosexuals wore pink. In addition to the 6 million Jews, 5 million others also died.

Each chapter begins on an edict dealing with what happened to that particular segment of the population. In her Postscript the author states that the Holocaust was not accomplished by Hitler alone, that "ordinary" citizens helped make it happen, and that "each of us has the responsibility to safeguard the rights of others." This well-written and thorough account will make readers aware of those who suffered in addition to Jews. The scope of Hitler's racial theories is evident here, and by tracing the roots of prejudice against Gypsies, homosexuals, and others, the author forces readers to examine their own prejudices and assumptions. There are a list of other books of interest and an index.

575 Gies, Miep, and Alison Leslie Gold. *Anne Frank Remembered: The Story of the Woman Who Helped to Hide the Frank Family.* Illus. with photos. Simon & Schuster 1988, P $7.95 (0-671-66234-1). 252pp. Nonfiction.

This is a compassionate book about Holland during World War II. Miep Gies was born in Vienna, Austria, but has lived most of her life in the Netherlands. Otto Frank arrived in Amsterdam in 1937, from Frankfurt, Germany, and his family a short time after that. Miep worked for his company testing foods.

When the Germans conquered Holland and the anti-Jewish laws became severe, the Frank family went into hiding. The Dutch people helped keep over 20,000 people in hiding during the occupation. Someone betrayed the Frank family, and everyone was sent to a concentration camp. Miep Gies was the one who found Anne's diary. She did not read it until she could hand it over to Mr. Frank, who was the only member of the family to survive. Not 1 in 20 of the Jews deported from Holland returned, and those who did had lost everything they owned. Otto Frank moved in with Miep and her husband. Amsterdam had become too modern; no longer was it a friendly town.

Along with the story of the Frank family, the author tells of Holland's struggle during the war years. She states that she was not a heroine. The book was written as a story of "ordinary people during extraordinarily difficult times." She notes that it is imperative that all "ordinary people" ensure that these times do not happen again. Whether or not they read *Anne Frank: The Diary of a Young Girl*, young adults will be caught up in this account of a cruel episode in history.

576 Harris, Jonathan. *The Land and People of France.* Illus. with photos. SERIES: Portraits of the Nations. HarperCollins 1989, LB $14.89 (0-397-32321-2). 244pp. Nonfiction.

This is one of the first revised editions of a well-known series, Portraits of the Nations. It begins with a world map based on a projection developed by Arthur H. Robinson, which redefines the shapes and sizes of countries and continents. Eighty-one pages cover French history through 1988. The rest of the book focuses on pertinent areas of interest, from population groups and the economy to the arts and sciences. There is information on the Channel Tunnel. There is even a page on the EuroDisneyland near Paris, opening in 1991.

Alongside emphasis on the positive aspects of life in France, there are several pages on the country's problems, including expressions of anti-Semitism and other forms of prejudice. Students will find this different from most texts that ignore the human dimension in favor of just the facts. Yet there are facts, including a section of "Mini-Facts" for those who want a quick summary. The book includes a long list of suggestions for further study via print materials, films, and videocassettes, phonorecords, and audiocassettes.

577 Lander, Patricia Slade, and Claudette Charbonneau. *The Land and People of Finland.* Illus. with photos. SERIES: Portraits of the Nations. HarperCollins 1989, LB $14.89 (0-397-32358-1). 212pp. Nonfiction.

Like others in the series, this book is clear and well organized. Some of the black-and-white photographs should be clearer than they are, and a few could use explanations beyond the captions. For example, a picture on page 96 leads readers to wonder how the bobbins were processed and what was flying around. There is a lot of information about the Samis (Lapps) and their problems after the Chernobyl disaster, which contaminated the land and harmed the reindeer. How to use a sauna, how to learn some Finnish, and other specialized information are parts of the book that are set off in prominent boxes. There are an extensive bibliography, a list of related films, a discography, and an index. A large "Mini-Facts" section is useful for those who want information in a hurry.

578 Meltzer, Milton. *Rescue: The Story of How Gentiles Saved Jews in the Holocaust.* HarperCollins 1988, LB $12.89 (0-06-024210-8). 168pp. Nonfiction.

There were men, women, and children who risked their lives and the lives of their families to rescue Jews during the Holocaust. As few as these rescuers were, they must be remembered. Sources include autobiographical reports, biographies, memoirs, interviews, journals, diaries, periodicals, letters, and historical studies. After providing a general background of the era, the book offers other chapters that contain specific accounts of events. Sometimes churches and whole villages hid Jews. Each chapter concentrates on a country where people found ways to circumvent edicts. In Denmark almost the whole Christian population rescued all but a few of Denmark's Jewish people and sent them to Sweden by all types of boats. In Bulgaria the Christian authorities refused to cooperate with Nazi orders to hand over the Jews of that country. Thoughtful readers will be concerned with the issues involved in defending the rights of others. Why did only certain people care? What were the costs to them and to their families? Why did most people ignore what the Nazis were doing? How did ordinary citizens help to carry out the Nazi plans? In what ways have the courageous rescuers been honored, years after their heroic acts?

Each chapter has a map showing locations of countries and towns where people were assisted. There are an extensive bibliography, which lists additional sources, and an index.

579 Newth, Mette. *The Abduction.* Trans. from Norwegian by Tiina Nunnally and Steve Murray. Illus. by Polar Inuits. Farrar, Straus & Giroux 1989, HB $13.95 (0-374-30008-9). 248pp. Fiction.

From the mid 1600s to the mid 1700s, approximately 50 Greenlanders were abducted to Bergen, Norway, or Copenhagen, Denmark. Even though this novel takes place long ago, minorities in Europe have many times since been subjugated and treated cruelly, both physically and emotionally.

The Abduction is a graphic, realistic novel. It alternates between the stories of Osuqo, an Inuit girl, and Christine, a white child with a disability. Osuqo's father has been murdered. Osuqo and Poq, the young hunter she has fallen in love with, are kidnapped by European adventurers seeking them as specimens for medical experiments. During the voyage she is brutally raped by several men, who see her as nothing more than an animal. In Norway, Christine awaits her sailor father's return, but he has been killed on the voyage home. She and her mother are now servants of Master Mowinckel. Life is hard for them. Master Mowinckel makes her guard and care for the Inuit captives. It is Henrik, the master's son, who champions them, as do Christine and her mother. The book ends with Osuqo and Poq able to escape, and they set out to sea in a kayak with only a slim hope of returning alive to their native land.

This is a sad, dramatic story of distinct cultures and their problems, hardships, and changing lives. Osuqo and Poq are treated cruelly, and many aspects of their treatment parallel the Nazis' persecution of the Jews and others. Only a few people—including a mother and daughter victimized by poverty and societal prejudice against the disabled—are willing to risk their lives to help what they alone realize are other human beings.

The artwork is of vignettes drawn by Polar Inuits from Alaska, Canada, and Greenland between 1900 and 1925. The book opens and closes with Eskimo poetry.

Ozer, Steve. *The Netherlands.*
See entry 565, Grades 7–9.

580   Philpott, Don. *The Visitor's Guide to Iceland.* Illus. with photos. SERIES: Visitor's Guides. Hunter Publishing 1989, P $14.95 (1-55650-192-7). 252pp. Nonfiction.

Even though flights to Iceland are available from several U.S. airports, it still arouses thoughts of a remote and frozen place. This guidebook provides an in-depth description of the country's history, geography, cities, and remote areas. It is almost a step-by-step, mile-by-mile guide and will inspire the nonadventurous to traverse Iceland. Visitors may want to stay in the populated areas, which are remarkably warm and highly developed. There are warnings against exploring certain areas without a guide and against the dangers of driving away from main roads. All fishing equipment brought in from abroad must be sterilized; there is a reindeer driving school; and there are no snakes, frogs, or other reptiles on the island. The chapter on Greenland contains quite a bit of travel information. There are an important "Code for Visitors" and an index. This book will be enjoyed by someone needing information for a school report as well as by the traveler.

581   Reichel, Sabine. *What Did You Do in the War, Daddy? Growing Up German.* Illus. with photos. Hill & Wang 1989, HB $19.95 (0-8090-9685-4). 214pp. Nonfiction.

The author is heir to an unwanted legacy, the feeling of guilt. Born in Germany right after World War II, she asks if anyone can understand the experience of growing up among people with that gruesome past. She wrote this book in English to use this language as a protective wall; only in the United States is she able to risk writing the book. This is about a daughter's rebellion tinged with guilt and anger against the older generation, the generation she believes to be responsible for the greatest crime against humanity in modern history. Reichel pressed her father, a singer and entertainer, to reveal what he did in the war, and he told her he helped some in the resistance. But five out of ten people said they were in the resistance. How could the Third Reich have survived with so many working against it? How could so many innocent people have been murdered?

Later she interviewed her mother, and coming through that interview were mainly personal problems—years of marital trouble and her mother's struggle to build an independent life after the eventual collapse of the marriage. Still unsatisfied, Reichel kept talking to Germans who lived through the war as she sought encounters, information, and answers. In this honest, thought-provoking testimonial, Reichel is very direct in her emotions and demands. Young adults can gain a perspective of what it means to face guilt for the Holocaust even if those directly involved came from a previous generation.

Roberts, Elizabeth. *Europe 1992: The United States of Europe?*
See entry 567, Grades 7–9.

Rossel, Seymour. *The Holocaust: The Fire That Raged.*
See entry 568, Grades 7–9.

582 Sullam, Joanna. *Villages of France.* Illus. with photos by Charlie Waite. Rizzoli Intl. 1988, HB $27.50 (0-8478-0927-7). 160pp. Nonfiction.

Visions of France fill this oversize book. The information, descriptions, and numerous photographs prove that there is more to France than populous cities and grapevines. The villages are arranged alphabetically by name, with their department. The book explores the many changes since World War II. Small villages have been abandoned as people have sought the amenities offered by modern towns. Sophisticated newcomers have arrived in many villages, however. Mostly middle class, they have come for a *résidence secondaire*, a second home for retirement or recreation away from the hectic city life. In many cases, they have restored older houses to their former grandeur, and readers interested in architecture can view the results of the restoration process. Browsers and those dreaming of a small village of their own will enjoy wandering through this book.

Vinke, Hermann. *The Short Life of Sophie Scholl.*
See entry 572, Grades 7–9.

583 Watkins, Paul. *Night over Day over Night.* Knopf 1988, HB $17.95 (0-394-57047-2); Avon 1990, P $7.95 (0-380-70737-3). 294pp. Fiction.

This adult book is about war and life confused by love, friendship, sexuality, brutality, and conflict. Mature readers will find small bits of compassion amidst the horrors.

Shortly after his father is killed on the Russian front in 1944, young Sebastian Westland joins the S.S. This is his story and the story of how the men of the German army were trained to fight and to destroy. Along with the cruelty of combat there is the cruelty of relationships. The spirit of world war rages throughout the novel. In contrast to its madness are Sebastian's friendship with the disabled Benjamin and their escapades. Sebastian's last thoughts are devastating. This dramatic novel is a frightening story of war and of Hitler's power. A graphic, believable account of a vulnerable teenager's first experience with death and evil, it is best suited to mature young adult readers, who will be able to handle its subject matter and frank language.

10

SOUTHERN EUROPE

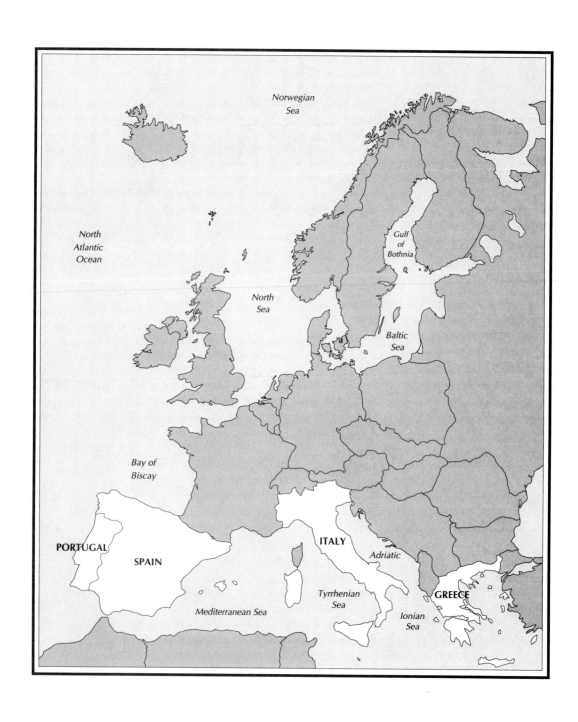

Norwegian
Sea

North
Atlantic
Ocean

Gulf
of
Bothnia

North
Sea

Baltic
Sea

Bay of
Biscay

PORTUGAL

SPAIN

ITALY

Adriatic

Tyrrhenian
Sea

GREECE

Mediterranean Sea

Ionian
Sea

10

SOUTHERN EUROPE

by Judy Fink

Recent publishing for children and young adults about Southern Europe (defined here as Greece, Italy, Portugal, and Spain) is dominated by series nonfiction. Translations with an ethnic flavor are few, as are individual nonfiction titles. Fiction makes use of recent events in history, particularly wars, and many of the books feature American or English characters. Overall, the available resources on the cultures of these four countries are limited, a situation that is surprising when we consider the number of Americans who trace their heritage to this part of the world. Portugal is particularly poorly represented. While they fall outside the scope of this bibliography, two series about immigrants, Lerner's "In America Books" and Chelsea House's "The Peoples of North America," will prove useful for those interested in the cultures more than the nations.

Parameters were established before beginning the compilation of this bibliography. A publication period of 20 years was set, although two books, *Wildcat Under Glass* by Alki Zei and *I, Juan de Pareja* by Elizabeth Borton de Trevino were published in the mid 1960s. Historically, this bibliography covers basically the period of the Spanish Civil War to the present, since repercussions of the events of the 1930s are still evident today in that part of Europe. Some books about the Spanish Inquisition—that "other" event of 1492—have been included, because they provide a counterpart to the celebration surrounding Columbus's voyage and give insight into the brutal methods that were soon to be used against the native peoples of the Americas. Even today, despots in Latin America have adopted tortures used first against Jews and other "infidels" during the Inquisition. Folklore has not been included because several excellent indexes, namely, Margaret Read MacDonald's *The Storyteller's Sourcebook* (Neal-Schuman, 1982) and *Index to Fairy Tales, 1978–1986, Fifth Supplement* by Norma Olin Ireland and Joseph W. Sprug (Scarecrow, 1989), have been compiled by folklorists.

Books included in this chapter had to do more than simply state that the setting was in Southern Europe; they had to relate something about life there. Likewise, translated books without geographic specificity in their stories, such as those by Bruno Munari and Mario Mariotti, have also been omitted. Unfortunately, this leaves the number of translated books at a handful. Many of the available nonfiction series that serve as a general reference to a country have been included. In only one case—Childrens Press's Enchantment of the World series—has more than one book from a particular series been included; there was a great difference in tone and photographic quality between the two authors chosen, who each wrote two books on this area of Europe.

War is a prominent theme in both fiction and nonfiction books about this area of Europe. Alki Zei, Billi Rosen, and Nicholas Gage all wrote moving portrayals of life in Greece during times of war, times when neighbors turned against neighbors and children became involved in the daily survival of their family. Edward Fenton, translator of both of Alki Zei's books, wrote about life in Greece during the period that preceded its achievement of democracy in 1974. The Spanish Civil War has been written about numerous times, but not as effectively for both children and young adults as it has been in the two nonfiction books included here—William Loren Katz's and Marc Crawford's *The Lincoln Brigade: A Picture History* and Don Lawson's *The Abraham Lincoln Brigade: Americans Fighting Fascism in the Spanish Civil War*. Repercussions of earlier conflicts can be felt in Jason and Ettagale Laure's *Jovem Portugal: After the Revolution* and Eva-Lis Wuorio's *Detour to Danger*.

Several novels feature contemporary life in these countries, with the stories often about Americans traveling or temporarily living there. The emphasis seems to be on the exotic aspects of the Mediterranean region. *Lily and the Lost Boy* by Paula Fox, the story of an American family living in Greece, is by far the most informative of these books. Two other books—one nonfiction, one fiction —use dilemmas over career choices to give elementary-age youngsters a sense of the country's culture. Allen Say's *El Chino* is a true account of a rather unusual Chinese-American engineer who gave up his career to become a bullfighter in Spain. Ingeborg Lippmann's *A Fisherboy of Portugal* presents the author's own photographs of Portuguese youngsters to illustrate the fictional tale of a boy who does not want to follow in his father's footsteps and become a fisherman. There are very few picture books, but those available effectively portray Southern European cultures. *Barmi: A Mediterranean City Through the Ages* by Xavier Hernandez and Pilar Comes as well as Robert Moore's *Living in Venice* use highly detailed illustrations to tell about those cities.

The nonfiction series books provide a cursory view of the countries, each telling in text and photographs something about a country's geographic makeup, history, government, and elements of ordinary life. Whereas most of the series devote only two pages to any subject, they do provide enough name recognition that readers will come away with the names of people, places, and events to look for more detailed information about. The longer books—those from Childrens Press, Dillon, and Chelsea House—include more detailed information but still are unable to provide more than a framework for further investigation. Several series—Gareth Stevens's Children of the World, Franklin Watts's Living Here, and Lerner's A Family in . . .— present the countries by focusing on individuals through interviews and detailed visits to homes. The books included are all fairly current, having been published no earlier than the mid 1980s.

The annotations for the two books about the Abraham Lincoln Brigade were written by my co-worker Deborah J. Langerman.

584 Calders, Pere. ***Brush.*** Trans. by Marguerite Feitlowitz. Illus. by Carme Sole Vendrell. Kane/Miller 1986, HB $10.95 (0-916291-05-7). 24pp. Fiction.

It was the last straw when Turco the dog ate Señor Sala's hat; he would have to go. The gardener's daughter would keep Turco at her house, and the Salas were free from trouble. But poor Little Sala was heartbroken, for he needed a pet to love. At last he found a suitable substitute: Up in the attic was a huge brush that had been banished from the broom closet. If he closed his eyes and ran his hand over the bristles, Sala could truly believe he was petting a real dog. At bedtime Sala noticed a strange thing: Brush was warm and was snuggling up to him. Turning on the light, Sala found that Brush was moving around like a real dog! The next day he tried to tell his parents but they just laughed. That is, until Brush alerted Sala and his parents to the burglar in the house. Saving the day, Brush is finally accepted as a worthy pet, just as Little Sala knew all along.

Wide-eyed expressive faces peer out from the pages of *Brush*. The book contains watercolor illustrations that depict life in a financially well-off Spanish family. Little Sala's reactions to the banishment of his dog, the finding of Brush, and the discovery of life in Brush are universal and well portrayed. Dayal Kaur Khalsa is another author who also wrote about the desire for a dog and the use of a substitute in *I Want a Dog* (Crown, 1987). Children will enjoy seeing Brush in action and may even seek one out at home for their own.

585 Delton, Judy. ***My Uncle Nikos.*** Illus. by Marc Simont. HarperCollins 1983, LB $10.89 (0-690-04165-9). 32pp. Fiction.

Every other Friday afternoon in the summer, Helena takes the bus from Athens to her uncle's small village. There is much work to be done for her uncle. Shopping for dinner requires stops at the baker, the butcher, and the grocer. With a raisin bun to hold them until they return home, Helena and Uncle Nikos take a taxi to her uncle's tiny house. Helena sets the table, noting that the house is so small that the beds are in the kitchen, or else the kitchen table is in the bedroom. After dinner, the two check on the garden. At the end of this long day, Helena brushes her teeth at the outdoor pump and climbs into a feathery-soft bed, to rest up for work in the garden the next day.

A wonderful celebration of family and simple life, *My Uncle Nikos* presents life in a small village where many homes do not have the conveniences we are accustomed to. Uncle Nikos has no running water or electricity but gets along well without them. Many villagers use a taxi or walk; they don't have cars. Marc Simont's bright watercolor illustrations reflect the joy and pride conveyed by the text.

586 DePaola, Tomie. ***Tony's Bread: An Italian Folktale.*** Illus. by the author. Putnam 1989, LB $13.95 (0-399-21693-6). 32pp. Fiction.

Tony, a bread baker, has the opportunity to realize his dream of owning a bakery in Milan and becoming the most famous baker in northern Italy when a nobleman from Milan passes through his small village and falls in love with his daughter, Serafina. After a visit to Milan, however, Tony feels that he cannot compete with the bakeries there. Angelo, the nobleman, and Serafina suggest things to add to his already wonderful bread to make it the best anyone has ever had. The result: the rich, fruit-filled, *panettone*, or "pan di Tonio," Tony's bread.

DePaola offers a simplified and modified version of the creation of *panettone*, a traditional Christmas sweet. In an introductory note, he conjures up a vision of Milan, including a café that exports the bread to the United States. DePaola's usual rosy-cheeked, round-bodied characters fill the pages. He has styled the three black-clad *zie* (aunties), the eyes and ears of the village, as they may very well be in real life.

587   Haskins, Jim. ***Count Your Way Through Italy.*** Illus. by Beth Wright. SERIES: Count Your Way Books. Lerner/Carolrhoda 1990, LB $11.95 (0-87614-406-7). 24pp. Nonfiction.

Elements of Italian culture and history are presented in the text and brightly colored illustrations of this counting book. The numbers one to ten have been matched with the appropriate number of the point being made. For example, for *tre* (three), Columbus's three ships are featured. Some of the associations seem a stretch, but this is an effective and nonthreatening approach to teaching language and culture.

Hubley, Penny, and John Hubley. ***A Family in Italy.***
See entry 596, Grades 4–6.

588   Kraus, Robert. ***The Gondolier of Venice.*** Illus. by Robert Byrd. Dutton 1976. 32pp. Fiction. o.p.

Gregory, a mouse, loves Venice and loves to show it off to visitors. He takes them to such places as the Basilica of Saint Mark, the Doge's Palace, and the Clock Tower, all by way of gondola. Gregory knows all the facts about his beloved city, including the sad fact that it is slowly sinking into the sea. After fruitless consultations with the other gondoliers and even the wise Signore Fellini, Gregory comes up with the idea of keeping Venice afloat by stuffing corks, soap, and other floatables under all the buildings. However, this does not help the situation and the plan is abandoned, but Gregory goes on loving his city despite its problem.

Detailed pen-and-ink drawings present the sights of Venice. Children will enjoy looking at the buildings, particularly when they are floating on the canal and have to be lassoed in place. This story offers the possibility for investigation of the reasons why Venice is sinking and what is being done in actuality.

589   Lye, Keith. ***Take a Trip to Portugal.*** Illus. with photos. SERIES: Take a Trip. Franklin Watts 1986, LB $10.90 (0-531-10196-7). 32pp. Nonfiction.

Young students will find the basic information they need for reports in the Take a Trip series. Each volume covers the history, geography, education, government, economy, and recreation of the particular country. A one-page layout of the country's money and stamps is also a standard feature. The typeface is large and bold and averages three inches of text per page (approximately three sentences); the remainder of the page contains a photograph.

"Quick facts" pages and indexes add to the usefulness of the series. Many facts are simplified to the point of generalization, and the reasons and actions behind many events are avoided.

590   Orstadius, Brita. *The Dolphin Journey.* Trans. by Eric Bibb. Illus. by Lennart Didoff. R & S Books; dist. by Farrar, Straus & Giroux 1989, HB $12.95 (91-29-59138-4). 29pp. Fiction.

Pia and Ianni travel with their families from Sweden to an island of Greece to visit Ianni's relatives. The airplane ride is exciting, especially when the plane approaches Greece. Pia is struck by the beauty of the colors of things she sees—the white houses, the green fields, and the blue, blue sea. Everyone welcomes them to the island and to Greece upon their arrival. The visitors settle in, and Pia, Ianni, and Ianni's older brother Niko go off to the beach, where they play in the sand and water. Over the course of a few days, a dolphin saves Niko, and he in turn saves the dolphin when it becomes beached. Villagers say this is the fulfillment of two legends, those of a dolphin helping a boy and a boy helping a dolphin. A celebration is held on the beach after these two events.

Large and vibrant cut and torn paper collage illustrations fill the pages of this story. The text reads choppily, however, with many short sentences. The story seems far-fetched; perhaps the retelling of the legend of Arion and the dolphin would be better served on its own instead of being set within the context of a contemporary family vacation.

GRADES 4-6

Cross, Esther, and Wilbur Cross. *Portugal.*
See entry 603, Grades 7-9.

De Skalon, Ana, and Christa Stadtler. *We Live in Portugal.*
See entry 604, Grades 7-9.

591   Fox, Paula. *Lily and the Lost Boy.* Orchard 1987, LB $12.99 (0-531-08320-9). 149pp. Fiction.

Everything had been going well until they met Jack. The Corey family was spending a few months on the island of Thasos while Mr. Corey finished writing a book. Contact with other Americans was minimal, and 11-year-old Lily and her brother, 13-year-old Paul, had grown close, closer than they had ever had a chance to be back home. Then Jack came along and spoiled everything, Lily thought. He was independent and defiant, and he took Paul away. His father was a dancer and left Jack to himself; that was all he would tell them. Even when a tragic accident occurred, resulting in the death of a Greek child, Jack remained distant. That was when Lily discovered that Jack was lost, emotionally if not physically, and that no one could help him because he would not let anyone do so.

A detailed, intimate look at Greek village life and an American family's successful adaptation to it surrounds this well-written story about throwaway children. Described in detail are the tasks the Coreys learn to do, such as shopping daily for their meals, using the kitchen sink for all washing, and baking in a communal oven. Their Greek neighbors are largely fishermen and shopkeepers, living the way their families had for generations and adopting little of modernity's ways. When an exhibit of German appliances is placed in a store, people flock to see it. Mr. Corey and another non-Greek temporary resident reflect on the interest shown by the Greek residents, knowing that few of their homes have adequate electrical capacity for these items. They also know these will soon be modernized.

592   Griffiths, Helen. *The Last Summer: Spain 1936.* Illus. by Victor Ambrus. Holiday House 1979, HB $7.95 (0-8234-0361-0). 160pp. Fiction.

The summer of 1936 was to be Spain's last summer of freedom for over 40 years. Eduardo was to spend part of it studying for his exams, under the watchful eye of his father while at his father's country estate outside Madrid. Between study sessions, Eduardo becomes acquainted with grounds keeper Baltasar and the old mare Gaviota. It is through Baltasar that Eduardo learns about his Aunt Angeles and her career as a horseback-riding bullfighter. Gaviota had been her horse and is well cared for in her mistress's memory. It is Gaviota who helps keep Eduardo alive when war breaks out and his father and Baltasar are killed. Weeks pass as Eduardo rides to safety with his mother in Galicia. Along the way, he is sometimes helped and sometimes hindered by many people, all of whom take an interest in Gaviota. Eduardo finally arrives in Galicia, but he has to leave Gaviota behind.

Gaviota's indestructible spirit makes this an intriguing horse story. It also portrays well the brutality of the Spanish Civil War. Unfortunately Eduardo and his family are flat characters and seem stereotypical of the wealthy with their self-centered attitudes. Eduardo's fierce attachment to Gaviota rises above this, which makes the story an exciting work of historical fiction. A one-page appendix briefly explains the events of the summer of 1936.

593   Hernandez, Xavier, and Pilar Comes. *Barmi: A Mediterranean City Through the Ages.* Trans. by Kathleen Leverich. Illus. by Jordi Ballonga. Houghton Mifflin 1990, HB $14.95 (0-395-54227-8). 59pp. Nonfiction.

While no city called Barmi has ever existed outside the pages of this book, numerous cities in the Mediterranean coastal zone share its history. The introduction explains that Barmi is a composite of the cities of this region, and the rest of the book traces the patterns of physical, economic, and political development common to Mediterranean cities founded in pre-Roman times. Each of the 14 sections presents Barmi at a particular period in its evolution. A double-page spread, similar to those done by Mitsumasa Anno, offers a panoramic view of the city and the surrounding area. The following two pages present an overview of life in the city, using text and illustrations and citing architectural, economic, and political events and developments. Aspects of the city receive further explanation through numbered and annotated maps and detailed drawings of individual buildings.

The intricate illustrations, done entirely in pen and ink, fill the pages, making them somewhat overwhelming. The History of Everyday Things series, by Giovanni Caselli and published by Peter Bedrick Books, uses a similar but full-color format.

Since Barmi is a prototype city, it will take some adult explanation for younger readers to understand that the fictional aspect does not make the information less valid; older students should be able to internalize this.

594 Hirokawa, Ryuichi. *Greece.* Illus. with photos by the author. SERIES: Children of the World. Gareth Stevens 1988, LB $12.45 (1-55532-269-7). 64pp. Nonfiction.

The Children of the World series seeks to show what it is like to be a child growing up in different countries of the world by focusing on an individual child and following his or her daily life in text and pictures. Ten-year-old Katerina lives on Mykonos with her parents and brother. Home life, school, special events, and activities are all portrayed. Katerina's parents own a toy store and operate a ferrying business for tourists, thus offering the reader a view of life in a family not engaged in the more traditional Greek forms of employment. Italy and Spain are other countries in the region covered in this series.

595 Hollinger, Peggy. *Greece.* Illus. by Malcolm Walker with photos by Jimmy Holmes. SERIES: Countries of the World. Franklin Watts 1990, LB $12.40 (0-531-18305-X). 48pp. Nonfiction.

A brief survey of basic facts about Greece, the title emphasizes the Greek people and the various aspects of their lives, such as education, religion, leisure, and family life. Boldface type is used to indicate words that appear in the glossary, and small boxes contain chronologies, statistics, and quick facts. Large, clear photographs capture life in Greece's cities and villages.

596 Hubley, Penny, and John Hubley. *A Family in Italy.* Illus. with photos. SERIES: Families the World Over. Lerner 1987, LB $8.95 (0-8225-1673-X). 32pp. Nonfiction.

Like Gareth Stevens's Children of the World series but less extensive, the Families the World Over series seeks to answer the question "What is it like to live in . . . ?" In *A Family in Italy*, the focus is on an 8-year-old girl and her parents, looking at their daily activities and special occasions. More general facts are woven into the description of their lives. Up-to-date color photographs help to make the book, and this family, come alive.

597 Lippmann, Ingeborg. *A Fisherboy of Portugal.* Illus. with photos by the author. Julian Messner 1971. 63pp. Fiction. o.p.

Thirteen-year-old Joaquim goes to the Fisherman's School, where he learns the skills necessary to become a skilled sailor and navigator in addition to studying regular academic subjects. During his brief Christmas break, he has the opportunity to go fishing with his father. Senhor da Trindade is a fisherman and is often away from home. Joaquim has always assumed that he, too, will become a fisherman, but with everything he is learning at school, he is not sure. Maybe he would like to do something else, perhaps be a metalworker. His parents, too, begin to wonder if fishing is right for their son, who is small for his age. Since an apprenticeship had to be arranged soon, a decision had to be made. Joaquim hopes not to disappoint his parents with his idea, and they hope not to disappoint him with theirs. At Mardi Gras, when they discuss his future, everyone is pleasantly surprised.

Black-and-white photographs lend a documentary feeling to this story. It provides a good view of village life, the education system, and the early age at which career decisions are made and training arranged. The 1971 copyright and some minor elements of the story date the book, but do not invalidate it.

598 Roseman, Kenneth. ***The Cardinal's Snuffbox.*** Illus. by Bill Negron. Union of American Hebrew Congregations 1982, P $6.95 (0-8074-0059-9). 120pp. Fiction.

Roseman has synthesized the many ways that Jews of fifteenth-century Spain dealt with religious persecution by fashioning a choose-your-own adventure–style book. Choices have to be made by the reader as to whether to remain Jewish or to convert, as to whether to leave Spain or to remain, and about whom to trust. The title refers to an element in one of the successful paths. The "solution" can be found quickly, and there are many pathways to choose, both successful and tragic. Italicized words appear throughout and are defined in a glossary.

599 Say, Allen. ***El Chino.*** Illus. by the author. Houghton Mifflin 1990, LB $14.95 (0-395-52023-1). 32pp. Nonfiction.

Billy (Bong Way) Wong was born and raised in Arizona by Chinese immigrant parents. His parents emphasized to him and his siblings that they were free to try what they wanted to do in life; being Chinese was not to deter them. Billy dreamed of being a basketball star, but his high school basketball fame did not continue in college, for he was too short. So he became an engineer and after a time traveled to Europe on vacation. In Spain, Billy fell in love with bullfighting and made a decision: He would become a bullfighter. He enrolled in a bull-fighter's school, despite hearing that only Spaniards did this, and he did well. Yet no one would hire him for a fight because he was not Spanish. Billy decided to get a traditional Chinese costume, because he was indeed Chinese, and it was only then that he gained notice. Given a bullfight to perform at last, he earned his name and fame as El Chino.

Pride in one's heritage and belief in dreams come through in this true story of the first Chinese bullfighter. The process of becoming one is described succinctly but honestly, with the unfortunate deaths of some fighters mentioned, thus providing a balance to romantic notions about the sport.

600 Snyder, Zilpha Keatley. ***The Famous Stanley Kidnapping Case.*** Dell 1985, P $3.50 (0-440-42485-2). 212pp. Fiction.

The Stanley family, featured in *The Headless Cupid* (Atheneum, 1971), has taken up residence in Italy, outside Florence, for a year. After a few days in a cramped hotel, they find a house in the country. The family interacts very little with village residents during the summer, and as a result only Janie, a genius, learns the language well enough to conduct a conversation. In the fall, Janie attends the local school, but David and Amanda go to an English-language school in Florence. It is there that Amanda brags to classmates that her father is rich, news that leads to her and the other children's kidnapping. A number of attempts are made to escape, and at last they are freed, but not before Amanda's father, who is not rich, is contacted. He comes over from the United States and clears up the troubled relationship they have.

Stereotypes abound in this book: the precocious genius; the beautiful Italian girl; the Italian kidnapper mafiosi. The situations will appeal to middle graders, but they will get only a very small glimpse of Italy from this book. Readers will learn that it is possible to visit a country without speaking the language, although an attempt to learn it will make things easier.

Stein, R. Conrad. *Greece.*
See entry 613, Grades 7–9.

601   Tollhurst, Marilyn. *Spain.* Illus. by Borin van Loon and Ann Savage. SERIES: People and Places. Silver Burdett 1989, LB $14.98 (0-382-09821-8). Nonfiction.

Double-page spreads, illustrated with a mixture of photographs and colored pencil drawings, organize the facts into neat overviews of Spain's culture, history, and geography in this series title. Long captions for the illustrations are as helpful as the regular text. As a brief overview, there is little room for detailed description and analysis of events, leaving the reader with sketchy ideas about such things as the Inquisition and the Spanish Civil War. Regionalism, however, receives coverage in sufficient detail to indicate the problems and desire for autonomy of the Spanish people. Indexed. Other volumes in this series present Greece and Italy.

602   Trevino, Elizabeth Borton de. *I, Juan de Pareja.* Farrar, Straus & Giroux 1965, HB $12.95 (0-374-33531-1); 1987, P $3.50 (0-374-43525--1). 180pp. Fiction.

Juan de Pareja tells the story of his life as a slave, first of a merchant and then of Diego Velázquez, painter of the seventeenth-century Spanish court. Though his life was peaceful and free from cruelty, except for the period of time between these two owners, it is important never to forget that de Pareja was not a free man, and his life was at the mercy of his owner. In spite of his situation, he learned to read, write, and develop his talent, if secretly, as a painter. This internal story is surrounded by the tale of friendship and respect between de Pareja and Velázquez, the ultimate expression of which was de Pareja's freedom from enslavement.

In the afterword to this Newbery Medal book (1966), de Trevino explains some of the liberties she took in re-creating the lives of these two men, but she also notes that the respect and affection shown by Velázquez to his servant was very much real.

Woods, Geraldine. *Spain: A Shining New Democracy.*
See entry 614, Grades 7–9.

GRADES 7–9

603   Cross, Esther, and Wilbur Cross. *Portugal.* Illus. with photos. SERIES: Enchantment of the World. Childrens Pr. 1986, LB $23.93 (0-516-02778-6). 127pp. Nonfiction.

Featuring glossy, if not completely clear, photographs, this entry in the Enchantment of the World series, like the others, serves the research needs of students who need to know about the history, geography, and general aspects of life in Portugal. The parenthetical explanations of the contents of chapters, found in the table of contents, the minifacts pages, and the index, help to guide the reader in the use of this book, as do the subheadings within the chapters.

A book such as this does not have the space or intention to give detailed explanations of anything. Unfortunately, the result is the lack of evaluation of conflicts and changes in Portuguese society. The 1974 coup and the political turmoil that followed leave the reader unsure of the current situation (at the time the book was written). Changes in life-styles, as more women work and more people adopt the ways of the more developed Western nations, seem to be avoided. Greece, Italy, and Spain are also covered in this series.

604 De Skalon, Ana, and Christa Stadtler. *We Live in Portugal.* Illus. with photos. SERIES: Living Here. Franklin Watts 1987, LB $12.90 (0-531-18088-3). 60pp. Nonfiction.

In a departure from the usual expanded encyclopedia article format, the creators of the Living Here series present information about a country's economy, government, and culture through interviews with a cross section of the population. The result is a book with far more browsing potential than most nonfiction series books have. The interviewees in *We Live in Portugal* comment openly on the decreasing supply of fish in the waters off Portugal, which affects a large percentage of Portugal's population, who rely on the fishing industry for livelihood. Education, tourism, and the export value of products form the majority of the discussion topics. One quarter of the interviewees are women, and all except the student are employed. It is standard in this series to include in each volume only one youth. A fact page, glossary, and index conclude the book. Other volumes in this series focus on Greece and Italy.

605 Fenton, Edward. *Morning of the Gods.* Delacorte 1987. 184pp. Fiction. o.p.

After Carla's mother dies, her father decides to send her from the United States to Greece for the remainder of the school year and the summer, which he expects will help her to cope with the death. She is to stay with Greek relatives—the aunt and uncle who raised her mother after her mother's parents died. Aunt Tiggie and Uncle Theo live in a small village near Athens, and a tour reveals the simplicity of the life of its inhabitants. Things are not, however, as simple and peaceful as they appear; this is Greece in 1974 and the country is under the control of the Colonels, a military junta. Under suspicion are an exiled judge and Lefteris, a boy Carla's age, whose family fled the country but had to leave him behind. He and Carla form a guarded friendship, as they discuss the restrictions of life under the Colonels and the freedom of life in the United States. Carla gets an opportunity both to defy the restrictions by offering Lefteris some books and to take part in an act of defiance. She feels pride in her resistance and in her Greek heritage, but just as the country achieves democracy, she finds herself in the midst of a dramatic escape.

Fenton offers a contemporary story from the perspective of an American visiting a country under strict government rule. Carla takes chances by defying restrictions, something she learns that her mother and relatives have also done during long periods of dictatorship. While some of the plot elements work out far too smoothly and the characters are at times two-dimensional, readers may draw from this book some of the emotions felt not only in Greece during the rule of the Colonels but also today in the many nations of the world currently undergoing political change. It is to be hoped that the publisher will reprint the book in paperback.

606   Finkelstein, Norman H. *The Other 1492: Jewish Settlement in the New World.*
Illus. with photos. Scribner 1989, HB $12.95 (0-684-18913-5). 100pp. Nonfiction.

Two edicts were issued in the spring of 1492 by the rulers of Spain that have had profound effects on the history of the United States. One, the permission for Columbus to undertake a voyage to the Indies, is well-known. The other, the expulsion of the Jews, who had lived in Spain relatively peacefully and prosperously for several centuries, is a lesser-known enactment. Finkelstein begins with the expulsion edict and the reaction to it by the Jewish community, then provides a detailed survey of the Golden Age of the Jews in Spain, noting the assimilation into society not seen in many other places. The Inquisition, beginning in the late twelfth century, caused many Jews to convert, if only outwardly, to Catholicism. From this point on in the book, readers need to distinguish the difference between the Sephardim (Spanish Jews) and the New Christians, or Marranos (those who converted), and to read about the treatment of each group as two separate parts of Jewish history. The flight of Jews and New Christians to Portugal and to the Portuguese colonies of Brazil provided only temporary safety, and eventually Jews of Spanish descent arrived in New Amsterdam in 1654.

The information presented in *The Other 1492* is sound and generally clearly written, the only problem being the possible confusion between the treatment of Jews and the treatment of Marranos, mentioned above. One photograph, that of a prayer book that could be quickly concealed up a sleeve, is upside down. An extensive bibliography of books and articles will prove helpful to adults and older students. Indexed.

Fox, Paula. *Lily and the Lost Boy.*
See entry 591, Grades 4–6.

Hernandez, Xavier, and Pilar Comes. *Barmi: A Mediterranean City Through the Ages.*
See entry 593, Grades 4–6.

607   Katz, William Loren, and Marc Crawford. *The Lincoln Brigade: A Picture History.*
Illus. with photos. Atheneum 1989, HB $14.95 (0-689-31406-X). 84pp. Nonfiction.

This pictorial account of the 2,800 American volunteers who helped defend Spain's democratic government from fascist rebels in the Spanish Civil War from 1936 to 1939 is brought to life with striking, well-captioned never-before-published photographs on every page of its magazine layout format. The book is divided into three sections. The first part covers events leading up to the war and the economic conditions worldwide and in the United States that spurred volunteers from every country in the world to go to Spain. Detailed minibiographical sketches of many of the typical volunteers, including those of African-American heritage, render a humanity within their stories that is lacking in other accounts of the brigade.

The second part furnishes the reader with descriptions of all the major Spanish Civil War battles in which the Abraham Lincoln Brigade played a major role. This section of the book details not only the conditions of battle but also the military decisions that led to the eventual retreat and flight of the brigade from the war and eventually from Spain. Included are accounts of the efforts by Americans at home to support the brigade. The final part talks briefly about the problems that faced brigade members returning to a United States that remained suspicious of the idealistic young brigade members, who went to fight fascism before it was fashionable.

The authors traveled with the Lincolns in 1986 on their return to Spain to observe their fiftieth anniversary. They interviewed surviving Lincolns on old battlefields, and the accompanying photographs bring the Spanish Civil War home to the 1990s. Maps, an annotated bibliography, and an index are included.

D.J.L.

608 Laure, Jason, and Ettagale Laure. *Jovem Portugal: After the Revolution.* Illus. with photos by Jason Laure. Farrar, Straus & Giroux 1977, HB $13.95 (0-374-33934-1). 160pp. Nonfiction.

A bloodless coup on April 25, 1974, ended 50 years of dictatorship in Portugal. Not long after, that nation, once a world power during the age of exploration, lost its colonies in Africa, with the advent of the independence of Mozambique, Angola, and Portuguese Guinea. The newly democratic nation had much to promise its citizens, particularly its youth. Interviews were conducted with eight *jovem*, youth, ranging in age from 15 to 19. They are from diverse ethnic, economic, political, and geographic backgrounds. Each youngster speaks candidly about life and his or her hopes, reflecting on the new government and how the end of dictatorship opened up new opportunities and closed doors on others. The contrasts between the subjects' lives are striking. Seventeen-year-old Ines, who lives in a *barraca*, a shantytown, is the wage earner for her family. She is of Indian descent and dreams of being on her own, in a home she can invite friends to. Eighteen-year-old Luis is studying to be a priest and works with the mentally ill. Fifteen-year-old Henrique, whose family has lost much of its wealth with the independence of Angola, apparently still lives better than the majority of his countrymen, and his personal outlook and hopes seem least affected by the changes in Portugal.

Certain aspects of *Jovem Portugal* are dated, since the book was written just after the revolution, and the feelings expressed reflect the recency of that event. Other points are still valid. Life for teenagers is not so carefree as it is for their American counterparts. Living conditions, too, may not have improved for many. Black-and-white photographs capture everyday life and two other aspects of life at that time: political protests and militarism.

609 Lawson, Don. *The Abraham Lincoln Brigade: Americans Fighting Fascism in the Spanish Civil War.* Illus. with photos. HarperCollins 1989, LB $11.89 (0-690-04699-5). 160pp. Nonfiction.

The Abraham Lincoln Brigade is a meticulously researched history of the involvement of young volunteers from the United States who fought alongside other international volunteers in the Spanish Civil War from 1936 to 1939. The beginning of the book takes a brief look at the economic and political conditions of the Depression era in the United States, which helped to produce impassioned and idealistic antifascists. This is followed by a brief history of Spain, General Franco, and the rise of fascism under Hitler and Mussolini in other parts of Europe. The bulk of the account is a detailed description of the various battles fought by the Lincoln Brigade.

Interwoven with the battle descriptions are brief biographical sketches of key figures in the Spanish Civil War, such as General Franco and Dolores Ibarruri (La Passionaria) as well as leaders of the brigade itself, such as Robert and Marion Merriman. Considerable attention is also paid to the role of the International Communist Party (Comintern) in the development and organization of the International Brigades mobilized to fight with the Spanish Loyalists against the fascist Republicans. The book ends with a look at events following the Spanish Civil War, including the start of World War II, the unsympathetic reception given the returning Lincoln Brigade volunteers in the United States by a government that labeled them as "premature antifascists," and a glimpse of what Spain is like today under the constitutional monarchy of King Juan Carlos.

A map of Spain, photographs, an index, and a list of recommended readings make this book an excellent resource.   D.J.L.

Lippmann, Ingeborg. *A Fisherboy of Portugal.*
See entry 597, Grades 4–6.

610   Miller, Arthur. *Spain.* Illus. with photos. SERIES: Let's Visit Places and Peoples of the World. Chelsea House 1989, LB $13.95 (1-55546-795-4). 120pp. Nonfiction.

One of the most extensive and fact-filled general studies of a country can be found in the Let's Visit Places and Peoples of the World series. This is a revision of the Let's Visit books published in England by Burke Books from the 1960s to the 1980s. Unfortunately, *Books in Print* lists the old Burke ISBNs for some of the Chelsea House books on Greece, Italy, and Portugal.

The survey of Spain's history spans several chapters of this title, with a more detailed description of the Spanish Civil War and its political and economic aftermath than in any other survey book. The book's other chapters are devoted to the different regions of Spain and life therein, as well as the usual description of the government, the economy, and daily life. The photographs, mostly black and white with a center section of color photographs, are clear and illustrate many aspects of the country. The "facts at a glance" and "history at a glance" sections as well as the glossary and index facilitate use.

611   Moore, Robert. *Living in Venice.* SERIES: City Life. Silver Burdett 1986, LB $13.96 (0-382-09116-7). 45pp. Nonfiction.

Packaged in a deceivingly simple format, this slim volume is packed with details about the city of Venice—its history, the daily life of its inhabitants, and how it operates. A discussion of efforts to reverse or at least retard Venice's destruction form the final chapter, which includes diagrams of the proposed underwater barrier system.

Photographs capture Venetians at work and involved in recreational activities. There are so many of them that, combined with the small type and the double-column layout of the text, the book seems crowded. The subheadings within each chapter help to alleviate this feeling while reading.

612   Rosen, Billi. **Andi's War.** Dutton 1989, HB $13.95 (0-525-44473-4); Penguin/Puffin 1991, P $3.95 (0-14-034404-7). 136pp. Fiction.

War has not left Greece, even with the end of World War II. Hostility is still felt, not against foreign armies, but between countrymen. Andi does not understand it all, especially why her parents have left to join the partisans, or why the police chief's son calls her a communist. She does not even know what one is. Andi begins to learn, bit by bit, what one may safely say in public and to whom. Just as the adults take sides, so, too, do the schoolchildren, engaging in what would in any other circumstance be normal childhood pranks and fights, but in that time and place are much more. They are really battles between monarchists and partisans. And when real killing began to happen in the village, there is no denying Andi's involvement nor her feelings. In an epilogue, she tells of her family's fate. Her mother and brother have been killed, and Andi and her father have escaped to Sweden, where they will remain as refugees, waiting for the day when they can go home again.

Civil wars are known for splitting families and villages, with loyalties to political causes overruling blood. Andi tells a story, which may be autobiographical, of bravery, loyalty, and confusion amidst the need to live a normal life. This is a very personal story of how the civil war affected one family. It does not explain the war as one might expect from reading a history book, but it allows the reader to get involved and understand the pain of war and the loyalty to beliefs that is tested by such a war.

613   Stein, R. Conrad. **Greece.** Illus. with photos. SERIES: Enchantment of the World. Childrens Pr. 1987, LB $23.93 (0-516-02759-X). 127pp. Nonfiction.

As one of the volumes of the Enchantment of the World series, *Greece* follows the format of presenting the country in terms of its geography, history, economy, and culture. Stein is objective, commenting on the changes and problems that the late twentieth century poses for Greece. The terrorist activities that took place at the Athens airport in 1986 are mentioned, if briefly. Feminist challenges to traditional ways also receive coverage. The clear photographs illustrate the diverse sights a visitor might encounter. The "mini-facts at a glance" section provides much of the same information as an encyclopedia article, with the addition of some basic vocabulary, a time line, and a list of famous natives of the country. Indexed.

Trevino, Elizabeth Borton de. *I, Juan de Pareja.*
See entry 602, Grades 4–6.

614   Woods, Geraldine. **Spain: A Shining New Democracy.** Illus. with photos. SERIES: Discovering Our Heritage. Dillon 1987. 166pp. Nonfiction. o.p.

The different geographic regions of Spain are described in terms of their topology, economics, and history, with regional differences noted. Photographs are clear and varied. A general historical account marks the influences of the Romans and the Moors, the strength of Spain in exploration, and the long road to democracy. The arts receive more detailed description than in most series books, as do the education system and religious and secular celebrations. Unique, too, to series books are the inclusions of folktales, recipes, and the description of the life of people of Spanish descent living in the United States.

Appendixes provide both a guide to the pronunciation of Castilian Spanish and a list of the addresses of embassies and consulates in the United States and Canada. A glossary, bilbiography, and index conclude the book.

615   Wuorio, Eva-Lis. ***Detour to Danger.*** Delacorte 1981, HB $12.95 (0-385-28206-0); Dell 1987, P $2.95 (0-440-91732-8). 192pp. Fiction.

Fernando Herrera's Scottish Aunt Jane owns a villa in Andalusia, which her second sight tells her is in trouble. Nando grudgingly rearranges his trip home from his London school in order to go check on the house. Just as his aunt has suspected, something is amiss. But what, she could never have imagined: A group of neo-Nazis have taken over the villa next door and have spread into Aunt Jane's. Nando learns that a plan is under way to assassinate the king. He thwarts this attempt, but not before several people are hurt and killed.

While the premise of the story is exciting, its execution is so dependent on knowledge of the political situation in Spain in the late 1970s that the reader soon becomes confused trying to keep up with all the different political parties. In addition, the plot elements do not flow well; characters appear suddenly, and Nando, with the turn of a page, has a cast on his arm and leg. Still, the reader comes away with the knowledge that the stability of the government of Spain, or of other countries with a wide spectrum of political views, can be easily upset through terrorist activities.

616   Zei, Alki. ***Petros' War.*** Trans. from Greek by Edward Fenton. Dutton 1972. 236pp. Fiction. o.p.

Before Greece went to war with Italy, Petros was a carefree 10-year-old Athenian boy. Even after the war started, it all seemed so romantic, and it was expected that all the men who went off to fight, like Uncle Angelos, would come home heroes. But it was not to be. The Italians, and then the Germans, settled in Athens, and life changed for the worse. Petros was always hungry, for his father had lost his job, and food was scarce in the city even if there was some money. Petros's sister's friend got him involved with the resistance, painting messages on walls all over the city. When the war ends four years later, Petros has seen the horrors of starvation, death, and neighbors turning against neighbors. Unfortunately, the war's conclusion does not spell the end of such happenings, for a civil war will continue the fighting and despair.

The winner of the Mildred L. Batchelder Award in 1974, this novel, like Zei's first, *Wildcat Under Glass*, vividly relates both the overall situation and how it affects individuals. Readers share Petros's pain at seeing friends killed and his change in attitude about war as the war persists. His whole family becomes involved in the fight to exist: His mother bargains for food, his father transcribes and transports messages, his grandfather begs, and his sister, Antigone, begins to work for the resistance as well. It is interesting to note the reverential way in which Antigone is treated, in contrast to the way females were considered in the small village that Nicholas Gage describes in *Eleni*.

617   Zei, Alki. ***Wildcat Under Glass.*** Trans. from Greek by Edward Fenton. Holt 1968. 177pp. Fiction. o.p.

Family members find themselves with split loyalties when the fascists take control of Greece. Melia, Grandfather, the housekeeper, and Uncle Niko are all pro-democracy, whereas other family members pledge allegiance to the king and, subsequently, the fascists. This split causes secrets to be kept, especially about Niko, a freedom fighter wanted by the police. The stuffed wildcat kept in a glass case has always been a source of stories told by Niko, and it continues to be a way for him to communicate with Melia through notes left in its mouth.

Myrto, Melia's older sister, joins a fascist youth club at school and finds herself in a difficult situation when she is forced to spy on her family. Her accidental discovery of Niko's hiding place forces her to examine her affiliation with the club, but she makes a decision she can live with.

The rise of fascism in Europe during the 1930s forms the background for this story of family ties and individual beliefs. It provides insight into the different reasons why people aligned in the way they did: true belief, job security, admiration of a monarchy. The first half of the book reads a little slowly, but once the characters and setting have been established, the pace picks up, holding readers and asking them to think about what they would do in a similar situation. Winner of the 1970 Mildred L. Batchelder Award.

GRADES 10–12

618   Gage, Nicholas. ***Eleni.*** Random House 1983, HB $19.95 (0-394-52093-9); Ballantine 1985, P $5.95 (0-345-32494-3). 572pp. Nonfiction.

Nicholas Gage, a *New York Times* investigative reporter, used the skills he acquired during his years on the job to learn about his mother's murder on August 28, 1948, in a remote village in Greece during its civil war. Gage sought to learn the circumstances leading up to her death and who was responsible. He also wanted to know more about his mother and what she left for her children. This is a very moving, detailed account, not only of the effect of World War II and the Greek civil war on innocent people but also of their daily existence in times of war and peace. The reconstruction of the setting, the attitudes of people, their daily tasks, and their struggle to survive is remarkable (and unenviable). Gage occasionally steps into the story, but most of the writing is in the third person, even references to himself as a young boy.

As this was a male-dominated society, the men were often absent for long stretches of time while they traveled as peddlers. The women were left to take care of the farm and the children. Daughters were a liability, and Eleni had four before she had a son, a son her husband never met until the children went to the United States, where her husband had gone years before in search of better economic opportunities. It may be hard to reconcile the feeling that men abandoned their families and brought disgrace to them by having affairs with learning that it was the daughters of these men who were the ones blamed and shunned. *Eleni* is as much a study of a society as it is a dramatic account of a war.

A movie, available on videotape, was produced based on the book. Gage wrote about his new life in the United States after his mother's death in *A Place for Us* (Houghton Mifflin, 1989).

Katz, William Loren, and Marc Crawford. ***The Lincoln Brigade: A Picture History.***
See entry 607, Grades 7–9.

Laure, Jason, and Ettagale Laure. ***Jovem Portugal: After the Revolution.***
See entry 608, Grades 7–9.

Lawson, Don. ***The Abraham Lincoln Brigade: Americans Fighting Fascism in the Spanish Civil War.***
See entry 609, Grades 7–9.

Miller, Arthur. ***Spain.***
See entry 610, Grades 7–9.

Rosen, Billi. ***Andi's War.***
See entry 612, Grades 7–9.

619   Valencak, Hannelore. ***When Half-Gods Go.*** Trans. from German by Patricia Crampton. Morrow 1976, LB $12.88 (0-688-32077-5). 192pp. Fiction.

An archaeological expedition to Greece turns into a search for love and respect when Andreas and Barbara visit Greece together. Their relationship, never open or very solid, seems at its end when they argue in a museum and Barbara leaves. She soon meets Alexander, a Greek, who kindly offers her a ride and the sightseeing she craves. He gives Barbara what Andreas does not—respect and praise for her individuality and interests. Andreas, however, is not left behind; he joins Alexander and Barbara, and the threesome remain together, but always with Barbara just out of Andreas's reach, until the end, when he comes to see her in a different light.

A sophisticated love story, the setting is more than just background. The natural and historic sights visited are described in detail, almost functioning as a travelogue. Mythology also plays a part in the book, although much of its use is through allusion, and it is left to the reader to explore the meaning. The reading of this book is fairly slow, as if Andreas's gloomy and jaded attitude about the natural beauty of Greece has put a dark cloud over the book. This may be a function of the translation, the time the book was written, or the amount of the story that is alluded to but not fully explained.

620   Wain, John. ***The Free Zone Starts Here.*** Delacorte 1984, HB $13.95 (0-385-29315-1). 196pp. Fiction.

Inspired by the true story of the crash of a chartered plane full of English schoolchildren, the story here centers on the mourning families who have traveled to Lisbon for a memorial service. Seventeen-year-old Paul writes letters in his mind to his sister, Clare, who was on that plane, explaining his feelings and the observations of the adults around him, particularly his parents. His mother is an alcoholic, and both parents are cold and uncommunicative. Also a part of his inner dialogue is his fantasy world, the World Free Zone. Paul has been looking for acceptable adult role models for this utopia but has found none up to this point. With the advent of this trip, he comes to understand the impossibility of his ideals, and he gains some hope and insight into the existing world.

The Portuguese setting has very little to do with this coming-of-age story. The focus is, more than anything else, on Paul's inner conflicts and his dysfunctional family, which has been thrown into crisis by Clare's untimely death in a foreign land.

11

EASTERN EUROPE AND THE SOVIET UNION

Eastern Europe

Soviet Union and Republics

11

EASTERN EUROPE
AND THE SOVIET UNION

by Christine Behrmann

As the end of the twentieth century approaches, there can be only one word for an attempt to produce a bibliography of children's literature about Eastern European countries and the Soviet Union. That word is "frustrating."

The problem is not the lack of materials, but rather that, within the next few years, there will be so much more to reveal about the lives and surroundings of the children behind the now-disintegrating Iron Curtain. Especially to be antici-pated are the picture books and novels from writers whose talents have had little exposure even in their own country, much less abroad. As of 1990, we have had barely a taste, in the works of the Russians Baklanov, Likhonav, and Zheleznikov. We have heard little from other Eastern European countries, ex-cept for works produced by expatriates, and virtually nothing from the various republics within the Soviet Union itself.

Political divisions present another fascinating frustration. As of this writing, Eastern Europe is defined as Albania, Bulgaria, Czechoslovakia, Hungary, Po-land, and Romania. The Soviet Union is defined as one entity—but how long will that hold? Will perhaps the next writing, instead of literature from the Soviet Union, be literature from Russia, the Ukraine, Armenia, Estonia, Latvia, Lithua-nia, and so on? Certainly a thorough search of children's literature produced in the Soviet Union currently mandates a search under these areas as well. Will the world order soon follow the lead of the Library of Congress?

The greatest frustration, of course, lies in the relevance of the nonfiction. With each passing month, titles grow more and more outdated. Certainly events beginning with the autumn of 1989 rendered most previous history and geogra-phy titles virtually obsolete, especially those produced as part of the more ephemeral series. Now, no nonfiction title completely represents the political situation of the Eastern European countries and the Soviet Union, and, as the situation remains fluid, it is difficult to say when an accurate, up-to-date publica-tion about this area will be published.

What, then, is available from this geographical area? For fiction, there is little from Eastern Europe, except for the work of two Czechoslovakian writers living abroad when their works were produced. Iva Prochazkova was living in Ger-many when she wrote (in German) *The Season of Secret Wishes*, a moving story

353

about a young girl coming of age in a society that persecutes her artist father, mirroring events in her own life. Vit Horejs makes his home in the United States but tries to keep the traditions of Czechoslovakian folklore alive in his collection *Twelve Iron Sandals*, as well as his original stories about two characters from Czechoslovakian folklore, *Pig and Bear*. One Czechoslovakian writer who has continued to be published within his country is Milos Macourek, whose entertaining fantasy for younger children, *Max and Sally and the Phenomenal Phone*, was recently translated and brought to this country by the small American publisher Wellington Publishing Company. One other title from this area has been included, though it is not widely available. In 1972, *Fairy Tales & Legends from Romania* was produced in a cooperative effort between a Romanian and a British publisher and is now listed as being available from Irvington, an American publisher. This publication makes available a folkloric tradition, representing the ideals that the Romanian people identify as theirs, and as such it is an interesting voice in children's publishing history. It is perhaps significant that, with the exception of Prochazkova's book, written and published outside of its setting, realistic stories about children from Eastern European countries have not been seen.

English-language juvenile novels set in Eastern Europe do have realistic plots, but they are historical and they use, without exception, the Jewish experience in World War II. As such, they can be divided into two types—books based on the voice of actual experience, which contain a powerful resonance, and well-intentioned books based on research and a strong moral imperative, which ultimately fail. Into the first category, we may put Chester Aaron's *Gideon*, in which the author used interviews with Holocaust survivors and his own experiences as a liberator of concentration camps to give his story a concrete veracity, and the moving *Island on Bird Street* by Uri Orlev, which is based on his war experiences. Into the second category, we must regretfully put Jane Yolen's *The Devil's Arithmetic* and Christina Laird's *Shadow of the Wall*. While both books seek to make the harshness of the Holocaust real to the young reader, they descend too often into melodrama and poorly conceived characterization to tell their stories with a believable strength. Perhaps the Holocaust is too terrible ever to imagine effectively.

Fiction from the Soviet Union has begun to show tantalizing promise. In the early 1980s, Albert Likhonav's *Shadows Across the Sun* was published by Harper, which, as a publisher, has been a pathfinder in searching out authors of promise from the U.S.S.R. Likhonav's work and a more recent example, Vladimir Zheleznikov's *Scarecrow*, are unique in that they use the contemporary era as their settings. Both are well-done, sensitive treatments of young people facing serious situations. Likhonav writes of two teenagers who find love despite serious physical and emotional obstacles; Zheleznikov's story concerns the tyranny of peer pressure. Harper has also published works by Ephraim Sevela, originally written in Russian though he currently lives in the United States. The two juvenile novels he has had published here, *Why There Is No Heaven on Earth* and *We Were Not Like Other People*, have World War II as a setting. Both are thoughtful, passionate examinations of the struggle as it affected children. Another Harper publication is *Forever Nineteen*, by Grigory Baklanov. This story, for teenagers, is another World War II novel, powerfully written, which follows the experiences of a young soldier up to his final battle.

English-language fiction about the Soviet Union and its republics takes up World War II themes as well. In *Uncle Misha's Partisans*, Yuri Suhl presents one of the only books, fiction or nonfiction, about the Jewish partisan groups. Joan Lingard, in *Tug of War*, presents another rarely told story—this time about Latvian refugees. There are contemporary stories, but the two major examples, Neal Shusterman's *Dissidents* and Larry Bograd's *The Kolokol Papers*, remain, because of a pedestrian style and characterization, interesting curiosities rather than lasting contributions to the literature.

A sampling of the folklore published for an English-language audience permits a view of the Soviet republics. The dark story, *The Rumor of Pavel & Paali*, comes from the Ukrainian tradition, while the ironically amusing *A Drop of Honey* comes from Armenia. *The Sea Wedding*, a lovely collection of stories from Estonia, gives the reader a glimpse of the cultural tradition that inspired these evocative tales from the Baltic Sea.

Two recent books, cooperatively published in the United States and the Soviet Union, represent promising steps toward a more worldwide spectrum of materials available to children. *Here Comes the Cat!* by the American Frank Asch and author-artist Vladimir Vagin from the Soviet Union is a bilingual picture book that, in addition to an entertaining story, presents a slyly amusing anti–Cold War message. *Face to Face*, edited by Anatoly Aleksin and Thomas Pettepice, is a collection of short stories and excerpts from novels by outstanding children's authors of the United States and the Soviet Union. Both books offer the reader a chance to dip into two cultures at the same time, suggesting interesting comparisons and contrasts in ideas, ways of life, and approaches to solving life situations, thus becoming paradigms of the goal of a multiethnic approach to children's literature.

Not found was nonfiction produced in Eastern Europe or the Soviet Union and published for children in the United States. Nonfiction about these countries originates in English and falls into these broad categories: (1) biographies and autobiographies concerning the Jewish experience in World War II, (2) trade books on history and biography, and (3) series books of widely varying quality concerning the history, geography, and biography of the area.

The titles that treat the Holocaust are a particularly powerful group of books. Two biographies of Hannah Senesh, *In Kindling Flame* by Linda Atkinson and *Hannah Szenes* by Maxine Schur, give the reader some background information about anti-Semitism in Hungary prior to World War II and provide moving stories about heroism. The same can be said of Mark Bernheim's *Father of the Orphans*, about the Polish author and pediatrician who founded a home for orphans and, in the Warsaw ghetto, accompanied his young charges when the Nazis rounded them up for the death camps. The strongest books, however, are the memoirs by Ruth Sender, Aranka Siegal, Rose Zar, and Sara Zyskind, all of whom survived Nazi persecution, but at a terrible cost, losing family, home, and friends. Their stories give vivid images not only of the German persecutors but also of the Polish and Hungarian neighbors who were a part of the persecution. These books confront the older child with enormous ethical questions.

There have been few individual trade books published on nonfiction topics in this area. Madelyn Klein Anderson's *Siberia* is an interesting if not transcendent survey of this region so significant in Russian history. The late Samantha Smith's *Journey to the Soviet Union*, written in the pre-Gorbachev era, has been reduced by current events to the status of oddly touching historical curiosity. The best of the recent trade nonfiction has to be *A Tree Still Stands*, by Yale Strom. The author, a filmmaker and photographer, spent 12 weeks touring Eastern

Europe in early 1989 and interviewing Jewish children, many of them grandchildren of Holocaust survivors. The result is a timely and unique picture of societies in transition, as well as a somber echo of the transforming disaster that was the Holocaust.

The largest and most varied category of nonfiction is that of series books. As trade books on history, geography, and related topics have gone out of print, these, mounted by several publishers, have moved into the void with varying degrees of success. The bulk of the publications are mediocre at best, containing little more information than that found in an encyclopedia article, limiting discussions of large and divergent societies to collections of generalizations. Among the series that treat countries in this geographical area are Watts's Inside and Passport series and Silver Burdett's Countries and People and Places. For the younger set, Childrens Press offers a New True Books title on the Soviet Union and Watts, the Take a Trip books, both of which do little more than introduce their subjects to younger beginning readers. The Watts Families Around the World series, which covers the Soviet Union, and the Lerner Families the World Over, which covers Hungary, discuss each country by focusing on daily family life. They are readable by primary graders, though their information is dating quickly. The Franklin Watts Living Here series contains titles on Poland and the Asian and European areas of the Soviet Union. Its approach, which is to present a series of interviews of residents from several parts of the society covered, is useful as a source of added information, though the series, as is often the case, is not revised often enough to be current.

For older primary school children, Lerner's Visual Geography series, which so far covers only the Soviet Union, is useful. These books offer much information in a frequently revised format that includes many photos, maps, and charts. The Discovering Our Heritage series from Dillon Press has only one relevant title, again on the Soviet Union, and has a utilitarian emphasis on culture and daily life rather than on history and geography. The Enchantment of the World series from Childrens Press offers attractive and expensive books on Hungary, Poland, Romania, and the U.S.S.R. with good minireference sections, but recent Eastern European events have dated the titles badly. Watts's First Books series has one book on Poland, which has been rendered obsolete by recent events. This is also the problem with the Time-Life Books Library of Nations series that contains an otherwise useful title on the Soviet Union.

Some specialized series comprise titles concerning events in the Soviet Union and Eastern Europe. Rourke's Flashpoints series, which concentrates on major events in post–World War II history, has a title on the Hungarian uprising. Watts's Turning Points in World War II series has one on the invasion of Poland. The World at War series from Childrens Press offers a title on the siege of Leningrad. Silver Burdett's Rivers of the World series has a title on the Volga and one on the Danube. Lerner's series of ethnic cookbooks offers *Cooking the Hungarian Way*, *Cooking the Polish Way*, and *Cooking the Russian Way*. Watts's series on Great Disasters contains the title *The Chernobyl Catastrophe*, and its Gloucester Press series, Hotspots, has a title, *Soviet Union: Will Perestroika Work?* which presents some useful background to the interested older reader. While none of these books contains distinguished writing, they are effective within the prescribed limits of the subject of the series in which they are included.

Among the plethora of series books, some stand out. Chelsea House's Let's Visit Places and Peoples of the World is revised often. Utilitarian in its approach to discussing basic information on history, geography, politics, and economy, its major virtue is extensive coverage of the Eastern European area. It sometimes contains the only books available on a specific region. Covered are Albania, Bulgaria, Czechoslovakia, Hungary, Poland, Romania, the Union of Soviet Socialist Republics, and the Soviet republics of Armenia, Estonia, Georgia, Latvia, Lithuania, Moldavia, Russia, the Ukraine, and Uzbekistan.

Two series on immigration are particularly useful to the young reader. Lerner's In America Books give the middle-grade student useful background information about the countries from which many American citizens came. Volumes in the series focus primarily on achievements and contributions of ethnic group members. Although most titles were produced in the 1970s and early 1980s, the information they contain has not dated. For older children, Chelsea House produces a very comprehensive series, The Peoples of North America. These books, which are introduced by Senator Daniel Patrick Moynihan, include information about the historical and sociological background of various ethnic groups immigrating to the United States and Canada, the immigration experience itself, and the influence each group has had on the history, economy, and culture of the United States and Canada. All volumes include a well-done interior photo-essay in color and an analysis of the current situation of the group under discussion. Though more sensitive to world events and therefore more likely to become dated than the Lerner series, most titles are nonetheless worthwhile purchases for library collections. Relevant titles include *The Armenian Americans*; *The Bulgarian Americans*; *The Carpatho-Rusyn Americans*; *The Czech Americans*; *The Hungarian Americans*; *The Jewish Americans*; *The Polish Americans*; *The Romanian Americans*; *The Russian Americans*; *The Slovak Americans*; and *The Ukrainian Americans*.

Another useful series from Chelsea House is *World Leaders, Past and Present*, which contains biographies of personages throughout history who have had influence on world events. Each book contains an introductory essay by historian Arthur M. Schlesinger, Jr., and goes on to give a basic chronological consideration of events in the subject's life, concluding with a chapter that analyzes the person's importance in world history. Written in prose that is clear but neither inspiring nor thought provoking, these often compose the only biographical information available on their subjects. Eastern European statesmen covered in this series are Leonid Brezhnev, Alexander Dubcek, Mikhail Gorbachev, Wojciech Jaruzelski, Nikita Khrushchev, Tomas Masaryk, and Lech Walesa.

Some series contain individual titles that are above average in their capability to fill gaps in information about the Soviet Union and Eastern Europe. Jim Haskins's Count Your Way series, published by Lerner, gives usable information about the language and culture of Russia in an entertaining format. The Franklin Watts Impact Biographies series features *Nikita Krushchev*, by Michael Kort, a timely life story of the late leader, which relates his accomplishments to the goals of Mikhail Gorbachev. Several series contain biographies about the current Soviet leader. The Chelsea House book is mentioned in the preceding paragraph. The People of Distinction series from Childrens Press has *Mikhail Gorbachev: A Leader for Soviet Change* by Walter Olesky, which is a solid, if dry, summation of the events and ideas informing Gorbachev's actions and is current through the beginning of 1989. Younger readers would find *The Picture Life of Mikhail Gorbachev* by Janet Caulkins useful. A recent (1989) revision of the title, originally published in 1986, indicates that the publisher has a commitment to keeping this title current.

Children's books have never been produced in a vacuum. They reflect the world in which they are written and published; they mirror the societies that inspire and inform them. As this world and these societies face unprecedented change, the children's books that begin to appear will inevitably be affected. As these effects begin to appear, the possibilities they convey move the observer beyond frustration toward exhilaration.

PRESCHOOL–GRADE 3

621 Bider, Djemma. *A Drop of Honey.* Illus. by Armen Kojoyian. Simon & Schuster 1989, HB $14.95 (0-671-66265-1). unp. Fiction.

This is a picture book version of an Armenian folktale about a young girl who falls asleep after quarreling with her brothers and dreams of the incremental calamity caused when a drop of honey falls in the marketplace: A bee lands on the honey; a cat chases the bee; a dog seizes the cat; and so on until chaos reigns. The girl wakes up to conclude that small quarrels should be stopped before they lead to big troubles. The retelling is undistinguished but highlighted by full-page, panoramic spreads done in pastel shades of green, mauve, and purple. A recipe for baklava is included. The book is a fair example of Armenian folklore.

622 Haskins, Jim. *Count Your Way Through Russia.* Illus. by Vera Mednikov. SERIES: Count Your Way Books. Lerner/Carolrhoda 1987, LB $10.95 (0-87614-303-6); 1988, P $4.95 (0-87614-488-1). 24pp. Nonfiction.

This title is a part of a series in which the numerals 1 to 10 in a language are each given a page on which they are named in the language and, here, the alphabet of the country in which the language is spoken. The number is then integrated into a paragraph illustrating cultural, geographical, or historical information about the nation under discussion. The final page is a pronunciation guide for each number named. The picture book format allows a basic, though scattered, introduction to the heritage of the people speaking the language illustrated.

The Soviet Union is the only Eastern European country covered in this series.

Herman, Erwin, and Agnes Herman. *The Yanov Torah.*
See entry 630, Grades 4–6.

Hoffmann, Peggy, and Selve Maas. *The Sea Wedding & Other Stories from Estonia.*
See entry 631, Grades 4–6.

623 Horejs, Vit. *Pig and Bear.* Illus. by Friso Henstra. Four Winds 1989, HB $11.95 (0-02-744421-X). 40pp. Fiction.

Folk characters introduced in Horejs's *Twelve Iron Sandals* are featured in a collection of four original stories.

Both Pig and Bear are lovably foolish, but Bear is big, gentle, and phlegmatic, while Pig is small, feisty, and full of energy. They are forever making plans that do not work out—opening a pawnshop when they are not even sure what one is, planning a trip to the movies but getting distracted by an argument, getting a telephone for urgent messages that they have to invent so they can use the telephone.

The stories are sweetly entertaining but not particularly distinguished. The book is interesting primarily as an extension of characters rooted in Czechoslovak tradition.

Horejs, Vit. *Twelve Iron Sandals: And Other Czechoslovak Tales.*
See entry 632, Grades 4–6.

624 Kismaric, Carole, ed. *The Rumor of Pavel & Paali: A Ukrainian Folktale.* Illus. by Charles Mikolaycak. HarperCollins 1988, LB $13.95 (0-06-023278-1). 32pp. Fiction.

Twin brothers, described as living on the Great Plain, have opposing views of life. Paali believes in goodness; Pavel is a cynic. They test their beliefs in a wager one day. The first three people they meet will determine who is right; the loser will give the winner everything he owns. When Pavel wins, he exacts payment from Paali, even to his eyes when Paali's family begins to go hungry. Paali wanders into the Great Forest and accidentally overhears the Evil Spirits discussing cures for various misfortunes, including his blindness, which they willfully withhold. He uses his knowledge for good, amasses a fortune, and returns. When Pavel hears the reason for his brother's good luck, he enters the forest, but the Evil Spirits, angered at being defeated, force him to join them.

Kismaric retells this dark fable with simple eloquence, matched by Mikolaycak's dramatic, tapestry-like full-page paintings, which echo the folk art of the story's origins. This is a picture book folktale of unusual power.

625 Lye, Keith. *Take a Trip to Hungary.* Illus. with photos. SERIES: Take a Trip. Franklin Watts 1986, LB $10.90 (0-531-10105-3). Nonfiction.

This is part of a series of titles that, on a simple level, introduce the primary-level reader to basic historical and geographical facts about the nations of the world. Given to generalities that can mislead, the books have well-reproduced color photos that give a flavor of the areas under discussion but do little more. Index. Will be dated unless revised.

Other Eastern European countries covered are Poland, Romania, and Russia.

626 Macourek, Milos. *Max and Sally and the Phenomenal Phone.* Trans. from Czech by Dagmar Herrmann. Illus. by Adolf Born. Wellington Publishing 1989, HB $16.95 (0-922984-00-X). 84pp. Fiction.

This is one of the first publications of a small publisher who is seeking to bring current Czechoslovakian children's literature to the United States. The effort has begun promisingly. This attractive, picture book volume contains beautifully illustrated stories about a magic telephone that takes a boy, a girl, and a dog on adventures during which the dog is turned into a boy; they enter the body of a friend to battle the germs causing his strep throat; and they learn the dangers of feeding zoo animals.

Macourek is a well-regarded author of children's books that often contain elements of satire. His *Curious Tales* (Oxford Univ. Pr., o.p.) contains 14 cautionary stories about defying adults and could have been read as a social/political commentary as well as a collection of entertaining children's stories. This one is in a lighter vein and full of farcical humor as the young protagonists enter into the most bizarre of situations with attitudes of bemused, plucky wonder.

Macourek is aided by Born's colorful illustrations that burst across each page in shades of orange, green, and blue. Macourek's lightly sophisticated humor is a delight to introduce to younger readers; it is to be hoped that they will be able to read more of him.

627   Marshak, Samuel. ***The Pup Grew Up!*** Trans. from Russian by Richard Pevear. Illus. by Vladimir Radunsky. Henry Holt 1989, HB $13.95 (0-8050-0952-3). 32pp. Fiction.

Marshak, a beloved figure in Soviet children's literature, first published this funny poem in 1926. Radunsky, a Moscow native who recently came to live in New York City, now illustrates it with mildly surrealistic images in crisply rendered shades of black, red, and brown against stark white space. The story is simple: a demanding female passenger arranges to have household goods shipped on a train for her vacation, among them a tiny Pekingese. When the little dog is left behind, the staff at the next station realizes that a dog is missing from the inventory and replaces it with a Great Dane. When the lady insists on an explanation, the only one she receives is "Maybe/During the trip/Your little pup/Grew up!"

Both an entertaining nonsensical story and a satire on bureaucracy, this is a welcome introduction for American children to an author little known in the United States.

628   Vagin, Vladimir, and Frank Asch. ***Here Comes the Cat!*** Bilingual ed. Illus. by Vladimir Vagin and Frank Asch. Scholastic 1989, HB $12.95 (0-590-41859-9). unp. Fiction.

A Russian writer and an American illustrator cooperate to produce a picture book with a warmly amusing message.

A mouse floats in a balloon, swims, runs, and rides a bicycle through a varied landscape, all the while warning, in Russian and English, "Here comes the cat!" The car arrives, introduced by an enormous, menacing shadow—harnessed to a cart full of cheese.

An anti–Cold War message is slyly conveyed in the story and illustrations, but the real charm lies in the entertaining pictures, which, for the discerning reader, hold many chances to learn new words in Russian (or English) in captions and ballooned dialogue. The result is a promising signal for more East-West cooperation.

GRADES 4–6

629   Caulkins, Janet. ***The Picture Life of Mikhail Gorbachev.*** Rev. ed. Illus. with photos. SERIES: Picture Life. Franklin Watts 1989, LB $11.90 (0-531-10694-2). 64pp. Nonfiction.

This second edition of a series biography, originally published in 1986, essentially uses the first few pages to update the same information contained in the previous edition. The book now includes Gorbachev's seminal speech at the

1988 party conference; the meetings between Gorbachev and Reagan in 1986, 1987, and 1988; and the Soviet withdrawal from Afghanistan. Retained are the sketchy facts of Gorbachev's early life and rise to power. The final sections of the book have been rewritten to reflect current happenings (through early 1989), and new photos and political cartoons have been added.

This remains a very simplistic introduction to Gorbachev and the country of which he is in charge, written in textbook style. However, the frequency of revision makes it useful. The book has a glossary, a brief chronology, and an index. A fair geopolitical map precedes the text.

630   Herman, Erwin, and Agnes Herman. ***The Yanov Torah.*** Illus. by Katherine J. Kahn. Kar-Ben Copies 1985, HB $10.95 (0-930494-45-8); P $5.95 (0-930494-46-6). 48pp. Fiction.

The publisher of materials relating to Jewish heritage presents a simple but moving tale of the survival of the spirit.

As he is preparing to leave the Soviet Union, in the pre-perestroika era, a doctor tells of his journey, with his father, to visit an old friend in the city of Lvov. The frail old man blesses the doctor, using a tattered Torah in the process, and then tells the story of its survival, albeit in pieces, in a Nazi work camp during the Holocaust. At the end of the war, the men who worked to save the Torah restore it and leave it to be passed down in turn to the oldest surviving member of their group that remains in Lvov. The old man, the last survivor, gives it to the narrator, who, after tense moments at the Czech border, is able to bring it to America, though he must pay all of his money to Soviet guards in the process. In the concluding chapter, coauthor Erwin Herman, a rabbi, describes his meeting with the doctor and the purchase of the Torah by members of his community. The purchase enables the doctor to study for an American medical licensing examination and is made with the understanding that the Torah, once returned to the doctor, will have its story told wherever the doctor travels.

Kahn's stark pen-and-ink illustrations highlight this brief tale that salutes spiritual as well as physical courage.

631   Hoffmann, Peggy, and Selve Maas. ***The Sea Wedding & Other Stories from Estonia.*** Illus. by Inese Jansons. Dillon Pr. 1978. 104pp. Fiction. o.p.

The authors, one of them a native Estonian, present a lively collection of stories from this Baltic area. There are 12 tales, including the title story, which is about a young fisherman who meets the Queen of the Sea. She sadly informs him she must leave the Baltic, where she has been living, because Estonia will soon be under attack from "fierce warriors." Other stories include a droll tale about "Six Hard-Boiled Eggs"; "Mushroom Gold," concerning a greedy woman who finds a treasure under a mushroom; and "Forest Mysteries," a cautionary tale about seeking useless knowledge.

The stories are informally told and accessible to any grade-school child; their settings, softly evoked images of forest and sea, give the reader a picture of the land that inspired them.

Horejs, Vit. ***Pig and Bear.***
See entry 623, Grades PS–3.

632 Horejs, Vit. *Twelve Iron Sandals: And Other Czechoslovak Tales.* Illus. by James J. Spanfeller. Prentice Hall 1985, HB $11.95 (0-13-934159-5). 128pp. Fiction.

Born and brought up in Czechoslovakia, Horejs, now a U.S. resident, retells seven folk- and fairy tales from his native land. Included are versions of the familiar "The Twelve Months" and "The Firebird" as well as the title story, about a beautiful princess who must undergo terrible trials to save her husband from bondage to a cruel witch. The other stories are "The Fisherman's Clever Daughter," about a poor girl who consistently outwits a king; "The Wheel-maker's Son," who wins the princess with a kind heart and much persistence; "Krakonos," about the last giant left in Bohemia; and "How the Pig and the Bear Went into Business," spotlighting two characters Horejs later featured in a book of their own.

Horejs's voice is brisk, his language unadorned, his retellings to the point, plunging the reader directly into the stories but retaining the flavor of their origins in the process. Ironic wit abounds, especially in the characters' dialogue. The narration has the feeling of true oral tradition in its descriptions and interjections. This collection is a good example of a culture seen through the tales it tells to its children.

Macourek, Milos. *Max and Sally and the Phenomenal Phone.*
See entry 626, Grades PS–3.

633 Oleksy, Walter. *Mikhail Gorbachev: A Leader for Soviet Change.* Illus. with photos. SERIES: People of Distinction. Childrens Pr. 1989, LB $10.98 (0-516-03265-8). 152pp. Nonfiction.

Here is a clear but somewhat dry account of the life of the noted Soviet leader whose changes in his society have had such an impact on the world order.

Oleksy offers a brief summation of Gorbachev's early years and rise to power, concentrating most of the book on a discussion of his policies, the myriad consequences of their implementation, and the implications of their success or failure. Liberally quoting from Gorbachev's speeches and writings, the author presents a clear, concise discussion of the ramifications of reconciling Communist ideology with a more diverse economic and political system. He goes on to talk about the thawing of the Cold War between the United States and the Soviet Union, relating this phenomenon to the effects of Gorbachev's domestic policy.

Oleksy concludes by attempting to analyze Gorbachev, the man, but gets little further than contrasting quotes from observers and informed but generalized speculation. This precedes the recent dynamic political events in both the Soviet Union and Eastern Europe and does not really anticipate them. Still, as preliminary source material for upper elementary school readers, this is a solid work.

There are an excellent chronology and an index, with a brief section on chapter notes. There is no bibliography.

634   Orlev, Uri. ***The Island on Bird Street.*** Trans. from Hebrew by Hillel Halkin. Houghton Mifflin 1984, HB $13.95 (0-395-33887-5). 176pp. Fiction.

This account of survival in a ghetto in Poland during World War II is an adventure story laced with harsh realism as 11-year-old Alex waits alone for his father to return from a Nazi selection.

After his mother disappears, Alex and his father become a team, training to endure and survive the Nazi threat. When they are caught, a contingency plan is put into action; with the help of a friend, Alex makes a sudden dash for freedom, hiding in an abandoned house to await his father. With only his pet white mouse for company, he stays there for five months, during which his ingenuity is tested time and again. He raids tragically abandoned apartments for food, clothing, and books. He builds an aerie above the blocked-up windows and doors of the house, which can be entered only by rope. He watches life on the Polish side of the wall, trying to discern whom he can trust—knowledge that becomes valuable when he conceals a fighter wounded in a ghetto rebellion and must find a doctor to help. All the while, he continually refuses to leave, refuses to give up his faith that his father will return for him. Yet when his father does return, he finds his presence so difficult to believe that he almost fails to make himself known.

Orlev, who spent part of World War II hiding in the Warsaw ghetto, precedes his tale with an introduction during which he briefly describes his own experiences. The power of both introduction and story lies both in Orlev's ability to render believable the concrete realities of the daily existence he describes and in his depiction of the sense of adventure and accomplishment that his young hero feels along with his tragically inevitable anger, fear, and anguish.

635   Prochazkova, Iva. ***The Season of Secret Wishes.*** Trans. from German by Elizabeth Crawford. Lothrop, Lee & Shepard 1989, HB $12.95 (0-688-08735-3). 208pp. Fiction.

The daughter of a sculptor begins to come of age, politically and emotionally, when her family moves to a new neighborhood in Prague.

As the book opens, Kapka, 11, is exploring the wondrous new world around her: the new room that is hers alone, the wonderful view from the roof above her room, and her mysterious neighbors, who include a princess and a destitute woman who has a fur coat hanging in her closet. The discursive narrative is less a tightly plotted story than a series of episodes common to the lives of many girls Kapka's age but that take a softly bitter turn when her father is denied space in an officially sponsored show. Kapka's neighbors and friends band together to put on a street exhibition, which results in a brief period of detention for Kapka's father. As Kapka watches, her father's strength wavers, and it takes the healing love of her extended family, especially her plain-speaking grandfather, to begin to mend his overstressed nerves.

Written in Germany by the daughter of an author labeled "undesirable" because of his actions in the 1968 "Prague spring," this resonates with sardonic emotion. Not entirely successful as a rounded novel, it does work memorably as a character study of an 11-year-old whose emotions are universal but who faces challenges unique to her society.

636 Schur, Maxine. ***Hannah Szenes: A Song of Light.*** Illus. by Donna Ruff. Jewish Publication Society 1986, HB $10.95 (0-8276-0251-0). 106pp. Nonfiction.

The story of the martyred heroine is told for younger readers.

The Schur book covers the same territory as does Linda Atkinson's, *In Kindling Flame*, but, though Senesh's writings are interpolated into the text, the story is told without any documentation as to its source material. What results is a straightforward biography in a hagiographic format with the addition of undocumented dialogue and imagined thoughts. Schur tells her story with fervor, and, while not distinguished as a biography, the book weathers well as an introduction for younger people to this woman of honor.

Illustrated with black-and-white charcoal drawings that are uneven in their effect. There is neither index nor bibliography.

637 Smith, Samantha. ***Samantha Smith: Journey to the Soviet Union.*** Illus. with photos. Little, Brown 1985, HB $19.45 (0-316-80175-5); P $14.95 (0-316-80176-3). 119pp. Nonfiction.

Before Gorbachev and before glasnost, there was Samantha Smith, who, after less than a decade, seems a distant memory. The 10-year-old girl whose letter to the then Soviet leader Yuri Andropov inspired an invitation to visit his country was a natural for a news story in 1982, at the height of the Cold War: a lovely young girl from Maine reaching out in an innocent desire for world peace.

Samantha's visit was covered by news agencies from all over the world, and, with the help of her father, she talks about her trip, from the time of her first letter to her Moscow visit with a representative of the Soviet premier (who was suffering from his final illness). The text is in Samantha's voice, telling in a straightforward manner her impressions of the people she met and the places she saw. The book is filled with crisply reproduced pictures, some in full color and most of Samantha. It is an entertaining story that preserves the fresh, eager voice of its teller.

Shortly after her visit, Andropov died and was replaced by Mikhail Gorbachev. Samantha went on to become a minor celebrity and was making a television series when she was tragically killed, with her father, in an airplane crash. Seven years after her visit, the Berlin Wall fell and Samantha Smith became part of an obsolete era. No one would have liked that better than Samantha herself.

638 Sullivan, George. ***Mikhail Gorbachev.*** Illus. with photos. Julian Messner 1988, LB $10.98 (0-671-63263-9); P $5.95 (0-671-66937-0). 128pp. Nonfiction.

This prolific writer of juvenile nonfiction has done a straightforward biography of the Soviet leader, covering events through 1987. The basic facts of his early life and his rise to power are covered briefly, and there is a discussion of his policies, but little is explained in detail about their origins or ramifications. A brief closing chapter attempts to analyze the future but in no way anticipates recent events. In sum, this is a fair introduction for primary grades, but it is outdated and should be revised.

Included are a brief chronology, a bibliograhy, a pronunciation guide, and an index.

639 Yolen, Jane. ***The Devil's Arithmetic.*** Viking Kestrel 1988, HB $11.95 (0-670-81027-4). 160pp. Fiction.

Yolen surrounds a realistic account of a Jewish child's experiences in Poland during the Holocaust with a time-travel structure that, while an interesting idea in theory, only succeeds in undermining her plot.

Hannah, who is an American child of the 1980s, is abruptly plunged from a current Passover seder to a time and place nearly 50 years before. Opening the door for Elijah, she finds herself in Poland, among loving strangers who call her by her Hebrew name, Chayah. The time is suddenly 1942, and Chayah is on her way to the wedding of an uncle she does not know. On their arrival, however, the wedding party is greeted by a Nazi roundup, and Chayah is thrust into the heart of the Holocaust, riding in a boxcar to a concentration camp, where she desperately tries to keep alive with her friend, Rivka. Their efforts are futile, and in the end they join hands and walk into the gas chamber's darkness, whereupon Hannah arrives back into the present and discovers that Rivka is, in fact, her beloved Aunt Eva.

This book is a laudable attempt by Yolen to bring concrete reality to the unbelievable facts of the Holocaust. However, the structure of the book trivializes its plot. Hannah's continuing allusions to the culture of the 1980s jar rather than lend texture; the twist that allows her to travel back is never explained, and the entire exercise emerges as didactic, with melodrama replacing authenticity. While it is possible to mix fiction and fictional themes with this overwhelming historic event, as Chester Aaron and Uri Orlev do, the writing must be specific, immediate, and of overwhelming power. In this, despite her best intentions, Yolen does not succeed.

640 Zheleznikov, Vladimir. ***Scarecrow.*** Trans. from Russian by Antonina W. Bouis. HarperCollins 1990, LB $12.89 (0-397-32317-4). 160pp. Fiction.

Zheleznikov, a noted writer for children in the Soviet Union (two State Prizes of the Soviet Union and one prize each from Poland and Italy), here makes his English-language debut in a powerful story about the struggle of the individual against the group.

Lena Bessoltsev has come to live with her grandfather in a small town in Russia, where he has become the local eccentric, devoting most of his time to recovering the portraits his great-grandfather, a noted artist, once painted and hanging them in the family's ancestral home. Self-conscious about her appearance, Lena has little self-esteem, and when Dimka Somov, a leader in her new class at school, shows friendship, she becomes passionately loyal to him. She enthusiastically supports Dimka's idea that the class earn the funds for their planned outing to Moscow, but things take a disastrous turn when a teacher is absent and the entire class decides to use the resulting freedom for a trip to the movies. Lena overhears Dimka's reporting their transgression to the teacher, but, when everyone is eventually banned from the trip and class leaders try to find the one who told, Dimka remains silent, allowing Lena to take the blame. Things escalate until, finally, Lena confronts the class, including Dimka, flinging her ostracism into their faces, after which she and her grandfather leave the small town, the grandfather having decided to let the town have the house and its pictures as a museum.

The book was made into a movie that was popular in the Soviet Union and was described by Elena Bonner as "one of the greatest events of recent years in

Soviet life," apparently because of the strong stand it takes in favor of personal action in the face of group tyranny. It is written with vigorous authority but seems flawed by abrupt transitions in story line and characterization. The weakness of the authority figures, especially of the teacher who is talked to and about by her students as a rather dim equal, will seem surprising to Western readers, who will not know if this is a realistic depiction of the setting or a function of individual characterization. The whole emerges as more of a passionate fable than a fully realized novel; nevertheless, Zheleznikov's enthusiastic voice deserves a place in children's collections.

GRADES 7–9

641   Aaron, Chester. **Gideon.** HarperCollins 1982, LB $11.89 (0-397-31992-4). 181pp. Fiction.

A Holocaust survivor relates his experiences as a 15-year-old in the Warsaw ghetto and in Treblinka in a fictionalized memoir that carries the immediacy of truth.

Gideon is blond and blue-eyed; he and his family have lived as assimilated Jews in Warsaw until the German occupation. Their resultant persecution and exile into the ghetto cause his parents to become active—his father in resistance organizations and his mother in the orphanage run by Dr. Korczak. Gideon, however, is preoccupied with surviving and resents the Jewishness that has led to his plight. He joins a gang of smugglers and becomes involved with a Polish gang outside of the ghetto, helping his family but earning the distrust of those around him. As the Nazi noose tightens, Gideon sees his father killed during an act of rebellion against a Nazi soldier and his mother marched off to camp with the orphans. Consumed with hatred, he joins the Warsaw ghetto revolt, escaping at the last, only to be captured and sent to Treblinka. There he is part of the inmate rebellion and once again escapes. At the end of the war, he returns to Warsaw to find no one left alive in his family and so sets out to America to find a new life. In the book's moving conclusion, Gideon speaks directly to his wife and children, emphasizing the importance of his own testimony about his ordeal.

Aaron says in an introduction that, though he never underwent the experiences of his protagonist, he was among the American liberators at Dachau and based much of his story on interviews with survivors, on diaries, and on histories left behind. He has used this research to his advantage, as his first-person narrative, often in the present tense, carries a tension and a potency of felt circumstances. More important, Gideon remains a real person with believable, often less than admirable, emotions rather than a tragic symbol of oppression, which serves to bring home even more strongly the tragedies that befall him and those he has loved.

642   Anderson, Madelyn Klein. **Siberia.** Illus. with photos. Putnam 1987, HB $13.95 (0-396-08662-4). 148pp. Nonfiction.

The enigmatic wilderness that is the northern part of the Soviet Union is given a competent historical survey. Anderson begins with the mysterious explosion that took place in 1908 in the atmosphere above Siberia, using it as an example of the area's never fully explained past. She goes back to trace Siberia's background from earliest mankind to the 1917 revolution, including much about Russian history in the process. She then devotes chapters to the most famous role that Siberia has played in history—that of archetypal exile. She discusses the class system accorded the czarist exiles, with the politicals at the top and the Jews at the bottom, and describes the daily activities of those who lived out large portions of their life in banishment. She goes on to talk about the new system of punishment, under Stalin, during which the Gulags were created, and she finishes with the role of Siberia in the world today.

Though written before the rise of the current political situation, much of the information remains relevant and fascinating in and of itself. Anderson is a proficient prose stylist, telling her story clearly if not transcendentally.

The book is illustrated with photos that, because of their age and state of decomposition, do not always reproduce well. Includes index but no bibliography.

Atkinson, Linda. *In Kindling Flame: The Story of Hannah Senesh, 1921–1944.*
See entry 660, Grades 10–12.

643 Bernheim, Mark. *Father of the Orphans: The Story of Janusz Korczak.* Illus. with photos. SERIES: Jewish Biography. Dutton/Lodestar 1989, HB $14.95 (0-525-67265-6). 176pp. Nonfiction.

This biography of the noted pediatrician, educator, and author gathers strength as it goes on.

Born Henryk Goldszmit into an assimilated Jewish family in Poland, Korczak faced a lifelong conflict between his loyalty to the land of his birth and the anti-Semitism that was solidly rooted there. Bernheim depicts the biographee's unhappy childhood, examining its influence on his later life. Deciding to become a doctor, Korczak found his calling in service to "all children," becoming most famous as an author, under the name of Janusz Korczak, and as the founder of a system of orphanages called Children's Homes, in which orphaned and abandoned children became families amongst themselves, even governing themselves in a form of democracy that the doctor guided. Bernheim describes the building of the homes and the growing influence of his books, achievements which grew in irony as his hopes for a democratic Poland, free of anti-Semitism, faded with the years. Even as the Nazis attacked, he was making plans to remove his orphanages to Palestine.

Bernheim tells Korczak's story simply and clearly, with a minimum of invented dialogue and thought processes, letting events speak for themselves. Thus, when he reaches the most powerful part of the story—Korczak's refusal to abandon his orphans in the Warsaw ghetto, even though it meant deportation to a death camp—his quiet prose carries a somber weight.

The author adds an afterword, which discusses the significance of Korczak as a teacher. While this suffers from poorly reproduced photos and a lack of specific documentation, the book is still a biography that will speak to children of the significance of their great advocate. Includes an index and a list of Korczak's works.

644   Bograd, Larry. *The Kolokol Papers.* Farrar, Straus & Giroux 1981, HB $11.95 (0-374-34277-6). 196pp. Fiction.

Lev Kolokol tells the story of his life as the son of human rights activists who live precariously in Moscow until his father goes too far and is arrested. Lev and his mother keep a transcript of his father's trial. This, plus Lev's record of his life as recorded in the book, will be sent to the West to follow his mother and perhaps will help in her hitherto unsuccessful battle to free her husband.

Ten years old, this title has, at this point, some of the aspects of a historical novel, but its characters are not drawn with enough strength or intensity to truly evoke the period in which it was written, and so the result is more dated than historical.

645   Hintz, Martin. *Hungary.* Illus. with photos. SERIES: Enchantment of the World. Childrens Pr. 1988, LB $23.93 (0-516-02707-7). 128pp. Nonfiction.

This book is part of a series of attractive books giving general information on the major countries of the world. Each volume includes facts about the history and geography of the area and about the daily lives of the people. Brief biographies of famous residents are provided. The series is weakest on economic and political information but shines in its visual presentation, including detailed maps and the tables included in the "Mini-facts at a Glance" sections. Unfortunately, the books are not revised often enough to remain current. There is an index.

Other Eastern European areas covered are Poland and the Soviet Union.

646   Kort, Michael. *Nikita Krushchev.* Illus. with photos. SERIES: Impact Biographies. Franklin Watts 1989, LB $13.90 (0-531-10776-0). 160pp. Nonfiction.

This smoothly written biography of the great Soviet leader of the 1950s and 1960s has been written by an expert in Russian history who effortlessly presents Khrushchev's life against the backdrop of the times during which he lived.

Kort's approach is chronological, and he postulates that the year of Khrushchev's birth, 1894, was one that served as both a symbol of Russia's old problems and a harbinger of the changes to come. That year, when Nicholas II, the last czar, mounted the throne, was the same year that Lenin published his first political work and Stalin entered the seminary, which, paradoxically, began his political education. Kort goes on to describe Khrushchev's life, quoting liberally from his autobiography in order to add texture. He is honest about Khrushchev's ambition during Stalin's years, making it clear that he had a definite enforcer role. His rise to power after the dictator's death is depicted in strokes as quick and incisive as those of his subject in his ascent.

Most interesting is Kort's analysis of Khrushchev as leader—a man who understood the practical need of his people, but who handicapped himself by often blind adherence to Marxist doctrine and a whirlwind imperative to get things done. His decline is clearly explained, and his graciousness in defeat observed. Kort concludes by revealing the debt that the smoother and perhaps more politically astute Gorbachev owes him.

This is a timely biography that gives the reader a useful context in which to observe current events. There are chapter notes and an index but no bibliography.

647 Laird, Christa. ***Shadow of the Wall.*** Greenwillow 1990, HB $12.95 (0-688-09336-1). 144pp. Fiction.

This British author's first novel is an earnest but finally unsuccessful attempt to depict life in the Warsaw ghetto in 1942.

The hero of the story is Misha, 13, who is desperately trying to keep his mother and sisters alive, now that his father is dead. He and his sisters live in the famed Korczak orphanage; his mother struggles weakly to stay alive in a room nearby. Misha smuggles, hustles, and does what he can to keep things going, but events steadily work against him as things deteriorate in the ghetto. There is less and less food; his mother weakens and dies; selections begin. Before his mother's death, Misha manages to smuggle Elena, his younger sister, over the wall, but there is nothing he can do to help Rachel, his other sister, when the Nazis come for the orphans. Helpless, he watches her march to the death trains. Misha, now a determined fighter, is smuggled out of the ghetto to join the partisans.

Laird has apparently done her research, telling an accurate story, but her prose is not up to the demands of the plot. She describes events rather than evokes them. She does not maintain a consistent point of view, nor can she skillfully integrate historical information into the narrative. Dialogue is stiff and unbelievable, and few of the characters truly achieve believability. The result is a worthy but curiously unmoving book.

648 Lear, Aaron E. ***Albania.*** Illus. with photos. SERIES: Let's Visit Places and Peoples of the World. Chelsea House 1987, LB $14.95 (1-55546-166-2). 96pp. Nonfiction.

This volume is part of a series of basic geographies of "Nations, Dependencies and Sovereignties of the World," which discusses, on an introductory level, each area's history, geography, government, and economy and offers rudimentary sociological data on the population. Utilitarian in approach, the chief virtues of this series are its currency and the extensive number of localities covered. Includes maps, a glossary, an index, and a "Facts at a Glance" section. Revisions should keep the series current.

Other volumes in this series present Bulgaria, Czechoslovakia, Hungary, Romania, the Union of Soviet Socialist Republics, and the Soviet republics of Armenia, Estonia, Georgia, Latvia, Lithuania, Moldavia, Russia, the Ukraine, and Uzbekistan.

649 Likhanov, Albert. ***Shadows Across the Sun.*** Trans. from Russian by Richard Lourie. HarperCollins 1983, LB $10.89 (0-06-023869-0). 128pp. Fiction.

A well-known Soviet writer of books for young adults produces a moving story about two lonely teenagers finding love for the first time.

Fedya feels handicapped by the toll his father's drinking has taken on him and his mother. They endure sneers from the neighbors; his parents' relationship is steadily deteriorating; and his mother, upset by her life, has misplaced funds at her job. Lena, wheelchair bound after a bout with polio, feels that her entire life is constrained by her disability. As she habitually watches the world go by through her apartment window, she sees Fedya and his family and understands his situation. One day he looks up at her, and a hesitant relationship begins between them, one which blossoms more and more, even resulting in help for Fedya's mother.

Just as they begin to feel true joy with one another, a blow falls: Fedya's building is to be destroyed to make way for renewal. Lena is plunged into depression when she learns this, a feeling that deepens when she is told about the death of a friend. One day, when Fedya comes to visit from his new neighborhood, he discovers that Lena is gone. In despair, he releases his pigeons, which were his only comfort until his friendship with Lena, and burns their cote, an action that serves to bring him to his senses and make him realize that he must fight for their relationship. He finds Lena in the boarding school to which she has retreated, and, tentatively, they both begin to hope.

The story is told from the point of view of both main characters, usually in alternating chapters, and their sensitive, profound angst is symbolized by the title, based on the eclipse they watch together at the beginning of their friendship. The eclipse symbolizes their sharp sorrow at the realization of the brevity of everything, including their relationship, and their realization of the courage it takes to love in spite of it all. Likhanov writes with a precise understanding of his characters' emotions, allowing his story to transcend any cultural barrier.

650   Lingard, Joan. **Tug of War.** Dutton/Lodestar 1990, HB $14.95 (0-525-67306-7). 194pp. Fiction.

The noted author of books for young adults bases her nineteenth novel on events that happened to her husband and his family during World War II.

As the story begins, it is 1944 in Latvia, and, as the Germans retreat from Russia, the Petersons family is caught in the middle. Lukas Petersons, a scholar and a landowner, is on the Russian enemies list. Their only choice is to flee, with the German army, into Germany to stay with Zimmerman, an old family friend. The flight, however, is a confusing disaster from the start, soon compounded by the fact that 14-year-old Hugo becomes separated from the family. The bulk of the book alternates between Hugo's adventures and those of his family, as seen through the eyes of his twin, Astra.

Hugo, who has lost his sorely needed glasses and sustained a head wound, misses the train his family takes but, barely conscious, is helped onto the next by fellow refugees. Delirious from his wound, he rides until the passengers are forced to disembark and collapses on the track. He is near death when Herr Schneider, a signal man, discovers him and takes him home. In the meantime, his family arrives at a refugee camp and goes from there to Zimmerman's house, only to discover that he is dead and his widow has no room for them. They find refuge on a farm. Astra desperately searches for Hugo, who is being nursed back to health by the Schneiders. Upon his recovery, Hugo journeys to the Zimmerman's now-destroyed house. Assuming that his family is dead, he begins to make a new life with the Schneiders. Astra and the family, too, begin to rebuild their lives, though always searching for Hugo. They are about to reach their goal, to emigrate to Canada, when, accidentally, Astra and Hugo meet, and Hugo is faced with an agonizing choice: Should he leave with his family, or should he stay in Germany with the Schneiders and their daughter to whom he has become engaged? After much painstaking deliberation, he joins his family on the ship.

Lingard's telling of this tale is only intermittently moving. It lacks immediacy, all too often summing up events instead of evoking them. Some of the dialogue seems forced as well. Still, the author's rendering of the sheer calamitous confusion caused by war is effective, and her setting is an unusual one. In sum, this is a satisfying but undistinguished novel with a uniquely interesting background.

651 Navazelskis, Ina. ***Alexander Dubcek.*** Illus. with photos. SERIES: World Leaders, Past and Present. Chelsea House 1990, LB $17.95 (1-55546-831-4). 112pp. Nonfiction.

This volume is one of a series of biographies (157 as of 1990) of famous world statesmen and stateswomen, all of them preceded by an introductory essay by historian Arthur M. Schlesinger, Jr. Each biography flashes back from a dramatic point in the subject's life to a basic chronological consideration of the events leading up to and following it. The concluding chapter analyzes the importance of the biographee to world history (thus far).

Each volume has a brief bibliography and a detailed chronology as well as an index. Liberally illustrated with newsphotos, these biographies are utilitarian in nature, produced in prose that is clear but not inspiring or thought provoking. In most cases, however, they are the only full-length biographies available on the subjects, and, as such, they serve a useful purpose.

Other volumes in this series cover Leonid Brezhnev, Mikhail Gorbachev, Wojciech Jaruzelski, Nikita Khrushchev, Tomas Masaryk, and Lech Walesa.

Oleksy, Walter. ***Mikhail Gorbachev: A Leader for Soviet Change.***
See entry 633, Grades 4–6.

Orlev, Uri. ***The Island on Bird Street.***
See entry 634, Grades 4–6.

652 Pettepice, Thomas, and Anatoly Aleksin, eds. ***Face to Face.*** Putnam/Philomel 1990, HB $15.95 (0-399-21951-X). 233pp. Fiction.

As the editors state in their preface, this is the first collection of Soviet and American stories for young people in one volume published simultaneously in both countries. As such, it is a history-making book and also one of great interest in and of itself.

Those familiar with American children's and young adult literature will know both the authors and the works excerpted. The American contributions include excerpts from Robert Cormier's *The Chocolate War*, Cynthia Voigt's *The Runner*, Jean Fritz's *Homesick: My Own Story*, Scott O'Dell's *Carlota*, Katherine Paterson's *Park's Quest*, and Cynthia Rylant's *A Blue-Eyed Daisy*. In addition, Walter Dean Myers and Jane Yolen contribute original short stories, and Virginia Hamilton donates the title tale from *The People Could Fly*. All of the excerpts stand alone as short stories and give insight into their authors' works. The titles have been well chosen to give a variety of backgrounds and ideas, resulting in a multifaceted image of American children and the books written for them.

A similar point might be made for the Soviet choices, which come from Lithuania, Azerbaijan, and Latvia as well as Russia and have a variety of settings —rural, urban, provincial, modern, and historical (World War II). As pointed out by Hugh Downs in his paragraph-long introduction, perhaps the most accessible of these is "The Tubeteika Affair," about a boy's near-disastrous solution to the problem of having lost his father's souvenir from Kirghizia. All, however, carry the flavor of their sources and introduce readers to the riches of Soviet children's literature.

The main benefit to American readers is the introduction to Soviet writers; in addition, this is a handsome, well-produced title that gives interesting information about the authors of the contributions and Soviet publishing in general.

Prochazkova, Iva. *The Season of Secret Wishes.*
See entry 635, Grades 4–6.

Schur, Maxine. *Hannah Szenes: A Song of Light.*
See entry 636, Grades 4–6.

Sender, Ruth M. *The Cage.*
See entry 662, Grades 10–12.

653   Sevela, Ephraim. *We Were Not Like Other People.* Trans. from Russian by Antonina Bouis. HarperCollins 1989, LB $13.89 (0-06-025508-0). 224pp. Fiction.

This picaresque novel about the adventures of a boy, suddenly on his own during World War II, is a kaleidoscope of images, each revealing a different facet of wartime Soviet Union.

The book opens with two images from the narrator's wanderings, both challenging his idea of courage. In one, he chops off part of the hand of a fellow child laborer at the child's request and receives not thanks but blame. In the other, a year later, he cannot find it in himself to kill a fellow soldier who is mortally wounded and wants to be put out of his misery. When a comrade of his can, he is nauseated, but the comrade demands of the sky: "You be the judge."

This forms the leitmotiv of the entire book, as the unnamed narrator is presented with a variety of situations, the moral dimensions of which are never very simple. Before the war, his society demands that he turn disloyal citizens in, but that same society says his own father, an officer in the Red Army, is disloyal and takes him away. His only defender is the despised local drunk. When, later, he and his mother, a devout believer in little but communism, are about to be frozen to death, she calls on God, who seems to answer.

Still later, fleeing the Germans, the narrator awakes from injuries incurred during an attack on their train to find himself completely alone, and he spends the balance of the book trying to make his way through the confusing landscape. His first companions are his old teacher and his wife, upright relics of czarist times, who take him in and keep him alive. When the wife begins to fail, the husband goes for help; the wife dies in the narrator's arms, and the husband never returns. The story goes on, plunging the narrator from situation to situation, all described with earthy reality and none predictable in its outcome (including the end), until the narrator returns home to discover his entire family intact.

Bouis's translation preserves the down-to-earth poetry of Sevela's narration, but cannot camouflage a certain disjointedness that may confuse readers. Still, this is a forceful and evocative glimpse of the many faces of war.

654   Sevela, Ephraim. *Why There Is No Heaven on Earth.* Trans. from Russian by Richard Lourie. HarperCollins 1982. 224pp. Fiction. o.p.

The reason "why there is no heaven on earth," the narrator says, is that Berele Mats, his closest friend, is no longer on earth. The title refrain is repeated by the unnamed storyteller throughout the novel as he recounts his and his friend's life together on Invalid Street in the Jewish quarter of an unnamed Russian town.

Berele Mats is considered by most of the proper people in town to be a scoundrel and a thief, which he is. He is also a profoundly talented violinist, a loyal friend, and a consummate observer of others, seeing into their very hearts. Thus he finds a way to show the narrator that his distant father really loves him, giving him, in the bargain, the best day of his childhood. As he tells the often earthy tales of Berele Mats's adventures, he also gives a vivid picture of their life in pre–World War II Russia and the problems and personalities of the friends, neighbors, and occasional enemies who surround them. War comes, however, and the narrator escapes on a train, only to be separated from his family. When he returns, four years later as a grown soldier, it is with the joy of reunion with his family and with the sorrow that comes from learning of Berele Mats's death. After hiding from the Germans' deportation efforts, Berele and those with him were betrayed and shot.

Sevela spins his story in poetic rhythms, and large portions of it beg to be read aloud. Berele Mats is a Huckleberry Finn figure who remains with the reader long after the story is ended. In his first novel for young adults, Sevela shows a strong original and promising voice.

655 Shusterman, Neal. **Dissidents.** Little, Brown 1989, HB $13.95 (0-316-78904-6). 224pp. Fiction.

Derek Feretti, 15, is sent to live with his mother, the American ambassador to the Soviet Union, after his father is killed in an automobile accident. Filled with an anger he finds difficult to understand, much less control, he rebels against the constraints of his life, his efforts coming to a climax when he helps the daughter of a famous dissident to escape the authorities. In the process, he begins to face some hard truths about himself.

The Russian locale of the story is significant mainly as a backdrop to an average coming-of-age story; the setting is by no means an accurate reflection of the Soviet Union today.

656 Siegal, Aranka. **Upon the Head of the Goat: A Childhood in Hungary, 1939–1944.** Farrar, Straus & Giroux 1981, HB $14.95 (0-374-38059-7). 214pp. Nonfiction.

Beginning with the quote from Leviticus that recounts the origin of the idea of the scapegoat, this memoir relates the childhood of a Jewish girl as she watches the Nazis and their allies slowly tighten the noose around her people.

As the book opens, Piri is visiting her grandmother in the rural Ukraine and is prevented from returning to her home in Beregszasz, Hungary, by the beginning of war. Like many of her fellow Hungarians, Piri feels no special threat in this, but Babi, her deeply religious grandmother, wise in the ways of anti-Semitism, begins to urge an escape for Piri and her brother and sisters.

Once Piri is able to return home, things are different; her stepfather is away at war, and her mother, now solely responsible for the family, reveals depths of strength Piri had not realized she had. As the Germans gain in strength over the Hungarian government, life becomes harder and harder for the Jews, who become more and more isolated. There is no news of Piri's stepfather; Piri's older sister is taken away; a friend commits suicide rather than expose her family to the results of her political action; her beloved Babi is taken away from her farm and moved to a ghetto. Then the Germans assume control of the Hungarian government, and Piri's immediate family is also relocated. In the brick factory ghetto to which they are taken, Piri's adolescence blossoms fleetingly until the ghetto residents are relocated again—to Auschwitz.

The story's value is in Siegal's ability to make the reader see the speeding up of the juggernaut through the eyes of a child—and a people—innocent of the absolute evil confronting them. Thus the final line of dialogue, "Do you know what 'Auschwitz' means?" echoes with a residual horror long after the book is closed.

A brief afterword describes the fate of much of Siegal's family.

657   ***Soviet Union in Pictures.*** Illus. with photos. SERIES: Visual Geography. Lerner 1989, LB $11.95 (0-8225-1864-3). 64pp. Nonfiction.

This is one of a series of titles that concisely treat the geography, history, government, culture, and economy of each country covered. Special distinctions include an abundance of photos, accurate maps, and clearly rendered charts as needed. The series is updated with each reprint; the current title on the Soviet Union (thus far, the Soviet Union is the only Eastern European country available) reflects the beginnings of glasnost. The book is indexed.

658   Strom, Yale. ***A Tree Still Stands: Jewish Youth in Eastern Europe Today.*** Illus. with photos. Putnam/Philomel 1990, HB $16.95 (0-399-22154-9). 111pp. Nonfiction.

Strom is, among other things, a filmmaker, a musician, and a photographer. He spent 12 weeks traveling through Eastern Europe—East Germany, Czechoslovakia, Poland, Romania, Bulgaria, Yugoslavia, and Hungary—in 1989, talking to Jewish children, most of them grandchildren of Holocaust survivors. His report is incisive and timely, revealing the condition of societies awakening to the challenges and struggles of political change.

Strom divides his book into country sections, preceding each section with a brief overall impression. Each segment contains interviews with Jewish children, their quotes unadorned, though they seemed to have answered most of the same questions about their impressions of the Holocaust, their treatment by their neighbors, and their observance of Jewish religious tradition. The answers are diverse and throw interesting light on the countries in which the children live.

The Hungarian and Czechoslovakian children speak freely of their Judaism and the importance of learning about the Holocaust, as do the Yugoslavian children who worry, though, that their Jewish traditions are slowly dying out. All of the Polish children interviewed are products of Christian-Jewish marriages, and both they and the Bulgarian children mention anti-Semitism the most frankly. The Eastern German section is the shortest, reflecting the small number of Jews left in the country. It is here that one child speculates about the "mentality" of Jews who did not resist the Nazis.

The book is liberally illustrated with photos of the children interviewed. Sometimes they peer earnestly into the camera, and sometimes they are caught in the odd, candid moment. They look very much like their American counterparts. Author Sonia Levitin contributes an introduction that places the interviews into a world context.

Because this book captures a small, specific moment in time, it will not, paradoxically enough, date as much as if it had tried to be more comprehensive or less specific. As a children's book, it is like a fly in amber, holding a moment of anticipation forever between its pages. There is neither index nor bibliography.

Sturdza, Ioana, ed. *Fairy Tales & Legends from Romania.*
See entry 665, Grades 10–12.

659   Suhl, Yuri. *Uncle Misha's Partisans: The Story of Young Freedom Fighters in Nazi-Occupied Europe.* Shapolsky Publishers 1988, P $7.95 (0-933503-23-7). 211pp. Fiction.

The novelist and Jewish historian produces a fast-paced novel on a subject rarely discussed in children's books—those Jews who fought the Nazis in partisan groups.

As the book opens, 12-year-old Motele is discovered walking the back roads of the Ukraine in search of the legendary Uncle Misha's Partisans. A talented violinist and a member of the only Jewish family in his small village, he has come home from a music lesson to find his entire family murdered. Now nothing will do but revenge. Two partisans he meets on the road try to deflect him to a family group hiding in the forest, but Motele will not be turned back. They accompany him to his goal.

The balance of the book is devoted to a depiction of partisan life and Motele's role in two important missions. In the first, he poses as a violinist on his way to a wedding so that members of his group can seek medical aid for a wounded partisan. The partisan dies, and, instead of aid, they discover the captain of the local Ukrainian police, who has enthusiastically helped the Nazis. They kill him, burn the houseful of furniture, jewels, and clothing that he had looted from the Jews, and turn out his wife and two children. The second assignment is filled with suspense. Motele, again posing as a musician, is sent as a beggar into town to do reconnaissance. Instead, he is captured by the Nazis, mistaken for a Ukrainian musician, and hired by them to play. This gives the partisans the chance they need to attack the Germans from the inside, a mission in which Motele is to play a vital role.

The end of the story is abrupt; having had his revenge, Motele flees the exploding German headquarters. In this extreme situation, the most the partisans can do is light a lethal candle to their dead—a sudden, harsh ending, but a truthful one.

Suhl's story is action packed and full of tension, though his characterizations, except for Motele's, are not strong. Based on real-life events, the book could stand on its own as an adventure story. Suhl's telling of his tale, however, does not shrink from the tragic events that surround and inform it.

Sullivan, George. *Mikhail Gorbachev.*
See entry 638, Grades 4–6.

Zar, Rose. *In the Mouth of the Wolf.*
See entry 666, Grades 10–12.

Zheleznikov, Vladimir. *Scarecrow.*
See entry 640, Grades 4–6.

660 Atkinson, Linda. *In Kindling Flame: The Story of Hannah Senesh, 1921–1944.* Illus. with photos. Lothrop, Lee & Shepard 1985, HB $13.95 (0-688-02714-8). 224pp. Nonfiction.

Atkinson passionately tells the story of the courageous Hungarian Jew who parachuted into her country to try to rescue her people from the Nazis.

The book is divided into three parts: The first, and longest, discusses her childhood and youth in Hungary and her years in Palestine. The second part takes up her mission in the underground and her subsequent capture, imprisonment, and death. The third part, a few pages long, places her martyrdom in the contexts of (1) the unraveling of the Third Reich and the efforts of her people to survive by leaving records of their sufferings and (2) underground movements existing even in Auschwitz.

The power of the book lies in Atkinson's use of primary sources—Senesh's writings and interviews with survivors—to bring the subject vividly alive. More than a heroine, Senesh is a girl and, later, a woman searching for meaning to her life and also for companionship and understanding. Courageous and headstrong, sensitive and overbearing, her own impatience led to her capture. In the end, it is not the rescue mission she sought so desperately for which she is remembered. It is her quiet, steady valor in her final months in prison as, while hoping for life, she waited for inevitable death.

Atkinson's intense narrative involves the reader from the first page and is marred only by its punctuation with poorly reproduced photographs. Includes index and Suggestions for Further Reading.

661 Baklanov, Grigory. *Forever Nineteen.* Trans. from Russian by Antonina W. Bouis. HarperCollins 1989, LB $13.89 (0-397-32297-6). 176pp. Fiction.

The first of this celebrated Russian children's writer's books to be published in the United States, this is a brutally honest report of war as it is experienced by a 19-year-old lieutenant in the Soviet artillery during World War II.

When, 30 years after the war, a film crew uncovers young Volodya Tretyakov's body, they swiftly cover it over. The narrative then switches to Volodya alive, years before, traveling to the battlefront on a train. Baklanov then goes on to convey the confusion, the grit, the everyday discomfort and pettiness of army life during battle. Volodya is wounded, struggles to a hospital, and endures pain and inadequate medical care. As he recovers, he remembers scenes from his childhood and tries to come to terms with why he is fighting and undergoing such misery. During his recovery, he meets and falls in love with a girl but returns to the war to fight on grimly until he is wounded again. As he is taken away from battle, relieved and even joyous that he does not face amputation, the Germans attack, and he is killed.

"A star fades, but its magnetic field remains. People are like that, too," says one of the characters, who reads Tretyakov's inevitable death in his eyes. The quoted sentiment is small comfort amidst the vast senselessness of war conveyed by this strong novel, which simply and vividly depicts the experiences of one young man and, in him, the thousands and thousands of his brothers.

Bernheim, Mark. *Father of the Orphans: The Story of Janusz Korczak.*
See entry 643, Grades 7–9.

Kort, Michael. *Nikita Krushchev.*
See entry 646, Grades 7–9.

Lingard, Joan. *Tug of War.*
See entry 650, Grades 7–9.

Navazelskis, Ina. *Alexander Dubcek.*
See entry 651, Grades 7–9.

Pettepice, Thomas, and Anatoly Aleksin, eds. *Face to Face.*
See entry 652, Grades 7–9.

662   Sender, Ruth M. *The Cage.* Macmillan 1986, HB $13.95 (0-02-781830-6). 252pp.
        Nonfiction.

Sender's first book is a powerful, immediate memoir of her survival during the
Nazi Holocaust.

As the book begins, she is an adult, haunted by nightmares of her experiences, plunged back into them by a daughter's innocent question. In short,
staccato sentences, always in the present tense, she gives glimpses of her childhood in prewar Lodz, one of seven children of a widowed mother. With the
arrival of war, persecution begins, a relentless wearing down, as she is deprived
of friends, school, home, and, then, members of her family—first older siblings
who flee to Russia and then her mother. In the Lodz ghetto, she struggles to keep
the remnants of the family together, even getting appointed as her brothers'
legal guardian. But as the Nazis relentlessly empty the ghetto of its inhabitants, it
becomes useless to resist. Accepting deportation, she is finally separated from
her family at Auschwitz, surviving the war in Mittelsteine and Grafenort, two
labor camps, by her wits and by the spirit of hope conveyed in her poetry, which
speaks to both her captors and fellow prisoners. But when she returns to her
Lodz home, there is no one left, and only several years later is she reunited with
her siblings, who fled to the Soviet Union.

Sender's style is relentlessly direct, flinging events before the reader and
providing their significance in the narrative as she goes along. The results are not
subtle, but they are vivid and memorable, spoken in a voice that echoes with a
kind of vengeful hope.

663   Sender, Ruth M. *To Life.* Macmillan 1988, HB $14.95 (0-02-781831-4); Penguin
        1990, P $3.95 (0-14-034367-9). 240pp. Nonfiction.

The sequel to *The Cage* details Sender's return to Poland after her release from
Grafenort labor camp; her subsequent marriage and flight to a displaced persons'
camp in Germany; her search for her remaining siblings; and the struggles of the
family to emigrate to the United States.

664   Siegal, Aranka. *Grace in the Wilderness: After the Liberation, 1945–1948.* Illus. with photos. Farrar, Straus & Giroux 1985, HB $13.95 (0-374-32760-2); New American Library 1986, P $2.50 (0-451-14624-7). 220pp. Nonfiction.

This sequel to *Upon the Head of a Goat* concerns itself with the postwar experiences of Piri, first in a relocation camp and then in Sweden, where, while waiting for a chance to emigrate to the United States, she becomes attached to a Swedish couple who become surrogate parents, and she falls in love for the first time. As before, this book is based on Siegal's true life experiences, but is for an older audience than the previous title.

Siegal, Aranka. *Upon the Head of the Goat: A Childhood in Hungary, 1939–1944.* See entry 656, Grades 7–9.

Strom, Yale. *A Tree Still Stands: Jewish Youth in Eastern Europe Today.* See entry 658, Grades 7–9.

665   Sturdza, Ioana, ed. *Fairy Tales & Legends from Romania.* Trans. from Romanian by Ioana Sturdza, Raymond Vianu, and Mary Lazarescu. Illus. by Angi Tiparescu. Irvington Publishers 1972, HB $29.50 (0-8057-5655-8). 333pp. Fiction.

A collection of "fantastic tales," fairy tales with strong heroes and heroines, which, according to the introduction, depict "the moral and spiritual values of a nation, its aesthetic tenets, its canons of beauty . . . its ideals and aspirations."

This compilation was published in collaboration with the Eminescu Publishing House in Bucharest, Romania, and, in addition to a scholarly introduction, contains 19 stories presented in an informal and lively fashion. The stories are long, both epic and episodic, and contain brutalities akin to those in Grimm. The result is a particularly apt glance into a culture as it sees itself.

666   Zar, Rose. *In the Mouth of the Wolf.* Jewish Publication Society 1983, HB $10.95 (0-8276-0225-1). 224pp. Nonfiction.

This memoir has all the aspects of a suspense novel as the narrator tells of her adventures as a Jewish girl posing as a gentile in Poland during World War II.

In 1942, Zar's parents, facing certain deportation by the Nazis, made arrangements for her and her older brother, Benek, to leave their ghetto near Warsaw and hide with friends. The plans went awry, but the two escaped and, Rose, called Ruszka by her family but using the name "Wanda" among the Poles, began a long odyssey of survival by working in many menial jobs—once even as a housekeeper for an SS officer. Always threatened by the willingness of her fellow Poles to turn suspected Jews over to the Nazis, trusting few and keeping one step ahead of the gestapo, Zar held out until the end and even, briefly, found love.

Zar writes with humor and irony, in an entertaining, matter-of-fact style that does not conceal the horror of her experiences or the daily toll that living a lie to save her life took on her and others in her situation. This is a rounded, well-written autobiography that brings alive an awareness of what it must be like to live minute by minute in fear of betrayal.

667 Zyskind, Sara. *The Stolen Years.* Trans. from Hebrew by Margarit Inbar. Lerner 1981, HB $11.95 (0-8225-0766-8); New American Library 1983, P $3.95 (0-451-14339-6). 299pp. Nonfiction.

This is a strong memoir of a young Jewish girl's efforts to survive the Nazi occupation in Poland.

After the invasion, 11-year-old Sara and her family are immediately moved to the Lodz ghetto, where they struggle to keep going. Her mother soon dies, and her father begins to suffer from malnutrition, so that Sara is the only support for the two of them. Despite her best efforts, he dies, and Sara is driven to attempt suicide by running out of the ghetto in the hopes of being shot by a guard. Kept alive by the love of her friends, she nevertheless is soon deported to Auschwitz, where she manages to escape the line of those headed to the gas chambers. Eventually, she is sent to a work camp and struggles through 12-hour workdays of terror and starvation to the end of the war, when she returns home to find no one left. An epilogue describes her postwar flight to Israel.

Zyskind writes with skill, allowing her emotions to show but never to interfere with a clear, factual depiction of the situations, which enables readers to realize the innate horror of the events as they occur. The book is a valuable testimony.

668 Zyskind, Sara. *Struggle.* Lerner 1989, HB $16.95 (0-8225-0772-2). 288pp. Nonfiction.

The author of *The Stolen Years*, which related her experiences as a Jew in Poland during World War II, now describes those of her husband in a companion book of equal power.

Speaking in the voice of Luzer, her husband, she begins with early memories of his battles with anti-Semitic boys in his small town near Lodz. Swiftly progressing to the war years, she tells a tale of displacement, removal first to the Bzezin and then to the Lodz ghetto, and the day-to-day struggles to remain alive under increasing abuse from the Nazis. Luzer's mother and sister are taken in a selection, but he saves them, managing a two-year respite during which his sister turns into a scholar. When the Lodz ghetto is liquidated, he and his family try to hide, but they are discovered and taken to Auschwitz, where his mother and sister are immediately sent to the gas chambers.

His father loses the will to live, but Luzer battles to keep him alive and safe, ultimately to no avail. After making Luzer promise to live for all of them, his father allows himself to be taken away to be with the sick, and he soon dies. Luzer then escapes a selection, and, as the war draws to a close, he battles to survive work camps and death marches, finally being liberated from within the depths of Germany by the American army.

Zyskind tells the story with raw emotion but refines her words with the gift of poetry so well displayed in the previous book. Together, they form a moral epic.

12

THE MIDDLE EAST
AND NORTH AFRICA

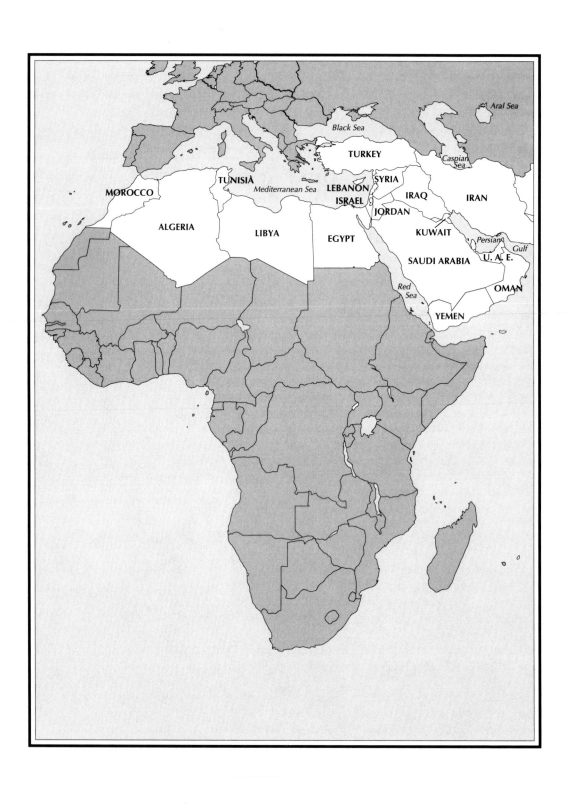

Black Sea

Aral Sea

Mediterranean Sea

Caspian
Sea

MOROCCO

TUNISIA

TURKEY

LEBANON

SYRIA

ISRAEL

IRAQ

IRAN

JORDAN

ALGERIA

LIBYA

EGYPT

KUWAIT

SAUDI ARABIA

Persian

Gulf

U. A. E.

Red
Sea

OMAN

YEMEN

12

THE MIDDLE EAST AND NORTH AFRICA

by Elsa Marston

As merchants, missionaries, and Marines, Americans have been active in the Middle East and North Africa since the birth of the United States. After World War I, the idealistic principles promoted by the United States gave hope to many Arabs as they faced a new form of European colonialism. Yet today most Americans know very little about the Arab-Muslim countries. At the same time, misperceptions and harmful stereotypes about the Middle East abound in many Americans' thinking. The more the United States is involved in this troubled area, the more essential it is that both government leaders and the American public have an accurate understanding of Middle Eastern countries, their histories, and their people.

What books are available for young Americans that will help balance the false impressions, offer background for understanding the news, and provide information on which to base intelligent judgment? Just as important, what books will excite interest in this fascinating part of the world?

Fortunately, there is no lack of nonfiction books about the Middle Eastern and North African countries. Several American publishers have introduced, expanded, or improved their series of "country books" in just the last few years, so that now there is at least one informative book about virtually every country. These books are quite impressive: accurate, well written, and attractive, with many striking photographs. They maintain a nonjudgmental attitude and usually touch on political problems lightly or only by implication. This skirting of controversy and criticism might be considered a weakness—but the general intent of these introductory books is to provide information that gives a positive image. In books for older readers, of course, the political discussion is somewhat more candid.

The Families the World Over series (Lerner) is particularly attractive for early readers, providing an intimate view of what people and their lives are really like in some little-known countries. Though impersonal in tone, the Take a Trip series published by Franklin Watts is another good choice for the youngest readers, with fine photographs. Lerner's Visual Geography series ("— in Pictures") presents concise, well-organized surveys of several countries. These books are prepared by the publisher's Geography Department, and what they lack in the "personality" that might come from an individual author's approach, they make up for in careful presentation (for middle grades and higher).

Chelsea House, drawing on some British publications, covers many countries, including the less well-known ones of the Arabian peninsula; some of these books are almost "fun" reading. For the middle school grades, the Enchantment of the World series (Childrens Press) provides solid information and excellent photographs, plus several useful pages of "mini-facts at a glance" and lists of important dates and persons. A weakness of the volume about Israel is that the indigenous Palestinian population is virtually ignored; and the outdated volume about Egypt seems far more concerned with ancient Egypt than the present. It starts, moreover, with the following sentence: "Throughout their long and unusual history, the people of Egypt have always worshiped the sun as a god"—which would certainly surprise any inhabitant of Egypt during the last 2,000 years. Fortunately, such off-the-mark statements are very rare in recently published books.

A chapter or section about Islam is standard in practically all of the books about predominantly Muslim countries, presented in a careful, straightforward way. Anyone concerned about finding reliable and interesting background books on Middle Eastern/North African countries, therefore, can take heart: They are available.

Nonfiction books also include some volumes on specific problems, above all, the Arab-Israeli conflict. These, too, deserve praise for their objectivity and the fairness with which information is presented, especially considering the severe bias with which this topic has usually been handled by the American media. Books originally published in Britain—for instance, David McDowell's *The Palestinians* and Paul Harper's *The Arab-Israel Conflict*—are particularly good in this respect.

Two Middle Eastern leaders have inspired several biographies: Golda Meir and Anwar Sadat. Other leaders, some generally considered admirable and others the object of much criticism in the West, are subjects of the excellent Chelsea House biography series, which presents history as well as biographical information in a meaningful, palatable form. The authors are well-qualified scholars and maintain a dispassionate tone and balanced view of the subject. Only the volume about Golda Meir should be criticized for excessive emotionalism and bias.

Franklin Watts has a series called Impact Books, which deals with a variety of controversial or timely topics. The books are of varying quality. A few, by the nature of their subjects, are outdated and therefore of "background" interest: *Iran and Iraq: Nations at War* by Lisa Mannetti (1986) and *East vs. West in the Middle East* by Peter L. Ferrara (see annotation). William Shapiro's book *Lebanon*, published in 1984, provides a thorough account of the Lebanese war, plus some historical background; it is a well-written, balanced book for the reader who wants the details of that immensely complicated struggle. *Libya and Qaddafi* by Don Lawson, published in 1982, is not a very satisfactory handling of the subject, with confusing organization and a highly journalistic approach. Golda Meir's biography (Mollie Keller—see annotation), though a very readable introduction to a fascinating subject, is distorted by prejudice.

Critical comments should be added about choice of illustrations and captions in some nonfiction books. Where pictures are used, particularly eighteenth- and nineteenth-century prints, something should be said about their source and the fact that they are, in most cases, the product of wildly romantic imagination. The inclusion of "portraits" of Mohammed is a regrettable error, since Islam traditionally forbids depiction of human beings, particularly Mohammed. Such a picture would be offensive to most Muslim readers. As for captions, since many readers get their first impressions from scanning the pictures, every effort should be made to have accurate, sensible captions. Better to say very little than to say too much and have it turn out misleading, inaccurate, or downright silly.

While nonfiction books provide factual background, it is fiction that offers the reader a glimpse into the heart and soul of a country, leaving the most enduring impression. Not surprisingly, children's novels and picture books about Israel outweigh those about all the other countries combined. Inevitably, the Arab-Israeli conflict is reflected in almost all books about Israel. The treatment of this pervasive and tragic problem, which affects all Americans whether they realize it or not, demands especially close attention.

A basic premise for evaluating children's literature (and it could be contrasted with adult literature in this respect) is that children's books should be positive and constructive. Books for young people should open eyes, increase understanding, broaden sympathies, offer hope. They should *not* arouse unthinking emotionalism, play upon fear and suspicion, reinforce prejudice, and, ultimately, teach hatred. They should not promote the idea that "other people," as a people, are base, vicious, or contemptible.

There is another type of book for young people inspired by political problems in the Middle East, and it deserves special note. This is the "hostage" story, in which a group of militants hold young citizens of Western countries hostage in order to dramatize their demands. Examples are *After the First Death* (Robert Cormier, Pantheon, 1979), *Call Back Yesterday* (James Forman, Scribner, 1981), *Zed* (Rosemary Harris, Faber & Faber, 1982), and *Captives in a Foreign Land* (Susan Rardin—see annotation). These are all outstanding books, highly recommended not only for the drama of the story but for the insights they offer into the mentality of Middle Easterners who feel frustrated by political conditions and have turned to acts of violence. Particularly interesting, too, are the intimate psychological and emotional relationships that develop between captor and hostage in each story. (Only one of these books is annotated here, because the others lack Middle Eastern settings or sufficient presence of the people of the country.)

In general, "archaeological" stories and mystery adventures, though appealing and often colorful, are beyond the scope of this selection. In most cases there is not enough focus on people and contemporary conditions in the country of the setting.

Unhappily, several of the very best novels are no longer in print. This is especially regrettable because they are of enduring appeal and relevance, and nothing similar has replaced them. Readers who succeed in finding copies will be rewarded for their efforts.

It will be noted that hardly any Middle Eastern authors for children appear on this list. Possibly this is because authors of Arabic background are not writing for young American readers. It may also be because most American publishers have not shown much enthusiasm for stories about Middle Eastern countries other than Israel, arguing that there would not be enough market for books about unfamiliar places. Whatever the reason, one must hope that good books in translation by Middle Eastern authors, offering "firsthand" experience of those countries, will start to appear.

There have been some exceptions to this pattern. One is Rafik Schami's outstanding young adult novel, *A Hand Full of Stars*, which achieved widespread success in Europe before being translated and published in the United States in 1990. The other exceptions are four books, published for adults and suitable for young adult readers, which are the works of Iranian writers. Three of these—Samed Behrangi's *The Little Black Fish and Other Modern Persian Stories*, Gholam-Hossein Sa'edi's *Dandil*, and *Modern Persian Short Stories*, edited by Minoo Southgate—are collections of short stories appropriate for use in high school classrooms. Children figure heavily in these stories, and often, as is common in the Iranian literary tradition, the world is viewed and presented through a child's eyes. A fourth work for advanced readers is Hadi Khorsandi's *The Ayatollah and I*, a collection of satirical stories and essays published by Reader's International, which specializes in works that have been banned in their country of origin. Interestingly, all of the above works by Middle Eastern authors examine religious conflicts (including conflicts over secularism), political oppression, and the enormous gap between rich and poor.

The annotations of the four books from Iran have been contributed by Brenda Naze, who is also a coauthor of the chapter "Sub-Saharan Africa." Homayoon Moossavi assisted her in the evaluation of the books and their translations.

PRESCHOOL–GRADE 3

669   Alexander, Sue. *Nadia the Willful.* Illus. by Lloyd Bloom. Pantheon 1983, LB $12.99 (0-394-95265-0). 32pp. Fiction.

Nadia, young daughter of the sheikh of an Arab tribe, is attached to her brother Hamed—favorite son of their father. When the boy becomes lost in the desert, she is desolate, while her father is so overwhelmed by grief that he forbids the uttering of Hamed's name. Nadia becomes more and more bad tempered and unhappy. At length she does start to talk about her brother and finds that not only she but also others in the tribe begin to feel happier. Her father, on learning this, is enraged, but Nadia helps him to see that by talking about the dead boy, they can "bring him back."

The illustrations, somewhat stylized but vigorous and reasonably accurate, suggest the sand deserts of North Africa or Saudi Arabia in "traditional" times. The story is timely for its presentation of bedouin society in a sympathetic light —and more so, for the universality of human emotion that it conveys. The young reader or listener can share emotional response across time and boundaries between radically different cultures.

Bennett, Olivia. *A Family in Egypt.*
See entry 681, Grades 4–6.

670   Burgoyne, Diane Turnage. *Amina and Muhammad's Special Visitor.* Illus. by Penny Williams Yaqub. Middle East Gateway 1982, $11.00. 58pp. Fiction.

A story within a story shows us both present-day city life in Saudi Arabia and traditional life of a few generations ago. The contrasts—and continuities—are illustrated by detailed, amusing drawings by a Canadian artist well-known for her distinctive depiction of Middle Eastern cultures. The simple tale of two children in a typical middle-class Saudi family and a boy who wants a camel provides a framework for plenty of information about Arabian family life and customs. (A supplement at the end discusses several topics suggested by the story, such as veiling and the role of women, religion, bargaining, and date farming.) The Saudi home's combination of modern features—the large bathroom, a vacuum cleaner—with traditional room arrangements and exotic oriental decoration adds interest.

The same artist and another writer, Juanita Will Soghikian, have produced an equally attractive and informative book, with hands-on activities for the reader, about the Arab-Islamic cultures of North Africa and the Middle East. *Lands, Peoples and Communities of the Middle East* (1980) is available from the International Book Center, P.O. Box 295, Troy, MI 48099.

Both books appear most appropriate for the middle elementary grades; the information and pictures may interest both younger and older children as well.

671   Chaikin, Miriam. *Aviva's Piano.* Illus. by Yossi Abolafia. Clarion 1986, HB $11.95 (0-89919-367-6). 48pp. Fiction.

Something good can result, in unexpected ways, from a bad thing. That idea comes across clearly in this "first chapter" book about a little girl, newly arrived in Israel. Her piano will not fit through the door of the second floor apartment on the kibbutz where she and her parents have settled. Then a rocket attack by "terrorists" blows a hole in the wall—and the piano slips through nicely.

It is a worthy theme for a story. What is troubling in *Aviva's Piano*, however, is the intimation that "terrorists"—faceless, nameless, purposeless bogeymen—constantly threaten this community. The menace of unexplained danger does not seem a healthy premise for a story for young children, and it certainly does not contribute to better understanding of life in Israel.

Illustrations are mild and pleasant but look very much like a typical American suburb.

Cohen, Barbara. *The Secret Grove.*
See entry 684, Grades 4–6.

Fakhro, Bahia, and Ann Walko. *Customs of the Arabian Gulf.*
See entry 685, Grades 4–6.

672   Heide, Florence Parry, and Judith Heide Gilliland. *The Day of Ahmed's Secret.* Illus. by Ted Lewin. Lothrop, Lee & Shepard 1990, LB $13.88 (0-688-08895-3). 32pp. Fiction.

Ahmed, a boy of about 9, delivers bottled gas to homes in the old part of Cairo. He is proud of his ability to do this work by himself and tells about his day's routine—all the while hugging a secret that he will share with his family in the evening. It is a secret that opens the door to Ahmed's future, even if only by a crack, and the reader cannot help rejoicing at the end of this sensitively told little tale.

The watercolor illustrations, blending realism with a touch of the exotic, give an unusually vivid and appealing picture of present-day old Cairo. The story, in a sense, is a touching and sympathetic portrayal of every Third World child who must forgo the luxury of childhood for the realities imposed by poverty. This book is a real contribution to appreciation of another culture, and, with its fine illustrations, can be enjoyed by persons of any age.

A similar picture book, by the same two authors and the same illustrator, will be published in 1992 by Clarion Books. Set in Beirut, it is entitled *Sami and the Time of the Troubles.*

673 Meir, Mira. ***Alina: A Russian Girl Comes to Israel.*** Trans. from Hebrew by Zeva Shapiro. Illus. with photos by Yael Rozen. Jewish Publication Society 1982, HB $7.95 (0-8276-0208-1). 48pp. Nonfiction.

Photographs, unusually natural and appealing, help tell the story of Alina, a young girl who has recently emigrated from Russia to Jerusalem. At first she feels strange and unwanted. The other children at school interpret her reactions as unfriendliness and call her stuck-up. In time she changes her hairstyle, becomes acquainted with the city, and gradually fits in. On a visit to a kibbutz, Alina experiences a rocket attack. The reason for the shelling is not hinted at—it is just a "fact of life." Nevertheless, this incident does not obtrude or detract much from the overall effect of the book. Along with the specifics of a family adjusting to a new life, the book has a universal theme: The newcomer learns how to deal with difference and overcome misunderstanding—and someday can offer help to a still newer arrival.

674 Morris, Ann. ***When Will the Fighting Stop? A Child's View of Jerusalem.*** Concept by Lilly Rivlin. Illus. with photos by Lilly Rivlin. Atheneum 1990, LB $13.95 (0-689-31508-2). 56pp. Fiction.

An Israeli boy whose family has lived in Jerusalem since his great-grandfather's time, Mishkin wanders through the old city looking for another child to play with. His friend Alya's father will no longer let her play much with him. The accompanying photograph of Alya with a woman in traditional Arab dress suggests that the time is the present, when tensions have risen to new heights.

Mishkin, about 7 years old, observes everyday life around him, including the soldiers. His path takes him briefly to three great religious sites: the Wailing Wall, the Dome of the Rock, the via Dolorosa. He tussles a bit with an Arab boy selling souvenirs: "This is *my* home!" he shouts. "This is *everybody's* home!" the boy shouts back. At last, lonely, tired, and hot, Mishkin accepts a drink at a well, from an Arab man.

The photographs are well-composed, interesting views of the old city and its inhabitants. But they are not sharply reproduced; in many there is a curiously dim, unfocused quality, as if we were "seeing through a glass darkly," in this city where, even for a child on a sunny day, life is full of uncertainty. This is a thoughtful, expressive book.

675 Sales, Francesca. ***Ibrahim.*** Trans. from Catalan by Marc Simont. Illus. by Eulalia Sariola. HarperCollins 1984, LB $11.89 (0-397-32147-3). 32pp. Fiction.

Ibrahim proudly starts to work with his father in the marketplace of the old city of Marrakech in Morocco. When a close friend decides to leave for a nomadic life, Ibrahim becomes restless and dissatisfied with his own lot. In dreams, he is first lured to the life of freedom in the desert but later is told that freedom is in the heart. He promptly stops yearning and lives out his life in the marketplace, telling stories.

Overwritten, with long rambling dialogue and much talk about "problems," *Ibrahim* conveys a puzzling message. Why is it better to give up hopes and dreams and settle for a routine, unchallenged life? Neither the goal of self-knowledge nor the idea of accepting what cannot be changed comes across clearly here, and one must question whether this philosophy would be meaningful for a small child. The illustrations—watercolor in a naive style—are appealing, though, and give some idea of a Moroccan environment.

676 Segal, Sheila. *Joshua's Dream.* Illus. by Juna Paiss. Union of American Hebrew Congregations 1985. 32pp. Fiction. o.p.

Joshua, a young American child, is fascinated by the story of his great-aunt who went to Palestine early in this century, and he dreams of taking part himself in the development of the land. With his mother he goes to Israel and plants a tree seedling in the Negev. The emphasis on caring for and enhancing the natural environment is appealing, but a child with no other knowledge about Israel could easily get erroneous impressions. The story implies that the land was utterly unpopulated wilderness when the first Jewish settlers arrived. One illustration shows an enormous pipe—a man's height in diameter—for irrigation, but no clue as to where such vast amounts of water might be found.

677 Steiner, Connie Colker. *On Eagles' Wings and Other Things.* Illus. by the author. Jewish Publication Society 1987, HB $12.95 (0-8276-0274-X). 32pp. Fiction.

As the biblical reference in the title suggests, this short book for young children is about the ingathering of people from many parts of the world in the first years of Israel's history as an independent state. Readers meet an orphan who has survived the war in Poland, a Yemeni boy, a boy from the ancient Jewish community in Tunisia, and an American girl who comes from a comfortable city background. With their families they settle in Israel to make a new life. The focus is entirely on this influx, in an idealistic context. The illustrative sketches are simple and appealing.

Stewart, Judy. *A Family in Morocco.*
See entry 690, Grades 4–6.

Stewart, Judy. *A Family in Sudan.*
See entry 691, Grades 4–6.

678 Stickles, Frances Copeland. *The Flag Balloon.* Illus. by Janet Townsley. American Educational Trust 1988, P $9.95 (0-937165-01-8). 40pp. Fiction.

The setting of the story is never mentioned by name, but obviously it is the occupied West Bank of Palestine. The people are planning a peaceful demonstration at which, contrary to the orders of the military forces in control, their national flag will be flown. With the help of her family, the young narrator makes a large flag out of various pieces of fabric, and it is displayed prominently in the village square. Soldiers destroy the flag and disperse the crowd, but the girl puts a sticker—a flag—on her balloon. Despite the soldiers' efforts to shoot it down, the "flag balloon" floats away, a symbol of hope.

The message is overtly political at the expense of basic literary qualities such as characterization, sound plot development, and good writing. When a child narrator says something like "The crowd let out a collective sigh of relief, but the spirit of the party was sobered," one can only wish the author had taken a few more pains to write appropriately. Nonetheless, the story is worthy of attention, and not simply because it appears to be the only children's story published in this country from the Palestinians' point of view.

Stickles's tale gives an indication of the daily trials faced by the people under a repressive military occupation that has gone on since 1967, and it does so without vilifying the enemy. There is none of the racist hate-preaching that is found in some books about Israel. The soldiers, though not explained, are shown as human. They are clearly following orders, harsh and arbitrary as those orders may be, and as individuals do not act with excessive brutality. The author appears to be saying that regardless of the intolerable political situation, hatred of the enemy as human beings is not a necessary or inevitable response.

The pen drawings are decidedly amateurish, but they do offer a picture of the Palestinians' lives and culture, for instance, the village square and the people's traditional costume. This book, even with its shortcomings, would have a valuable role in classroom discussion of Middle East problems and the broader question of popular resistance to oppressive rule.

679   Tames, Richard. *Take a Trip to Iran.* Illus. with photos. SERIES: Take a Trip. Franklin Watts 1989, LB $10.90 (0-531-10650-0). 32pp. Nonfiction.

Fine photographs of dramatic mountains and desert will attract the reader to this very simply written introduction to Iran. As with others in the series, the approach is factual and noncritical. Even such a subject as the Shah's regime is handled delicately: the Shah "tried to make changes which he thought were good for Iran. But he had lost touch with the people's feelings and needs." Geography, history, ethnic groups, agriculture, and the arts are all touched upon. The book ends with a picture of the *chador* (women's black covering) as a symbol of many people's wish to return to "customs of the past." There is an index.

Other books in this series, by the same author and of comparable quality, are *Libya, Iraq,* and *Lebanon* (all published in 1989) and by Keith Lye, *Saudi Arabia* (1984), *Turkey* (1987), and *Syria* (1988). Photographs are consistently attractive.

GRADES 4–6

680   Ashabranner, Brent. *Gavriel and Jemal: Two Boys of Jerusalem.* Illus. with photos by Paul Conklin. Putnam 1984, HB $11.95 (0-396-08455-9). 95pp. Nonfiction.

This photo-essay acquaints the reader with two boys in the old city—although they do not know each other. Jemal, a Muslim Arab, is a slight boy of 14, whose father lost a good vegetable business in the 1967 war; his father now runs a small canteen at a school for refugee girls. Gavriel, age 12, comes from a Jewish family in which the father is an accountant and the mother, in addition to raising 12 children, is a full-time social worker and writes at night. Both boys go to good schools, and both families are reasonably comfortable, even if pinched by inflation.

Positive in tone, focused on everyday human activity and the similarities among people, the book reveals awareness of tension but does not emphasize political attitudes or fears. The author concludes with the thought that these two boys, though "ground between the millstones of prejudice and fear" like all young Palestinians and Israelis, are growing up in loving, peaceful homes. If the conflict between their peoples is ever to be solved, Ashabranner says, it will have to be by people like them. A good book for its detailed and positive portrayal of family life, Jewish and Arab, in Israel.

681   Bennett, Olivia. *A Family in Egypt.* Illus. with photos by Liba Taylor. SERIES: Families the World Over. Lerner 1985, LB $8.95 (0-8225-1652-7). 32pp. Nonfiction.

This title presents a colorful look at Nile Valley village life, which has probably changed very little in many hundreds of years, or since 1985—except that now there is more plastic around. The focus is on 10-year-old Ezzat and his peasant family. Excellent photos show us the village, the home, crafts, the mosque, the famous camel market in Cairo, and many activities—an informative book with a good "feel" for Egypt.

Other countries included in this series—all of them very attractive and informative books—are Arab (Gulf), Israel (a kibbutz), Morocco, and Sudan.

682   Bergman, Tamar. *The Boy from Over There.* Trans. from Hebrew by Hillel Halkin. Houghton Mifflin 1988, HB $12.95 (0-395-43077-1). 192pp. Fiction.

The strength of this book, set in the late 1940s, is its vivid portrayal of life on a kibbutz. At the start, the many characters are confusing, but this reflects the nature of the kibbutz, where the collective predominates over the individual. Personality does emerge, and there is a lot of realistic squabbling among the children, as well as mutual support.

"The boy," Avramik, has been brought from Europe, where he somehow survived the war in hiding. As a newcomer he is timorous and antisocial. Two years later, when the children are about 9 or 10, Avramik is better accepted. During the fighting of 1948, he shows quiet leadership in helping the others to reach a safe place.

The reader should be warned that this book is badly marred by an extraordinarily negative image of the Palestinians. Without exception, Arabs are shown as hateful and hate filled. The only explanation of the Arabs' hostility comes in a Jewish adult's answer to the children: "Why? Simple. The Arabs think this whole country belongs to them. They don't want to share it with us." The book reinforces harmful stereotypes, encourages antipathy, and would not enlighten anyone as to the causes of conflict.

Burgoyne, Diane Turnage. *Amina and Muhammad's Special Visitor.*
See entry 670, Grades PS–3.

683 Chetin, Helen. *Perihan's Promise, Turkish Relatives, and the Dirty Old Imam.* Illus. by Beth and Joe Krush. Houghton Mifflin 1973. 140pp. Fiction. o.p.

Don't be put off by the mouthful of title. A delightful view of everyday life in a small Anatolian village, this experience in cross-cultural living is described in flip, funny language by a high-spirited Turkish-American girl of 14.

Perihan has promised her Turkish father, living in Canada, that she will keep a journal of her visit to his home village. She arrives full of enthusiasm; there is no problem in overcoming prejudice or apathy, nor is there any rejection on the part of the Turkish family. One of the connecting themes of the story is the approaching wedding of Perihan's cousin. The American teenager is somewhat dismayed by the early age of marriage and the restricted lives of women but reminds herself to accept things that seem strange—and to remember that it was just such a marriage that produced her beloved father.

The crazy old imam (Muslim religious leader) stands for extreme conservatism; at the same time, he decides he wants to marry Perihan. Then he nearly wrecks the cousin's wedding by announcing that a destructive earthquake is Allah's judgment on the young couple. One criticism of the book is that a more favorable view of Islam might have been included to balance the negative image of the ignorant and pathetic old imam.

With gusto (accompanied by unusually stylish, amusing, and informative pen drawings), Perihan describes such experiences as the family's house and toilet, the public bath, community dancing, men's competitions in oiled wrestling and ox-head throwing, the handsome itinerant mattress-fluffer, a circumcision ceremony, conflict between old attitudes and modern medicine, and of course the wedding. By the end of her stay, Perihan realizes that her world has broadened in another way as well; her antagonism toward her recently remarried American mother and stepfamily has softened. This book offers the reader both a vivid glimpse of a way of life that is doubtless fading and an exuberant argument for cross-cultural experience.

684 Cohen, Barbara. *The Secret Grove.* Illus. by Michael J. Deraney. Union of American Hebrew Congregations 1985, HB $7.95 (0-8074-0301-6). 32pp. Fiction.

Always the last to be chosen in soccer, Beni runs away from the group one day. In an orange grove he comes across a boy from the nearby Arab village. There is no contact between the Israeli and Arab villages, and the two boys are wary at first. They agree, however, to meet again in the grove. They chat, and each admits the injustice of the stereotypes he has been taught. As Beni says, "I didn't ask him if he would steal money from his mother. I knew such a question would make him as angry as the picture [a caricature in an Arabic schoolbook] had made me." The boys do not see each other again, but 20 years and two wars later, Beni still values that brief friendship.

The illustrations, though a little clumsy, are gentle and in keeping with this touching story. A good book for discussion of prejudice and possibility.

685 Fakhro, Bahia, and Ann Walko. *Customs of the Arabian Gulf.* Illus. Ann Walko 1978. 48pp. Nonfiction. o.p.

In brilliantly colored pictures by Arab schoolchildren, we see many aspects of life in the Gulf countries. The illustrations portray, for instance, traditional dress, the marketplace, wedding customs, social calls, the mosque and the pilgrimage to Mecca, musicians and their instruments, fishing and pearl diving, and Islamic and local festivals. The brief text is informative, and the drawings vividly reveal the "child's view" of life around him or her.

The authors undertook this unusual and charming book both to acquaint American children with life in the Gulf countries and to help preserve—for the people of these countries themselves—a record of traditional customs and scenes that are fast changing in a rapidly modernizing area.

Hassall, S., and P. J. Hassall. **Bahrain.**
See entry 708, Grades 7–9.

Al Hoad, Abdul Latif. **We Live in Saudi Arabia.**
See entry 709, Grades 7–9.

Hostetler, Marian. **Fear in Algeria.**
See entry 710, Grades 7–9.

Kristensen, Preben, and Fiona Cameron. **We Live in Egypt.**
See entry 714, Grades 7–9.

Lawton, Clive A. **Passport to Israel.**
See entry 716, Grades 7–9.

686   Lloyd, Norris. **The Village That Allah Forgot: A Story of Modern Tunisia.** Illus. by Ed Piechocki. Hastings House 1973. 128pp. Fiction. o.p.

The story takes place in a small, poor village in the hills of Tunisia, reachable only by a donkey path. Ali, about 10, has recently lost his father in the nationalist confrontations with the French at Bizerte (1961). Now he must support his mother and sister—and buy the traditional sheep for the "Big Feast." On the Tunis road he sells wildflowers, then eggs laid by the hen bought with his flower money, and then, amazingly, his own drawings. Meanwhile, more or less by accident, he gets the other boys organized into rival teams and builds a road from the village down to the Tunis highway. For the first time that Ali can remember, the old men of the village take an interest in something besides complaining.

Outsiders do come and help. One is a university student whose father grew up in the village and who now finds himself coming regularly to teach the children—girls as well as boys. A Tunisian artist notices Ali on the road and, discovering the boy's own drawings in the sand, gives him paper and crayons. But most important, as Ali and the others learn, Allah helps those who help themselves.

A great deal is packed into this gracefully written little book: description of the countryside, the mood of impatience during the first years of independence, ancient and recent history, village life and mentality, desire for education, attitudes toward progress, sympathetic views of Islam, a young boy's struggle for self-realization, and, not least of all, humor. It is a pleasure to read and deserves to be a minor classic.

687 McDowell, David. *The Palestinians.* Illus. with photos. Franklin Watts 1986, LB $10.40 (0-531-17031-4). 32pp. Nonfiction.

Though heavily illustrated, with short and simply written text, this book is not only for the older elementary grades but serves as a thought-provoking introduction to the subject for older readers as well. The author calls attention to some basic facts often overlooked in popular impressions about the Palestinians. For instance, "Today's Palestinians are descended from the earliest known inhabitants of the area" (p. 6) and the Balfour Declaration's stipulation that a Jewish "national home" should not inflict any harm on the resident population of Palestine. The author discusses the Jewish settlers, the partition plan, dispossession of the Palestinians, life in the camps and within Israel, the PLO, problems of terrorism and Israeli retaliation, the status of Jerusalem, and the outlook for peace in the near future (gloomy). Includes some chronology and a brief index.

688 Ofek, Uriel. *Smoke over Golan: A Novel of the 1973 Yom Kippur War in Israel.* Trans. from Hebrew by Israel I. Taslitt. HarperCollins 1979, HB $12.85 (0-06-024614-6). 185pp. Fiction.

Eitan, an 11-year-old boy living with his parents on an isolated farm near the Syrian border, becomes friendly with the soldiers at the military outpost. When fighting breaks out suddenly in October 1973, Eitan, left alone, seeks their help. With one of the young soldiers, he manages to capture a Syrian intelligence officer. But he does not forget another friend he has made—a boy in a nearby Arab village—and finds that they still have the possibility of comradeship.

There is some exciting action, along with a feeling for the hilly, barren country. Although the political background is not explained, the captured officer (who speaks Hebrew with only the slightest accent!) and the enemy in general are spoken of with restraint and even respect, rather than the dislike that might have been expected. This is a strong point in the book's favor.

Eitan, the narrator, seems a cheerful and generous boy, but the one significant weakness of the book is his voice. Whether the fault of author or translator, the language is far too adult and literary. For example: "She was in the last months of her pregnancy, and as she felt a kind of weariness, she decided to spend the few days until she gave birth in the city, where she would be near a hospital." Good, clear English—but not an 11-year-old boy speaking. As a result, Eitan never becomes as real as we would like, and it is hard to get fully caught up in the story.

689 Semel, Nava. *Becoming Gershona.* Trans. from Hebrew by Seymour Simckes. Viking 1990, HB $12.95 (0-670-83105-0). 153pp. Fiction.

Gershona is an immature 12-year-old girl, but in 1958 she is two years older than the country in which she lives—Israel. All around her in Tel Aviv buildings are being constructed and refugees from throughout the world are arriving at the port. One of the new arrivals is Gershona's blind grandfather, who is coming from America to patch things up with the family he deserted decades earlier, when Gershona's father was a little boy. He and Gershona's grandmother remarry, and they move into the same building as the mysterious Nimrod, with whom Gershona has fallen in love. Gershona's schoolmates Hemda and Avigdor tease her, but Nimrod proves to be a true friend. As Gershona matures, she sees her parents having sex and later learns that her mother, a Holocaust survivor, is going to have another child. She also discovers the origin of her strange name, for her mother had a younger brother, Gershon, who perished in the Holocaust.

The novel's greatest strength lies in its evocation of a place and time. The reader experiences Israel's newness, the lack of amenities such as cars, refrigerators, and television, and the struggle of people to build new lives after being scarred by the Holocaust. Semel presents Gershona's story as symbolic of the growing pains, frustrations, hopes, and achievements of the new country. Gershona herself, however, is a less appealing character than the society she represents; to some extent, she fails to make the transition from symbol to real person. The scene in which she sees her parents in bed is handled discreetly, but it is not well integrated into the plot. Minor characters—Nimrod, his father, Gershona's mother, and the self-assured know-it-all Hemda—seem more interesting, primarily because they add tension and flavor to Semel's portrait of urban life in Israel in the 1950s.   L.M.-L.

690   Stewart, Judy. *A Family in Morocco.* Illus. with photos by Jenny Matthews. SERIES: Families the World Over. Lerner 1986, LB $8.95 (0-8225-1664-0). 32pp. Nonfiction.

Malika, age 12, and her family live in a three-room house in the beautiful Moroccan port city of Tangiers. The father is a hand-weaver, struggling against the competition of factory-produced fabrics. Malika's mother, who wears the traditional gown and the veil below the nose "because of modesty," manages the home and seven children. We see, in excellent photographs, Malika and others preparing food and making bread, going to the public baths, visiting relatives in an isolated mountain village, serving tea with the highly prized English tea set—and watching their TV set! The book offers an attractive, sympathetic view of a still largely traditional way of life that is undergoing some change.

691   Stewart, Judy. *A Family in Sudan.* Illus. with photos by Jenny Matthews. SERIES: Families the World Over. Lerner 1987, LB $8.95 (0-8225-1682-9). 32pp. Nonfiction.

Here we meet 11-year-old Dawalbeit and his family in a village of western Sudan, a flat desert country. The polygamous Muslim family is presented in a sympathetic way, stressing equality of treatment, lots of kids to play with, and lots of grownups to administer discipline. The text is informal and chatty, describing home life, crops, food, school, and prayer. A vivid description of drought and its effects shows the uncertainty of life in this harsh land. With attractive photos, this book is a fine introduction to daily life in a little-known part of the world.

Stickles, Frances Copeland. *The Flag Balloon.*
See entry 678, Grades PS-3.

692   Taitz, Emily, and Sondra Henry. *Israel: A Sacred Land.* Illus. with photos. SERIES: Discovering Our Heritage. Dillon 1987, LB $12.95 (0-87518-364-6). 160pp. Non-fiction.

Volumes in this series give more space to cultural and social activities than do other series. Separate chapters are devoted to folkways and tales, holidays and food, school, sports, and family life. Another unusual feature is a chapter on immigrants to the United States; the discussion of attitudes toward Israelis who return or emigrate to this country is interesting. Arabs—Muslim and Christian—are given attention in the above-mentioned chapters. In the treatment of Israel's history, there are a few misleading statements; for example, the Arabs tried to get Britain to halt Jewish immigration because "they were afraid that they would lose their own influence in the Middle East if too many Jewish settlers came" (p. 49). But, generally, this sort of fault seems due more to oversimplification than intentional distortion. (A caveat worth adding here: Trying to put complex and highly sensitive subjects into very simple language can lead to dangerous misstatements, and both authors and editors should be vigilant.) The photographs are attractive, and the book includes a glossary, a bibliography, and an index.

Another book in this series is Kevin McCarthy's *Saudi Arabia: A Desert Kingdom* (1986).

Tames, Richard. *The Muslim World.*
See entry 724, Grades 7–9.

693   Thiebaut, Elisabeth. *My Village in Morocco: Mokhtar of the Atlas Mountains.* Trans. from French and adapted by Bridget Daly. Illus. with photos by Philippe Lefond. Silver Burdett 1985. 48pp. Nonfiction. o.p.

This Mokhtar (not to be confused with the head man in an Arab community!) is a boy of about 12 in a little-known part of Morocco, scarcely touched by modernization. His family are Berbers, people of mysterious origin who once populated all of North Africa and now retain their traditional ways only in remote localities. The photographs, though on the dark side, are fascinating for the glimpse they give of this wildly mountainous area and the villagers' life. We see Mokhtar gathering walnuts (the only crop the villagers can grow for income), rough-housing with his friends, crossing deep valleys, and attending prayers with the men on a mountain slope. The story is simple, but it provides the means for much information about the Berbers' customs and their particular blend of Islamic religion with ancient folk beliefs. This is a nicely written and handsome book.

694   Watson, Sally. *The Mukhtar's Children.* Holt, Rinehart & Winston 1968. 249pp. Fiction. o.p.

This story belongs in the realm of "wishful thinking." On its own terms, nevertheless, it offers excitement, a satisfying plot, and a glimpse into traditional rural Arab life.

The setting, in 1949, is a small, isolated Arab village near the northern border of Israel. There the mukhtar (head man), Moussa, tries to keep a correct but cool relationship with the kibbutz that is expanding in the valley below. His concern seems to be about the threat of new ways more than a resentment of the new state.

Moussa's lively 12-year-old twins, however, have other ideas. Khalil, attracted to violent action, takes a shot at an abrasive Israeli officer and wounds a younger man. In retribution, his father decides that the boy must work at the kibbutz for a while. Jasmin, who personifies the frustration of women under a repressive male-dominant society, also secretly finds her way to the kibbutz; she learns to read and soon is teaching other village girls. When their father learns of the growing contacts between the young people of his village and the young Israelis, he is furious—but soon must face the inevitability of change.

Watson, writing in a light, wryly humorous style, manages to achieve a reasonably fair balance in sympathies. The focus of the story is on the Arabs, and some aspects of their traditional culture are shown in a complimentary light: dignity, hospitality, enjoyment of leisure. (And the imam, the religious leader, is an enlightened man.) Overall, however, the impression is that these Arabs are backward and repressive (especially regarding women), badly in need of the Israelis' superior technology and modern attitudes. The question of how the kibbutz—and Israel—came to be there in the first place is ignored, aside from references to the Arabs' shock at being defeated. To sum up, the book, though essentially patronizing and not very realistic, is enjoyable and makes a certain contribution to understanding of the area.

695   Whitman, Doris. *The Hand of Apollo.* Illus. by Paul Hogarth. Follett 1969. 160pp. Fiction. o.p.

Although "archaeological adventures" are outside the scope of this selection, *The Hand of Apollo* illustrates the ongoing social significance of archaeological research, especially the conflict between the needs of science and the needs of ordinary people. As the mukhtar (head man) of this little Turkish village says, "We aren't ruins! We are today, the living, the life, the very pulse of the place."

Metin, the young hero, lives in a coastal village that has grown up among the ruins of a Greco-Roman city. He longs to find a marble hand, the only part still missing from a large statue of Apollo, and his interest in archaeology is quickened by a friendship with the son of an archaeologist from Ankara. Then the villagers learn of plans to move their community to another site so that archaeological excavation can proceed, and everyone is outraged.

Along with a sympathetic view of this Turkish village of the 1960s, the reader is shown a realistic attempt to reconcile opposing demands. The idea that young people of a developing country can be interested in archaeology is a good theme, and others are the growing assertiveness of rural people vis-à-vis the government and city people and the basic question of change versus preservation of tradition. The book is entertaining, informative, and thought provoking.

GRADES 7–9

696   Abodaher, David J. *Youth in the Middle East: Voices of Despair.* Illus. with photos. Franklin Watts 1990, LB $12.40 (0-531-10961-5). 112pp. Nonfiction.

One of only seven books by Arab authors reviewed here, *Youth in the Middle East* deserves particular attention both for that reason and for the intrinsic importance of its subject matter. There could be no more vital concern than the effects of war, poverty, and social disintegration on young people, and their response and prospects.

Unfortunately, the Lebanese-American author tells us practically nothing about the subject. Instead, the book is largely a historical background of the Middle East and of the Lebanese war and Arab-Israeli conflict. Little reference is made to young people, beyond the "meanwhile, children suffer" type of remark. In Egypt, the author describes a visit to the "City of Garbage"; even there, focus is on the efforts of a French nun working with the waste collectors.

Facts are amazingly garbled. We learn, for instance, that "as long ago as 4000 B.C., the Persians and Greeks had already left their mark on the Middle East" (p. 16). We are told that in AD 500 the Jews of Palestine, fed up with Roman rule, went to Europe (p. 70). The American University of Beirut, states the author, was established in the 1920s by Bayard Dodge (p. 28); actually it was founded by Daniel Bliss in 1866. And infinitely more "howlers." If the book is so riddled with blatantly erroneous information about well-known history, why should the reader have any confidence in the author's remarks about the present? For example, visitors who find themselves near the Nile Hilton in Cairo are far more likely to be pestered by a plump merchant of perfume than by the swarms of "thin, emaciated" boys the author describes.

Critical questions about youth in the Middle East must be pursued. In Lebanon, for instance, why do youngsters continue to join militias? What do they see as their future? On the West Bank, for instance, what psychiatric services exist for kids who have seen their parents shot? Who is trying to provide schooling that is not filled with bias and anger? Information and insights of this sort are highly appropriate for American young people to consider. But they will have to wait for another book on the subject.

Archer, Jules. *Legacy of the Desert: Understanding the Arabs.*
See entry 726, Grades 10–12.

Ashabranner, Brent. *Gavriel and Jemal: Two Boys of Jerusalem.*
See entry 680, Grades 4–6.

697 Banks, Lynne Reid. *One More River.* Simon & Schuster 1973. 288pp. Fiction. o.p.

When her businessman father decides on a radically different life—emigration to Israel and work on a kibbutz—Lesley storms and sulks. Why should she leave her near-perfect life in Saskatoon, Canada? Only after a secret meeting with her beloved older brother, Noah, banished from the family for his marriage and conversion to Christianity, does 14-year-old Lesley agree to prepare for the inevitable.

The first months in Israel are grueling. Lesley still resists, refusing to learn Hebrew. Her mother is dismayed by the disregard for religious law in the kibbutz kitchen; her cultivated father exhausts himself in dirty manual labor. Determined to "tough it out," however, Lesley gradually finds herself accepted by the other young people.

The kibbutz is on the Jordanian border. Right across the river Lesley sees, one day, an Arab farmer with his teenage son and donkey. The boy beats the donkey; this arouses Lesley's anger—and curiosity. Though other kibbutzniks warn her not to take an interest in the Arabs, finally Lesley does meet Mustapha and makes him promise not to beat the donkey anymore. But she begins to realize *why* he is cruel to the animal—and why his embittered father is cruel to him. Lesley awakens to some realities.

The time is 1967, and the Arab states are taking belligerent postures. Lesley's brother arrives, one among many volunteers who have come to defend Israel, and the family is at last reunited. Then the tables of war are turned. In Israel's victorious aftermath, Lesley joins the general rejoicing; now the Arabs will have to make peace, and now it will be possible to visit Cairo, Beirut, everywhere.

Touring the captured territory, Lesley runs into Mustapha again. Their meeting, conqueror and conquered, is at first bittersweet, and finally only bitter. But Lesley has hope and leaves Mustapha with the thought that, however humiliated and hurt, he is still a valuable human being.

Banks writes with humor and perception; her style is light, lively, even lyrical. The picture of the Jewish family fitting into a new life is fascinating, and it raises the question of "Who is a Jew?"—for these kibbutzniks are anything but religious. To a large extent the book seems a paean of success, and for Lesley's growth as a compassionate, courageous person, it is. But the heartbreaking last scenes jolt the reader back to reality. There is, in the words of the spiritual, still "one more river" to cross, and it is wide and deep: the barriers to mutual understanding, respect, and reconciliation between Israelis and Arabs.

698   Beaton, Margaret. *Syria.* Illus. with photos. SERIES: Enchantment of the World. Childrens Pr. 1988, LB $17.95 (0-516-02708-5). 128pp. Nonfiction.

Besides the standard presentation of geography, population, history, and economy, this book offers insights into Syrian character. Tradition bound and suspicious because of longtime foreign domination, Syrians generally do not have an "open" mentality, the author says; loyalties, focused on the family, do not extend to jobs or the government. Syria's future is uncertain, due to the shaky economy, waste of people's abilities, and the firm grip of an undemocratic regime. Good photographs accompany this thorough, objective country survey, which is indexed.

Also in this series are equally reliable and attractive books about Algeria, Israel, Libya, Morocco, and Tunisia.

699   Brill, Marlene Targ. *Algeria.* Illus. with photos. SERIES: Enchantment of the World. Childrens Pr. 1990, LB $17.95 (0-516-02717-4). 128pp. Nonfiction.

Algeria's colonial experience under France and bitter war for freedom left it a harsh legacy. One still troublesome area is the repressed status of women, which doubtless contributes to the severe problem of overpopulation. The average woman has seven to nine children! Along with accurate discussion of history and social conditions, the author analyzes Algeria's economic situation and the problem of misdirected policies. She rightly gives special attention to the importance of Islamic influence in this country. This is a well-written, informative book about a nation that has not been very accessible to observers during its formative years. The photographs are plentiful and striking. Includes index.

700 Brill, Marlene Targ. *Libya.* Illus. with photos. SERIES: Enchantment of the World. Childrens Pr. 1987, LB $17.95 (0-516-02776-X). 128pp. Nonfiction.

The author achieves a carefully balanced assessment of Libya under Qaddafi, giving the ruler and his revolutionary government a mixed review: material and social advances, but excessive controls on individual rights and a troublesome role in international affairs. The chapter on Islam is important because of Qaddafi's stress on an Islamic society in which religion and government are virtually the same. Other especially interesting sections of this informative book focus on the Barbary pirates and descriptions of the desert, ancient cities, and the position of women—liberated by education and at the same time more limited by religious restrictions. The book contains good photographs and an index.

Chetin, Helen. *Perihan's Promise, Turkish Relatives, and the Dirty Old Imam.* See entry 683, Grades 4–6.

701 Clayton-Felt, Josh. *To Be Seventeen in Israel: Through the Eyes of an American Teenager.* Illus. with photos. Franklin Watts 1987, HB $12.90 (0-531-10249-1). 96pp. Nonfiction.

This is a valuable book for American teenagers—if for no other reason than to highlight aspects of their own society in contrast with Israel's. But the young author's observations offer even more to think about.

Writing in simple prose with no attempt at lofty style, Clayton-Felt describes a remarkably healthy "model" society in the mid 1980s. Families are close, and young people actually like to do things with their parents; their friends are welcomed warmly. Divorce is very rare—and so are excessive drinking and use of drugs. The author attributes this to the responsibilities placed on teenagers, who in Israel are treated as adults. Only fast, "offensive" driving and heavy smoking stand out as social ills, in his view.

Along with the family, the army provides a vital institution for young people. Everyone must serve, and the experience hastens maturity. What are young Israelis' goals in life? Not money, fame, and power, but "being happy." Although during his visit Clayton-Felt stayed with a family in a working-class neighborhood, he feels that his observations are widely valid.

Little is said about the Arabs, beyond annoyance at the continued tension. But the author downplays the impression, commonly held in this country, that most Israelis live in constant fear and danger.

The book is a youthfully enthusiastic report. Other views of Israeli society are likely to be less glowing, and after three years of *intifada* (uprising), the picture is bound to be more complex. Nonetheless, the book provides food for any discussion of the "ideal society."

702 Cockcroft, James D. *Mohammed Reza Pahlavi, Shah of Iran.* Illus. with photos. SERIES: World Leaders, Past and Present. Chelsea House 1989, HB $17.95 (1-55546-847-0). 112pp. Nonfiction.

Anyone who reads this book will be enlightened as to some of the reasons why such intense anti-American feeling erupted with the overthrow of the Shah of Iran. The author does not spare the role of the United States in supporting the Shah's regime, and an embarrassing story it is. Though most biographies present a generally favorable view of their subject, the Shah emerges from these pages with very little to his credit other than modest success in modernizing the country. The tone, however, is dispassionate and sober, without diatribe; the author gives some weight to psychological strikes against the man, such as a miserable relationship with his father (a ruthless dictator) and his manipulation by the British. A companion biography in the same series is Matthew Gordon's *Ayatollah Khomeini* (1987), also a good, objective presentation. Includes bibliography, chronology, and index.

Other Middle Eastern subjects of biographies in this outstanding series are Yasir Arafat, Kemal Ataturk, David Ben-Gurion, the Gemayals (Pierre, Bashir, and Amin), Golda Meir, Gamal Abdel Nasser, Muammar Qaddafi, and Anwar Sadat.

703 DeChancie, John. *Gamal Abdel Nasser.* Illus. with photos. SERIES: World Leaders, Past and Present. Chelsea House 1988, LB $17.95 (0-87754-542-1). 112pp. Nonfiction.

Few people in Western countries realize that Nasser was the first truly Egyptian person to rule Egypt since the days of the pharaohs. As the author says, he "set Egypt free"; with his charismatic presence, he virtually personified Egypt—and Arab nationalism. At the same time, with his overweening ambition and lack of realism, he got his country into all sorts of trouble. DeChancie weighs Nasser's formidable strengths and his failings, in a well-written objective biography that sheds light on the stormy mid-century decades of Egyptian and Arab history. Includes bibliography, index, and chronology.

704 Docherty, J. P. *Iraq.* Illus. with photos. SERIES: Let's Visit Places and Peoples of the World. Chelsea House 1988, LB $14.95 (0-7910-0094-X). 96pp. Nonfiction.

One of the world's oldest centers of civilization, Iraq today is a troubled country, with wealth as well as heavy debt due to the long war with Iran. But, says the author, "No one complains, because no one is allowed to do so."

The book offers a good historical survey, a description of cities and culture, and attention to ethnic groups such as the interesting Marsh Arabs. The author, apparently well acquainted with Iraq, writes with enthusiasm, but closer editorial polishing would have helped. The photographs add to the appeal, and, though dated, the book is a solid introduction to a country that Western people need to understand better. Includes index.

Other countries included in the same series are Iran, Israel, Kuwait, Lebanon, North Yemen, Oman, Syria, United Arab Emirates, and the West Bank/Gaza Strip.

Ferrara, Peter L. *East vs. West in the Middle East.*
See entry 729, Grades 10–12.

Forman, James. *My Enemy, My Brother.*
See entry 730, Grades 10–12.

705   Fox, Mary Virginia. ***Tunisia.*** Illus. with photos. SERIES: Enchantment of the World. Childrens Pr. 1990, LB $17.95 (0-516-02724-7). 128pp. Nonfiction.

Many parts of Tunisia are idyllic, and the tourist industry flourishes. Pros and cons of this controversial emphasis in the national economy would have been an interesting addition, as would a lengthier discussion of women's prospects— and the problem of enough jobs for educated youth, one of the country's significant social problems. Tunisia's long, fascinating history is well presented and includes balanced assessment of twentieth-century French rule and Bourguiba's regime.

The book is very attractive, and Fox's enthusiasm evident as she takes the reader on a tour of cities and countryside, where majestic Roman ruins rise among the rolling hills. It may encourage more Americans to visit this country, which has had a relatively peaceful existence since independence and tries to play a moderating role in regional politics. Includes several pages of "mini-facts" and an index.

Gilmore, Kate. ***Remembrance of the Sun.***
See entry 731, Grades 10–12.

706   Goldreich, Gloria. ***Lori.*** Holt, Rinehart & Winston 1979. 183pp. Fiction. o.p.

Lori, a rebellious New York teenager, is sent to live with an Israeli family that raises greenhouse flowers for export, and she quickly makes warm friendships. Her love affair with the son of the family, Danni, has a counterpart in the engagement of Danni's sister to an Ethiopian Jewish soldier. But here some intra-Israeli prejudice arises; the father looks down on the latecomer "black ones."

Other interesting individuals among the well-drawn cast of characters include Udi, the embittered son who was crippled in the 1973 war, and a German girl who has come to work in Israel as personal atonement for her country's crimes. Lori's host family is friendly with an Arab family whose daughter wants to study agriculture. A guerrilla attack, led by a cousin of the Arab family, produces a crisis and a sane resolution.

The theme of peace and reconciliation runs throughout the book. Unfortunately, there is no recognition of the cause of the Palestinians' hostility; we are told that the Arabs had nothing to fear and no reason to leave—an assertion that flies in the face of historical fact. This and the description of a pet given to Lori by the Arab family—a "tiny" 4-month-old camel, which she holds and cuddles in her arms—are false notes in an otherwise appealing story. (Cuddling a young camel would be harder than cuddling a Great Dane.)

Plot is not a strong point here; rather, the book is a good account of cross-cultural experience and the heroine's growing up.

707   Harper, Paul. ***The Arab-Israeli Conflict.*** Illus. with photos and cartoons. SERIES: Witness History. Franklin Watts 1990, LB $12.90 (0-531-18294-0). 64pp. Nonfiction.

Heavily illustrated with photos, maps, and—an unusual feature that should interest young readers—political cartoons, this book presents a compelling discussion of the problem. The author touches all bases in a smoothly written, concise, balanced presentation, in easily comprehended two-page sections. Topics include the following: "East meets West" before 1917; the rise of Zionism and the Zionists' choice of Palestine; the arbitrary dividing up of the Middle East and the beginnings of Arab nationalism; the Holocaust and its effect on both Jewish determination and Western support; the end of British-French dominance in the area and the involvement of the United States; Arab reactions; the "myth of Israel's invincibility"; the PLO, including its many nonmilitary activities; and so forth, to the Palestinian uprising in late 1987. One section discusses the "war of words" in the United Nations, another the lethal blend of religion and politics. The author's tone is careful and objective; the photographs are well reproduced. Includes a glossary and chronology, brief biographies, bibliography, and index.

If only one book on the Israeli-Arab conflict could be chosen, this is probably the one with strongest reader appeal. Two others would also be excellent choices, although they are somewhat dated—Geoffrey Regan's *Israel and the Arabs* (Lerner, 1986) and Richard Worth's *Israel and the Arab States* (Franklin Watts, 1983).

708   Hassall, S., and P. J. Hassall. ***Bahrain.*** Illus. with photos. SERIES: Let's Visit Places and Peoples of the World. Chelsea House 1985, HB $13.95 (0-222-01093-2). 96pp. Nonfiction.

Bahrain means "two seas"; sweet-water springs emerge at the floor of the sea. (Pearl divers used to tap the fresh water by means of long leather tubes.) Springs also bubble up in the northern part of this island in the Gulf, with resulting lush vegetation. The same unusual geological structure that brings the fresh water produces the oil wealth that has changed Bahrain to a dramatically modernizing country. The history of civilization on this island goes back 5,000 years; today the country's main problem seems to be the possibility of overpopulation. The book, with good photographs and a smooth presentation of facts, is a pleasure to read. Includes index. This is one of the Burke Books' Let's Visit series, published in England and distributed in the United States and Canada by Chelsea House. Other Let's Visit books present Algeria, Egypt, Sudan, and Turkey.

709   Al Hoad, Abdul Latif. ***We Live in Saudi Arabia.*** Illus. with photos. SERIES: Living Here. Franklin Watts 1987, LB $12.90 (0-531-18089-1). 60pp. Nonfiction.

Some aspects of Arabian culture may seem troubling to young American readers, such as the strict limitations placed on women and the harsh punishments for certain crimes. But these interviews with Saudi Arabians reveal a range in attitude and practice (for instance, women do practice medicine and meet the public in this context) and, apparently, widespread acceptance of family, social, and religious rules for behavior. The reader will gain a broad acquaintance with life in present-day Saudi Arabia by meeting all sorts of individuals: a builder of dhows (traditional wooden boats), the first Arab Muslim astronaut, schoolchildren, a nurse who specializes in diabetes, a soccer player, a newspaper editor, a restaurant manager, and many more. The photographs are fine, and the writing enjoyable. The book offers insights that could never be derived from a standard, descriptive text, and it certainly offers substance to counter stereotyped thinking. Includes index.

Also in this series are *We Live in Egypt* (1987) and *We Live in Israel* (1983).

710   Hostetler, Marian. *Fear in Algeria.* Illus. by James Converse. Herald Pr. 1979, P
$3.95 (0-8361-1905-3). 128pp. Fiction.

This story takes place in the early years of Algeria's hard-won independence
from French rule, perhaps the late 1960s or early 1970s, and there is a climate of
suspicion and defensiveness. Into this situation comes 14-year-old Zina, the
daughter of American missionaries, who is visiting the land where she was born.
She finds her hostess, an American teacher, under threat of expulsion along with
other foreigners.

Zina manages to avoid expulsion herself until after she and another young
American teacher have had a chance to drive through quite a bit of the country,
including a visit to the remote village where her parents once worked. The
picture of the mountainous land is intriguing, and the ordinary Algerians are
portrayed sympathetically; the book is informative in that respect. Zina's story
ends much too abruptly, however, as the author's own experiences in Algeria
may have. The book unfortunately does not provide enough background information to shed light on the Algerian government's hostile, xenophobic attitude.

The pen illustrations are stylish and attractive, with an air of authenticity.

711   Johnson, Julia. *United Arab Emirates.* Illus. with photos. SERIES: Let's Visit Places
and Peoples of the World. Chelsea House 1987, LB $14.95 (1-55546-178-6).
96pp. Nonfiction.

The "UAE," with evidence of advanced agricultural techniques 5,000 years old,
and a government still in the hands of traditional ruling families, is a very new
country. It was formed in 1971 from seven smaller "princedoms." Positive in
tone and pleasantly written, the book provides a lot of information that will
impress the reader about this rapidly developing "welfare state," where children
are provided not only free schooling but also pocket money. Smartly uniformed
policewomen handle cases involving women and children, schools for the
bedouin are arranged so as not to interfere with their traditional life-style, and
agricultural innovation holds promise of self-sufficiency in raising vegetable and
wheat crops—in a desert environment. And one of the emirates boasts the first
falcon hospital in the world! (Falconry and camel racing are still the men's
favorite sports.) The book may, though, make this Gulf country sound a little too
idyllic and isolated from regional problems. Includes index.

712   *Jordan in Pictures.* Illus. with photos. SERIES: Visual Geography. Lerner 1988, LB
$9.95 (0-8225-1834-1). 64pp. Nonfiction.

The population of Jordan presents a paradox: The Jordanians themselves, largely
of bedouin origin, are outnumbered by Palestinian refugees, both in camps and
in offices. The emphasis on education and health services (by the Jordanian
government and UNRWA, the United Nations agency concerned with Palestinian refugees) hastens rapid population growth. Other chapters discuss the land;
history from ancient times until 1986, including Jordan's involvement in the
Palestinian-Zionist conflict; and economic growth. Most of the numerous photos
are of excellent quality. A concise, readable, and accurate introduction, which
includes an index.

713   Keller, Mollie. ***Golda Meir.*** Illus. with photos. SERIES: Impact Biographies. Franklin
        Watts 1983, LB $12.90 (0-531-04591-9). 119pp. Nonfiction.

No one can deny that Golda Meir's life story is truly remarkable. From her oppressed childhood in czarist Russia to her youth in the United States, where she showed zest for social action at a very early age, to her role as a Zionist leader in Palestine from 1921 on, Golda Meir was a force to be reckoned with. Keller's account does justice to the talent and determination of this architect of Israel's creation and early decades.

The book does not, however, present Zionist aims and activities in a broader framework that would help explain the complexities of the situation in Palestine. Rather, the author describes the Zionists as totally right in all respects and the Arabs totally in the wrong—and, moreover, reprehensible. We are told, for instance, that the Egyptian government, while under combined attack by Britain, France, and Israel in 1956, saw fit to equip its soldiers with copies of *Mein Kampf* (p. 91). Why this author, and others, felt it necessary to indulge in hate-mongering is indeed puzzling. Even though Meir was a hard-liner in her policies toward the Arabs, her story has enough strength to stand without the prop of untruth and gross exaggeration about those who opposed her single-minded pursuit of the Zionist goal. The book has an index.

It is difficult to recommend a biography of Golda Meir. The subject matter is fascinating, and all four books reviewed are well written. But all are marked by an extraordinarily hostile attitude toward Arabs. Particularly offensive is the repeated Zionist claim that "nobody else wanted the land," that there was, in effect, "nobody" in Palestine—except a handful of venal landlords and miserable peasants. These books do very little to encourage constructive thinking on the Arab-Israeli conflict. Nor do such mudslinging and distortion of the truth display a responsible approach to literature for young people.

The most temperate of the books on this subject is David Adler's *Our Golda: The Story of Golda Meir* (Viking, 1984). Other biographies are Margaret Davidson's *The Golda Meir Story* (Scribner, 1976) and Karen McAuley's *Golda Meir* (Chelsea House, 1985).

714   Kristensen, Preben, and Fiona Cameron. ***We Live in Egypt.*** Illus. with photos by
        Preben Kristensen. SERIES: Living Here. Franklin Watts 1987, LB $12.90 (0-531-
        18087-5). 60pp. Nonfiction.

Part of the Living Here series, this unusual book presents present-day Egyptian life through individual interviews, each with attractive photos showing the subject in his or her work and general environment. We meet such persons as a camel dealer in Cairo, an Egyptologist, a Nubian housewife, the chairman of the State Information Service, a bedouin "supermarket" owner, a carpet factory worker, a fisherman, a schoolgirl, a belly dancer, and many others. Each speaks of his or her life and work, hopes and problems. The first-person language is a bit too literary, but it is still readable and informative.

The book provides an excellent introduction to Egypt today and incorporates accurate information about past and present in a very enjoyable manner. Includes index.

715 Kyle, Benjamin. *Muammar El-Qaddafi.* Illus. with photos. SERIES: World Leaders, Past and Present. Chelsea House 1987, LB $17.95 (0-87754-598-7). 112pp. Nonfiction.

An outstanding quality of the World Leaders series is the skillful interweaving of information about the subject and his or her time and place, so that the reader gains a sense of how the individual was shaped, sometimes even "trapped," by events and how at the same time he or she played a crucial role in determining them. The volume about Qaddafi appears an exception, simply because Qaddafi's role has overwhelmed just about every other influence in his country's recent history. From his bedouin, desert origins, where his high intelligence and revolutionary drive were evident at a very young age, to his seizure of power in September 1969, Qaddafi cuts an admirable figure. Since then, he has distributed the benefits of oil wealth in order to upgrade the living standards of his people and thus ensure himself a certain popularity. But he has also achieved an astonishing record of unpredictable and often bizarre behavior.

A coldly sober book about Qaddafi is hard to imagine, because the outrageous things he has done—or that have been attributed to him—command so much attention. The author of this biography has nonetheless resisted the sensationalist approach in order to present the material in a calm, straightforward manner. Includes bibliography, chronology, and index.

716 Lawton, Clive A. *Passport to Israel.* Illus. with photos. SERIES: Passport to. . . . Franklin Watts 1987, HB $12.90 (0-531-10494-X). 48pp. Nonfiction.

With a large, attractive format and many good photographs, this book contains a great deal of factual information about Israeli life. A special feature are the two-page spreads of imaginatively presented "fact files"—statistics and comparisons on land and population, home life, economy and trade, government and Israel's international role. As an introduction to the country it is almost entirely positive, but students of middle school age may wonder why virtually nothing is said about social and political problems. Includes index.

717 *Lebanon in Pictures.* Illus. with photos. SERIES: Visual Geography. Lerner 1989, LB $9.95 (0-8225-1832-5). 64pp. Nonfiction.

Lebanon is one of the world's most photogenic countries, and views of snow-tipped mountains, astonishing ancient ruins, and fruit orchards make the place appear a paradise. In recent years, however, these kinds of photos have given way to photos of destruction. This volume emphasizes not only Lebanon's problems that have been brought on by the dreadful war that started in 1975 but also the people's resilience. Chapters discuss the land and cities, as well as history and government, and they include a clear account of Lebanon's entanglements with Palestinian fighters and Israel in the years preceding the war.

The chapter on people describes the various religious groups but does not give sufficient recognition to Lebanese women's high status and achievements in education, business, and the professions. In addition, it is worth noting that student enrollment at the American University of Beirut has *not* dropped, as stated.

Along with good photographs, this basically solid introduction to the country includes many maps and charts on a wide variety of subjects, along with an index.

McDowell, David. *The Palestinians.*
See entry 687, Grades 4–6.

718 Marston, Elsa. *The Cliffs of Cairo.* Beaufort Books 1981; New American Library 1982. 174pp. Fiction. o.p.

Tabby, an American teenager living in Cairo with her family, is fascinated by the past, particularly the medieval times, when Cairo was truly the city of the "Arabian Nights." Her quest for the exotic takes her to an ancient mosque, a crumbling palace, and Khan el-Khalili, the famous old bazaars. At a tiny antique shop she buys a wooden ikon and soon discovers that other people desperately want to get this unimpressive small painting away from her.

Fascination with the old blends in with problems of the present—such as preservation of valuable ancient buildings in a country where there is not enough money for schools—and theft of important artifacts from archaeological sites. Scenes of home and non-American school life, encounters with many "ordinary" Egyptians, street activity, and a rowing excursion on the Nile add to the authenticity of the setting. The rise of Islamic fundamentalism, along with the tensions this has produced in Egyptian society, is foreshadowed. Despite the many books about ancient Egypt and archaeology, to date this appears to be the only American novel for young people that accurately portrays life and cross-cultural experience in contemporary Egypt.

719 Messenger, Charles. *The Middle East.* Illus. with photos. SERIES: Conflict in the 20th Century. Franklin Watts 1988, HB $12.90 (0-531-10539-3). 64pp. Nonfiction.

A political/military history from World War I on, with reference to social currents and conditions, this is a useful volume for its concise and balanced presentation. Originally published in London, the book inevitably focuses on British involvement but does not plead Britain's case. Photos are dramatic, and maps indicate military campaigns—the Suez crisis (1956), the Six-Day War (1967), the October 1973 war, and Israel's invasion of Lebanon (1982). Includes index and several appendixes on personalities, oil, mini-accounts of major conflicts, and even the Lebanese factions.

720 Rardin, Susan Lowry. *Captives in a Foreign Land.* Houghton Mifflin 1984, HB $12.95 (0-395-36216-4). 218pp. Fiction.

A thrilling, provocative, profoundly moving story, this book takes us to an unnamed "foreign land" that can be identified as Libya. Here six American youngsters are held hostage after being kidnapped in Rome, where their parents are participating in an international conference on nuclear disarmament. The Arab kidnappers are a small, essentially idealistic group that demands that the United States—as chief offender and at the same time moral leader—disarm its nuclear arsenal unilaterally. Though not cruel to the youngsters, the kidnappers do want to make things tough for these "soft American kids" and eventually come to admire them for not crumbling.

In time, the children are rescued from the mountain hideout and taken back to their families. But they have grown, changed, and learned too much from their experience to continue to accept simplistic chatter about "good old American ways" and "Arab terrorism." As individuals they now have greater faith in themselves and a determination to struggle for what they believe is right.

The main characters are 15-year-old Matt, son of a liberal U.S. senator and a peace activist in his own right, and 7-year-old Steven, timid and frail, all too aware of his parents' impending divorce. Each voice is true and compelling, and each character in the story—the other youngsters and the Arab captors alike— grows into a solid, believable individual.

The four American boys are put to work, along with their guards, on a project to catch water in the *wadi* (dry streambed) so that the local bedouin can cultivate grain. Relationships grow from this. Particularly touching is Steven's friendship with his "boss," a fatherly man who is later killed in the rescue, leaving the boy desolate. When Sidney, a Jewish boy who has spent time in Israel, rescues his work partner from a sandslide, one of the other youngsters asks if he "likes" Sadik. The boy blurts out: "He's a terrorist and Arab kidnapper. How could I like him?" But then, why rescue him? Thoughtfully, Sidney answers. "Sadik and I . . . we moved a lot of stones together."

As a survival story, *Captives in a Foreign Land* grips the reader; as an escape story it is almost as effective. The picture of the hostile desert environment is fascinating. But the greatest strengths of this outstanding book may be the exploration of human motivation, the psychological intricacies, and the hint that "moving stones together" may bring the possibility of greater understanding between adversaries.

721 Richard, Adrienne. ***The Accomplice.*** Litte, Brown/Atlantic Monthly Pr. 1973. 174pp. Fiction. o.p.

Fifteen-year-old Benjy, whose mother was killed in an accident for which he still blames his father, has come to Israel to join his father, a famous archaeologist. On top of his own emotional needs and conflicts, he finds himself drawn into the acute dilemma faced by Israeli Arabs.

A teenage Arab boy from the nearby village that contributes many of the archaeological workers becomes Benjy's friend as they work together on the site. Fawzi invites the young American to visit his family. There Benjy discovers that Fawzi's family is unwillingly sheltering a cousin, Jameel, who is a terrorist. Fawzi's village was not hurt by the fighting in 1948 and wishes to keep out of trouble. Jameel, on the other hand, lost his home, witnessed acts of Zionist terrorism, grew up in a refugee camp, and wants to fight for a state in which Jews and Arabs will be equal. If Jameel is discovered by the Israeli authorities, his relatives' homes will be blown up and the whole village will suffer.

Benjy, alarmed but sympathetic toward the young man, is unwittingly embroiled in a plot to create an explosion at the archaeological site. When questioned by the police, he wrestles with a painful moral dilemma.

This is a gripping novel, well written and rich in provocative themes. The archaeological description alone would fascinate many readers. In addition, there is a cast of vividly drawn characters, including a tough old Catholic priest who becomes a vital support for Benjy. The boy's own coming to terms with questions of loyalty and love; the Israelis' attitudes toward the Arabs and their desire to preserve their history through archaeological research; and perhaps above all, the revealing view of the Arabs in Israel make *The Accomplice* one of the most powerful fictional introductions to Middle Eastern problems in recent juvenile literature.

722 Rosen, Deborah Nodler. *Anwar el-Sadat: Middle East Peacemaker.* Illus. with photos. SERIES: People of Distinction. Childrens Pr. 1986, LB $11.95 (0-516-03214-3). 152pp. Nonfiction.

Sadat, though not universally revered in Egypt today, has inspired great admiration in the West because of his initiation of diplomatic relations with Israel, certainly a courageous and optimistic act. As successor to the dynamic leader Nasser, whom he served as a yes-man, he had to assert himself and at the same time institute a more liberal regime. With the October '73 war, his status at home soared, but repressive measures followed. As the author says, "Egyptians who found it harder to afford bread resented their modern pharaoh" (p. 136). Not a "workaholic" like his predecessor, Sadat gradually withdrew from an active role following the Camp David accords. The author presents, very readably, an honest assessment of Sadat's career and personality from his revolutionary youth, marked by hatred of the heavy British hand in Egypt, to his shocking death by assassination in 1981. This is an excellent book, with chronology and index.

The following biographies of Sadat are also highly recommended: Patricia Aufderheide's *Anwar Sadat* (Chelsea House, 1985) and *Sadat: The Man Who Changed Mid-East History* by George Sullivan (Walker, 1982).

Schami, Rafik. *A Hand Full of Stars.*
See entry 736, Grades 10–12.

Semel, Nava. *Becoming Gershona.*
See entry 689, Grades 4–6.

Spencer, William. *The Land and People of Turkey.*
See entry 738, Grades 10–12.

723 Stefoff, Rebecca. *West Bank/Gaza Strip.* Illus. with photos. SERIES: Let's Visit Places and Peoples of the World. Chelsea House 1988, LB $14.95 (1-55546-782-2). 104pp. Nonfiction.

This historical overview, from very ancient times to the establishment of Israel and thereafter, stops just short of the outbreak of Palestinian resistance in late 1987 and Jordan's severance of administrative ties with the West Bank. Separate chapters describe life in the West Bank, where the situation is particularly inflamed because of illegal Jewish settlements, and in the less complicated but terribly overcrowded Gaza Strip.

The author's approach is careful and evenhanded. More emphasis on the Palestinians' high level of education—from the start of this century to the present—and other evidence of a distinctive Palestinian culture, such as traditional dress and the women's famous needlework, would have helped give a more accurate picture of these people. Includes index.

Taitz, Emily, and Sondra Henry. *Israel: A Sacred Land.*
See entry 692, Grades 4–6.

724 Tames, Richard. *The Muslim World.* Illus. with photos. Silver Burdett 1985. 48pp. Nonfiction. o.p.

A particularly dramatic aerial photograph of hundreds of thousands of pilgrims at Mecca will give the reader an inkling of what Islam means to its followers. This lavishly illustrated volume covers many aspects of Islam, from the life of Muhammad to topics such as marriage, Sufism, Islamic art, and scientific inventions and discoveries made by Arabs in medieval times, when the Muslim world far surpassed Europe in learning. Unfortunately, the photographs, though well chosen, suffer poor color reproduction. Smoothly written, highly informative, and straightforward in approach, Tames's book is an excellent introduction to this world religion.

725 Tilley, A. F. *Oman.* Illus. with photos. SERIES: Let's Visit Places and Peoples of the World. Chelsea House 1987, LB $14.95 (1-55546-172-7). 96pp. Nonfiction.

Another little-known area, Oman is a ruggedly mountainous country on the southeastern edge of the Arabian peninsula. Since ancient times, intricately designed channels have brought water down from the heights for agriculture, and copper was produced by an advanced technology as early as 3000 B.C. Most Omanis follow a distinct sect of Islam that encourages independence and self-confidence. The author presents a sympathetic and attractive view of this rapidly developing "oil country," where a hereditary ruler sets progressive policies— and some remote villages can still be reached only by foot. With excellent photographs and index.

GRADES 10–12

Abodaher, David J. *Youth in the Middle East: Voices of Despair.*
See entry 696, Grades 7–9.

726 Archer, Jules. *Legacy of the Desert: Understanding the Arabs.* Little, Brown 1976. 214pp. Nonfiction. o.p.

This explanation of Arab history, from pre-Islamic times to the mid 1970s, provides an excellent introduction to the area for junior-high-age to adult readers. The book opens with a description of recent acts of terrorism by Arab groups, a device that points out the need for Americans to seek a far better understanding of why violence seems to be endemic in the Middle East. Then comes an objective, detailed, and accurate presentation of Arab history, culture, and character, revealed thorough research and information that goes beyond the scope of the usual survey. Numerous quotations enliven the text and illustrate points. Possibly the generalizations about oppression of women are too sweeping, but recognition is given to differences among countries and advances in women's status.

While wishing to avoid "special pleading," the author says his aim is to redress the imbalance of information about Arabs and to help young Americans understand the Middle East, "since it is they who will influence our foreign policy in the Middle East tomorrow." Even though published before the Lebanese civil war, the *intifada*, and other tumultuous events, this book is a solid, timely contribution toward that objective, and it makes fascinating reading besides. Includes extensive bibliography and index.

Banks, Lynne Reid. *One More River.*
See entry 697, Grades 7–9.

727   Bedoukian, Kerop. *Some of Us Survived: The Story of an Armenian Boy.* Illus. with photos. Farrar, Straus & Giroux 1978, HB $13.95 (0-374-37132-6). 242pp. Nonfiction.

The Armenian massacres at the time of World War I are history, but anyone who reads this book will understand why even today Armenian groups forcefully publicize the story of their holocaust and continue to demand recognition of Turkey's guilt.

This is the author's personal account of what he, as a boy, and his family went through from 1915 to 1926. Though writing 50 years after the events, the author's recall of detail is astonishing. He takes us on a forced march from central Turkey into what is now Syria, with death everywhere, and describes unbelievable cruelty on the part of Turkish and Kurdish guards and villagers. Kerop's tough and resourceful mother keeps her family alive, taking charge of many other remnants of families as well. All the men have been systematically shot.

For a while, having reached comparative safety in a small Syrian city, the family survives by weaving; during the harsh last winter of the war they live on little more than a daily handful of raisins. From there they migrate to Aleppo, and Kerop manages to be taken into a school. He observes the sad irony of well-meaning efforts by Armenian-American volunteers, who have rounded up Armenian children living with adoptive Turkish families, only to compound them in miserable orphanages with no resources or plans for the future. Even after the war is over, attack by Muslim mobs is a constant possibility. Kerop's family moves on to Beirut, Constantinople, Bulgaria, Liverpool, and finally to North America.

Kerop records all that he has seen—degradation, death, and slaughter—with a childlike detachment. This tone of dispassionate observation, at times almost a grim humor, is one of the most remarkable aspects of the book and could be called the one thing that makes such an account of horrors tolerable. As the author says of that awful winter of 1917, "If I had not forced myself to keep my curiosity and interest alive, I would have followed our neighbors to heaven." The insights into the ability of the human being to endure and the mental attitudes that contribute to survival are among the book's most impressive strengths. For mature readers, *Some of Us Survived* offers an unforgettable experience of history and appreciation of the human spirit.

Another book about the Armenian massacres and deportation, moving but less horrific, is David Kherdian's *The Road from Home: The Story of an Armenian Girl* (Greenwillow, 1979).

728   Behrangi, Samad. *The Little Black Fish and Other Modern Persian Stories.* Trans. from Farsi by Eric Hooglund and Mary Hegland. Three Continents Pr. 1976. 106pp. Fiction. o.p.

Samad Behrangi's collection of powerful short stories gives significant insights into the lives of the poor in Iran, in both urban and rural settings. Behrangi, himself a rural teacher, is a kind of folk hero, that image having been strengthened after his untimely death by drowning at age 29.

Throughout his life Behrangi lived and worked with "ordinary" people, mainly in rural areas. Traveling from village to village he sought to educate the peasants, expanding their world and fostering pride in themselves and their lives. By writing about the poor, Behrangi hoped to reach educated urban dwellers, giving them an accurate picture of life in rural Iran. In this way he served as a bridge between the two groups. To both he stressed the importance of each person's responsibility for improving the social, political, and economic disparities and problems in society.

Of the five stories in this collection, "The Little Black Fish" is the most famous and perhaps most loved of Behrangi's stories. Through the eyes of the little black fish we leave home, taking a journey downstream to learn a number of life's lessons through a variety of individuals and circumstances. The final lesson of the story is that all groups in society are to be recognized and given a voice and, further, that each of us should both strive for the courage to understand those different from ourselves and be willing to struggle against all oppression and injustice.

Another story in the collection, "24 Restless Hours," is told by a young village child about his final 24 hours in Tehran, where he has come with his father, who sells produce. Behrangi includes a short note to the reader to explain the story's purpose, ". . . that you become better acquainted with your fellow children and think about solutions to their problems." Through the dreams and eyes of the child as victim (a recurring theme of Behrangi's), we become aware of the questions, problems, pain, loneliness, humiliation, and hunger he sees and experiences as he wanders the streets of Tehran.

"The Little Sugar Beet Vendor" tells the story of the life and family of a 12-year-old sugar beet vendor through the eyes of a teacher who had taught in the one-room school of the boy's village. We learn about the pride of the boy's poverty-stricken family in refusing to accept extra pay from a man who hopes to attract the boy's sister for his own "dishonorable intentions."

All the stories in this collection are readily adaptable and easy to read and could be used to explore a variety of social and political themes in order either to gain understanding of a child's life in Iran or similar "developing" countries or simply to examine our own view of people different from ourselves.

Children and teens will enjoy "The Little Black Fish" and "The Bald Pigeon Keeper," a folktale about a king, his daughter, and their neighbor. The other stories in the collection are best used with teens.   B.N.

Clayton-Felt, Josh. *To Be Seventeen in Israel: Through the Eyes of an American Teenager.*
See entry 701, Grades 7–9.

Cockcroft, James D. *Mohammed Reza Pahlavi, Shah of Iran.*
See entry 702, Grades 7–9.

DeChancie, John. *Gamal Abdel Nasser.*
See entry 703, Grades 7–9.

729 Ferrara, Peter L. *East vs. West in the Middle East.* Illus. with one map. SERIES: Impact Books. Franklin Watts 1983, LB $12.90 (0-531-04543-9). 90pp. Nonfiction.

The author states that forcing the East-West Cold War conflict on Arab leaders, most of whom seem firmly committed to nonalignment, will only sour American relations with the Arab world. The truth of this has been amply proved since the days of the Baghdad Pact, the first "official" involvement of Arab countries in the U.S.-Soviet standoff. Specific topics include Nasser's arms deal, the Nixon doctrine of reliance on Saudi Arabia and Iran, oil politics, arms sales, and the Arab-Israeli conflict. The presentation is balanced and well written, though densely. While the book predates drastic change in both Israel and East-West relations, it is useful as a history of critical events. However, the index, which should be an important tool in such a book, is not sufficiently thorough.

730 Forman, James. *My Enemy, My Brother.* Meredith Pr./Hawthorne Pr. 1969; Scholastic 1970. 250pp. Fiction. o.p.

This superbly written novel affects the reader deeply with its insights into what the founding of Israel meant for both Jews and Arabs. It dramatizes the complexity of the issues and the psychology of both sides better than any other book reviewed and makes a unique contribution toward the reader's understanding of the problem.

The story focuses on Dan, a boy of 16 who, with his grandfather, has survived a concentration camp in Poland because of his mechanical skills. Liberated by the Russians, the two are left to wander back to Warsaw and eventually find the means to work and endure. The desolation of the present is sharpened by scenes in which Dan remembers his happy childhood—and his parents' death in the courageous Jewish uprising in Warsaw.

At a nearby camp where Jews are being helped to make their way to Palestine, Dan meets three other young people—the hardened partisan fighter Gideon, the tough but warmhearted girl Hanna, and the saintlike idealist Sholem. Together they set off to walk to the coast, where they hope a boat will take them—illegally, of course—to Palestine. The story of their exodus from Europe presents a wrenching picture of these people who have suffered terribly and are now being thwarted in their efforts to rebuild their lives.

Separated from the others, Dan manages to reach the shores of Palestine and is saved from drowning by an Arab fisherman. Though pressured because of his ability to make explosives, he refuses to serve in the Irgun. Like Sholem, he wants only a peaceful, agricultural life. On a kibbutz, he finds Hanna and Gideon once more. While watching sheep in the hills, he meets Said, son of the mukhtar of the nearby Arab village. Dan becomes friendly with Said's family, who are educated and progressive—and sadly resigned to what they know is coming.

As partition approaches, the Jewish fighters become increasingly militant. Knowing an attack is planned against Said's village, Dan warns the mukhtar. The Irgun's attack is no mere threat, and Dan is horrified to see the Arabs slaughtered in cold blood, an unequivocal act of terrorism. Dan's story ends, with blood on his own unwilling hands, in a mood of deep sorrow and determination to keep trying to make a decent life.

Once more we meet Said, a few years later. Now a fighter in the Arab Legion, he returns to visit his mother in a bleak refugee camp. The author leaves little ground for optimism. The Israelis face continued hostility and tension; the

Palestinians face a life of grief and deprivation until "Allah wills" justice. The only hope lies in the sensitivity and civilized intentions of individuals such as Dan and Said.

731   Gilmore, Kate. ***Remembrance of the Sun.*** Houghton Mifflin 1986, HB $13.95 (0-395-41104-1). 246pp. Fiction.

In the last year of the Iranian Shah's reign, an American girl goes to Tehran with her family. Through her eyes the reader has a view of the city and beautiful mountainous countryside, a glimpse of the people and Persian customs, and some awareness of the growing political agitation. The girl, Jill, develops a friendship with a handsome Iranian boy, a fellow student at the American high school, and spends most of her time with him, cruising around in his MG, until her family has to flee from Iran. Knowing that he is a leader of student demonstrations against the Shah, she can only hope that one day they will meet again.

The book should offer an excellent introduction to the country and better understanding of Iran's political and social turmoil, as well as a touching cross-cultural love story. Unfortunately, these aspects are smothered in endless talk—in a relentlessly clever, glib, adult style—about Jill's passion for the Iranian boy. Shaheen sounds totally American, and Jill, the narrator, like a literary intellectual. The self-conscious writing slows down the pace of the story and levels the emotion, so that no one emerges as a real person. Explorations of cultural conflict and attempts toward understanding, development of character, revelation of growth and change, and serious commitment are themes that are sadly neglected. What results is little more than a romance.

Goldreich, Gloria. ***Lori.***
See entry 706, Grades 7–9.

Harper, Paul. ***The Arab-Israeli Conflict.***
See entry 707, Grades 7–9.

732   Khorsandi, Hadi. ***The Ayatollah and I.*** Trans. from Farsi by Ehssan Javan. Reader's International 1987, HB $14.95 (0-930523-36-9); P $7.95 (0-930523-37-7). 159pp. Fiction.

"Laugh and the world will laugh with you." However, if you happen to be from a country that has suffered through years of political repression, mass executions, and war, how much laughter can you muster? Hadi Khorsandi's answer is "quite a bit." Continuing in the tradition of Iranian political black humor, this London-based veteran satirist has managed to publish 250 issues of his *Asghar Agha* paper over the past ten years.

Writing in simple, yet varied, styles (verse, essays, etc.), Khorsandi chronicles the experiences of postrevolutionary Iran with biting observations. He has created such fictitious characters as the everyman, Asghar Agha (Mr. Asghar), and the know-nothing simpleton high school student, Sadegh Sadaghat (the name literally translated means Honest Honesty), through whom he demystifies the Iranian government's propaganda and reveals the greed, corruption, and lack of concern for human life that underlie its revolutionary rhetoric.

Sadegh Sedaghat in his school essay on the age-old question, "Knowledge or wealth, which is better?" discovers a surprising new twist: ". . . we had an uncle who was very knowledgeable and used to read books all the time . . . they came over from the Komiteh [armed neighborhood-based revolutionary militia] and took his books and beat him up so badly he fainted. But we had another uncle who was very rich . . . they took him to the Komiteh and took his money from him and they also beat him up and he too fainted. We therefore conclude that the Komiteh is better." In other words, neither knowledge nor wealth can protect one against the Islamic revolutionary government and the zealotry it has unleashed; the only rational choice is to conform.

Khorsandi does not spare the opposition forces or Iranian intellectuals. "Perhaps one of our misfortunes in Iran was the oversupply of intellectuals . . . I myself was an intellectual for a few weeks—all for the price of a magazine." His satire, though unsophisticated at times, has proved to be a hit with the Iranian exile community and has become a way of venting frustration and pain for its readers.

The language of this collection is simple enough to be understood by most young adult readers. A general knowledge of postrevolutionary Iran is necessary to grasp the humor and significance of certain events, although there are many observations by Khorsandi that are universal.   B.N.

Kyle, Benjamin. *Muammar El-Qaddafi.*
See entry 715, Grades 7–9.

733   Lange, Suzanne. *The Year.* S. G. Phillips 1970, HB $16.95 (0-87599-173-4). 188pp. Fiction.

Like *Lori*, this title is based on the author's own year in Israel. Particularly interesting is the exploration of college-age Anne's motivation for going, which highlights conflict in attitude among American Jews, as well as "age gap." Her life on the kibbutz is described in detail. Conflict among the Americans and the Sabras (native-born Israelis) adds a lively and realistic note.

Unlike *Lori*, this book displays a consistently hostile attitude toward all Arabs, starting with the following stereotypical remark: "There we saw our first Arab, complete with flowing headdress and three wives following him on foot as he rode a tiny donkey" (p. 28). The Arabs are The Enemy, with no hope of reconciliation or understanding. Moreover, heavy speeches abound, didactic discourses about Israel being the sole hope of the Jews. Anne, the narrator, takes herself very seriously. The valuable description of kibbutz life is offset by the self-important main character—and the unfortunate air of propaganda.

734   Rohr, Janelle, ed. *The Middle East: Opposing Viewpoints.* Rev. ed. Illus. SERIES: Opposing Viewpoints. Greenhaven 1988, LB $15.95 (0-89908-428-1); P $8.95 (0-89908-403-6). 238pp. Nonfiction.

A new version of the 1982 volume edited by Bruno Leone, this is a valuable tool for classroom discussion. Topics covered are the following: conflict areas, including Lebanon and Iran; Islamic fundamentalism; the U.S.-Israeli alliance and the role of the United States in the Middle East; Palestinian rights; and prospects for peace. Selections, from a variety of sources, are scrupulously balanced. Each section features a different activity in critical thinking.

The book includes a detailed chronology from 1881 to June 1987, plus an extensive bibliography and a list of U.S. organizations concerned with the Middle East. Includes index.

735   Sa'edi, Gholam-Hossein. ***Dandil: Stories from Iranian Life.*** Trans. from Farsi by Hasan Javadi et al. Random House 1981. 239pp. Fiction. o.p.

Censorship and repression have been mainstays of Iranian life for the better part of the last 50 years. To combat them, Iranian writers have devised an elaborate style of coded stories. The late Gholam-Hossein Sa'edi, Iran's foremost dramatist, was the master of such coding. Whether in a play or a short story, he created a world at once real and metaphorical, in which an allegorical theme would be fleshed out without reducing its subjects and characters to triviality.

Written from the point of view of a young boy living in the slums of southern Tehran, "The Game Is Over" conveys the message that poverty and repression turn individuals into petty tyrants (in their own small realm), and poor children, by virtue of being at the bottom of the social pyramid, become the ultimate victims.

Hassani, a mischievous boy, lives with his beastlike father and ineffectual mother in the slums near the city dump. He is savagely beaten and humiliated by his father every day. His only respite from this hell is his friendship with the narrator of the story. One day, after a particularly harsh beating, Hassani plots with his friend to take revenge on his father. The plan backfires and leads to a second and desperate plan by Hassani to fake his own death. He believes that by doing so his parents will realize how much they love him and when he reappears will shower him with the love he has been denied. Sa'edi's harsh and desperate universe leaves no room for such a fairy tale ending.

"They call this Dandil. Everybody's down and out. We just want a mouthful of bread to hold our stomach together and give us the energy to drag the corpses." Set in the red-light district of a small provincial town, *Dandil* is a rundown neighborhood where dingy buildings are populated by shabby people with small hopes, fears, and dreams. An air of excitement takes over when a beautiful young woman is brought to one of the brothels. In pursuit of the most suitable and profitable patron for her, everyone's attention focuses on an American from the nearby army base. What the residents of Dandil expect from the American, and what actually happens, is the contradiction that symbolically represents the relationship between the United States and Iran through the 1960s and the 1970s. Given the setting of the story, its language is occasionally explicit, but this by no means takes away from its strength or the insight it provides.

The three stories and two novellas that make up this collection demonstrate Sa'edi's immense indignation at social injustice as they transcend mere representations of ordinary suffering. The introduction by Hasan Javadi puts Sa'edi's work in its proper historical and intellectual context.

The short stories in this anthology are suitable for young adults because of their content, length, and the effort the translators have given the work so as to make a glossary of Farsi terms unnecessary.   B.N.

736 Schami, Rafik. *A Hand Full of Stars.* Trans. from German by Rika Lesser. Dutton 1990, HB $14.95 (0-525-44535-8). 197pp. Fiction.

Reflecting on this novel, the reader may be surprised to realize that nowhere is the narrator named. Yet such a vibrant, rounded personality has emerged in the pages of this teenage boy's journal that a personal name is scarcely needed. A remarkable book, and virtually unique in that it is written by an Arab for young readers in Western countries, *A Hand Full of Stars* gives us an inkling of what it feels like—from the inside—to be a youth growing up in a politically repressive, confused Middle Eastern society—Syria in the mid 1960s.

The boy, 14 when he starts his journal, is a Christian living in the ancient part of Damascus. Written with spirit and humor, the entries made during the first year of the journal reveal a rambling, realistic, possibly overlong account of the boy's daily life. He talks about school, friends, family, his father's bakery, the old streets and "mud houses" of the poor quarter where he lives, his growing passion for a neighbor girl and determination to defy her secret-police father, and, throughout, his special friendship with Uncle Salim. This illiterate old coachman's wisdom, warmth, and good stories have made him the soul of the neighborhood. In fact, the title of the book refers to Uncle Salim's guiding hand.

The narrator's interest in writing begins to bear fruit in the succeeding years of his journal. Encouraged by a teacher, he submits poems to an editor and eventually sees them published and praised. He is rescued from the drudgery of working in his father's bakery by Habib, a journalist, who gets him a job in a bookstore. With Habib, who is embittered by the restraints imposed by the repressive regime, and his childhood friend Mahmud, the narrator starts a subversive underground "newspaper." The devious means by which the boys contrive to disseminate their paper are described with humor, but humor becomes more precious as the narrator's mission becomes increasingly serious and dangerous. Ultimately, Habib is arrested, and the boys know there is no hope for their friend and mentor; all they can do is continue their underground struggle in his memory.

Other important people in the young man's life are his good-natured mother, his girlfriend, and a pathetic madman whose eccentricity conceals profound wisdom. The reader gains a view of working-class life in Damascus and the people's growing disgust with the successive military rulers. The narrator's namelessness is perhaps symbolic of his need for anonymity in the police state. Boyish, funny, sardonic, thoughtful, idealistic, he is a superb example of the young person who tries to do what he can to resist oppression.

737 Southgate, Minoo, ed. *Modern Persian Short Stories.* Trans. from Farsi by Minoo Southgate. Three Continents Pr. 1980, P $10.50 (0-89410-033-5). 228pp. Fiction.

In this collection, Minoo Southgate has gathered works by some of the most important contemporary writers of Iran. The majority of these stories were written during the 1960s and early 1970s, a time that saw the transition of Iran from a traditional rural agrarian society into an urban society with a capitalist economy. Themes of social and political repression, alienation, and the collapse of traditional ways of life dominate the collection. Given the developments in Iran, with the resurgence of Islam and traditional Islamic values, this book provides a valuable background for understanding the basic contradictions that fueled the revolution of 1979 and events since then.

The stories by Simin Daneshvar, Jalel Ale-Ahmad, and Gholam-Hossein Sa'edi should be of special interest to young adult readers.

In "A Land Like Paradise," Simin Daneshvar, the most important and successful woman writer of Iran, portrays the disintegration of a traditional merchant household through the eyes of the family's son. The story follows the strong bond that develops between the young boy and a black woman servant-slave. As forces of history quicken the decrease of the family's socioeconomic standing, the lines of loyalty and love prove too frail to forestall impending tragedy and unhappiness. Daneshvar succeeds in relating the brutal and ambiguous master-servant relationship with subtlety and power. The story is multi-layered, bringing forth subjects such as the status of women, betrayal, and human suffering in a fully realized universe.

Set against the backdrop of forced modernization and the gimmickry of Reza Shah's regime in the 1930s, "The Joyous Celebration" tells the story of a boy who is confronted with the cruelty of his father, coming to terms with the pressure of the outside world that undermines the traditional religious ways of his family. Ale-Ahmad's young protagonist lives in a house that is empty of love and affection, where everyone is brutalized by another. The situation is exacerbated when the father receives an invitation requesting that he and his wife attend "a joyous anniversary of . . . the Day of Women's Liberation." The invitation implies that his wife should be dressed in a modern fashion for the occasion, or, as the father screams out, "bare headed and bare bottomed." Ale-Ahmad draws parallels between the brutal nature of the traditional family and that of the government.

The stories in this anthology offer an unsentimental look at hopes, fears, frustrations, and tragedies of the human condition in Iran. The glossary of Farsi terms, biographical notes, and bibliography that Southgate has included enhance readers' understanding. At times the book suffers from an unimaginative translation that indicates a lack of affinity for the English language and its cultural specificities; this is the one major flaw in an otherwise valuable book for classroom use and independent reading in the upper high school grades.

B.N.

738 Spencer, William. *The Land and People of Turkey.* Illus. with photos. SERIES: Portraits of the Nations. HarperCollins 1990, LB $14.89 (0-397-32364-6). 208pp. Nonfiction.

The longest of the "country" books, this is written in adult—but not heavy-handed—style by an author well acquainted with Turkey. The section on ancient history, especially the history of the Hittites, is interesting, and the achievements of Ataturk and political developments since World War II are carefully appraised. The author notes that in view of the deplorable economic conditions at the end of Ottoman rule, Turkey has made dramatic advances. But there is a black chapter in Turkey's twentieth-century history—the massacres and deportations of the Armenians—and this is rightly given emphasis. Spencer's book is sufficiently readable to be enjoyed for itself, not used just for school assignments. The main disappointment is in the photographs, many of which appear drab and do not give sufficient view of the land. The book has an index, as well as a bibliography that includes sources of Turkish folk music.

13

SUB-SAHARAN AFRICA

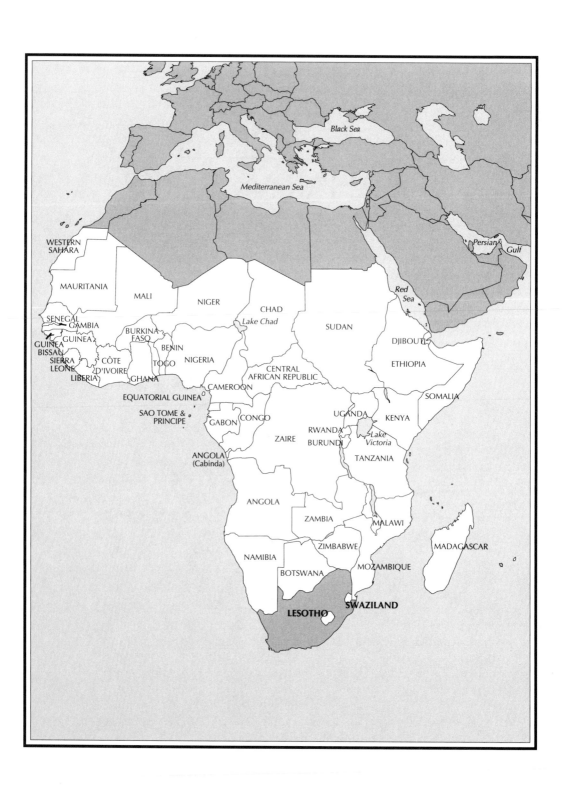

WESTERN
SAHARA

MAURITANIA

MALI

NIGER

CHAD

Lake Chad

SUDAN

Red
Sea

DJIBOUTI

ETHIOPIA

SOMALIA

SENEGAL
GAMBIA

GUINEA
BISSAU

SIERRA
LEONE

LIBERIA

GUINEA

CÔTE
D'IVOIRE

GHANA

BURKINA
FASO

BENIN

TOGO

NIGERIA

CENTRAL
AFRICAN REPUBLIC

CAMEROON

EQUATORIAL GUINEA

SAO TOME &
PRINCIPE

GABON

CONGO

ZAIRE

UGANDA

RWANDA
BURUNDI

Lake
Victoria

KENYA

TANZANIA

ANGOLA
(Cabinda)

ANGOLA

ZAMBIA

MALAWI

MADAGASCAR

NAMIBIA

ZIMBABWE

BOTSWANA

MOZAMBIQUE

LESOTHO

SWAZILAND

Black Sea

Mediterranean Sea

Persian
Gulf

13

SUB-SAHARAN AFRICA

by Michael Afolayan, Patricia Kuntz, and Brenda Naze

Children's books about Africa became available in the United States and Canada in large numbers in the 1960s. Until the 1960s most African countries were still British, French, or Portuguese colonies, but as one after another gained independence, Americans participated in the Peace Corps, the Agency for International Development, and the foreign service with assignments in African countries. Many travelers and government employees have recorded their impressions in children's books over the past three decades. Although most of these books have been characterized by poor research and a patronizing tone and approach, several photo-essays and works of nonfiction have distinguished themselves in terms of quality.

Another, more recent, impetus for writing and publishing books about Africa has been the rise in ethnic consciousness among African Americans. During the late 1960s and early 1970s, a number of small presses produced children's books, but in most cases the presses closed and the books went out of print. A few major presses participated in the trend; among the mainstream press books that came from this period and tradition and that remain in print are Eloise Greenfield's *Africa Dream* and Muriel Feelings's *Moja Means One*. Beginning in the late 1980s there has been a resurgence of publication of books with an emphasis on African heritage, and new small presses, such as Just Us Books—the publishers of *Afro-Bets Kids*—have entered the field.

Few African authors have participated in the children's literature genre, although African-American authors have written and illustrated some of the more significant and noteworthy titles set in Africa. Children's literature in Africa traditionally has been oral rather than written; thus few writers have considered writing for children, as opposed to writing about children in a literature that is principally for adults. Furthermore, the uncertainty of markets in Africa has discouraged African writers from producing children's literature. American publishers who might consider commissioning an African writer to create a children's story find that many African writers are not familiar with the American child, the educational curricula, or the market in general.

Some works by adult authors have been considered suitable for young adults and are therefore included in this bibliography. However, the lack of works for children by African authors is one reason for the generally poor quality of juvenile books set in this region. The problems are myriad. First, many writers fail to specify a country, nation, or group of people in their works, leading readers to assume their books are valid for the entire continent. Several fine African-American writers and publishers have fallen into this trap, among them Greenfield. Another otherwise good work marred by this problem is the *Afro-Bets First Book about Africa*.

Second, in treatments of Africa, there tends to be an emphasis on the exotic. Margaret Musgrove's *Ashanti to Zulu: African Traditions*, published in the late 1970s, focuses on each group's most unusual features. More recently, Jim Haskins's *Count Your Way Through Africa* uses Kiswahili as the unifying element and presents customs and beliefs out of the Swahili context. Other books show only the most picturesque and insignificant ethnic groups. Since young children are not able to discriminate between a small population and a large population, books for this level that feature only the exotic groups, such as the Masai, San, Mbuti, and Khoi, create misconceptions and stereotypes.

A third problem has to do with language, which reveals the author's sensitivity, or lack thereof, for the characters or peoples. Pejorative language often reveals a racist tendency. Examples of insensitive language include the term "tribe," for ethnic group, "Bushmen" for the San and "Hottentots" for the Khoi, and the words "hut," "native," and "scars" (the latter term itself referring to a custom that is far from universally practiced).

A fourth problem is one of illustration. Besides reinforcing stereotypes in the text, illustrations can create their own. Most illustrated fiction about Africa portrays rural villages and ways of life that are fast disappearing. Some of the better ones that do this are Ann Grifalconi's *The Village of Round and Square Houses* and Karen Lynn Williams's *Galimoto*, but they need to be balanced by works set in cities and towns. Nigel Gray's *A Country Far Away*, illustrated by Philippe Dupasquier, not only reinforces the rural stereotype but also exaggerates the facial features of the Africans in a way that might be interpreted as ridiculing them. Those who use books about Africa with children should be wary of illustrations that either minimize or exaggerate facial features or that make African subjects appear unattractive, exotic, or otherwise strange.

Folktales continue to dominate in the publishing of books about Africa. This in itself is a statement about U.S. perceptions of the region, for a body of literature that is predominantly folktale emphasizes the exotic, the traditional, and the safe, and a contemporary portrait usually leaves the non-African author open to more criticism. Although folktales are beyond the scope of this bibliography, several have been included here, as they reveal something of contemporary culture in the region of their origin. Among the most noteworthy are John Steptoe's beautifully illustrated folktale-based story *Mufaro's Beautiful Daughters*, and Veronique Tadjo's *Lord of the Dance*, a poetic rendition of the Senufo tales of her home country, la Côte d'Ivoire. Other books—for example, the volumes in the Dillon Press Discovering Our Heritage series, include folktales within the text; these are more useful in teaching about the countries of the region, as they put the oral tradition into a context.

Besides folktales, another type of book that tends to prevail are books about animals. Few have been included here; the argument against including them is that people are rarely included in the text. Young readers conclude that African countries are inhabited by wild animals. In fact, few countries have wild animals except on game preserves or in zoos. The chances of seeing an elephant, lion, or hippopotamus, even on the preserves, are not great, and poachers have reduced the animal population considerably. If young readers insist on an animal book, Joyce Powzyk's *Tracking Wild Chimpanzees in Kibira National Park* is recommended for content and realism. Barbara Margolies's *Rehema's Journey*, another highly recommended work, raises the issue of wildlife preservation within the context of a Tanzanian child's vacation with her father, a tour guide in a wildlife preserve.

Early books of fiction and nonfiction for younger readers revolved around Europeans', Euro-Africans', or Americans' adventures in an African country. For instance, Lillian Gould's *Jeremy and the Gorillas* (1970s; o.p.) portrays the adventures of a young Euro-African boy in Uganda. While Gunilla Lundgren's photo-essay, *Malcolm's Village*, presents a 7-year-old Swedish youngster living near Mount Kilimanjaro, the emphasis is on cross-cultural relationships and a child's first encounter with death. The focus of the story is the African family's response to Grandma's death, and Malcolm and his family are there to learn rather than to teach. Books in the 1990s, however, are focusing on the adventures of African children. *Rehema's Journey*, also a photo-essay, documents a young girl's trip to Arusha, Tanzania; although Rehema comes from a rural village, the reader is treated to a portrait of town life and a view of various ethnic groups living and working together. Despite its rustic setting, *Galimoto* describes the resourcefulness of its African protagonist, who builds a car from pieces of wire. For older readers, *Story for a Black Night*, by Clayton Bess, presents a family's tale of terror, disease, and sacrifice, and Sonia Levitin's *The Return* features an Ethiopian Jewish girl who leads her frail younger sister to safety and freedom in Israel.

An unusually large proportion of the books set in sub-Saharan Africa, excluding South Africa, are picture books. (In the case of South Africa, one sees the opposite trend, with almost no picture books and a wealth of young adult materials or adult materials suitable for young adults.) Counting books are popular for the young child. *Moja Means One* has been reprinted due to popular demand, and *Count Your Way Through Africa* is a recent issue. Both books introduce the counting numbers in Kiswahili. *Moja Means One* maintains the East African environment, while Haskins throws in ten countries that do not use Kiswahili. Haskins's weak title should not be confused with Claudia Zaslavsky's *Count on Your Fingers, African Style* and *Africa Counts*, two books that touch upon the origins of counting systems and mathematics in various African cultures. Unfortunately, both of the Zaslavsky books are out of print and difficult to find.

Another type of book for elementary-age students is the language book. The language of choice is Kiswahili. Muriel Feelings's *Jambo Means Hello*, Leila Ward's *I Am Eyes—Ni Macho*, and Katherine Klyce's *Kenya, Jambo* present basic Kiswahili. These three books are positive contributions to school systems. As more districts consider offering Kiswahili as a language program, students with knowledge about the language will be potential participants.

Older elementary-age children and middle schoolers are often interested in craft and cooking books. Several books have been published to fulfill this interest; they contain historical and cultural information as well as instructions and recipes. The best of these is Constance Mabwere's *Cooking the "African" Way*, which contrasts the cuisines of various areas of East and West Africa.

Beyond the middle school level, students interested in fiction and nonfiction set in Africa should read works by African authors. Among the ones especially recommended for older teenagers are Buchi Emecheta's *The Moonlight Bride*, Nafissatou Diallo's *A Dakar Childhood*, and Ben Okri's *Flowers and Shadows*.

Nigerian-born Okri at the age of 19 wrote his story of upper-class corruption and intergenerational conflict.

Numerous series books cover the countries of Africa, and new ones emerge each year. Increasingly authors and editors realize that books with African content must involve an Africanist consultant. Errors in facts, language, sensitivity, and interpretation are no longer excusable. (Articles that document these errors are listed in the Reference section of this book.) The U.S. Department of Education funds nine centers of African studies and language to inform citizens about Africa. Series and other nonfiction books not using the services of a consultant should be considered suspect. Two geography series that use consultants or area specialists, with a consistently better product as a result, are Enchantment of the World, published by Childrens Press, and Portraits of the Nations (a revision of the Land and People series), published by HarperCollins. For beginning researchers, the Discovering Our Heritage series furnishes interesting cultural information, although topics are not explored in nearly as much depth as in the series recommended above.

The annotations have been prepared by a team from the African Studies Program at the University of Wisconsin under the guidance of Outreach Director Patricia Kuntz, who wrote this introduction. In addition to Kuntz, individual entries were contributed by Nigerian educator Michael Afolayan and Brenda Naze, a secondary English teacher. One entry, that for *Malcolm's Village*, was contributed by Bojana Vuyisile Jordan, author and professor of African studies at the State University of New York at Albany.

PRESCHOOL–GRADE 3

739   Ellis, Veronica Freeman. ***Afro-Bets First Book about Africa: An Introduction for Young Readers.*** Illus. with photos. Just Us Books 1989, P $4.95 (0-940975-03-3). 32pp. Nonfiction.

A classroom situation is used as a device to explore Africa in this unique small press book. The teacher, Mr. Amegashie, brings the whole of Africa to the Afro-Bets Kids in a vivid and remarkably detailed way. The kids learn about the geography of the continent, its cultural and linguistic diversity, its fascinating history from prehistoric to contemporary times, and its traditions of art, music, warfare, dress, kingship, and natural endowments. Mr. Amegashie surveys the animals of Africa by means of a folktale that holds the Afro-Bets Kids spellbound, and he concludes his narrative with a few steps of an African dance.

The book is well illustrated with color drawings featuring the trademark Afro-Bets Kids and photos. With its glossary of words and difficult concepts, the book provides a valuable resource for older children doing first reports and exploring the continent on their own. At times, the writing is marred by outdated terminology, for instance, the use of the word "tribe" to refer to ethnic groups, and some Africanists have argued that Liberian author Ellis has featured the most exotic and insignificant of Africa's ethnic groups. Still, respect for the continent and its people is communicated throughout, from the presence of the African teacher to the emphasis on diversity in presenting the continent to the linkage made between Africa and students of African-American heritage.

M.A.

740   Feelings, Muriel. ***Jambo Means Hello: A Swahili Alphabet Book.*** Illus. by Tom
Feelings. Dutton/Dial 1981, P $4.95 (0-8037-4428-5). 46pp. Fiction.

Following her two-year trip to Uganda, where she taught high school in
Kampala, Muriel Feelings wrote two books that focus on different aspects of
Kiswahili. The first and shorter book, *Moja Means One: A Swahili Counting Book*
(1971), won Tom Feelings a Caldecott Medal. The second book, *Jambo Means
Hello: A Swahili Alphabet Book*, introduces elements of everyday life in East
Africa through the national language of Uganda, Kenya, and Tanzania,

Both books are sensitive to young readers and teachers. A map is provided to
locate countries. A description of Kiswahili prefaces the text with a brief linguistic explanation for teachers. For each Kiswahili word there is a pronunciation
insert. Finally, Tom Feelings provides a detailed illustration of each term and a
second sketch to place the word in context. The three- or four-sentence description elaborates on the importance of the word in Swahili or East African culture.
Both books focus on the urban setting where Kiswahili is a medium of communication. Unlike similar books of this format, Muriel and Tom Feelings include
people on nearly every page. Young children can hear and see the importance of
relationships.

These two books are models for future children's books. They demonstrate
the positive nature of a major African language, the impact of a culture, and the
importance of people. As more large school districts offer Kiswahili among their
language programs, children in the elementary school will need this type of
introduction. Muriel Feelings is also the author of *Zamani Goes to Market* (Africa
World Pr., 1989), a book for older elementary school students.   P.K.

741   Gray, Nigel. ***A Country Far Away.*** Illus. by Philippe Dupasquier. Orchard 1989, LB
$12.99 (0-531-08392-6). 32pp. Fiction.

This book means well. Its sparse text describes a day in the life of two boys—one
from a developed country in the West and one from rural Africa. The illustrations, of the African boy above the text and the Western boy below, show how
their daily activities are at the same time both different and essentially similar as
both boys help their parents, attend school, ride their bike, play with their
friends, go shopping, celebrate the birth of a baby sister, and read a book about
another boy in a faraway land.

Having young children point out both the similarities and differences in the
boys' lives has appeal. Children can observe the variety of experiences, cultures,
and ways of life. However, this presentation is not without its problems. The
white middle-class boy who lives in the suburbs and the African child who lives
in a semiarid rural area are portrayed as representing all of "the West" and
"Africa," when the two places are in themselves quite diverse. In the case of the
African child, this plays into common preconceptions; even the bicycle, one of
the more "modern" features, is a particularly old-fashioned and rickety model.
In another picture, a railroad track and train have fallen into disrepair. Of more
concern, though, are the illustrations of humans, which caricature black people
and might be used to ridicule them. (The ones on the front and back covers are
among the worst in this respect.) A more sensitive treatment would have used
photographs or another style rather than Dupasquier's cartoonish watercolors.
When on the next-to-last page the two boys look at pictures of each other, one
cringes to think of the misconceptions and stereotypes each has absorbed.

L.M-L.

742   Greenfield, Eloise. ***Africa Dream.*** Illus. by Carole Byard. HarperCollins 1977, LB $12.89 (0-690-04776-2). 32pp. Fiction.

This story is the fantasy of an African-American child who finds herself in the Africa of the past. Her "dream adventure" takes her to the marketplace, where she buys delicate items such as perfume and pearls. She reads some strange words in old books and rides through a huge crowd on a donkey. Arriving at the dream village, she meets her grandfather of "long ago," whom she identifies through her memory of her father's face. He plants a magical plant that produces delicious mangoes. Dressed in a long costume, she participates in ritual dances to the rhythm of her uncle's drums, and she sings in a circle with cousins from all over Africa. Finally, she tires. She turns into a baby and falls asleep in the arms of her "long-ago grandma."

Greenfield's is a nostalgic presentation of Africa, an imaginary journey that tries to make a connection between that world and African Americans today. Byard's grayish pencil illustrations give the story a realistic flavor, although, in truth, the world visited by the protagonist is quite idealized. Young readers will delight in the fun activities and warm familial love experienced by the little girl; the sense of heritage communicated by Greenfield is perhaps the book's greatest contribution. However, as the title itself suggests, the beauty of the rendition does not negate the fact that the Africa portrayed here is a dream bearing only the slightest resemblance to the reality of the continent, past or present.

M.A.

743   Grifalconi, Ann. ***Darkness and the Butterfly.*** Illus. by the author. Little, Brown 1987, HB $14.95 (0-316-32863-4). 32pp. Fiction.

This picture book, the second of Grifalconi's works about Osa, explores Osa's fear of the dark. An energetic, active child by day, Osa is so frightened at night that she cannot even eat in the dark. One day, she wanders into the woods and cannot find her way home. An old woman and a yellow butterfly come to her rescue and lead her home. Later she has a dream recalling the butterfly leading her to safety; when she tells the Wise Woman about her dream, the Wise Woman pronounces her cured of her fear.

This work accurately reflects the emotions and responses of any child afraid of the dark. In that sense, the story is a universal one. However, it is set in Africa and is based to some extent on the spiritual beliefs and folklore found there, although Grifalconi does not specify a place or a particular culture.

Users of the book should be cautioned that the supernatural events do not reflect reality—a fact understood when reading works based on familiar Western folklore but one that cannot be taken for granted when the culture is a distant and unfamiliar one—and that spiritual beliefs are presented in the most general terms; they cannot be said to characterize any one African culture. Given these caveats, this charming book, with its vivid, warmly rendered color illustrations, will appeal to children who have at some point themselves been afraid of the dark.

M.A.

744   Grifalconi, Ann. ***Osa's Pride.*** Illus. by the author. Little, Brown 1990, HB $14.95 (0-316-32865-0). 32pp. Fiction.

This short tale represents a recollection by the African girl Osa, encountered in two earlier works by Grifalconi. Here, she recalls a time in which she showed excessive pride and foolishness. After her father's death in the war, she invented a story depicting him as a hero. Ignoring other people's feelings and the fact that the other children, too, may have lost their fathers, she pestered everyone with her make-believe story. Finally, her grandmother stepped in, telling Osa a highly graphic and didactic tale of a proud girl who goes to the market and finds herself humbled. This restored Osa's sobriety and made her realize pride will lead her nowhere.

Osa's Pride is very didactic, reminiscent of African folktales, particularly those intended for younger audiences. The style is interesting, as the author presents one story that concludes another one. The stories describe the universal experience of childhood fantasy and call attention to the African child's experience of the agony of war and its consequences.

The colorful artwork contributes to the overall linguistic and didactic effect of the text. However, more sophisticated readers will question whether what we read in Osa's life is really an expression of pride rather than a young child's normal reaction to the loss of her father. The story does not indicate if Osa realizes her father will never come back; rather than exploring these emotions, the author displaces them, producing what is ultimately a shallow and frustrating work.

M.A.

745   Grifalconi, Ann. *The Village of Round and Square Houses.* Illus. by the author. Little, Brown 1986, LB $14.95 (0-316-32862-6). 32pp. Fiction.

Grifalconi traveled to the isolated community of Tos in Cameroon, where she gathered data for this book. During her visit she learned about the custom in which men live in square-shaped houses and women and children live in round-shaped ones. Her illustrated book explains the origins of this custom. This practice is unique and not representative of other Cameroon communities. Unfortunately, the reader does not learn about the actual location of Tos or the background of the "nation" of which the citizens of Tos are a part.

The story itself is interesting and the illustrations provide a positive image of this community. Grifalconi describes food preparation and children's responsibilities. She illustrates the storytelling of the grandmother, which becomes a reward for completion of the children's work.

This book is Grifalconi's best production so far. *Darkness and the Butterfly* (1987) describes the efforts of a child to overcome fear of the darkness. Although the book is considered by the publisher to be an "African" story, no content about any African country or people is contained in the book. The sequel, *Osa's Pride* (1990), lacks a strong story line. The practice of generalizing about Africans, African Americans, and Afro-Caribbeans only confuses children. In order to repair the damage that stereotyping has done in the past, books must project honest appraisals of specific situations, as this first Grifalconi title has done.

P.K.

746   Haskins, Jim. *Count Your Way Through Africa.* Illus. by Barbara Knutson. SERIES: Count Your Way Books. Lerner/Carolrhoda 1989, HB $11.95 (0-87614-347-8). 24pp. Nonfiction.

The Count Your Way Books is an excellent idea—a holistic approach to learning to count in a foreign language and to discovering another culture. Here, the Swahili numbers from 1 to 10 are used to introduce the reader to the history, geography, and cultures of Africa. However, rather than focus on items from the Swahili culture or cultures where Kiswahili is an official language, this book uses examples from a variety of non-Swahili people. The people of Zimbabwe speak Shona, Ndeble, or Chichewa, not Swahili. The San (misstated as the "Bushmen") consist of a population of 1,000 in South Africa and Namibia. Swahili culture and language have little similarity to these people.

Stereotyping is prominent in this book. Not only are pejorative words used, such as "native" or "tribal," but the images are exotic. The text reads paternalistically. Scarification is a practice among some nations in West Africa, but this custom would never be practiced by Muslim Swahili. The traditional Watusi dancers could speak Kiswahili; however, their dress is ceremonial only.

The author provides an inaccurate phonetic transcription of the Swahili numbers. "Moja," the Kiswahili word for "one," is written [mojah] rather than [mo-dyah]. Either the author does not know Kiswahili or he is transcribing nonstandard Kiswahili.

The book does not portray Africa or the Swahili culture or language positively. Children reading this book will confuse Africa as a country with only the language of Kiswahili. Unfortunately, this book has not reversed stereotypes about Africa, which American children hold from exposure to inaccurate media. Although the illustrations are adequate, they portray a negative, false image.

M.A./P.K.

Jacobsen, Karen. **Zimbabwe.**
See entry 766, Grades 4–6.

747   Klyce, Katherine Perrow, and Virginia Overton McLean. **Kenya, Jambo!** Cassette included. Illus. with photos and drawings. Redbird 1989, HB $15.95 (0-9606046-4-2). 32pp. Nonfiction.

"Jambo" is a Kiswahili word meaning anything within the range of "hello," "how are you?" "how are things?" and so on. As a traditional and contemporary manner of conveying one's greetings, wishes, and concern to others, "jambo" has become synonymous with the Swahili culture all over East Africa and particularly in Kenya and Tanzania. The title of this book is thus an appropriate metaphor for introducing a child to the language and culture of East Africa.

By narrating the experiences of two fictitious American children, aged 5 and 10, who journey to Kenya, the authors present basic information about that nation's cities, peoples, languages, traditions, and wildlife. The cassette contains a few Swahili words and songs that augment the text. The drawings and photographs are well done, adding color and lucidity.

While the volume is informative and readable, its major weakness is excessive focus on rural Kenya; to expose Americans to Swahili culture would require a presentation on the coastal towns of Malendi, Mombasa, and Lamu. Here, readers are deprived of an opportunity to understand the modern-day urban cultures of a country that is, in reality, highly urbanized. This flaw, shared by most books on sub-Saharan Africa, reinforces the stereotype that the region consists of little more than wild animals, unruly people, small farms, drums, hunting, and traditional songs and dances.

M.A.

748   Knutson, Barbara. **How the Guinea Fowl Got Her Spots: A Swahili Tale of Friendship.** Illus. by the author. Lerner/Carolrhoda 1990, HB $12.95 (0-87614-416-4). 32pp. Nonfiction.

Knutson's work is an etiology tale from the Swahili people of East Africa, one that explains how the guinea fowl got its spotted and colorful feathers. The guinea fowl, Nganga, and Cow were good friends and protected each other from their common enemy, Lion. Through two heroic acts, Nganga saved Cow's life, and Cow in turn camouflaged Nganga's feathers by spraying milk over them, giving them their speckled appearance. When vindictive Lion returned, the camouflage helped to save Nganga.

The narrative flows smoothly and holds the reader's attention as each event quickly leads to another. Illustrations add to the clarity of the tale, and Knutson's brilliant palette will appeal to young readers. Concluding the book is a picture of Nganga and Cow standing together, glancing at each other, with the Kiswahili inscription "Asante sana," meaning "Thank you very much." The acknowledgment of mutual gratitude and interdependence implied in this conclusion is rooted in East African culture and reflects a typical response to this kind of situation. Knutson's sympathy with Swahili culture is evident in her lively and colorful rendition.   M.A.

Lester, Julius. **How Many Spots Does a Leopard Have? And Other Tales.**
See entry 768, Grades 4–6.

749   Lundgren, Gunilla. **Malcolm's Village.** Trans. from Swedish; originally published in Sweden, 1983. Illus. with photos by Lars Jacobsson. Annick 1985, HB $6.95 (0-920303-28-5). 37pp. Nonfiction.

Malcolm's Village is a story that nearly reflects the thoughts and observations of children in a typical African village near the base of Mt. Kilimanjaro in East Africa as well as the thoughts of Malcolm, a Swedish youngster living in the village with his parents. The acacia tree, referred to as "the green roof of Africa," and the termite hill or anthill as the "red tower of Africa," are common scenes on the landscape and are used to interpret African beliefs and cultures.

The distribution of power and work among the termites as they build the hill ("some of them are soldiers, others collect food; some termites are nurses and many are builders") is just what is usually taught to the village youngsters by the elders. The village children also learn ways and means of cooperation among themselves and division of duties as future citizens. The presence and influence of Grandma among the people and the nursing she is given when sick are characteristic of the care and respect of elders. Though the weeping and grieving of elders when Grandma dies surprise Malcolm, who only "feels a lump of worry in his throat," this is a commonplace reaction among Africans, especially when an elder dies. Malcolm picks acacia blossoms for Grandma; later they are put with other flowers in Grandma's coffin. Acacia trees grow all over, and antelopes and bees feed on them. When an antelope eats the seeds of the tree, the seeds travel with the animal in its stomach and finally drop to the ground, thereafter to sprout and grow into a huge acacia tree that becomes a delight to the whole savannah. The entire story of Malcolm's village shows how almost each thing on earth is dependent on another thing.

Malcolm is a 7-year-old white child growing up and appreciating the wonders of nature with local African children, merging together with them and their ways in the same way that the products and people of nature are interdependent: acacia tree, termite hill, antelope, the good earth, and Grandma, buried and adorned with flowers nurtured by the savannah.

Striking color photographs capture the beauty of the surroundings. Highly recommended for both younger and older elementary school students, this photo-documentary is a sensitive portrait of a cross-cultural living experience and a child's first encounter with death. B.V.J.

750 Margolies, Barbara. *Rehema's Journey: A Visit to Tanzania.* Illus. with photos by the author. Scholastic 1990, HB $13.95 (0-590-42846-2). 32pp. Nonfiction.

Nine-year-old Rehema is traveling with her father from her village in the mountains of Tanzania to the town of Arusha and then to a nearby game park. Her real-life experiences are captured in pictures by Margolies, who presents in photo-diary form Rehema's firsthand impressions of what she sees on her trip. Rehema welcomes the reader with the Kiswahili greeting "jambo," then describes herself and her family. As she tells the reader, her family grows maize, bananas, and beans and gathers wood for cooking. Her father also works as a tour guide.

Taking the bus to Arusha, Rehema observes the passing scenery. She is struck by the contrasts between the town and her small village. In particular, the noises startle her. She attends her first church service and witnesses infant baptisms and confirmations. Going to the market, she sees all kinds of merchandise. At a nearby park, her father introduces her to the wide variety of animal species and tells her about the problems of poaching and the dangers that have driven some of the animals into extinction. For the first time, she visits people of other ethnic groups—the Waarushaa and Maasai peoples—and she learns the Maasai word for "goodbye."

Unlike other books on Africa, this one allows Tanzanians to speak for themselves, thereby offering a more authentic view of the culture. Margolies does not attempt to present all of Africa but rather focuses on the experience of one rural Tanzanian girl. Nonetheless, Rehema's experiences on vacation enable readers to see other sides of Tanzania, such as the larger town, the wildlife preserve, and other ethnic groups. Her journey shows vividly how many Africans—young and old, city people and village dwellers—do not have to travel far to see wild animals and a different way of life.

Because the author does not set herself up as the mouthpiece for a foreign culture, the book is free from the stereotypes that mar other treatments. Rather, her full-color photography and her sensitive editing of Rehema's narrative allow the reader to empathize with the youngster and to experience her world from her perspective. M.A.

751 Musgrove, Margaret. *Ashanti to Zulu: African Traditions.* Illus. by Leo Dillon and Diane Dillon. Dutton/Dial 1976, LB $15.89 (0-8037-0358-9); 1980, P $4.95 (0-8037-0308-2). 30pp. Nonfiction.

Nearly every school district in the United States holds a copy of *Ashanti to Zulu.* In addition to receiving a Caldecott Medal for the illustration, this book has won many other awards. Musgrove studied in Ghana in preparation for writing this book. The Dillons have illustrated several African-related children's books, including *Why Mosquitoes Buzz in People's Ears* (1976) and *Behind the Back of the Mountain* (1976).

Musgrove's format, which uses the English alphabet to describe one of 26 African "nations," is attractive to elementary school teachers. A map at the end of the book highlights the specific country in which each of the 26 "nations" mainly reside.

Unfortunately, few African languages contain the 26 letters of the English alphabet. This format provides an overly simplistic introduction in English to a continent that uses more than 2,000 different languages. English is the official language in only 16 of the 55 African countries.

Africanist educators have criticized this "acclaimed" picture book and continue to do so. In summary, the book focuses on traditions more characteristic of early-twentieth-century rural communities. It fails to look at the current traditions and urban cultures. This would not be so bad except that these stereotypes are perpetuated through the media and in textbooks. Consequently, children are presented with quaint, exotic misrepresentations of a people, and they continue to believe the errors into adulthood.

A more useful activity would be to focus on one African language and one culture. Several books on or about Swahili on the East Coast have followed the format. The two Feelings books (*Moja Means One* and *Jambo Means Hello*) are cases in point, as is Katherine Klyce's and Virginia McLean's *Kenya, Jambo!*

P.K.

752   Powzyk, Joyce. ***Tracking Wild Chimpanzees.*** Illus. by the author. Lothrop, Lee & Shepard 1990, LB $13.88 (0-688-06734-4). 32pp. Nonfiction.

This attractive and informative book chronicles the adventures of two Americans who observed and helped to protect the endangered chimpanzees in Kibira National Park in Burundi, a country in East Africa. Powzyk, an illustrator and photographer, traveled to Burundi to meet with her old college classmate, Pete, a wildlife conservationist trying to save the chimpanzees from the loss of their habitat due to deforestation. Upon her arrival, Powzyk was captivated by the exotic scenes of the marketplace and by the customs of the people, manifested in their flamboyant dress and methods of marketing. Names of small towns also caught her attention. From Pete she learned about the history of the park and the behavior of the wild chimpanzees. Finally, after braving a two-day downpour, she saw the chimpanzees close up, as well as a number of other animals that inhabit the park.

Powzyk's personal account is well written, and the illustrations of every major encounter with humans and animals make the book vivid, appealing, and real. Readers will be fascinated with the richness of life in this East African national park. Although occasional archaic and stereotypic words, such as "jungle," mar the presentation, the language is, in general, more appropriate and sensitive than that found in most books of this type. Again, the focus is on the "exotic" aspects of African life, but the author does include environmental issues of significance. The glossary at the end helps to simplify some difficult concepts.

M.A.

753 Price, Leontyne. ***Aida.*** Based on the opera by Giuseppe Verdi. Illus. by Leo Dillon and Diane Dillon. Harcourt Brace Jovanovich 1990, HB $16.95 (0-15-200405-X). 32pp. Nonfiction.

Leontyne Price, opera diva known for her stage portrayal of Aida, retells Verdi's tragic love story of the Ethiopian princess torn between love for her country and love of her country's great foe, Radames, captain of Egypt's army. This classic love story, in which the lovers can be together only in death, is embellished by Leo and Diane Dillon's illustrations, which are of Caldecott quality. Each page is framed with what appear to be staffs decorated with lotuses and lily designs. The designs are mainly in royal purples and blues and are embossed with gleaming golds and bronzes that look as though they could leave gold dust on browsers' fingers. Marbleized paper adds richness and depth.

Price's retelling is poetic yet brief. Children may have difficulty following it because of their lack of familiarity with the names. This is not a book children will find on their own. Teachers, librarians, and family members will need to introduce it and possibly explain much, but it is an important contribution to children's literature for several reasons: It introduces not only an opera (though not necessarily a historically accurate one) about Africa but also an important African-American opera singer as well. It shows a major art form; creative educators may want to play the music of the triumphal march from the opera as children arrive for the story. Also, in a folklore tradition filled with Aryan princesses, it is time children see that there are dark-skinned ones just as beautiful and unforgettable. The only other title that conveys this is John Steptoe's *Mufaro's Beautiful Daughters* (Lothrop, Lee & Shepard, 1987).   A.H.

754 Steptoe, John. ***Mufaro's Beautiful Daughters.*** Illus. by the author. Lothrop, Lee & Shepard 1987, LB $13.88 (0-688-04046-2). 32pp. Nonfiction.

Steptoe's acclaimed work is a Zimbabwean tale that follows the hero-villain motif of the African folk tradition. It touches upon the tradition of animal totems in the indigenous culture and also shows both the traditional law of retribution for wrongdoing and the reward of charity that are central to the beliefs of the African people. In the story, two sisters, beautiful and well brought up, had opposite temperaments. One was ill-mannered, jealous, and contemptuous. The other was kind, well mannered, and humble. A nearby king wanted to marry, and it was the duty of all beautiful girls in the community to compete for the king's hand. Despite trickery, the arrogant Manyara lost to her sister, Nyasha, and as punishment became Nyasha's and the king's servant.

Like any African tale, this is a didactic one, showing that while beauty has its place in the making of a successful woman, good character is far more important. The names of the characters are significant, as they are in African culture in general, reflecting parents' wishes and expectations for the child. In the Shona language of Zimbabwe, Mufaro means "happy man," Nyasha means "mercy," and Manyara means "ashamed." Steptoe's faithful representation of these traditions is one of the reasons for the praise this book has received. The illustrations are another reason. Though rooted in their African setting, the rich, detailed drawings reveal an element of fantasy that is also present in the oral tradition. For instance, wild animals appear tame and friendly in the presence of the good characters. The girls' beauty is evident in the illustrations, but also there is the intangible element that sets Nyasha and Manyara apart.

This book is a must for any collection on Africa, though if it is used in classes with younger children, teachers should point out the elements of fantasy that form part of the oral tradition but are not characteristic of everyday life in Africa. Children who recognize those elements in a Western fairy tale such as Cinderella may not do so when the story is from a distant culture. The "competition call," made by the beautiful women of the region to the king, is one such example of an imaginary device. M.A.

755 Tadjo, Veronique. *Lord of the Dance: An African Retelling.* Illus. by the author. HarperCollins 1988, LB $12.89 (0-397-32352-2). 32pp. Nonfiction.

Tadjo's book is a poetic rendition of the story of the Senufo of the Côte d'Ivoire. The Senufo immortalize their traditions and cultural heritage through their arts. The masks and their usages are central here; they are vessels that the Senufo believe their ancestors inhabited. It is therefore of paramount importance to them that these masks survive across ages and at all costs. The masks are used at various occasions; they express the people's feelings and are constant reminders of their heritage. Representations of these masks are drawn by the people everywhere—on papers, clothes, and carved wood—and at times they are worn by specially designated people accompanied by music and dancing.

All of these themes appear in Tadjo's poems. She illustrates the story with bright ink drawings, and the reader can feel the rhythm of the drum in the writing of the poem. Though not herself Senufo, Tadjo hails from the Côte d'Ivoire, and her work shows a sense of intuition and a familiarity with the culture. She not only gives details of the mask but in fact renders illustrations that are very much characteristic of Senufo art. Her ability to do so is a credit to her artistic talent and creativity.

The book's only difficulty is that Tadjo's presentation of the mask may be understood by younger readers in its literal context. As a repetitive device, the word "mask" appears so frequently that its underlying symbolic implication gets lost. Thus it would be of value for teachers to explain to very young readers that the mask symbolizes the spirit of ancestors in Africa, and the voice heard through it is not physical but metaphysical. Still, this is an exemplary work of writing and illustration. Readable and comprehensible, it is a valuable resource for any collection on African mythology and the oral tradition. M.A.

756 Ward, Leila. *I Am Eyes—Ni Macho.* Illus. by Nonny Hogrogian. Scholastic 1989, P $3.95 (0-590-40990-5). 32pp. Fiction.

Although this book contains a Kiswahili title, it contains no other Kiswahili words or references. One wonders why the writer could not have written the book bilingually since the sentences are designed for beginning readers. This device would have tied the title with the message of the book. In addition, it would have provided the reader with the knowledge that an African language can be as communicative as English.

The format of the book is simple. It contains a sentence "I see . . . and . . ." Usually the two items begin with the same letter or contain a similar sound. All the items are plants or animals of a generic African countryside. Unfortunately, the author makes no reference to people or Swahili speakers of East Africa. In fact, some of the plants and animals are not indigenous to the Swahili coast of East Africa. No people are referred to in this book, which gives the impression that Africa contains only wild animals and tropical plants. Consequently, the author perpetuates a stereotype held by many children and adults about African countries.

This book illustrates a major problem in children's literature about Africa. Not only is the author apparently uninformed about African countries, but the publisher encourages half-truths. Until authors, publishers, teachers, and parents can be educated about the continent of Africa, these stereotypes and pieces of misinformation will continue to prevail in the classrooms of the United States.

P.K.

757   Williams, Karen Lynn. *Galimoto.* Illus. by Catherine Stock. Lothrop, Lee & Shepard 1990, LB $13.88 (0-688-08790-6). 32pp. Fiction.

Seven-year-old Kondi wants a toy "galimoto," as a car is called in Chichewa, a language of Malawi. His older brother discourages him from the idea of ever owning one, but the determined youngster searches his village for materials to make one. He trades his knife to his friend for some wires and begs his uncle for more wires. Still short, he tries some village women and other sources. Finally, he gets what he needs. He fashions a fine galimoto, which his friends and his pessimistic brother admire. He thinks he will transform the galimoto into an ambulance, an airplane, or a helicopter the following day.

This story of a young boy's inventiveness is well written and illustrated. It shows the reward of hard work, persistence, and following a dream. The author demonstrates that while Malawi children may not necessarily have access to store shopping the likes of which their Western counterparts enjoy, they also have the same need for playthings and can often create toys that are even more durable, flexible in their uses, and appreciated. In fact, wire vehicles and other toys are common in rural southern Africa and can be quite elaborate. However, though this book provides a perspective on Malawi for young readers who are learning about the region for the first time, the impression it gives is a one-sided one. American children may think that their familiar Western toys are not available to Malawi or other African children. This is not true, for in larger cities, the standard toys are available. Even the village marketplace features commonly found playthings of plastic and metal, and large chain stores have outlets in the big cities. Therefore, while this book may teach overindulged youngsters a valuable lesson and provide some interesting details of village life, its portrayal requires cautious handling and clear explanations.

M.A.

758   Yoshida, Toshi. *Young Lions.* Illus. by the author. Putnam/Philomel 1989, HB $14.95 (0-399-21546-8). 32pp. Nonfiction.

Yoshida's book is an excellent work of art and a well-written introduction to one of the major animals inhabiting the savannas of East African game parks. She traces the adventures of three young and energetic lions who head into the woods to have a taste of their first hunt ever. Although their efforts prove unsuccessful, they encounter a variety of other animals—rhinos, water buffaloes, zebras, impalas, cheetahs, vultures, hyenas, gnus, and, finally, a leopard whose stare chases the young lions back to their pride (herd) with empty stomachs.

Written in a straightforward narrative style, the book uses a fictional technique to expose young readers to the varied wildlife of Africa. There is much information about the lions' behavior. For instance, readers will learn how the male lion watches over the younger ones at a distance but always within range of rescue, and how young lions embrace their mothers after being separated for a time. Simple sentence constructions and logically arranged facts make this a good choice for beginning readers, but older elementary school students will also appreciate the book and its nonstandard approach to the teaching of African wildlife. Yoshida's *Elephant Crossing* (Putnam/Philomel, 1989) uses a similar approach to present elephants, but its overly complicated and diffuse fictional plot makes it a less successful work. M.A.

759 Zaslavsky, Claudia. *Count on Your Fingers African Style.* Illus. by Jerry Pinkney. HarperCollins 1980. 34pp. Nonfiction. o.p.

In an age when science and technology are the major disciplines being pursued, it is sad that two excellent books on African counting systems are out of print. Children's writers and publishers could contribute significantly by producing more books following Zaslavsky's model. As a math teacher, Zaslavsky chose counting systems for her research in Africa. *Africa Counts: Numbers and Patterns in African Culture* (1970) and *Count on Your Fingers African Style* provide a positive and realistic application of several "nations."

This particular book explains the practices of counting systems among the Mende of Sierra Leone, the Zulu of South Africa, and the Masai, Kamba, and Taita of Kenya. She includes the numbers in the various languages. Consequently, students not only learn systems of counting and thought, but they also learn linguistics and language. Her comparison of the three Kenyan groups is most interesting. To her credit, she compares U.S. counting systems with those of the six African groups.

Pinkney's award-winning illustrations maintain the authenticity of each group at a market scene. The only criticism is the lack of a map to help students locate the specific areas of the six groups. P.K.

GRADES 4–6

760 Bailey, Donna, and Anna Sproule. *We Live in Nigeria.* Illus. with photos. SERIES: Where We Live. Steck-Vaughn 1990, LB $9.96 (0-8114-2557-6). 32pp. Nonfiction.

Bailey's and Sproule's book is a brief depiction of the occupations, daily activities, ceremonies, festivals, and major religion of the city of Kano, in the northeastern part of Nigeria. Narrated by young Mallam, who first introduces himself and his friend Bala, the book follows the sequence of an imaginary journey from Mallam's house through the entire city of Kano and back again. The tour introduces the reader to the details of the buildings' architecture, manners of dressing, the dynamics of the Muslim family in that area, the use of camels, the tie-and-dye industry, pottery, open barbecues, and various entertainments.

The book is easy to read; full-color photos add vividness to the text. Unfortunately, most of the topics of discussion address the exotic and traditional life more illustrative of the early twentieth century. Rather than contrasting Hausa traditional dress with contemporary clothing, the authors focus on the traditional clothing and its construction. Traditionally the Kano dye pits were the location where all cloth was dyed; however, today these pits are used for ceremonial clothing and for tourists' admiration. The emir of Kano does wear elaborate celebratory clothing and ride a horse, frequently at a polo match. However, the authors fail to show the emir in his automobile and at the office handling city problems.

What is stated and illustrated in the book does occur; however, the authors fail to clarify the uniqueness of these situations. Hausa students in the United States are offended by stereotypes of traditional Kano. The selection on animals perpetuates the stereotype that Americans hold about Nigeria. In actual fact, in Kano snakes and hyenas would appear no more often than they would in New York or Chicago outside a zoo. Because of these misrepresentations, this book should be used with caution.

Another volume in the series, by the same authors, presents Kenya.

M.A./P.K.

761   Bess, Clayton. *Story for a Black Night.* Houghton Mifflin 1982, HB $12.95 (0-395-31857-2). 96pp. Fiction.

Story for a Black Night is a mournful, heavy-hearted, wonderfully written story told by a father to his young son, Smallboy. The setting is the town of Kakata, some distance from Monrovia, Liberia.

One night when a storm cuts off the electricity to the town, the father seizes the opportunity to gather his son and other children around the kerosene lamp to tell them a sad and tragic story from his childhood. The father begins with the time when he was a Smallboy. His own father had been killed by a snake bite and he was living with his mother (Ma), grandmother (Old Ma), and baby sister (Meatta).

The father begins to describe that one night blind Old Ma "saw" a leopard come too close to their house and predicted that evil would soon follow. That very night there was a knock at the door. Old Ma warned Ma not to open the door, but when Ma heard the voices of an old woman, a young woman, and a crying baby, she could not resist. The following morning the young woman and her mother were gone, but the baby, who was a victim of smallpox, had been left behind. Although Old Ma tried to convince Ma to leave the smallpoxed baby in the bush for the leopard or to take it to the river to drown, Ma could not follow her advice. The gloomy tragedy that followed and the crucial role of Ma's sister in it create feelings of sympathy for all of the characters.

The skillful use of language and the storytelling method employed entice and captivate readers of *Story for a Black Night*. This fairly short novel will grab the interest of older elementary and young adult readers and can be used in a variety of ways. Reading it orally to or with students would be engrossing because of the use of dialect and the storytelling structure of the novel.   B.N.

762   Brooke-Ball, Peter, and Sue Seddon. *Southern Africa.* Illus. with drawings and photos. SERIES: People and Places. Silver Burdett 1989, LB $11.97 (0-382-09797-1). 46pp. Nonfiction.

Although this series contains 27 titles, many of the non-European titles represent regions rather than countries. Silver Burdett has lumped seven southern African countries into a 46-page book. The two authors certainly could have prepared a more comprehensive book on each southern African country. The format itself reinforces the stereotype that African countries have little value and status.

In addition to the format problems, the authors continue to use pejorative terms that have been shunned by Africans and Africanists since the 1960s (huts, tribes, bushmen). The time and effort expended in the preparation of this text do not justify its use in elementary or middle schools.   P.K.

763   Chiasson, John. **African Journey.** Illus. with photos by the author. Bradbury 1987, LB $16.95 (0-02-718530-3). 55pp. Nonfiction.

After completing a Peace Corps tour in Burkina Faso, John Chiasson worked in Niger on a film. Subsequently, he traveled through West Africa as correspondent for *Gamma Liaison.*

His experiences during his five years of professional employment in West Africa form the impetus for this book. *African Journey* documents various locations and groups of people: WoDaaBe and Twaregs of Niger; the Bozo and Bambara of Mopti, Mali; Dakar and the Lébou of Touba Diallow in Senegal; Eritrea, Ethiopia; and the Yoruba of Gbobjé in Benin. The text and photos depict the food, religion, clothing, occupation, and entertainment of a specific people. Moreover, Chiasson alludes to the political struggles of each group. Many of the portrayals represent one of several minority or refugee groups located within the boundaries of countries. This fact is not stated, and yet it could have been a strength of the book. A map helps the reader locate the precise area of each group.

Although this photo-journalist's presentation is informative and attractive, several errors do occur. Many of the problems derive from pejorative terminology. Chiasson's insensitive description of Islam fosters the stereotypes of Muslims, Islam, and the Qur'an. A case in point is a reference to a mosque as a "Moslem church."   P.K.

764   Corwin, Judith Hoffman. **African Crafts.** Illus. by the author. SERIES: Crafts. Franklin Watts 1990, LB $11.40 (0-531-10846-5). 48pp. Nonfiction.

Although this book generalizes about the art of Africa, the author as illustrator has provided an interesting and practical book for young students, which complements some of the older "African arts/crafts" books—*African Crafts for You to Make* by Janet and Alex D'Amato (1969) and *Getting Started in African Crafts* by Jeremy Comins (1971). Corwin has selected a variety of traditional items that have a practical application for children. In addition to containing items to make, this book includes several recipes and caters to the senses of vision, touch, and taste.

The author's focus is primarily on the West African tradition. Unfortunately, the book does not contain a map, which would help children locate the different countries and nations. In addition, many of the designs do not have identification. These two problems promote the stereotype that Africa is a "country" rather than a continent of 55 distinct countries.   P.K.

765   Gibrill, Martin. **African Food and Drink.** Illus. with photos. SERIES: Food and Drink. Franklin Watts 1989, LB $12.40 (0-531-18296-7). 50pp. Nonfiction.

Gibrill, a Sierra Leonean, gives an interesting explanation of cuisine in West Africa. This book provides readers with an introduction to the history of crop production and marketing. He discusses the variation of food preparation among different West African nations. The text includes a map to help identify foods and crops.

The title of the text, however, misrepresents the contents of the book and confuses students about the diversity of the continent as a whole. Far more specific in its identification of recipes and customs, for both East and West Africa, is Nabwire's and Montgomery's *Cooking the African Way* (Lerner, 1988). Captions to pictures should be specific and personalized as well. For instance, the King Jimmy Market is in Freetown, Sierra Leone. Although the author is a Sierra Leonean, he projects a pejorative tone in his writing.   P.K.

766   Jacobsen, Karen. ***Zimbabwe.*** Illus. with photos. SERIES: New True Books. Childrens Pr. 1990, LB $9.95 (0-516-01110-3). 48pp. Nonfiction.

Childrens Press recognizes the need for factual information about African countries. The recent series New True Books provides beginning readers with an introduction to geography and history. *Zimbabwe* describes the physical and cultural geography of the Mashona and Matabele nations. Nearly half of the book portrays contemporary Zimbabwe and explains the successes of this independent country.

The colorful pictures provide a realistic portrait of the country. Following the text is a short glossary of important terms. A small map assists students in locating important places, and the captions to the pictures are informative.

P.K.

767   Kleeberg, Irene Cumming. ***Ethiopia.*** Illus. with photos. SERIES: First Books. Franklin Watts 1986, LB $10.40 (0-531-10115-0). 65pp. Nonfiction.

Franklin Watts has revised its format for the series First Books. This series appears to examine information by country only. Another recently revised volume covers South Africa.

Ethiopia is a land of contrasts. The country's droughts and political activities in both the south and the north have contributed to these contrasts. Traditionally Ethiopia (Abyssinia) has been open to various beliefs and cultures, and Christians, Muslims, and Jews have lived in relative harmony with those believers of traditional religions. Kleeberg outlines some of the issues of overpopulation, overgrazing, and overcultivation, which have contributed to Ethiopia's economic struggle and to ethnic and religious conflict.

Some problems occur in the text. Although the author provides a map, several maps with greater detail would help students obtain an understanding of the diversity of the country. Since the photos are black and white, the pictures are not clear. The glossary is helpful. A supplementary list of books would strengthen this work.   P.K.

768   Lester, Julius. ***How Many Spots Does a Leopard Have? And Other Tales.*** Illus. by David Shannon. Scholastic 1989, LB $13.95 (0-590-41973-0). 72pp. Nonfiction.

Since Julius Lester is an African American of Jewish ancestry, he has assembled oral narratives from both "African" and Jewish traditions. *How Many Spots Does a Leopard Have?* contains 12 stories, of which 10 represent traditions from ethnic groups throughout the continent. Each story is a didactic explanation of a specific feature of life or a phenomenon of the environment.

All of the stories have been edited from other texts. For instance, several of the "African" tales derive from collections edited by Harold Courlander. Lester has justified his selection and editing by the interests of young children and the concerns of parents.

This collection lacks continuity and purpose. The stories do not appear to have any unifying thread. Rather they seem to be a collection of tales. Lester does not link the "African" selections with his "Jewish" ones. Since a Jewish population did exist and still exists in many current countries, the linkage could have occurred. Examples abound from North Africa, Ethiopia, Liberia, and South Africa. The two Mende and Hausa tales are similar; however, Lester does little with the tales. In addition, he does not provide a description of the ethnic tradition. Without a map to identify these groups, the reader gains little from this collection.

The idea of this collection is worth the effort; however, the author needs to give the reader additional information and more coherent links.　　　P.K.

Levitin, Sonia. **The Return.**
See entry 775, Grades 7–9.

Lundgren, Gunilla. **Malcolm's Village.**
See entry 749, Grades PS–3.

Nabwire, Constance, and Bertha Vining Montgomery. **Cooking the African Way.**
See entry 777, Grades 7–9.

769　　Pelnar, Tom, and Valerie Weber. **Tanzania.** Illus. with photos by Haruko Nakamura. SERIES: Children of the World. Gareth Stevens 1989, LB $12.95 (1-55532-210-7). 64pp. Nonfiction.

Unlike most nonfiction books, this series is an "autobiography" of a child from the designated country. Rajabu Juma, age 12, introduces the readers to Swahili life in Tanzania. The narration describes not only the family but also school, festivals, work, and responsibilities. The photographer, Nakamura, has captured the realistic life of Tanzanians living in Moshi along the border of Kenya.

The strengths of the book include the support materials. The Swahili glossary is helpful for children. The bibliography and list of follow-up activities assist the instructor in developing a unit on Tanzania. A reference section presents the geography, history, economy, and government. In many state social studies curricula, Tanzania is often studied.

The major weaknesses are stereotypic terminology and misinformation. Dodoma is now the capital of the country, replacing Dar es Salaam. Some of the vocabulary is pejorative: "tribes, huts, etc." The name Rajabu Juma is Kiswahili. It is unusual for a Swahili family to live in Moshi (a non-Swahili community) without an explanation. Indeed Kiswahili is the official and national language of Tanzania; however, in the home, most working-class families would continue to communicate in one of the parents' first language. Islam is an important component of a Swahili family. This text does not mention Islam.

Despite these weaknesses, the format helps young readers become familiar with same-aged children from a Tanzanian community. The instructor should develop a unit based on some of the ideas outlined in the appendix.

Additional titles in this series present children in Burkina Faso, Nigeria, South Africa, and Zambia. P.K.

Powzyk, Joyce. *Tracking Wild Chimpanzees.*
See entry 752, Grades PS–3.

Stark, Al. *Zimbabwe: A Treasure of Africa.*
See entry 781, Grades 7–9.

GRADES 7–9

770 Baynham, Simon. *Africa from 1945.* Illus. with photos. SERIES: Conflict in the 20th Century. Franklin Watts 1987, LB $13.90 (0-531-10319-6). 62pp. Nonfiction.

The desire of African countries for independence from European governments became critical following World War II (1945). Many of the men and women of British, Belgian, French, Portuguese, and Italian colonies demanded independence and self-rule. *Africa from 1945* documents the long struggle from the time of the partition of the continent at the Berlin conference. The text traces the transition of governments and ends with a chapter discussing issues of the twenty-first century. Because of rapid growth, modernization, and the problems of economic distribution, health care, education, and agricultural development, many countries have experienced 30 years of instability.

As a British military scholar Baynham focuses on the repercussions of military activities. Africans opposed colonization and organized resistance groups throughout the twentieth century. *Africa from 1945* enumerates some of the major efforts to destroy the colonial government efforts, which include Mau Mau, the Suez Canal, the Algerian War, the Boer War, Zaire, FRELIMO, MPLA, the ANC, and SWAPO. The author suggests that the military has held key roles in the formation of independent and self-sufficient governments due to the nature of the independence struggle. Countries that have not experienced military rule are rare in Africa. Unlike many books and U.S. government documents, the author includes examples from all African regions, including North Africa.

The text does contain errors that detract from its value. First the map confuses Portuguese and Spanish colonies. Second, the terminology is sometimes pejorative and reflects a lack of sensitivity: Africans and Africanists no longer use terms of degradation for the Mbuti, San, and Khoi. P.K.

Bess, Clayton. *Story for a Black Night.*
See entry 761, Grades 4–6.

771 *Cameroon in Pictures.* Illus. with photos. SERIES: Visual Geography. Lerner 1989, LB $11.95 (0-8225-1857-0). 64pp. Nonfiction.

This volume on Cameroon appears to be one of the weaker works in the series. In the first place, it recycles pictures (principally of the slave trade) found in previously published books on Ghana, Nigeria, and Senegal. There is an over-emphasis on village life and the village marketplace, while the modern urban centers of Bula, Douala, Yaounde, Bamenda, Tiko, and Limbe receive short shrift. Although basic historical information is presented clearly, there is no treatment of Nigeria's role in Cameroon's development, of a comparison be-tween the colonial rule of the British and French (the British were seen as more liberal, hence the migration from the French section to the British one), or of the border problems as a legacy of colonialism. The writing, on the whole, is condescending to Africans, a problem not generally found in this series and a major reason that this one volume cannot be recommended.

Other books in the series present the sub-Saharan African countries of Botswana, Central African Republic, Côte d'Ivoire, Ethiopia, Ghana, Kenya, Liberia, Madagascar, Malawai, Mali, Nigeria, Senegal, South Africa, Tanzania, and Zimbabwe. All volumes include an index but no bibliography.   M.A.

Cheney, Patricia. *The Land and People of Zimbabwe.*
See entry 782, Grades 10–12.

Emecheta, Buchi. *The Moonlight Bride.*
See entry 784, Grades 10–12.

772   James, R. S. *Mozambique.* Illus. with photos. SERIES: Let's Visit Places and Peoples of the World. Chelsea House 1988, LB $14.95 (1-55546-194-8). 103pp. Nonfiction.

Chelsea House has taken on the challenge of producing a text on every African country to replace the dated Childrens Press series Enchantment of Africa. The text follows a format that includes a time line, a brief list of facts about the country, and a glossary. The nine chapters describe Mozambique's physical geography, history, education, and economy. A small section of color photos provides a realistic view of contemporary Mozambicans. This particular volume tends to avoid such controversial issues as South Africa's role in the destabiliza-tion of the leftist FRELIMO government, and the book was published before the suspicious deaths of President Samora Machel and most of his cabinet in a plane crash near the South African border. Machel's death highlights the difficulty of keeping a series current when things change so quickly. In addition, each volume in the series is written by a different author, with different biases and approaches; some are more willing to tackle controversial issues than others. This volume suffers from a lack of maps to help students orient themselves in the country. Includes index but no bibliography. Among the books in this series is one on the illegal homeland of Venda, which was established as part of South Africa's apartheid policy.   P.K.

773   *Kenya in Pictures.* Illus. with photos. SERIES: Visual Geography. Lerner 1988, LB $11.95 (0-8225-1830-9). 64pp. Nonfiction.

Of the Visual Geography books dealing with African countries, this is one of the best. The volume discusses the contrasts between rural and urban life and the problem of mass migration to the cities, particularly Nairobi, with the poverty, overcrowding, and inadequate social services that result. The role of tourism in Kenya's economy is presented succinctly and in a balanced way. Those using the book should be aware of recent changes, both positive and negative, and use additional articles and more current books to supplement, though this volume does provide a solid basic introduction. Another one of the better books in the series, and one which has been revised more recently, is *Botswana in Pictures* (1990).   M.A.

774   Laure, Jason. ***Zimbabwe.*** Illus. with photos. SERIES: Enchantment of the World. Childrens Pr. 1985, LB $17.95 (0-516-02704-2). 128pp. Nonfiction.

In the 1970s, Childrens Press published a series of books, with each African country represented. This series was the only one at the time that provided a book for the 50 continental countries of Africa. Students interested in Gabon, Guinea Bissau, and Djibouti could find equal treatment with the Anglophone countries of Nigeria, South Africa, Egypt, and Kenya.

Rather than updating the Enchantment of Africa series, the editor chose to select a few major countries to revise. From a list of 75 countries, Childrens Press includes 14 African countries (Algeria, Angola, Egypt, Ethiopia, Gabon, Ghana, Kenya, Libya, Malawi, Morocco, South Africa, Tunisia, Zambia, and Zimbabwe). The authors of each book in the current series Enchantment of the World follow a specific format similar in scope to the previous series. The texts include history, geography, education, economics, and current politics. Each book has an Africanist and reading consultant to maintain authenticity and readability.

One of the strengths of this series is the consistent inclusion of maps. The book provides a realistic perspective of regional, physical, and political geography. Another asset of this series is the involvement of Africanists in public education. Few scholars take time to collaborate with editors and authors on materials that will be most likely the only source of information on an African country. The result is an accurate treatment that utilizes the most up-to-date interpretations and terminology.

This book does contain faults, however. The most significant of these is the discussion of Zimbabwean literature, which is actually a discussion of African literature in general. A photo of Nigerian author Wole Soyinka accompanies this discussion.   P.K.

775   Levitin, Sonia. ***The Return.*** Atheneum 1987, HB $12.95 (0-689-31309-8); Fawcett/Ballantine 1988, P $2.95 (0-449-70280-4). 180pp. Fiction.

An ALA Best Book for Young Adults, *The Return* by Sonia Levitin is an engaging story of flight from one homeland to another.

The story is told by Desta, an adolescent girl who lives with her 9-year-old sister, older brother, and aunt and uncle in a small village in Ethiopia in the early 1980s. Desta and her family are among the remaining few thousand Jewish people restricted to living in remote mountainous areas of Ethiopia. Certainly not willing to convert to Christianity but forbidden to leave Ethiopia to go to Israel, these outcast and captive Jews maintain a close-knit, loyal community.

By tradition, Desta has been betrothed at a young age to the son of the village priest. The boy, Dan, has a grandmother who hopes to die in Israel, and who has a dream that a return to Israel is imminent. Following a series of events, Dan's father decides his family will attempt the journey. Since Desta is to become Dan's wife, it is decided that she and her siblings will also make the journey, leaving behind their elderly aunt and uncle.

Preparation for the journey to Israel with the social, political, and cultural traditions and values of Ethiopian Jews and the dangerous trip itself compose the main text of this novel. Some of the issues and topics addressed include coping with the loss of loved ones, facing the unknown future, confronting the rules of one's faith and historical tradition, and exploring one's identity as an adolescent.

This novel is captivating and informative and could be used to teach about one African group's life-style and culture, to present the plight of Ethiopian Jews, or to examine the issues and roles facing adolescents in another culture.

B.N.

776   Milsome, John. *Sierra Leone.* Illus. with photos. SERIES: Let's Visit Places and Peoples of the World. Chelsea House 1988, LB $14.95 (0-7910-0106-7). 96pp. Nonfiction.

Although the first and last few pages of John Milsome's series book on Sierra Leone seem misplaced in that they resemble a tourist brochure telling "visitors" about hotels, beaches, and suitable clothing, the rest of the book gives a fairly accurate portrayal of modern-day Sierra Leone. A general history of the country is provided, as is information on ethnic distribution, industry, wildlife, and art. Overall the photographs, both color and black and white, are adequate in number, informative, and accurate, adding clarity to the written material.

B.N.

777   Nabwire, Constance, and Bertha Vining Montgomery. *Cooking the African Way.* Illus. with photos by Robert L. Wolfe and Diane Wolfe. SERIES: Easy Menu Ethnic Cookbooks. Lerner 1988, LB $9.95 (0-8225-0919-9); 1990, P $5.95 (0-8225-9564-8). 50pp. Nonfiction.

This book represents the collaboration between a home economics teacher and a Ugandan-American social worker from the Minneapolis public schools who have selected several dishes from specific countries of West and East Africa. The map locates not only the countries but also the major crops and animals. In addition, the authors provide a daily menu from both regions so that students can compare the different ingredients for similar dishes. Photographs of the final products entice the reader to try a recipe.

Although this book is designed for middle school students, university classes of anthropology or language (Kiswahili, Twi, Yoruba, Tigre, Amharic, and so forth) could use these recipes to try foods of their target-language culture. This book should be in both juvenile and adult library collections.

778   Negash, Askale. *Haile Selassie.* Illus. with photos. SERIES: World Leaders, Past and Present. Chelsea House 1990, LB $14.95 (1-55546-850-0). 111pp. Nonfiction.

Since the military committee of Mengistu Haile Mariam took power over Ethiopia in 1974, U.S. contact with Ethiopia has diminished. The news that Americans do hear focuses on famine and war. This book examines the leadership of one of the longest-ruling kings of the twentieth century. Askale Negash has provided readers with a study in the evolution of Ethiopia as a model for self-determination and independence. *Haile Selassie* explains the conflicts among different nations within Ethiopia—Oromo, Amharic, and Tigre. Negash describes the control that the Ethiopian Coptic church exerts over the peasant farmer. The Jewish and Muslim citizens hold little political power. Finally, Negash portrays an elder leader who fought the Italians in 1936 and established the Organization of African Unity in 1963. Although Haile Selassie's actions were not always admirable, this book brings to light many of the accomplishments that an African leader emerging from colonialism could achieve.

This biography contains many insights into Ethiopia by its culturally sensitive Ethiopian-American author. The series as a whole provides numerous historical photographs of the leaders. The maps, time line, and bibliography assist students in comparing one country with another. Other African leaders in the series include Cleopatra, Jomo Kenyatta, the Mandelas, Hosni Mubarik, Robert Mugabe, Gamal Abdel Nasser, Kwame Nkrumah, Muammar El-Qaddafi, Anwar Sadat, and Jan Smuts. Of the collection, only Smuts is not an indigenous African. Although Africa has numerous women leaders and queen mothers, to date only Cleopatra has been selected for this series.

779   ***Nigeria in Pictures.*** Illus. with photos. SERIES: Visual Geography. Lerner 1988, LB $11.95 (0-8225-1826-0). 64pp. Nonfiction.

This book summarizes basic information about the economy, politics, history, and culture of Nigeria. Photos and other visual material are well reproduced and enhance the text. However, much of the information, particularly statistics and information about ethnic groups, is out of date, and little attention is given to recent concerns about rural-to-urban migration and desert encroachment.

M.A.

780   ***Senegal in Pictures.*** Illus. with photos. SERIES: Visual Geography. Lerner 1988, LB $11.95 (0-8225-1827-9). 64pp. Nonfiction.

High-quality pictures and copious maps are the strengths of this series volume. Much space has been devoted to Senegal's history and government, but the treatment is quite Eurocentric, favoring the French, who colonized the country. Absent is a discussion of some of the grimmer aspects of colonial rule and of the role of an indigenous Senegalese resistance. If used, this book should be balanced by works of Africans involved in the independence struggle, such as the poet Leopold Senghor, who became the country's first president.   M.A.

781   Stark, Al. ***Zimbabwe: A Treasure of Africa.*** Illus. with photos. SERIES: Discovering Our Heritage. Dillon 1986, LB $12.95 (0-87518-308-5). 160pp. Nonfiction.

Zimbabwe is one of the success stories on the continent of Africa. Stark documents the struggle for self-government by the majority population. He personalizes his text to meet the expectations of young readers. He obviously likes the Zimbabweans, and his overall tone is positive.

This book caters to the interest of students. Included in the chapter on traditional activities are recipes. Education is explained in detail. Unfortunately, the author did not include artifacts of school—class schedules, books, exams. He does include addresses for the Zimbabwe Embassy, a list of Shona words and phrases, and a glossary. Most of the books listed in the bibliography are for adults and are not specific to Zimbabwe.

This book will provide a beginning in exploring Zimbabwe for older elementary and middle school students.   P.K.

782 Cheney, Patricia. *The Land and People of Zimbabwe.* Illus. with photos. SERIES: Portraits of the Nations. HarperCollins 1990, LB $15.89 (0-397-32393-X). 242pp. Nonfiction.

In *The Land and People of Zimbabwe,* Patricia Cheney provides a fairly comprehensive history of the land that is now Zimbabwe. The book opens with journal entry descriptions from December of 1979. The London setting for the signing of the paper that gave birth to Zimbabwe comes first, a description of and a conversation by a black family about the new Zimbabwe follow, and finally there are a description of and a conversation by a white family reacting to the end of Rhodesia. This opening is a clue to the fact that many perspectives are offered throughout the book, from that of early African rulers to the white settlers. Short personal narratives of common people, notable figures in Zimbabwe's history, "minifacts," poetry, chronologies, and information on language, food, and the arts appear in sidebars throughout the book. At times these enhance the historical background; however, these bordered areas are excessive, and they interrupt the text on almost every page. For some young adult readers, particularly less capable ones, this could be a major frustration.

A bibliography, which is quite extensive, and an index follow the text. Additional volumes in this series present Kenya and South Africa.   B.N.

783 Diallo, Nafissatou. *A Dakar Childhood.* Trans. by Dorothy S. Blair. Longman 1982. 134pp. Nonfiction. o.p.

A Dakar Childhood is an autobiographical account of the childhood and adolescence of Nafissatou Diallo, who was raised in Senegal in the 1940s and 1950s. Growing up under the security and at times too strict and overbearing care of a large Muslim family, Diallo shares both her childhood rebellion and her love of tradition and adherence to Islam.

In an easy-to-read, free-flowing style, Diallo gives descriptions and vivid accounts of the physical environment, cultural traditions, familial roles, rituals and ceremonies, and personal relationships and responsibilities she encountered while growing up in Dakar.

Much of the action and events revolve around Diallo's domineering father, who is the leader of the family, and her grandmother, who served as Diallo's mother. In fact, the book is dedicated to the author's father and grandmother, "without whom neither my life nor this work would have had any meaning."

Diallo, who is now a wife, mother, midwife, and child welfare nurse in Senegal, wrote her autobiography during short breaks in the afternoons at her job at the Maternity and Child Welfare Center in Ouagon-Niane. Her purpose in writing her autobiography was to provide Senegalese youth with a picture of childhood 30 to 40 years ago. However, this book can be used with young people outside of Senegal to teach about and give insights into a different way of life, one in which extended family, religious, and community values reign.   B.N.

784   Emecheta, Buchi. *The Moonlight Bride.* George Braziller 1983, LB $7.95 (0-8076-1062-3); P $4.95 (0-8076-1063-1). 77pp. Fiction.

Told through the voice of a 12-year-old girl named Ngbeke, *The Moonlight Bride* is the story of a marriage preparation and its impact on daily life in a Nigerian village.

Through Ngbeke and her 13-year-old cousin, Ogoli, the reader becomes acquainted with family structure, men's and women's roles, children's roles, and styles of clothing, food, and housing in one Nigerian village. Tradition, ritual, and the excitement of preparing the marriage are shown on both individual and community levels.

Ngbeke and her cousin are determined to make the most beautiful lamps and earthenware pots to present to the new bride, who will be joining their homestead. The two of them venture into the forbidden "bad bush" for clay. There they encounter a python, which is later killed by the young men and used ceremonially in the wedding.

The secret of which man from the village will marry and the mystery of the "somehow different" bride provide the thread uniting action, events, and sequencing in this short novel.

Cultural sensitivity and discussion will be necessary to deal with the traditional, stereotypic roles with respect to women and to statements such as Ogoli's response to a younger girl about the aging of men and women, "Don't you know it is not permitted to say that a man is ugly? The words ugliness and old age apply only to women, not to men."

Although brief and lacking in complexity in terms of the dynamics of personal relationships involved, *The Moonlight Bride* is useful in providing a glimpse of life in one village of Nigeria. The novel could supplement teaching about "traditional" village life or could be used in a unit on African literature. Young readers will easily relate to the narrator and the mischievous behavior she is coaxed into by her daring cousin.   B.N.

Negash, Askale. *Haile Selassie.*
See entry 778, Grades 7–9.

785   Okri, Ben. *Flowers and Shadows.* Longman 1989, P $9.95 (0-582-03536-8). 266pp. Fiction.

At the age of 19, Nigerian-born Ben Okri wrote *Flowers and Shadows*, in which corruption, dishonesty, deceit, hatred, and cruelty abound, as do innocence and naïveté.

The central figure in the novel is 19-year-old Jeffia Okwe, who lives with his parents in a wealthy neighborhood of Lagos. The story revolves around the corrupt business practices and final destruction of Jeffia's father. Also at the heart of the novel is the coming of age of Jeffia as he responds to his father, mother, and others during the crisis in which his father's past abuses are exposed.

Unfolding in often blatantly predictable ways, this novel introduces readers to a less than attractive segment of Nigerian society. Major focus is on the cruel, obsessive men, mainly wealthy businessmen, who will stop at nothing to gain power, control, and authority. The impact of their behavior on the lives of other people, including workers, servants, and their own family members, is revealed.

Many of the Nigerians in this novel are confused, corrupt, revengeful, or downtrodden. Those like Jeffia and the kind young woman he meets struggle with how to pick up the pieces and go on with life under seemingly hopeless circumstances. Their honesty, love, and innocence provide hope and a dream for a more just future society.

Flowers and Shadows is an interesting story but one that should not be used as a central text for teaching about Nigeria, since its focus is too narrow. It could be used as a supplement to other works on Nigeria that center on different segments of the society and on adolescents in life situations and experiences outside of the sometimes corrupt, wealthy elite class.   B.N.

14
SOUTH AFRICA

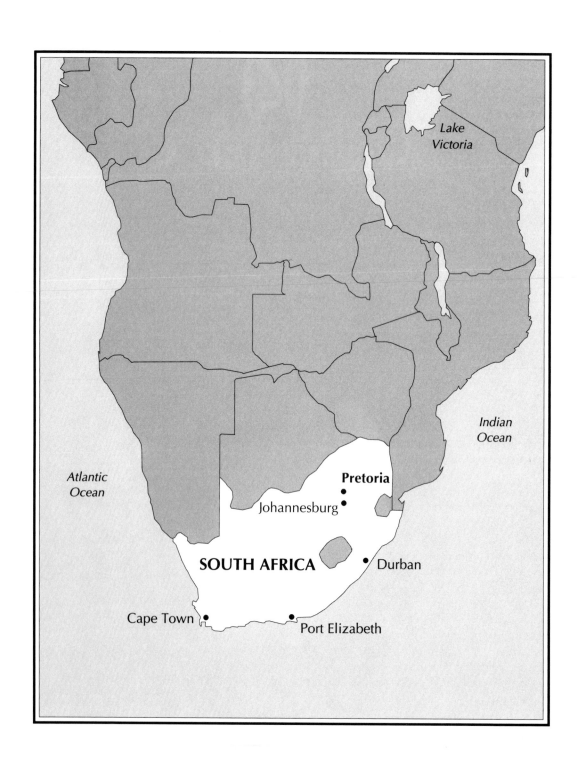

Lake
Victoria

Indian
Ocean

Atlantic
Ocean

Pretoria

Johannesburg

SOUTH AFRICA

Durban

Cape Town

Port Elizabeth

14

SOUTH AFRICA

by Patricia Kuntz and Lyn Miller-Lachmann

Books on South Africa are the largest group of those on any African country, and for that reason they have been given a separate chapter. Virtually all the books contain some reference to the apartheid policies of the white minority government. Reports on apartheid and opposition to it both within South Africa and throughout the world have appeared in the news media since the 1976 Soweto student uprising. Publishers have responded with nonfiction and fiction for both adults and children.

In contrast to books on the rest of Africa, books on South Africa are directed almost exclusively to a young adult or adult audience. There are very few picture books or even those for the middle grades; however, the various series for these age groups do contain works on South Africa. Picture books on South Africa tend to be nonconfrontational. Niki Daly's *Not So Fast, Songololo* contains no inflammatory information in the text, which tells of a black child's shopping trip to the city with his grandmother. Only in the illustrations does the reader see evidence of a segregated and unequal society. *Armien's Fishing Trip* by Catherine Stock contains an introduction describing the government's plan to resettle the multiracial inhabitants of Kalk Bay; otherwise, the story is a universal one with characters from all ethnic groups. Although Hugh Lewin, author of the Jafta books, was imprisoned and exiled because of his antiapartheid activities, the books themselves are a portrait of a rural black family whose life could be that of rural people anywhere.

Beginning with literature for the middle grades, one sees treatment of life under apartheid. Two fine novels for this age group—Sheila Gordon's *The Middle of Somewhere* and Beverley Naidoo's *Journey to Jo'burg*—present black youngsters who become aware of the impact that the policies of the white minority government have on their lives. In the former book, young Rebecca is faced with the forced relocation of her family and friends from their ancestral village to a distant and desolate "homeland." Naidoo's now-classic story tells of two children's journey from their village to Johannesburg to inform their mother that their younger sister is seriously ill. This crisis opens young Naledi's eyes to the poverty that she, her family, and her people must endure simply because they are black.

While fiction for the middle grades presents children who come to recognize the forces beyond their control that affect their lives, young adult novels show black teens who try to change the system. In *Chain of Fire*, the sequel to *Journey to Jo'burg*, Naledi and her brother protest their removal to a "homeland." Although their efforts are in vain, one knows they will continue to struggle for justice. In Gordon's earlier novel, *Waiting for the Rain*, the black farmhand Tengo draws away from his Afrikaner friend because he knows that, without an education, he will always be the subordinate. When the education is revealed as inferior, he too joins the movement.

Though marred by flaws in writing, two novels for young adults examine white teenagers' loss of innocence. The better of the two, Margaret Sacks's *Beyond Safe Boundaries*, is an authentic portrayal of a Jewish teen's coming of age and her relationship with her older sister, who has become an antiapartheid activist. Toecky Jones's *Skindeep* presents an interracial relationship and examines the deception that results from a racial classification system not unlike that of the Nazi era. Interestingly, all of the authors of young adult fiction (as well as the editor of the outstanding short story collection for teenagers *Somehow Tenderness Survives*) are white South Africans who live in exile. It is to Gordon's and Naidoo's credit that, although white, they ably portray the lives of black South Africans with credibility, authenticity of detail, and sympathy. Among other things, they do not present the "generic African" but rather identify their characters as members of specific ethnic groups, with their specific language and culture.

Juvenile trade nonfiction (not part of publishers' series) on South Africa tends to suffer from a Eurocentric point of view at odds with the sensibilities and experiences of black South Africans. The most notorious example is K. C. Tessendorf's *Along the Road to Soweto*, which contains factual errors, gross insensitivities in text and illustration, and an overwhelming concern for the heritage and history of whites. Carolyn Meyer's *Voices of South Africa* reflects her limited access to black South Africans; virtually all of her interviewees are white, although whites make up less than a quarter of the country's population. Elaine Pascoe's treatment in *South Africa: Troubled Land* is dry but more balanced. Biographies of black leaders are generally superior despite some flaws. Diane Stanley's and Peter Vennema's *Shaka: King of the Zulus* does contain errors in details, but its treatment of the Zulu leader is more respectful and balanced than Tessendorf's, which can only be characterized as diatribe. Other trade biographies focus on Nelson and Winnie Mandela at the expense of other black leaders, but they do present Winnie Mandela as a leader in her own right.

An even larger number of books have been written for adults but feature teenagers and coming-of-age themes. Many of these works are not novels but rather autobiographies of works of drama. Several are by black South African authors. In Sipho Sepamla's novel *A Ride on the Whirlwind*, a group of teenage activists in the Soweto school boycott join forces with a professionally trained guerrilla. Among the many fine autobiographies is Mark Mathabane's *Kaffir Boy*, the story of his coming of age in the squalor of Alexandra township, his conflicts over political commitment, and the ultimate realization of his childhood dream of living in America. Don Mattera's *Sophiatown* chronicles the author's conversion from gang leader to antigovernment activist as a result of the piecemeal bulldozing of his urban neighborhood to make way for white settlement. Other autobiographies, particularly Molapatene Collins Ramusi's *Soweto, My Love* and Bojana Vuyisile Jordan's *We Will Be Heard*, reflect the sensibilities of an older generation that grew up in rural rather than urban areas, were educated in rigorous mission schools rather than under the demeaning "Bantu Education," and attempted to combine their traditional cultures with modern-day activism.

Notable white authors who have portrayed the effects of apartheid on both whites and blacks include Andre Brink, Athol Fugard, Nadine Gordimer, and Donald Woods. Brink's *A Dry White Season* portrays an Afrikaner teacher moved to action when a black school custodian is murdered by the police. Fugard's acclaimed drama *Master Harold . . . and the Boys* shows how institutionalized racism poisons the mind of even the most well-meaning whites. Gordimer's *My Son's Story* is the sensitive coming-of-age tale of a mixed-race teenager and his relationship with his activist father, whom he comes to see as an imperfect human being. Donald Woods's biography of Stephen Biko, *Biko*, and his autobiographical work, *Asking for Trouble*, chronicle a white journalist's struggle to overcome racism, his friendship with the martyred black leader, and his failed attempt to determine the truth of Biko's death and to bring the killers to justice.

Books of photographs and art, in addition to anthologies of South African literature, round out the offerings for older high school students. The most well-known of these works are Peter Magubane's collections of black-and-white photos—*Magubane's South Africa, Black Child,* and *Soweto.* These give a comprehensive portrait of black life over the past four decades. Another useful collection is *From South Africa,* edited by David Bunn and Jane Taylor. Teachers of high school English classes will find an assortment of poems and short stories, many of which are by hitherto unknown black writers.

Three types of series books—geographical, biographical, and current events—feature volumes on South Africa. The geography series feature entries for all age groups, as do the biography series. For younger elementary-age students, the recommended series volumes are the New True Books volume on South Africa published by Childrens Press and that publisher's Picture-Story Biographies title on Desmond Tutu. For older elementary-age students, the Childrens Press People of Distinction series focuses more on the life of the individual biographee, whereas the Gareth Stevens series People Who Have Helped the World concentrates on the society in which the person lived.

The middle or junior high age group claims the largest number of South African texts. Current events works appear for this age group, and the best one of these is a British publication, Sarah Harris's *Timeline: South Africa.* Franklin Watts distributes both British and American series books, and the ones written from a British perspective, such as Michael Evans's entry for the Issues series, tend to be superior. An especially weak book, because of its excessive focus on white South Africans and its avoidance of any controversy, is *We Live in South Africa,* part of Watts's Living Here series. In its Let's Visit Places and Peoples of the World series, Chelsea House has produced a volume on the illegal "homeland" of Venda in addition to its volume on South Africa. The most highly recommended geography text on South Africa is Jonathan Paton's *The Land and People of South Africa,* part of HarperCollins's Portraits of the Nations series. Paton is himself South African, the son of the acclaimed author Alan Paton.

Among recommended series biographies for junior high students are Milton Meltzer's *Winnie Mandela: The Soul of South Africa,* published as part of Viking's Women of Our Time series, and the biography of Nelson and Winnie Mandela in the Chelsea House series called World Leaders, Past and Present. High school students who are interested in biography should read Donald Woods's *Biko,* Mary Benson's biography of Nelson Mandela, and Shirley du Boulay's *Tutu:*

Voice of the Voiceless, as well as the speeches and writings of the biographees themselves.

The authors of this chapter would like to acknowledge the advice of Daniel Kunene, Harold Scheub, and Barbara Ellery. All opinions and errors are, however, our own.

PRESCHOOL–GRADE 3

786 Daly, Niki. *Not So Fast, Songololo.* Illus. by the author. Macmillan 1986, LB $13.95 (0-689-50367-9). 32pp. Fiction.

When Malusi's elderly grandmother, Gogo, begins her trudge up the village road for her shopping trip to the city, Malusi's mother sends him out to accompany her. Malusi puts on his battered sneakers, called "tackies," that have been handed down from his brother. The two ride the bus in and then window-shop on their way to the OK Bazaars, a low-price department store similar to K-Mart or Wal-Mart. After making her purchases, Gogo stops at a shoe store, where Malusi has admired some new red tackies, and she buys them for him. Proud of his new shoes, he walks ahead of her, and she has to ask him to slow down, calling him by her pet name for him, Songololo. They laugh when she looks at her old shoes and says, "Maybe if I had red tackies with white stripes I would walk as fast as you."

Though the book steers clear of political questions, it presents a positive view of the black family and the black community. Daly has captured the life-style of poor township residents who help each other and maintain pride in themselves and their heritage. The aging process is presented with humor and affection. Aspects of apartheid appear in the form of segregated buses, street scenes where both whites and blacks are present but do not mix, and the shoe store where Malusi and Gogo are helped by a friendly black salesperson. One minor criticism is that the illustrations show the traffic moving on the right, whereas in South Africa, as in Britain, the traffic moves on the left. This raises the question of whether the author-illustrator does not know South Africa that well or else has "Americanized" her presentation. On the whole, however, this is an attractive and well-written picture book, one that shows everyday realities in a way a young child can understand and enjoy, without being preachy or heavy-handed.

P.K./L.M-L.

Greene, Carol. *Desmond Tutu: Bishop of Peace.*
See entry 790, Grades 4–6.

787 Lewin, Hugh. *Jafta—The Journey.* Illus. by Lisa Kopper. SERIES: The Jafta Collection. Lerner/Carolrhoda 1983, LB $9.95 (0-87614-265-X). 24pp. Fiction.

The Jafta series, written by Hugh Lewin, a white South African living in exile in England, and illustrated by Lisa Kopper, features the activities of a black South African boy living in a rural village. This series is a nonconfrontational introduction to a particular way of life in that country, designed to appeal to beginning readers. In fact, the text is generic in its scope and treatment of the setting. Few details about the family and the country are revealed; this could be about a boy in Botswana or Zimbabwe, or Pakistan or Argentina for that matter. Kopper's two-color illustrations provide the reader with an impression of the rural village, yet one does not get a concrete sense of where or when the events take place. This is especially disappointing given Lewin's personal experience as an antiapartheid activist and as the author of the acclaimed *Bandiet*, a book for adults about his strife-torn country. One would think that he could have provided more details and realism in this work for children.

In contrast to other books for this age group, particularly *Armien's Fishing Trip* and *Not So Fast, Songololo*, this volume contains no introduction with supporting information about South Africa. There are no maps to help the reader locate the action nor leads into further curricular activities.

Besides this volume, there are five others in the series. Four of them are available in paperback.   P.K.

Stanley, Diane, and Peter Vennema. *Shaka: King of the Zulus.*
See entry 794, Grades 4–6.

788   Stock, Catherine. *Armien's Fishing Trip.* Illus. by the author. Morrow 1990, LB
$13.88 (0-688-08396-X). 32pp. Fiction.

The fishing village of Kalk Bay is located at the southern tip of South Africa. Originally settled by Southeast Asians, Pacific Islanders, and Europeans, it remains a multiethnic community in spite of a much-resisted effort by the South African government to declare the area all-white.

After giving readers this expository information at the beginning, Stock proceeds to tell a story about a young boy who, while visiting his aunt and uncle in Kalk Bay, stows away on his uncle's fishing boat early one morning. Young Armien (pronounced AH-min) has always wanted to be a fisherman like his uncle. When he brags about going with his uncle, his friends taunt him, and his uncle refuses to take him along. On the day he sneaks aboard, there is a terrible storm in the bay, and after fighting off seasickness Armien saves the life of a crew member who is washed overboard.

This story of a boy's defiance and unexpected heroism could be set anywhere. Yet Stock's soft watercolor illustrations depict a multiethnic society in which people of all colors live and work together. Armien himself has a Muslim name; his heritage is most likely East Indian. His friends include white and brown-skinned boys. This is not unrealistic in South Africa today, as children of all races often play together until they are teenagers and become aware of the system that separates them. By choosing her material in this way, Stock does avoid the social and political implications of a story set in South Africa (except for her short introduction about the Kalk Bay fishing village), but in many ways this tale embodies hopes for a nonracial society, in which the personal dilemmas of growing up are more important than the obstacles and restrictions imposed by outside powers.   L.M-L.

Denenberg, Barry. *Nelson Mandela: "No Easy Walk to Freedom."*
See entry 795, Grades 7–9.

Evans, Michael. *South Africa.*
See entry 796, Grades 7–9.

789   Gordon, Sheila. *The Middle of Somewhere: A Story of South Africa.* Orchard
1990, LB $13.99 (0-531-08508-2). 154pp. Fiction.

Nine-year-old Rebecca and her best friend, Noni, play with the secondhand
white doll that Rebecca's mother has brought her from the "Madam" and
discuss the possibility that the entire village will be bulldozed, its inhabitants
moved to the remote settlement of "Pofadderkloof." At night, Rebecca has
nightmares of bulldozers and snakes (the "pofadder" is the deadly puff adder
snake). Her older brother, John, cannot attend school because there are not
enough teachers and classrooms for the less able students; he grows more angry
and sullen by the day. Then John and Papa join the group to resist relocation;
painting placards and distributing posters, John gains confidence in his intellectual abilities for the first time. But many villagers, including Noni's family, leave,
and, after a demonstration, Rebecca's Papa is jailed. Despite support from other
villagers, her teacher, and the interracial antiapartheid committee, Rebecca is
lonely and depressed. She hears of "worldwide attention" that is being focused
on the village's plight; eventually that attention leads to her father's release, the
release of Nelson Mandela, and the probable end to the relocation threat.

Gordon's portrayal of black family life is positive, authentic, and moving.
Despite the odds—two working parents, including a mother who is a live-in
servant with precious few days off; overcrowded and inadequate schools; and
grinding poverty—the family members give each other strength and love. The
community, too, is a source of strength, as the teacher tells the class of Rebecca's
father's heroism, and the other children go out of their way to cheer her up. Like
Beverley Naidoo's *Journey to Jo'burg* (HarperCollins, 1986), this story is told from
a child's point of view, although the children, having been exposed directly to
the injustices of the white minority government, are far less innocent than
Naidoo's protagonists. Gordon presents with honesty the hatred that many
blacks feel toward whites and Rebecca's confusion when she sees some whites
helping her family. When Noni's Aunt Miriam buys Rebecca a black doll, she
does not throw away the white doll; as her father returns from prison and
Mandela is freed, her decision becomes symbolic of hopes for equality, justice,
and reconciliation. As a result of events in the country of her birth, Gordon is
more optimistic here than in her earlier novel, *Waiting for the Rain* (Orchard,
1987).   L.M-L.

790   Greene, Carol. *Desmond Tutu: Bishop of Peace.* Illus. with photos. SERIES: Picture-
Story Biographies. Childrens Pr. 1986, LB $8.95 (0-516-03634-3). 32pp. Nonfiction.

This Childrens Press *Desmond Tutu* has the same limitations of many biographies of Africans. It confuses the biographee's personal history and activities
with those of the countries. The book becomes a testimonial of apartheid rather
than a witness of an individual.

Although the text attempts to weave the Tutu history with apartheid, the
photos do not. Few pictures illustrate Desmond Tutu or his family. The photos
portray South African resistance; they do not illustrate the activities of Tutu.

This text lacks a map of either South Africa or southern Africa. The personal-
ization of the text through maps and content would help a child become more
involved with the actual racial struggle.   P.K.

Kristensen, Preben, and Fiona Cameron. *We Live in South Africa.*
See entry 802, Grades 7–9.

791   McKenna, Nancy Durrell. *A Zulu Family.* Illus. with photos. SERIES: Families the
World Over. Lerner 1986, LB $9.95 (0-8225-1666-7). 32pp. Nonfiction.

Eleven-year-old Busisiwe lives in a dry, dusty town in the "homeland" of
KwaZulu, where her family has been forcibly relocated. She and her siblings live
with her grandmother. Her mother is dead; her father works in distant Johannesburg and can come home only once a year.

 This volume in the Families the World Over series shows the hardships faced
by one black family as a result of the apartheid system. It differs in this respect
from most of the volumes in the series, which adopt a nonconfrontational point
of view. The color photos are effective in capturing the poverty of the rural
community, its contrast to thriving Johannesburg, and the inhabitants' sense of
togetherness, pride, and struggle. There is little treatment of what is uniquely
Zulu (principally a reference to the great king Shaka); rather the emphasis is on
the shared difficulties and challenges of the black majority in South Africa.

                                                                          L.M-L.

792   Meltzer, Milton. *Winnie Mandela: The Soul of South Africa.* Illus. by Stephen
Marchesi. SERIES: Women of Our Time. Viking 1986, LB $10.95 (0-670-81249-8).
54pp. Nonfiction.

Often the women behind the famous men have conquered as many challenges;
yet few authors describe the wife's efforts to fight for a cause. *Winnie Mandela*
describes the personal sacrifices that the subject made with her two daughters
and some female friends. The black women and some white women are the
strength of the antiapartheid cause. Meltzer has synthesized much of this information into the biography.

 Meltzer's sensitivity allows him to focus on the actions of Winnie Mandela
rather than on the complicated history evolving since 1640. Illustrator Marchesi
has made a major contribution to the book with realistic drawings.

 Missing in the book are a map to identify important locations where Mandela
and her daughters lived. In addition, a time line of political events and the
Mandelas' activities would help readers, as would a bibliography for additional
reading.   P.K.

793   Naidoo, Beverley. *Journey to Jo'burg.* Illus. by Eric Velasquez. HarperCollins 1986,
LB $11.89 (0-397-32169-4); P $3.50 (0-06-440237-1). 96pp. Fiction.

When their baby sister falls ill, 13-year-old Naledi and her 9-year-old brother
Tiro undertake a 300-kilometer journey from their rural village to Johannesburg,
where their mother works as a domestic servant. On the way there they learn a
great deal about their country, their fellow blacks, and the system that keeps
blacks in poverty. Among those whom they meet on the way are Grace, a young
Soweto woman who puts them up for the night and tells them about the 1976

demonstrations, her older brother's arrest, and his decision to become a freedom fighter.

The next day, Naledi's and Tiro's mother returns to the village with them, just in time to get baby Dineo to the hospital. While they wait on line at the hospital, the children see other malnourished babies and witness the death of a little boy. Although Dineo survives, she will need milk and fresh fruits—things the family cannot afford—to avoid falling ill again.

This well-written, moving story is told in the third person, but the focus is on the two children, whose observations and perceptions never fail to ring true. Beginning their journey as innocents, they have their eyes opened, but they do not become instantly committed, as weaker treatments would have it. Rather, Naledi pledges to keep in touch with her new friends, and she thinks she will try to befriend the older students at her school, who might be impressed with her trip and help her to make sense of her world. She also dreams of becoming a doctor and making a difference, a common childhood dream made more poignant by the magnitude of the forces against her. Naidoo, a white South African living in exile in England, describes vividly the sights and sounds of the journey and the emotions of children traveling alone for the first time.

In all respects, this is an outstanding book, one that will appeal to both older elementary and middle school students. L.M-L.

794 Stanley, Diane, and Peter Vennema. *Shaka: King of the Zulus.* Illus. by Diane Stanley. Morrow 1988, LB $14.88 (0-688-07343-3). 38pp. Nonfiction.

This book traces Shaka's rise from an insignificant place in his clan to the highest position—king of the Zulu nation. The theme here is that Shaka overcame life's vicissitudes and attained his ultimate dream to become undisputed leader of his people by dint of hard work, intelligence, and perseverance.

Shaka grew up as a cattle herder and underwent punishment from other boys for infringement on set rules for herdboys; after one such occasion, he and his mother, who had spoken up for him, were thrown out of their Bulawayo home. His mother's clan was too poor to accommodate them, so they moved on and found accommodation with another clan. As a herdboy, Shaka soon proved his boldness and prowess by killing a leopard that had tried to attack him and the cattle. For this he earned the respect of his peers, who regarded him as their leader and hero.

The ruler and chief of the Zulu nation, Chief Dingiswayo, the Great One, soon recognized and took note of him. Shaka joined the regiment of other boys who were trained to fight other clans to extend and enlarge the Zulu Empire. He soon showed his expertise as a military genius by devising the art of using short spears in warfare, which gave his side an advantage over those who used long, clumsy spears. Unlike other leaders who watched from afar, Shaka fought side by side with his men. Because of his popularity he was chosen by the Great One to be king of the Zulus.

European historians have called Shaka Black Napoleon, Julius Caesar, and Alexander the Great. However, Shaka was an *African* military genius and was not regarded as "often cruel," as the author suggests. He provided everything his people needed—food, clothing, land, and cattle.

Certain aspects of the illustrations present a Eurocentric view. For example, the pictures of Zulu boys wearing sandals could not have occurred in Shaka's time. Only elders wore sandals, and the soldiers whom Shaka deprived of their sandals had earned them when they graduated into adulthood.

This is otherwise a fine and fairly accurate account of a great African warrior. From reading this, young people should begin to gain a sense of history about an oft-neglected area of the world. Includes bibliography.   B.V.J.

Stewart, Gail. *South Africa.*
See entry 808, Grades 7–9.

Winner, David. *Desmond Tutu: The Courageous and Eloquent Archbishop Struggling Against Apartheid in South Africa.*
See entry 811, Grades 7–9.

GRADES 7-9

795   Denenberg, Barry. *Nelson Mandela: "No Easy Walk to Freedom."* Illus. with photos. Scholastic 1991, HB $12.95 (0-590-44163-9); P $3.95 (0-590-44154-X). 176pp. Nonfiction.

This is the first Mandela biography to be published since his release from prison in 1990. It balances an account of Mandela's life with information about modern South African history and the history of the anti-apartheid movement, and, as a result, broader issues receive more attention than Mandela himself. Denenberg's writing is straightforward and somewhat dry; he includes brief quotes from the Freedom Charter, Mandela's speeches, and other primary-source documents. Winnie Mandela receives some attention, but there is no mention of recent accusations made against her by the South African authorities with respect to the death of one of her teenage bodyguards. Although the black-and-white photographs are few and not well reproduced, they are well chosen and enhance the treatment of the subject. Despite its shortcomings, this work is a sympathetic and useful presentation of Mandela's life within the context of the modern anti-apartheid movement. Includes chronology, bibliography, and detailed index.

L.M-L.

796   Evans, Michael. *South Africa.* Illus. with photos. SERIES: Issues. Franklin Watts 1988, LB $11.90 (0-531-17056-X). 32pp. Nonfiction.

In this book Evans reviews the history of Euro-African migration into the interior of "South Africa." The book has a clear explanation of the homelands, which are similar to U.S. Native American reservations.

Evans demystifies the characteristics of apartheid in the 1990s. The continuous color-coding of the four "ethnic" groups reminds readers of the inequality of government policies. White, "Coloured," Asians, and blacks are juxtaposed through discussion of education, land rights, employment, unions/clubs, socializing, recreation, religion, economics, and politics.

The author has corrected most of the problems evident in previous writing on African military history. The maps project a visual illustration of different conflicts. Although the book was published prior to Nelson Mandela's release, it remains an excellent introduction to the situation in South Africa. The book could be strengthened by listing organizations from which students could obtain additional information about apartheid in South Africa. A bibliography of books and videos would also add to the work. An index is included. Despite these weaknesses, this series book is a valuable addition to a middle school library and one that older elementary school students will profit from reading as well.

P.K.

797 Gordon, Sheila. ***Waiting for the Rain: A Novel of South Africa.*** Orchard 1987, LB $12.99 (0-531-08326-8); Bantam 1990, P $2.95 (0-553-27911-4). 224pp. Fiction.

At 10 years old, Tengo, a black farmhand, and Frikkie, the white farm owner's nephew, are best friends. Their relationship begins to change soon afterward, for Tengo does not want to spend his life as a farm worker, even though Frikkie has promised him the job of "boss boy" once Frikkie inherits the farm. While Tengo dreams of getting an education, Frikkie hates school and counts the days until he will finish. Eventually, Tengo goes to school in faraway Soweto; he leaves without even telling Frikkie goodbye. But Soweto is a squalid place, full of poverty, crime, and unrest. Try as he might, Tengo cannot avoid political involvement, especially when the school is closed after the student strike and he is unable to take his exams. He becomes ever angrier as he sees the results of discrimination and repression, and one day, at a demonstration, his anger explodes. He comes face-to-face with a white soldier, who turns out to be none other than his old friend, Frikkie, with whom he has lost contact. He holds Frikkie's gun and the power to kill him; nonetheless he spares his ex-friend's life after they confront each other with their rage.

Gordon captures brilliantly the sense of tragedy in this relationship, as a state's bigotry destroys two boys' innocence and friendship and comes close to destroying their humanity as well. Both Tengo and Frikkie are fully realized characters, and it is to Gordon's credit that she develops the reader's empathy for Frikkie, who is both prisoner and perpetrator of an evil system. The attitude and prejudices—both overt and hidden—of white Afrikaners are revealed.

Tengo's strength and resolve inspire the reader's admiration, and Gordon shows convincingly how he is gradually moved to throw stones at a demonstration and even considers taking a life. The setting—a remote farmstead ultimately threatened by a disastrous drought (hence the title)—is well rendered and symbolic of the situation faced by a divided and tormented nation today. Sophisticated older teenagers may find the final confrontation between Tengo and Frikkie to be somewhat contrived, but younger teens will be drawn into the story and the very real emotions that are expressed here.

L.M-L.

798 Harris, Sarah. ***South Africa: Timeline.*** Illus. with photos. SERIES: Weighing up the Evidence. Dryad Pr. 1988, LB $19.95 (0-85219-724-1). 64pp. Nonfiction.

Harris, a British writer, has focused on the current development of South Africa. The dedication to the more than 4,000 children detained in South African prisons is a testimony to her effort to explain the history that resulted in students' defying the minority government rule through apartheid. Her appeal to British and American students to consider this political and economic situation is pointed.

Unlike other books on comparable topics, Harris utilized first-person source information. The black-and-white photos and illustrations underscore the stark reality of the current struggle. Throughout the text she raises questions for students to consider and suggests activities to clarify ambiguities of history. Her text demonstrates her sensitivity for various groups of South Africans. Unlike some authors, she does not use derogatory terms or a patronizing style. Page footers provide a time line for students as a constant reminder.

Harris includes a glossary of South African terms and acronyms. Her list of further readings is categorized by topic for easy reference. The most useful feature is her time line, juxtaposing events in Britain, Africa, and South Africa. Students could add U.S. events as an activity.

In a short amount of space, Harris has captured issues of South Africa and has managed to challenge the reader. This book is commendable. No school system should hesitate to purchase this British text.   P.K.

799   Haskins, Jim. **Winnie Mandela: Life of Struggle.** Illus. with photos. Putnam 1988, HB $14.95 (0-399-21515-8). 179pp. Nonfiction.

When she was 27, with two tiny girls at home, her husband was arrested, tried, and sentenced to life in prison. Nonetheless, Winnie Mandela, who had avoided politics as a teenager in order to study and to become South Africa's first black medical social worker, now emerged as a major spokesperson against apartheid in her own right.

Haskins's biography portrays a woman of incredible courage, who consciously chose a life of hardship and struggle so that her people and her country could attain freedom and justice. Among the highlights of this work are the details of her rejection of an arranged marriage to a Xhosa chief and to a chief's son, Kaiser Matanzima (later a collaborator in the South African government's notorious homelands policy), in favor of Matanzima's uncle, Nelson Mandela, as well as Haskins's description of her imprisonment, under the most deplorable conditions, in Pretoria Prison.

Interspersed with Winnie Mandela's personal story are brief discussions of South Africa's history and society. Though they are well integrated into the text, there are some inaccuracies in these background presentations; students will need to look elsewhere for a history of South Africa. However, the biographical information is accurate, with a balance between personal information geared to spark the reader's interest and a consideration of Mandela's role in the anti-apartheid struggle. Above all, this biography shows that women with families have not been invisible but rather have played a significant role in the struggle.

                                                                                L.M-L.

800   Hayward, Jean. **South Africa Since 1948.** Illus. with photos. SERIES: Witness History. Franklin Watts 1989, LB $12.90 (0-531-18262-2). 63pp. Nonfiction.

When the National Party of South Africa won the 1948 election, a system of apartheid (separateness) became law. This book documents the factors contributing to this legislation and the efforts of non-Euro-Africans to resist its restrictions. The content and themes covered are similar to Michael Evans's *South Africa*, also distributed by Franklin Watts. The Hayward book utilizes quotes from legal proceedings to illustrate the South African administration's repression. The citations, maps, illustrations, and photographs help the reader comprehend the degree of degradation imposed upon the non-Euro-African. The list of prominent leaders representing several factions in the struggle for majority rule clarifies some of the issues. Hayward includes a time line and a glossary of terms.

South Africa Since 1948 focuses on current events prior to Nelson Mandela and other ANC members' release from prison. This book represents an American point of view in contrast to Evans's British interpretation. The use of primary sources, combined with the author's background information and explanations, makes this an especially useful resource for the classroom.   P.K.

801   Jones, Toeckey. **Skindeep.** HarperCollins 1986, LB $12.89 (0-06-023052-5). 250pp. Fiction.

Eighteen-year-old Rhonda is obsessed with boys and with going to London, where she can read racy books without worrying about censorship. While chasing her "Handsome Hulk," she meets Dave, whose most noticeable physical feature is a shaved head. Dave is secretive about his head, but he and Rhonda become close friends nonetheless. In fact, Dave becomes a friend of Rhonda's bigoted 8-year-old brother, Mark, whom he consoles when Mark's dog is run over; he even brings Mark a new puppy for his ninth birthday.

Tensions arise in the relationship when Rhonda wants more physical contact and Dave backs off. She even suspects her boyfriend is gay (which her Handsome Hulk turns out to be). After their first sexual experience, Rhonda arranges to take Dave to Cape Town, where an unfortunate encounter reveals the truth. Dave is of mixed race but is passing as white. Seeing his mother and siblings in dire circumstances in Cape Town, he decides to be reclassified as Coloured, drops out of university, and joins the anti-apartheid struggle. Returning to Johannesburg, alone, Rhonda too takes up the cause despite, or rather because of, her broken heart.

Were this a better-written book, it would have received a recommendation. It certainly raises the important issue of interracial relationships in a racist society. Dave's initial reluctance to have sexual relations with Rhonda rings true; he is attracted to her but fears the consequences of his deception. As the narrator, Rhonda is less sympathetic, and her flippant tone trivializes the issues. Particularly offensive is the treatment of homosexuality; younger readers might also find the racial slurs upsetting. Despite the author's use of South African English slang, the dialogue seems forced and wooden. Finally, the ending, in which Dave discovers his mother after she approaches him, begging for alms, in Cape Town, is contrived, and the story of how he has managed to live as white all those years, unnecessarily complicated.   L.M-L.

802   Kristensen, Preben, and Fiona Cameron. **We Live in South Africa.** Illus. with photos. SERIES: Living Here. Franklin Watts 1985, LB $12.90 (0-531-18005-0). 60pp. Nonfiction.

Few books on South Africa describe the lives of ordinary people. The biographies available in most series focus on the highly publicized lives of Nelson or Winnie Mandela and Desmond Tutu. *We Live in South Africa* juxtaposes 26 individuals and compares their lives and dreams. These first-person interviews illustrate the diversity found in South Africa; it is the first series to include the lives of "Asians/Indians" and "Mixed-race."

The book has several positive characteristics. First, it contains color photographs of the interviewees and aspects of their work. It provides a map to help readers locate the homes of the interviewees and includes a brief description of South Africa followed by a glossary of terms.

Despite its positive features, *We Live in South Africa* exhibits some flaws. Of the 26 individuals included in the text, only 11 are non-Euro-Africans. The book maintains a positive tone, avoiding many of the conflicts and controversies surrounding apartheid and other policies of the minority government.   P.K.

Magubane, Peter. *Magubane's South Africa.*
See entry 822, Grades 10–12.

803   Meyer, Carolyn. *Voices of South Africa: Growing Up in a Troubled Land.* Harcourt Brace Jovanovich/Gulliver 1986, HB $14.95 (0-15-200637-0). 244pp. Nonfiction.

In 1985 Meyer toured South Africa from Cape Town, up the eastern coast, and inland to Johannesburg. Along the way she visited schools and families and met a variety of people, both black and white. Dozens of those people appear here, including a white anti-apartheid activist, whites who embrace the system that has provided for them one of the highest living standards in the world, and blacks who appear fearful and demoralized even as they dream of success and struggle to create a more just society. A recurrent theme is suspicion of Meyer and her motives, particularly among whites who see the United States as their country's enemy and among blacks who fear their words will one day be used against them.

By presenting as wide a range of perspectives as possible, Meyer provides an overview of the country, its many cultures, and the diverse attitudes that exist. Unfortunately, her approach leads to a certain lack of depth, as no single point of view is explored fully. Whites do not come off well. About half are overt racists who spew vicious opinions and slurs (quoted in the text); the prejudices of the rest exist just below the surface. Among the latter group are the ostensibly liberal members of a Johannesburg church group who do not want changes to occur too quickly so as to affect their way of life.

Meyer's access to blacks was limited, and it shows; the reader has virtually no sense of the life and personality of any of the black interviewees. The book's value lies in its depiction of white intransigence and Meyer's often frustrating research experience, but those who want more substance should bypass it in favor of the better works of autobiography and fiction.   L.M-L.

804   Naidoo, Beverley. *Chain of Fire.* Illus. by Eric Velasquez. HarperCollins 1990, LB $12.89 (0-397-32427-8). 242pp. Fiction.

On his way to the village tap, 11-year-old Tiro notices someone painting numbers on the houses. He points it out to his 15-year-old sister Naledi, and the government worker tells them they are to be moved from their village to Bophuthatswana, the "tribal homeland" they have never seen. "Bop" is arid and far from work and schools, and the children wonder if they can do anything to stop the forced removal.

South African exile Naidoo's second novel continues the story of Naledi, Tiro, and Dineo, whom readers met in her noteworthy *Journey to Jo'burg*. Here, the children do become committed to political action. Naledi befriends an older schoolmate, Taolo Dikobe, the son of an activist and former political prisoner sent to the village as part of his banning order. At his first demonstration, Tiro is bitten by a police dog and barely escapes arrest. Then the youngsters are betrayed by fellow blacks. Their chief, the father of Naledi's best friend, has sold the land to the whites, and black policemen prove to be as brutal as the whites. There is tragedy, as Taolo's father is killed and he returns to Soweto with his mother as the bulldozers are demolishing the village and trucks are taking Naledi's family and other families to a bleak camp in the "homeland."

Again, Naidoo's portrait of young people in crisis is unerring in its authenticity. The children in this story have many reasons for not getting involved—Naledi, for instance, takes care of her ill grandmother and shoulders additional family duties as well—yet they risk their lives to protect what little they have. Only gradually do they become aware of the consequences of their actions, but they realize in the process that by standing together they can be strong. Even in failure, they have achieved a victory, for by supporting each other they continue the struggle another day. Young teenagers will empathize with Naledi and Tiro, whose inspiring, action-filled story will command their attention up to the final page.   L.M-L.

Naidoo, Beverley. *Journey to Jo'burg.*
See entry 793, Grades 4–6.

805 Pascoe, Elaine. *South Africa: Troubled Land.* Illus. with photos. Franklin Watts 1987, LB $12.90 (0-531-10432-X). 128pp. Nonfiction.

Pascoe draws the reader into her survey of South African history by contrasting the lives of fictional black men and white men. The reader gets a sense of the injustices of apartheid, and Pascoe's history tells clearly, though somewhat dryly, how that system evolved. The book succeeds in conveying the diversity of ethnic heritages among blacks, whites, and those classified as Coloured, as well as more recent ideological and political divisions. The language is as neutral and objective as possible, but the outrage does come through. The achievements of black leaders such as the Mandelas and Desmond Tutu are highlighted. The history ends in 1986, and the conclusion features a brief discussion of the pros and cons of economic sanctions.

There are a bibliography, a glossary of key terms and concepts, a chronology, and an index. This is a useful introduction for middle schoolers and those needing a short, easy-to-read introduction, but more advanced students should read recently published histories published for adults.   L.M-L.

Paton, Jonathan. *The Land and People of South Africa.*
See entry 825, Grades 10–12.

806 Rochman, Hazel, ed. *Somehow Tenderness Survives: Stories of Southern Africa.* HarperCollins 1988, LB $12.89 (0-06-025023-2); 1990, P $3.25 (0-06-447063-6). 192pp. Fiction.

As a reviewer of young adult books, South African–born writer Hazel Rochman's name is familiar to librarians, teachers, and many parents. This anthology of ten short stories—five by black authors and five by white authors—presents the range of experiences and emotions in the country of her birth, a country torn apart by racial division and injustice. Neither blacks nor whites live in peace. In black writer Peter Abrahams's "Crackling Day," a black youth fights back when three white bullies insult him and call his dead father a baboon. Later the white boys come to his house with a white man, who forces the protagonist's uncle to beat him in punishment. Conversely, in Ernst Havemann's "A Farm at Raraba," a white officer fighting black guerrillas in Namibia (known by him as South-West Africa) spends a night talking with Adoons, a guerrilla he has wounded and trapped. When he lets Adoons escape, he fears that the man, or another captured guerrilla, will one day inform to his superiors about his act of humanity. Other stories portray an Indian Muslim wife who duplicates anti-apartheid leaflets after her daily chores are done, a Jewish family who confronts a group of Afrikaner men and women abusing a black child, and a teenage white boy whose love for the black servant's daughter leads to her pregnancy, the child's murder, and his humiliation.

The stories introduce teenagers to the work of notable African authors, including Abrahams, the first major black writer to emerge from South Africa; Mark Mathabane; Dennis Brutus, from whose poem the collection's title comes; Nadine Gordimer; and Doris Lessing. The selection has been made with a young adult audience in mind, and there is not a superfluous work in the bunch. A brief but eloquent introduction sets the tone. The stories are short enough to be used in a variety of classroom settings, and the depth and variety of themes and situations make this a crucial book for any study of South Africa on the junior high or high school level. L.M-L.

807   Sacks, Margaret. ***Beyond Safe Boundaries.*** Dutton/Lodestar 1989, HB $13.95 (0-525-67281-8); Penguin/Puffin 1990, P $3.95 (0-14-034407-1). 156pp. Fiction.

Eleven-year-old Elizabeth Levin's life begins to change in 1958 when her father brings home the woman who is to be his new wife—Elizabeth's stepmother. But for this Jewish girl growing up in South Africa not all the changes she experiences are on a personal level. While she accepts and becomes close to her new stepmother, her rebellious older sister, Evelyn, resents her father's new wife and becomes withdrawn and secretive. Elizabeth witnesses problems involving the black servants and a mixed-race employee of her father's, problems that include an arrest on a pass-law violation, a crime in the local area, and the employee's alcoholism. Only gradually, however, does she realize these events—as well as the privileges she has taken for granted—are the result of a fully developed, legalized system of racial discrimination. In the meantime, Evelyn has become involved with a Coloured student leader, the son of her father's demoralized employee. She takes part in meetings and demonstrations, and, during one fateful visit by Elizabeth to her university apartment, Evelyn is unwittingly betrayed. The young man dies under interrogation, his father commits suicide, Evelyn must flee the country, and Elizabeth realizes too that her future is elsewhere, away from the hatred and inhumanity.

Sacks conveys effectively a child's loss of innocence. As Elizabeth becomes more aware of her world, that world becomes more menacing, on both personal and political levels. The plot structure is episodic and somewhat disjointed, which prevents the tension from building as well as it should, and some of the scenes (such as a dinner-table discussion early on with right-wing Afrikaner neighbors) seem manufactured to give information to the reader. The writing is fairly clumsy; even so, images and emotions do come through. This autobiographical first novel is an authentic portrayal of the experiences of a white Jewish girl in South Africa, growing up with privileges and an emerging sense of guilt, and for this reason it is a valuable complement to other fiction and nonfiction accounts geared to young adult readers.   L.M-L.

808   Stewart, Gail. **South Africa.** Illus. with photos. SERIES: Places in the News. Crestwood House 1990, LB $10.95 (0-89686-539-8). 48pp. Nonfiction.

This series of 12 titles includes two concerning African issues—*South Africa* and *Ethiopia.* (Crestwood House should consider books on Liberia and Morocco, which have also been in the news.)

Stewart has written the text for both of the mentioned titles. The format of *South Africa* is one that raises issues for discussion about race, prejudice, laws, education, resistance, and apartheid. Many of the issues discussed in *South Africa* can also be compared with issues in the United States.

Stewart traces the historical evolution of South African apartheid, focusing on the events of Sharpville and Soweto. She examines the effects of boycotts and world sanctions on the lives of South Africans. One missing issue is the impact of the U.S. political and economic policy on South Africa.

The writing is clear and relatively simple, as the series is geared to reluctant readers; photos and other visual materials add interest and aid in the comprehension of the text.   P.K.

809   Tessendorf, K. C. **Along the Road to Soweto: A Racial History of South Africa.** Illus. with maps, prints, and photos. Atheneum 1989, HB $14.95 (0-689-31401-9). 194pp. Nonfiction.

Though published in 1989, this book's approach and tone are more reminiscent of histories published 30 or more years earlier. The author seeks to tell the story of South Africa's development through the various "races" that are in conflict today—blacks, Coloureds, Asians, Afrikaners, and English. Each individual group receives attention both for itself and in regard to its interaction with other groups.

The problem with this work lies in its white-oriented perspective. Most of the attention is directed at the development of Afrikaner and English settlement and the conflicts between these two groups. Of the black groups, only the Xhosa and Zulu seem to rate mention; the author ignores completely the Ndebele, Sotho, Tswana, Venda, and other groups who settled in the region and make up its population today. Asians are treated only briefly, and the Coloured, many of whom trace their origins to the Khoikhoi and San peoples, receive rather disparaging treatment. The antiquated and racist terms "bushmen" and "Hottentots" are used to refer to the San and the Khoikhoi, and, up until the last chapters of the work, blacks are referred to as the "Bantu." The Wars of Dispossession are referred to by their Afrikaner name, the "Kaffir Wars," "kaffir" being in South Africa a term equivalent to "nigger."

Tessendorf revels in descriptions of atrocities committed by Shaka and other black African rulers, here relying upon testimonials by admitted white supremacists while explaining away acts of brutality committed by both English and Afrikaner forces during the Boer War. Visual materials, particularly early prints, depict blacks as hideous-looking savages with exaggerated physical features.

There are problems with more contemporary chapters as well. Tessendorf recycles white South African arguments that justify the denial of equal rights and majority rule—the history of American racial oppression against blacks and Native Americans, the brutal and treacherous history of the "Bantu," the influence of communism on African nationalism, and the failure of other African nations to end ethnic warfare and establish viable economies and societies.

When the material discusses black leaders today, only Nelson and Winnie Mandela receive mention; equally eloquent and capable leaders such as Desmond Tutu are ignored. While the discussion of the contemporary situation is more balanced than the preceding chapters, this book cannot be recommended. Even if one wished to present the white South African side, the book's overall lack of sensitivity—as evidenced by the visual materials and the insulting tone of the text as it relates to the earlier history of black South Africans—would make it an exceedingly poor choice. Includes index, bibliography, and source notes.   L.M-L.

810 Wepman, Dennis. ***Desmond Tutu.*** Illus. with photos. SERIES: Impact Biographies. Franklin Watts 1989, LB $12.90 (0-531-10780-9). 157pp. Nonfiction.

Since Desmond Tutu won the Nobel Peace Prize, many books for adolescents have described his life and his fight against apartheid in South Africa. He has modeled nonviolent resistance against the minority government. Wepman documents this slow move to world recognition. Unlike many leaders who receive recognition, Tutu insisted on living with the ordinary working-class people of the townships. By choosing this route, he retains the respect of the African population and the Euro-African administrators. He works systematically to improve the conditions of Africans by fund-raising tours in the Americas and Europe, and church leadership in South Africa has become a significant force; Wepman helps readers understand how religion can be one avenue for equality, justice, and social change.

The book's format is scholarly. It lacks charts and graphs that are usually characteristics of other nonfiction texts. The black-and-white photos underscore the racial confrontation. Wepman provides a bibliography, a time table, and citations. This book is a valuable addition to a middle school library. Another book in this series is *Nelson and Winnie Mandela*, by Dorothy and Thomas Hoobler.   P.K.

811 Winner, David. ***Desmond Tutu: The Courageous and Eloquent Archbishop Struggling Against Apartheid in South Africa.*** SERIES: People Who Have Helped the World. Gareth Stevens 1989, LB $12.45 (0-8368-0459-7). 68pp. Nonfiction.

One of the trends of books about Desmond Tutu is that his biography becomes lost in the history of the antiapartheid struggle. A reader anticipates learning about the career and family of Tutu but finds that the text deals with the history from 1640 until the present. The time line is a case in point. Rather than beginning with the birth of Desmond Tutu in 1931 and documenting his life, some authors document the political activities of the various factions in South Africa.

One of the problems of U.S. readers is their failure to identify with South Africans in everyday struggles. Because of media coverage of Tutu's visits to the United States, many children have seen him. This book captures the reader's initial interest by showing the impact of apartheid on Desmond Tutu and his family. Unfortunately, the powerful beginning is not followed up as effectively.

In addition to copious color photos, the text includes lists of additional books and organizations for further information. The glossary provides definitions of terms. A simplified version of this biography for younger elementary-age students is being published as part of Gareth Stevens's People Who Have Made a Difference series.

P.K.

GRADES 10–12

812   Benson, Mary. *Nelson Mandela: The Man and His Movement.* Illus. with photos. Norton 1986, P $8.95 (0-393-30322-5). 269pp. Nonfiction.

This biography presents the facts of Nelson Mandela's life, but its primary focus is on the movement with which he has been identified. Benson examines the history of the antiapartheid movement and the formation of the African National Congress, discussing the role played by black, Coloured, Asian, and white leaders, most of whom she mentions by name. Special attention is given to the decision by Mandela and others to abandon nonviolent tactics in the face of state repression, to Mandela's 1964 trial that resulted in his life prison sentence, and to the conditions of his imprisonment. Benson shows how Mandela and other black leaders coped in prison, their resolve strengthening rather than being weakened.

The book is carefully researched, with heavy reliance on primary sources of all kinds. Benson shows why Mandela became a leader and a symbol of the antiapartheid movement at the same time as she acknowledges the role played by other capable and articulate leaders. She does not shortchange Winnie Mandela, who is portrayed as a powerful symbol and spokesperson in her own right, as well as a source of strength for her family. Although events such as Mandela's release from prison must await an updating of this biography, the title's greatest assets are the history and context that it provides. High school students will need to do some background reading before tackling this book, but its clear writing and sophisticated presentation make it one of the best biographies of Mandela for older teens as well as adults.

L.M-L.

813   *Beyond the Barricades: Popular Resistance in South Africa.* Illus. with photos. Aperture 1989, P $24.95 (0-89381-375-3). 144pp. Nonfiction.

Hundreds of black-and-white photos, taken by photographers from all ethnic backgrounds, illustrate resistance to apartheid in South Africa during the 1980s. In addition to explanatory captions there are excerpts from poems, speeches, and firsthand accounts. The result is a powerful portrait of life, death, and struggle in black communities throughout the country. More journalistic and more focused on political events than Peter Magubane's *Black Child* (Knopf, 1982) or *Magubane's South Africa* (Knopf, 1978), this work provides visual documentation of blacks' quest for equality and of brutal repression on the part of police and township vigilantes, many of whom are affiliated with the Zulu organization Inkatha. As major participants in the resistance, children and teenagers are highly visible, both in the photos and in the accompanying testimonials.

L.M-L.

814   Biko, Steve. *I Write What I Like.* HarperCollins 1979, P $7.95 (0-06-250055-4).
153pp. Nonfiction.

This is a collection of anti-apartheid activist Steve Biko's writings, published after his death at the hands of South African prison authorities. The founder of the South African Students' Organisation and the Black Consciousness Movement, Biko articulates here the definition, purposes, and goals of Black Consciousness and strategies for nonviolent opposition to apartheid. His essays on multicultural education are particularly interesting for high school students and teachers. Some of the essays were published before Biko's death, while others are taken from his trial testimony. This is a useful primary-source document for the high school researcher, and teens will find parallels between Biko's observations of race relations in South Africa and issues facing blacks and whites in the United States today.   L.M-L.

815   Brink, Andre. *A Dry White Season.* Penguin 1980, P $7.95 (0-14-006890-2).
316pp. Fiction.

After a black school custodian's son, and then the custodian himself, die in detention, Afrikaner schoolteacher Ben Du Toit confronts his own people in search of the truth. His social-climbing wife is unsupportive, as is his eldest daughter; his friends persuade him to be silent; and the authorities obstruct his efforts at every turn. An investigation into the custodian's death rules it a suicide, for the doctor who found signs of foul play has been arrested and is unable to testify. Another prisoner defends police authorities in exchange for his freedom, and those who support Du Toit meet with terrible fates. In search of understanding, Du Toit has an illicit affair with a journalist who is subsequently expelled from the country; photographs of them naked are circulated to his wife and the school's headmaster. He is fired, his wife leaves him, a daughter who had supported him withdraws, and he learns that his eldest daughter is spying on him. Only his teenage son remains loyal. When he visits the black taxi driver who has urged him to continue the struggle, the man is gone (escaped the country, he is told), and township residents chase him away with stones. Finally, the desperate Du Toit is murdered, run down in the street, but not before delivering the notes for his life story to the anonymous writer who tells it.

Afrikaner author Brink presents the attitudes of his people with brutal honesty. Convincingly, he shows how the previously apathetic Du Toit comes to take a moral position and how his decency is seen as high treason by his peers. While the Afrikaner authorities kill off the black characters one by one, Du Toit is tortured, for his well-meaning efforts lead to their suffering, and at every step he sees the hopelessness of his actions. In this hellish world, his growing paranoia reflects his real experience as he is, literally, hounded to death.

This gripping story has been made into a feature film. A major literary novel by one of South Africa's finest writers, its tight plotting, style, and presentation of the process and consequences of political commitment upon the teacher and his family make it a valuable work for the advanced high school student.
                                                                       L.M-L.

816   Bunn, David, and Jane Taylor, eds. ***From South Africa: New Writings, Photo-graphs, and Art.*** Illus. Univ. of Chicago Pr. 1988, HB $43.00 (0-226-08035-8); P $16.95 (0-226-08036-6). 501pp. Fiction.

Originally published as a double edition of the literary magazine *TriQuarterly*, this volume contains poems, short stories, novel excerpts, speeches, black-and-white photos, and graphics, all of which show the response of progressive intellectuals of all races to the injustices of apartheid and the struggle for liberation in South Africa. Although all of the contributors are from South Africa, many must live in exile; others are in prison or dead. Most of these works are not available to be read within the country. Nonetheless, in addition to reflecting and analyzing the present situation, the works express hope for a nonracial society. Readers will become acquainted with the work of many lesser-known writers and artists featured here, and particularly valuable for the high school curriculum are works of poetry by Dennis Brutus, Sipho Sepamla, and other noted black writers.   L.M-L.

817   Du Boulay, Shirley. ***Tutu: Voice of the Voiceless.*** Illus. with photos. Eerdmans 1988, HB $22.50 (0-8028-3649-6). 304pp. Nonfiction.

In 1984 the Nobel Peace Prize was awarded to the first black Anglican bishop for Johannesburg, Desmond Tutu. Since then, Tutu has been chosen as Archbishop of Cape Town, the highest Anglican post in South Africa. Du Boulay's biography captures the essence of this remarkable man, whose philosophy and achievements have been compared with those of Dr. Martin Luther King, Jr.

Tutu is portrayed as a man committed to nonviolence in a violent society. Du Boulay traces the development of his beliefs and his career up to 1987. He emerges as a three-dimensional human being, with flaws as well as strengths. Charges of financial mismanagement in organizations he has led, raised by South African authorities to discredit him, are dealt with honestly and thoroughly. Du Boulay presents the positions of those who oppose Tutu—both conservative whites and more militant blacks—and she details his response to the insults and threats of the former and the violent actions of the latter; for instance, she describes vividly the times he has interceded to protect accused township spies from being "necklaced" during demonstrations.

The account reflects a solid knowledge of Christian beliefs and church organization, and, thus, the author is able to give substantive treatment to Tutu's career and role as a religious leader. Although information about Tutu's family life appears, the principal focus is on his emergence as a leader in the struggle for social justice, equal rights, and reconciliation in South Africa.   L.M-L.

818   Finnegan, William. ***Crossing the Line: A Year in the Land of Apartheid.*** HarperCollins 1986, HB $22.95 (0-06-015568-X); 1987, P $10.95 (0-06-091430-0). 418pp. Nonfiction.

While journeying around the world, Finnegan, a surfing enthusiast from California, found himself in South Africa. Interested in seeing what was going on and in financing his further travels, he took a job in a mixed-race secondary school in the Cape Flats, a dusty, overcrowded suburb of Cape Town set aside for those designated as Coloured. Over the next year (1980), he taught English and geography to young teenagers, took part in a two-month school boycott, and toured the country with a politically aware student in her final year at the school.

His autobiographical account is filled with vignettes of the teachers and students and with background information about the school, the Cape Flats community, and South Africa as a whole. Emerging is a picture of a second-rate school where students fail more often than they experience success and where bleak prospects for further education and advancement demoralize all but the most committed.

Although many teenage and adult readers may find this book somewhat overwritten, others will relish the details of the students' and teachers' lives and Finnegan's own efforts to become an effective teacher. One of the most interesting parts of Finnegan's account is his discussion of the school boycott. Teachers who supported the boycott gave alternative lessons that told the truth about apartheid. Even so, he argues, its effects were not positive on the whole; the action went on far beyond its usefulness as a tactic, disrupting the students' education while producing few concrete results. Other aspects of his book will spark further thought and discussion as well, among them choices made by various students and teachers to seek or to avoid activities that might get them arrested. This work is most useful as that of an outsider observing the South African situation and, in doing so, raising issues that we, his fellow North Americans, may ponder.   L.M-L.

819   Fugard, Athol. ***Master Harold . . . and the Boys.*** Knopf 1982, HB $11.45 (0-394-52874-3); Penguin 1984, P $4.95 (0-14-048187-7). 60pp. Fiction.

As the two black waiters at St. George's Park Tea Room, Sam and Willie, practice waltz steps for Willie's upcoming competition, 17-year-old Harold (Hally), the owners' son, comes in. Willie and Hally both have personal problems. Willie has recently quarreled with his girlfriend and partner in the competition, and he does not believe they will be able to perform well enough to win. Hally's disabled, alcoholic father is in the hospital, and Hally does not want him to come home. For a while, the three share memories of Hally's childhood, when Sam and Willie treated the lonely, neglected youngster as a younger brother or son. But when Hally's mother calls, putting his father on the phone, and Hally does not have the guts to tell his father he does not want him home, Hally turns on Sam. He insults the two black men and demands that Sam call him Master Harold. Although there is a partial reconciliation, the damage is done. Hally sees the depth of his racism. He has lost a friend, perhaps his only one, and has one more reason to feel ashamed of himself.

This realistic and poignant work of drama has much to say to teenagers about families, friends, and the situation in South Africa. One of the tragedies of apartheid is that friendships between whites and blacks do not continue past childhood, once racism becomes so ingrained and the obstacles to togetherness so great that the two are forever divided. At the time the play takes place, in 1950, Sam cannot even legally sit on a bench with the crying Hally in order to comfort him. Further, because of his prejudice, Hally refuses to accept Sam's understanding and wisdom when faced with a family crisis. Hally's sense of isolation will ring true to many teens and, in addition to providing a personal view of apartheid, will perhaps encourage them to examine their own biases and assumptions.   L.M-L.

820   Gordimer, Nadine. *My Son's Story.* Farrar, Straus & Giroux 1990, HB $19.95 (0-374-21751-3). 277pp. Fiction.

Several months after his political activist father's release from prison, 15-year-old Will, a Coloured youth, sees his father leaving a movie theater with a white woman. The woman is a human rights activist who has helped the family in the past, but Will's disillusionment in the face of his father's imperfections and treachery takes the form of a sullen resentment that binds him to his father at the same time as it repels him. Through Will's eyes, we learn of his father, Sonny's, career, first as a ghetto schoolteacher reluctantly pushed into the anti-apartheid movement and then as a middle-level leader and spokesperson for the movement. Over the next six years, Sonny finds himself eased out of the inner circle as his daughter, Baby, Will's older sister, and his wife, Aila, are moved to risk their own lives for the cause. Only Will remains aloof—observing, recording, and ultimately writing his family's tormented history, the book he "can never publish."

This novel is at once a coming-of-age story and an exploration of the dynamics and costs of political commitment. Things are never simple, or what they appear to be on the surface, and it is to Gordimer's credit that she can write about an atrocity such as apartheid without losing sight of the complexity of human thought and experience. Characters are compelling and multidimensional; despite the differences between his experiences and theirs, teenagers will empathize with Will's struggle to accept the life—and family—he has been given.

This is a challenging work, one which, because of its intricate style, frank language, and discussion of sexual issues, is most appropriate for mature high school students. Those who do read it will long remember this work, considered perhaps the finest by one of the world's most important contemporary authors. Among other recommended novels by Gordimer that deal, at least in part, with coming-of-age themes are *Burger's Daughter* (Viking, 1979) and *A Sport of Nature* (Knopf, 1987).

L.M-L.

821   Gordimer, Nadine, and David Goldblatt. *Lifetimes Under Apartheid.* Illus. with photos by David Goldblatt. Knopf 1986, HB $30.00 (0-394-55406-X). 115pp. Nonfiction.

Goldblatt's black-and-white photographs and excerpts from Gordimer's writings between 1953 and 1986 depict the lives of blacks and whites and relations between them from the 1960s to the 1980s. We see blacks and whites in rural and urban settings, at home and at work. The focus is exclusively on black and white, as those two groups embody the sharpest conflict. Asians and those of mixed race are not pictured. The final section, the most political, ends with a photo of a black teenager released from prison with a cast on each arm; the photo's moving quotation is from Gordimer's 1979 novel *Burger's Daughter*.

Sections of mostly descriptive quotations alternate with sections of briefly captioned photos; they do not correspond exactly. Still, the relationship between the textual and the visual, in the South African context, makes this an excellent work for interdisciplinary study on the high school level. The book is also an introduction to two significant white South African artists who have chosen through their work to challenge the apartheid system.

L.M-L.

Hayward, Jean. *South Africa Since 1948.*
See entry 800, Grades 7–9.

Jones, Toeckey. *Skindeep.*
See entry 801, Grades 7–9.

822   Magubane, Peter. *Magubane's South Africa.* Illus. with photos by the author.
       Knopf 1978. 118pp. Nonfiction. o.p.

Black South African photographer Peter Magubane has given readers a detailed portrait of life and resistance in his country. The book begins with a brief autobiographical essay highlighting Magubane's early life growing up in the doomed black township of Sophiatown, his struggle to become a photographer (including his efforts to perfect his craft), his reactions to police brutality against his people, his own run-ins with the police, which included imprisonment and banning, and his experiences documenting the uprisings in Sharpeville and Soweto. Once he had to hide his camera inside an empty milk carton; at other times he had to avoid both police bullets and beatings by demonstrators who feared being photographed.

The black-and-white photos themselves are vivid testimony to the conditions under which black South Africans live, while others show the many faces of struggle against the apartheid system. Taken over a period of two decades, the photos show changes in the manner and appearance of the demonstrators as a younger generation has come to the fore. Concise, well-written captions explain the pictures and often provide background information.

This collection is an excellent visual introduction to South Africa—especially to the black majority ignored by standard tourist photos—and to the work of one of the country's finest photographers. Magubane's work is the focus of two other books: *Black Child* (Knopf, 1982), which documents the process of growing up black under apartheid, and *Soweto: The Fruit of Fear* (Africa World Press, 1986), the story, in pictures, of the 1976 demonstrations in Soweto, Alexandra Township, and throughout the country.   L.M-L.

823   Mathabane, Mark. *Kaffir Boy: The True Story of a Black Youth's Coming of Age
       in Apartheid South Africa.* Macmillan 1986, HB $19.95 (0-02-581800-7); New
       American Library 1988, P $8.95 (0-452-25943-6). 354pp. Nonfiction.

At 6 years old, his earliest memories were of the police's ransacking the tiny shack where he lived and taking his father and mother away. They returned after a short while, though his father's spirit was broken by repeated arrests, humiliations, unemployment, and crushing poverty. Young Johannes (who later renamed himself Mark) vowed that such a fate would never happen to him, even if it meant leaving his home and family and coming to America.

This moving autobiography traces Mathabane's life from his first memories to the realization of his dream, when, at the age of 19, he arrives in the United States on a tennis scholarship. Along the way, he sees and experiences incredible brutality perpetrated by white South African authorities and the black policemen who have sided with the forces of oppression. He refuses to take the easy way out—to sell his body to itinerant workers for food money or to join one of the criminal gangs prowling the black township. Criticized for pursuing education over activism and for playing tennis at white clubs, he also participates in demonstrations against the demeaning system of Bantu education. He is honest about his conflicts with his father, which include differences over career goals and traditional values.

Mathabane's true story is vivid and gripping, commanding the reader's attention from the very first page. At times harsh in his judgment of himself and others, the author emerges as a complete person, worthy of our empathy and admiration. Overcoming daunting obstacles that would have crushed a less driven person, he is faced with his final agonizing choice—to leave behind his family and community in pursuit of an individualistic dream of freedom at odds with both his traditional culture and the collective struggle for freedom going on in his country. Teenage readers may debate his decision, but they cannot help but have the most profound respect for the young man who has written so eloquently about his struggle.

Mathabane's story continues in *Kaffir Boy in America* (Macmillan, 1989), which chronicles his efforts to build a new life in the United States and to bring his family to freedom. L.M-L.

824   Mattera, Don. ***Sophiatown: Coming of Age in South Africa.*** Beacon 1989, HB
        $15.95 (0-8070-0206-2). 151pp. Nonfiction.

South African poet Mattera narrates his coming of age in the tough multiracial neighborhood known as Sophiatown, which was bulldozed block by block between 1955 and 1962 to make room for pristine white neighborhoods. Of mixed race (including a paternal grandfather who immigrated from Italy), Mattera describes the process of "classification," through which, by the stroke of a pen, a person could be declared white and come into a life of opportunity or declared black and shipped off to a distant "location."

Though a good student, the neglected youngster became, at the age of 14, a gang member and quickly rose to leadership. Almost killed numerous times, he went to jail for the murder of a rival, only to have the charges dropped. Several experiences—most notably the influence of a white liberal priest, the example of an elderly convict, the birth of his first child, and the beginning of Sophiatown's destruction—turned the young criminal into a political activist. The final pages of the book eloquently document Mattera's conversion and the slow death of his community.

The chapters in this short memoir are self-contained and may be read separately. The language is both graphic and poetic. Mattera's portrayal of a troubled youngster trying to find his identity (as opposed to the "Coloured" identity the white government has decreed for him) will appeal to many inner-city teens who are struggling to make choices in their own life, at the same time as it reveals to them the particular brutality of South Africa's apartheid system. A variety of cultures are interwoven into the narrative, as Mattera's grandfather and father maintain elements of their Italian heritage, and Tswana, Zulu, Muslim, and Chinese neighbors express their cultures as well. L.M-L.

825   Paton, Jonathan. ***The Land and People of South Africa.*** Illus. with photos. SERIES:
        Portraits of the Nations. HarperCollins 1990, LB $14.89 (0-397-32361-1). 288pp.
        Nonfiction.

HarperCollins has embarked on a second edition of this series. Currently, the new series includes coverage of Ethiopia, Kenya, South Africa, Zambia, and

Zimbabwe. For South Africa, the Paton family has been instrumental in presenting the country. The renowned author Alan Paton wrote the first edition, and now his son Jonathan Paton has written the revision.

In this volume Jonathan Paton has tried to be as evenhanded as possible in the presentation. His interest in the arts and humanities is evident in the poems and songs used to illustrate points. The chapters are divided into geography, history, and issues of apartheid.

One of the strengths of this series is its sensitivity to students and teachers. The editor includes maps in sufficient detail to be useful for study. The original documentation provides realism. The photographs are clear. The bibliography by topic rather than chapter is helpful. Unlike other series, this one includes a list of records and films/videos to support the text. Of the numerous series books on South Africa, this one is the most useful and comprehensive.

With the second printing of the book, at the end of 1990, information on the release of Nelson Mandela and other prominent black leaders has been included.   P.K.

826   Ramusi, Molaptene Collins. **Soweto, My Love.** Henry Holt 1989, HB $22.95 (0-8050-0263-4). 262pp. Nonfiction.

Born in Molemole in the northern Transvaal, the author grew up knowing little of the world outside his Babirwa clan and his tribe, the Batlokwa. His traditional upbringing included an African initiation and work as a shepherd. However, after a cousin arranged for him to attend a mission school at the age of 14, his thirst for education could not be satiated. To earn money for tuition, he sought work as a laborer and for the first time had to confront legalized racism. Another cousin, Ramusi's "guardian angel," helped put him through university, where he trained to be a social worker and a lawyer. At the university he found others who had shared similar humiliating experiences and who desired to see justice in South Africa; among his many associates were Nelson Mandela and the founder of the Pan-Africanist Congress, Robert Soboukwe. An early member of the PAC, Ramusi defended blacks against racist laws and later used an official position in the "tribal homeland" of Lebowa to denounce apartheid and the homelands policy. He spent many years in the United States, first as a student with a young family and later as a lonely exile, stripped of his position in Lebowa and far away from his family; during this latter period, his militant eldest son was killed by police, and his wife died as well.

Ramusi's first-person account is passionate and tragic. More than in other autobiographies, the reader gets a sense of African traditions and relationships; while these sustain Ramusi, they make it all the more painful for him when he must choose between exile or death. Even so, there is hope amidst the sadness. The reader sees tiny victories—a township resident allowed to keep her house, families permitted to remain together, intrepid black leaders testing the system and getting away with previously unimaginable words and deeds—and the result is a portrait of heroic individuals trying in every way possible to triumph over an evil and powerful adversary.

There is much food for discussion as well in Ramusi's observations about the Americans he met and the policies of the U.S. government toward South Africa.
                                                                                   L.M-L.

Rochman, Hazel, ed. ***Somehow Tenderness Survives: Stories of Southern Africa.***
See entry 806, Grades 7–9.

827 Sepamla, Sipho. *A Ride on the Whirlwind.* SERIES: African Writers. Heinemann
1984, P $7.50 (0-435-90268-7). 224pp. Fiction.

A professionally trained guerrilla, Mzi, slips into Soweto township with the
express mission of assassinating a black policeman who has betrayed many to
the white authorities. Making local contacts, he falls in with a group of teenage
organizers of the Soweto student uprising. The youths, led by the handsome,
intelligent, and charismatic Mandla, are captivated by Mzi, who has received
training elsewhere in Africa and in the Eastern Bloc. Under Mzi's tutelage, they
take part in the assassination and manufacture homemade bombs. The youngsters—boys and girls—are sheltered and cared for by Sis Ida, who works in
distant Johannesburg.

Through fictional newspaper clippings and through the eyes of various
characters—the students, Sis Ida, Mzi, other township residents, white security
officers, and the hated (and doomed) policeman—Sepamla weaves a tense story
of struggle, violence, retribution, and hope. A bomb-making accident in Sis Ida's
kitchen reveals the group to authorities, and many are arrested. Mzi is hastily
smuggled out by a white activist; Mandla too escapes to join the guerrillas being
trained abroad. Sis Ida is arrested and tortured, and in the end she learns that one
of her teenagers has died in detention.

Best suited to mature readers because of its style, language, and content, this
novel explores the issue of terrorism. In a society founded upon injustice, racism,
and state-sponsored violence, is a violent response justified? What if innocent
civilians are killed? When does one's innocence end and one's responsibility for
injustice begin? The novel is based on black writer Sepamla's own experiences
during the Soweto uprising and was originally published clandestinely in South
Africa in 1981. Mature teenagers will be captivated by the action and drawn in
by the experiences of politically committed youngsters living on the run, dealing
daily with questions of life and death. This thought-provoking book presents a
terrifying world in vivid detail, challenging our assumptions about life, security,
and morality.   L.M-L.

828 Williamson, Sue. ***Resistance Art in South Africa.*** Illus. St. Martin's 1990, HB $35.00
(0-312-04142-X). 159pp. Nonfiction.

White South African artist Sue Williamson has presented the works of dozens of
her fellow artists, both black and white, in this attractive and well-produced
volume. Included are painters, graphic artists, sculptors, and others; T-shirts,
graffiti, and cartoons complement the presentation. One can see the variety of
influences that have contributed to political art in South Africa. Captions give
the reader a brief biography of the artist and some interpretive material, usually
in the artist's own words. High schools that combine the teaching of social
studies with the humanities will find this book an especially valuable resource.
                                                                                L.M-L.

829 Woods, Donald. ***Biko.*** Henry Holt 1987, HB $19.95 (0-8050-0655-9); P $4.95 (0-8050-0385-1). 448pp. Nonfiction.

This work—half biography, half autobiography—chronicles the friendship between Woods and Biko and Woods's efforts to determine the truth about Biko's death at the hands of South African prison officials in 1977. As described here, the first encounter between the white journalist and the black leader was not an entirely friendly one, for Woods had criticized Biko's Black Consciousness Movement as a kind of reverse racism. The dialogue between the two men increased Woods's understanding of the movement and of the forces that gave rise to it, and in the process he gained an enormous amount of respect for the young activist and theorist. After Biko's death, Woods risked his career and his newspaper's future by demanding an inquest. Pages of testimony documenting Biko's last days in captivity are reproduced in this book. Nonetheless, the murder was covered up. Woods concludes with a reasoned condemnation of the apartheid system, indicting the white minority government for its crimes against humanity.

Woods's narrative is gripping. The testimony of the inquest is particularly powerful, revealing as it does the indifference and cruelty of prison officials; this is a matter-of-fact account of the torture that goes on daily in prisons in South Africa and throughout the world. At the same time, Woods's relationship with Biko embodies the hope that whites and blacks can overcome differences, understand each other, and one day establish a nonracial society in South Africa. Unfortunately, as Woods details in his autobiography, *Asking for Trouble* (Atheneum, 1980), he and his family were forced to flee the country, his manuscript of *Biko* smuggled out in his bag to prevent it from being destroyed by white authorities.

The events of *Biko* and *Asking for Trouble* have been combined to make the feature film *Cry Freedom*, which documents Biko's life, the friendship between the two men, and Woods's bold escape.   L.M-L.

15

SOUTHERN
AND
CENTRAL ASIA

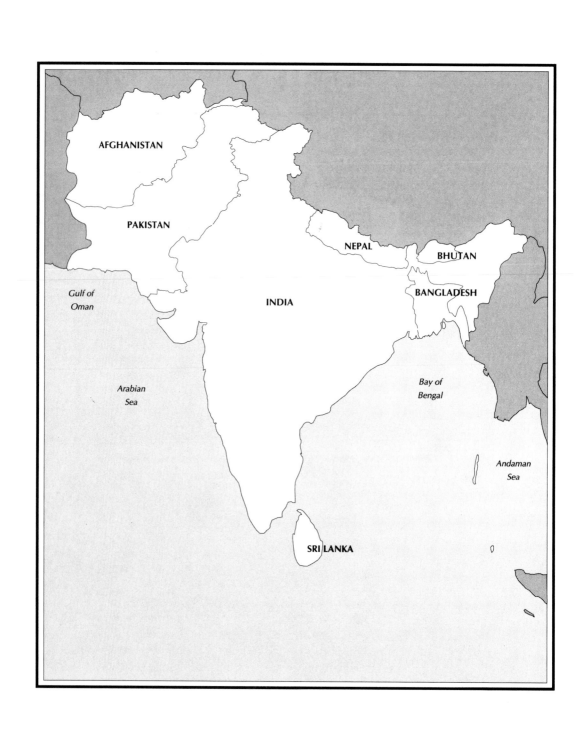

15

SOUTHERN AND CENTRAL ASIA

by Melinda Greenblatt

Situated between the Middle East and East Asia, the countries of Afghanistan, Bangladesh, Bhutan, India, Maldives, Nepal, Pakistan, and Sri Lanka have been grouped into the category of Southern and Central Asia. The countries themselves represent a diversity of geography, languages, religions, and cultures. Several were British colonies granted independence in the middle of the twentieth century; Pakistan further divided in 1971, with Bangladesh becoming an independent country. Most of the nations of Southern and Central Asia have been the scene of ethnic strife, and in 1979 Afghanistan was invaded and occupied by a foreign power.

The goal of this chapter is to create a picture of life in Southern and Central Asia as it is lived today. A few of the books give some historical perspective, particularly those that deal with the political history of India's independence movement. Excluded from the chapter are books that have a strong focus on the English experience in the region; this has been done in order to place the emphasis squarely where it belongs—on the people who are indigenous to this part of the world.

Although one of the main purposes of this bibliography is to highlight contemporary fiction, it has been difficult to find appropriate picture books and juvenile novels for the region. India has always dominated the region in the Western publishing world, and it is relatively easy to find nonfiction books on India and even on many of the other countries of the region. Most picture books, however, depict unspecified times in the past. Very few children's or young adult novels about the region have been published in the past 20 years and remain in print. *Shabanu: Daughter of the Wind* is a notable exception. It was named a Newbery Honor Book for 1989 and richly deserves the accolade. It is one of the finest novels published in the United States about a young person from another culture. The realistic text marks the evolving nature of traditional cultures not only on the Cholistan Desert of Pakistan but also in many parts of the world.

The role of women in this region is an interesting one and is the theme of *Shabanu* and several other works of fiction and nonfiction. While the Islamic, Buddhist, and Hindu cultures of the region have all tended to restrict women's opportunities, one finds that women are finally making their mark in today's society. Biographies of three important women can be found in this chapter. Indira Gandhi, Benazir Bhutto, and Mother Teresa (long associated with India, though she was not born there) are world figures in spite of the obstacles placed in their way. Political considerations aside, the biographies of these three incorporate much of the political and social history of the region.

The lives of Mahatma Gandhi and Jawaharlal Nehru are intertwined with the Indian independence movement, and the life stories of these two leaders are integral to any comprehensive study of India. The 1982 Academy Award–winning film *Gandhi* inspired a new group of biographies of the Mahatma, the great soul whose philosophy of *Satyagraha*, or Soul Force, succeeded in India and influenced other freedom movements throughout the world, including the civil rights movement in the United States. Several books about Nehru, Gandhi's close associate, are also available.

Storytelling is still a living art in India, often associated with the many festivals that are celebrated throughout the year. *Seasons of Splendor: Tales, Myths, and Legends of India* succeeds in placing the folklore within its cultural context. Interested readers may want to find out more about the great Indian epics, the *Ramayana* and the *Mahabharata*, the bases for much of Indian art and culture. Early in 1991, a film adaptation of the *Mahabharata*, directed by Peter Brook, was shown on public television. A video of the performance could be used with older students.

Although there is a dearth of literature for children and young teens, adult works that can be appreciated by mature readers are very much in evidence. Books recommended for the very sophisticated "special reader" include *Midnight's Children*, by Salman Rushdie, and the trilogy by V. S. Naipaul, whose titles are listed in the reference section. Works recommended for a broader cross section of older teenagers are listed in the chapter itself. Ruth P. Jhabvala, a European married to an Indian, has lived in India for over 25 years and has written stories and novels about the lives, passions, and foibles of both Indians and Europeans in India. Although most of her books are accessible to older teens, a recent collection of stories, *Out of India*, may be a good introduction to this keen observer of life in present-day India.

Raj, by Gita Mehta, is the story of Jaya, an Indian princess who lives through the turbulent years of India's struggle for independence and who finds herself drawn into the idealism of the time. The autobiographical writing of Ved Mehta can be found in such volumes as *Daddyji*, *Mamaji*, and *Vedi*. The tension and upheaval as traditional village India becomes contemporary urban India are skillfully conveyed through Mehta's memories. Malgudi, a fictional town in South India, is the creation of R. K. Narayan. Readers who are enticed to enter this quietly comedic world will be rewarded by a growing familiarity with the human relationships and rhythms of life depicted there in *The Painter of Signs* and other works.

Two well-known titles, not included in this volume because they were published before 1970, should be mentioned because they fit into the spirit of this bibliography—Kamala Markandaya's *Nectar in a Sieve*, the story of a traditional woman in rural India, and *Train to Pakistan*, by Khushwant Singh, a novel about the partition of India and Pakistan. For those who are interested in an individualistic view of the British withdrawal from India, the *Raj Quartet* volumes and the companion novel, *Staying On*, all by Paul Scott, offer an expansive slice of Anglo-Indian history. Although not reviewed in this chapter because of their emphasis on the British in India, they remain a wonderful literary experience for those who choose to read the entire five volumes.

Most of the nonfiction about Southern and Central Asia is published as part of the various series that are available for elementary and junior high school readers. The Enchantment of the World series (Childrens Press), represented in the chapter by the volume on Bhutan, is one of the most comprehensive in its coverage of the basic topics of history, geography, and culture. Its format is more attractive to middle school audiences than the Visual Geography series (Lerner; see *Afghanistan in Pictures*). For junior and senior high students, the Portraits of the Nations series (HarperCollins; see *The Land and People of Afghanistan*) is worthy of consideration, but as of this writing, no other volume covering the region exists. Young children, starting with those in the second grade, will enjoy the photo-essays found in the Families the World Over series (Lerner) and the Families Around the World series (Franklin Watts). Both series use the title *A Family in . . .* and are fairly similar in content. The Lerner series is far more extensive by virtue of the countries presented, covering India, Pakistan, and Sri Lanka in this region. The Children of the World series (Gareth Stevens; see *India*) also covers Afghanistan, Bhutan, and Nepal. This photo-essay series, with its more extensive reference section, can be very useful for several elementary grades. The Discovering Our Heritage series (Dillon), here represented by a volume on Bangladesh, has also published volumes on India and Pakistan. The books in this series for upper elementary and middle school include recipes, folktales, and other cultural information not contained in other series books.

Biograhies are often published in series format as well. The Picture-Story Biographies (Childrens Press) are good choices for younger biography readers. The Women of Our Time series (Viking) is useful for middle graders. Chelsea House's World Leaders, Past and Present series is most useful for junior high students. Some sixth-grade readers can probably handle the books because there is extensive use of photos, and reluctant high school readers may also appreciate them.

PRESCHOOL–GRADE 3

830 Bonnici, Peter. ***The Festival.*** Illus. by Lisa Kopper. Lerner/Carolrhoda 1985, LB $9.95 (0-87614-229-3). unp. Fiction.

Bonnici grew up in India, and after living in London for many years, he returned for a six-month stay. This picture book is a mixture of his childhood memories and his adult experiences. It tells a simple story about Arjuna, a city boy who is bored in his grandmother's small village until festival time draws near. For the first time, Arjuna is treated like a man. His mother gives him a *lungi*, the traditional cloth worn by men in South India. His Uncle Raju takes him to bathe in the river, and at the festival he sits among the men and is invited to dance with them. Then the embarrassing incident occurs—his *lungi* falls down (an experience the author had as an adult). His uncle rescues him, and the night continues with feasting and storytelling.

A lovely evocation of one night in a child's life, there are lots of details in the text and pictures that could be explored through conversation and research. The brown and gray paintings are stylized, yet each face belongs to an individual. The feelings of family affection and community warmth are evident. The artist also illustrated the Jafta books about a young boy in South Africa. *The Rains* is another book about Arjuna, done by the same author-illustrator team; in that volume, Arjuna can hardly wait for the monsoon season to begin.

831   Davis, Emmett. ***Clues in the Desert.*** Illus. by Julie Downing. SERIES: Adventure Diary. Raintree 1983, LB $14.65 (0-940742-29-2). 32pp. Fiction.

Although this picture book has a didactic quality, the story about a Pakistani boy and his archaeologist aunt who visit the site of the ancient city of Mohenjo-daro could inspire child interest in several topics. Although not explicitly discussed, the role of women in Pakistan could be explored. Is Aunt Leela's profession an unusual one in Pakistan? As Asif, the young boy, must make his own decision about education, so readers could try to find out about educational opportunities in Pakistan. The topic of archaeology and the city of Mohenjo-daro could be researched, although some of the children who might enjoy *Clues in the Desert* would find this difficult at their reading level.

While the text is sometimes choppy and stilted, the illustrations are inviting, with intricate borders around pictures and text. The details of clothing, modes of transportation, and architecture will draw the attention of readers at several age levels.

Greene, Carol. ***Indira Nehru Gandhi: Ruler of India.***
See entry 843, Grades 4–6.

832   Haskins, Jim. ***Count Your Way Through India.*** Illus. by Liz B. Dobson. SERIES: Count Your Way Books. Lerner/Carolrhoda 1990, LB $11.95 (0-87614-414-8). 24pp. Nonfiction.

Small tidbits of information about India are presented in a counting book format. The Hindi language is introduced, and readers will learn to count to ten in the national language of India (but only one of many spoken in the country). This title, one of a growing series, can serve as a motivational resource in introducing a unit on India or can be enjoyed by individual browsers in a library setting.

833   Kamal, Aleph. ***The Bird Who Was an Elephant.*** Illus. by Frane Lessac. HarperCollins 1990, LB $14.89 (0-397-32446-4). unp. Fiction.

Although the text of this bird's-eye view of Indian village life fails on several levels to address its intended audience, the illustrations readily draw readers into an exploration of a small village with its streets, shops, train station, temples, and movie theater. The device of using a bird as a guide to the village sights falls flat. A very simplistic explanation of reincarnation is tied in with the title. According to a palmist, the bird was once an elephant in a former life. During the course of the book, the bird visits with the Palmist, the Snake (from the Snake Charmer's basket), the Sacred Cow, and the Sadhu (a holy man), but there is no significant action.

Although the elements of Indian life emphasized by Kamal may seem stereotyped, the engaging, naive-style paintings offer a wealth of detail that will give children many opportunities to formulate their own questions about India, and thus they will serve as an impetus to find out more about the country. The design of each two-page spread is quite lovely. The full-page painting on the left and the text on the right are surrounded by identical borders embellished with motifs drawn from the paintings. For example, the marketplace with its fruit stands is echoed in the golden borders with a design of local fruits. The author's note contains a glossary defining the Hindi words used in the text. The region of India depicted in the book is not mentioned, however.

834   Lye, Keith. ***Take a Trip to Nepal.*** Illus. with photos. SERIES: Take a Trip. Franklin Watts 1988, LB $9.40 (0-531-10557-1). 32pp. Nonfiction.

Intended as a first nonfiction book for children in the early grades, this volume is one of several from this extensive series that covers South Asian countries. *India, Pakistan,* and *Sri Lanka* are available, and all include color photos on every page and a simple text. The reader would gain a superficial knowledge of Nepal and its geography from this book. In spite of the advertising copy on its back cover, there is little of interest to young children, such as the interior of a classroom, the active celebration of a festival, or children playing games would be. This volume might be used in conjunction with other, more child-oriented materials, but it does little on its own for the very audiences that need easy nonfiction to excite them about the many countries of the world.

835   Mathieson, Feroza. ***The Very Special Sari: A Story Set in India.*** Illus. with photos by Prodeepta Das. SERIES: Wide World. A & C Black; distributed by Childcraft Education Corp. 1988, LB $10.95 (0-7136-3064-7). 25pp. Fiction.

This book, presented in photo-essay style, is an intimate look at a little girl's relationship with her mother as they shop for a new sari for the mother to wear to a wedding. The photographs depict their shopping expedition as they select red and silky material, beads, gold and silver thread, mirrors, and sequins and then bring everything to Mrs. Nayak's shop, where the sari will be beautifully embroidered. As she accompanies her mother, Gita, a 6-year-old, wishes for a new outfit of her own. Finally, the sari is ready, and when Mum picks it up, she gets a surprise for Gita—a new *shalwaar kameez* (Anglicized as shalwaar chemise)—the traditional outfit of a long tunic and pants worn in some parts of India and Pakistan. Gita goes to the wedding too in her wonderful new clothes.

Although the photographs show lots of interesting details such as the interiors of the shops, the mixture of English and one of the many languages used in India on the shop signs, and different rooms of Gita's house, the reader does not get a full view of Gita or her mother in their new outfits. The text is stilted, but a teacher or parent could use the visuals to help young children tell a story based on the photos. There are several other stories set in South Asian countries in the series, including *Lost at the Fair.*

836   Wettasinghe, Sybil. ***The Umbrella Thief.*** Originally published in Japan under the title of *Kasa Doroboh* in 1986. Illus. by Cathy Hirano. Kane/Miller 1987, HB $11.95 (0-916291-12-X). unp. Fiction.

Kane/Miller is a unique publishing institution, set up several years ago by a sister and brother team who wanted to bring books from all the world to an American audience. Their small list is growing, and they are trying to find books from Asia, Africa, Latin America, and Australia to add to their first European titles to make this a truly international venture. The tale of *The Umbrella Thief* is set in Sri Lanka but was originally published in Japan. It has a folkloric quality, but the setting is in contemporary times.

Reminiscent of *Caps for Sale* by Esphyr Slobodkina, this is the story of Kiri Mama, a man from a small village in Sri Lanka who brings back a new invention, the first umbrella any of the villagers have ever seen, after a visit to the town nearby. Before he can share this wonderful new convenience, a thief steals it. Kiri Mama buys another and another, but before he can show them off, they are stolen again. Finally, Kiri Mama foils the robber-monkey and finds all his umbrellas. He proudly opens a shop so that the villagers can enjoy their new umbrellas.

The book's illustrations contrast the small village and the larger town, and the flat graphic style is enhanced by a wonderful textural quality. The patterns on the umbrellas, saris, and *longhis* in the town scenes and the illustrations of the rural coffee shop with its displays of fruits and sweets are particularly attractive. Without a hint of didacticism, this engaging picture book will introduce young children to another culture.

GRADES 4–6

Amin, Mohamed. *We Live in Pakistan.*
See entry 854, Grades 7–9.

837   Bahree, Patricia. *The Hindu World.* Illus. with photos. SERIES: Religions of the World. Trafalgar Sq./David & Charles 1989. 45pp. Nonfiction. o.p.

Information about many aspects of Hindu life is packed into this volume, one of five in a series that includes *The Buddhist World* and *The Muslim World*. The two-page spreads on such topics as festivals, sacred books, Hindu weddings, rites of passage, Hindu gods, and other matters pertaining to Hindu philosophy give readers basic explanations and some interesting details about each topic. The format has a choppy appearance with its pictures of differing sizes, extended captions, and double-column text, and some readers might find it difficult to follow. For the most part, the author avoids the usual tendency to compare every aspect of this major religion with Christianity, and the text is accessible to upper-grade elementary students. Though varied and interesting, the color photos have a slightly washed-out look, perhaps due to the matte texture of the paper used.

Another Religions of the World series (Franklin Watts) also covers Buddhism and Hinduism and may also appeal to children at slightly lower reading levels. The print is larger, and the photos are on glossier stock. Many of the same topics are covered but in less detail. The author of *Buddhism*, John Snelling, uses a more personal approach, inviting readers to try to meditate or to answer philosophical questions for themselves. Both series offer glossaries, bibliographies, and indexes.

838   Bennett, Gay. *A Family in Sri Lanka.* Illus. with photos by Christopher Cormack. SERIES: Families the World Over. Lerner 1985, LB $9.95 (0-8225-1661-6). 32pp. Nonfiction.

Nimal's family lives in a small farming community near the southern tip of Sri Lanka. His family's everyday routines are photographed and described in this book, which is from a series that also includes volumes about Indian and Pakistani families. Niman is 12 and he attends school during the week and, for religious training, the local Buddhist temple on Sunday. He also helps his family by selling produce in the market and peeling cinnamon branches. (His town of Dorala is in the heart of the world's most important cinnamon-growing area.)

The emphasis here is on work and family life, not on children's recreational interests. The color photos are clear and amplify the text. Although the one-page history mentions the Sinhalese and the Tamils, it says nothing about their conflicts, which have intensified since 1985, when the revised edition of the book was published. Children will need additional sources of information about Sri Lanka, but this photo-essay will pique their interest in learning about this island country.

839   Cumming, David. *India.* Illus. with photos by Jimmy Holmes. SERIES: Countries of the World. Franklin Watts 1989, LB $12.40 (0-531-18271-1). 48pp. Nonfiction.

This series features an introductory, readable approach for the child just beginning to do research projects on other countries. Short chapters (usually two to four pages in length) deal with topics such as history, wildlife, education, food and drink, and growing up in a city and growing up in a village. Large, easy-to-read print and an abundance of color photos will appeal to many children at different reading levels. The index, glossary, and bibliography (all fairly recent children's books, although most are published or distributed by Franklin Watts) are useful features. *Pakistan* (1989) is also available.

840   Das, Prodeepta. *Inside India.* Illus. with photos by Prodeepta Das et al. SERIES: Inside. Franklin Watts 1990, LB $11.90 (0-531-14045-8). 32pp. Nonfiction.

Very similar in format to *India* (Countries of the World) by David Cumming, this book covers such subjects as history, towns and cities, family life, and the future. The text is brief and sometimes so generalized that readers will have to go elsewhere for in-depth information on most aspects of Indian life, but the attractive color photographs placed on each page will be of interest to middle-grade students. The book by David Cumming has more information about such topics as city and country life, food and drink, and sports and recreation, whereas this volume has a clearer map, and the "Facts About India" page has a good graphic comparing India's size and population with those of other nations.

Davis, Emmett. *Clues in the Desert.*
See entry 831, Grades PS–3.

841 Giff, Patricia Reilly. ***Mother Teresa: Sister to the Poor.*** Illus. by Ted Lewin. SERIES: Women of Our Time. Viking 1986, HB $10.95 (0-670-81096-7); Penguin/Puffin 1987, P $3.50 (0-14-032225-6). 58pp. Nonfiction.

This is one volume of a biographical series that has been well received by reviewers, librarians, teachers, and children themselves. Although it lacks such research aids as an index, bibliography, or a list of important dates, this book will appeal to young readers who may read it for assignments or just to satisfy their own curiosity about a woman who has gained the respect and admiration of private citizens, government leaders, and religious figures throughout the world. The life of Mother Teresa is presented in a simple but moving narrative. Lewin's ink and wash paintings are a cut above most illustrations that usually accompany biographies for the elementary grades.

842 Glubok, Shirley. ***The Art of India.*** Illus. with photos. Macmillan 1969. 48pp. Nonfiction. o.p.

Glubok has written extensively about the art of many of the world's cultures. She brings together history, religion, and art to give young people an understanding of why the people of this region created the sculptures, religious structures, and paintings illustrated in the book. All photos are black and white. While the sculpture pieces are effectively presented, the paintings suffer without the brilliant colors that are usually used. This book could be supplemented with an adult book on Indian art that has the advantage of full-color illustrations.

843 Greene, Carol. ***Indira Nehru Gandhi: Ruler of India.*** Illus. with photos. SERIES: Picture-Story Biographies. Childrens Pr. 1985, LB $8.95 (0-516-03478-2). 32pp. Nonfiction.

Greene gives us an introductory biography of the woman who was to consolidate India's role as a world power. Although intended for children as young as 7, the book does present Indira Gandhi's positive and negative actions. The text is sometimes choppy, due to the "easy-to-read" nature of the series, but fictionalized incidents are not used. Black-and-white photos (sometimes printed on a beige background, giving them a dated look) are found on almost every page. There is a simple chronology but no index. *Mother Teresa: Friend of the Friendless* has been written by the same author for this series.

844 Harkonen, Reijo. ***The Children of Nepal.*** Illus. with photos by Matti A. Pitkanen. SERIES: The World's Children. Lerner/Carolrhoda 1990, LB $14.95 (0-87614-395-8). 48pp. Nonfiction.

Striking color photos of Nepalese children, adults, and various scenes in different parts of the country are not well served by the text of this series book imported from Finland. The translation is awkward and does not emphasize children, as should be expected from the title. Included are a map, pronunciation guide, and index. This book is not recommended as an individual resource, but the photos could be used to spark interest in Nepal.

845   Hunter, Nigel. *Gandhi.* Illus. with photos and paintings. SERIES: Great Lives. Franklin Watts 1986, LB $11.90 (0-531-18093-X). 32pp. Nonfiction.

This straightforward text avoids the fictionalized dialogue often used in biographies intended for fourth- and fifth-grade audiences. Undistinguished color illustrations are mixed with historical photos. The author has included the highlights of Gandhi's life, but there is a lack of depth to the explanations given for some of his actions and feelings. A chronology, glossary, bibliograhy, and index are included. A volume on Mother Teresa is also available in this series, though it should not be confused with the more recent biograhy of her in the Lifetimes series.

846   Jacobsen, Peter, and Preben Kristensen. *A Family in India.* Illus. with photos. SERIES: Families Around the World. Franklin Watts 1984, LB $11.90 (0-531-03788-6). 32pp. Nonfiction.

Similar in scope and format to the Families the World Over series (Lerner), each book in this series also focuses on one family. The style differs, and that has both positive and negative aspects. The authors start the book with their journey to the village of Mehendwara, near New Dehli. The experiences of two Europeans begin to take on more importance than the family that is the subject of the book. However, this also allows the members of the family to speak directly to the reader, as they are interviewed. (The Lerner series uses a third-person narration.) The Kaushik family are farmers, but a change is taking place. Sri Chand Kaushik wants to educate his children so that they can find other employment. A fact page, a short glossary, and an index are included.

847   Jaffrey, Madhur. *Seasons of Splendor: Tales, Myths, and Legends of India.* Illus. by Michael Foreman. Atheneum 1985, HB $15.95 (0-689-31141-9); Penguin/Puffin 1991, P $7.95 (0-317-62172-6). 128pp. Nonfiction.

The author, who grew up in a well-to-do household in Delhi, has selected stories that were told by her family in honor of the various festivals held throughout the year in India. She introduces each story or group of stories with a childhood memory. As she explains the significance of each holiday, Jaffrey personalizes the information with the telling of an appropriate anecdote. Many of the stories are from the great Indian epics, the *Ramayana* and the *Mahabharata*. Others are traditional folktales, and a few may have been created by family members.

This is a handsome book, with Foreman's full-page paintings alternating with smaller drawings and paintings. Foreman's artwork is sometimes reminiscent of both Indian religious and secular images. When, in other illustrations he allows his imagination free rein, fantastical demons and unusual perspectives take over. There is an excellent glossary with extensive notes on pronunciation and good definitions, although the origins of the stories should have been identified in greater detail. Nonetheless, this is a winning combination of intriguing tales and a description of the social framework in which they were actually told.

848   Kapoor, Sukhbir Singh. *Sikh Festivals.* Illus. with photos. SERIES: Holidays and Festivals. Rourke Publications 1989, LB $12.23 (0-86592-984-X). 48pp. Nonfiction.

Heavily illustrated with both black-and-white and color photographs, this book, originally published in Britain, offers a wealth of information on Sikh history, traditions, religious beliefs, holy days, and celebrations. The ways that holidays are observed in Britain are often described in addition to the Indian customs. North American Sikhs are only briefly mentioned. Perhaps because it was written for a largely Christian British audience, there is an element of ethnocentrism in its frequent comparisons between Sikhism and Christianity. *Hindu Festivals, Buddhist Festivals,* and *Muslim Festivals* are also available. *Hindu Festivals* focuses more on celebrations held in India and uses almost exclusively color photographs.

849   Knowlton, MaryLee, and David K. Wright, eds. *India.* Illus. with photos by Uchiyama Sumio. SERIES: Children of the World. Gareth Stevens 1988, LB $12.95 (1-55532-208-5). 64pp. Nonfiction.

The *Children of the World* series is a hybrid. Originally published in Japan, the first part of the book is a photo-essay, usually concentrating on one child and his or her immediate environment. The second section has been added in the U.S. edition and gives children the kind of information needed for most school projects, similar to the approach used in an encyclopedia article. The text of the information section is more difficult than the text about the individual child, and the book can be used on several levels.

Vikram (nicknamed Viku) Singh, the subject of the volume on India, is not a typical Indian boy. He is the son of a Maharajah's personal secretary and a member of India's small upper class. One of the criticisms often leveled at books like these is that the children are not always representative of the country. It is my feeling that several books should be used when studying about any country and that the lives of people living at different economic levels should be discussed. The color photos and child-oriented text will entice children, but additional information will be needed to place Viku's life into the context of the rest of India's population. A small attempt has been so made in the presentation of a short chapter on Kiran, a young boy who goes to a small village school about 10 miles from Viku's city of Jodhpur in Northern India. The caste system, mentioned several times throughout the book, is an issue that should probably be discussed by teachers or other adults. Children may also need more information on the historical events leading up the partition of India and Pakistan. The text is very weak on this subject. Activities, some resources, and an index add to the usefulness of this volume for school and public libraries.

McClure, Vimala. *Bangladesh: Rivers in a Crowded Land.*
See entry 862, Grades 7–9.

850   Rosen, Mike. *The Conquest of Everest.* Illus. with photos; additional illustrations by Doug Post. SERIES: Great Journeys. Franklin Watts 1990, LB $11.90 (0-531-18319-X). 32pp. Nonfiction.

The challenge to climb Mount Everest, the tallest mountain in the world, has excited expeditions since 1921. This book, abundantly illustrated with photos of varying quality and impressionistic paintings that have a heavy, leaden feeling, details many of the expeditions before and after 1953, as well as the successful climb by Tenzing Norgay, the Nepalese Sherpa, and Edmund Hillary in that year. A few pages are devoted to the Sherpas—the people who live in the foothills of Everest, or Chomolungma, as the mountain is known locally—and the important role that the Sherpas have played as guides is mentioned. A two-page spread on "Women on Everest" may be interesting to display during Women's History Month in March.

851 Scarsbrook, Alisa, and Alan Scarsbrook. *A Family in Pakistan.* Illus. with photos. SERIES: Families the World Over. Lerner 1985, LB $9.95 (0-8225-1662-4). 32pp. Nonfiction.

This series volume is a detailed photo-essay of life in a Pakistani village near Rawalpindi, a city in the northern part of the country. Assim Mahmood's farm family is the focus of this book, one of several in this series that are about South Asian countries. (*A Family in Sri Lanka* and *A Family in India* are also available.) Although Assim lives in a small village, he goes to school in the city, and he shops in the market there. The reader gets an opportunity to see urban and rural life in action, as 14-year-old Assim also visits another village for a festival and the larger city of Lyallpur, where his uncle lives. Unfortunately, we do not get enough of a sense of Assim as a young teenager in terms of his interests, friends, sports, and games. The book's short section on Pakistani history and facts will give the reader some limited background information.

Staples, Suzanne Fisher. *Shabanu: Daughter of the Wind.*
See entry 865, Grades 7–9.

852 Tames, Richard. *Mother Teresa.* Illus. with photos. SERIES: Lifetimes. Franklin Watts 1989, LB $11.90 (0-531-10847-3). 32pp. Nonfiction.

Biographies for elementary and middle school readers are increasingly being presented in photo-essay style. This format seems to have originated in Great Britain and with the influx of nonfiction books being imported to the United States, has established itself on this side of the Atlantic. Short, one-page "features" on topics such as the Loreto Order, Bengal and Bengali, and leprosy interrupt the text regularly. Some of this information should have been part of the main text, which can best be described as adequate. The many photos in black and white and color are usually appropriate, although a striking photo of the republic of Montenegro does not show the shrine mentioned in the text. Several maps show Mother Teresa's early travels and are of interest in setting the scene. The glossary words could have been defined within the text. Important dates, books, and addresses may help on a research project, but no U.S. addresses are given. Includes index.

853   ***Afghanistan in Pictures.*** Rev. ed. Illus. with photos. SERIES: Visual Geography. Lerner 1989, LB $11.95 (0-8225-1849-X). 64pp. Nonfiction.

This is a standard introduction to Afghanistan, a country still trying to forge its own identity after centuries of invasions from all directions. Geography, history, economic issues, and cultural topics are covered in a mundane, yet accurate style. The revised editions in this series contain a greater number of color photographs, and the many small black-and-white photos are of varying quality and clarity. Several new colorful graphs on safe water and hashish and opiate production are of interest. This book, like others in the series, such as *Pakistan in Pictures*, *India in Pictures*, and *Sri Lanka in Pictures*, will be useful for school assignments but will probably not be chosen voluntarily by readers.

854   Amin, Mohamed. ***We Live in Pakistan.*** Illus. with photos. SERIES: Living Here. Franklin Watts 1985, LB $9.49 (0-531-03817-3). 60pp. Nonfiction.

Government official, student, police officer, newscaster, copper artisan, pilot, museum director—these are but a few of the many people interviewed for this book. Each person tells readers about his or her job, family, and education (or lack of it) and usually imparts some additional information on social, political, and religious issues. Women talk about traditional and nontraditional roles. A few of the interviews refer to political figures and issues that are no longer current; however, political conflicts and concerns do receive treatment in this volume. Most people make nationalistic statements about Pakistan and Islam, but this volume and *We Live in India* give readers a look behind the scenes of history and geography at the people of each society. A page of general facts, a glossary, and an index are included. A close-up of each interviewee, together with general photos of the milieu in which the person lives, works, or studies, complements the text.

Clifford, Mary Louise. ***The Land and People of Afghanistan.***
See entry 867, Grades 10–12.

855   Doherty, Katherine M., and Craig A. Doherty. ***Benazir Bhutto.*** Illus. with photos. SERIES: Impact Biographies. Franklin Watts 1990, LB $13.90 (0-531-10936-4). 144pp. Nonfiction.

The political history of Pakistan since its independence and partition from India in 1947 and up to early 1990, when this book was published, is viewed through the Bhutto family's participation in government affairs. Though Benazir Bhutto is the focus, her father's political career is thoroughly explored, and her mother's activities are also explained. Benazir Bhutto is presented as a very admirable person—a strong woman, an able speaker, a fighter for democracy, a diplomat, and the first woman to have a baby while leading a modern nation. There is little criticism of her. Unfortunately, the book was published before Bhutto's latest round of political difficulties began in 1990. It must be supplemented by newspaper and periodical articles to continue to be of value. A short reading list and an index are included. A volume entitled *Indira Gandhi*, by Nayana Currimbhoy, appeared in this series, but it is now out of print. The format of this series is traditional, with some black-and-white photos scattered throughout the text.

856 Faber, Doris, and Howard Faber. ***Mahatma Gandhi.*** Illus. with photos. Julian Messner 1986, LB $10.98 (0-671-60176-8). 122pp. Nonfiction.

The coauthors introduce and end this book with information about the sources they used in their research. While they credit the movie *Gandhi* as an inspirational force and recommend that readers view it, they acknowledge the difficulty of making dramatic movies that are totally accurate. The Fabers state that Gandhi's story of his own life (*An Autobiography: The Story of My Experiments with Truth*, Beacon Press, 1957) was their principal source, and other sources included the writings of people who knew him personally. It is important that young people both realize the importance of accurate sources of information and be able to distinguish between primary sources, such as those the Fabers have used, and secondary sources.

The Fabers have fashioned a readable text in a traditional format. Gandhi's whole life is covered, and a short postcript ties his ideas to other struggles for freedom, including the civil rights movement led by Martin Luther King, Jr. There are both a bibliography of adult sources and an index.

857 Finck, Lila, and John P. Hayes. ***Jawaharlal Nehru.*** Illus. with photos. SERIES: World Leaders, Past and Present. Chelsea House 1987, LB $17.95 (0-87754-543-X). 112pp. Nonfiction.

This is one volume in an extensive series of international biographies. Indira Gandhi and Mohandas Gandhi are also featured. Each volume begins with the same essay by Arthur M. Schlesinger, Jr., a name certainly intended to lend credibility to the series. Because the link between the two men was so great, Gandhi seems almost to overshadow Nehru in some parts of the biography (many photos of him are scattered throughout), but Nehru's life is competently described. The struggle for India's independence, led by these two very different personalities, is of paramount importance in the text, but the chapters covering Nehru's years as prime minister after independence are informative. Photos, detailed captions, quotes (many by Nehru himself), and text are arranged in varied ways to maintain interest, but some readers may find the format too busy. The graphic embellishment around two sides of each quote is unnecessary.

858 Foster, Leila Merrell. ***Bhutan.*** Illus. with photos. SERIES: Enchantment of the World. Childrens Pr. 1989, LB $23.93 (0-516-02709-3). 127pp. Nonfiction.

The Enchantment of the World series has become one of the more comprehensive, readable, and accurate series available today. From its origins in the older Enchantment of Africa and Enchantment of South America series, this new grouping of books has become less stereotypical, more accurate, and certainly far more attractive. This volume on Bhutan is similar to others in the series but unique in its extensive coverage of this small nation. Detailed chapters about history and current developments are well written, and a chapter on geologic history, although very specialized, may interest students in learning more about this topic. The balance between traditional life and careful, well-planned development is one of the most important aspects of current-day life in Bhutan, and this volume ably explores the issue. The color photos are often striking. The "mini-facts" section is useful, but the print (smaller than the regular text) is difficult to read. Unfortunately, the author, who happens to be a United Methodist minister, makes a somewhat disparaging remark in her discussion of

Bhutanese festivals, stating, "Of course, many of the audience do not under-stand the details of the dances and the religion, but they believe it is more important to have faith than to understand."

859 Herda, D. J. ***The Afghan Rebels: The War in Afghanistan.*** Illus. with photos. Franklin Watts 1990, LB $12.90 (0-531-10897-X). 128pp. Nonfiction.

Herda makes no bones about the fact that he admires the Afghan rebels who fought against Soviet occupation of their country. He intersperses chapters that factually recount events throughout the 1980s with an account of a *mujahad*, a resistance fighter who is a composite figure, created from personal accounts made by many individuals. Herda spent time in Central Asia during this period, and he states that all experiences related in the book are true.

Unfortunately, the chapters about Abdul Ahad do not fit well within the context of the book. Perhaps it is the author's style in creating what is essentially a fictional character in the guise of a realistic treatment; the interviews and stories of the many people with whom Herda came into contact might have been more effective. Still, this serves as a useful introduction to a protracted struggle that has parallels in other countries. Includes bibliography and index.

860 Hooper, Neil. ***Maldives.*** Illus. with photos. SERIES: Let's Visit Places and Peoples of the World. Chelsea House 1988, LB $14.95 (0-7910-0160-1). 93pp. Nonfiction.

This is one volume of an extensive series that covers many countries all over the world. Other South Asian nations available are *Afghanistan, India, Nepal, Pakistan*, and *Sri Lanka*. Possibly the only book for children on the Republic of Maldives, it includes information on history and geography, as well as environment and social life in the capital of Male and on the inhabited islands. There is also a discussion of tourism, development, and the future of this island nation. The author speaks somewhat condescendingly of the "strangest thing" about traditional island life being the high frequency of divorce. The text patronizes the island residents elsewhere as well. Small color and black-and-white photos throughout the book vary in quality. Some look washed out, while some photos showing the region's fish and the beautiful beaches are arresting.

861 Laure, Jason, and Ettagale Laure. ***Joi Bangla: The Children of Bangladesh.*** Illus. with photos by Jason Laure. Farrar, Straus & Giroux 1974. 154pp. Nonfiction. o.p.

While covering the independence of Bangladesh in 1971, Jason Laure became interested in the fate of the children of the new nation. He returned to the country in 1972 and began to photograph and, in collaboration with his wife, to write about the life of nine children from different communities in Bangladesh. The young people, who range in age from 11 to 16, work and/or go to school. They are members of the dominant Muslim group, the minority Hindu group, and the Bihari group, a Muslim minority from the state of Bihar in northeastern India who came to what was then considered East Pakistan in 1947. Many crave the opportunity to go to school while they spend long hours working as flower sellers or beggars. They all think about marriage, a reality for most young people in Bangladesh during their late teens. The war is still fresh in their minds, and there are many references to young women who were raped and taken away by Pakistani soldiers. The black-and-white photos are expressive and stand up well by themselves. Yet they also help to bring an immediacy to stories that are now 20 years old.

Is this book still valid? The young men and women of Bangladesh still face many of the realities that their counterparts (and now parents) faced in the early 1970s. The reaction of these children and adolescents to war and upheaval in their country is central to understanding the contemporary history of Bangladesh. It would be interesting to compare one or two of these profiles with a comparable piece about a child growing up today, but perhaps because this book was written for an older audience, it discusses issues with a sensitivity and an open, frank quality that eludes most of the texts of other photo-essays about children around the world today. The interviewing skills of the Laures are evident throughout. Includes glossary.

862   McClure, Vimala. **Bangladesh: Rivers in a Crowded Land.** Illus. with photos. SERIES: Discovering Our Heritage. Dillon 1989, LB $14.95 (0-87518-404-9). 127pp. Non-fiction.

A folktale, recipes for Bangladeshi snacks and sweets, a profile of an unusual woman—Captain Yasmin Rahman, her nation's "first and only woman to work as a commercial airline pilot"—and a chapter on Bangladeshis in the United States make this volume stand out from other books that focus more on history, geography, and political issues. These topics are covered too, but the books in the Discovering Our Heritage series, including *India* (1985), give young readers a fuller picture of what life is like for young people today in the countries under discussion. "Fast Facts" pages, an extensive glossary, an index, and bibliography of adult materials are included in each volume. The quantity of color photographs has increased in the newer books in the series.

863   Madavan, Vijay. **Cooking the Indian Way.** Illus. with photos and drawings. SERIES: Easy Menu Ethnic Cookbooks. Lerner 1985, LB $9.95 (0-8225-0911-3). 48pp. Nonfiction.

Recipes that can be used to create Indian meals for different occasions and times of the day are presented in an attractive, easy-to-follow format. The photos are inviting, and an excellent introduction places the dishes in their appropriate social and cultural milieu. For those students who want a little more background on food in India, try *Food in India* (International Food Library, Rourke Publications, 1989) by Sharon Kaur.

864   Nicholson, Michael. **Mahatma Gandhi: The Man Who Freed India and Led the World in Nonviolent Change.** Illus. with photos. SERIES: People Who Have Helped the World. Gareth Stevens 1988, LB $12.48 (1-55532-813-X). 68pp. Nonfiction.

Written in a format similar to a lengthy magazine article, this biography may appeal most to reluctant readers in junior or even senior high school. The brief text is punctuated by subheadings and heavily illustrated with archival photos and color stills from the movie *Gandhi*. Extensive photo captions and quotes from Gandhi's writings and those of other writers and officials are placed in the wide outside margins. Although some may feel that the page design is too busy, this material should encourage youngsters to read the entire text. Gandhi's full career and his philosophy are presented. The end matter added to the U.S.

edition (the series was first published in England) has a helpful chronology, but the bibliography includes many titles that are out of date or not appropriate for the audience. An index is included. A volume on Mother Teresa is also available.

Rosen, Mike. *The Conquest of Everest.*
See entry 850, Grades 4–6.

865   Staples, Suzanne Fisher. *Shabanu: Daughter of the Wind.* Knopf 1989, LB $13.99 (0-394-94815-7). 256pp. Fiction.

This novel is one of the best children's or young adult books about contemporary childhood and adolescence set in a region outside North America. Although Shabanu's problems may be different from those of teens living in the United States or Canada, the conflict between adapting to life in conventional adult society and young people's desires to make their own decisions is a shared one.

Eleven years old when we first encounter her, Shabanu is the daughter of a nomadic family in Pakistan. She loves the free life of a camel herder and knows her animals intimately. Her older sister, Phulan, is 13 and about to be married according to time-honored customs. Shabanu knows that her father will arrange a wedding for her, too, in the near future. Although she accepts the inevitability of the event, she wonders whether she will be happy.

Most of the adult characters follow the traditions of the people of the Cholistan Desert. However, Shabanu has one aunt, Sharma, who has broken away from the strict rules that govern relationships. She has become an independent woman, herding her own camels after leaving her abusive husband. Although Sharma's life-style is highly unusual, she is admired by some, including Shabanu. The young girl is envious of Fatima, Sharma's daughter, who will never be forced to marry against her will. Throughout the novel, Sharma offers words of wisdom that guide Shabanu in developing her own outlook on life.

When Shabanu's boldness contributes to the death of Phulan's husband-to-be, the family must flee to protect the two sisters from the sexual grasp of a rich landowner. Eventually, Shabanu is promised to Rahim, the landowner's brother, to smooth things over. Rahim is a powerful local politician who admires Shabanu's youthful spirit. Yet she does not want to marry this older man and be the fourth wife in his household, as Islamic law allows. She wants to maintain the freedom of her childhood years. She tries to run away, but her father finds her and beats her. She then comes to a decision: She will marry Rahim, but she will always keep some aspect of herself private, her own internal strength, as Sharma has wisely advised.

The desert, unforgiving in its harshness, yet familiar and dear to its inhabitants, is more than a backdrop to the story. Its beauty and its terrors are described in rich detail. Each character has a distinctive personality; though not stereotypes, most represent traditional viewpoints. Such scenes as the wedding ceremonies and the camel fair offer a taste of life among some of Pakistan's people, but it is the insights into a young girl's feelings about herself and her place in her own culture that will draw readers below the surface of this very special book. The author lived in Pakistan for many years as a journalist and came to know the people of the Cholistan Desert; her story of Shabanu is authentic, realistic, and compelling throughout.

866 Traub, James. ***India: The Challenge of Change.*** Rev. ed. Illus. with photos. Julian Messner 1985, LB $10.29 (0-671-60460-0). 167pp. Nonfiction.

Though it must be supplemented with updated political information, this is a well-organized study of modern India for middle school students. The book was published just as Rajiv Gandhi was coming to power in 1984, after his mother's assassination. The Bhopal incident is mentioned briefly in a discussion of the place of large-scale industry in the scheme of India's economic development. Information on development and the economy is especially well presented. The chapter on political life in India gives a very positive view of Nehru and his leadership qualities. The negative aspects of Indira Gandhi's career are emphasized, and the author takes a "wait and see" attitude on Rajiv, necessary because of the timing of the book's release. The chapter on religion tries to place each major belief system within a historical context. The black-and-white photos are mundane, but the text is accessible. *India: Now and Through Time* (Houghton Mifflin, 1980) is similar in scope and interest level, but its information is even more dated.

GRADES 10-12

867 Clifford, Mary Louise. ***The Land and People of Afghanistan.*** Illus. with photos. SERIES: Portraits of the Nations. HarperCollins 1989, LB $14.89 (0-397-32339-5). 225pp. Nonfiction.

Serious junior high or high school history students will be interested in this title's comprehensive information on the succession of empires and dynasties that occupied Afghanistan throughout the centuries. Less interested readers may be put off by the genealogical tables, language charts, and dense text. Excerpts from Afghan literature, sidebars about India, Greece, and Persia (three of the early invading countries), many types of maps, and an annotated bibliography complement the text. The contemporary situation is also covered. Several chapters on daily life and culture are included. Although the book has a recent publication date, the author flounders when writing about the current political situation after Soviet withdrawal, because events are still unfolding. Students will have to use newspaper and magazine articles for updates.

Doherty, Katherine M., and Craig A. Doherty. ***Benazir Bhutto.***
See entry 855, Grades 7–9.

Herda, D. J. ***The Afghan Rebels: The War in Afghanistan.***
See entry 859, Grades 7–9.

868 ***India.*** Illus. with photos. SERIES: Library of Nations. Time-Life 1986, LB $25.93 (0-8094-5315-0). 160pp. Nonfiction.

Armchair travelers and students working on projects will find this volume in the Library of Nations series visually inviting and interesting. Reminiscent of National Geographic publications, this large-size book gives readers a detailed picture of life in today's India. Both urban and rural life are depicted in general chapters about city and village living and in photo-essays about the family of a Calcutta clerk and the village of Harmara in Rajasthan. An extensive discussion of Hinduism and its influence on Indian life today includes a thorough exploration of the caste system, outlawed but still very much practiced. The other major religions are not treated in depth. Chapters on history and geography round out this attractive volume. Political updates will have to be located in other sources. Includes bilbiography and index.

869 Jhabvala, Ruth Prawer. ***Out of India: Selected Stories.*** William Morrow 1986, HB $16.95 (0-688-06382-9); Simon & Schuster/Fireside 1987, P $7.95 (0-671-64221-9). 288pp. Fiction.

This short story collection covers the Indian period of Jhabvala's writing career. Originally from Central Europe, she married an Indian architect and spent many years in India before eventually settling in the United States. Her long association with India, strengthened by family ties, has spawned many works dealing with Indian life. Among her themes are how Europeans and North Americans are changed by their relationships with India, India's spiritual life in all its myriad forms, and Indian sexual and romantic partners.

In the introductory essay of this collection, she writes about her own experiences as an inhabitant of a country that is not her native land. Although the essay contains statements that seem stereotypical and ethnocentric on the surface, one recognizes that she cares deeply about her adopted home and plays the devil's advocate as she writes about some difficult truths she has faced in adapting to life in India. Sophisticated readers will appreciate this essay and will be able to read between the lines.

Some of the stories will appeal more to young adult readers than others. "My First Marriage" is about a Westernized, upper-class young woman who leaves her very proper existence to follow a young man with no social standing but with a philosophy of his own. The relationship between another young woman, her wheeler-dealer husband, and the father who has reluctantly brought them together is the subject of "On Bail." "The Interview" is about the younger brother in an extended family who cannot find a job worthy of his interests. In reality, he does not really want to work, but to live the imaginary life of a movie hero. "A Spiritual Call" and "How I Became a Holy Mother" take a somewhat satirical look at Europeans searching for religious truths and romantic relationships with their Indian gurus.

Irony and wit, a high degree of realism, and clear insight into the human heart are all at play in Jhabvala's writing. The young adults who use this collection as a stepping-stone to her other works will find themselves looking at a multilayered view of India and Indians.

870 Mehta, Gita. ***Raj.*** Simon & Schuster 1989, HB $19.95 (0-671-43248-6). 479pp. Fiction.

The word *raj*, or reign, is often used to refer to the British colonization of India, but this book is about the royal kingdoms that also existed at the time. These kingdoms were "independent" of British India but were still influenced by the British political officers assigned to each ruler.

This is Jaya's story, the epic tale of a girl born a princess at the turn of the century in a kingdom in northern India. She is trained in the traditional feminine arts by her mother and the women of the court and educated in the royal science of government at her father's command. She enters an unhappy, arranged marriage with a prince from another kingdom, who cares only for his extramarital affairs. But Jaya is fortunate to have developed a degree of self-reliance and confidence that stand her in good stead in both Indian and Western society, although she much prefers the Indian way of life over the wealthy-European life-style.

Wanting her son to ascend to the throne when he comes of age, Jaya stays within her unhappy marriage. But she is also aware of the struggles going on in British India. The history of the independence movement and Gandhi's work are integrated into the story in a very positive way, through the characters of a woman tutor and a male friend who is a Nationalist leader. Jaya lives through some of the great events of the twentieth century—two world wars and India's independence. When royal India finally becomes part of the new republic, she decides to become a candidate for public office. Her education and her association with both the Nationalist leader and an English friend temper her royalist sentiments and propel her into the future.

This long novel will attract readers who enjoy entering a different world for an extended period of time. The writing is sometimes slow going, but it offers young adult readers a bit of everything—war, politics, history, romance, a coming-of-age story, and a chance to experience the struggle for Indian independence from the viewpoints of the maharajahs and maharinis of the various Indian kingdoms. There is little here about the great majority of the Indian people, but for those who want to learn how history affected the highest social classes, *Raj* serves as a good introduction.

871   Mehta, Ved. ***Daddyji.*** Norton 1989, P $8.95 (0-393-30562-7). 195pp. Nonfiction.

Daddyji is the story of a self-made man, affectionately told by his son. It is but one chapter in the saga of the Mehta family, engagingly chronicled by world-renowned author Ved Mehta. Ved Mehta makes his appearance in this biography, as he tells of the bout with meningitis, which blinded him; in his autobiography *Vedi* (Norton, 1987), he presents his own experiences of growing up sightless. Mehta's several books about his family are filled with the kind of details and warmth that will appeal to some young adult readers, and the documentaries based on these family memoirs are also suitable for viewing by high school students.

Although primarily the story of Amolak Ram Mehta, who is Ved's father, *Daddyji* is also about the larger history of the Mehta family as it changed from a traditional village family to an urban, professional one. The transformation began when Amolak's father left the village to become a tax collector. One by one, his sons were sent off to live with relatives in the city and to go to school. The various stages of Amolak's education in India, England, and the United States are recounted, as are his efforts to become a doctor and to finance his younger brothers' education. The conflicts between Amolak's Western ideas and the more traditional values held by his wife (the subject of another biography entitled *Mamaji*, Norton, 1988) are similar to those of many young couples who were married during the early part of the twentieth century, as more men became exposed to higher education and life outside India.

The story of Ved's illness and his father's inability to prevent his blindness, in spite of advanced medical training, are dispassionately related. The reader wants to admonish Daddyji for his mistakes in not recognizing the disease and to comfort him at the same time. It constitutes a powerful chapter. On the whole,

Ved Mehta has done justice to his family's story, and he succeeds in giving readers some sense of the changing mores in India in this century.

872 Narayan, R. K. ***The Painter of Signs.*** Viking 1976, HB $16.95 (0-670-53567-2); Penguin 1983, P $5.95 (0-14-006259-9). 183pp. Fiction.

R. K. Narayan has invented a southern Indian city and peopled it with characters created during a 55-year writing career. His men and women are thoroughly Indian, yet they display universal emotions and personality traits. Social commentary is his specialty, always written with a deft, quiet, comedic tone.

Raman, the painter of signs, is a bachelor in his 30s when he is smitten with love for Daisy, an outspoken advocate of population control who has just been assigned to a post in Malgudi, Narayan's fictional city. Narayan's working men are always originals, and Raman is no exception. He is proud of his professionalism and his artistry, his pastime is reading esoteric texts purchased from the used bookseller in the marketplace, and he is immersed in a wide circle of men from every social and economic class in the city. He is comfortable as a single man, living with his maiden aunt, who takes care of all the household duties. Through her example, the reader becomes familiar with the life of an orthodox Hindu woman, in great contrast to Daisy.

Daisy is a completely independent young woman who has cut herself off from all family ties because she did not want to comply with her family's marriage arrangements. Educated and intensely committed to her work, she is representative of a new generation of Indian women. Raman is willing to marry Daisy under any circumstances, even giving up any hope of a child in deference to Daisy's strong ideological bent. Although it seems as though Raman and Daisy will live together happily as husband and wife, the crusader decides not to give up her hard-won freedom. She goes off to a desert village to continue her campaign.

Narayan's work, of which this is but a small and interesting sample, may not appeal to all young adult readers, even those who are ready for more mature novels by world-renowned writers. Those who can appreciate the small touches of humor, the unassuming stories of ordinary people, and the loving picture of modern India will want to read this and the other novels and stories about the conflicts that arise between the citizens of Malgudi, a fictional city as vividly realized in its own way as is Faulkner's Yoknapatawpha County.

873 Russell, Malcolm B. ***The Middle East and South Asia 1989: 23rd Annual Edition.*** Adapted, rewritten, and revised annually from a book entitled *The Middle East and South Asia 1967.* Illus. with photos. SERIES: The World Today. Stryker-Post Publications 1989, P $5.50 (0-943448-50-6). 178pp. Nonfiction.

Issued annually in August, this is a comprehensive, yet relatively inexpensive research tool for students. Historical background on the whole region is followed by separate chapters on each of the countries in the area. History and the current political and economic situation are emphasized. The political analysis tries to be evenhanded, but the short paragraphs on the future are often proved wrong by unforeseen events. This is a good starting point for some research projects, but not as useful for reports requiring cultural and social information. All of the South Asian nations are represented, including the Maldive Islands and Bhutan.

16

EAST ASIA

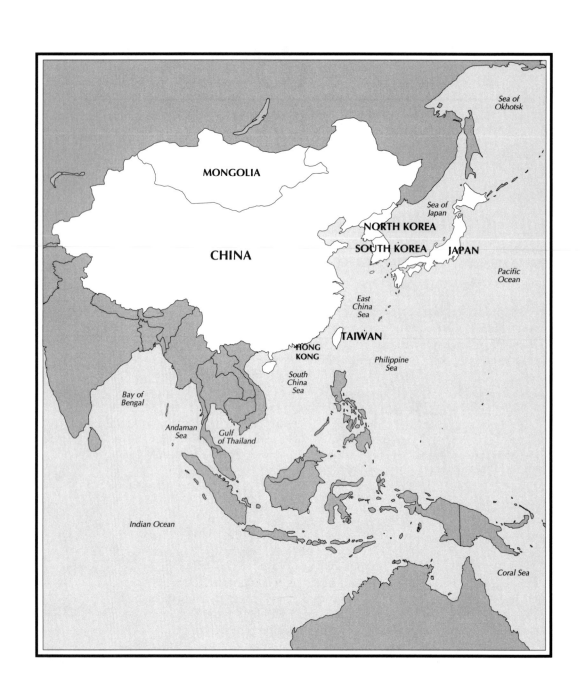

16

EAST ASIA

by Ginny Lee, Suzanne Lo, and Susan Ma

Asia is not the only area of the world to bear the often well-intentioned misconceptions and stereotypes of the modern West. Perhaps because of the long traditions of Asian countries of remaining sequestered from the world, these stereotypes have become exaggerated and abetted by xenophobia and misinformation. Much of the aim of this bibliography is to dispel those cultural mix-ups and wrong notions born of mid-century fears and ignorance and, more recently, simply a lack of informed contact.

Readers in the United States are just beginning to be able to rely on the fact that updated published material will reflect the essence of modern countries. A selection of material that focuses on the social and political being of each country enables the rest of the world to understand each cultural group on its own terms. This humanizing factor also helps children from these countries to feel proud of their heritage and helps us to go beyond stereotypes in working with these children.

In the last decade, publishers in the United States have made a great effort to challenge stereotypes. In the past, books on other countries have focused mainly on historical dates, lists of rulers, major rivers, and major products. Now they attempt to portray the daily lives of people and especially the lives of children at a level to which children can relate. Modern photography techniques and equipment are employed to make us believe that those children in the pictures are alive and real in the world today. They could be our neighbors. The pictures are not simply musty and antiquated photos that give a feeling of the remote past.

Photography has changed our attitudes as well. Children today enjoy so much fast-paced, quick-changing color in TV, videogames, and commercials that they associate black and white and sepia with the past. The exposure to faraway nations that these books provide is an important part of giving readers the feeling that these are modern people living in the world today, that we all belong to the same world. In the same way that TV and modern communications make the world into a global community, these books work both to elicit the feeling of the oneness of the world and to help us take off our social blinders. At the same time, color photography helps us to focus on the unique characteristics of these countries and even on differences between various social and cultural groups within each country.

We have used only the books directly available to us for review. We discussed thoroughly the ones we found especially helpful or else flawed. We looked first for cultural authenticity but also for literary merit and photographic and artistic clarity, reality, and enhancement of the text. There is no place for artistic misinformation, even when the illustration is used only as decoration.

The publication date of a book does not necessarily reflect its quality. Many good books have come out within the past five to ten years. What makes them good is often their revised attitude, historical perspective, and up-to-date, catchy photos. However, for basic understanding of a culture via its own history and literature, especially when this can be seen extended into today, often a classic from earlier in this century remains the best work. We have tried to mention a few of those.

The bulk of the books listed here are not folktales, although those are much of what is published. This listing will focus on the modern nations of China, Japan, Mongolia, North and South Korea, and Taiwan, using material that sheds light on why they have become what they are, both socially and politically. At times this may include mythology or ancient history, but more often there will be a photographic and journalistic commentary on the country, as seen in many of the series books.

There are a great variety of series books. Some deal with history (Life and Times series, Twentieth Century World History series, Focus Books, Conflict in the Twentieth Century series, and First Book series, e.g., *Ancient Japan and Its Influence on Modern Times*), and some maintain a specific cultural focus (Easy Menu Ethnic Cookbooks series and Count Your Way series), but the majority deal with a modern-day description of the culture, the people and how they live, language, religion, arts, politics, and history.

Reading levels vary. A few appeal to the very young (New True series, Take a Trip series, Count Your Way series, Step Into series), being more general, wider in scope, or written simply in large print. Many reach a middle grade level (Rivers of the World series, Families the World Over series, Children of the World series, and Looking At series), with photos and essays on how people live, food and clothing, entertainment, art, and history.

Another handful appeals to the junior high and high school levels, and the better ones are also useful to the average interested adult (The Land and Its People series by Silver Burdett, Passport series by Franklin Watts, the Portrait of the Nations series by HarperCollins, Cultures of the World by Cavendish, and Enchantment of the World series by Childrens Press). The last three are particularly well laid out and readable, with informative detail and eye-catching photos. The HarperCollins series uses black-and-white reproductions of art with a few black-and-white photos that are nevertheless intriguing. The other two (Cavendish and Childrens Press) employ more color photos.

Of the ones that deal primarily with history, several give quite detailed and thought-provoking accounts and even include study questions. The Twentieth Century World History series is particularly adaptable to the classroom in this respect.

There are many beautifully rendered books now available from Asian publishers, but for the present purpose we will deal only with material republished in the United States or Canada. It is hoped that U.S. publishers will soon reprint more of those books to enable Asian countries to speak to us in their own voice.

While valuable in giving us a window on Asian countries, there are some problems with these books, which publishers will need to be aware of in making them ready for an increasingly enlightened U.S. reading public. Though the illustrations are colorful and wonderfully presented, many worthy of framing, at times they seem included for the mere sake of color and extravagance and either do not enhance the text at all or misrepresent the story. Moreover, after a while they all begin to look alike, as though all were drawn by the same person. It became difficult to pinpoint an individual style. The style is all more or less that of traditional Chinese ink paintings, which of course comprises many schools.

Another problem with books published in Asian countries is that in preparing them for export, publishers have translated virtually literally an already terse text—somewhat reminiscent of newspaper headlines—into uninteresting English. Lack of literary quality does not prevent the story itself from being of value, but a more beautiful retelling could have turned a common stone into a gem.

Of the picture books published originally in the United States—most of them by American authors—there is a tendency to focus on universal values, such as pride (*Three Strong Women*) or the interdependence of mankind and nature (*The Gift of the Willows*), with Asian countries as physical and cultural backdrops. Though often well rendered, the text and illustrations do contain errors. Here, the emphasis is almost uniformly on traditional societies and cultures, and young children will come away with stereotypes newly reinforced unless these works are supplemented with more contemporary portrayals, such as Riki Levinson's documentary-style story of Hong Kong, *Our Home Is the Sea*.

The chief noticeable lack in the literature from and about Asian countries is in the area of literature itself. Other than prolific writers such as Katherine Paterson, Laurence Yep, Lensey Namioka, and Florence Uchida, who write realistic novels set in modern or historical Asian countries or which may bring their Asian characters over to the New World, not many writers have reached into themselves to find that universal something that wells up from within and that has importance and value both for the author and for the world. What is needed is not a contrivance but a good story that might reflect a certain culture without being overly self-conscious about the fact that it hails from that culture.

Most of the literature coming from Asian and Asian-American sources in English for children lacks depth of character and profundity of thought. The novels are not strong enough to hold their own on the shelf next to Virginia Hamilton, Madeline L'Engle, Mildred Taylor, and Cynthia Voigt. In addition, sometimes books written about children are not written for children. In spite of the beautiful black-and-white scroll painting that tops many of its pages, *Chi Po and the Sorcerer* contains very adult sarcasm and esoteric humor; besides, the many attempts to be Chinese are so un-Chinese as to be bothersome. However, *The Moon Bamboo*, which also could be considered to be written at an adult level, chiefly in its underpinnings, can be read by young people too, like *Alice in Wonderland*, and is thoroughly consistent with Vietnamese culture.

For close to two centuries there have been Western missionaries in China. Today there are a myriad of adults who were born and raised in China during very interesting times. This large and largely silent group is represented by a few writers who have made twentieth-century China come alive for us with their own personal and poignant memoirs. Jean Fritz wrote *Homesick*, about her childhood in Shanghai just after World War I, and *Homecoming*, which covers her return to China as an adult in 1950 just after the Communist liberation. Betty Vander Els wrote *Bomber's Moon*, which follows her and her little brother to

India under the protection of their school for two years during World War II. Her story continues with *Leaving Point*, which clarifies somewhat the emotional political scene in China that accompanied the Communist rise to power in 1949.

Into this category also fall a few of the old classics, such as A. J. Cronin's *The Keys of the Kingdom*, about a Scottish priest who spends most of his life as a missionary in China, and *Inn of the Sixth Happiness*, about the daughter of a missionary.

A few other authors are also writing their own enlightening and very readable stories. Margaret and Raymond Chang's *In the Eye of War* describes the daily life of a young boy in Shanghai during World War II, when war was happening all around but only peripherally affecting him. Yoko Kawashima Watkins's *So Far from the Bamboo Grove* follows a young Japanese girl (herself) and her family in their trek from northern Korea to the South and thence to Japan as escapees and refugees at the end of the war.

The materials in the bibliography for the chapters on East Asia and Southeast Asia were gathered and examined in conference by Ginny Lee, Suzanne Lo, and Susan Ma, all librarians in the San Francisco Bay Area. The annotations and introduction were written by Ginny Lee.

PRESCHOOL–GRADE 3

874 Baker, Keith. *The Magic Fan.* Illus. by the author. Harcourt Brace Jovanovich 1989, HB $14.95 (0-15-250750-7). 18pp. Fiction.

This eye-catching, colorful, and beautifully illustrated story is not entirely accurate in its presentation of the traditional Japanese culture and life-style. For instance, in Japan it is the fabric and the clothing that are ornately patterned, not the roofs. However, much detail as well as style is based on the Japanese stages of the Tokaido woodcut series, and the colors are Japanese—muted with black. The story is about a carpenter who makes everything for the village. When he runs out of things to make, a fan appears in the sea and shows him some interesting things for which the villagers have no use. The villagers ridicule him. Lastly, the fan tells him to build a great rainbow bridge over the town, which at first the villagers dislike, but they change their minds when it saves them from a tidal wave. When the carpenter loses his fan, he realizes that the magic lay all the time within himself, like Dumbo who learned he could fly without his magic feather. The fan itself appears open on each double-page spread and carries the illustrations, while the text surrounds it. With each turn of the "fan" page, the story is furthered, an ingenious arrangement and delightful for children.

875 Demi. *The Empty Pot.* Illus. by the author. Henry Holt 1990, HB $15.95 (0-8050-1217-6). 32pp. Fiction.

In order to choose a successor, the emperor gives each of the children a handful of seeds to see who can grow the most beautiful flowers. When the seeds fail to sprout, everyone else goes out to buy beautiful flowers to present, but one little boy simply presents his empty pot. The emperor has boiled the seeds, so he knows none will sprout. Only the boy with the empty pot is proved honest and therefore worthy of being emperor. This is truly a beautifully drawn fairy tale, one that will appeal to children and adults alike.

While this story is relevant to the idea of development of moral character, it has nothing to do with actual Chinese history. We would rather see books with true relevance to Chinese history and literature given more attention by publishers and librarians. This book does not fill the gap. No little boy who was honest and wise ever had a chance to become emperor simply for being honest and wise, especially not in the Tang Dynasty. If the author-illustrator was going to present the characters in Tang Dynasty clothes, then the story should have been an accurate representation of the Tang Dynasty. Since it was done otherwise, children are likely to come away from this book with new misconceptions about China.

876 Evans, Doris Portwood. ***Breakfast with the Birds.*** Illus. by Tony Chen. Putnam 1972. 44pp. Fiction. o.p.

It is the emphasis on tourists and what a foreigner would notice about Hong Kong that gives readers the sense that this book was written by a foreigner who has been there. The conversation about chop suey and egg rolls sounds more relevant to an American Chinatown. "A man in a gray robe" implies a monk, yet the illustration does not show a monk—and the clothes are orange. However, the story is interesting. A boy and his pet mynah tell fortunes to earn money from tourists in front of big hotels and restaurants. The boy is arrested for working without a license, but the judge has a sense of humor and lets him go. A generous gentleman gives him a Hong Kong ten-dollar bill so he has enough money to treat his bird to breakfast at the special teahouse where old gentlemen take their birds in cages in the morning, an old tradition that still persists. The black-and-white line drawings, sometimes with color added, are also very good. They are representative of Hong Kong, although a few items seem to have been thrown in for good measure. For instance, pigs and geese do not run loose in Hong Kong streets, especially not near a traffic circle. But most of it rings true, from the designs on the protective iron grates in front of the doors to the juxtaposition of Western and Chinese buildings.

877 Fisher, Leonard Everett. ***The Great Wall of China.*** Illus. by the author. Macmillan 1986, HB $11.95 (0-02-735220-X). 32pp. Nonfiction.

Stark and powerful in black and white and shades of gray, the illustrations in this historical rendition of the infamous building of the Great Wall reflect the cruel determination of the First Emperor. Chin Shih Huang Ti (lit. Chin's first emperor) indeed did many wonderful things for China. He was the first to unite the many little states into one empire. He standardized the writing, the system of weights and measures, and the length of axles on carts so that the ruts (driving lanes) in the roads would all be the same. And he connected the many walls, which had been built in centuries past, in order to continue to keep at bay the "barbarians" to the north, who were a constant threat to the new country.

Chin Shih Huang Ti was notorious as well for his inhumanity and pride. He had all the books burned for fear people would read and think and rise against him. This picture book tells the story of the construction of the wall, the terrorizing of the workers, regulations against rest and runaways, and the burying of dissidents alive in the rocks of the wall. The connected wall served its purpose. For 1,000 years it kept out intruders and still stands as a lasting tribute to China's unrestful beginnings.

Each double-page spread is graced by a caption in Chinese calligraphy and a red square "chop" (seal), which is the Chinese counterpart to the Western official signature and is often added to paintings and used on documents and letters. The translations for these are given at the end. There is a simple map in the front, silhouetting modern China and indicating both the route of the wall and the original positions of the many small states that unified to become China.

This book can be used as a dynamic and graphic introduction to a discussion of the relative worth of an individual—or thousands of individuals—and the good of the country as a whole. Is it valid, for instance, to execute common criminals as a token to discourage civil misbehavior? This has been done in many countries throughout history and is still done in China today. Young readers can evaluate for themselves Chin Shih Huang Ti's role and the qualities that make a good or a bad leader.

878   Friedman, Ina R. ***How My Parents Learned to Eat.*** Illus. by Allen Say. Houghton Mifflin 1984, HB $12.95 (0-395-35379-3). 32pp. Fiction.

Allen Say's intricacy of detail in his line drawings provides us with good feelings about Japan, about the tender awkwardness of a Japanese trying to be American, and about an American trying to be Japanese. A young Japanese girl wants to impress an American sailor with her facility in the use of Western eating utensils, and he likewise wants to impress her. Each struggles in secret to learn the other's way. The mix-up between British and American eating styles provides enough laughter to break the ice. The story is told by their little girl, shown on the first page in Japanese dress with Japanese food and chopsticks, and on the last page in Western dress with Western food and knife and fork. For her, it is natural.

Here is a springboard for discussion of just what is natural and what is not: Is it natural to live in a mansion? To paint your house? To live in a house at all? Can we adjust our idea of what is natural in order to be more welcoming and accommodating to the peoples of the world? Can we adjust initial impressions of "silly customs" by realizing that what is natural to one group might not be natural to another?

879   Garrison, Christian. ***The Dream Eater.*** Illus. by Diane Goode. Bradbury 1978, HB $10.95 (0-87888-134-4). 28pp. Fiction.

Here is a story to solve everyone's nightmare problems. Yukio has nightmares, but no one will listen to him because all the villagers have nightmares of their own to deal with. But all is well when Yukio saves the life of a Baku who eats dreams and is especially fond of consuming nightmares. One by one, the Baku eats up all the nightmares in the village. Everyone sleeps peacefully, and the Baku is contentedly full.

The illustrations, elaborately elegant in gold ochre and green, portray properly fearsome dragons and other nightmares in a remote countryside filled with butterflies and dragonflies and plum blossoms. The Baku himself is a gentle and lovable monster, and Yukio is a boy we can all identify with, though he is also definitely Japanese.

Georges, D. V. ***Asia.***
See entry 904, Grades 4–6.

880   Gerstein, Mordicai. ***The Mountains of Tibet.*** Illus. HarperCollins 1987, LB $12.89
(0-06-022149-6); 1989, P $4.95 (0-06-443211-4). 26pp. Fiction.

The simplicity of the telling belies the profundity of this tale. Inspired by a
reading of the Tibetan Book of the Dead, the story of a little boy who lives in
Tibet and loves kites is told in a few lines and a few pages. He dies happily of old
age and is given a choice of whether to become one with the universe or live
another life. A lengthy series of choices leads him improbably but certainly right
back to Tibet, where this time he decides to see what it is like to be a girl who
loves kites. Reminding us of the story of the Bee Man of Orn who is given a
chance to make something better of himself in a new life and becomes the same
thing he was before, this tale also invites us to wonder whether there may be
some odd factor calling us to become who we are, though we appear to be given
free choice. The illustrations, also deceptively simple, reflect Tibet and at the
same time are universal.

881   Haskins, Jim. ***Count Your Way Through Japan.*** Illus. by Martin Skoro. SERIES: Count
Your Way Books. Lerner/Carolrhoda 1987, LB $10.95 (0-87614-301-X). 20pp.
Nonfiction.

This is an interesting little series and includes volumes on China and Korea.
There is an introductory note on the language, then ten double pages of the first
ten numerals. A colorful drawing portrays an appropriate item from the culture
to represent each number on one page; a paragraph explaining the item is on the
facing page along with the number in the target language and as an Arabic
numeral. In all three books in the series, some items are quite apropos, while
others either stretch the point for the sake of filling in the number or miss a good
opportunity to exemplify the culture. It seems that a little more thought and
effort might have produced a better representation of the culture, but this is a
good idea. The books are appealing, and the items chosen will do.

882   Johnston, Tony. ***The Badger and the Magic Fan: A Japanese Folk Tale.*** Illus. by
Tomie dePaola. Putnam 1990, HB $13.95 (0-399-21945-5). 28pp. Fiction.

This is a retelling of a Japanese folktale. The story is of three Japanese goblin
children called Tengu, who have a magic fan that can make noses grow shorter
or longer. A mischievous badger steals the fan and uses it to play tricks on a
princess to win her hand. In a lax moment, however, he loses it back to the
Tengu children, who make the badger's nose grow so long it is used as a bridge
pole in the sky by some heavenly workers.

   Both story and illustrations stretch our credibility, as well as our noses, and
the drawings border on the stereotypical. However, the story is well told, and the
drawings are appealing to children. This will be a popular story-hour item, and
the many details of Japanese culture provide discussion topics that could better
elucidate the essence of Japan.

883   Levinson, Riki. ***Our Home Is the Sea.*** Illus. by Dennis Luzak. Dutton 1988, LB
$13.95 (0-525-44406-8). 26pp. Fiction.

Here is another way of looking at life, from the other side of the world. We see a
young boy on his way home from school. He lives in Hong Kong, so all the sights

and sounds that present themselves along the way are very much typical of Hong Kong. We feel the artist must have spent a great deal of time on the streets of that city in order to give us so balanced a representation. We see the tall, congested buildings, the painted trams, the markets, the "international flags" (laundry hanging out from windows and balconies on poles), the old men practicing ancient exercises in the park, and the men out for a walk with birds in cages. Finally, we see through the pictures, rather than being told outright, that our young guide's home is on a boat in the harbor. What must it be like to live one's whole life on a boat? Here we have a glimpse. The boy lets us in on his life's ambition: not to have to go to school but to go to sea and be a fisherman with his father, like his father's father before him.

The pictures are large and impressionistic, covering sometimes a page and a quarter of the facing page. They give us much information about what it is like to live in Hong Kong, mostly from a child's perspective. The text is simple and clear, and so is the message. The book provides good discussion material on the relative values of formal schooling and learning through direct experience of a way of life.

884 Lifton, Betty Jean. *Joji and the Dragon.* Illus. by Eiichi Mitsui. Linnet Books 1989, HB $15.00 (0-208-02245-7). 64pp. Fiction.

At first appearing too washy and splashy, the black ink brush drawings that illustrate this story are actually full of character. The writing is simple but clever. An adult will chuckle at some of the lines, enhancing the enjoyment for small children. The story is of a scarecrow that does not scare crows. In fact, he lives in peace with them. They have promised to eat worms instead of grain. The farmer of little faith advertises for someone who will do a better job: "Straw men need not apply." A fierce dragon gets the job, but in the end proves no match for the wily Joji and his friends the crows. It is the story that is interesting, rather than the fact that it is Japanese, but the Japanese qualities do come through in the details of the illustrations.

McDearmon, Kay. *Giant Pandas.*
See entry 906, Grades 4–6.

885 Mason, Sally. *Take a Trip to China.* Illus. with photos by the author. SERIES: Take a Trip. Franklin Watts 1981, HB $9.40 (0-531-04317-7). 32pp. Nonfiction.

Large text and large color photos, some including children or portraying a child's interest, offer us a few tidbits of information on each page about some aspect of life in China. No sections are delineated, but the topics are the familiar ones: arts, food, shopping, agriculture, town and country, the people, their work. Simple but interesting, for a younger child this is a good introduction to a country. The series also covers Japan. Includes index.

Mattingley, Christobel. *The Miracle Tree.*
See entry 907, Grades 4–6.

886 Morimoto, Junko. ***My Hiroshima.*** Illus. with drawings by the author and historical photos. Viking 1987, HB $12.95 (0-670-83181-6). 30pp. Nonfiction.

Here is a personalized account, through a child's eyes, of daily life in Japan before World War II, the increasing obsession, even among schoolchildren, with militarism and military tactics during the war, the suddenness and horror of the atom bomb, and the contrast of the past with the present. The author, then a high school student, and her family survived. In telling this story, she is determined that the horror not be repeated and that children be taught to love peace and revere life. The drawings are a delicate and detailed pen and ink with a color wash, and they are interlaced with black-and-white photos of the devastation and a few color photos of modern Hiroshima rebuilt. Nothing is belabored or explained—just stated as simple facts. This provides the account with a subtle power, though it does not satisfy any thirst for details of survival or life immediately after or for profound thoughts and pleas for the future. A note to parents and teachers on the inside back cover offers a few details, such as the fact that children in school were also trained for war and "taught that suicide came before surrender." It is here that Morimoto asks us to consider the mistakes of war and the greater value of life and peace.

The book consists mostly of drawings and photos with a few lines of text, delicately and forcefully presented. It could be used both to elicit discussion about whether war is ever justified and to generate feelings of compassion for the myriad individuals who suffer for the ambitions and conflicts of a few adults.

887 Paterson, Katherine. ***The Tale of the Mandarin Ducks.*** Illus. by Leo Dillon and Diane Dillon. Dutton/Lodestar 1990, HB $14.95 (0-525-67283-4). 34pp. Fiction.

This slim book is a masterpiece of both illustration and storytelling. The story is set in ancient Japan, where the Mandarin ducks, symbols of conjugal felicity, attract the attention of a greedy emperor. He captures the male duck for the brilliant plumage but soon tires of him, as the duck begins to droop in grieving for his mate. The emperor loves things only so long as they are beautiful. A kitchen maid frees the duck, infuriating the emperor, who blames it on a servant. In their innocence and honesty, maid and servant fall in love, further enraging the emperor. He condemns them to death, but they are saved ("It is never foolish to show compassion to a fellow creature") by the ducks' impersonating imperial messengers. The story ends with the rescued couple living happily in a poor hut in the woods, bearing many children and living to a ripe old age. "Trouble can always be borne if it is shared," they reason. The conjugal felicity of the ducks is reflected in this couple and contrasted with the selfish and greedy emperor.

The illustrations are based on Japanese Ukiyo-E woodcut prints in rich, muted Japanese color and are held together by the flowing, delineating black line. The tidbits of human wisdom throughout, the Japanese detail and eye for natural beauty, and the richness of both story and painting will make this treasure a classic. It is good for a special story hour or for independent reading throughout the elementary grades.

888 Pittman, Helena Clare. ***The Gift of the Willows.*** Illus. by the author. Lerner/Carolrhoda 1988, HB $12.95 (0-87614-354-0). 30pp. Fiction.

It is the old Japan of flowing robe, flowing black hair, and flowing line so common to Japanese art that is evoked in these refreshing illustrations. A few details are amiss; for instance, husband and wife would probably not have embraced in public. However, this does not prevent the book from being a beautiful evocation of life in the Japanese countryside. The tale is of a potter for whom life is contentment as he works on his pots and lives close to nature. Life becomes joy when he marries. A couple of willow seedlings begin to grow by a river. Years pass. When drought comes, life is hardship for both man and willows. The potter waters the trees from the river. Later, when the river floods, one of the trees, now full grown, falls and provides a bridge for the escape of the man, his wife, and their newborn son. Life comes full circle as the family moves back in and sets up shop again. The fallen willow sprouts anew. This attractive book is a charming, nondidactic way of showing the cycle of life, the interdependence of man and nature, and the need to care for the environment.

889   Roy, Ronald. *A Thousand Pails of Water.* Illus. by Vo-Dinh Mai. Knopf 1978, LB $4.95 (0-394-93752-X). 26pp. Fiction.

A small boy who lives in a remote Japanese fishing village cannot understand why his father must kill whales. "It is what he knows," his grandfather tells him. It is how everyone in the village makes a living. One day a great whale is washed ashore and caught in the rocks as the tide goes out. Our little hero is the only one who sees him. "I will help you, sir," he says and takes his little pail to fetch water from the ocean to keep the whale wet. He knows that the whale will die in the sun if he is not kept wet. A little pail does not cover a great whale with enough water, but love and determination can accomplish a good deal in this world. "I will pour a thousand pails of water on you before I quit," he tells the whale. Late in the afternoon, with aching arms and legs and back, the boy finally collapses in the sand. The villagers find him and help him pour water on the whale. They soak their jackets in the sea and cover the whale to keep him wet. The whale survives to swim out with the next tide. No mention is made of why the villagers help the whale out to sea rather than take advantage of an easy kill, since this is how they live. Is it not sporting? Was the whale too old? Too young? Wrong size? Wrong sex? Nevertheless, the lessons in kindness, in the oneness of all living things, and in the villagers' sticking together and coming to the rescue of the one leap to the fore. It is a tender portrait of a small boy's concern for a living being.

The book is small and the drawings nicely rendered but not powerful enough to carry a large audience. Even so, it may make for children a very nice story hour in support of a study of whales or a discussion of environmental issues.

Sadler, Catherine Edwards. *Two Chinese Families.*
See entry 910, Grades 4–6.

890   Say, Allen. *The Bicycle Man.* Illus. by the author. Houghton Mifflin 1982, HB $12.45 (0-395-32254-5); 1989, P $3.95 (0-395-50652-2). 40pp. Fiction.

Unlike some of the picture books coming from Japan, this one does give a good impression of the unique culture of the country. The writing is lyrical and readable, and the line drawings are full of the intricate detail of a Japanese country school. The characters border on comic but are endearing, and the details of daily life allowed by this intricate style are abundant. The story is of a sports day in a rural Japanese school. Parents attend, bringing tiered basket lunch boxes wrapped in large carrying "kerchiefs." The sportsmanship decreed by the principal is recognizable by those in the West: "Whether we win or lose, let us enjoy ourselves." In the midst of the festivities, two U.S. soldiers appear. The children had heard of but never had seen red hair (on the one) and black skin (on the other). But the soldiers are smiling, so fears melt. With gestures the soldiers ask to ride the children's bicycle. The black man is a comic, hotshot rider, entertaining all. The commentary among the children is delightful.

The whole story is a wonderful ice-breaking, humorous, peacemaking story with which to initiate discussion about the differences between cultures and peoples. Those differences need not mean quarrels. Through this book, children can identify attitudes on the parts of key individuals that promote mutual understanding.

891   Snyder, Dianne. ***The Boy of the Three Year Nap.*** Illus. by Allen Say. Houghton Mifflin 1988, HB $14.95 (0-395-44090-4). 32pp. Fiction.

Here is another of Allen Say's wonderfully illustrated picture books. A hardworking widow has a lazy son who, it is said, would sleep for three years if no one woke him. But he is clever, too, and it is his cleverness that is his undoing. When a rich merchant with a beautiful daughter moves in next door, lazy Taro devises a trick to win the daughter in marriage and thus be ensured of enough money so he will not have to work. His trick backfires, and he finds himself working for his father-in-law—and even enjoying it.

With a touch of humor now recognizable as Allen Say's trademark both in the text and in the illustrations, the plot gradually unfolds, revealing Taro's mother to be his match in cleverness. The ending is satisfying, with a happy marriage, a new house for the mother, and a relieved father-in-law. If the whole thing seems a bit improbable, requiring a belief in and a healthy fear of ghosts, it is still a well-told, gripping tale, excellent for a story hour. Young children will love it. The illustrations, in muted Japanese color and ink, are mostly full page in a relatively large book. They are full of the detail of Japanese life, architecture, daily routines, clothing, and household items.

892   Stamm, Claus. ***Three Strong Women: A Tall Tale from Japan.*** Illus. by Jean and Mou-sien Tseng. Viking 1990, HB $12.95 (0-670-83323-1). 30pp. Fiction.

On a humorous note and lightly poking fun at the pride of a strong man who thinks too much of himself, this picture book will be well received as a read-aloud by those at a variety of age levels. With almost cartoonlike caricature, the line drawings extend the humor of the text. Our mighty hero is brought down to size by a jolly girl who turns out to be a great deal stronger than he, and her mother and grandmother are even more powerful. They pluck up trees by the roots and hurl them over mountains. After living with this demanding trio for some time, our hero not only learns a little humility, but has worked so hard that he becomes nearly as strong as they are, which is to say, impossibly stronger than anyone else in Japan. Finally, in a wrestling match, he proves himself worthy of the admiration of the court, but by then he has relinquished most of his pride. He becomes a simple farmer, adopting both the hardworking life and the simple values of Maru-me, the jolly girl. There are some Japanese qualities to the drawings; they are attractive because of the delicious way they depict the downfall of pride. This adaptation is a good source for lighthearted but pointed lessons.

893   Svend, Otto S. ***Children of the Yangtze River.*** Illus. by the author. Pelham Books 1982. 29pp. Fiction. o.p.

This charming book truly captures the essence of life in a Chinese Yangtze River village. A large, thin book filled with detailed drawings, it tells the story of the flooding of a village along the river through the eyes of a couple of small children, Mei Mei and Chang. We see their tiered rice farms lying against the slope of the steep hills that line the river, the farmers with carrying poles, the water buffalo, the ever-present animals—geese, chickens, pigs—the fishermen, the schoolhouse, the birds in cages that Mei Mei keeps, and Chang's pet pig. We see the familial relationship between the people of the village, the good-natured joking, and the spirit of working together. When the rains come, everyone works to move the village to higher ground. Pigs, birds, old people, and other precious things are carried in arms and on backs. After the river sweeps away the houses, all work together to carry cement from the boats to build a new village. The villagers celebrate their new homes with fireworks and lanterns and good luck couplets by their doors. This realistic tale is a real treasure for story hour or for one-on-one.

894   Takeshita, Fumiko. ***The Park Bench.*** Bilingual ed. Trans. from Japanese by Ruth A. Kanagy. Illus. by Mamoru Suzuki. Kane/Miller 1988, HB $11.95 (0-916291-15-4); P $6.95 (0-916291-21-9). 33pp. Fiction.

We hardly need the text, which is in both Japanese hiragana, for the benefit of beginning readers, and English. The full-page illustrations carry the whole story, which is a vignette of a day in the life of a park seen through the eyes of a white park bench. The day begins with a misty, chalky, pastel dawn and brightens into primary colors and interesting characters who people the park. The chief human role is filled by the park employee who is seen working in the background on nearly every page. It is difficult to pinpoint the characters as Japanese or the place as Japan. The park and its people seem universal, but, then, so does modern Japan. The day ends with a misty, muted twilight, and the park worker takes leave of the bench and the park. It is easy to get lost in these pointillistic pictures with one hundred children on every other page. Charming details abound.

895   Tompert, Ann. ***Grandfather Tang's Story.*** Illus. by Robert Andrew Parker. Crown 1990, LB $12.95 (0-517-57272-9). 30pp. Fiction.

The tangram is Chinese, as are the many different configurations possible, and the Chinese have used tangrams to help tell stories in the way demonstrated here. This story is of two foxes who chase each other, changing from one animal into another, each change accompanied by a different tangram. The story is acceptable, though not as well told as the author's *Little Fox Goes to the End of the World,* which is a gem. However, the story does not need the pony of tangrams to carry it. The tangrams chosen are not even the best ones possible. If the point is to make up a story including many of the various tangram figures, the author comes nowhere near exhausting the possibilities. The drawings of the animals are engaging, the tangrams do decorate the story nicely, and it was a good idea to use tangrams in the traditional way to illustrate a story, but a different emphasis in illustration and greater attention to literary quality would have given us a story with greater impact.

896   Tsuchiya, Yukio. *Faithful Elephants: A True Story of Animals, People, and War.* Trans. from Japanese by Tomoko Tsuchiya Dykes. Illus. by Ted Lewin. Houghton Mifflin 1988, HB $13.95 (0-395-46555-9). 32pp. Nonfiction.

The intention of this picture book is to strike the horror of war into the hearts of children by means of their natural empathy for the elephants and the other animals in the zoo that were ordered to be killed during the war for fear they would escape during a bombing and run loose in the streets. However, the horror lies more with the zookeepers and their inability to come to a definite decision for the sake of the animals. The dwelling on the process of death is overdone, and it is unfortunately the main focus of the book. Sentiments at the end are closer to disgust than to peace. Being starved to death has not much to do with faithfulness. The watercolor paintings realistically portray the animals in muted purples and pinks and the zookeepers in olive drab, as though they themselves were the soldiers who condemned the elephants to death. First written in the early 1950s, this book still carries the feeling of that era.

897   Tsutsui, Yoriko. *Anna's Secret Friend.* Illus. by Akiko Hayashi. Viking 1987, HB $10.95 (0-670-81670-1). 32pp. Fiction.

The excitement and trepidation of moving to a new house in a new town, the packing and unpacking of boxes, the sadness of leaving old friends, and the joy of meeting new ones are all presented very much from a little girl's point of view, both in the bold print text and in the large pastel drawings. Someone is leaving little presents in the mailbox, and it is not the mailman. Flowers, a note, a handmade paper doll appear. Who could it be? It turns out to be another little girl, as shy as Anna and just her age. The whole story turns on this simple and evocative theme. Nearly impossible to place the setting, we feel the universality of the story and delight in the humanity of the theme. This book is excellent for a preschool or kindergarten story hour and lends itself easily to a follow-up discussion of how one feels about moving to a new place and having to find new friends.

898   Tsutsui, Yoriko. *Before the Picnic.* Illus. by Akiko Hayashi. Putnam/Philomel 1987, HB $10.95 (0-399-21458-5). 24pp. Fiction.

This is a simple story, told in just a few words on each page, of a little girl who is endearingly helpful but who makes a mess of everything. The story line is actually carried in the bright and colorful line drawings, which also convey the parents' love for and patience with their charming, if troublesome, little one. Little Sashi's genuine desire to be of good service and her uplifting, cheerful little face make the book a delight. Any parent will identify. The drawings are not particularly Japanese except here and there, as in a table full of sushi, oriental vegetables, and chopsticks and in the shoes laid out on the step before the front door. Nonetheless, it tells us something about modern Japan in its increasing resemblance to Western industrialized nations; the trend toward homogeneity is very much in evidence here.

899 Winthrop, Elizabeth. *Journey to the Bright Kingdom.* Illus. by Charles Mikolaycak. Holiday House 1979, LB $7.95 (0-8234-0357-2). 40pp. Fiction.

More than just a fairy tale, this small book is an exquisitely written story that illuminates several facets of the Japanese character, insofar as a nation can be said to possess a character. It illustrates appreciation of the details in nature and art, devotion to a group—family, company, or nation—and long-suffering patience. It is the story of a woman who was an artist and delighted in painting the little creatures of the fields and forests. "She makes us see things we never saw before," say the people. But one day she goes blind and learns how to do everything by touch. When she has a baby girl, her greatest desire is to see the baby's face. As the girl grows, she befriends the field mice, who bring her and her blind mother to Kakure-sato, the magical land where no one is ever unhappy or sick—or blind—to show them again how beautiful the world can be. There the mother can gaze upon the face of her daughter and hold on to that image to carry her through her darkness. "As long as I can see you, I am not truly blind."

The black-and-white drawings, which use a strong flowing line, large areas of pattern, and blank space, faintly reminiscent of the ukiyo-e woodcut prints, are as delicately executed as the writing and are most evocative of Japan.

GRADES 4–6

Chang, Margaret, and Raymond Chang. *In the Eye of War.*
See entry 919, Grades 7–9.

900 Clement, Claude. *The Painter and the Wild Swans.* Illus. by Frederic Clement. Dutton/Dial 1986, HB $12.95 (0-8037-0268-X). 21pp. Fiction.

Strikingly blue and cold and effectively evocative of winter, the illustrations are what first call attention to this thin and rather unusual book. Done partly in Japanese triptych style, they tell the story of a painter who falls in love with the beauty of wild swans in winter. He follows them and eventually becomes one of them, not knowing whether he is a swan dreaming of being a man or a man dreaming of being a swan. The text expounds on a poem written in Japanese calligraphy alongside each painting, also telling the story. Thus the story is told four times, each version enhancing the others: in the Japanese poem, written again in full at the end, in the English translation, in the English text, and in the haunting paintings. This is a good gift for adult-minded friends, but one wonders whether young children will appreciate the idea that it is enough to have seen such rare beauty; the artistic expression of such beauty does not, finally, matter.

901 Elkin, Judith. *A Family in Japan.* Illus. with photos by Stuart Atkin. SERIES: Families the World Over. Lerner 1987, LB $9.95 (0-8225-1672-1). 32pp. Nonfiction.

This is an innocuous, superficial description of life in a Japanese family. It presents the daily routines, school life, likes and dislikes, special activities, and outings of a small boy. Festivals, temples, and Grandmother's doll collection are also given space. More space is devoted to the large color photos of the smiling faces and smart modern life than to the large-print text. Enough detail is provided to make this a good introduction to Japan for early to mid-elementary school, and the personalized photos encourage a child reader to believe that the children in the book are as real and as close as a next-door neighbor. However, real problems are not presented. A glossary and a few facts conclude. Other volumes in this series present children and their families in China, Hong Kong, South Korea, and Taiwan.

902 Els, Betty Vander. ***The Bombers' Moon.*** Farrar, Straus & Giroux 1985, HB $11.95 (0-374-30864-0). 167pp. Fiction.

What was it like to be children of missionaries in China just before World War II? Ruth and Simeon grew up speaking both Chinese and English, playing with the children of their servants, listening to the calls of the street vendors, eating Chinese food, and becoming familiar with the local customs and festivals. When the Japanese invaded, the children were sent to a special school to be safe. Homesick and unhappy with their severe teachers, they looked after each other in the way of many siblings, with much bickering and quarreling. From that school they were moved across the Himalayas to India. It was two years before they returned.

The excitement of the journeys, the frustration of censored letters from home, the worries about war, the school delights, and the mishaps are all viewed through the eyes of a feisty little girl 6 years old at the beginning and 8 on the return home. Amid her school mischiefs, Ruthie ponders the war, considers "the wicked Hitler," and befriends a German girl who loves Hitler "because he loves little children." This book would make an unusual and stimulating insert into a biography lesson and would be good reading for a better understanding of China in this century. The story explains the relationship between teachers and students and what goes on in the minds of children caught in a war and removed from their parents.

Farley, Carol. ***Korea: A Land Divided.***
See entry 922, Grades 7–9.

Fisher, Leonard Everett. ***The Great Wall of China.***
See entry 877, Grades PS–3.

Fritz, Jean. ***China Homecoming.***
See entry 924, Grades 7–9.

903 Fritz, Jean. ***Homesick: My Own Story.*** Putnam 1982, HB $9.95 (0-399-20933-6); Dell 1984, P $3.25 (0-440-43683-4). 176pp. Fiction.

Jean Fritz grew up in China speaking Chinese as well as English, attending a British school, resisting the British anthem, teasing her amah (maid) by giving her the wrong English words to learn, pondering with her best friend Andrea over the best way to bring love into a family, and having little side adventures in the Chinese community, where she was not supposed to wander. This part of her life's story takes place in the late 1920s, when the Communists and the Nationalists were in the midst of their struggle for power. It would be 20 more years before the Communists established control, but the skirmishes between the various political groups, including the warlords, affected the citizens and even the foreign community, which tried to keep pretty much to itself. However, this was a time when foreigners were not popular in China, and eventually they were forced to leave. Jean longs to go "home" to America, where she can roller skate (roller skating to her representing the essence of growing up American); she feels out of place as a foreigner in China, though it is clear that she also has a great love for China. Indeed we see her fiercely defending China once she gets to the United States as a 12 year old, just as she defended the United States while living in China. Her story is another step toward understanding China as well as being the heartwarming story of a feisty and caring little girl on her way to maturity.

904   Georges, D. V. **Asia.** SERIES: New True Books. Childrens Pr. 1986, HB $12.95 (0-516-01288-6). 48pp. Nonfiction.

Very large print distinguishes this book for readers in the lower grades of elementary school, although the color photographs do not feature children or even a child's view. Maps on each country and many relatively small landscape and geography photos punctuate each section. Very brief facts and small-scale photos probably appeal more to an adult than to a child. Japan is also covered in this series. Includes glossary and index.

905   Johnson, Neil. **Step into China.** Illus. with photos by the author. SERIES: Step into. Julian Messner 1988, LB $9.50 (0-671-64338-X); P $5.95 (0-671-65852-2). 32pp. Nonfiction.

Color photographs by the author allow us to see the daily lives of individual Chinese people and become acquainted with them as though they were our own neighbors. Especially appealing to young children, many of the photos are from a child's point of view, and many are of children. On each double-page spread, large photographs surround a paragraph or two of text on a particular subject: school, marketplace, games, work, silk, language (including calligraphy), culture, family, and more. In such a brief book, the information cannot be presented in depth, but for children this title is an excellent introduction to a culture. The photos are appealing and well selected, and the writing is geared to the elementary level.

Lye, Keith. **Inside China.**
See entry 928, Grades 7–9.

906   McDearmon, Kay. **Giant Pandas.** Illus. with photos. Dodd, Mead 1986. 62pp. Nonfiction. o.p.

A symbol of China, these picturesque creatures are everybody's favorite and have been offered by China to zoos throughout the world. We follow a pair to their new home in the United States. But the species is also endangered. In the last decade or two, there has been a natural dying out of the type of bamboo they subsist on. Moving down the mountains to find new sources of food, they either starve or run into civilization. The Chinese government and people are at work to help them survive. This book explains their plight, their habits and habitats, the attraction they have, and a bit of their history in relation to people. Black-and-white illustrations and photographs abound. This is a small but useful book for mid to upper elementary grades, one that presents some of the underlying environmental issues as well as the animals themselves.

907 Mattingley, Christobel. ***The Miracle Tree.*** Illus. by Marianne Yamaguchi. Harcourt Brace Jovanovich/Gulliver Books 1985, LB $11.95 (0-15-200530-7). 32pp. Fiction.

The true miracle lay in the patience and devotion of the three people whose quiet lives revolved around the tree: the gardener who tended it, the old woman who came by to greet him twice a year, and the young woman who watched the two from the window of her hospital room. The young woman, Hanako, had been badly injured in the atomic blast at Nagasaki, and her beauty was no more. Before the blast, Hanako had gone against her mother's wishes by marrying the gardener, and for 20 years afterward she had cooped herself up in her room, afraid to show herself. One Christmas, on the brink of death, Hanako wrote a poem about the gardener and the old woman, folded it into a paper crane, and sent it flying down to them. The gardener recognized the handwriting, and the reunion of the three—mother, daughter, and husband—was joyous. Hanako had folded a thousand paper cranes for a wish to see her husband and mother one more time. Together they went to the church to present the thousand cranes to the Christ Child for the baby Hanako would never have.

This is not only an inspirational piece but also one indicative of Japanese traditional family devotion, as well as Christian forgiveness. The destruction of nuclear war and the paper cranes, a symbol of life, are woven into the tale. Black-and-white graphite drawings are quietly well done, but they decorate rather than enhance the story.

Morimoto, Junko. ***My Hiroshima.***
See entry 886, Grades PS–3.

Neff, Fred. ***Lessons from the Samurai: Ancient Self-Defense Strategies and Techniques.***
See entry 930, Grades 7–9.

908 Patent, Gregory. ***Shanghai Passage.*** Illus. by Ted Lewin. Clarion 1990, HB $13.95 (0-89919-743-4). 115pp. Fiction.

It takes a while to figure out who the characters are and what is going on in this book. The first person turns out to be a young boy of mixed parentage. His mother is Iraqi; his father, Russian. He was born in Britain and is living in Shanghai along with his extended families on both sides. No reason is given for both families' having immigrated to China. We might guess it was to escape persecution.

The language does not flow as it might for a professional writer, and transitions between passages and ideas are sometimes less than graceful. Nonetheless, the story is interesting. We find out something about China and its position during the war, and we learn what it was like to be a young foreign boy living in Shanghai in the 1940s. Most of the political happenings are presented as seen through the innocent and often uncomprehending eyes of the young boy, leaving us often as confused as he must have been as to exactly what was going on in China. Nonetheless, it is interesting to have this "You were there" personal involvement in such events as Chiang Kai-shek's triumph and downfall, Mao Tse-tung's success as a political hero, and the Communist domination of Shanghai.

The black-and-white ink illustrations are more of a "general scene" nature than they are specific to the story, except in a few cases. Though well done and revealing of life in China, they appear to be too general to help a child enter into the story.

Paterson, Katherine. **The Tale of the Mandarin Ducks.**
See entry 887, Grades PS–3.

909   Pitkanen, Matti A., and Reijo Harkonen. **The Children of China.** Illus. with photos by Matti A. Pitkanen. SERIES: The World's Children. Lerner/Carolrhoda 1990, LB $14.95 (0-87614-394-X). 40pp. Nonfiction.

This book is an example of a new series entitled The World's Children. Each book takes us through the daily routine in the life of children living in a certain country. The descriptions are applicable to the society as a whole as well as specific to the children and their families; thus they are filled with details that would be of interest to youngsters, allowing them to compare the facets of their own lives with those of children living a much different life-style. Color photos lavishly illustrate the geography as well as the people and their lives. History and geography are presented briefly, interlaced with the general descriptions, not under headings of their own. The outlying province of Tibet is given attention in the last few pages, also with color photo portraits of people and views of Lhasa.

910   Sadler, Catherine Edwards. **Two Chinese Families.** Illus. with photos by Alan Sadler. Atheneum 1981, LB $9.95 (0-689-30865-5). 70pp. Nonfiction.

Slightly odd romanizations of the two family names are the only apparent problems in this little book. Wider than it is tall, every other page sports a full black-and-white photo with a couple of paragraphs of text on the facing page. Intriguing photos are candid and give us a feeling of being right there with the individuals in these two families as they go through their day-to-day lives. Often the children are a focus, but there are also some adult-oriented photos. Geared to elementary school youngsters, this work is good for presenting lots of detail of family life in Guilin, a small town in southern China.

Say, Allen. **The Bicycle Man.**
See entry 890, Grades PS–3.

911   Say, Allen. **The Feast of Lanterns.** HarperCollins 1976. 57pp. Fiction. o.p.

Bozu and Kozo are not running away from home. They love their little fishing village and their little island just off Japan. From there they can see the mainland, hear the train, watch it snaking along the coast, and long to ride it someday and be part of its magic. But they have never been to the mainland. Uncle Toji goes over there and comes back with stories about that "better place." Father will take them "someday" but not soon enough. So they take a small boat and set out to explore that "better place" for themselves.

The place they find is as foreign to them as it is to readers here. Seeing it through their eyes, we realize that half of what is foreign to the children in the story is simply what is modern, like the dragon of a train, but the other half is unfamiliar also to us—the Japanese celebration of the Feast of Lanterns, the hawkers, the congestion, the sights and sounds of even so small a city. The older boy explains to the younger, and also to readers, about various aspects of both modernity and traditional Japan that he has heard from his uncle. The two small boys are both impish and innocently delightful as they ponder how to get something to eat without money, how to make friends with a group of clowns, what to do with a self-appointed pet monkey, how to avoid bullies and policemen, and how to get back home. We share with father and boys their unbridled joy when they find each other—even amid fires, fireworks, and festivities.

The comic line drawings and the text descriptions of Japanese daily life and the Feast of Lanterns are as enticing as the glimpse into the lives of these two unspoiled island boys. The book is as useful for its cultural information as for its insight into the minds of small children.

912   Schlein, Miriam. ***The Year of the Panda.*** Illus. by Kam Mak. HarperCollins 1990, LB $12.89 (0-690-04866-1). 83pp. Fiction.

In view of the status of the panda as an endangered species particular to China, this story is an attempt to familiarize people with the problems it faces in its natural habitat. Every 60 years the type of bamboo it feeds upon dies out, and it must come down from the mountains in search of food. This was not so great a problem in centuries past, but now, with the expansion of the human population, it finds farms and villages instead of bamboo. The government asks farmers at some elevations to evacuate so that the land can return to the wild, aiding the starving pandas, who normally eat only bamboo. Resistance is bound to be met, but the Chinese themselves are familiar with famine and, in this story, eventually empathize.

The story is told through the eyes of a young boy, Lu Yi, who finds a baby panda during one of the species' 60-year migrations and keeps it to raise. His tender care of his pet and the understanding of the government workers who help him to ease it back into wildlife via a government-operated Panda Rescue Center gently assure us that China has the situation under control. We also see the isolated life and traditional attitudes in back-country Chinese farming villages and their own movement into the twentieth century, represented by Lu Yi's leaving the farm to study to become "a scientist who works with animals." He is encouraged in this aim by the very workers who run the Panda Rescue Center. Large print and short chapters give this book special appeal to a mid-elementary school level, but those of all ages will read with interest this story of a boy and his panda.

913   Shui, Amy, and Stuart Thompson. ***Chinese Food and Drink.*** Illus. with photos and drawings. SERIES: Food and Drink. Franklin Watts 1987, LB $11.90 (0-531-18129-4). 48pp. Nonfiction.

Although this book is on cuisine and does provide several typical recipes, it is not primarily a recipe book. Preliminary sections discuss China's history and people and the differences between various regions, pointing out the many minority groups (one featured on the cover) that live primarily in Western China. The following sections present food in history, cultivation, processing and preserving, markets, meals, and family etiquette. Chinese medicine and related beliefs concerning food are briefly but interestingly introduced. Kitchen tools and exhortations for safety are discussed, as is the variety of restaurants and customs connected with eating out and with tea, soup, alcohol, and special food for festivals. All sections are brief and simplified but presented in a manner interesting enough to satisfy initial curiosity and to pique further interest for delving into these many subjects in greater depth. A glossary, bibliography, and index are included.

914   Talan, Sally, and Rhoda Sherwood. *China.* Illus. with photos by Yasuhiko Miyazima. SERIES: Children of the World. Gareth Stevens 1988, LB $12.50 (1-55532-207-7). 64pp. Nonfiction.

In this series volume, we follow an 11-year-old Chinese girl and her parents through their day, through their city, to school, to work, to festivals, and to visit other places, discussing the roles of religion, communism, and daily life and mores. The color photos are child centered and pull us into the world described. A few minor faults and inaccuracies with this series in general and with this title in particular make us wonder how well researched they are. To cite only two examples from the several here, the girl's name, Chunz, does not sound Chinese. Probably it is meant to be in two syllables: Chun Zi, meaning spring. Also, the term Peking is the Taishanese pronunciation of the capital, not a Western approximation of Beijing. Many Chinese immigrants to this country were Taishanese, so it is natural that we should be familiar with their pronunciation of the names in their homeland. Still, the use of this form is very much out of date.

The usual 14 pages at the end provide the teacher with the country's background information and data in great variety. Research projects and further activities also add interest to an already interesting book. There are a map and an index.

Tang, Yungmei. *China, Here We Come! Visiting the People's Republic of China.* See entry 935, Grades 7–9.

915   Timpanelli, Gioia. *Tales from the Roof of the World: Folktales of Tibet.* Illus. by Elizabeth Kelly Lockwood. Viking 1984, HB $11.95 (0-670-71249-3). 53pp. Nonfiction.

Four unusual and uniquely Tibetan folktales—tales of karma and luck, magic and love, comeuppances and forgiveness—are presented with Buddhist symbols gracing the borders of each page. Notes at the end reveal the significance of these symbols. Tibetans have always been deeply religious, and both men and women make pilgrimages to Buddhist temples on top of mountains. Traveling slowly, the journey is twofold—inner and outer. An intriguing preface invites us not only to take the outward journey but also to look within at what these tales say to us and to take a journey inside ourselves as well.

916   Tung, S. T. *One Small Dog.* Illus. by Ted Lewin. Dodd, Mead 1975. 160pp. Fiction. o.p.

There have been many times in China's history when poverty, unrest, and famine have sent many into the streets begging, starving, and dying. In the mid 1950s, only a few years after Mao's rise to power, idealism was rampant, and everyone was determined to raise China's standard of living. In order to save food for the people, and also, by the way, to provide it, the government ordered that all dogs be killed. There were also campaigns to kill cats, flies, and sparrows, but in this book it is the dogs that are under fire, in particular, one little black dog named Lucky. His owner, a young boy named Sung, is determined to save him. A few incidents with soldiers' hunting of dogs, dog meat for sale in the market-place, and large posters everywhere proclaiming the undesirability of dogs in society are enough to convince Sung that he must travel with his uncle to the South with a herd of pigs, taking Lucky along in order to leave him with someone who would care for him in Hong Kong.

Finally his mother agrees, giving Sung her silver hairpin to sell in dire need, the only item of value left in the household. Many ordeals and adventures befall Sung and his uncle en route, all common enough for those who must live in the streets. Thieves steal a few pigs, a few fights start, and at one point Sung must sell his only shirt to pay for something to fill his stomach. Worse, Lucky is stolen. Sung finds him in the hands of a one-man traveling circus act. His uncle convinces him Lucky is safer and happier there than loose on the streets of Hong Kong, though Sung still has to struggle with his feelings of longing for the dog. On his return home, he finds Mao's Great Leap Forward under way. People are turned out of their homes so that everyone will live equally in communes and farm and do work communally. Sung finds his mother working in one place and his father sent off to another city. Not only is this book the compelling story of a boy and his dog, but it also provides readers with a simple version of what was happening in China in the 1950s, presented in terms comprehensible to a child. The author's opposition to Mao's policies is clear, and his passion drives the story; nonetheless, plot and character development are not sacrificed. Black-and-white line drawings add flavor to this interesting and thought-provoking book.

We Live in China.
See entry 938, Grades 7–9.

Winthrop, Elizabeth. **Journey to the Bright Kingdom.**
See entry 899, Grades PS–3.

GRADES 7–9

917   Bell, William. **Forbidden City: A Novel of Modern China.** Bantam 1990, HB $14.95 (0-553-07131-9); Bantam 1990, P $3.50 (0-553-28864-4). 208pp. Fiction.

Seventeen-year-old Alex Jackson is a history buff, with a special interest in China. When his father, a cameraman for the Canadian Broadcasting Corpora-tion, is unexpectedly sent to China, Alex jumps at the chance to go along. It is March 1989, and trouble is brewing. Alex begins to learn Chinese and obtains a secondhand bicycle to tour Beijing on his own. He also befriends the journalists' interpreter and guide, Lao Xu. Xu allegedly spies for the government, but Alex enjoys his company anyway. Over the next two months, Alex witnesses the students' hunger strike and the massive demonstrations in Tienanmen Square in support of democracy. He meets several pro-democracy students, one of whom saves his life (and dies in the process) during the massacre. Alex also witnesses the death of Lao Xu, who cannot believe his beloved People's Liberation Army would turn its guns on the people; Xu dies begging the soldiers not to shoot the students. Alex escapes with videos and photos of the slaughter as well as with nightmares that haunt him long after his return home.

Bell's novel is based upon first-hand accounts of the demonstrations and the massacre. Alex's voice is authentic, as is his limited understanding of and perspective upon the events. We learn little of the Chinese students themselves, their goals, or the process by which the protests developed. On the other hand, the official response, including Lao Xu's change of heart, is more developed, as it would be when viewed from the lens of foreign journalists who do not know Chinese. Although most of the minor characters are portrayed sketchily, Alex is a full and compelling individual. His first-person narrative will draw readers in, and the suspenseful, fast-paced plot will keep them turning the pages. While readers will get more complete information from a work of nonfiction, this novel successfully presents the emotions of a young outsider caught up in a tragic historical event. L.M-L.

918   Blumberg, Rhoda. *Commodore Perry in the Land of the Shogun.* Illus. Lothrop, Lee & Shepard 1985, LB $13.00 (0-688-03723-2). 144pp. Nonfiction.

Detailed and personalized, this rendition of Perry's opening of Japan reenacts the drama that began when Perry's black ships sailed into Shimoda harbor in 1853. Almost moment by moment we watch the unfolding of the mutual impressions of foreigners, the doubts, the curiosities, the fears, and the hopes that each side had in regard to the other. Reproductions of Japanese artists' portrayal of Americans fill the pages, as do black-and-white drawings, maps, historical photos, and woodcuts. At times amusing, at times thought provoking, this chronicle delights in revealing all the mistakes, faux pas, and cultural misconceptions rampant on both sides. If we have ever asked, with Robert Browning, "Would some god the giftie gie us to see ourselves as others see us," this delightful account also satisfies that longing.

Five appendixes detail letters and gifts from each side to the other and the treaty of Kanagawa. Detailed notes on chapters follow. The book includes a bibliography and an index.

919   Chang, Margaret, and Raymond Chang. *In the Eye of War.* Macmillan 1990, HB $13.95 (0-689-50503-5). 197pp. Fiction.

With World War II going on all around them, including the Japanese atrocities at Nan Jing and elsewhere, middle-class Chinese families living in Shanghai experienced an uneasy calm, as if they lived in the eye of a storm. There was enough to eat, and though they could hear bombing, they were never directly affected. The picture we are given in this loosely autobiographical novel is of such a family and of daily life as seen through the eyes of a young boy, Shao-Shao. His father is involved in resistance activities, but his own life revolves around candy, crickets, and kung fu novels. The people next door are Japanese sympathizers, but their little girl is his friend, and he winces as a mob of boys, of which he is, inexplicably, a part, throws mudballs and turnips at her house. Later, conflict arises between him and his father when he captures and shelters a bird. His father appears harsh in punishing him and demanding the bird be freed, and Shao-Shao wishes he had his girlfriend's father, who is far more sympathetic to his plight. This contrast between the fathers, symbolic of their political allegiances, provides much food for thought, as does the protagonist's own concerns and actions during these troubled times. The Changs' portrayal is vivid and realistically rendered, giving readers of older elementary and middle school age a clear sense of very ordinary lives in extraordinary times.

920 De Lee, Nigel. ***Rise of the Asian Superpowers: From 1945.*** Photos by Stefor Chubluh. SERIES: Conflict in the 20th Century. Franklin Watts 1987, LB $12.90 (0-531-10407-9). 62pp. Nonfiction.

In a newspaper reporting style, with maps and photos and charts of the movements of armies, the book covers recent upheavals in South Asian and East Asian countries. The Maoist revolution in China—beginning with the fall of the Ching Dynasty in 1911 and proceeding through Japan's occupation of China and the Chinese war in Korea, Mao's Long March, the Great Leap Forward, and the cultural revolution—covers half the book. Reconstruction in postwar Japan and religious and political wars on the Indian subcontinent cover the other half. Lengthy appendixes present key personalities, various war tactics used by the Chinese, details of violence in India by group, a comparison of the Indian army and the Pakistani army, and a chronology from 1921 to 1984. Includes an index and a bibliography.

Els, Betty Vander. ***The Bombers' Moon.***
See entry 902, Grades 4–6.

921 Els, Betty Vander. ***Leaving Point.*** Farrar, Straus & Giroux 1987, HB $12.95 (0-374-34376-4). 212pp. Fiction.

This book continues the story of Ruth and Simeon, children of missionary parents in China. The writing in this title is considerably improved. The crux of the story is Ruth's forbidden friendship with a slightly older Chinese girl, Chuin Mei, who is caught up in the vehemence and idealism of the politics surrounding the Communist party's dominance of China in 1949. The friendship is forbidden on both sides. The Chinese, who refer to the missionaries as political spies and American robbers, out of their fear of foreign influence, forbid all interaction between Chinese and foreigners. Ruthie's parents, for fear that Chuin Mei might be an informer and could jeopardize their chances of leaving, consider the friendship an unnecessary risk.

The Chinese, in times of such turmoil, have been known to execute foreigners, or anyone else who draws their anger or suspicion, rather than permit them to leave the country. Politics and daily life both turn topsy-turvy, and no one knows where truth lies. Mr. Hilary, the children's teacher, says, ". . . the revolution will be brutal ... dislocating China from its ancient enduring past and thrusting it into the modern industrial present. And probably we're the scapegoats for some of the humiliations the West has heaped on China." But it is Chuin Mei who facilitates their final leaving, who "bravely warns us behind the disguise of harsh criticism," and though Ruth clarifies for young readers much of the ambiguity of the Chinese revolution, she leaves behind many mysteries and questions of her own. This is a gripping story, one that skillfully combines issues of growing up with real and significant conflicts in the world outside.

Eunson, Roby. *The Soong Sisters.*
See entry 943, Grades 10–12.

922 Farley, Carol. *Korea: A Land Divided.* Illus. with photos. SERIES: Discovering Our Heritage. Dillon 1983, HB $10.95 (0-87518-244-5). 143pp. Nonfiction.

This is a general-purpose introduction to Korean culture. It uses relatively large print and is aimed at readers at older elementary and middle school levels. The chapters present a simple history, discussing the division between North and South as one might honestly discuss a divorce with a child. Interesting tidbits about language, religion, holidays, and leisure activities fill the book. The chapter on home life presents several Korean recipes. Another recapitulates a few basic folktales. There is a final chapter on Korean Americans and problems earlier this century that affected all Asians in America. Both black-and-white and color photos intrigue and complement. An appendix lists Korean consulates in Canada and the United States. Two pages in front give fast facts. Also included are maps, a glossary, a bibliography, and an index.

923 Friese, Kai. *Tenzin Gyatso, the Dalai Lama.* SERIES: World Leaders, Past and Present. Chelsea House 1989, LB $17.95 (1-55546-836-5); 1990, P $9.95 (0-7910-0676-X). 111pp. Nonfiction.

Written interestingly enough to appeal to nearly any age group, this book is full of little-known information about the Dalai Lama, the origins of the office with the Mongols, the mystic and state-upholding search for each new one, the exile of the present one to India, and the persecution by the Chinese of the Tibetans in this century. Tenzin Gyatso, the present Dalai Lama, whose writings have already received worldwide attention, has set up a little Tibet in India in order to preserve the language, the customs, and the Tibetan religion of Lamaism. He has tremendous support among his people, both in India and in Tibet, where people come out by the thousands to view and pay homage to his brothers. India, wanting to stay on the good side of China, is caught in the middle, allowing him to stay, but not doing much overtly to help.

The book's unassuming black-and-white photographs, including many historical ones, aid in giving a graphic impression both of the gentle and imposing figure of the Dalai Lama, who now stands as an international symbol of peace, and of his people, the hardy Tibetans. Quotes in the margins and extensive comments with each photograph help to summarize and hold together the history. A list for further reading, a chronology, and an index are provided at the end. Other books in this excellent series present Deng Xiaoping, Hirohito, Kim il-Sung, Mao Zedong, Zhou Enlai, Chiang Kai-shek, Genghis Khan, Kublai Khan, and Sun Yat-sen.

924 Fritz, Jean. *China Homecoming.* Illus. with photos by Michael Fritz. Putnam 1985, HB $12.95 (0-399-21182-9). 143pp. Nonfiction.

Who says you "can't go home again"? Mixed in with nostalgic personal remembrances of her own childhood in China, Jean Fritz gives us anecdotes and explanations of the whys and wherefores of China itself: the history, the stories of emperors, the mysteries of the Forbidden City, and a picture of Mao Zedong and his reasons for the Cultural Revolution.

Returning to China "not just to recognize, but to find out" after 55 years of absence, Fritz's impressionistic descriptions of the country are of the sights that any Westerner might be impressed with, but are laced so delicately with her feelings of tender and powerful attachment to her birthplace—Wuhan on the Yangtse River. Her admiration of the length of Chinese history comes forth again and again; every time she mentions it, we learn a little something more about what makes China tick. Descriptions of the nationwide "chain" of youth-leisure-time recreation and art centers called Cultural Palaces as well as visits to Chinese schools and special schools like the Foreign Language Middle (High) School will appeal to young readers. In addition, the author describes the difficulties of life in modern China, including the plight of some young couples who must live in different cities because they are not allowed to change jobs, and people in their 30s who missed their education due to the cultural revolution. She visits communes where the peasants' lives have become as organized hierarchically as those of the city people and the 2,400-year-old temple of the Marquis Yi, who had buried with him everything he would need in his next life, including 21 young women to play music for him, his little pet dog, and two well-stocked picnic baskets.

But it is her discovery of the very house she lived in as a child and her warm welcome by its present inhabitants that will touch everyone who reads this book. Old feelings come flooding back as she visits her old school and discovers she can still be angry at a classmate. The old church has become an acrobatic school. The graveyard where her baby sister is buried has become a children's playground, the old foreign gravestones having been turned into park benches upon which tired grandmothers now rest.

Several pages of notes, a chronology of Chinese history, and an intriguing and useful bibliography are included in this informative and heartwarming book.

925   Fritz, Jean. ***China's Long March: 6,000 Miles of Danger.*** Illus. by Yang Zhr Cheng. Putnam 1988, HB $14.95 (0-399-21512-3). 124pp. Nonfiction.

Full of humor and empathy, these anecdotes, gleaned from conversations with the survivors of the Long March, are put together so well that they all read as one story. Although the book reads like fiction, the stories are all real. Maps accompany the vignettes, which proceed in chronological order, creating the effect of a single tale with many heroes. The yearlong trek of the Red Army from Southeastern China to the west and then north was to join other factions and to escape the Nationalist forces. Along the way the marchers spread among the peasants their passion, their hopes for a new China, and their determination to maintain the Red Army. Gathering supporters and participants as they went, they finally reached Bao An, where they were able to make successful plans to kidnap Chiang Kai-shek and to turn the tide of the civil war in their own favor. A chapter at the end discusses Mao's intentions (and mistakes) in initiating the cultural revolution two decades later. Black ink paintings capture the spirit of the march. Notes, a bibliography, and an index are included.

Fritz, Jean. ***Homesick: My Own Story.***
See entry 903, Grades 4-6.

926 Haugaard, Erik Christian. *The Samurai's Tale.* Houghton Mifflin 1984, HB $12.95 (0-395-34559-6). 234pp. Fiction.

Japan of the sixteenth century was in a turbulent time of unrest and struggle for power known as the Period of the Civil Wars. In this novel readers do not learn the overall history or see what came before (Muromachi era) nor glimpse what came after (Edo era), but they do see the ruthlessness of various factions battling to exterminate not only enemy generals but also their entire families. No one was safe. Into this period Taro was born. His samurai father was killed in battle. Therefore his whole family was killed soon after, but the small boy was spared and went to live in the house of an enemy samurai. His lord became the object of his admiration and he desired nothing more than to emulate him, work his way up in station to become a samurai like his father, and serve his lord, all of which he accomplishes, and more. The tale ends with a battle that removes horribly most of the main characters, including his lord, from the story.

A suggestion of a love story is made toward the end and makes the novel more widely appealing. The author seems to imply that there will be a forthcoming sequel to this story in which we will see the young samurai married to his lady and continuing his battle. Throughout we see the nobility of the samurai and the code of honor between enemies and friends alike. Despite the lack of background and context, the teenage reader is easily drawn into this tale and kept turning the pages until its cataclysmic end. This may be an excellent choice for more able reluctant readers, and it may pique their curiosity about Japanese history and cultural traditions as well.

927 Kalman, Bobbie. *Japan: The Land.* Illus. with photos. SERIES: Lands, Peoples, and Culture. Crabtree 1989, LB $14.95 (0-86505-204-2); P $7.95 (0-86505-284-0). 32pp. Nonfiction.

Each country in this series is represented by three separate books: one for the Lands, one for Peoples, and one for Cultures. Contained within each are mostly beautiful color photos and some drawings. The Culture book is useful for program ideas. There is a lot of detail in brief paragraphs, each devoted to another aspect of life, history, culture, or art. The selection and clarity of the photographs are high points. Includes glossary and index.

928 Lye, Keith. *Inside China.* Illus. with photos. SERIES: Inside. Franklin Watts 1989, LB $11.40 (0-531-10833-3). 32pp. Nonfiction.

Many large color photos, both of the geography and of the people, complement sections in relatively large-print text discussing a variety of subjects ranging from history to the arts, from farming to industry, and from family life to food. Presentations of changes from the pre-Communist era through Mao Tse-tung's revolutionary policies and modern developments help to make the book interesting. Maps, a page of facts, and an index add to its usefulness. Though mostly adult in its point of view, it is more likely to appeal to a wide range of children and grade levels than other series for the middle school level. Though the reading level is fairly high, the large pictures and large print will appeal to younger children and reluctant readers. This series also includes coverage of Japan.

Major, John S. *The Land and People of Mongolia.*
See entry 945, Grades 10–12.

519
GRADES 7-9

929 Namioka, Lensey. *Island of Ogres.* HarperCollins 1989, LB $13.89 (0-06-024373-2). 197pp. Fiction.

A samurai novel set in sixteenth-century Japan has great possibilities for making Japanese history come alive for young people, but this one emphasizes more the feistiness of teenagers and their courtship battles. This is a tale of intrigue, of spies and struggles for power, of convenient marriages, and of a crazy old daimyo lord in exile on an island. Some clever turns of events contribute to a gripping plot, although the writing is inexact. Woven together we find mistaken identity, a couple of budding love affairs, a mighty suspicious nunnery, traitors within the ranks of the trusted, and a masquerade of ogres that the naive villagers and even the readers are not quite sure whether or not to believe in until the end.

With a few changes, the setting could be ancient Greece or modern Nicaragua. The plot is more important than the Japaneseness, but the plot is good and will hold interest. It is a Japanese Gothic novel for young teens.

Lensey Namioka has written other swashbuckling tales of the wild East such as *The Samurai and the Long-Nosed Devils, Valley of the Broken Cherry Trees, Village of the Vampire Cat,* and *White Serpent Castle.*

930 Neff, Fred. *Lessons from the Samurai: Ancient Self-Defense Strategies and Techniques.* Illus. with photos by Bob Wolfe. Lerner 1987, LB $9.95 (0-8225-1161-4); P $4.95 (0-8225-9531-1). 112pp. Nonfiction.

More than just another how-to-do-it karate book, although there is certainly that element as well, this book delves into the history and philosophy behind the art. The emphasis is on discipline, persistence, and redirecting energy from worry into action. Not a bad philosophy for some of the rest of us as well! Carefully examined movements and paragraphs on types of advances, throws, and escapes complement the descriptions of the specific techniques. Conditioning the body, using the mind, and incorporating safety features are all important aspects of this learning. This is a wonderful source for adding depth to your karate fanatics. Includes index.

Patent, Gregory. *Shanghai Passage.*
See entry 908, Grades 4–6.

931 Rau, Margaret. *Holding Up the Sky: Young People in China.* Illus. with photos. Dutton/Lodestar 1983, HB $12.50 (0-525-66718-0). 136pp. Nonfiction.

Under the auspices of discussing young people in China, a great deal of historical and cultural ground is covered, from the cultural revolution to factory concern for air pollution. Each chapter presents a different young person going about daily life and gives a detailed description of various jobs and the national concerns represented there. Weddings, the Tang Shan earthquake, life in remote areas, visits to national historic sites, and several minority cultures are each personalized through the eyes of a teenager or young adult. Black-and-white photos complement the narratives. By the time one finishes the book, one has met many young people and through their understandings of their country has absorbed a good deal of cultural detail.

932   Rau, Margaret. ***The Minority Peoples of China.*** Julian Messner 1982, LB $9.95 (0-671-41545-X). 128pp. Nonfiction.

Ranging from Tibet and Chinese Turkestan, now called Xin Jiang, and the desert land of Turfan (the second-lowest place in the world), across to Mongolia and down to the southwestern cultures, which resemble the minorities of Indochina and include other religious groups such as the Muslims, this book gives us a personal picture of what life is like for a young person in each culture. Details of games, clothing, food, courtship, joys, and sadnesses are mixed with just enough history to whet the palate and to give us a well-rounded picture of many of the non-Han peoples who live in China. (The Han are the historical Chinese majority people.)

The black-and-white photos are less than inviting, but the lively, easy-to-read text draws us into the cultures for which, then, the photos are somewhat helpful.

Shui, Amy, and Stuart Thompson. ***Chinese Food and Drink.***
See entry 913, Grades 4–6.

933   Stefoff, Rebecca. ***Mongolia.*** SERIES: Let's Visit Places and Peoples of the World. Chelsea House 1986, HB $11.95 (1-55546-153-0). 96pp. Nonfiction.

Emphasizing the transition from the ancient and traditional ways of life to the modern infiltration of Western civilization in the form of skyscrapers, large apartment complexes, and city life, this book presents a readable account of the history, culture, life-style, and economics of Mongolia. Stefoff focuses on the wide-open land of ever blue skies, home to the nomadic shepherds, to Genghis Khan, who led his armies over most of Asia, and to all the other khans who continually threatened the northern borders of China. A brief mention is made of communism, but only a scant attempt is made to discuss Mongolia's relations with its two powerful neighbors, Russia and China, between whom it lies sandwiched and by whom it has historically been disputed. The illustrations are both black-and-white and color photos, some unusual and interesting, others uninspiring. Index. China, Japan, North Korea, South Korea, and Taiwan are also part of this series.

934   Tames, Richard. ***Japan: The Land and Its People.*** Rev. ed. Illus. with photos. SERIES: Countries. Silver Burdett 1986, LB $15.96 (0-382-09256-2); P $6.95 (0-382-09463-8). 47pp. Nonfiction.

A great variety of subjects and detailed information are packed in tiny print into this high and wide but very thin volume. Each section (one per double page) is accompanied by many large color photos, drawings, charts, or maps, so that the effect of the whole is one of isolated comments and captions. Sections include several on history, festivals, industry, shopping, family life, cooking, schools, nature, theater, resorts, and sports. The format makes for fascinating browsing as well as a good resource. Includes gazetteer, index, and maps. There is also a volume on China in this series.

935 Tang, Yungmei. *China, Here We Come! Visiting the People's Republic of China.* Illus. with photos. Putnam 1981, HB $9.95 (0-399-20826-7). 64pp. Nonfiction.

Thirteen-year-old American students go to visit China, having earned their own money and having been sponsored by their parents. They meet Chinese young people, learn songs, trade cultural items, visit schools and communes, parks, and national historic sites, keep individual diaries, and take photos. The text is told in the first-person plural and is full of their personal thoughts and actions. The black-and-white photos give readers an idea both of China and of the delight of this group in being there. Wonderfully provocative for ideas and issues within readers' own group, it might encourage students and teachers elsewhere to organize a similar trip.

Timpanelli, Gioia. *Tales from the Roof of the World: Folktales of Tibet.*
See entry 915, Grades 4–6.

Tung, S. T. *One Small Dog.*
See entry 916, Grades 4–6.

936 Walker, Richard L. *Ancient Japan and Its Influence in Modern Times.* Illus. with photos. Franklin Watts 1975. 86pp. Nonfiction. o.p.

Chapters of scholarly, descriptive essays highlighted with striking black-and-white photographs give insight into the history of Japan. Enmeshed in these historical chapters are art, religion, literature, and the elements comprising traditional Japanese life. A relatively short book, its small print and high reading level make it suitable for background and interest reading at the high school level. A chronology, bibliography, and index are included.

937 Watkins, Yoko Kawashima. *So Far from the Bamboo Grove.* Lothrop, Lee & Shepard 1986, HB $10.25 (0-688-06110-9). 183pp. Fiction.

A story all the more haunting because it is based on truth, this is the exorcising of the terror of events that World War II in Korea became for a little Japanese girl. Her family lived in northern Korea, and her father worked as a Japanese official just across the border in Manchuria. This did not endear them to the Koreans when war broke out and Japan invaded Korea. The girl and her family had to leave to save their lives. They were to have taken a train in the middle of the night, but they missed it and walked most of the length of Korea, all the while evading Korean soldiers. They were shot at from all sides, hiding, hungry, and constantly terrified of being attacked and abused by the angry Korean soldiers. Always they left messages carved on walls in train stations where her older brother might find them, messages telling him where they had gone next. Her mother did not survive the ordeal, but the girl and her sister were eventually reunited with their brother. She now lives in the United States with her own family.

Details of her story are vividly rendered. Among the most memorable are the pain of being wounded, the constant search through garbage for food, and posing as boys so as not to be molested as girls. Also coming through are the family members' devotion to each other and the level of courage they had to maintain in order to stay alive. All of these loom up like scenes from a nightmare that need to be shown over and over again before they can be truly understood, long after the book is closed. This is a personal, vivid, and unforgettable rendering of a historical era and what it means to be a refugee.

938 *We Live in China.* Illus. with photos. SERIES: Living Here. Franklin Watts 1984, LB $12.95 (0-531-04779-2). 64pp. Nonfiction.

More than two dozen people (one per double-page spread) in a great variety of professions from ivory carver to opera teacher and from bus driver to zookeeper tell about their jobs and their lives, what they think, and what life is like for them in the People's Republic of China. As is usual in this series, controversial issues are avoided. Color photos, not particularly inspiring but at least informative, complement the interesting text. Both photos and text are aimed at an adult interest level, though the reading level is appropriate for upper elementary grades. A page of facts, a glossary, and an index help to make this book useful. An additional volume presents interviews with citizens of Japan.

939 Wolf, Bernard. *In the Year of the Tiger.* Illus. with photos by the author. Macmillan 1988, HB $14.95 (0-02-793390-3). 124pp. Nonfiction.

Close personal detail in the text and in the striking black-and-white photographs gives the reader a lasting impression of both the unending sameness and the startling changes in way of life in a tiny 1,000-year-old village of south China. It is a farming village. We watch individual families at their meals, at their work, fixing machinery, at the market, and with children, and we see a wedding ceremony, all in graphic detail, which makes us feel as though we were there. The text discusses the continuity of the past 1,000 years and also the newness brought in by the Communists. We hear comments from the villagers about various aspects of their lives. The book was written and photographed by Bernard Wolf, a photojournalist who lived for three months in this village with its people. The result is an attractive, very personal work that will make a small place in China real for middle- and high-school-age readers.

940 Yep, Laurence. *Mountain Light.* HarperCollins 1985, LB $11.95 (0-06-026759-3). 282pp. Fiction.

Continuing Yep's saga begun in *The Serpent's Children*, Squeaky Lau, a young man in China around the turn of the century, determines to join the "noble" revolution against the Manchu Dynasty and is disappointed to find only flea-bitten, quarreling looters. He teams up with a spunky Cassia, who hails from a family in a nearby village, which is feuding with his own. Underconfident at first, Squeaky longs to prove himself manly and brave. His method of fighting Manchus, feuders, and even friends is with humor. He is a comic and an acrobat. Cassia is uncompromisingly serious and devoted to the revolution. Sometimes one tactic works, sometimes the other. Learning from each other how to joke and how to be serious, they struggle against the unreasonable and fearful mob in the forms of Manchu soldiers, farm communities, and, finally, for Squeaky alone on his journey to the United States, the gold seekers in California. Along with the immigrants from China small family feuds are also transferring to the United States and reigniting in the new land.

Laurence Yep has written a handful of other novels about Chinese young people, both in China and in the United States, beginning with *Dragonwings* and

Child of the Owl. He has also written some fantasy based partly on Chinese mythology and legend. Like his other works, this action-filled adventure will appeal to teenage readers and give them a sense of China's history in the previous century.

GRADES 10–12

941   *All Japan: The Catalogue of Everything Japanese.* Morrow 1984, P $14.95 (0-688-02530-7). 224pp. Nonfiction.

Greatly informative, finely researched, scholarly, and beautifully written essays characterize this unassuming reference work, which is ideal for the student researcher as well as for teachers. Wonderfully aesthetic color photos adorn each double-page-spread essay. Pertinent lists in boxes also make this an invaluable research item. Not for younger children, this book is indispensable to acquiring a solid background in the fine art of Japanese daily living for anyone aspiring to understand or to explain Japan to children. Essays range from poetry to photography, gardens to garnishes, calligraphy to clothing, and music to medicine. The book contains a bibliography, an 11-page source list, and an index.

Bell, William. *Forbidden City: A Novel of Modern China.*
See entry 917, Grades 7–9.

Blumberg, Rhoda. *Commodore Perry in the Land of the Shogun.*
See entry 918, Grades 7–9.

942   Covell, Jon Carter. *Korea's Cultural Roots.* Illus. with photos and drawings. Hollym International 1982, HB $18.95 (0-930878-32-9). 132pp. Nonfiction.

Bases of shamanism hailing from the entire Altaic arc across Asia still provide a foundation for Korean art, culture, symbolism, religion, and tradition. A discussion of these traditions forms the basis for the first part of this book. The second part traces the influences of Buddhism, and the third, neo-Confucian vestiges. The book is a good source for answering detailed questions such as "Why does the Buddha hold his hands in that position?" as well as providing a broader background.

Margin notes and illustrations enhance the text, and full-page drawings and photographs, in both color and black and white, add greatly to the interest of this book. Although concentrating on the religious roots, the book is also a good source for information on literature, calligraphy, painting, poetry, and history. Includes index.

Els, Betty Vander. *Leaving Point.*
See entry 921, Grades 7–9.

943   Eunson, Roby. *The Soong Sisters.* Illus. with photos. Franklin Watts 1975. 136pp. Nonfiction. o.p.

Can one person change the flow of history? Certainly the history of China in this century would be different if Charlie Soong's three beautiful and talented daughters had not lived. All three were educated in the United States during an era when it was not considered advantageous for a woman to be either educated or exposed to radical Western ideas. Eling, the businesswoman, married H. H. Kung, the international business tycoon. Ching-ling, serious and shy and devoted to her ideals, which became those of the common people of China, became Madame Sun Yat-sen. May-ling, who usually got what she wanted, became Madame Chiang Kai-shek and worked beside her husband all her life politically and socially, unwilling to retire to a life of tea parties. All three generously devoted their time, energy, money, and most of their lives to orphanages, hospitals, and the liberation of China's women, to say nothing of personally stepping in to help and even to rescue their husbands in time of need. This book parallels the more ambitious *Soong Dynasty*, written for adult readers, and includes a good bibliography for further reading. Entertaining as well as eye-opening, this book offers insights into the changing status of women in China and is a personal political history of China in this century.

Friese, Kai. ***Tenzin Gyatso, the Dalai Lama.***
See entry 923, Grades 7–9.

Fritz, Jean. ***China's Long March: 6,000 Miles of Danger.***
See entry 925, Grades 7–9.

Haugaard, Erik Christian. ***The Samurai's Tale.***
See entry 926, Grades 7–9.

944 Lee, C. Y. ***The Second Son of Heaven: A Novel of Nineteenth Century China.***
William Morrow 1990, HB $19.95 (0-688-05140-5). 340pp. Fiction.

The first part of this book reveals all the little details of peasant farm life in China of the last century, complete with turns of phrase translated roughly into English, rural beliefs and superstitions, and old wives' tales. Among them are courtship customs, auspicious omens at birth, the communal forces holding a village together, and the particulars of meat and drink, which were then just as colorful as they are now. All of these are viewed through the perspective of the son of a poor farmer whose village believes him destined to be an emperor and who hopes to pass the imperial exams and become at least an official.

Though this is essentially an adult novel, the characters begin the story as children. We follow them briefly struggling through adolescence and really get to know them as young adults, lively and passionate (explicitly) and in their 20s. Still, this novel could hold the interest of a sophisticated high school student.

We follow not only the details of the life of this young man, Hung Shiu-Ch'uan, but also the bent of his thought, which we suppose must have been common among young Han men wanting to see the Manchu (Qing) Dynasty fall so that China could become Chinese again.

In this particular peasant uprising in the mid 1800s, opium brought in by foreigners was a direct cause, and many secret societies became organized against both the foreign imperialists and the Manchu government. The hero of this story is the man who proclaimed himself the second son of God and attempted, finally unsuccessfully, to overthrow the dynasty, leading the famous Taiping Rebellion. The bulk of the book contains anecdotes of war and intrigue, following Taiping leader Hung Shiu-Ch'uan and a complex network of major and minor characters. It is a long, thoughtful, and painstaking rendering of an uncomfortable story and one that successfully blends fact and fiction.

945 Major, John S. *The Land and People of Mongolia.* Illus. with photos. SERIES: Portraits of the Nations. HarperCollins 1990, LB $15.95 (0-397-32387-5). 200pp. Nonfiction.

This series book is stark and scholarly but readable, especially for someone already interested in the field. It is illustrated with black-and-white photos and drawings, some quite striking, although a touch of color might have made the book more appealing to a reluctant researcher. Special interest essays in boxes add to the appeal. Detailed and in-depth discussions focus on Mongolia's people, land, history, religion, arts, daily life in a variety of settings, and changes in this century. Following the text is an impressive, extensive chapter-by-chapter bibliography. Includes index. Major is also the author of *The Land and People of China* (1989), which was being revised at the time of publication to include information on the Tienanmen Square massacre.

946 Nahm, Andrew. *A Panorama of 5000 Years: Korean History.* Illus. Hollym International 1983, HB $19.95 (0-930878-23-X). 125pp. Nonfiction.

A straightforward history of Korea from its beginnings, with prehistoric archaeological artifacts up to modern times, this account is lavishly illustrated with color photos, maps and charts, drawings and paintings, historic photos, and art items from museums. Essentially a political history, it also includes comments on art, economy, religion, science, and language. Includes index.

947 *Pictorial Encyclopedia of Japanese Culture: The Soul and Heritage of Japan.* Trans. from Japanese by Richard De Lapp. Illus. with photos. Gakken Co., dist. by Kodansha International 1987, HB $29.95 (0-87040-752-X). 130pp. Nonfiction.

Profusely illustrated with color photos depicting religious and cultural artifacts and art items, the format of this encyclopedia is one topic per double-page spread. There is a wealth of information here, just enough to incite interest, but not in enough depth to provide a really encyclopedic grasp of each subject. Though not one of the better sources for student researchers, therefore, the book is still wonderful for browsing. Its arrangement is roughly chronological, a fact that is not immediately obvious. A 20-page section at the end in nonglossy pages provides information on personal attitudes, etiquette, and some statistics. A glossary of paragraph-long descriptions of cultural and historic items takes the place of an index.

948 Roberson, John R. *Japan: From Shogun to Sony, 1543-1984.* Illus. with photos. Atheneum 1985, HB $13.95 (0-689-31076-5). 198pp. Nonfiction.

The focus of the first half of this book is an excellent rendering of the opening of Japan. The book offers a glimpse of pre-Western Japan, and the first impressions that Portuguese traders made on Japan and the subsequent infatuation with "Dutch learning." A detailed political history takes us almost up to the present era. The second half of the book deals with the inner development of a strong Japan. When Japan became a major power in the Far East, there were many invasions and many clashes with foreign armies. When Hirohito became emperor, there were discussions about the place of the emperor in Japan.

The emphasis of the book is on politics and war and on the opening of Japan for trade, on the development of the economy, and on Japan's relations with both the Soviet Union and China. Effective details take us through the 1950s. A brief chapter at the end attempts to bring Japan into the modern world scene, but it does not mention how rich Japan has become, nor is much said about the lives of the people other than that they have to work hard to get ahead both in school and in work. The title, therefore, is somewhat misleading, for it promises a more recent history and analysis. A glossary at the beginning helps, and there are a good bibliography and an extensive index at the end.

Walker, Richard L. *Ancient Japan and Its Influence in Modern Times.*
See entry 936, Grades 7–9.

949   Wang, Anyi. *Baotown: A Novel.* Trans. by Martha Avery. Norton 1989, HB $17.95 (0-393-02711-2). 144pp. Fiction.

A novel of love and life, of birth and death, the story of this tiny village in the hinterlands of China is a microcosm of life anywhere and yet very specific to its time and place. It is set at the beginning of the cultural revolution, when Mao Zedong's Communist regime initiated radical measures to make a New China. The village is located on the floodplains near the Yellow River, which is notorious for its ravaging of the land. Life is a struggle there. The land is hard to work. People are poor. Traditions are strong and hard to break. But they do get broken. It is accepted that a woman must go and live in her husband's house and serve her mother-in-law, but Second Aunt takes a younger man into her home. He is called Picked-up because the woman who raised him picked him up somewhere in her travels north to find food in lean times. The town founder's youngest boy, Dregs, bonds with an old man who has lost his grandson, the last of his line, to tuberculosis. The two are inseparable and even die together when the river in flood after heavy rains finally spills over the dam. Cultural revolutionaries looking for models of heroism pluck up the story of the two, pad it, and sell it to the people as an example of self-sacrifice for socialism. Little Jade goes as a child bride to live and serve in the household of her husband-to-be but falls in love with his younger brother. A man, at 40, takes a second wife, who begins to give him the children he has longed for. He hides her to keep her from the party's Birth Control Committee.

Each portrait is carefully and poignantly drawn, and the modern attitudes of the New China are seen slightly skewed through the old lens of village eyes. Written for adults but with many young characters and definite appeal to high-school-age youngsters, Wang's work is an illuminating and thought-provoking account of China old and new as well as a brilliantly written and touching novel.

Watkins, Yoko Kawashima. *So Far from the Bamboo Grove.*
See entry 937, Grades 7–9.

Wolf, Bernard. *In the Year of the Tiger.*
See entry 939, Grades 7–9.

Yep, Laurence. *Mountain Light.*
See entry 940, Grades 7–9.

950   Yoo, Yushin. *Korea the Beautiful: Treasures of the Hermit Kingdom.* Golden
Pond 1987, HB $24.95 (0-942091-01-9). 226pp. Nonfiction.

A very readable traversing of the whole country, this work covers physical
geography, industry, ten major parks, the history, the arts, the religions, the
language, and a variety of customs and traditions, all profusely illustrated with
color photos, museum pieces, copies of paintings, drawings, and charts and
maps. Each category is given equal attention, making this a well-balanced as
well as thorough treatment of Korean culture. Of all the general nonfiction on
Korea, this one most approaches a coffee table book, being the 1988 Olympic
Games Commemorative Edition. Includes index.

951   Zhao, Ji, Guang-mei Zheng, and Wang Hua-dong. *The Natural History of China.*
Illus. with photos. McGraw-Hill 1990, HB $29.95 (0-07-010752-1). 224pp. Nonfic-
tion.

This reference work begins with chapters on basic facts and historical and
natural geography. Filling out the visually appealing book are exquisite color
photos accompanied by detailed information on the flora and fauna of each
region, including forests, rivers, lakes, sea coasts, mountains, grasslands, and
deserts. A final chapter focuses on conservation and natural protection. Appendixes on typical animals of each region are included, as is an index.

17

SOUTHEAST ASIA

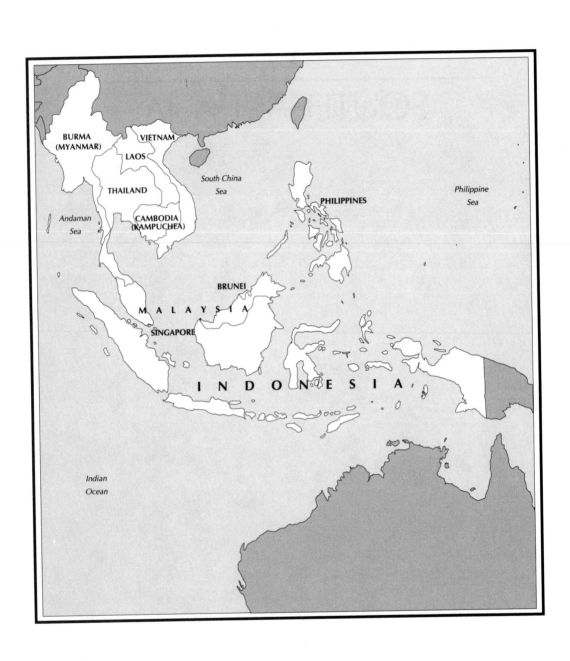

17

SOUTHEAST ASIA

by Ginny Lee, Suzanne Lo, and Susan Ma

With the influx to the United States of immigrants from many places in Asia during the past decade, we begin to become more aware of the differences in the various ethnic groups and cultures represented. We begin to recognize names, styles of dress, and cultural accompaniments, such as the Hmong embroidered story cloths.

As educators, such as librarians, teachers, museum guides, and parents, we need to read copiously in the background materials available to us, seeking to notice and understand the differences between the peoples rather than simply lumping them together. We notice that we can pick out identifying features for each culture. We can identify by last name, by pattern of weaving or embroidery, by language. Of course, not everyone will become an expert in Southeast Asian cultures, but just being aware of the types of differences is a big step forward.

It is also important not to jump to all-embracing conclusions based on information about one particular ethnic group. If we learn that a group has no written language, this does not mean that no group has a written language. In fact, some ethnic languages have recently gained written form.

Minority groups have made their home in various Southeast Asian countries without much regard for international borderlines. A group living in Laos or Thailand, for instance, may not be Lao or Thai but have its own identity. In Appendix 1, Professional Sources, there is a section on this chapter that lists books that discuss a few of these cultures.

Though Southeast Asians have been coming to North America in droves, books about them are just beginning to appear. The material available consists mostly of personal accounts, current events, accounts of the Vietnam War, and a few folktales and legends.

What type of material do we want to look for in the coming decade? We hope for works that will help us to better understand each culture and its people. *Kim Tong and the Moneylender*, for instance, is a very interesting story, but the illustrations, which are largely abstract, look more Chinese oriented than Vietnamese. Does this book really help us to understand Vietnam?

Many of the series books discussed in other chapters now extend their coverage to Southeast Asia. The Portraits of the Nations series (called The Land

and People of . . . , put out by HarperCollins, now has four new books: Cambodia, China, Korea, and Mongolia. The one on Cambodia is more pointedly political, but the others include a fine array of daily life, history, and fine arts in combination with the political. Black-and-white photographs and historical prints are interesting, but they add to the somewhat intimidating (to a middle school student) scholarly appearance of the book. Biographies and other special interest items in boxes make wonderful browsing material and help to isolate usable material for younger students. These are excellent books with a great deal of information packed into their pages.

On the same level, with well-selected but all black-and-white photographs, both historical and recent, is the World Leaders, Past and Present series, which gives young readers portraits of over 150 world leaders. The volumes present the leaders' private lives and thoughts and place them in their historical and political milieu. Arthur Schlesinger's excellent essay "On Leadership" introduces every volume, pondering whether an individual can make a difference in the history of the world, what makes a leader, and what the various types of leaders are. The titles for Southeast Asia include *Ho Chi Minh, Prince Sihanouk, Sukarno,* and *Corazón Aquino.*

The two reference books we offer on Southeast Asia are quite different in nature. One is an atlas, full of historical, political, and cultural commentary with accompanying maps, charts, and graphs. The other is an aesthetic and emotional photographic essay on Vietnam, an attempt to reconcile the reality of Vietnam with the image of that country in the minds of people who think only of war in connection with the name.

Offering more depth, insight, and information than the photographic essays is the title *Vietnam* in the Enchantment of the World series (Childrens Press). This book will appeal more to a younger middle school student than books in the Portraits of the Nations or the World Leaders series because of the format, which presents short, easily graspable sections and color photos.

The series Cultures of the World, represented here by *Singapore*, concentrates on modern daily life, with color photos, maps, and special interest information in boxes interspersed among essays on such topics as dance, music, language, religion, family, ethnic groups, economy, government, history, food, and celebrations.

For the lower grades there are several series portraying the daily lives of children as a major emphasis. For the mid-elementary grades, the Children of the World series (Gareth Stevens), here represented by *Burma*, takes us through a child's daily life, highlighting aspects of school, religion, and a different way of life. Fourteen pages of valuable information, facts, and maps end each book. It is an appealing series, but we have noticed a few mistakes and misleading language in the main sections.

Also in this category is the Families the World Over series (Lerner), here represented by *Singapore*. This series does not provide either the breadth or depth of information that Children of the World does, but it is well done and appealing to young readers.

For the very young there is the Take a Trip series (Franklin Watts), here represented by *Indonesia*. Appealing and informative color photos bring us right into the country, and the few bold lines of text per page give young children all they can probably absorb about a new country.

The Mekong represents a series for mid and upper elementary school children, presenting rivers of the world. Color photos abound. The text is informative and readable and contains an interesting presentation of ideas.

Cookbooks about Asia are numerous. On Southeast Asia there is the series of Easy Menu Ethnic Cookbooks (Franklin Watts), here represented by *Cooking the Vietnamese Way*. It demonstrates well the difference between Chinese and Vietnamese cooking. Recipes are easy to follow, but a child would need adult help.

Finally, there is a group of books that are essentially folktales, but which include in them enough informative material on history, religion, and culture to justify their inclusion here. These are not series books. Each one stands on its own. Representing Laos is *The Encircled Kingdom*. Cambodian folk stories from the Gatiloke contain 20 pages of historical information at the end. *The Moon Bamboo* features a Buddhist world view of the interconnectedness of all life, presented through modern fairy tales calculated also to represent the present plight of the Vietnamese people.

Picture books include *Ba Nam* from Vietnam, *A Trip to Cambodia*, and *Tuan*. Even so, this is an area to which more attention should be given by publishers.

Personal accounts are collected in *Dark Sky, Dark Land*, tales of escaping and emigrating told by members of a Hmong Boy Scout troop. *Fighters, Refugees, and Immigrants* recounts the memoirs of an American doctor working in a Hmong refugee camp in Thailand. *The Land I Lost* is a collection of poignant reminiscences of a boyhood in the hills of central Vietnam. Two first-person accounts written for adults but of interest to older teenagers—*Haing Ngor: A Cambodian Odyssey* and *To Destroy You Is No Loss*—reveal the horrors of life in Cambodia under the Pol Pot regime.

Rice without Rain stands alone as a moving novel of Thailand, portraying the struggles of trust and mistrust between young revolutionaries who want their country to move into a more modern way of thinking. It tells of freedom and equality and of traditional farming villagers who are content to watch their crops grow and do not wish violence or bloodshed even for the sake of liberation.

We cannot expect there to be a lot of material yet. In most public libraries there are only a handful of books on Southeast Asia. University libraries have more, but that is chiefly for background reading and adult reference. Writers, publishers, librarians, educators, parents, and young people themselves must work together to bring the story of the various Southeast Asian peoples to light.

PRESCHOOL–GRADE 3

952 Blia, Xiong. ***Nine-in-One Grr! Grr! A Folktale from the Hmong People of Laos.*** Adapted by Cathy Spagnoli. Illus. by Nancy Hom. Children's Book Pr. 1989, LB $12.95 (0-89239-048-4). 32pp. Nonfiction.

Traditionally, Hmong embroidery tells a story. The Hmong, mountain people who live in the more remote areas of several Southeast Asian countries, notably Laos, have carried the tradition of embroidery through their migrations from northern points centuries ago. The more recent story cloths spell out details of the horror and humiliation of having one's hometown and one's home and hearth invaded by foreign soldiers. Many of the older story cloths depict the movements of the Hmong, their daily lives, and the people, animals, and mythical beasts of their folktales and myths.

In this brief tale, the land is in danger of being overrun by tigers who have been given the blessing by a god of having nine cubs every year if Tiger remembers "Nine-in-one, Grr! Grr!" At that rate, the other animals will have no chance of survival. A clever bird tricks Tiger into saying "One-in-nine, Grr! Grr!" and saves the land.

The illustrations are the prime feature of this book. Based on traditional Hmong embroidery motifs and styles, the paintings portray the animals as we hear about them in the tale. This small book would make a good retelling for a story hour, though its size makes it unlikely to hold the attention of a very large group.

953 Boholm-Olsson, Eva. *Tuan.* Trans. by Diane Jonasson. Illus. by Pham van Don. R & S Books/Farrar, Straus & Giroux 1988, HB $11.95 (91-29-58766-2). 23pp. Fiction.

The pastel watercolors are done by a popular Vietnamese artist, and the book seems to be a vehicle for displaying his work, which is representative of Vietnam and affectionately done. The story, however, misses several chances to help bring Vietnam within the realm of understanding by a Western audience. The first part of the story is a good portrayal of village life in the Vietnamese countryside. But the introduction of a mad dog that suddenly bites the boy seems a contrivance. Then we wonder why a 5-year-old boy can be wandering along a road when his grandmother was supposed to be watching him, and it just happens that his mother comes along. Perhaps it is natural, due to the small size of the village, but it is not very well explained.

There arises a fear of rabies because of the dog bite and a close call about whether there will be medicine or not. This section is long, drawn out, and a bit overdone for young children. Then suddenly all is well, and everyone celebrates on the last page a month later with the Children's Festival, which seems incongruous. This festival would have been a good subject for enlargement and explanation, but it is passed over in a couple of sentences. The cover illustration is of the festival, which should have been but was not the focus of the book.

954 Lee, Jeanne M. *Ba Nam.* Illus. by the author. Henry Holt 1987, HB $13.95 (0-8050-0169-7). 30pp. Fiction.

A couple of really good ideas here would have benefited greatly from a better rendition. The story could have been a wonderful chance to introduce the festival called Thanh-Minh in Vietnam (Ching Ming in China), an important time when believers visit the graves of their ancestors, clean them, offer flowers and special foods, launch firecrackers, bring along a picnic, and have a good time together. It is like Easter in terms of the lightness of color and feeling, and it too takes place in spring. However, in this book, readers get a dark, somber, and even scary feeling, more reminiscent of Halloween.

The story is of a little girl, Nan, who goes with her family to celebrate Thanh-Minh, about which she oddly knows very little. An 8-year-old Western child would not have to ask what a Christmas tree is for. Her questions are undoubtedly for the benefit of the reader. She is afraid of the graveskeeper, an old woman with blackened teeth. Nan wanders off with her older cousin, they get lost, a storm comes up, and Nan is rescued by the old woman, her cousin having inexplicably abandoned her.

The idea of an old person being scary to a young child because of certain traditional characteristics and then turning out to be a helpful friend is a good theme, but this festival is not a good setting for it. The illustrations do not enhance the feeling of lightness associated with Thanh-Minh, the drawings of the people seem awkward, and the sudden spring shower is more like a dark autumn storm. The great tree falling right next to the old woman and the little girl seems improbable and contrived. There are good possibilities here, but they are neither well thought out nor appropriately illustrated.

955   Lye, Keith. *Take a Trip to Indonesia.* SERIES: Take a Trip. Franklin Watts 1985, HB $9.40 (0-531-04940-X). 32pp. Nonfiction.

Although this small book is aimed at the lower elementary level, the focus is adult. In a few lines of large, bold text, very simple, terse facts describe the color photos, one per page. The photos range from interesting to uninspired but manage to present a great variety of subjects ranging from transportation to entertainment, geography to ethnic composition, and schools to markets. Includes index. Other volumes in this series take trips to Malaysia, the Philippines, Singapore, and Thailand.

956   Tran Khan-Thuyet. *The Little Weaver of Thai-yen Village: Co Be Tho-Det Lang Thai-yen.* Bilingual ed. Trans. by Christopher N. H. Jenkins and Tran Khanh Thuyet. Illus. by Nancy Hom. SERIES: Fifth World Tales. Children's Book Pr. 1987, HB $12.45 (0-89239-030-1). 24pp. Fiction.

A little girl lives happily in her village in Vietnam until the war comes too close, killing her mother and grandmother and wounding her with bomb fragments. She is taken to the United States to be treated in a hospital. Attempts are made to make her feel comfortable, but she does not respond. She is confused by the fact that it is Americans who both wounded her and are helping her. She dreams of the ancient spirit bird who in time of war has always come to urge her people to resist the invader. She resolves to live and to help her people. She longs to return to Vietnam but is taken in by a kindly American family. Thinking of the blankets she used to weave with her grandmother, she decides to weave blankets with the spirit bird on each one to send back to people struggling to survive in Vietnam.

    The story, presented in Vietnamese and in English, is patronizingly political, and the illustrations hail from the 1960s and early 1970s, when radical posters drawn in this style were in vogue. For these reasons, this book is less than appealing, although, told with a more gracious attitude and illustrated less garishly, the story would have had some merit.

GRADES 4–6

957   Carrison, Muriel Paskin. *Cambodian Folk Stories from the Gatiloke.* Retold from a translation by The Venerable Kong Chhean. Charles E. Tuttle 1987, HB $15.95 (0-8048-1518-6). 139pp. Nonfiction.

The Gatiloke is to Cambodia what the Mabinogian is to Wales: the original collection of oral folk legend. An extensive introduction gives background information on Cambodian folk stories, most of which are Buddhist moral teaching tales. One of the sections tells something about the Buddha and Buddhism and how these tales relate to the real world of Cambodian beliefs and attitudes. Cultural and historical notes following each tale offer insight into both the tale and the people. Interesting for a few very un-Western turns, some of these stories end with "the culprit free and happy, living with his stolen goods, while the victim suffers." It is understood that he will be properly punished in a future life. Others poke fun at the rascals' innocent victims who are so stupid as to think unwisely or to believe some farfetched line. Cruel or greedy hunters are outwitted by kind and clever animals. People are always exhorted to be kind and compassionate.

A lengthy appendix (20 pages) gives historical, geographical, and cultural background information. A five-page glossary is further enlightening. The tales are readable and make good read-alouds for story hours, but the additional information in this book makes it useful in a more scholarly way as well.

958   Chan, Anthony. *Hmong Textile Designs.* Illus. by the author. Stemmer House 1990, P $5.95 (0-88045-113-0). 43pp. Nonfiction.

The body of this work comprises the unannotated designs themselves. Some of them contain the captions for the stories, but notes on the plates follow the introduction. All the designs are black and white, intricate, and wonderfully expressive of life-style and culture as well as the appreciation of beauty in nature.

The size of a child's coloring book, this work is a good reference for analyzing the beautiful Hmong embroideries and for creating special drawings, displays, or other materials of one's own. The introduction by Norma Livo is a fine treatise on Hmong history and beliefs, as well as a discussion of the textile designs. Much information is crammed into two pages. This is a good reference work that can be viewed with interest by readers at almost any level.

Coburn, Jewell Rienhart. *Encircled Kingdom: Legends and Folktales of Laos.*
See entry 967, Grades 7–9.

959   Goom, Bridget. *A Family in Singapore.* Illus. with photos by Jenny Mathews. SERIES: Families the World Over. Lerner 1986, LB $9.95 (0-8225-1663-2). 32pp. Nonfiction.

Twelve-year-old Chor Ling and her family are the focus of this series title that presents the highly urbanized island nation of Singapore. Goom explores the contrast between the old and the new, showing, for instance, Chor Ling's father eating with chopsticks while the rest of the family uses forks and the family's occasional trip to McDonald's. The book is short, with copious photos, and therefore topics are not presented in much depth. However, the photos are attractive and do give readers a concrete sense of life in this land. Also included in this series is a volume on Thailand.

960   Huynh, Quang Nhuong. *The Land I Lost: Adventures of a Boy in Vietnam.* Illus. by Vo-Dinh Mai. HarperCollins 1982, LB $9.89 (0-06-024593-X). 115pp. Nonfiction.

If *Lassie-Come-Home, Where the Red Fern Grows,* and *The Yearling* exemplify the outpouring of affection between a child and a pet, usually a dog, this one from

Vietnam paints just as tender a portrait of a boy and his water buffalo, though it is of less ambitious length and in simpler writing style. The style is anecdotal, one vignette following another with varying degrees of connection. Similar to the family narratives of Walt Disney, complete with his poignancy and humor, these anecdotes are held together by the backdrop of a small Vietnamese mountain village and the Tom Sawyer–like boyhood of the author, who alternately regales and horrifies us with descriptions of events and the colorful characters who people his life. We see not only that there are a multitude of fine points about Vietnamese village life so far removed from our own experience that we never could have guessed at them but also that human affection, sorrow, indignation, and regret are universal. We easily identify with the characters portrayed.

Since the book is a biography and most readable, it can be used to entice upper elementary students into an interest in the sort of truth that can be more powerful than fiction, as well as to vividly introduce a country through the eyes of one of its children.

961   Knowlton, MaryLee, and Mark Sachner, eds. ***Burma.*** Illus. with photos by Takashi Morieda. SERIES: Children of the World. Gareth Stevens 1987, LB $12.45 (1-55532-159-3). 64pp. Nonfiction.

For the most part a very attractive series, some of its titles do have a few minor misleading ideas or unexplained items. On the cover of this book, a young smiling boy has white paintbrush marks on his cheeks. Inside we are told about a face-painting ritual in which boys are initiated as monks, but this does not seem to describe the more intricate white designs portrayed on the cover. Moreover, other people in daily life scenes also have the white-paint-brushed cheeks. We are never told what it is for.

With its focus very much on the child, both in color photos and in the simple text, the aim is definitely to interest children in the way of life of a child in another culture. We follow a young boy through his day, seeing the inside of his house in great detail, watching his parents at their work, meeting his friends at school, and playing in the neighborhood. A good portion of the text is given to the description of the ritual that all boys go through to become a monk for a short time. Some boys remain monks their whole life. We watch them "splash each other silly" at the water-splashing festival in April, for the New Year celebration. A visit to Rangoon, the capital (now called Yangon), and some of its temples concludes the section.

Fourteen pages at the end provide facts, figures, and historic and cultural information for adult reading. Map, research projects and activities, and index are found at the end.

Since the publication of this book, the country has been renamed Myanmar; it is not known whether the volume will be revised to incorporate this fact or other recent developments. Other volumes in this series present children and their families in Indonesia, Malaysia, the Philippines, Singapore, Thailand, and Vietnam.

962 Lepthien, Emilie U. *Corazón Aquino: President of the Philippines.* Illus. with photos. SERIES: Picture-Story Biographies. Childrens Pr. 1987, LB $8.95 (0-516-04170-3). 32pp. Nonfiction.

This volume in the Picture-Story Biographies series for the middle elementary grades presents the housewife and political wife who became her country's president after her husband's assassination. Lepthien's narrative is straightforward and clearly written, but it lacks the tension that would keep young readers turning the pages. Much of the emphasis is on Aquino as a person, and the biography ends with her electoral triumph and dictator Ferdinand Marcos's reluctant departure. Thus, youngsters will receive a personal view and a hopeful ending. Family and news photos add interest, and there is a time line but no index or bibliography.

While this book may appeal to younger readers, older ones will be much better served by Howard Chua-Eoan's biography of Aquino (1988), part of Chelsea House's World Leaders, Past and Present series. Filled with well-reproduced news photographs, the Chua-Eoan biography does a much better job of developing and maintaining tension and establishing a balance between Aquino's personal history and contemporary events in her country. That book does include an index, a time line, and a short bibliography.

Yet another biography of Aquino is Margaret Scariano's *The Picture Life of Corazón Aquino* (Franklin Watts, 1987). While written in a lively, appealing manner, this series book is oversimplified even for its older elementary school audience. Aquino appears as a saint who can do no wrong, whereas Marcos is portrayed as a lying, cheating, corrupt villain whose only supporters had to be paid to back him.

963 Lightfoot, Paul. *The Mekong.* SERIES: Rivers of the World. Silver Burdett 1981, HB $11.95 (0-382-06520-4). 67pp. Nonfiction.

Following the river down from its source in Tibet and commenting on each culture it touches along its way to the sea, the author also garnishes his thought-provoking and information-packed text with intriguing better-than-average tourist photographs. We meet the hill tribes in northern Thailand, the saffron-robed monks in their ornate temples in Luang Prabang, the flat lands and rice fields, the larger cities of Vientiane and Phnom Penh, the refugee camps of Thailand, the temples of Angkor Wat, and soldiers in the Delta. A helpful glossary concludes with a page of facts and figures, bibliography, index, and map. This is a good book for a variety of age levels, though its core readership will be older elementary school students.

Nguyen, Chi, and Judy Monroe. *Cooking the Vietnamese Way.*
See entry 974, Grades 7–9.

964 Sechrist, Elizabeth Hough. *Once in the First Times: Folk Tales from the Philippines.* Illus. by John Sheppard. Macrae Smith 1969. 213pp. Nonfiction. o.p.

Humor and human wisdom prevail in these tales from the Philippines, giving us an idea of the mores and cultural attitudes of the peoples who told them. A short preface gives a sketchy history of the islands, and small, scattered black-and-white ink paintings decorate the text. The stories flow in a conversational tone, making good read-alouds, and some of them are very familiar.

GRADES 7–9

965 Brown, Marion Marsh. *Singapore.* SERIES: Enchantment of the World. Childrens Pr. 1989, LB $17.95 (0-516-02715-8). 126pp. Nonfiction.

This book presents a more popular than scholarly approach to another culture. There are chapters on history and government, but the focus of the book is on culture: people, life-style, leisure, food, religion, and music. Full of interesting information and appealing color photos, it could also serve as a good tourist guide. Special interest items in boxes add greatly to the appeal and usefulness. Adults might be more attracted to this book than children, but the reading level is appropriate for upper elementary, junior high, and high school. Includes map and index. Other volumes in this series present Laos, Malaysia, the Philippines (updated), Thailand, and Vietnam.

966 Canesso, Claudia. *Cambodia.* Illus. with photos. SERIES: Let's Visit Places and Peoples of the World. Chelsea House 1989, LB $16.95 (1-55546-798-9). 96pp. Nonfiction.

Cambodia's recent troubled history is but one aspect of this series book, which tries to communicate the ancient traditions and cultural diversity of the country. The treatment is concise, readable, and balanced, but most of the photos are pre-1970 or have no date at all. More up-to-date pictures of the country, especially of Phnom Penh, after the Vietnamese takeover would have enhanced the work. Useful front and back matter include facts at a glance, a glossary, and an index; a bibliography for further reading would have been helpful, though. The recently revised volumes in this series focus on Brunei, Laos, the Philippines, and Vietnam. Other volumes on Southeast Asia are part of the less current and less successful Burke Books series, which Chelsea House is distributing until new volumes are produced.

Carrison, Muriel Paskin. *Cambodian Folk Stories from the Gatiloke.*
See entry 957, Grades 4–6.

Chan, Anthony. *Hmong Textile Designs.*
See entry 958, Grades 4–6.

Chandler, David P. *The Land and People of Cambodia.*
See entry 979, Grades 10–12.

967 Coburn, Jewell Rienhart. *Encircled Kingdom: Legends and Folktales of Laos.* Illus. by Nena Grigorian Ullberg. Burn, Hart & Co. 1979, HB $10.00 (0-918060-03-6). 80pp. Nonfiction.

Among these folktales and anecdotes of Laos are explanatory essays about some of the country's customs, festivals, and peoples. The folktales themselves are traditional ones, most of which we do not see repeated in theme in the tales of other countries.

The book is prefaced by a map of Laos and an essay describing the country and its people and providing a brief historical background. The essays interspersed throughout the book provide interesting information on the silver necklaces of the Hmong, which represent freedom. Others are on the Baci, which are ceremonial strings of friendship tied to the wrist, the Lao New Year celebration, the Buddhist belief in good deeds, and the fireboat festival.

The illustrations, which are pencil drawings in black and white, do a good job of calling up the feeling of Laos. Sprinkled throughout, also, are Lao proverbs, which add to the spice of the book.

968   Garland, Sherry. *Vietnam: Rebuilding a Nation.* Illus. with photos. SERIES: Discovering Our Heritage. Dillon 1990, LB $14.95 (0-87518-422-7). 127pp. Nonfiction.

This is a colorful, critical description of Vietnam today as it recovers from a long history of war and occupation by foreign powers. Legends about the country's beginnings, open discussions of the advantages and disadvantages brought to it by the various foreign groups, and the impact of the Vietnam War are followed by sections on modern daily life, including recipes and information on festivals, school, and sports. A chapter at the end describes painfully the refugee camps, the boat people, and the immigrants to the United States. Color photos bring the country and its people to life. Two pages of facts in the beginning and a glossary, bibliography, and index at the end enhance the usefulness of this book. This series volume is a good springboard for discussions about war, immigration, occupation, and other problems involving interactions between cultures.

969   Goldfarb, Mace. *Fighters, Refugees, Immigrants: A Story of the Hmong.* Illus. with photos. Lerner/Carolrhoda 1982, LB $9.95 (0-87614-197-1). 40pp. Nonfiction.

A poignant and very personally involved commentary on a Hmong refugee camp in Thailand and the recent history of the Hmong predicament in Southeast Asia, this thin but powerful book gives readers the feeling this is a book of memoirs more than a case study. It was written by a doctor who left a comfortable practice with modern facilities to serve in a place where his skills would make a real difference. His eye-opening account of Ban Vinai, the refugee camp, paints for us a picture of loving, caring individuals who were forced to flee their homeland, of the life-in-a-small-town quality of the camp, and of the problems facing the Hmong in having to abandon not only their homeland but also their life-style and their families, each of utmost importance to them. The warfare skills of the men do not transfer well to the refugee camps or to life in the United States, so it is difficult for them to maintain their positions of respect and prestige in both the family and the community. Families must often be separated, since polygamy, common in Hmong culture, is illegal in the United States. This is an odd and uncomfortable trial for the new immigrants, as they revere the family above all else.

The author was impressed by the spirit and vitality, the drive for hard work and independence, and the desire to educate their children that he saw among the Hmong, and his total sympathy for his subjects comes through. Large color photos illustrate the local color and the paradoxical gaiety of this halfway place in tropical Thailand.

970 Ho, Minfong. *Rice without Rain.* Lothrop, Lee & Shepard 1990, HB $12.95 (0-688-06355-1). 236pp. Fiction.

Tradition vies with science and new ideas, feudalism with freedom and new ways of life, witch doctors' chants with modern medicine. Ned, a university student, comes to the village to transform it into a twentieth-century community. Are the villagers and their concerns just "symbols of feudal oppression" to him? The author does a good job of jarring us out of our complacency and making us feel, along with the villagers, all the indignation against both the unfairness of feudalism and the impersonality of the new politics. The villagers themselves are beset by a period of drought and famine, and they want to be treated as human beings rather than as either animals or symbols. Jinda, the village girl, admires Ned but is uncertain of his motives. He urges the villagers to pay less than the traditional half of rice for the rent of their fields, resulting in the arrest of Jinda's father on a trumped-up charge. He dies in prison, leaving us feeling as much rage and frustration against the system as Jinda does. We see through Jinda's eyes—first hopeful, then horrified—a controlled student political rally that turns into an unruly and violent mob scene. Jinda and Ned finally part ways, he to join the Thai Communist forces in the north to fight violently for the goals he could not gain peacefully, and Jinda to live in peace with the land and her village. After the tragedies she has witnessed, she wants to "grow things," because the tangible feel of soil and seed are things she can live for. Their last conversation expresses the paradoxical doubts and questions of those innocent idealists (both Jinda and Ned) who want a better world, peopled with honesty and fairness and with enough rice for all, but who cannot find a single best and certain road to lead to that paradise.

Each of these fully realized characters will continue the struggle in his or her own way. And each will be right. This remarkable young adult novel is powerful reading for anyone seeking a deeper level of understanding of the civil rights movement, Kent State, the Chinese cultural revolution, the Sandinistas, guerrilla movements throughout the Third World, or the whys and wherefores of any attempt, however misguided or failed, to stand up for a better life for a people.

Huynh, Quang Nhuong. *The Land I Lost: Adventures of a Boy in Vietnam.* See entry 960, Grades 4–6.

971 Ignacio, Melissa Macagba. *The Philippines: Roots of My Heritage: A Journey of Discovery by a Filipina American Teenager.* Filipino Development Associates 1977. 172pp. Nonfiction. o.p.

How do you know what your heritage is unless you travel to the land of your parents? This firsthand account was written by a Philippine-American teenager who spent a year living in the Philippines seeking her heritage. The literary quality is on a par with junior high school English writing assignments. It is a simplistic, fact-by-fact description of the day-to-day events of the author during her year's stay. She makes an effort to include background on politics, history, religion, and the fine arts. Considering the age of the author, it is informative, quite readable, and well put together. But the true beauty of the book lies in what it is: a journey alone into the world to seek the nature of one's own being. One may compare this work to the Native American teenager's vision quest alone into the wilderness to seek a name or an animal spirit. It is the sort of quest that lets you know you are equal to the demands of the world, and it is something young people should be required to undertake in their early teens in order to be initiated into the adult world. The last chapter on Melissa's impressions, including questions asked of her about the United States by her Philippine friends and those about the Philippines by her U.S. friends, is more than informative. It is revealing of the attitudes and misconceptions on the parts of both cultures. We could wish that this chapter had been more developed. Nonetheless, this book is a good source of information and inspiration for young people.

972   Lloyd, Dana Ohlmeyer. ***Ho Chi Minh.*** Illus. with photos. SERIES: World Leaders, Past and Present. Chelsea House 1986, HB $17.95 (0-87754-571-5); 1989, P $9.95 (0-7910-0576-3). 116pp. Nonfiction.

Representing the excellent series on World Leaders, Past and Present, the story of Ho Chi Minh is also a history of Vietnam in this century. Educated in a French school, Ho received a solid, basic knowledge of Western thinking. For a century, the French had occupied his country and eventually dominated it, imposing Christianity, both government and military control, and the Western alphabet instead of Chinese characters to represent the Vietnamese language. At times occupied by the Chinese and the Japanese as well, the people of Vietnam simply wanted to be rid of foreigners and allowed to live their own lives. Ho Chi Minh's revolutionary notions were to make Vietnam utterly and only Vietnamese. Toward that end he worked fanatically for his whole life. Appealing to the peasants for his backing, he became known as Bac Ho (Uncle Ho) and was admired and venerated by his people.

Each volume in this series is introduced with an essay on leadership by Arthur Schlesinger, Jr. Well-selected black-and-white photographs with ample captions themselves provide a good background of the era. Additional quotes from historians and historical characters add flavor as well as information. A brief bibliography, chronology, and index end the book. Other titles in the series pertaining to Southeast Asia include *Corazón Aquino, Ferdinand Marcos, Pol Pot,* and *Prince Sihanouk.*

973   Moore, David L. ***Dark Sky, Dark Land: Stories of the Hmong Boy Scounts of Troop 100.*** Illus. by Tim Montgomery. Tessera Publishing 1989, P $14.95 (0-9623029-0-2). 191pp. Nonfiction.

A troop of Boy Scouts in Minneapolis finds itself made up of Hmong boys, each of whom has his own story to tell of life in Laos and Thailand. The themes they touch upon include their escape from war, the uncertain "middle ground" of refugee camps, and their struggle to adjust to a new life in a new country. Each boy's story is prefaced by a sensitive pencil sketch portrait, and the stories themselves bring home the horrors of being uprooted from home and family, as well as war-related traumas, often involving the death of family members. These are stories that most of us can only wince at; even those of us who have experienced death and uprooting firsthand have not likely experienced anything close to what these youngsters have gone through. The least we can do in their honor is to read their stories and try to understand. After the stories, a chronology of Hmong history follows, as does a bibliography for further reading.

974 Nguyen, Chi, and Judy Monroe. *Cooking the Vietnamese Way.* Illus. with photos by Robert L. Wolfe and Diane Wolfe. SERIES: Easy Menu Ethnic Cookbooks. Lerner 1985, LB $8.95 (0-8225-0914-8). 48pp. Nonfiction.

Several pages of introduction give geographical background on the whys and wherefores of Vietnamese cuisine and some tidbits about holiday feasts. A page or two describing utensils and methods is helpful for the uninitiated. Recipes, which compose the main portion of the book, are easy to follow but do require adult supervision, particularly for younger chefs. Many call for interesting, exotic, or hard-to-find ingredients, but nonetheless give a very delicious impression of Vietnamese food and what makes it different from Chinese. Interesting historical or cultural comments on each dish add to the flavor. Tips for the careful cook, a metric conversion chart, and an index top off the meal.

Nhat Hanh, Thich. *The Moon Bamboo.*
See entry 985, Grades 10–12.

Sechrist, Elizabeth Hough. *Once in the First Times: Folk Tales from the Philippines.*
See entry 964, Grades 4–6.

975 Terada, Alice M., ed. *Under the Starfruit Tree: Folk Tales from Vietnam.* Illus. by Janet Larsen. Univ. of Hawaii Pr. 1989, HB $15.95 (0-8248-1252-2). 136pp. Nonfiction.

The introduction to these folktales and the notes following each story tell us a great deal about the beliefs, mores, attitudes, and culture of the Vietnamese people. The narrative of the tales sounds suspiciously like translation, but the awkwardness does not seem excessive unless one has just read beautiful flowing prose. The stories are intriguing. Some we have heard before but appreciate in a new format. Others have a familiar ring, and still others are brand-new. In many we see the influence of Chinese culture on that of Vietnam. The illustrations are plain black-and-white sketches, sometimes bordering on the grotesque, which unfortunately lend neither beauty nor information to these compelling tales.

976 *Thailand in Pictures.* Illus. with photos. SERIES: Visual Geography. Lerner 1989, LB $11.95 (0-8225-1866-X). 64pp. Nonfiction.

Maps, charts, and photos, some in vivid color and most relatively well reproduced, fill this straightforwardly written series volume. The text presents information on Thailand's land, history, government, ethnic and religious composition, art, and economy. The treatment is objective, with attention given to the issue of economic growth and the government's concern over unrest in the neighboring nations of Cambodia and Burma (Myanmar). Political conflicts within Thailand itself have not been ignored, though the emphasis is on the positive resolution of those conflicts. Includes index. Other volumes in this series present Indonesia, Malaysia, and the Philippines.

977   Walsh, John E. *The Philippine Insurrection, 1899–1902.* Illus. with photos. SERIES: Focus Books. Franklin Watts 1973. 74pp. Nonfiction. o.p.

Primarily a political history of the few years mentioned in the title, this book attempts to provide background and rationale for the U.S. presence in the Philippines. Illustrations are black-and-white historical sketches as well as photographs, for the most part quite well selected, which nicely complement the readable text. Personalized with anecdotes about Emilio Aguinaldo, the charismatic leader of the insurrection, the book is an interesting presentation of a very specific time and place. Though of limited appeal, this book definitely fills a place in Asian history. A bibliography and index are included.

978   Wright, David K. *Vietnam.* SERIES: Enchantment of the World. Childrens Pr. 1989, LB $17.95 (0-516-02712-3). 128pp. Nonfiction.

The first half of the book is largely political history, focusing on the French and then the U.S. occupation of Vietnam. The second half deals more with the issues of current daily life of the people—farming, crops, city living, mountain dwellers, religion, and fine arts. Several biographies are included, as is a section on the various cities. Several pages at the end presenting minifacts contain a great deal of information, a date line, a map, and an index. Color photos make the book appealing, but it still would not be used below the upper elementary school level. Photos concentrate on adults rather than children. This is a detailed and well-balanced survey and a good source book for junior high and high school reports.

GRADES 10–12

979   Chandler, David P. *The Land and People of Cambodia.* Illus. with photos. SERIES: Portraits of the Nations. HarperCollins 1991, LB $17.89 (0-06-021130-X). 224pp. Nonfiction.

A good deal of prehistory and ancient history in an interesting and readable format occupies the first third of the book, providing for us the connection between the Cambodian culture and the Indian. The last 500 years are examined in some detail, and the present century is emphasized in the last part, with much political detail of the past 20 years and their repercussions on the daily life of modern citizens, both those in Cambodia and the tens of thousands who have emigrated to Western countries. Benefiting from discussions with Cambodians themselves, the descriptions draw us into people's lives. The black-and-white photos and other illustrations in this series are well selected and both aesthetic and scholarly, but they lack the splash of color. Special interest boxes and individual biographies add interest as well as information and help to bring the level of the book from scholarly back down to popular. This title dwells more on the historical and political, partly because that is what has appeared in the media; cultural information receives much less attention here. There are an extensive bibliography and an index.

980 Clifford, Geoffrey, and John Balaban. ***Vietnam: The Land We Never Knew.*** Illus. with photos. Chronicle Books 1989, HB $29.95 (0-87701-597-X); P $18.95 (0-87701-573-2). 144pp. Nonfiction.

Chiefly a volume of stunning color photography, this book provides us with an emotional view of the Vietnam that the soldiers serving there never came into contact with. An introduction of some 20 pages offers a combination of historical perspective and personal commentary. The rest of the book consists of sections of photographs accompanied by essays on Rivers & Mountains, People, Leaders, and War & Post War. A bibliography is included.

981 Criddle, Joan D., and Teeda Butt Mam. ***To Destroy You Is No Loss: The Odyssey of a Cambodian Family.*** Little, Brown/Atlantic Monthly 1987, HB $17.95 (0-87113-116-1). 289pp. Nonfiction.

Teeda Butt was 15 years old when the Khmer Rouge marched into Phnom Penh, where she and her family lived a privileged existence. Her initial relief at the end of the war turned to fear when soldiers announced the evacuation of the city's 3 million residents, who were to find new homes in rural villages. On the way to the village her family had chosen, Teeda's father was pointed out as a member of the deposed government. He disappeared. In the village, Teeda and her extended family became little more than slaves. Near starvation and death from disease and overwork, they began to hear of other relatives and friends who were being murdered and dumped into mass graves. Teeda's sister and her husband watched helplessly as their oldest child was taken from their home and moved into a nearby children's compound for indoctrination. The Khmer Rouge were determined to erase all aspects of Cambodian culture and heritage and to build a new society from scratch. The 1979 Vietnamese invasion made escape possible. Teeda, now 19 and newly married to 21-year-old Vitou Mam, joined her family in a treacherous journey to Thailand. When the Thais deported them, they were forced to retrace their steps to freedom.

As written by Joan Criddle (who helped sponsor the family in America), Teeda Butt Mam's story is a gripping narrative of a girl who had spent her adolescence under the most horrifying of conditions. Her feelings at the time of the Khmer Rouge victory and her grappling with suicide as a way out of the torment ring true, as does the determination that ensured her survival then and her success in America today. The narrative gives readers some information about the rich Cambodian culture that existed before 1975; although the discussion of rural life uses some pejorative terminology, such as the word "backward," in describing the peasantry of the hill areas, the diversity of the country and age-old tensions between rural and urban residents receive coverage. This highly recommended work will give older teenagers personal insight into one of the century's great atrocities, through the eyes of one of their own.

Ho, Minfong. ***Rice without Rain.***
See entry 970, Grades 7–9.

982   Lewis, Paul, and Elaine Lewis. *Peoples of the Golden Triangle: Six Tribes in Thailand.* Illus. with photos. Thames & Hudson 1984, HB $35.00 (0-500-97314-8). 300pp. Nonfiction.

Large color photos and fine print detail the life-styles of six different hill peoples in northern Thailand. This is an encyclopedic work covering many aspects of these rich cultures. Silver and other ornaments, clothing, portraits, and life in the village are pictured in the multitude of photos. Essays discuss language, history, mythology, religion, death, dress, villages and their leaders, houses, households, courtship and marriage, sickness and curing, and social relationships. This is a profusely illustrated, very readable, engrossing anthropological study. There is a final chapter on musical instruments and baskets. The book includes a two-page bibliography, a distribution map, and an index.

Lloyd, Dana Ohlmeyer. *Ho Chi Minh.*
See entry 972, Grades 7–9.

983   Lue, Vang, and Judy Lewis. *Grandmother's Path, Grandfather's Way: Hmong Preservation Project: Oral Lore—Generation to Generation.* Zellerbach Family Fund 1984. 197pp. Nonfiction. o.p.

This is a rather detailed reference work, which nevertheless is useful for its many retellings of Hmong folk stories. Sections also include proverbs, songs, poetry, and a detailed, scholarly essay on language and the connection between language and music. Essays on crafts, needlework, and life-style, especially as revealed in the embroideries, conclude the book, along with lengthy subject bibliographies. An interested teacher could make good use of the information presented here, though the book would not likely be used by children themselves below the high school level.

984   Ngor, Haing, and Roger Warner. *Haing Ngor: A Cambodian Odyssey.* Macmillan 1987, HB $19.95 (0-02-589330-0). 478pp. Nonfiction.

The 1984 feature film *The Killing Fields* documented the atrocities of the Khmer Rouge dictatorship, as experienced by Dith Pran, the Cambodian assistant to *New York Times* reporter Sidney Schanberg. The part of Dith Pran was played by another Cambodian refugee who had survived the Khmer Rouge horrors—Dr. Haing Ngor.

As a doctor, Ngor was considered suspect by the Khmer Rouge, who distrusted all those with education and foreign contacts. The Khmer Rouge glorified the illiterate peasants, although in reality peasants were treated no better than anyone else under their rule. Shortly after the fall of Phnom Penh, Ngor's parents and most of his family were executed. He and his wife were turned out of their comfortable home and sent to a rural work camp, where he had to disguise his previous identity and practice medicine in secret. Ironically, he could not save his wife, who died in childbirth, along with their baby. Three times he was arrested, interrogated, and tortured. After the Vietnamese invasion, he rejoined the remnants of his family and shortly afterward escaped to Thailand with his niece.

Ngor's story is graphic and powerful testimony to one of the most brutal regimes of the twentieth century. Nonetheless, his experience shows the capacity of individuals to endure humiliation, hardship, deprivation, and the loss of loved ones at the hands of other people and still retain their humanity. Teenagers will also appreciate reading about the process by which Ngor slowly rebuilt his life in the United States, changing professions from doctor to professional actor, a field for which he had had no training. This book is a useful companion to the movie, providing depth for the scenes and events in *The Killing Fields*. An index is included to help readers identify themes and individuals.

985   Nhat Hanh, Thich. ***The Moon Bamboo.*** Trans. from Vietnamese by Vo-Dinh Mai and Mobi Ho. Illus. by Vo-Dinh Mai. Parallax Pr. 1989, P $12.00 (0-938077-20-1). 179pp. Fiction.

Not all stories about children are for children. This one dwells so much on political confrontations and religious insight that it is more likely to be appreciated by a very select group of socially and theologically aware people than by young people in general. The main premise of the four modern fairy tales told herein is that there are different ways of seeing Truth, and the Truth propounded here is that of the interconnectedness of all life. In the first story, a rocky mountain peak that witnesses much pain brought by humans onto themselves materializes as a boy who takes care of a blind girl—until she regains her sight and does not need him any more. She mourns his disappearance, but he will always be with her and within her, and now she plays her flute for peace in the world. The plight of the boat people, attacked by pirates and denied a place to land, is addressed in another story. A young girl, raped and flung into the sea, is rescued by a little girl who is really a magical pink fish roaming the seas in search of people to save. "Give all your energy to those people suffering in the camp," exhorts the fish. In the title story, a young woman is torn between two husbands and two sets of children—one family on earth, one on the moon. Finally she divides herself and becomes two people. Have we not all at one point desired to be in two places at once? In the last story, a young boy's critical illness affects both uncle and father, who ruminate on the similarity of precepts in science and in Buddhism. Written by a monk to get the attention of adults through tales ostensibly for children, these stories will have the success he aims for with a very limited audience, although young adults in general will appreciate the stories on a fairy tale level.

986   Ulack, Richard, and Gyula Pauer. ***Atlas of Southeast Asia.*** Macmillan 1989, HB $85.00 (0-02-933200-1). 171pp. Nonfiction.

Not only a book of maps, this volume offers chapters on physical geography and resources, history and politics, culture (including language and religion), regional population, and urban change, accompanied by color photos, charts, graphs, and various types of explanatory maps and illustrations. Each of the ten nation states then has its own chapter of cultural and historical information along with color photos, charts, and graphs in addition to the maps. Major city maps are included as well. An adult reference book, with definite usefulness on the high school level, this atlas does provide much useful background information on Southeast Asia. A lengthy bibliography and an index are included.

18

AUSTRALIA, NEW ZEALAND, AND THE PACIFIC

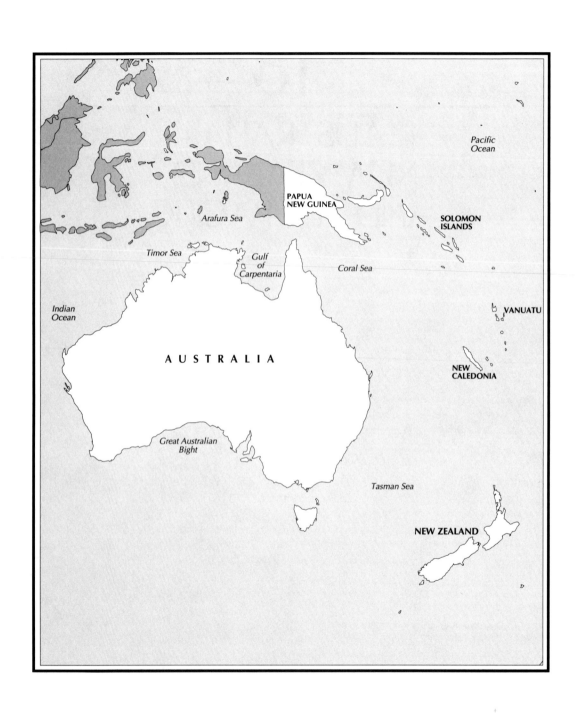

Pacific
Ocean

PAPUA
NEW GUINEA

Arafura Sea

SOLOMON
ISLANDS

Timor Sea

Gulf
of
Carpentaria

Coral Sea

Indian
Ocean

VANUATU

AUSTRALIA

NEW
CALEDONIA

Great Australian
Bight

Tasman Sea

NEW ZEALAND

18

AUSTRALIA, NEW ZEALAND, AND THE PACIFIC

by Melinda Greenblatt

Because Canada and the United States share the English language with Australia and New Zealand, there is an easy literary exchange that is not stifled by translation problems. The idiomatic expressions and contemporary slang particular to Australia and New Zealand enrich the books that come from "down under" and allow North American readers to stretch their imaginations and language skills. Authors such as Patricia Wrightson, Ivan Southall, Colin Thiele, and Margaret Mahy have become known throughout the English-speaking world, and Patricia Wrightson has won the coveted Hans Christian Andersen prize for the body of her work. This award is given by the International Board on Books for Young People, and the winners are selected from a worldwide group of nominees.

The earlier nonfiction books that filled school and public library shelves in the 1950s and 1960s often had distorted views of Australia and New Zealand, emphasizing the outback or the New Zealand sheep farms at the expense of any information about urban areas. The treatment of the Aborigine and the Maori was usually stereotypical, particularly in the case of Australia. The Aborigines were often treated with little respect in written material, in the same way as they were discriminated against in most real-life situations.

Most of the books included in this chapter reflect a more diverse and accurate portrayal of life in today's Australia and New Zealand. Although the Australian outback still remains intriguing as Robyn Davidson makes her way across it in *Tracks*, and a New Zealand sheep farm locale is the setting of Alexia's search for an unusual mammal in *A Rumor of Otters* by Deborah Savage, many other environments are presented, from large cities to mining communities, seaside villages, and small country towns.

The majority of the novels take place in recent years, but a few are set during World War II or in the years right before the war. *Jacob's Ladder* by Alan Collins deals with Jewish refugees who escaped from Europe and emigrated to Australia. *McKenzie's Boots* by Michael Noonan is about a young Australian's military experiences, and *The Other Side of the Family* by Maureen Pople is about one of the English children sent to Australia to escape the war in Great Britain.

Patricia Wrightson uses Aboriginal folklore in modern-day settings to create an awareness of the importance of the Aboriginal stewardship of the land. Bruce Chatwin, in *Songlines*, dramatizes this issue in his account of a trip through the central area of Australia to explore the Aboriginal relationship to the land. In *Where the Forest Meets the Sea* by Jeannie Baker, there is a hint of the original inhabitants of the endangered rain forest in the highly original collages that illustrate the simple text.

Contemporary Aboriginal young people play important roles in *Fire in the Stone* by Colin Thiele and *The Ice Is Coming* by Patricia Wrightson, but North American youngsters will also want to read some nonfiction books on this subject, such as *An Aboriginal Family* by Rollo Browne, a photo-essay on one family that has lived both in a larger city and in a more traditional community.

For high school students, the current political situation is highlighted in *The Australians* by Ross Terrill. Robyn Davidson's *Tracks* and Bruce Chatwin's *Songlines* can be read for a more intimate view of the problems facing Aboriginal people today. Dick Roughsey, an Aboriginal artist, and Percy Tresize, who worked with him for many years, are represented in the chapter. *The Giant Devil-Dingo* by Roughsey is a folktale detailing events in the Dreamtime, the mythical era when the Ancestors inhabited the continent and were transformed into all of the landforms, so important in Aboriginal folklore and spiritual ceremonies. *The Peopling of Australia* by Tresize is a combination of legend and history, which could serve as an introduction to the study of Australian history —a history begun too often in older texts with the exploration of Australia by Europeans.

The Maori experience in New Zealand differed from that of their neighbors in Australia, but both peoples are struggling to regain their land rights and keep their spiritual heritage alive. *Flight of the Albatross* by Deborah Savage and *The Bone People* by Keri Hulme both include instances of an elder passing on special knowledge of Maori history and the guardianship of religious objects to a younger Maori. *The Maoris* by Charles Higham is useful for background reading.

Physical survival is an important theme that recurs in many of the novels. In *Shadow Shark* by Colin Thiele, two children battle a great white shark and keep their father and uncle alive on an island off the southern coast of Australia. Robyn Davidson's *Tracks* details one woman's solitary journey across Australia by camel and on foot. Alexis survives several days in the mountains after being cut off by a snowstorm in Savage's *A Rumor of Otters*.

The multicultural population of Australia is beginning to be recognized. *My Place* by Nadia Wheatley, one of the best books reviewed in this chapter, tells the history of Australia by introducing a child from each decade between 1988 and 1788. Most of the major immigrant groups are represented. This book, with its detailed illustrations and enticing maps of the local area made to look as if the child of each decade had drawn one, will help children find out much about the social history of Australia. *Acacia Terrace* by Barbara Ker Wilson tries to cover some of the same ground but is not as successful.

Where the Forest Meets the Sea is another outstanding picture book. The conflict of increased tourism and commercial development versus the preservation of the rain forest is beautifully presented for children. The collages created with natural materials are fascinating, and the issue presented is one of global importance.

One Woolly Wombat by Rod Trinca and illustrated by Kerry Argent is pure fun —a counting book that uses many of the unique Australian animals. Young children can also take a quick trip around Australia by reading *Possum Magic* by Mem Fox.

It was particularly disappointing to learn there remains a dearth of material about the Pacific Islands. While this has been true for a number of years, it seems that the many new country series that are currently being published are ignoring this part of the world. Picture books and novels have also been difficult to locate. Many nonfiction books in adult library collections that were written in the early 1970s are out of print and are not current enough to include in this chapter. Periodical and newspaper articles will be needed for any substantive study of this area.

Recent informational series books are not very different in scope from their predecessors. Rather, it is their point of view, their format, and their generous use of high-quality color photographs that distinguish them from earlier editions. Most authors have steered away from the stereotypical generalizations, chauvinistic statements, and derogatory comments about cultural mores that often marred books in the past. Today, information is usually accurate. The major problems have to do with bland writing styles and the necessity of giving children and young adults a vivid picture of a country in a text often limited to 32, 48, or 64 pages.

Many books currently on the market offer children a rich selection of pictorial materials, but their texts suffer from the constraints of their brevity and rigid formats. The Inside series and the Take a Trip series, both published by Franklin Watts, are examples of books that might be used as supplementary resources but that cannot be used alone. Their short, simple texts cannot give children a full picture of a country, although they try to cover many topics. The Passport series and the Countries of the World series, also published or distributed by Franklin Watts, have many photos as well, with two- or four-page spreads on most subjects, and their texts are more comprehensive.

Upper elementary and middle school students seeking information for research projects will find the volumes in the Discovering Our Heritage series (Dillon) and the Enchantment of the World series (Childrens Press) most useful. The Discovering Our Heritage books usually include folktales and recipes, interesting features that go beyond the more traditional approach of the Childrens Press titles, with their emphasis on history and geography.

Children who want more of a feel for the people of an individual country will enjoy the Families the World Over series, published by Lerner, and the Families Around the World series, distributed by Franklin Watts. These can be used for school projects, but if they are attractively displayed, children may choose to read them on their own.

Each of the titles in the Living Here series (Franklin Watts) includes interviews with 25 people in different schools and occupations. These books give readers an inside look at the economic and social factors that affect the citizens of each country.

Junior and senior high students will need a greater variety of resources for their research projects, including periodicals, but they may want to start with the concise information available in the Visual Geography series (Lerner) and a regional survey, the annual volume of the World Today series (Stryker-Post). The Library of Nations (Time-Life) is probably the most attractive series for young adults. These books give readers good background information and also convey a strong sense of a country's contemporary situation. The Let's Visit

Places and Peoples of the World series (Chelsea House) contain some disappointingly old-fashioned and stereotyped works on this region. Steck-Vaughn's new series, World in View, is adequate but not very detailed. It may be useful for reluctant readers.

Young people who want to learn about Australia and New Zealand have a wealth of informational material from which to choose, but there is also a rich selection of literature. Many excellent titles have been cited here, but several books stand out for their intriguing style. These books may not be the most culturally specific ones included in this chapter, but *Josh* by Ivan Southall and *Memory* by Margaret Mahy are wonderful coming-of-age stories set in different decades and settings—a small Australian town in the 1930s and a large New Zealand city today. These novels allow readers to enter the minds of two adolescents growing up halfway across the globe and to experience their lives in a special way that most informational books cannot come close to portraying.

PRESCHOOL–GRADE 3

987   Baker, Jeannie. *Where the Forest Meets the Sea.* Illus. by the author. Greenwillow 1988, LB $13.88 (0-688-06364-0). unp. Fiction.

Rain forests and their destruction by modern society have become a topic of concern the world over. Baker has used a variety of natural materials gathered at the site of the Daintree Wilderness in North Queensland, Australia, to construct a series of collages that are strikingly beautiful, mysterious, and incredibly detailed. Without a hint of didacticism, they illustrate a story about development that may be harmful to the environment.

Arriving by a small boat, a young boy and his father spend a perfect day in this tropical rain forest. They are alone and can explore this wondrous place without seeing others. The boy wanders into the forest, dark and dense, yet teeming with life—birds, lizards, snakes, and even the shadows of dinosaurs that once lived here too. He wonders about the Aborigines who may have inhabited the forest, and several figures are pictured throughout the pages of the book. He walks back to the beach, eats the fish caught by his father and cooked over a fire, and thinks about the changes that might occur in this place of great natural beauty, even in the very near future. Shadowy images of hotels, Coke cans, children watching television, swimming pools, and four-wheel-drive vehicles appear in his imagination. Is this what will happen?

The author clearly wants children to think about the consequences of large-scale tourism and other development, and this concept can be explored in discussions and research projects, but the book transcends this classroom-oriented activity. Readers will want to pore over its illustrations again and again, and may be inspired to try to make their own collages using leaves, paper, clay, twigs, and other materials.

Browne, Rollo. *An Aboriginal Family.*
See entry 999, Grades 4–6.

Browne, Rollo. *A Family in Australia.*
See entry 1000, Grades 4–6.

988   Burns, Geoff. ***Take a Trip to New Zealand.*** Illus. with photos. SERIES: Take a Trip. Franklin Watts 1983, LB $10.90 (0-531-03761-4). 32pp. Nonfiction.

This title is meant for the younger student, the second or third grader who is just starting to do "research." There are bits of information to be gleaned about the geography and economy of New Zealand, but the text has little of real interest for its intended readers. The simple sentences on different topics and color photos on each page do not add up to a vivid picture of New Zealand. Includes index.

989   Cawthorne, W. A. ***Who Killed Cockatoo?*** Illus. by Rodney McRae. Farrar, Straus & Giroux 1989, HB $13.95 (0-374-38395-2). Fiction.

The birds and animals of the Australian bush inhabit this adaptation of the traditional English nursery rhyme, "Who Killed Cock Robin?" The poem was adapted around 1870 by an Australian teacher and artist. It was probably one of the first children's picture books to be written and published in Australia. Rodney McRae has used bold colors and stylized images of animals and Aboriginal designs to create a very contemporary picture book, one that may attract adults even more than children. Interwoven within the tapestry of animals are some of Australia's famous buildings and monuments, including Sydney's famous opera house, but North American readers may be unfamiliar with the others, and they are not identified.

990   Eugene, Toni. ***Koalas and Kangaroos: Strange Animals of Australia.*** Illus. with photos. SERIES: Books for Young Explorers. National Geographic Society 1981, LB $13.95 for set of 4 assorted titles (0-87044-408-5). 32pp. Nonfiction.

The large high-quality photographs of many Australian birds and animals, including echidnas, bandicoots, wombats, and the ubiquitous koalas and kangaroos, are the trademark of National Geographic publications. The text is simple, little more than captions for the photos. This volume is sold only as part of a set of four, with other animal titles unrelated to Australia. The society also publishes a very appealing pop-up book called *Wonderful Animals of Australia* (sold only with *Whales: Mighty Giants of the Deep* for $21.95).

991   Fox, Mem. ***Possum Magic.*** Illus. by Julie Vivas. Harcourt Brace Jovanovich/Gulliver 1990, HB $13.95 (0-15-200572-2). 32pp. Fiction.

Young children often come to know Australia through its singular animals. There is a growing body of appealing picture books by Australian authors and illustrators that are being picked up by American publishers, and they often use animal characters. While opossums are also found outside of Australia, the other animals in *Possum Magic*—the dingoes, wombats, kookaburras, and kangaroos —are found only on the island continent. The rhythms and word repetitions that make Mem Fox's books excellent read-alouds are here in this tale of innocent sorcery. Grandma Poss has made her granddaughter Hush invisible by means of a magic spell. Although it is lots of fun to slide down kangaroos, Hush eventually wants to be visible, but Grandma cannot undo the spell. She finally remembers that some kind of people food is required.

  The pair set off to locate the right dish, and they circle Australia in their search, tasting such local delicacies as Anzac biscuits in Adelaide, pumpkin scones in Brisbane, and pavlova, the quintessential Australian dessert, in Perth. Finally, a combination of foods make Hush visible once again. A map of Australia and a description of each of the Australian foods mentioned in the text appear on the last page.

It would be fun to make one or two of the dishes and celebrate Hush's birthday as she does every year with a Vegemite sandwich, a piece of pavlova, and half a lamington. Julie Vivas's soft watercolors are quietly humorous. Her little sketches of various Australian locales could be linked to photographs of the real sites. Among many other books, Fox has also written *Koala Lou* (Gulliver, 1989), about the relationship between a koala and her mother, and *Wilfred Gordon McDonald Partridge* (Kane/Miller, 1985), a moving picture book about a little boy who helps a senile neighbor to remember her earlier life.

Georges, D. V. **Australia.**
See entry 1002, Grades 4–6.

Gunner, Emily, and Shirley McConky. **A Family in Australia.**
See entry 1003, Grades 4–6.

992 Roughsey, Dick. **The Giant Devil-Dingo.** Illus. by the author. Macmillan 1973. unp. Fiction. o.p.

Dick Roughsey is an Aborigine who has written down and illustrated some of the traditional tales of his people. This book has won several of the most prestigious Australian children's book awards, for example, the Children's Book Council of Australia Picture Book of the Year Award and the 1974 commendation of the Commonwealth Visual Arts Board.

Roughsey was born on an island in the Gulf of Carpentaria near Cape York on the northern coast of Australia. This particular legend about the devil-dingo is from the Cape York region. Dingoes—hunting dogs—were supposedly brought to Australia by one group of Aborigines when they migrated from Southeast Asia, perhaps 7,000 to 10,000 years ago. Although many Aborigines believe that birds and animals had human forms in the Dreamtime—the time when the Ancestors lived on the earth—the dingo is the only one that has always been an animal. *The Giant Devil-Dingo* tells one story of how dingoes became useful friends of the Aboriginal people. Within the story, there are other explanations of natural phenomena, such as the fact that butcher-birds have long beaks representing the long spears that they (in human form) had used to kill the giant devil-dingo.

The Dreamtime is the most important concept in the Aboriginal belief system. The land is sacred today because of the Ancestors who traversed that land and who are embodied in the rocks, mountains, rivers, plants, and animals that are found in Australia. The legends of the Aborigines are central to their traditional way of life. Today's Aborigines, whether they live in urban areas or on their own lands, are trying to preserve their stories and their beliefs. Roughsey's colors—the red clay of the earth, the subtle greens of the wooded areas, and the red eyes of the devil-dingo—convey a strong sense of the Australian bush. His strong images of people, animals, and the landscape make this a good choice for sharing at a picture book session or for individual reading.

993 Tresize, Percy. ***The Peopling of Australia.*** Illus. by the author. Gareth Stevens 1988, LB $11.95 (1-55532-950-0). 32pp. Nonfiction.

In picture book format, the author-illustrator tells the history of Australia from its beginnings as part of the supercontinent Gondwanaland up until 1788, when members of the Eora clan saw the ships of the First Fleet sailing into a bay near where the city of Sydney stands today.

The author-illustrator worked for many years with Dick Roughsey, an Aboriginal artist who wrote *The Giant Devil-Dingo*, until Roughsey's death in 1985. Their styles are very similar, although Roughsey's palette is more subtle.

It is difficult to tell where legend ends and history begins, although the introduction claims that the book "incorporates both the Aboriginal and modern archaeologists' and paleontologists' view of Australia's ancient history." Children will be excited by the sight of prehistoric dinosaurs and then of the marsupials and other animals found only in Australia. The author states that the first people arrived more than 100,000 years ago, although most texts affirm that the Aborigines arrived about 30,000 years ago. The relationship of the people to the land and the animals is explored beautifully as the people respond to the climatic changes.

The strength of the book lies in its Aboriginal perspective. It can be used by several different age groups and could be read effectively to groups of students, but some additional research and/or explanation by a teacher or librarian may be necessary.

994 Trinca, Rod, and Kerry Argent. ***One Woolly Wombat.*** Illus. by Kerry Argent. Kane/Miller 1985, LB $11.95 (0-916291-00-6). 32pp. Fiction.

This is a wonderfully original counting rhyme that employs Australian animals as its characters. From "one woolly wombat sitting by the sea" to "nine hungry goannas wondering what to cook" to "fourteen slick seals sailing out to sea," young children have a chance to learn their numbers and Australian zoology in one easy lesson.

Two- and 3-year-olds will have kookaburras and echidnas rolling off their tongues. The illustrations are softly shaded yet definitely accurate pictures of the animals in settings that are sometimes surrealistic and usually humorous, and children and adults will enjoy them. Look for the map of Australia on the koala's tea cozy.

Kerry Argent also illustrated *Sebastian Lives in a Hat* (Kane/Miller, 1990) by Thelma Catterwell. This won the award for the Best Children's Book in the 1985 Whitley Awards given by the Royal Zoological Society of New South Wales. It was also short-listed for the Australian Picture Book of the Year Award in 1986.

Sebastian is a baby wombat whose mother has been killed. The author writes simply, but movingly, about Sebastian's new home, in a brown wool hat in Ms. Catterwell's house. Although Australia cannot simply be introduced as the place where kangaroos, koalas, and wombats live, beautiful picture books such as these make the country-continent accessible to very young children who should be able to continue their acquaintance with the country through the growing body of literature from Australia written for all ages.

995   Wheatley, Nadia. *My Place.* Illus. by Donna Rawlins. Australia in Print 1989, HB $14.95 (0-7328-0010-2). unp. Fiction.

Children can learn more from this picture book about the history of Australia and the many different kinds of people who have lived there than from several of the usual kinds of nonfiction books published for elementary school students. From 1988 back to 1788, every decade is marked by a two-page description of life in that year as told by a child of the era. The children are connected from decade to decade by the fact that they all live in the same place, near Sydney on the land between a great tree and a creek. As the reader travels back in time, the wonderful maps, drawn and annotated as if done by the children themselves, tell the story of the changes in the neighborhood.

From Bangaroo, an Aboriginal child whose life has not yet been changed by the English colonists, to Sam, a young English convict deported to Australia, to Benjamin Franklin, an American boy whose father came to Australia for the gold rush in the 1850s, to children from German, Chinese, Irish, and Greek families who move to the community, these young people tell the story of Australia in a very direct manner. Events such as the Great Depression, World Wars I and II, and the Vietnam War are all brought into the children's stories. Political parties and social movements are also briefly mentioned.

History comes full circle as Laura, an Aboriginal child of contemporary times, moves into "my place." Her family has put up a flag symbolizing that the house is on Aboriginal land. As an interesting sidelight, all the children mention the tree that has been allowed to stand there through the centuries and the creek that has become a polluted canal. Environmental issues have become a priority in Australia today, as they have in many countries.

The illustrations, done in soft but vibrant pastels, lovingly evoke the various eras. The various details—"Feed the World" T-shirts in 1988, Beatles' posters in 1968, and the Chinese New Year dragon in 1878, seen by 10-year-old Heinrich Muller (mentioned again in 1908 when Evelyn notes that "Mr. Muller says when he was a boy, the dragon lived across the creek")—make the pictures ring true.

There are hints about the negative side of Australian history—prejudice against the Chinese (called "Heathen Savages" by a "proper" German mother), the mistreatment of the convicts that made up much of Australia's initial European settlements, and evictions during the 1930s depression. The situation of the displacement of Aborigines from their land is handled more obliquely, but it is really at the foundation of the whole historical cycle.

Children could do further research on various periods and try to fill out the stories of the various children or draw parallels between Australian and North American history. The maps could serve as wonderful inspiration for all kinds of mapmaking projects.

996   Wilson, Barbara Ker. *Acacia Terrace.* Illus. by David Fielding. Scholastic 1990, HB $13.95 (0-590-42885-3). 40pp. Fiction.

Wilson and Fielding give young readers a picture book perspective on Australian history from the mid-nineteenth century to the present, as seen through the story of one family and one group of houses built on Acacia Terrace in Sydney. Some of the events mentioned are World War I and the battle of Gallipoli, the capture of Ned Kelly, the depression of the 1930s, and the Vietnam War. Different waves of immigration are represented.

The jewellike, intense colors and the fine details of the illustrations, done by a painter whose work has been exhibited in several countries, will attract children and adults. The text is sometimes a bit stilted and the story's ending surprisingly similar to that of the children's classic *The Little House* by Virginia Burton, in which the great-great-great-granddaughter of the original owner wants to buy the house to save it from destruction.

The book can be used as a stepping-stone to research on different eras in Australian history, but *My Place* by Nadia Wheatley covers a longer period and has more appeal with its emphasis on the children in each generation.

GRADES 4-6

997   Armitage, Ronda. *New Zealand.* Illus. with photos by Chris Fairclough and Stefan Chabluk. SERIES: Countries of the World. Franklin Watts 1988, LB $12.40 (0-531-18158-8). 48pp. Nonfiction.

Two- or four-page spreads on the usual topics such as history, family life, culture, and the arts offer upper elementary school students, including those who are reluctant readers, an introduction to New Zealand. The many attractive photos and the large typeface used will keep students reading even after they finish the sections needed for their report. Current issues facing New Zealand are mentioned, such as unemployment, Maori rights, and differences with the United States over allowing ships with nuclear warheads to enter New Zealand ports.

Information on Pacific Islanders and Maoris is included in chapters on education, shopping and food, and culture and the arts, although the focus on New Zealand's strong British influence is certainly evident. *Australia* (1988), another title in the series, also tries to stress the multicultural nature of Australian society today. There are an index, glossary, and short bibliography.

998   Arnold, Caroline. *Australia Today.* Illus. with photos. SERIES: First Books. Franklin Watts 1987, LB $10.40 (0-531-10377-3). 96pp. Nonfiction.

The usual mix of history, geography, natural resources, and the people of Australia, including the Aborigines, the English settlers, and the newer immigrants from many countries, are handled in competent, but prosaic, fashion. Run-of-the-mill black-and-white photos, a chronology of important dates, and an index fill out this series volume.

Baker, Jeannie. *Where the Forest Meets the Sea.*
See entry 987, Grades PS–3.

Ball, John. *We Live in New Zealand.*
See entry 1020, Grades 7–9.

999   Browne, Rollo. *An Aboriginal Family.* Illus. with photos by Chris Fairclough. SERIES: Families the World Over. Lerner 1985, LB $9.95 (0-8225-1655-1). 32pp. Nonfiction.

This is a representative title of one of the more attractive series available for children in the middle elementary grades. A contemporary family is the focus of each photo-essay. Lynette Joshua is 11 years old and lives in the Northern Territory of Australia in a small community of Aborigines. Lynette's family has also lived for a short time near the Aboriginal Teacher Education College in a larger town near Darwin, one of the major Australian cities along the northern coast. Her father is the president of their community. Young readers can get a sense of the traditional life of the Aborigines through the presentation of information about religious ceremonies, kinship relationships, and hunting and gathering activities. Current issues, such as lack of employment opportunities and distance from medical facilities, are also discussed in the text. Information about children's activities, such as school and games and recreation, is found in the text and in color photos. This is one of several books in the series that have been named as Notable Children's Trade Books in the Field of Social Studies.

1000   Browne, Rollo. *A Family in Australia.* Illus. with photos by Chris Fairclough. SERIES: Families the World Over. Lerner 1987, LB $9.95 (0-8225-1671-3). 32pp. Nonfiction.

David Baker, age 12, lives near Cape Arnhem, which is on the northern coast of Australia, in the mining town of Nhulunbuy, which in turn is located on land leased from the Arnhem Land Aboriginal Reserve. The town is isolated, yet David's life seems similar to that of other young Australians: he attends a modern school (there is a picture of David in the computer lab), boats, surfs, swims, and plays team sports (David plays rugby). Although Aborigines are mentioned throughout the book in different contexts, none are pictured in the otherwise excellent photos. *An Aboriginal Family* (Lerner) should be used as a companion volume.

1001   Garrett, Dan, and Warrill Grinrod. *Australia.* Illus. with photos. SERIES: World in View. Steck-Vaughn 1990, LB $15.95 (0-8114-2429-4). 96pp. Nonfiction.

One of the newest series books on Australia, this book will be mostly useful for the report writer in grades 5–7. History and geography are adequately treated, although there is no depth or detail. The Aborigines are described both historically and today in a positive manner; for example, Aboriginal land rights are discussed, and the authors mention that today's Australians need to learn from the Aborigines' relationship with the environment. A chapter on cities tries to dispel the notion that most Australians live in rural areas. Comparisons concerning many issues are made with both Britain and the United States. The arts are given short shrift. The black-and-white color pictures vary in quality and interest. Index included.

1002   Georges, D. V. *Australia.* Illus. with photos. SERIES: New True Books. Childrens Pr. 1986, LB $13.27 (0-516-01290-8); P $4.95 (0-516-41290-6). 48pp. Nonfiction.

Titles in the New True Books series are purchased for many school and public library collections because they cover a wide variety of science and geography topics in a format for students who are just beginning to tackle nonfiction in short chapter books. The print and the simplicity of the sentence structure resemble basal readers. The texts usually sound quite stilted, and this volume on Australia is no exception. This is basically a geography book, with very little information about the people of Australia.

The Aborigines have been given a chapter, in one caption of which they are compared with other "primitive tribes." The photographs are usually superior to the texts. There are an index and a glossary.

1003 Gunner, Emily, and Shirley McConky. *A Family in Australia.* Illus. with photos by the authors. SERIES: Families Around the World. Franklin Watts 1985, LB $11.90 (0-531-03824-6). 32pp. Nonfiction.

Similar in format to the Families the World Over series, published by Lerner, this volume describes a sheep-farming family with two girls aged 10 and 12 and a baby boy. The style is a bit different from other series, as the authors describe their visit to the King family farm in a personal way, quoting liberally from their "conversations." There are no surprises here, except for the fact that the two girls have their own motorbikes that they use when they round up sheep. There is also no sense here of the multicultural society that Australia has become, but this family portrait could be used in conjunction with other materials to explore contemporary Australia.

1004 Hereniko, Vilsoni, and Patricia Hereniko. *South Pacific Islanders.* Illus. with photos. SERIES: Original Peoples. Rourke 1987, LB $15.33 (0-86625-259-2). 48pp. Nonfiction.

Although the authors mention other islands, they state that this volume will emphasize Fiji, Western Samoa, and Tonga, three of the larger island countries in the region of Oceania. The book suffers from generalizations about Pacific cultures. Many photographs are not properly identified. The various forms of cooperation among the Pacific Islands are briefly noted, but economic and political alliances with other countries such as Australia and New Zealand are not discussed in detail. More books on this region are needed, but this one is inadequate.

The Maoris of New Zealand and *Aborigines of Australia* are also titles in the series. The book on Maoris treats the current daily life of Maoris in a fairly comprehensive manner, but students will learn more details about their past in *The Maoris* by Charles Higham.

1005 Higham, Charles. *The Maoris.* Illus. with drawings and photos. Lerner 1983, LB $8.95 (0-8225-1229-7). 48pp. Nonfiction.

This thorough history of the Maoris uses archaeological evidence to shed light on Maori society as it developed in Aotearoa, the "land of the long white cloud." Higham presents the Maori people, the fact of their probable arrival from other Pacific islands, and their life-style and customs as they were practiced. He writes objectively about encounters with Europeans or Pakehas beginning in 1642, when Abel Tasman first sailed into a New Zealand bay.

Historical works of art, some original black-and-white drawings, and photos (of varying quality and clarity) help tell the story. Only a page or two is devoted to contemporary life. There are a glossary and an index.

1006 James, Ian. ***Australia.*** Illus. with photos. SERIES: Inside. Franklin Watts 1989, LB $11.40 (0-531-10759-0). 32pp. Nonfiction.

Many series books today depend on their colorful photos as their main selling points, and this book fits into that category. Although this volume covers the high points about Australia, its brief texts on many subjects, including geography, family life, the arts, and industry, lack any real depth. Students may enjoy browsing through this book, but they will need additional materials to do any real research. Index included.

1007 Klein, Robin. ***Hating Alison Ashley.*** Viking 1987, HB $11.95 (0-670-80864-4). 182pp. Fiction.

This first-person narrative skillfully employs the very natural language of an Australian sixth grader. The contemporary slang, the expressions that are unique to Australia, and the way in which Erica Yurken (nicknamed Yuk) tells her story are intriguing and amusing. Although readers may have to puzzle out the meaning of a few words, Yuk's feelings will be very familiar.

Barringa East Primary School is in a working-class neighborhood. It is classified as a Disadvantaged School and therefore receives extra funding, but teachers do not want to stay, and wealthier families would rather send their children elsewhere. One year the zoning changed, and a new girl from an upper-middle-class family enters Erica's class. Alison Ashley is perfection personified—beautiful, gorgeous clothes, well behaved, intelligent, and artistic. And Yuk cannot help but hate her. Before Alison arrived, Yuk had believed herself to be the best, most creative student at Barringa East, head and shoulders above anyone else. But Alison seems to shine at everything, including photography, one of Yuk's special talents, or so she thought.

Yuk is a surprisingly appealing protagonist in spite of her regular outbursts of hypochondria and her ridiculous tall tales about herself and her family. Her disarming manner, her humorous descriptions of school and family life, and her very real ambition to be recognized for some special ability all ring true.

Alison Ashley has her own problem—a mother who does not seem to care enough. Although it seems natural that Alison should be a snob, in reality she is quite happy to be Yuk's friend, if only Yuk stopped being so defensive. Their friendship begins at the end of the annual summer camp week for sixth graders, when Yuk realizes that her talent for inventing stories can be directed into writing plays. Although she wants to be the star of the Drama Night Play, she finally realizes that her talents may best flower behind the scenes. Only then, secure in her own glory as a playwright, can Yuk accept Alison as a real friend.

Laurie Loved Me Best (Viking, 1988), a story of two friends at a private girls' school who fall in love with the same boy, has some of the same qualities as this book, but it is for a slightly older junior high audience. Klein is an engaging storyteller. Her characters are real, solidly set in their own neighborhoods in Australia's cities, yet familiar in their activities and emotions. Yuk's narrative will make the reader laugh out loud and wish for a sequel.

1008 MacDougall, Trudie. ***Beyond Dreamtime: The Life and Lore of the Aboriginal Australian.*** Illus. by Pat Cummings. Coward, McCann 1978. 64pp. Nonfiction. o.p.

This is a handsome book designed and illustrated by an artist who has since become well-known for her picture books on African-American themes. The text includes several legends and descriptions of Aboriginal life in different regions of Australia. These glimpses are rich in detail, but they are the author's re-creations of the way that she imagines people lived before Europeans came to Australia's shores.

The regional differences are well defined: the difficult life of day-to-day survival in the desert, the lush landscape and more plentiful food supplies in the northern coastal areas, and the mountainous areas of Western Australia with their kangaroo hunting grounds.

Fishing, hunting, the creation of bark paintings, the gathering of food, and other aspects of life are described. The initiation ceremony of one boy is presented, but circumcision (usually part of initiation ceremonies in Australia and many other parts of the world) is not mentioned.

A short chapter deals with the changes brought about by the Europeans, who first settled in 1788. It ends with some indication of the paths that today's Aborigines are following. But the author realistically states that "Their traditional world has changed forever."

The description of the Dreamtime is marred by the use of the term "semihuman beings" to describe the legendary Ancestors of the Aboriginals. The four legends that follow are economically told.

The illustrations, in dark brown on cream backgrounds, are dramatic and expressive. Different, but accurate facial types, muscular rounded bodies that leap out of some of the flatter, more stylized landscapes, and the varied placement of the illustrations on the pages recommend this book as a supplementary resource on Aboriginal culture.

1009   Park, Ruth. *Playing Beatie Bow.* Atheneum 1984, $12.95 (0-689-30889-2); Penguin/Puffin P $3.95 (0-14-031460-1). 196pp. Fiction.

Winner of the 1981 award for the best Australian children's book, this time-travel story takes place in Sydney, in the nineteenth and twentieth centuries. It is one of the few Australian novels picked up by North American publishers that has an urban setting.

Abigail Kirk is an unhappy adolescent living in contemporary Sydney. Her father left her mother years before, but has recently returned. Abigail seems to have no friends of either sex but wants to know when she will find love and romance. She even begins to fight with her mother, a manifestation of her disturbance over the possibility that her mother will return to a relationship with the man who deserted them both.

One day, after watching the children in the playground engaging in an unfamiliar game called Beatie Bow, she follows a strange little girl who turns out to be the Beatie Bow named in the singing game. She goes up a flight of stairs near her big apartment building and suddenly finds herself in the world of one hundred years ago. She hurts herself, and Beatie's family takes her in. As she recovers, she learns more about the family and life in the last century. The family is from the Orkney Islands, near Scotland, and their speech and customs reflect their origins.

The working-class existence, the dirt, the poverty, the lack of educational opportunities for girls, the household chores, and the work involved in runnning a candy shop (owned by Mr. Bow) are described through Abigail's eyes. She has additional frightening experiences when she tries to return to her real home and is captured by a brothel keeper. Beatie's grandmother has a vision of Abigail and sends her grandson Judah to rescue her. The family believes that Abigail has a role to play in the unfolding of an old prophecy, and, indeed, Abigail does save the life of the youngest child in the family. She falls in love with Judah but accepts that he is already betrothed to his cousin. When finally she returns to her own time, her experiences have changed her. Four years later, she meets a descendant of Judah Bow and falls in love once again, this time with a boy of her own time. The development seems a bit trite, but it allows Abigail and the reader to find out about events that befell the Bow family after Abigail's return to the present.

This is an absorbing novel that brings the past to life. The supernatural aspect of the prophecy is an interesting plot element. Abigail's twentieth-century sensibilities and emotions color her view of the past, thus making it more accessible to today's young people.

1010   Pepper, Susan. *Australia.* Illus. with photos. SERIES: Passport to . . . Franklin Watts 1987, LB $12.90 (0-531-10270-X). 48pp. Nonfiction.

Fairly similar in format and content to two other series published by Watts and Bookwright Press (distributed by Watts)—the Countries of the World series and the Inside series—the Passport to . . . series is slightly more sophisticated in its approach and is probably more suitable for the fifth to sixth grader than the two series mentioned earlier. Smaller print allows for more detailed information on each topic, but most subjects are still covered in two pages. The four "fact file" double-page spreads include attractive graphs and charts that should encourage children to sharpen their skills in reading and interpreting these informational aids. The many pictures will keep students browsing, but additional resources will be needed by anyone doing an extensive research project.

1011   Phipson, Joan. *A Tide Flowing.* Atheneum 1981. 156pp. Fiction. o.p.

Most Australians live in the major cities near the coast—Sydney, Melbourne, Perth, Brisbane, and Adelaide. Often, however, the Australian fiction published in the United States is about children and young people who live in more rural settings. This realistic novel about a boy growing up in a Sydney suburb will give its readers some insight into a typical middle-class life-style that includes great emphasis on sailing and racing. Interest in sports and competition among adolescents exists in many countries, but because of its island geography, many Australians have a special relationship with the ocean.

Mark's relationship with the water is a bit different from his cousins' enthusiastic embrace of the weekly races. As the story opens, Mark and his mother (estranged from his father) are sailing to Sydney from Tasmania, off the southern coast of the mainland. One night in a storm, his mother falls off the boat, and no one knows whether her death is an accident or a suicide. Although Mark had been on his way to his maternal grandparents' home in England, he is now brought to his father's parents' house in the Sydney area. Mark is despondent, unable to join in the activities his robust grandparents have planned for him. He feels abandoned by both his parents, and he longs to go to England to finally meet his mother's family.

As his depression lifts, he begins to participate in weekend activities with his relatives in Sydney, but he never feels any real kinship with them. His only positive thoughts center on an albatross, a huge white seabird, seen as dawn came up on the morning after his mother's death. He associates it with his mother on her way to a new life. Throughout the next four years, as he grows from 10 to 14, he longs to see it again.

Mark finds it difficult to make friends at school, but he finally meets someone with whom he can communicate. Connie, an older teenager, is a quadriplegic, injured in a car accident that killed her father. After seeing each other regularly during her daily walks, Mark saves her from greater injury as her wheelchair rolls away from her mother. After that, they begin a friendship that is satisfying to both of them. Mark gives her great pleasure by taking her sailing, and they enjoy both their time together and the natural beauty of the region near Sydney. Mark shares his reminiscence of the albatross with her, and she too begins to feel that it is a symbol of freedom, a way for her thoughts to soar beyond her physical limitations. One day, she believes that she has seen the bird, and although she weakens and dies soon afterward, she is content. Mark is more emotionally mature as he faces the second death of someone close to him and understands that he is still tied to his mother and Connie in the same way that the albatross remains connected to the sea and sky.

The Australian background is intrinsic to the story, but the novel's themes are universal. It will appeal more to the special reader who can understand the nuances of Mark's and Connie's emotions as they deal with their feelings about life in a world from which they both feel alienated.

1012 Rau, Margaret. ***Red Earth, Blue Sky: The Australian Outback.*** Illus. with photos by the author. HarperCollins 1981, HB $12.95 (0-690-04081-4). 118pp. Nonfiction.

Although the majority of Australians live in the coastal areas, the people of the outback, the large central region of deserts, mines, sheep stations, and remote towns, often come to mind when outsiders think of Australia. The author, who has traveled through parts of the Northern Territory and South Australia, has tried to give readers a picture of contemporary life in the isolated railroad sidings, Aboriginal settlements, cattle and sheep stations, and opal mining towns by reporting on her experiences and quoting her new acquaintances, both children and adults.

She starts with a history of the land and its first human inhabitants, the Aborigines, and continues with a short introduction of the European settlers. In each subsequent chapter, a different aspect of life in the outback is described in a way that will draw children's interest. Details about the way children learn and play, the responsibilities that even young children have in this rural environment, the way sheep and cattle are mustered (rounded up), and the unique social services that Australians have developed, including the Flying Doctor Service and the School of the Air, enliven the text.

Unfortunately, the sections about Aboriginal children and families often seem to be overgeneralized and stereotypical in their approach. This sometimes happens when Rau mentions social problems, such as alcoholism, that also affect the white population. There are not enough individual portraits of Aboriginal families. The black-and-white photos are often too small or unclear to be of much interest. Even so, chapters of this book might be effectively used with other resources.

Roughsey, Dick. *The Giant Devil-Dingo.*
See entry 992, Grades PS–3.

1013   Spence, Eleanor. *The Devil Hole.* Lothrop, Lee & Shepard 1977. 215pp. Fiction.
o.p.

The Mariners were an ordinary, happy, close-knit family living in a small coastal town in Australia. Their lives were caught up with school, the operation of a general store and post office, and the typical water sports enjoyed by people living near the ocean. Douglas, the middle child, is a bit of a loner, and it is mostly through his eyes that we view the changes that occur in the family when Carl, the new baby, is born. Kenneth, the eldest brother, a popular athelete, and Adrienne, the little sister, a charming extrovert, are affected by the birth of this new baby, who shows signs of being different from his first weeks. But it is Douglas who feels that he may have caused Carl's premature arrival by getting lost during a fire. He worries that his mother's fears may have brought on her labor, an impression that his older brother encourages with a chance remark.

As Carl grows, it becomes clear that his crying and destructive behavior are very serious problems. Douglas and his mother take the baby to a doctor in Sydney, but the diagnosis is not very clear. Eventually, the family moves to Sydney so that Carl can attend a special school. It is only then that autism is mentioned specifically, although the symptomatic behaviors of this condition are described throughout. Douglas seems to be the only one who can sometimes break through the barrier of Carl's isolation with his singing, but Douglas too is overwhelmed by the problems caused by Carl.

The move to Sydney changes the life of the entire family and allows the author to describe some of the differences between living in a small Australian town and living in a suburb of the largest city. Douglas, a music student, is lucky enough to attend a special school where he can develop his talents, but Kenneth is alienated by their move and becomes a fringe member of a hippie commune with religious undertones.

When their mother says, "He could be worse than Jenny Weber" (a reference to their neighbor's retarded child), the contemporary reader may feel this is a stereotypical remark. One wishes an explanation of autism had been inserted here instead of at the very end of the novel. However, the doctor's diagnosis may not have been specific at that point. One of the problems that families face is not having enough information about their child's disability.

The author works in a school for autistic children, and her treatment of the difficulties faced by families with autistic children is realistic. The Australian setting is well integrated into the story, and the characters, especially Douglas, are fully rounded in a way that does not always happen in "problem novels."

1014   Thiele, Colin. *Fire in the Stone.* HarperCollins 1974. 305pp. Fiction. o.p.

A remote mining town in South Australia is the locale for one of Thiele's many novels about his home state. Ernie Ryan, abandoned by his mother and barely acknowledged by his alcoholic father, lives in the opal fields in a rude dugout. During his school vacation, he decides to try his luck mining someone's old claim. After several weeks of hard work, Ernie finds some opal, but his good luck soon runs out as a thief finds both the opal pieces hidden in Ernie's dugout and his mine itself.

Ernie is determined to find the thief, and in his search he is aided by two friends. Nick, a son of Greek immigrants; Willie, an Aborigine boy from the reserve near the town; and Ernie, a "white Australian," form a microcosm of the town itself. The new European immigrants who came to Australia after World War II in search of political freedom and economic opportunities, the urban Australians searching for riches (just as their ancestors did in the gold rush of the nineteenth century), and the Aborigines, given a little piece of barren land on the continent that once was all theirs, are uneasy neighbors in this town. Although the town is far from the urban population centers of the Australian coast, crime, alcoholism, and racism are prevalent, and children sometimes need to grow up very quickly.

The three young teenagers struggle to survive, and they sometimes triumph in their conflicts with their environment. An unusual car accident, a mine explosion, a flood, and some good detective work will keep readers glued to the page. Ernie is the only character whose emotional development is evident. Willie remains a one-dimensional character, although his bravery and knowledge of the land are intrinsic to the plot. Nick also lacks any real depth. He goes along with the other two for the adventure and excitement.

In contrast to the characters, the site of the story is strongly realized, in both physical and sociological terms. One short scene involves a discussion of the effect of tourism and development in the town and throughout Australia. The issue of racism comes up throughout the book. Although the author portrays a friendship between Ernie and Willie that becomes stronger in the course of the book, there is an element of paternalism that seems pervasive, particularly in relationship to the adult Aborigines, who appear as minor characters. This could become a point for discussion.

The book was an Edgar Allan Poe Special Award winner, a prize given by the Mystery Writers of America.

1015   Thiele, Colin. *Shadow Shark.* HarperCollins 1988, LB $12.89 (0-06-026179-X). 214pp. Fiction.

Loyalty and survival are important themes in Thiele's novels, and they figure prominently in one of the author's newest works. Set on the coast of South Australia, *Shadow Shark* has some of the elements of both *Jaws* and *Robinson Crusoe* as it tells a strong story of the growing friendship and commitment between two cousins—a boy and a girl just entering their teens.

Like the situations of other Thiele characters, Joe's immediate family has been dissolved. His mother left when he was young, and his father has recently died. His aunt and uncle have taken him into their home in Cockle Bay, a small coastal town that is very different from the big city of Melbourne, where he grew up. Maureen and Meg are his cousins, and Joe and Meg, who share the same birthday, begin the process of learning about each other.

The beginning of the book is devoted to a description of life in the small town and its various inhabitants—the fishermen and the others who work in the town. The mix of ethnic groups, including Greeks and Germans, is briefly noted in the names of the characters, but this aspect of Australian life and recent history is not emphasized. Sheep raising, still an important part of Australia's economy, plays a part in the novel, although the family's sheep do their grazing on a small island off the coast, not on a large inland ranch. The young people's love of the sea—their natural environment—is woven into the story from the very first pages, but it is the sea, the sharks who swim into the sheltered bay, and the boating disasters that will provide Joe and Meg with the most fearful experiences of their lives.

Down-to-earth characters, a realistic setting in a very specific region of Australia, and adventurous exploits that sometimes strain the boundaries of belief are the hallmarks of this very readable book. Colin Thiele is well-known in his own country and throughout the world. Some of his other works include *Storm Boy* (Harper, 1978), *Fight Against Albatross Two* (Harper, 1976), and *Farmer Schulz's Ducks* (Harper, 1988), a picture book for younger children.

Tresize, Percy. *The Peopling of Australia.*
See entry 993, Grades PS–3.

Wheatley, Nadia. *My Place.*
See entry 995, Grades PS–3.

Wilson, Barbara Ker. *Acacia Terrace.*
See entry 996, Grades PS–3.

Wrightson, Patricia. *Balyet.*
See entry 1032, Grades 7–9.

1016   Wrightson, Patricia. *The Ice Is Coming.* Atheneum 1977. 223pp. Fiction. o.p.

This is one of Wrightson's earlier books, about the spirits from Aboriginal folklore. It concerns the battle between fire and ice, between good and evil. It is also about the responsibility of the People (the Aborigines) for the land. In this allegory, the Happy Folk (the coastal Australians) are characterized as having little real feeling for the land and the environment. The Inlanders (the people of the interior who live on the sheep stations and in other rural areas) are more dependent on the land, but even they are not sensitive enough to notice the changes in the land as the ice released by the Ninyas starts to spread.

Wirrun, a young Aboriginal man who lives among the Happy Folk near the eastern coast, sees the ice first in the center of the country near Ayers Rock, one of the sacred places in Aborigine tradition that he is visiting in an effort to learn more about the land. He becomes caught up in a superhuman effort to stop the ice from taking over the continent and bringing about a new ice age. It becomes his job to find the Eldest Nargun, a primordial fire spirit. He travels with the Mimi, a rock spirit who starts out shy and cowardly but shows her true mettle as the journey and the struggle progress. In each chapter, Wirrun and the Mimi meet new spirits who help or hinder them, and the suspense grows until the scene of the final battle.

The tension between contemporary concerns and the ancient traditions of the stewards of the land, the Aborigines, is at the core of this novel. Fantasy enthusiasts will find a new world to explore, but the book's appeal should be wider.

1017   Yanagi, Akinobu. *Australia.* Illus. with photos by the author. SERIES: Children of the World. Gareth Stevens 1988, LB $12.95 (1-55532-222-0). 64pp. Nonfiction.

Scott Lowe, a 10-year-old boy, lives on the grounds of the largest zoo in Australia because his parents work there. His life is similar to that of other middle-class, surburban children throughout Australia. He lives in a comfortable house, goes to a well-equipped school, and has lots of opportunities for sports and family barbecues. The zoo setting adds extra child interest to this nicely photographed pictorial essay.

Titles in the Children of the World series also include a reference section, written at a slightly higher reading level than the first part of the book. All of the standard topics necessary for assignments are covered, although some of the information is superficial due to the section's brevity. A short reading list, a glossary, ideas for research projects and activities, and an index are included. There is also a volume on New Zealand.

GRADES 7–9

1018 ***Australia in Pictures.*** Illus. with photos. SERIES: Visual Geography. Lerner 1990, LB $11.95 (0-8225-1855-4). 64pp. Nonfiction.

This series volume provides a succinct survey of the history, geography, culture, and economy of Australia. Though it reads like an expanded encyclopedia article, it may be more palatable than earlier editions by dint of the new color photos. Above all, the book is most useful for school assignments. Includes index. Another recently revised volume features New Zealand.

1019 Ball, John. ***Fiji.*** Illus. with photos by Chris Fairclough. SERIES: Let's Visit Places and Peoples of the World. Chelsea House 1988, LB $14.95 (0-222-00984-5). 96pp. Nonfiction.

There are few recent books on the Pacific. This volume from the extensive Let's Visit series, originally published by Burke Books and distributed by Chelsea House, covers the history, geography, and current daily life of Fiji. The many color photos will appeal to report writers and armchair travelers alike, but the text is often superficial or sensationalistic. The author's calling a chapter on history "Cannibals, Chiefs and Parliament" places undue emphasis on this particular aspect of earlier Fijian society, especially when the chapter itself mentions it within only one of its sentences.

Australia, New Zealand, and New Guinea are also represented in the series. The volume on New Guinea is particularly stereotypical. Chapter titles such as "Curious Customs" and the continual use of the word "primitive" are reminiscent of books from the 1950s, not the 1980s. It is hoped that Chelsea House will replace the Burke Books titles (those with the ISBN prefix 0-222) with more sensitive, in-depth materials.

1020 Ball, John. ***We Live in New Zealand.*** Illus. with photos by Chris Fairclough. SERIES: Living Here. Franklin Watts 1982, LB $9.49 (0-531-04781-4). 64pp. Nonfiction.

Similar to its counterparts in this series, this is a compilation of almost 30 interviews with New Zealanders from many walks of life. Maoris, people of European descent (Pakehas), and Pacific Islanders are represented, and their occupations range from Member of Parliament to bus driver to alpine guide. Women seem to be underrepresented, but this approach gives readers some insight into the New Zealand economy and contemporary society. One interview does require some further explanation: the teacher of Maori crafts retells the traditional legend concerning the Maoris' arrival in Aoteraroa as a historical event. Archaeologists believe that the arrival date is earlier than the 1350 AD that is cited in the legend.

1021 Collins, Alan. *Jacob's Ladder.* Originally published in 1987 by Univ. of Queensland Pr. under the title *The Boys from Bondi.* Dutton/Lodestar 1989, HB $13.95 (0-525-67272-9). 149pp. Fiction.

Jacob was born in the late 1930s into a Jewish community in Australia that swelled with the refugees ("reffos" in Australian slang) from Hitler's Germany. He has been brought up with the bare minimum of Jewish education, but when he and his younger brother, Solly, are orphaned, they are placed in a Jewish home for children, populated with refugee children. As Jacob grows to manhood, he wrestles with his feelings about his religion, his weakening relationship with his brother, and his first sexual experiences.

After he leaves the home, he is apprenticed to a printer. In his free time, he attends meetings at two different groups, a communist youth organization where he meets Peg, and a Zionist group where he encounters Ruti again, a young woman with whom he had grown up in the children's home. Peg is a fun-loving radical, and Ruti is well meaning and motherly, but both characters remain wooden and flat.

Solly, the younger brother, who has attached himself to the mother of one of his friends and gone off to live with them, comes back into contact with Jacob when Solly is sentenced to the State Home for Boys for a minor infraction. At the trial, Jacob makes a hasty decision and tells Solly to make a run for it. As they both dash to the ferries that transport people in Sydney's harbor, the younger brother accidentally falls into the water and dies. Although Jacob experiences the deaths of all three of his family members, his emotional responses to these events fall within a very narrow range.

Like the United States and Canada, Australia is a land of immigrants, and so this treatment of one of the minority cultures within the European community is important to understanding Australia's multicultural society. The anti-Semitism, expressed in the mocking, off-the-cuff remarks of many minor characters, is a realistic undercurrent. Unfortunately, this first novel by an Australian journalist, which seems to have some autobiographical elements, does not fully bring its characters to life. It is about an aspect of Australian life that is not well-known to many Americans, but the social milieu of the novel is stronger than its characterizations.

Garrett, Dan, and Warrill Grinrod. *Australia.*
See entry 1001, Grades 4–6.

1022 Germaine, Elizabeth, and Ann Burckhardt. *Cooking the Australian Way.* Illus. with photos by Robert L. Wolfe and Diane Wolfe. SERIES: Easy Menu Ethnic Cookbooks. Lerner 1990, LB $9.95 (0-8225-0923-7). 52pp. Nonfiction.

The attractive photos, easy-to-follow recipes, and informative introduction to food customs in Australia will invite readers into the kitchen to try out these dishes. As in other books in this series, a number of dishes that can be used to put together typical lunches or dinners are presented. Although Australian cuisine has broadened as immigrants from many nations have come to the continent, the dishes included are mostly those with some British origins.

Higham, Charles. *The Maoris.*
See entry 1005, Grades 4–6.

1023   Hinton, Harold C. *East Asia and the Western Pacific 1989.* First appeared as a book entitled *The Far East and Southwest Pacific 1968.* Illus. with photos. SERIES: The World Today. Stryker-Post 1989, P $6.50 (0-943448-48-4). 138pp. Nonfiction.

This series provides a useful, relatively inexpensive source of current facts and political information on this region of the world. Each volume in the series is revised annually to include current events. The short chapters on Australia and New Zealand will aid report writers, but information on the smaller islands of the Pacific is very limited. It is disappointing to find that these nations and dependencies are not covered adequately by a series that usually has more information on even the smallest nations in each region.

1024   Lepthien, Emilie U. *Australia.* Illus. with photos. SERIES: Enchantment of the World. Childrens Pr. 1982, LB $23.95 (0-516-02751-4). 128pp. Nonfiction.

Although comparable in scope to the other books in this comprehensive series for upper grades and intermediate school students, the text of this volume is sometimes choppy. The chapter on history exemplifies this negative quality. Bold headings, followed by short paragraphs, break up the flow of historical information. The two chapters that cover the different states and territories of Australia include appropriate details and read more easily. This work will be most useful for report-writing assignments, with its "mini-facts at a glance" section that has almost as much information in six pages as other books contain in 32 or 48, because of the small typeface used. In addition to history and geography, chapters on Aboriginals, the economy, and contemporary life and culture are included. There is an index.

Mahy, Margaret. *Memory.*
See entry 1037, Grades 10–12.

1025   Noonan, Michael. *McKenzie's Boots.* First published in 1987 by Univ. of Queensland Pr. Orchard 1988, LB $13.99 (0-531-08348-9). 249pp. Fiction.

Although Rod is only 15, he enlists illegally in the Australian army and is sent to New Guinea, where he distinguishes himself for his bravery. But his is an unconventional war story, and in it Rod begins to think about the true nature of the enemy that he has been sent to fight.

Rod's reasons for joining up are complicated. He is extremely large for his age and seems to feel out of place. He is having difficulties with his alcoholic mother, and his father is already in the army. He would like to win the affection of his childhood friend, Brenda, and when her mother mentions that he would look handsome in uniform, he is ready to enlist. The army's first efforts to reject him only strengthen his resolve.

By the time Rod is in the army, he is dedicated to the cause. He is ready to kill Japanese because they are the enemy, but he never figured that he would meet a Japanese soldier face-to-face, while they were both hunting for butterflies. Although Rod later assists in the capture of Ohara, at the insistence of his superiors, and accompanies the prisoner back to Australia for interrogation, he cannot get over his feelings of sympathy and friendship for the man, even as other Australians show their hostility.

This relationship affects Rod for the next few years of his short life. He witnesses both Japanese and Australian atrocities. Although he continues to hold fast to his conviction that not all Japanese are barbarians, most of the other Australian characters voice the opposite opinion.

There is a subtheme about homosexuality as it concerns one of Rod's former teachers, who shows up as an intelligence officer in New Guinea. The attitude toward homosexuality is almost as negative as the attitude toward the Japanese, and although it may be realistic in terms of the times, it seems overdone today.

The boots that figure in the title are mentioned often in the text, and although they serve as an important part of the end of the novel, the frequent references tend to be boring. The prologue and epilogue concern Rod's best friend in the service, Nugget Bates, and his contemporary business associations with the Japanese, indicative of Australia's current relationship with its former enemy.

This book will give readers a slightly different viewpoint of the war and Australia's participation in the conflict. It may lead to discussion of the stereotypes that are perpetuated in wartime. As an aside, it should be noted that the people of New Guinea, where much of the action takes place, are pejoratively referred to as "natives" in several sentences. The landmarks of Sydney provide a realistic background for many of the chapters.

Park, Ruth. *Playing Beatie Bow.*
See entry 1009, Grades 4–6.

1026 Phipson, Joan. *Hit and Run.* Macmillan 1985, HB $12.95 (0-689-50362-8); 1989, P $3.95 (0-02-044665-9). 123pp. Fiction.

Survival has always been an important theme in Australian life. Roland Fleming, a pampered young man from a wealthy family, could hardly expect to find himself in a situation where he had to fight for his life, but one day his irresponsible actions place him in difficult circumstances. Roland is a teenager who must prove himself. Although he craves the love of his parents, he does not feel that they really love him. When he is teased by two young garage mechanics, his pride gets the best of him, and he steals a Ferrari. As he careens through town, he hits a baby carriage and keeps on going.

Constable Gordon Sutton tries to catch him. They wind up on the rough terrain of an Australian cattle station, far from any outside help, and each must battle alone and together to stay alive until help arrives. This frightening incident—first the loss of control in the car accident itself, then the almost automatic urge to drive away from the scene, the feeling of being hunted down, and finally the struggle with the land and the elements—helps Roland to take a positive step in his own process toward maturity. He decides to help Constable Gordon, after the police officer falls and hurts himself badly, even though it will mean his capture and the notification of his father.

The spoiled young man decides that he is guilty and must serve time for the accident, although his father tries to get him acquitted. This is another step in Roland's emotional growth.

The land is almost another character. Phipson's hand is very sure as she describes the dirt road away from the highway and the scrub-covered hills as well as the valley where Roland finally finds a short refuge. The remoteness of the Australian bush country envelops the characters right after they leave the road.

Phipson is an established Australian novelist who has published many books in the United States. Her prose is taut and controlled, and the rapid pace of the novel builds with each page. The growing relationship between Roland Fleming and Gordon Sutton helps Roland to move beyond his own needs and to recognize the importance of others.

1027 Pople, Maureen. *The Other Side of the Family.* Henry Holt 1988, HB $13.95 (0-8050-0758-X); Knopf 1990, P $3.25 (0-394-83854-8). 176pp. Fiction.

During World War II, some English children traveled to Australia (as they also did to Canada and the United States) to escape the dangers and privations of war. In this novel, Kate Tucker, age 15, is sent halfway around the world to Sydney, Australia, to live with her maternal grandparents, the Dawsons. But the war catches up with her, as this safe haven begins to feel threatened by Japanese submarines. Kate's grandparents want to send her deep into the countryside to "the other side of the family," her father's mother, although no one has had any communication with her for years.

When Kate arrives at Parsons Creek, she finds out that family history differs from the version she has been told. Her grandmother, Mrs. Tucker, is not a rich, selfish woman who refused to accept the bride her son had chosen. It takes a while for Kate to understand the circumstances of her grandmother's eccentric life. She seems to live in poverty. The older woman is also deaf, but Kate does not realize this fact and sometimes believes her grandmother is a madwoman. When old family friends help her understand the situation and her grandmother's reasons for not telling Kate about it in the first place, they also give her some insight into the relationship between Mrs. Tucker and her only son. Kate finds out that her grandmother was never wealthy and that her father had become embarrassed about his modest origins when he met the young woman destined to become Kate's mother.

Once the air is cleared, Kate and her grandmother realize that they enjoy each other's company, and at the end of her school vacation Kate vows to return to Parsons Creek again. She has made other friends as well, including the mother and son of the Italian family next door. They have been branded as enemies, although they are Australian citizens, but Kate resourcefully finds a way to help the townspeople cease their xenophobic behavior.

The wonderful characterizations of Kate, the people of Parsons Creek, and the Dawson grandparents, as well as the evocation of the atmosphere of the World War II era in Australia, set this first-person narrative apart. Pople has also written *A Nugget of Gold* (Henry Holt, 1989), is which chapters about a contemporary Australian girl alternate with the story of a girl who lived during the gold rush.

1028 Savage, Deborah. *Flight of the Albatross.* Houghton Mifflin 1989, HB $14.95 (0-395-45711-4). 258pp. Fiction.

A New York City teenager visits her mother on a small island off the coast of New Zealand's North Island and meets a Maori boy. More than a simple intercultural girl-meets-boy tale, this novel has several strong themes that will capture the reader's attention and encourage reflection on the issues presented. Sarah is a musician and interested in perfection and excellence. She is envious of her mother's position as a world authority on birds and resentful that she and her father were abandoned years before. Although Pauline has invited Sarah to spend the summer vacation with her, she has no time to re-create the broken relationship. Sarah is left to her own devices and begins to form friendships with three other women on the island—Mari Harris, her neighbor, a Maori married to a Pakeha; Daphne, the island's visiting nurse; and Hattie, an old Maori woman who wants to reconcile the differences between the Maoris and the Pekahas. Sarah finds a wounded albatross, a rare bird, and she and Hattie work together to nurse it back to health. Sarah finds it strangely satisfying to be involved in the same work as Pauline, without her mother knowing anything about it.

Her relationship with Mako, son of Mari and a Maori activist (who also abandoned his family years before) is troubled at first. They dislike each other, are resentful of each other's worlds, but grow to love one another. Hattie's powers cement their love, as Mako finally learns about his own destiny to become a leader of his people.

The old woman passes on her teachings to Mako, as well as the pendant of green jade, representing the Maori culture, and gold, representing the European culture. She tells Sarah and Mako of the curse that blights the lives of both Maoris and Pakehas, the curse that can be lifted only by one who can make the two groups live in peace with each other and the land. The albatross, finally flying on its own once again, soars to the heavens and carries the hopes and dreams of the three of them.

1029 Savage, Deborah. *A Rumor of Otters.* Houghton Mifflin 1986, HB $12.95 (0-395-41186-6). 160pp. Fiction.

Kept by her traditionalist father from going on the winter roundup, or muster, of sheep on her New Zealand homestead, Alexia decides to go on a journey of her own. She will go to a high mountain lake to search for otters, mammals that have never been seen in New Zealand, according to all scientific evidence. (Very few mammals are indigenous to this island country.)

She undertakes her quest because Billy, an older Maori man, has told her that he has seen them. The trip is more difficult than she could ever have imagined but more rewarding than anything she has ever done before. Her fight for survival and her feelings of exhilaration and understanding when she finds the wondrous otters make this both an exciting adventure story and a thoughtful novel of a young woman's very personal rite of passage.

Tod, Alexia's brother, is the focus of a subplot. He has been allowed to go with the other men on his first muster, and he has his own experiences that test his skills. Both Alexia and Tod are perfectly at home in their rural environment and have strong relationships with their horses and their dogs, but Alexia has made a break with the past. She is a contemporary young woman who wants to make her own decisions. She will not be content to be the wife of the owner of a sheep ranch, as her mother was. She is probably representative of a growing number of young people who want a different life in today's New Zealand.

The book is filled with descriptions of the natural beauty and the animal life of New Zealand. Although there are some references to Maoris throughout the book, and Billy is certainly a respected figure, readers are given very little background information about Maoris.

1030   Southall, Ivan. *Josh.* Macmillan 1988, LB $12.95 (0-02-786280-1). 179pp. Fiction.

Josh is a stylistic tour de force—an evocation of five days in a boy's life in rural Australia, written with humor, suspense, and a strong sense of adolescence. Although the time period of the story is probably the 1930s, it could probably have taken place in any of the decades since then. The differences between urban and rural youth have probably decreased, but there still may be tensions when a strange city boy shows up in a small town.

Josh has come from Melbourne to Ryan Creek to visit his Aunt Clara, the only relative who has remained in the town established by his great-grandfather. His older cousins have all told him about the town and he is eager to see it. However, he is not prepared for the kind of negative welcome that he receives from the children of the locality nor for the strict rules of behavior laid down by his very proper aunt.

Josh has a hard time with certain rural activities, like trapping rabbits and even just watching Laura (who's trying hard to win his affection) make a dangerous jump off the railway bridge into the dam below. He is beaten up by one of the town boys because of a dispute concerning his participation in a cricket match. And in between all these disturbing incidents, Josh talks to himself about his problems in relating to everyone in the town, including his aunt. The trip that started out being so much fun turns into an unmitigated disaster.

Josh won the Carnegie Medal in England. Southall writes about the origins of the story in a book of essays entitled *A Journal of Discovery: On Writing for Children* (Macmillan, 1976). It is interesting to read about how the author has transformed several personal experiences into this fine novel.

1031   Stark, Al. *Australia: A Lucky Land.* Illus. with photos. SERIES: Discovering Our Heritage. Dillon 1987, LB $14.95 (0-87518-365-4). 151pp. Nonfiction.

The comfortable home life in Australia's cities and suburbs, the very different life-style in the outback—where students receive their education through a combination of home schooling, two-way-radio contact with professional teachers, and occasional days spent with other students in the larger towns—and a chapter on Australians who have become famous in Europe and America are included, in addition to chapters on history, Australian celebrations, and the natural environment. The glossary of Australian slang is an interesting supplement, but the book lacks an adequate discussion of the Aborigine situation today.

Thiele, Colin. *Fire in the Stone.*
See entry 1014, Grades 4–6.

1032 Wrightson, Patricia. *Balyet.* Macmillan 1989, HB $12.95 (0-689-50468-3); Penguin/Puffin 1990, P $3.95 (0-14-034339-3). 132pp. Fiction.

Patricia Wrightson is probably one of the best-known Australian novelists for children and young adults in her own country and around the world. In 1986, she won the prestigious 1986 Hans Christian Andersen Award, given by the International Board on Books for Young People to authors for the body of their work. In many of her novels, Wrightson uses Aboriginal folklore and traditions as the foundations for her own original and intriguing stories. She incorporates this authentic material with a great sense of responsibility, and as she says, in the author's note of *Balyet*, "this is not the story of Jo, Terry, Lance or Kevin," the young white children and adolescents who enter Balyet's world, the world of the Australian hills. Not only is Patricia Wrightson knowledgeable about Aboriginal legends, but she also pays homage to the very strong relationship that Aboriginal people have always had with the land.

Jo is a young girl who hides in Mrs. Willet's car so that she can encounter a certain classmate at his camping site. Mrs. Willet, her next door neighbor and an Aboriginal Clever Woman, a keeper of the traditions, is going to visit the sacred sites and sing the ancient songs as her teacher taught her long ago. She is surprised to find Jo but tolerates her presence, as they have almost a grandmother-granddaughter relationship. Once in the hills, Jo joins Terry and Lance, the older brother, and flirts with both of them. This foreshadows the story that will unfold about Balyet, the girl who lived thousands of years ago and who was condemned to remain alone because she broke the laws of her people. She fell in love with two blood brothers who killed each other because of jealousy.

Balyet is still alive and longs for companionship. She calls through the hills and tries to summon people to her, for her own people have condemned her to an everlasting solitary life. First she calls Kevin to her, a little boy for whom Jo is babysitting, but Mrs. Willet succeeds in finding him before he is harmed. But then Jo is drawn to Balyet, who seems so much like herself.

Mrs. Willet and Jo fight over Balyet. The older woman is strong in her feeling that Balyet disobeyed the law, but Jo finally convinces her to feel some sympathy for the young girl, suddenly cut off from all human contact. Mrs. Willet brings some resolution to the story by summoning her wise teacher from the spirit world. He and the other spirits of the people release Balyet from her living hell, and her human form is transmuted into the natural surroundings of the hills, just as the spirits of the ancient ones who lived in the Dreamtime became all the natural features of the land known today as Australia.

This is a haunting story that may invite interested readers to read more about Aboriginal folklore, but Wrightson's novel stands on its own as a compelling piece of literature for older children and young teenagers.

Wrightson, Patricia. *The Ice Is Coming.*
See entry 1016, Grades 4–6.

1033 ***Australia.*** Illus. with photos. SERIES: Library of Nations. Time-Life Books 1986, LB $25.93 (0-8094-5165-4). 160pp. Nonfiction.

Created by a team of writers and editors and intended primarily for the armchair traveler, this volume, like others in the series, is an informative and readable description of the island continent. The large format of the book allows room for the many impressive photographs. The five chapters are each followed by pictorial essays, including one on the Aborigines and another on the recreational pleasures of Australia's coastline. The chapter on history is a solid account of the country from the time the Aborigines arrived up until the 1980s. Australia's contemporary society is described with some emphasis on its increasingly multicultural makeup. Although some myths about the old independent sheep shearers and the like are debunked, stereotypical characterizations of the Australians as the new hedonists are included in the text. Teenagers with some sense of perspective will learn a lot of useful information and probably want to visit Australia at the earliest opportunity. Includes index, extensive bibliography, and references to periodical articles.

1034 Chatwin, Bruce. ***The Songlines.*** Viking 1987, HB $18.95 (0-670-80605-6); Penguin 1988, P $8.95 (0-14-009429-6). 293pp. Nonfiction.

Bruce Chatwin is a most unusual travel writer. While providing a series of amusing and sometimes ironic portraits of the individuals he met on a journey through central Australia, he also gives readers the opportunity to ponder the nature of nomadic life. Having traveled with nomadic groups in Iran, Afghanistan, Mauritania, and other countries, Chatwin visits Australia to learn about the Songlines, the ancient tracks of the Dreamtime, created with words and musical notes, that traveled the continent from coast to coast. The Songlines were both boundaries and connecting points between the different Aboriginal groups.

This is a book for mature readers with a philosophical bent. Chatwin includes excerpts from his notebooks, written over a number of years. Quotes from philosophers and scholars, notes taken on his many trips, and other writings on a variety of subjects lead the reader to question the differences between those who settle in one place and those who constantly change their location, living usually as hunter-gatherers, such as was the case with most Australian Aborigines. Although most Aborigines today live in more permanent settlements, their nomadic traditions sometimes still play a part in daily life, and the skills, stories, and customs of earlier times remain important.

Chatwin is an excellent writer, and the vignettes that he sketches are insightful, sometimes satiric, and full of realistic details about human behavior. He is concerned about Aboriginal rights and critical of the European majority's treatment of the original inhabitants and their land, but he is never didactic. He clearly takes pleasure in making friends, and his book enables readers to meet a host of memorable people from the Australian outback.

Collins, Alan. ***Jacob's Ladder.***
See entry 1021, Grades 7–9.

1035 Davidson, Robyn. ***Tracks.*** Illus. with photos. Pantheon 1983, P $6.95 (0-394-72167-5). 256pp. Nonfiction.

Camels were first imported to Australia in the 1850s to assist in the development of the desert that covers much of the central and western areas of the continent. There is still a wild population in those areas and a few domesticated camels that are used for tourist rides in towns like Alice Springs. It is there that Robyn Davidson began her quest to learn all about camels and planned her trip westward across the outback to the coast, riding and walking with four camels and a dog.

During her two years of preparation and training, she met many Aboriginal people who knew the survival skills necessary to life in the outback. Davidson was an outspoken young woman with an unusual dream. Although a monetary advance from the National Geographic Society helped her economic situation, the successful completion of her trip was due mostly to her own determination and her growing knowledge of her animals and the desert. She was welcomed in Aboriginal communities and cattle stations along the way and describes with realism and respect the people that she met.

Older teenagers will be attracted to Davidson's story on several levels. It is an animal story, an adventurous tale of survival, the diary of an unusual woman, and a realistic description of Aboriginal life today in the outback.

1036 Hulme, Keri. ***The Bone People.*** Louisiana State Univ. Pr. 1985, HB $19.95 (0-8071-1284-4); Penguin 1986, P $8.95 (0-14-008922-5). 450pp. Fiction.

A complex, poetic novel that may be read only by a small audience, this is the story of three people whose lives intersect on the coast of New Zealand's South Island. Kerewin Holmes (a very autobiographical character), an artist, a loner, part British and part Maori, lives in a tower of her own creation. Simon, a child rescued from the sea, without any real identification, and adopted by a Maori man, Joe Gillayley, invades Kerewin's tower and brings her into contact with people again. Simon, who has not spoken since his rescue several years before, is believed to be autistic. His adoptive father, Joe, has not been the same since his wife and baby son died. He drowns his sorrows in alcohol and vacillates between abuse and indulgence in his relationship with Simon.

These three people form a new grouping—almost a family—in which they slowly open up to the love and companionship of each other. But these feelings get wrecked by violence—the boy and the father are caught up in a cycle of destruction, and eventually Kerewin is touched by it also. Joe almost kills Simon and is sent to jail. Although he begins to recover physically, Simon becomes more withdrawn without Joe and Kerewin, who has run away from the situation. Eventually, the three are drawn together again to make a new beginning.

Maori culture pervades the novel. Phrases and conversations in the Maori language are translated in the extensive glossary. Objects made by Maori craftspeople are prized. Near the end of the novel, Joe is taken in by an old man who is guarding the symbol of the Maori life force. He imparts his tales and knowledge to Joe and then dies, willing Joe his land and the job of watching over what the elder considered to be the soul of Aotearoa. After this somewhat magical encounter, Joe becomes whole once again. He can face his son and the woman he loves.

The stream-of-consciousness style of writing in many of the sections of the novel is daunting, but once the reader masters the rich language and enters this world of three tormented people and their struggle to understand the wisdom of the past, the rewards are worthwhile. This book won the 1985 Booker McConnell Prize for the best novel of the year published in Great Britain.

1037 Mahy, Margaret. *Memory.* Macmillan 1988, HB $13.95 (0-689-50446-2); Dell 1989, P $3.25 (0-440-20433-X). 277pp. Fiction.

In the English-speaking world, Margaret Mahy is probably the best-known author of children's and young adult books from New Zealand. Her style and themes vary greatly from humor to the supernatural (*The Haunting* and *The Tricksters*) to science fiction (*Aliens in the Family*). *Memory*, one of her most recent books, is yet another type of novel.

Realistic, but with some expressionistic touches, this is the story of Jonny Dart's search for the truth concerning his sister's death. Jonny is now 19, a currently unemployed, unskilled young man who was once on his way to becoming a child star. His older sister and tap-dancing partner had died five years before, falling off the cliffs into the sea below.

Three people were in that seaside park when Janine fell to her death—Jonny, Janine, and Bonny, their friend. Jonny feels that he must now find Bonny, the only person who can tell him if his memories of that night are true. Jonny feels that he may have been responsible for the death, that he may have accidentally pushed Janine. Although he has lost touch with Bonny, he manages to find her family. They are reluctant to give her address to this young man, who shows up drunk and with fresh bruises on his face, the result of a pub brawl.

Driven back to the city, he wanders through the night, searching for a sign that will mean something to him. He finds Sophie, an older woman suffering from Alzheimer's disease, "someone with a whole history, but a broken memory." Sophie seems to recognize Jonny as a long-lost cousin and allows him to come home with her. Although Jonny is repulsed by the terrible condition of her house and frightened by her inability to care for herself, he is touched by her humanity and gives himself the task of caring for her. His own growing concern about another person begins to break down the shell that has grown around his feelings.

Somehow his odyssey has also brought him back to Bonny, for she lives next door. His subconscious memory must have led him to the part of town where she was living. She confirms his innocence but rejects his amorous advances. However, Jonny may not need her anymore. Although his memories of her as a magical being—a "Pythoness" who looked into the future and gave him direction—are strong, he is now ready to meet life on its own terms.

This very personal story is set against a backdrop of life in a New Zealand city in the 1980s. The fight for Maori land rights, urban renewal, social welfare issues, and class conflicts are woven seamlessly into this novel, the strength of which lies in its relationships and its movement between the past and present. Mahy is a masterful stylist, and this book will appeal to readers who can follow the intricate twists and turns of Jonny's interior thoughts.

Noonan, Michael. *McKenzie's Boots.*
See entry 1025, Grades 7–9.

Phipson, Joan. *Hit and Run.*
See entry 1026, Grades 7–9.

Savage, Deborah. *Flight of the Albatross.*
See entry 1028, Grades 7–9.

Savage, Deborah. *A Rumor of Otters.*
See entry 1029, Grades 7–9.

1038 Terrill, Ross. *The Australians.* Simon & Schuster/Touchstone 1988, P $8.95 (0-671-66239-2). 354pp. Nonfiction.

The politically astute senior high school student should find this overview of contemporary Australia revealing. Written by a former Australian who now lives in the United States, it exposes the views of a great many inhabitants of Australia on a variety of subjects, including politics, labor, immigration, multiculturalism and its converse—racism—Aboriginal land rights, and the arts.

The people who were interviewed for the book range from high government officials, both past and present, to cabbies, scholars, students, and pub patrons. The language is sometimes blunt, but the mosaic of opinions will give readers some insight into Australian society as it exists today. Some of the information about political parties and politicians may be difficult to wade through without prior background, but several of the chapters can be read individually, depending on the reader's interests. The first chapters involve Terrill's own memories about Australian life in the 1940s and 1950s, as well as his reactions to the changes that occurred in the ensuing years.

Although there is no formal bibliography, there are several pages dealing with "Notes on Sources," from which many references can be gleaned. Includes index.

Appendix 1

PROFESSIONAL SOURCES

Each contributor has compiled a list of additional resources to assist teachers, librarians, and others who work with children. Many of these resources provide background information on the country, region, or ethnic group, or explore themes in the books that have been included in the main section of this bibliography. Other resources provide more up-to-date information on current issues. Some cite other bibliographies, and some list resources in other media, such as films, videos, and music. The lists corresponding to each chapter differ, for each reflects the personal interests and recommendations of its contributor.

CHAPTER 1. UNITED STATES: AFRICAN AMERICANS

[April Hoffman, Sandra Payne, and Reeves Smith]

Books

Adams, Russel L. *Great Negroes Past and Present*. 3rd ed. Edited by David P. Ross, Jr. Chicago: Afro-Am Publishing Co., 1984. A collective biography of 177 men and women, this is an ideal reference source for teachers and librarians seeking information on African Americans whose contributions have been overlooked in other sources.

McCann, Donnarae, and Gloria Woodard. *The Black American in Books for Children: Readings in Racism*. 2nd ed. Metuchen, N.J.: Scarecrow Pr., 1985. A collection of essays focusing on criteria for selection and the avoidance of stereotypes; major contributions to this work have been made by members of the Council on Interracial Books for Children.

McKissack, Patricia, and Fredrick McKissack. *The Civil Rights Movement in America: From 1865 to the Present*. Chicago: Childrens Pr., 1987. A textbook, suitable for middle and high schools, that provides a comprehensive history not only of the civil rights movement but also of African Americans as a whole in the last 150 years, from the perspective of African Americans themselves.

Sims, Rudine. *Shadow and Substance: Afro-American Experience in Contemporary Children's Fiction*. 2nd ed. Chicago: NCTE/ALA, 1982. Provides an important theoretical framework for the evaluation of picture books and juvenile fiction about African Americans.

Periodicals and Other Publications

The Black Experience in Children's Literature. New York: New York Public Library, Office of Children's Services, 1989. A list, with brief annotations, of outstanding books, both recent publications and classics, for readers up to the age of 14.

Books for the Teen Age. New York: New York Public Library. An annual list of outstanding fiction and nonfiction for young adults, with sections devoted to books about the black experience.

Celebrating the Dream. New York: New York Public Library, Office of Young Adult Services, 1990. An annotated list of recommended books about the black experience, including recent publications and classics, books published for young adults, and adult books suitable for young adults.

Interracial Books for Children Bulletin. New York: Council on Interracial Books for Children, 1969–1986, 1988– . Publishes critical essays and reviews about multicultural literature in general.

Multicultural Children's and Young Adult Literature. Madison, Wis.: Cooperative Children's Book Center, 1989. An annotated list of recommended titles published since 1980; although the focus is on multicultural books in general, a significant proportion of the books included deal with the heritage and experience of African Americans.

CHAPTER 2. UNITED STATES: ASIAN AMERICANS

[Ellin Chu and Carolyn Vang Schuler]

"Asian Americans in Children's Books." *Interracial Books for Children Bulletin*, vol. 7, nos. 2–3, 1976, p. 3. This article provides specific questions for evaluating the literature and examines older works on Asian Americans that were seen as perpetuating stereotypes and misconceptions about the various cultures in question.

Jenkins, Esther C., and Mary Austin. *Literature for Children about Asians and Asian Americans: Analysis and Annotated Bibliography, with Additional Readings for Adults.* Westport, Conn.: Greenwood Pr., 1987. This extensive annotated bibliography provides detailed information about books intended for young people; groups included are the Chinese, Japanese, Koreans, and some cultural groups of Southeast Asia. Not included are Pacific Islanders and Asian Indians. Most useful are both the listing of criteria librarians should use for selecting books and a discussion of the rationale for introducing the literature of these ethnic groups into the curriculum. A major drawback is that no titles published after 1985 are included, although there has been an explosion in publishing about these groups since that time.

Sue, Stanley, and Nathaniel Wagner, eds. *Asian Americans: Psychological Perspectives.* Palo Alto, Calif.: Science and Behavior Books, 1973. Though an older study, this scholarly work gives some insight into the themes and conflicts touched upon in literature for children and young adults about Asian Americans.

Takaki, Ronald. *Strangers from a Different Shore: A History of Asian Americans.* Boston: Little, Brown, 1989. The sagas of both the older immigrant communities and the newest arrivals from all over Asia are covered in this outstanding Pulitzer Prize nominee. This is the most authoritative, eloquent, and complete volume yet written. Advanced high school students as well as adults will appreciate this work.

Wang, Helen, comp. "China and Chinese Culture: A Selected Booklist to Promote a Better Understanding, Grades K–8." Greater Mid-Atlantic Chapter, Chinese

American Librarians' Association (CALA), 1990. This is one of the more recent bibliographies of children's literature by and about China and Chinese Americans.

579

PROFESSIONAL
SOURCES

CHAPTER 3. UNITED STATES: HISPANIC AMERICANS

[Oralia Garza de Cortes]

Allen, Adela Artola. *Library Services for Hispanic Children: A Guide for Public and School Librarians*. Tucson, Ariz.: Oryx Pr., 1987. Deals primarily with professional issues related to library services for Hispanic children, including ways of evaluating programs and materials. There is an annotated booklist of materials in Spanish and in English, which is especially useful for the Spanish-language materials. The resource list in English includes books about Mexican-American youngsters.

Martinez, Julio, and Francisco Lomeli, eds. *Chicano Literature*. Westport, Conn.: Greenwood Pr., 1985. Contains essays on Chicano literature, including children's literature and adult authors whose works may be suitable for young adults.

Moore, Opal, and Donnarae MacCann. "Paternalism and Assimilation in Books about Hispanics." *Children's Literature Association Quarterly* 12 (Summer 1987). Provides an overview of the history of publishing children's books about Hispanic Americans, with emphasis on the theme of assimilation and how it has been treated.

Schon, Isabel. *A Hispanic Heritage: A Guide to Juvenile Books about Hispanic People and Culture*. 3rd ed. Metuchen, N.J.: Scarecrow Pr., 1988. An annotated bibliography of children's and young adult books in English from every Spanish-speaking country in the world, including the United States and Spain. Entries are in alphabetical order rather than by grade, making it especially difficult to track P–6 titles amidst the mass of young adult material, most of which is nonfiction. Many titles are university-press published. Annotations focus primarily on diacritical errors and on the negative stereotypes of Hispanic culture. Includes author-title index and an author's introduction.

CHAPTER 4. UNITED STATES: NATIVE AMERICANS

[Elaine Goley; with notes compiled by Brenda Naze and Lyn Miller-Lachmann]

Coltelli, Laura. *Winged Words: American Indian Writers Speak*. Lincoln: Univ. of Nebraska Pr., 1990. Contains interviews with contemporary Native American writers. Although none of the authors interviewed writes expressly for children or young adults, the authors raise many issues facing Native American writers in general, and some of the authors included write adult fiction that may be suitable for young adults.

Crosby, Alfred W., and Helen Nadler. "The Voyages of Columbus: A Turning Point in World History." *ERIC Clearinghouse for Social Studies* (Oct. 1989): 1–43. This article is well-timed for the 500th anniversary of Columbus' voyage to the Americas. It is a reconsideration of traditional teaching about Columbus, and it provides some alternatives for presenting the history of the time.

Hill Witt, Shirley. "Pressure Points in Growing Up Indian." *Perspectives: The Civil Rights Quarterly* (Spring 1980): 24–31. Examines issues and problems facing Native American youngsters today as they navigate between two worlds.

Marriot, Alice, and Carol K. Rachlin. *American Indian Mythology*. New York: Harper and Row, 1968. An introduction to the principal Native American myths throughout the Americas. This is a fairly sophisticated presentation, more suitable for adults than for high school researchers.

Slapin, Beverly, and Doris Seale. *Books Without Bias: Through Indian Eyes*. Berkeley, Calif.: Oyate Pr., 1988. Native American authors, educators, and others discuss issues of concern in books about the Native American experience, including criteria for selection.

Zvirin, Stephanie. "Growing Up Native American." *Booklist* (Nov. 1, 1987): 468–469. A list of recommended titles for older children and young adults. Includes folklore, mythology, and poetry as well as fiction and nonfiction. Recommendations include brief annotations.

CHAPTER 5. CANADA

[Joan McGrath]

Books

Between Two Worlds: The Canadian Immigrant Experience. Edited by Milly Charon. Dunvegan, Ont.: Quadrant Editions. A collection of short stories and personal narratives by immigrants who made the decision to come to Canada—contemporary and of the recent past.

Hawkins, Freda. *Canada and Immigration: Public Policy and Public Concern*. 2nd ed. Kingston, Ont., and Montreal, Que.: Institute of Public Administration of Canada, McGill/Queen's Univ. Pr., 1988. A history of government policy since World War II and the first full-length treatment of Canadian policy in fifteen years.

The Illustrated History of Canada. Edited by Craig Brown. Toronto, Ont.: Lester and Orpen Dennys, 1987. The history of Canada, from the remote past to the present day, as recounted by six of Canada's most respected historians: Ramsay Cook, Desmond Morton, Christopher Moore, Arthur Ray, Peter Waite, and Graham Wynn. Beautifully illustrated.

Landsberg, Michele. *Michele Landsberg's Guide to Children's Books: With a Treasury of More Than 350 Great Children's Books*. New York: Penguin, 1985. A personal, engaging, and idiosyncratic overview of children's literature in Canada, by an author renowned for her double interests in social issues and the welfare of women and children in particular, as well as in the promotion of the best in children's literature.

Saltman, Judith. *Modern Canadian Children's Books*. New York: Oxford Univ. Press, 1987. A scholarly view of Canadian children's literature, under the headings of Writing and Publishing, Picture Books and Picture-Story Books, Fiction, Historical Fiction, The Oral Tradition and Poetry.

Encyclopedias

The Canadian Encyclopedia. 4 vols. Edited by Jim Marsh. Edmonton, Alta.: Hurtig, 1988. The source for information on matters Canadian in all disciplines, with particular attention to Canada's literature and creative artists.

The Junior Encyclopedia of Canada. 5 vols. Edited by James H. Marsh. Edmonton, Alta.: Hurtig, 1990. Lavishly illustrated junior version of the *Canadian Encylcopedia*, with great youth appeal; emphasis on subjects of pop culture of particular interest to readers aged 13–18.

Periodicals

CCL: Canadian Children's Literature/Littérature canadienne pour la jeunesse. Guelph, Ont.: Canadian Children's Literature Association. A journal of criticism and review, in-depth studies, and reviews, often with a thematic approach to issues of children's literature, both historically and in present-day publishing.

C.M.: A Reviewing Journal of Canadian Materials for Young People. Canadian Library Association.

Quill & Quire. Toronto, Ont. Read by publishers, booksellers, librarians, writers, and teachers across Canada. Features, news, columns, and reviews of happenings in Canada's world of print. Twice annually; includes *Canadian Publishers Directory*; a necessity in any Canadian office or library.

CHAPTER 6. MEXICO AND THE CARIBBEAN

[Heather Caines and Oralia Garza de Cortes]

The Black Experience in Children's Books. New York Public Library. This work is an annotated bibliography of books on the black experience. It is arranged geographically and then, within this arrangement, by topic or genre subdivision, with such categories as Picture Books, Stories, Folklore, and People and Places. The geographical areas covered are the United States, South and Central America, the Caribbean, Africa, and England. The work is compiled by the Black Experience in Children's Books Committee and is revised periodically. "This bibliography is intended for use by those studying children's literature and the Black Experience in children's books and may be used with all children from preschool through junior high school."

Books for the Teenage. New York Public Library. This work is similar in scope and purpose to *The Black Experience in Children's Books.* However, it focuses on books suitable for and of interest to the teenager. It is also compiled by a committee and is issued annually. A useful source for tracking materials for the young adult.

Celebrating the Dream. New York Public Library, 1990. Similar in approach to *The Black Experience in Children's Books,* but focusing on young adult literature about black youngsters in the United States and elsewhere.

Meyer, Michael C., and William L. Sherman. *The Course of Mexican History.* 3rd ed. New York: Oxford Univ. Pr., 1987. An encyclopedic work, over 700 pages long, detailing the history of Mexico throughout the different periods of its history, from pre-Columbian times to the present. The book reads easily and explores historical subjects and themes in depth.

Schon, Isabel. *A Hispanic Heritage: A Guide to Juvenile Books about Hispanic People and Culture.* 3rd ed. Metuchen, N.J.: Scarecrow Pr., 1988. See annotation in sources for Chapter 3, United States: Hispanic Americans.

CHAPTER 7. CENTRAL AND SOUTH AMERICA

[Lyn Miller-Lachmann]

A good single-volume introduction to the countries of Central and South America is *Modern Latin America,* by Thomas E. Skidmore and Peter H. Smith (New York: Oxford Univ. Pr., 1984). For a basic discussion of the geography, history, and culture of each individual country, there is the Area Handbook Series, published by the U.S. Government Printing Office. The series is revised every five to ten years and is quite thorough, though reflecting a U.S.-centered perspective.

Since books cannot present the most up-to-date information for a rapidly changing region, periodicals are often the best sources of information. In addition to newspapers such as the *New York Times*, good sources include the bimonthly *Report on the Americas*, published by the North American Congress on Latin America (NACLA, 475 Riverside Drive, Room 454, New York, NY 10115, subscription, $22/yr.) and the weekly *Latin America Press* (Apartado 5594, Lima 100, Peru, subscription $40/yr.; ask for English version).

Much current nonfiction has focused on the environment. Adrian Cowell's *Decade of Destruction* (New York: Arcade, 1990) is the book version of the four-part documentary presented on PBS in fall 1990, dealing with the destruction of the Amazon rain forest. The video version is also available and highly recommended for classroom use.

Two opposing perspectives of the Nicaraguan revolution are contained in *Nicaragua in Revolution*, edited by Thomas Walker (New York: Praeger, 1981), which contains articles by scholars mostly sympathetic to the Sandinistas, and Shirley Christian, *Nicaragua: Revolution in the Family* (New York: Random House, 1985), which supports the Reagan Administration.

Testimonials give a personal perspective of events; among the most gripping are Jacobo Timerman's *Prisoner Without a Name, Cell Without a Number* (New York: Knopf, 1981), the harrowing account of a principled Jewish journalist's arrest and imprisonment during Argentina's "dirty war"; *Victor: An Unfinished Song* (London: Jonathan Cape, 1983), Joan Jara's story of her life with one of Chile's foremost musicians, who was killed in the 1973 coup; and *I, Rigoberta Menchu* (New York: Routledge, Chapman & Hall, 1985), the autobiography of a Mayan Indian woman in Guatemala who became politically active when the army destroyed her traditional community.

The Latin American literary "boom" of the past four decades has produced many fiction writers of note. Among those who have written extensively about the region, its culture, and its problems are Isabel Allende (Chile), Manlio Argueta (El Salvador), Miguel Angel Asturias (Guatemala), Julio Cortazar (Argentina), José Donoso (Chile), Mario Vargas Llosa (Peru), Gabriel García Marquez (Colombia), Manuel Puig (Brazil), Sergio Ramírez (Nicaragua), and Marta Traba (Colombia). A particularly accessible introduction to the genre of magical realism, as embodied by these authors, is Isabel Allende's *The House of the Spirits* (New York: Knopf, 1985).

Films are among the most effective ways of showing places and events. Recent feature films, widely available, that are set in Central and South America and are recommended are *El Norte* (1983, 139 minutes), the story of a brother and sister, Mayan Indians, who escape certain death in Guatemala to rebuild their lives in Los Angeles; *Missing* (1982, 122 minutes), which tells of a U.S. businessman's attempts to find his son after the military coup in Chile; and *The Official Story* (1987, 110 minutes), about an upper-middle-class Argentine woman's growing awareness that her adopted daughter was kidnapped from a "disappeared" couple.

CHAPTER 8. GREAT BRITAIN AND IRELAND

[Elaine Goley]

The Cambridge Historical Encyclopedia of Great Britain and Ireland. Edited by Christopher Haigh. New York: Cambridge Univ. Pr., 1990. Seven chapters of 50 pages each address as many periods of British and Irish history from 100 B.C. to 1975. Each chapter has sections on government and politics, warfare and international relations, economy, society, and culture, with special sections on Ireland, Scotland, and Wales and their relationships with England.

Lynch, James. *Multicultural Education in a Global Society.* New York: Falmer Pr., 1989. Via this theoretical work on multicultural education and curricula from a British perspective, Lynch posits that increased sensitivity to human rights issues is the goal of a multicultural educational program. Although he presents criteria for evaluating resources, he does not cite examples of multicultural children's literature published in England.

O'Malley, Padraig. *Biting at the Grave: The Irish Hunger Strikes and the Politics of Despair.* Boston: Beacon Pr., 1990. O'Malley examines the ongoing conflicts between Catholic and Protestant Irish and with the British through the prism of the dramatic hunger strikes that resulted in the deaths of Bobby Sands and nine other men in 1981.

Twentieth-Century Children's Writers. 3rd ed. Edited by Tracy Chevalier. Chicago: St. James, 1989. This massive reference work contains biographical entries for many of the significant twentieth-century English-language writers of children's books. Each entry gives biographical information, a list of the author's publications for children, a short note by the author on why he or she writes for children, and a brief essay on the author's themes and development of a career in children's literature. An appendix offers similar entries for some of the most famous nineteenth-century children's authors, such as Lewis Carroll. Virtually all of the nineteenth-century authors featured are British.

CHAPTER 9. WESTERN EUROPE

[Annette C. Blank]

Announcement of the Mildred L. Batchelder Award publicity release from the Public Information Office, American Library Association, Chicago, Illinois. Dated January of each year. The announcement of this award is made annually, at the American Library Association Midwinter Conference. This announcement gives information about the award, as well as the list of previous winners, with brief annotations. Over the years, most of the Batchelder winners have been translated books from Scandinavia and Western Europe.

Bradburn, Frances. "Middle Books." *Wilson Library Bulletin* (December 1989): 111–112. Fifteen series are reviewed for scope, special features, and uses, all in the area of social studies. These are suggested as replacements for outdated titles.

Kruse, Ginny Moore. "One Planet, Many Voices: Books in Translation." *Children's Book Bag* (Winter 1990). The annotations for this list are fuller than those on the longer list in *Booklist*. The Mildred L. Batchelder Award is highlighted. Books for all ages are on the list, but it is especially useful for books for junior and senior high school readers.

Kruse, Ginny Moore. "Translated Children's Books." *Booklist* (April 1, 1989). This list has short annotations of translated picture stories, fiction, nature books, history and people, and folklore, all of which are recommended for school and library purchase.

CHAPTER 10. SOUTHERN EUROPE
[Judy Fink]

Area Handbook Series. Washington, D.C.: U.S. Government Printing Office. These studies, researched by specialists, are extremely thorough. Their time lines, statistical appendixes, and bibliographies are very complete and useful. A list of the available studies is included in each volume.

Gillespie, John T., and Corinne J. Naden, eds. *Best Books for Children: Preschool through Grade 6.* 4th ed. New York: R. R. Bowker, 1990. Literature for this age group has been arranged by subject. Short, helpful annotations accompany each entry, which includes author, title, and subject/grade level indexes.

Schon, Isabel. *A Hispanic Heritage: A Guide to Juvenile Books about Hispanic People and Cultures.* Metuchen, N.J.: Scarecrow Pr., 1980. A more extensive, less date-restrictive bibliography covering Hispanic literature in English from Spain and other Spanish-speaking areas.

CHAPTER 11. EASTERN EUROPE AND THE SOVIET UNION
[Christine Behrmann]

In addition to standard sources, such as *The Children's Catalog* (19th edition and supplements, available from Wilson), the latest edition of *Best Books for Children* (now in its fourth edition, edited by John T. Gillespie and Corinne J. Naden, available from Bowker), lists in the American Library Association periodical *Booklist*, back issues of *Phaedrus* (the international annual covering the history of children's literature but now no longer being published), and the New York Public Library's subject indexes, the following were found to be helpful in preparing this bibliography.

Gilbert, Martin. *Macmillan Atlas of the Holocaust.* New York: Da Capo, 1984. A valuable basic resource, giving accurate data as well as a clear geographic overview of the persecutions of Jewish individuals during World War II. Since so much of Eastern European literature concentrates generally on World War II, and specifically on Jewish experiences, this gives useful background.

Povsic, Frances. *Eastern Europe in Children's Literature: An Annotated Bibliography of English-Language Books.* New York: Greenwood Pr., 1986. The basic reference source for English-language books in the field, this covers children's material originally written in English or translated into English about Albania, Bulgaria, Czechoslovakia, Hungary, Poland, Romania, and Yugoslavia through the early 1980s. A volume on the Soviet Union is in preparation. The annotations are lengthy and critical; grade levels are included. Povsic covers traditional literature (folklore) as well as fiction and nonfiction. Unique and extremely useful.

Stejskal, Vaclav. *Czech and Slovak Books for Children.* Prague: Circle of Children's Book Lovers, 1975. This bibliography is currently the only English-language source from one of the countries in this section. While little of the material listed is available here, it is interesting for background in the field.

[Elsa Marston]

Two lists proved helpful in compiling this bibliography.

Corsaro, Julie. "Arab Culture: Books for Children and Young Adults." *Booklist* (September 1, 1989). A useful selection that covers a wide range of nonfiction and fiction, including some forms not dealt with here, such as folktales, recent "Arabian Nights" stories, a few filmstrips, books about Arab Americans, and a Lebanese cookbook; with brief annotations.

Maehr, Jane. "The Middle East: An Annotated Bibliography of Literature for Children." ERIC Clearinghouse on Early Childhood Education, 1977. This gives an idea of what was available in the 1950s to mid-1970s in fiction and nonfiction. Unfortunately, most can no longer be found easily, but some are well worth the effort.

For background reading on the Middle East in general and the Arab-Israeli problem in particular, there is a great wealth of material. The following are just a selection, well recommended.

Adams, Michael, ed. *The Middle East.* Handbooks to the Modern World, Facts on File Publications, 1988. This large volume provides all the information anyone could possibly want. Each country of North Africa and in the Middle East is covered thoroughly for basic facts, then discussed at greater length by individual writers. Eminent authorities have contributed articles on a host of topics covering general background in addition to political, economic, and social questions.

Antonius, George. *The Arab Awakening: The Story of the Arab Nationalist Movement* (first published 1938; still in print, from International Book Centre, P.O. Box 295, Troy, MI 48099). For anyone unfamiliar with nineteenth- and early twentieth-century Middle Eastern history, this is the great "awakener"—a classic, and very interesting.

Chapman, Colin. *Whose Promised Land?* Batavia, Ill.: Lion, 1985. Chapman examines many ideas about the creation and history of the state of Israel, with particular focus on biblical prophecy.

Ellis, Harry B. *Israel: One Land, Two Peoples.* New York: Thomas Y. Crowell, 1972. In this book, suitable for young readers as well as adults, Ellis has made a scrupulous effort to be objective and balanced.

Flapan, Simha. *The Birth of Israel: Myths and Realities.* New York: Pantheon Books, 1987. An Israeli writer and scholar scrutinizes several commonly believed assertions about the way Israel came into being and the dispersal of the Arab population.

Khouri, Fred. J. *The Arab Israeli Dilemma.* 3rd ed. Syracuse, N.Y.: Syracuse Univ. Pr., 1985. Widely respected for its objectivity and throroughness, this is a fundamental history of the question.

McDowall, David. *Palestine and Israel: The Uprising and Beyond.* Berkley: Univ. of California Pr., 1989. By a noted British writer, another of the most highly regarded of all histories and analyses of the Arab-Israeli conflict.

Nolte, Richard, ed. *The Modern Middle East.* Englewood Cliffs, N.J.: Prentice Hall, 1963. Articles by noted authorities on several historical and social topics, for readers seeking deeper background.

Pearson, Robert P., ed. *Through Middle Eastern Eyes.* Rev. ed. New York: Praeger, 1975, rev. ed. 1985. From many sources, these selections give an idea of how Middle Easterners feel about their life and the world. Readable.

Said, Edward W. *The Question of Palestine*. New York: Times Books, 1979. A personal, impassioned discussion of the whole question, by an eminent professor of literature at Columbia University.

Good sources for the purchase of books about the Middle East, at significantly discounted prices, are:

American Educational Trust, P.O. Box 53062, Washington, DC 20009. Americans for Middle East Understanding, Room 241, 475 Riverside Drive, New York, NY 10015.

CHAPTER 13. SUB-SAHARAN AFRICA

[Michael Afolayan, Patricia Kuntz, and Brenda Naze]

Books

Gunner, Elizabeth. *A Handbook for Teaching African Literature*. Portsmouth, N.H.: Heinemann Educational Books, 1984. This is an excellent African literature study and teaching resource for texts, novels, plays, poetry, prose, and other materials written by Africans and others. Curriculum guides and teaching ideas on a number of novels are included, as is a section on common themes in African literature.

Hall, Susan J. 1978. "Tarzan Lives! A Study of the New Children's Books about Africa." *Interracial Books for Children Bulletin* (9/1):3–7.

_____. (1978). "What Do Textbooks Teach Our Children about Africa?" *Interracial Books for Children Bulletin* (9/3):3–10.

Kuntz, Patricia S. 1980. *Books about the Middle East for Adolescents and Youth*. Madison, Wis.: Department of Public Instruction.

_____. (1978). *Books about Africa for Adolescents and Youth*. Madison, Wis.: Department of Public Instruction.

Rich, Evelyn Jones. 1976. "Mark My Word!" *Africa Report* (Nov./Dec.):52–56.

_____. (1974). "Mind Your Language." *Africa Report* (Sept./Oct.).

Schmidt, Nancy. 1990. *Africans as Primary Actors in Their Own Lives and Lands: Validating African Curriculum Materials*. Baltimore, Md.: African Studies Association paper.

_____. (1981). "Children's Fiction about Africa in English." *Conch*.

_____. (1979). *Supplement to Children's Books on Africa and Their Authors: An Annotated Bibliography*. New York: Africana.

_____. (1977). "Children's Literature and Audio-Visual Materials in Africa." *Conch*.

_____. (1975). *Children's Books on Africa and Their Authors: An Annotated Bibliography*. New York: Africana.

Seguin, Clare. 1991. "The Search for Multiculturalism in Children's Books: An Interview with Kathleen Horning of the Cooperative Children's Book Center." *Rethinking Schools* 5/4 (Jan./Feb.):16–18.

Van Ausdall, Barbara Wass. 1988. "Images of Africa for American Students." *English Journal* (Sept.):37–39.

Periodicals

Africa Report, African-American Institute, 833 United Nations Plaza, New York, NY 10017. Bimonthly.

Africa Today, Graduate School of International Studies, University of Denver, Denver, CO 80208. Quarterly.

African Arts, James S. Coleman African Studies Center, University of California, Los Angeles, CA 90024–1310. Quarterly.

African News, P.O. Box 3851, Durham, NC 27702. Biweekly.

West Africa, 43–45 Coldharbour Lane, Camberwell, London, SE5 9NR, England. Weekly.

African Studies Centers

Boston University, African Studies Center, 270 Bay State Rd., Boston, MA 02215. 617-353-7303.

Indiana University, African Studies Program, Woodburn Hall 221, Bloomington, IN 47405. 812-855-6825.

Michigan State University, African Studies Center, 100 International Center, East Lansing, MI 48824-1035. 517-353-1700.

Stanford University, Center for African Studies, Institute for International Studies, Littlefield Center, 300 Lausen St., Stanford, CA 94305-5013. 415-723-0295.

University of California, James S. Coleman African Studies Center, 10244 Bunche Hall, Los Angeles, CA 90024-1310. 213-825-3686.

University of Florida, Center for African Studies, 427 Grinter Hall, Gainesville, FL 32611. 904-392-2183.

University of Illinois, Center for African Studies, 1208 W. California, Room 101, Urbana, IL 61801. 217-333-6335.

University of Wisconsin, African Studies Program, 1454 Van Hise Hall, 1220 Linden Drive, Madison, WI 53706. 608-262-9689.

Yale University, Council on African Studies, 85 Trumbull St., Box 13A, New Haven, CT 06520. 203-432-3437 or 3438.

CHAPTER 14. SOUTH AFRICA

[Patricia Kuntz and Lyn Miller-Lachmann]

A number of excellent books have been published on the situation in South Africa, and new ones come out each year; thus any recommendations for contemporary analyses risk becoming dated rather quickly. However, one source of background information that explores the attitudes of white racists and obstacles to change is *Move Your Shadow: South Africa, Black and White* (New York: Times Books, 1985), written by *New York Times* reporter Joseph Lelyveld.

Little attention has been given in juvenile series books to South Africa's relations with neighboring African countries. Joseph Hanlon's study, *Apartheid's Second Front: South Africa's War Against Its Neighbors* (New York: Penguin, 1987), documents South Africa's economic, political, and military interventions in Angola, Mozambique, Zimbabwe, and other countries.

Current information about South Africa may be found in a number of periodical sources. The *New York Times* contains regular coverage. Also useful are many of the sources cited in the reference section for Sub-Saharan Africa, such as *Africa News*, *Africa Report*, and *Africa Today*. In the area of children's and young adult publishing, *Booklist* features regular bibliographies compiled by Hazel Rochman, whose edited short story collection, *Somehow Tenderness Survives*, has been recommended in the chapter. Rochman also writes occasional essays evaluating individual titles.

CHAPTER 15. SOUTHERN AND CENTRAL ASIA

[Melinda Greenblatt]

Among the books published for adults that can be used by teachers, librarians, and high school researchers are the following.

The Area Handbook Series, published by the U.S. Department of the Army and sold through the U.S. Government Printing Office. This is a good source for background information. Because of its official uses, this series always covers the armed forces and national security issues in the country under discussion, but geography and social issues receive some coverage as well. Countries covered in the series include Afghanistan, Bangladesh, India, Pakistan, and Sri Lanka.

Robinson, Francis, ed. *Cambridge Encyclopedia of India, Pakistan, Bangladesh, Sri Lanka, Nepal, Bhutan, and the Maldives*. New York: Cambridge University Press, 1989. An excellent reference tool covering most of the countries of Southern and Central Asia, with the exception of Afghanistan (included in a companion volume on the Middle East). A variety of historical and cultural topics are covered in signed articles that focus on the region as a whole, with many references to specific countries.

Among the many sources treating exclusively India are the following.

Gandhi, Mohandas K. *An Autobiography*. Boston: Beacon, 1957. The classic primary source for Gandhi's life and philosophy. Selections may be used with classes in junior and senior high school.

Wolpert, Stanley. *A New History of India*. 3rd ed. New York: Oxford University Press, 1989. A detailed and sophisticated presentation of India's history and recent politics, though, like all books of its kind, it needs supplementation with newspaper and periodical sources.

Although the works of several authors for adults have been included in the section for grades 10–12, two additional authors—Salman Rushdie and V. S. Naipaul—deserve mention. Rushdie's first published novel, *Midnight's Children*, is a "magical mystery tour" through the first 31 years of India's life after independence. For lovers of language and those who want to see history from an original viewpoint, this novel can be a door into an India seldom glimpsed elsewhere. Naipaul's trilogy of books set in India provide a critical perspective on life and politics there.

CHAPTER 16. EAST ASIA
CHAPTER 17. SOUTHEAST ASIA

[Ginny Lee, Suzanne Lo, and Susan Ma]

Many of the works annotated for grades 1–12 in the chapters on East Asia and Southeast Asia are excellent reference sources for teachers and librarians as well. They provide background geographical, historical, and cultural information that can be supplemented by newspaper and periodical articles on current events.

Several other annotated bibliographies are also available that cover the countries of East Asia and Southeast Asia, as well as the Asian-American experience. Most notable among them is *Literature for Children About Asians and Asian Americans: Analysis and Annotated Bibliography, with Additional Readings for Adults*, by Esther C. Jenkins and Mary Austin (Greenwood Press, 1987). This bibliography appears to be quite comprehensive, but the annotations are simply descriptive and are not critical enough of some of the problems of misrepresentation in otherwise attractive books.

Japan Through Children's Literature, by Yasuko Makino (Greenwood Press, 1985), does a nice job of explaining why a book is recommended or not recommended. *Recommended Readings in Literature, Kindergarten Through Grade Eight* (prepared by the California State Department of Education, 1988) provides a checklist of basic multicultural reading materials in a number of genres.

Two books—Patricia Beilke's and Elaine Sciara's *Selecting Materials For and About Hispanic and East Asian Children and Young People* (Library Professional Publications, 1986) and *Marjorie H. and Peter Li's Understanding Asian Americans: A Curriculum Resource Guide* (Neal-Schuman, 1990)—explore the backgrounds of various Asian-American immigrant groups and suggest curriculum activities, teaching methods, and means of evaluating a multicultural program. The volume by the Lis has an especially useful list of resources for adults.

CHAPTER 18. AUSTRALIA, NEW ZEALAND, AND THE PACIFIC

[Melinda Greenblatt]

Jameyson, Karen. "News from Down Under." *Horn Book* Mar./Apr., 1991:237–40. Jameyson's column on children's literature on Australia is a regular feature in *Horn Book*. This article focuses on several 1990 picture books and gives background on the development of picture books in Australia.

Larson, Jeanette. "An Australian Celebration." *School Library Journal* Sept., 1987:131–33. An excellent bibliography highlighting Australian authors. Almost 30 titles are listed, including some books published in Australian editions only. The listing of U.S. distributors of Australian books is useful.

Wrightson, Patricia. "Deeper Than You Think." *Horn Book* Mar./Apr., 1991:162–70. An article adapted from a speech delivered at the University of British Columbia on May 18, 1990, at Serendipity '90 conference. A reading of this article on the long roots of Aboriginal Australian life and folklore will lead to a fuller understanding of Wrightson's work.

Appendix 2

SERIES TITLES

The series titles are listed under the following areas: Geography; Biography; Ethnic Groups and Immigration; Current Events; and Fiction. All member titles of each geography series will be listed, with books receiving annotations indicated with an asterisk (*) preceding the individual title. In the case of Biography series and series focusing on ethnic groups and immigration, only those titles within the series that are multicultural and within the scope of this bibliography (such as biographies of African Americans or books on Native Americans or Asian and Hispanic immigrants) will be listed, with those receiving annotations indicated with an asterisk (*). Since most members of Current Events and Fiction series will not fall within the scope of a multicultural bibliography, only those titles that are annotated will be listed here. Again, an asterisk (*) will precede the title.

The *principal* grade level of each series (P–3, 4–6, 7–9, or 10–12) will be indicated as well, following the name of the publisher of the series. If a series covers two grade levels equally, both will be indicated.

The purpose of the full listing is to indicate the relevant multicultural series and titles within series that do exist. For reasons of space, not all can be annotated in the bibliography. In many cases, contributors have mentioned, and perhaps have provided brief evaluations of, additional series titles within the annotation of one title. Typically, annotations of geography or ethnic and immigration series have mentioned other titles within the same series. Annotations of biographies frequently mention other series that present the same person. A book that is only mentioned, without a full entry, does not receive an asterisk in the listing below, nor does it appear in the indexes.

Children of the World (Gareth Stevens/grades 4-6)
*Australia; Bhutan; Bolivia; Brazil; *Burma; *China; Costa Rica; Cuba; Czechoslovakia; El Salvador; England; Finland; France; *Greece; *Guatemala; Hong Kong; *India; Indonesia; Italy; Japan; Jordan; Malaysia; Mexico; Nepal; New Zealand; Nicaragua; Philippines; Singapore; South Africa; South Korea; Spain; Sweden; *Tanzania; Thailand; Turkey; USSR; West Germany; Yugoslavia.

City Life (Silver Burdett/grades 7-9)
*Living in Venice

Count Your Way Books (Lerner/grades P-3)
*Count Your Way through Africa; Count Your Way through the Arab World; Count Your Way through Canada; Count Your Way through China; *Count Your Way through Germany; *Count Your Way through India; Count Your Way through Israel; *Count Your Way through Italy; *Count Your Way through Japan; Count Your Way through Korea; *Count Your Way through Mexico; *Count Your Way through Russia.

Countries (Silver Burdett/grades 7-9)
Australia; Belgium and Luxembourg; Brazil; The Caribbean; China; Eastern Europe; France; *Great Britain; Greece; Italy; *Japan; Mexico; The Middle East; The Netherlands; Nigeria; Southern Africa; The Soviet Union; Spain; The United States of America; *West Germany.

Countries of the World (Franklin Watts/grades 4-6)
Australia; Canada; *The Caribbean; China; *France; Great Britain; *Greece; *India; Italy; Japan; The Netherlands; *New Zealand; Pakistan; Spain; The United States; West Germany.

Discovering Our Heritage (Dillon/grades 7-9)
Argentina; *Australia; *Bangladesh; *Brazil; Canada; Chile; El Salvador; France; Germany; Greece; Indonesia; *Ireland; *Israel; *Korea; New Zealand; Nicaragua; Pakistan; Saudi Arabia; Soviet Union; *Spain; *Switzerland; Thailand; *Vietnam; *Zimbabwe.

Enchantment of the World (Childrens Press/grades 7-9)
*Algeria; Angola; Argentina; *Australia; Austria; *Belgium; *Bhutan; Bolivia; Brazil; Burma; Canada; *Chile; China: A History to 1949; Colombia; *Cuba; Ecuador; Egypt; El Salvador; *England; Ethiopia; Finland; France; Gabon; Ghana; *Greece; Greenland; Hong Kong; *Hungary; Iceland; India; Iran; Iraq; Israel; Italy; Japan; Kenya; Korea; Laos; *Libya; Luxembourg; Malawi; Malaysia; *Mexico; Morocco; The Netherlands; New Zealand; Norway; People's Republic of China; The Philippines; Poland; *Portugal; The Republic of Ireland; Romania; Russia: A History to 1917; Scotland; Singapore; South Africa; Spain; Sweden; Switzerland; *Syria; Thailand; *Tunisia; The Union of Soviet Socialist Republics; *Venezuela; *Vietnam; Wales; West Germany; Yugoslavia; Zambia; *Zimbabwe.

Families Around the World (Franklin Watts/grades 4-6)
*A Family in Australia; *A Family in Iceland; *A Family in India.

Families the World Over (Lerner/grades 4-6)
*An Aboriginal Family; An Arab Family; *A Family in Australia; A Family in Bolivia; *A Family in Brazil; A Family in Chile; A Family in China; *A Family in Egypt; A Family in England; An Eskimo Family; A Family in France; A Family in Hong Kong; A Family in Hungary; A Family in India; *A Family in Ireland; A Kibbutz in Israel; *A Family in Italy; *A Family in Jamaica; *A Family in Japan; A Family in Kenya; A Family in Liberia; *A Family in Mexico; *A Family in Morocco; A Family in Nigeria; *A Family in Norway; *A Family in Pakistan; A Family in Peru; *A Family in Singapore; A Family in South Korea; *A Family in Sri Lanka; *A Family in Sudan; A Family in Taiwan; A Family in Thailand; A Family in West Germany; *A Zulu Family.

Inside (Frankin Watts/grades 4–6)
*Australia; *China; France; Great Britain; *India; Israel; Italy; Japan; Mexico; *The Netherlands; Soviet Union; Spain; United States; West Germany.

Let's Visit Places and Peoples of the World (Chelsea House/grades 7–9)
Afghanistan; *Albania; Algeria; Andorra; Angola; Antarctica; Argentina; Armenia; Australia; Austria; Bahamas; *Bahrain; Bangladesh; Barbados; Belgium; Bermuda; Bhutan; Bolivia; Botswana; *Brazil; Brunei; Bulgaria; Burkina Faso; Burma; Burundi; *Cambodia; Cameroon; Canada; Chile; China—People's Republic; *Colombia; Comores; Congo; Cuba; Cyprus; Czechoslovakia; Danish Dependencies; Denmark; Dominican Republic; East Germany; Ecuador; Egypt; *El Salvador; England; Ethiopia; *Fiji; Finland; France; French Overseas Departments and Territories; Gabon; Gambia; Ghana; Gibraltar; Greece; Grenada; Guam; Guyana; Haiti; Hong Kong; Hungary; Iceland; India; Indonesia; Iran; *Iraq; *Ireland; Israel; Italy; Ivory Coast; Jamaica; Japan; Jordan; Kenya; Kuwait; Laos; Lebanon; Lesotho; Liberia; Libya; Liechtenstein; Luxembourg; Macao; Madagascar; Malawi; Malaysia; *Maldive Islands; Mali; Malta; Mauritius; Mexico; Monaco; *Mongolia; Morocco; *Mozambique; Namibia; Nepal; *The Netherlands; Netherlands Antilles; New Guinea; New Zealand; Niger; Nigeria; North Korea; North Yemen; Northern Ireland; Norway; *Oman; Pacific Islands; Pakistan; Paraguay; Peru; Philippines; Poland; Portugal; Puerto Rico; Qatar; Romania; Russia; Rwanda; St. Lucia; San Marino; Saudi Arabia; Scotland; Senegal; Seychelles; *Sierra Leone; Singapore; Somalia; South Africa; South Korea; Soviet Georgia; *Spain; Sri Lanka; Sudan; Suriname; Swaziland; Sweden; Switzerland; Syria; Taiwan; Tanzania; Thailand; Togo; Trinidad and Tobago; Tunisia; Turkey; Uganda; Ukraine; Union of Soviet Socialist Republics; *United Arab Emirates; United Kingdom Dependencies; Uruguay; Uzbekistan; Vatican; Venda; Venezuela; Vietnam; Wales; *West Bank/Gaza Strip; West Germany; *West Indies; Yugoslavia; Zaire; Zambia; Zimbabwe.

Library of Nations (Time-Life/grades 10–12)
*Australia; *India.

Living Here (Franklin Watts/grades 7–9)
*We Live in Belgium and Luxembourg; *We Live in Chile; *We Live in China; We Live in East Germany; *We Live in Egypt; We Live in Indonesia; *We Live in Mexico; *We Live in New Zealand; *We Live in Pakistan; *We Live in Portugal; *We Live in Saudi Arabia; *We Live in South Africa; We Live in Switzerland; *We Live in the Caribbean; We Live in the Netherlands; We Live in the Philippines.

New True Books (Childrens Press/grades 4–6)
Africa; Argentina; *Asia; *Australia; Brazil; Chile; China; Cuba; Egypt; Europe; Greece; Japan; Kenya; Korea; Laos; Mexico; South Africa; South America; The Soviet Union; Thailand; *Zimbabwe.

Passport to. . . (Franklin Watts/grades 4–6)
*Passport to Australia; Passport to China; Passport to France; Passport to Great Britian; *Passport to Israel; Passport to Italy; Passport to Japan; Passport to Mexico; Passport to Soviet Union; Passport to Spain; Passport to West Germany.

People and Places (Silver Burdett/grades 4–6)
*Argentina; Australia; Brazil; Canada; The Caribbean; Central America; China; France; Germany; Greece; India; Ireland; Israel; Italy; Japan; Mexico; Middle East; Pakistan and Bangladesh; *Southern Africa; Southeast Asia; *Spain; U.S.S.R.; United Kingdom; U.S.A.

Portraits of the Nations (HarperCollins/grades 10–12)
*The Land and People of Afghanistan; *The Land and People of Argentina; *The Land and People of Bolivia; *The Land and People of Cambodia; The Land and People of Canada; The Land and People of China; *The Land and People of Finland; *The Land and People of France; The Land and People of Kenya; The Land and People of Korea;

The Land and People of Malaysia and Brunei; *The Land and People of Mongolia; The Land and People of the Netherlands; *The Land and People of Scotland; *The Land and People of South Africa; The Land and People of the Soviet Union; *The Land and People of Turkey; The Land and People of Venezuela; *The Land and People of Zimbabwe.

Rivers of the World (Silver Burdett/grades 4-6)
*The Mekong.

Step Into (Julian Messner/grades 4-6)
*Step into China.

Take a Trip (Franklin Watts/grades P-3)
*Take a Trip to Argentina; *Take a Trip to Austria; *Take a Trip to China; Take a Trip to Cuba; Take a Trip to East Germany; *Take a Trip to England; Take a Trip to Finland; Take a Trip to Haiti; Take a Trip to Hungary; *Take a Trip to Indonesia; *Take a Trip to Iran; Take a Trip to Iraq; *Take a Trip to Jamaica; Take a Trip to Lebanon; Take a Trip to Libya; *Take a Trip to Mexico; Take a Trip to Morocco; *Take a Trip to Nepal; *Take a Trip to New Zealand; Take a Trip to Nicaragua; *Take a Trip to Panama; Take a Trip to Peru; *Take a Trip to Portugal; *Take a Trip to Puerto Rico; Take a Trip to Romania; Take a Trip to Sri Lanka; Take a Trip to Syria; Take a Trip to Thailand; Take a Trip to Turkey; Take a Trip to Venezuela; Take a Trip to Wales; Take a Trip to Yugoslavia; Take a Trip to Zimbabwe.

Visitor's Guides (Hunter/grades 10-12)
*The Visitor's Guide to Iceland.

Visual Geography Series (Lerner/grades 7-9)
*Afghanistan in Pictures; *Argentina in Pictures; *Australia in Pictures; *Bolivia in Pictures; Botswana in Pictures; Brazil in Pictures; *Cameroon in Pictures; Canada in Pictures; Central African Republic in Pictures; Chile in Pictures; China in Pictures; Colombia in Pictures; *Costa Rica in Pictures; Cote d'Ivoire in Pictures; Cuba in Pictures; Denmark in Pictures; Dominican Republic in Pictures; Ecuador in Pictures; Egypt in Pictures; El Salvador in Pictures; England in Pictures; Ethiopia in Pictures; Ghana in Pictures; Guatemala in Pictures; Guyana in Pictures; Haiti in Pictures; Honduras in Pictures; India in Pictures; Indonesia in Pictures; Iran in Pictures; Iraq in Pictures; Ireland in Pictures; Israel in Pictures; *Jamaica in Pictures; Japan in Pictures; Jordan in Pictures; *Kenya in Pictures; Kuwait in Pictures; *Lebanon in Pictures; Liberia in Pictures; Madagascar in Pictures; Malawi in Pictures; Malaysia in Pictures; Mali in Pictures; Mexico in Pictures; Morocco in Pictures; Nepal in Pictures; New Zealand in Pictures; Nicaragua in Pictures; *Nigeria in Pictures; Northern Ireland in Pictures; *Norway in Pictures; Pakistan in Pictures; Panama in Pictures; Paraguay in Pictures; Peru in Pictures; Philippines in Pictures; Puerto Rico in Pictures; Saudi Arabia in Pictures; Scotland in Pictures; *Senegal in Pictures; South Africa in Pictures; South Korea in Pictures; *Soviet Union in Pictures; Sri Lanka in Pictures; Sudan in Pictures; Sweden in Pictures; Syria in Pictures; Taiwan in Pictures; Tanzania in Pictures; *Thailand in Pictures; Tunisia in Pictures; Turkey in Pictures; Uruguay in Pictures; Venezuela in Pictures; Wales in Pictures; Zimbabwe in Pictures.

World in View (Steck-Vaughn/grades 4-6)
*Australia.

The World Today (Stryker-Post/grades 10-12)
*East Asia and the Western Pacific 1989; *The Middle East and South Asia 1989.

The World's Children (Carolrhoda/grades 4-6)
*The Children of China; The Children of Egypt; *The Children of Nepal; The Grandchildren of the Incas.

BIOGRAPHY

Alvin Josephy's History of the Native Americans (Silver Burdett/grades 4-6)
Geronimo; Hiawatha; King Philip; *Sequoia; *Sitting Bull; Tecumseh.

American Women in Science Biography (The Equity Institute/grades P-3)
Engineer from the Comanche Nation, Nancy Wallace; *Scientist from Puerto Rico, Maria Cordero Hardy; Scientist from the Santa Clara Pueblo, Agnes Naranjo Stroud-Lee; *Scientist with Determination, Elma Gonzalez.

Black Americans of Achievement (Chelsea House/grades 7-9)
Muhammad Ali; Richard Allen; Louis Armstrong; Arthur Ashe; Josephine Baker; James Baldwin; Benjamin Banneker; Amiri Baraka (Leroi Jones); Mary McLeod Bethune; George Washington Carver; Paul Cuffe; Frederick Douglass; Charles R. Drew; W.E.B. DuBois; Paul Laurence Dunbar; Duke Ellington; Ralph Ellison; Ella Fitzgerald; Marcus Garvey; Dizzy Gillespie; *Matthew Henson; Chester Himes; Billie Holiday; Lena Horne; *Langston Hughes; Zora Neale Hurston; Jesse Jackson; Jack Johnson; James Weldon Johnson; Scott Joplin; Martin Luther King, Jr.; Joe Louis; Malcolm X; Thurgood Marshall; Ronald McNair; Elijah Muhammad; Jesse Owens; Charlie Parker; Gordon Parks; Sidney Poitier; *Adam Clayton Powell, Jr.; A. Philip Randolph; Paul Robeson; Jackie Robinson; Bill Russell; John Russwurm; Sojourner Truth; Harriet Tubman; Nat Turner; Denmark Vesey; Madame C.J. Walker; Walter White; Richard Wright.

Cambridge Topic Books (Lerner/grades 7-9)
*St. Patrick and Irish Christianity.

Creative Minds Biographies (Lerner/grades 4-6)
*What Are You Figuring Now: A Story about Benjamin Banneker; Between Two Worlds: A Story about Pearl Buck; A Pocketful of Goobers: A Story about George Washington Carver; Raggin': A Story about Scott Joplin; Shoes for Everyone: A Story about Jan Matzeliger; Walking the Road to Freedom: A Story about Sojourner Truth; *Go Free or Die: A Story about Harriet Tubman.

First Biography (Holiday House/grades P-3)
*Jackie Robinson.

First Books (Franklin Watts/grades 4-6)
*George Washington Carver; *Martin Luther King, Jr.

Great Lives (Franklin Watts/grades 4-6)
World leaders from 19th and 20th centuries only: Winston Churchill; *Ghandi; Mother Teresa; Queen Victoria.

Hispanic Stories (Raintree/grades 4-6)
Luis Alvarez; Simon Bolivar; *Sor Juana Ines de la Cruz; Hernando de Soto; David Farragut; *Carlos Finlay; *Miguel Hidalgo y Costilla; Queen Isabella; Benito Juarez; Luis Munoz Marin; *Jose Marti; Vilma Martinez; *Pedro Menendez de Aviles; Diego Rivera; Junipero Serra.

The History of the Civil Rights Movement (Silver Burdett/grades 7-9)
Ella Baker; Stokeley Carmichael; Fannie Lou Hamer; Jesse Jackson; Martin Luther King, Jr.; Malcolm X; Thurgood Marshall; Rosa Parks; A. Philip Randolph.

Impact Biographies (Franklin Watts/grades 7-9)
Marian Anderson; *Benazir Bhutto; W.E.B. DuBois; *Nikita Khruschev; Martin Luther King, Jr.; Nelson and Winnie Mandela; *Golda Meir; *Satchel Paige; Joseph Stalin; Harriet Tubman; *Desmond Tutu.

Jewish Biography (Dutton/grades 7-9)
*Father of the Orphans.

Let's Celebrate (Silver Burdett/grades P-3)
*Harriet Tubman and Black History Month.

Lifetimes (Franklin Watts/grades 4-6)
*Mother Teresa.

Makers of America (Facts on File/grades 10-12)
*Martin Luther King, Jr. and the Freedom Movement.

On My Own Books (Lerner/grades P-3)
*Martin Luther King Day.

People in Focus (Dillon/grades 7-9)
From Prisoner to Prime Minister: A Biography of Benazir Bhutto; An Unbreakable Spirit: A Biography of Winston Churchill; *Senor Alcalde: A Biography of Henry Cisneros; Up with Hope: A Biography of Jesse Jackson; Madam Prime Minister: A Biography of Margaret Thatcher.

People of Distinction (Childrens Press/grades 4-6; 7-9)
Hans Christian Andersen: Teller of Tales; Joan Baez: Singer with a Cause; Mary McLeod Bethune: A Great American Educator; Simon Bolivar: South American Liberator; Pablo Casals: Cellist of Conscience; *Frederick Douglass: The Black Lion; Paul Laurence Dunbar: A Poet to Remember; *Mikhail Gorbachev: A Leader for Soviet Change; Martin Luther King, Jr.: A Man to Remember; Lenin: Founder of the Soviet Union; Nelson Mandela: South Africa's Silent Voice of Protest; *Diego Rivera: Mexican Muralist; Sacagawea: Indian Interpreter to Lewis and Clark; *Anwar el-Sadat: A Man of Peace; Margaret Thatcher: First Woman Prime Minister of Great Britain; Jim Thorpe: World's Greatest Athlete; Oprah Winfrey: TV Talk Show Host.

People Who Have Helped the World (Gareth Stevens/grades 7-9)
Oscar Arias; The Dalai Lama; *Mahatma Gandhi; Bob Geldof; Mikhail Gorbachev; Martin Luther King, Jr.; Mother Teresa; *Sojourner Truth; *Desmond Tutu; Lech Walesa; Raoul Wallenberg.

People Who Made a Difference (Gareth Stevens/grades 4-6)
Bob Geldof; Mahatma Gandhi; Martin Luther King, Jr.; Mother Teresa; Sojourner Truth; Desmond Tutu.

Picture Life (Franklin Watts/grades 4-6)
The Picture Life of Bill Cosby; The Picture Life of Charles and Diana; The Picture Life of Corazon Aquino; The Picture Life of Dwight Gooden; The Picture Life of Michael Jackson; *The Picture Life of Mikhail Gorbachev; The Picture Life of Whitney Houston.

Picture-Story Biographies (Childrens Press/grades 4-6)
Everett Alvarez, Jr.: A Hero for Our Times; *Corazon Aquino: President of the Philippines; *Cesar Chavez and La Causa; Evelyn Cisneros: Prima Ballerina; *Henry Cisneros: Mexican-American Mayor; Diana, Princess of Wales; *Indira Nehru Gandhi: Ruler of India; Carolina Herrera: International Fashion Designer; Ishi: The Last of His People; James Weldon Johnson: Lift Every Voice and Sing; Barbara Jordan: The Great Lady from Texas; Martin Luther King, Jr.; Leontyne Price: Opera Superstar; Mother Teresa: Friend of the Friendless; *Desmond Tutu: Bishop of Peace; Harold Washington: Mayor with a Vision; Andrew Young: Freedom Fighter.

Raintree Stories (Raintree/grades P-3)
Booker T. Washington; Hiawatha; *Matthew Henson; Pocahontas; Sacagawea; Sequoia.

Rookie Biographies (Childrens Press/grades P-3)
Hans Christian Andersen: Prince of Storytellers; Martin Luther King, Jr.: A Man Who Changed Things; Pocahontas: Daughter of a Chief; Jackie Robinson: Baseball's First Black Major Leaguer.

Taking Part (Dillon/grades 4-6)
Bill Cosby: Making America Laugh and Learn; Sarah Ferguson: The Royal Redhead; Samantha Smith: A Journey for Peace.

Trailblazers (Lerner/grades 4-6)
*Space Challenger: The Story of Guion Bluford; *Arctic Explorer: The Story of Matthew Henson; Native American Doctor: The Story of Susan LaFlesche Picotte.

What Was It Like? (Childrens Press/grades 4-6)
Jackie Robinson; *Harriet Tubman.

Women of Our Time (Viking/grades 4-6)
*Mary McLeod Bethune: Voice of Black Hope; Diana: Twentieth Century Princess; *Winnie Mandela: The Soul of South Africa.

World Leaders, Past and Present (Chelsea House/grades 7-9)
Contemporary leaders: Konrad Adenauer; Salvador Allende; Corazon Aquino; Yasir Arafat; Hafez al-Assad; Clement Attlee; Menachem Begin; David Ben-Gurion; Willy Brandt; Leonid Brezhnev; Fidel Castro; Winston Churchill; Moshe Dayan; Charles de Gaulle; Deng Xiaoping; *Alexander Dubcek; François and Jean-Claude Duvalier; Faisal; Francisco Franco; Indira Gandhi; Mohandas K. Gandhi; The Gemayels; Mikhail Gorbachev; *Ernesto "Che" Guevara; *Tenzin Gyatso—Dalai Lama; Hirohito; Adolf Hitler; *Ho Chi Minh; Hussein; Wojciech Jaruzelski; Jomo Kenyatta; Ayatollah Khomeini; Nikita Khruschev; Martin Luther King, Jr.; Nelson & Winnie Mandela; Mao Zedong; Ferdinand Marcos; Golda Meir; Hosni Mubarak; Robert Mugabe; Benito Mussolini; *Gamel Abdel Nasser; *Jawaharlal Nehru; Daniel Ortega; *Mohammad Reza Pahlavi; Peron; Pol Pot; *Muhammar el-Qaddafi; Anwar Sadat; *Haile Selassie; Prince Norodom Sihanouk; Joseph Stalin; Sukarno; Mother Teresa; Margaret Thatcher; Josip Broz Tito; Lech Walesa; Zhou Enlai. *Past leaders—19th and 20th centuries*: Kemal Ataturk; Bismarck; Leon Blum; Simon Bolivar; Chiang Kai-shek; Georges Clemenceau; Eamon De Valera; Benjamin Disraeli; Giuseppe Garibaldi; William Gladstone; Paul von Hindenburg; *Benito Juarez; Vladimir Lenin; David Lloyd George; Tomas Masaryk; Klemens von Metternich; Napoleon Bonaparte; Nicholas II; Nkrumah; Charles Stewart Parnell; Sun Yat-sen; Toussaint L'Ouverture; Leon Trotsky; Queen Victoria; Chaim Weizmann; Emiliano Zapata.

ETHNIC GROUPS AND IMMIGRATION

American Century series (Hill & Wang/grades 10-12)
*The New Chinatown.

America's Ethnic Heritage (Facts on File/grades 7-9)
*The Chinese-American Heritage.

Crafts (Franklin Watts/grades 4-6)
*African Crafts.

Easy Menu Ethnic Cookbooks (Lerner/grades 7-9)
*Cooking the African Way; *Cooking the Australian Way; Cooking the Austrian Way; Cooking the Caribbean Way; Cooking the Chinese Way; Cooking the English Way; Cooking the French Way; Cooking the German Way; Cooking the Greek Way; Cooking the Hungarian Way; *Cooking the Indian Way; Cooking the Israeli Way; Cooking the Italian Way; Cooking the Japanese Way; Cooking the Korean Way; Cooking the Lebanese Way; Cooking the Mexican Way; Cooking the Norwegian Way; Cooking the Polish Way; Cooking the Russian Way; Cooking the Spanish Way; Cooking the Thai Way; *Cooking the Vietnamese Way.

First Books (Franklin Watts/grades 4–6)
The Apaches and Navajos; *Australia Today; *Ethiopia; The Iroquois; The Seminoles; *The Shoshoni; *The Sioux; The Totem Pole Indians of the Northwest; The Tragedy of Little Bighorn.

Food and Drink (Franklin Watts/grades 4–6)
*African Food and Drink; Australian and New Zealand Food and Drink; British Food and Drink; Caribbean Food and Drink; *Chinese Food and Drink; Italian Food and Drink; Japanese Food and Drink; Jewish Food and Drink; Mexican Food and Drink; Middle Eastern Food and Drink; Southeast Asian Food and Drink; *West German Food and Drink.

Holidays and Festivals (Rourke/grades 4–6)
*Sikh Festivals.

In America (Lerner/grades 7–9)
The American Indians in America, Vol. I; The American Indians in America, Vol. II; The Blacks in America; The Chinese in America; The East Indians and Pakistanis in America; *The Filipinos in America; The Japanese in America; The Koreans in America; *The Mexicans in America; The Puerto Ricans in America; The Vietnamese in America.

Indians of North America (Chelsea House/grades 7–9)
The Abenaki; The Apache; The Arapaho; The Archaeology of North America; The Aztecs; The Cahuilla; The Catawbas; The Cherokee; The Cheyenne; The Chickasaw; The Chinook; The Chipewyan; The Choctaw; The Chumash; The Coast Salish Peoples; The Comanche; The Creeks; The Crow; Federal Indian Policy; The Hidatsa; The Huron; The Innu (Montagnais-Naskapi); The Inuit (Eskimo); The Iroquois; *The Kiowa; The Kwakiutl; The Lenapes; Literatures of the American Indian; The Lumbee; The Maya; The Menominee; The Modoc; The Nanticoke; The Narragansett; The Navajos; The Nez Perce; The Ojibwa; The Osage; The Paiute; The Pima-Maricopa; The Potawatomi; The Powhatan Tribes; The Pueblo; The Quapaws; The Seminole; The Tarahumara; The Tunica-Biloxi; Urban Indians; The Wampanoag; Women in American Indian Society; The Yakima; The Yankton Sioux; The Yuma.

My Best Friend (Julian Messner/grades 4–6)
*My Best Friend Duc Tran: Meeting a Vietnamese-American Family; My Best Friend Mee-Yung Kim: Meeting a Korean-American Family; *My Best Friend Martha Rodriguez: Meeting a Mexican-American Family.

New True Books (Childrens Press/grades 4–6)
The Apache; Aztec Indians; The Cherokee; The Cheyenne; The Chippewa; The Choctaw; The Crow; The Hopi; The Inca; Indians; The Mandans; *The Maya; The Mohawk; The Navajo; The Nez Perce; The Pawnee; The Seminole; The Seneca; The Shoshoni; The Sioux; The Tlingit.

Original People (Rourke/grades 4–6)
*Plains Indians of North America; *South Pacific Islanders.

The Peoples of North America (Chelsea House/grades 7–9)
*The Afro-Americans; The American Indians; The Arab Americans; *The Central Americans; The Chinese Americans; The Cuban Americans; *The Dominican Americans; *The Filipino Americans; The Iberian Americans; The Japanese Americans; The Korean Americans; The Mexican Americans; The Pacific Islanders; The Peoples of the Arctic; The Puerto Ricans; *The South Americans; The West Indian Americans.

Recent American Immigrants (Franklin Watts/grades 4–6)
Asian Indians; Chinese; *Filipinos; Mexicans.

Religions of the World (Trafalgar Square/grades 4–6)
*The Hindu World.

The Texians and the Texans (Univ. of Texas Institute of Texan Culture/grades 7-9)
*The Mexican Texans.

CURRENT EVENTS

Conflict in the 20th Century (Franklin Watts/grades 7-9)
*Africa from 1945; *The Middle East; *Rise of the Asian Superpowers.

Flashpoints (Rourke/grades 7-9)
*The Irish Question.

Hotspots (Franklin Watts/grades 7-9)
China: A New Revolution?; *Colombia: The Drug War; Eastern Europe: The Road to Democracy; *Europe, 1992: The United States of Europe?; Ireland: A Divided Country; Soviet Union: Will Perestroika Work?

Impact Books (Franklin Watts/grades 7-9)
Cuba and the United States: Troubled Neighbors; *East vs. West in the Middle East; El Salvador: Country in Crisis; The New Philippines.

Issues (Franklin Watts/grades 7-9)
*South Africa.

Opposing Viewpoints (Greenhaven Press/grades 10-12)
*The Middle East.

Places in the News (Crestwood House/grades 7-9)
*South Africa.

Weighing up the Evidence (Trafalgar Square/grades 7-9)
*South Africa.

Witness History (Franklin Watts/grades 7-9)
*The Arab-Israeli Conflict; *South Africa Since 1948.

FICTION

Adventure Diaries (Raintree/grades 4-6)
*Clues in the Desert.

Adventures in Canadian History (Lorimer/grades 7-9)
*The Curses of Third Uncle.

African Writers (Heinemann/grades 10-12)
*A Ride on the Whirlwind.

Discoveries (Latin American Literary Review Press/grades 4-6)
*The Enchanted Raisin.

Flying Fingers Club (Gaullaudet/grades 4-6)
*The Secret in the Dorm Attic.

I Can Read Books (HarperCollins/grades P-3)
*Chang's Paper Pony.

The Jafta Collection (Lerner/grades P-3)
*Jafta—The Journey.

Kipling Press Library of American Folktales (Kipling Press/grades P-3)
*John Henry.

Sweet Dreams (Bantam/grades 7-9)
*One Boy at a Time.

Sweet Valley High (Bantam/grades 7–9)
*Out of Reach.

Time of Our Lives (Lorimer/grades 4–6; 7–9)
*Camels Can Make You Homesick and Other Stories; *The Minerva Program; *My Name Is Paula Popowich; *Storm Child.

Walker's American History Series for Young People (Walker/grades 7–9)
*Out from This Place.

Wide World (A & C Black/grades P–3)
*The Very Special Sari.

Appendix 3

DIRECTORY OF PUBLISHERS

Africa World P.O. Box 1892, Trenton, NJ 08607

Aladdin 866 Third Ave., New York, NY 10022

Algonquin Books of Chapel Hill P.O. Box 2225, Chapel Hill, NC 27515

American Educational Trust P.O. Box 53062, Washington, DC 20009

Annick Press 15 Patricia Ave., Willowdale, ON M2M 1H9 Canada

Applause Theater Book Publishers 211 W. 71 St., New York, NY 10023

Arte Público Press University of Houston, Houston, TX 77204-2090

Atheneum Publishers 866 Third Ave., New York, NY 10022

Avon Books 105 Madison Ave., New York, NY 10016

Ballantine/Del Rey/Fawcett/Ivy Books 201 E. 50 St., New York, NY 10022

Bantam Doubleday Dell Publishing 666 Fifth Ave., New York, NY 10103

Basil Blackwell 3 Cambridge Ctr., Cambridge, MA 02142

Beacon 25 Beacon St., Boston, MA 02108

Bilingual Education Services 1607 Hope St., South Pasadena, CA 91030

Black Butterfly P.O. Box 461, Village Station, New York, NY 10014

John F. Blair 1406 Plaza Dr., Winston-Salem, NC 27103

Bradbury Press 866 Third Ave., New York, NY 10022

George Braziller 60 Madison Ave., Suite 1001, New York, NY 10010

Carolina Wren Press P.O. Box 277, Carrboro, NC 27519

Center for Migration Studies 209 Flagg Pl., Staten Island, NY 10304-1199

Chelsea House Publishers 95 Madison Ave., New York, NY 10016

Children's Book Press 1461 Ninth Ave., San Francisco, CA 94122

Childrens Press 5440 N. Cumberland Ave., Chicago, IL 60656

Chronicle Books 275 Fifth St., San Francisco, CA 94103

Clarion Books 215 Park Ave. S., New York, NY 10003

Coward, McCann 200 Madison Ave., New York, NY 10016

Creative Arts 833 Bancroft Way, Berkeley, CA 94710

Creative Education P.O. Box 227, 123 Broad St., Mankato, MN 56001

Crowne Publications P.O. Box 688, Southbridge, MA 01550

Delacorte   666 Fifth Ave., New York, NY 10103

Dell Publishing   666 Fifth Ave., New York, NY 10103

Dillon Press   242 Portland Ave. S., Minneapolis, MN 55415

Doubleday   666 Fifth Ave., New York, NY 10103

Douglas & McIntyre   1615 Venables St., Vancouver, BC V5L 2H1 Canada

Dryad Press   Trafalgar Square, David & Charles, P.O. Box 257, North Pomfret, VT 05053

Dutton   375 Hudson St., New York, NY 10014

Eagle Dancer/Raincoast Books   112 E. Third Ave., Vancouver, BC V5T 1C8 Canada

Eakin   P.O. Drawer 90159, Austin, TX 78709-0159

Editorial Justa   P.O. Box 9275, Berkeley, CA 94702

Eerdmans   255 Jefferson Ave. S.E., Grand Rapids, MI 49503

The Equity Institute   P.O. Box 30245, Bethesda, MD 20814

Facts on File   460 Park Ave. S., New York, NY 10016

Farrar, Straus & Giroux   19 Union Square W., New York, NY 10003

Fearon Teacher Aids   500 Harbor Blvd., Belmont, CA 94002

Feminist Press   311 E. 94 St., New York, NY 10128

Firefly   250 Sparks Ave., Willowdale, ON M2H 2S4 Canada

Four Winds Press   866 Third Ave., New York, NY 10022

Gage Jean Pac: Gage Educational Publishers   164 Commander Blvd., Agincourt, ON M1S 3C7 Canada

Gallaudet University Press   800 Florida Ave. N.E., Washington, DC 20002

David Godine   Horticultural Hall, 300 Massachusetts Ave., Boston, MA 02115

Greenhaven Press   P.O. Box 289009, San Diego, CA 92128-9009

Greenwillow Books   105 Madison Ave., New York, NY 10016

Douglas & McIntyre Groundwood Books   26 Lennox St., 3rd Floor, Toronto, ON M6G 1J4 Canada

Harbinger House   2802 N. Alvernon Way, Tucson, AZ 85716

Harcourt Brace Jovanovich   6277 Sea Harbor Dr., Orlando, FL 32887

HarperCollins   300 Reisterstown Rd., Baltimore, MD 21208

Hastings House   141 Halstead Ave., Mamaroneck, NY 10543

Heinemann   361 Hanover St., Portsmouth, NH 03801

Henry Holt & Co   115 W. 18 St., New York, NY 10011

Herald Press   616 Walnut Ave., Scottdale, PA 15683

Hill & Wang   19 Union Square W., New York, NY 10003

Lawrence Hill   520 Riverside Ave., Westport, CT 06880

Holiday House   40 E. 49 St., New York, NY 10017

Holt, Rinehart, & Winston   City Center Tower II, Suite 3700, Fort Worth, TX 76102

Houghton Mifflin   One Beacon St., Boston, MA 02108

Hunter Publishing   300 Raritan Centre Parkway, Edison, NJ 08818

Irvington Publishers   522 E. 82 St., Suite 1, New York, NY 10028

Jewish Publication Society   1930 Chestnut St., Philadelphia, PA 19103-4599

Just Us Books   301 Main St., Suite 22-24, Orange, NJ 07050

Kane/Miller Book Publishers   P.O. Box 529, Brooklyn, NY 11231-0005

Kar-Ben Copies   6800 Tildenwood Lane, Rockville, MD 20852

Kids Can Press   585$\frac{1}{2}$ Bloor St. W., Toronto, ON M6G 1K5 Canada

Kipling Press   496 LaGuardia Place, New York, NY 10012

Alfred A. Knopf Inc   201 E. 50 St., New York, NY 10022

Latin American Literary Review Press
2300 Palmer St., Pittsburgh, PA 15218

Left Bank Books   4142 Brooklyn Ave.
N.E., Seattle, WA 98105

Lerner Publications Co.   241 First Ave. N.,
Minneapolis, MN 55401

Lester & Orpen Dennys   78 Sullivan St.,
Toronto, ON M5T 1C1 Canada

Little, Brown   34 Beacon St., Boston, MA
02108

Lollipop Power Books   P.O. Box 277,
Carrboro, NC 27510

Lorimer   35 Britain St., Toronto, ON
M5A 1R7 Canada

Lothrop, Lee & Shepard   105 Madison
Ave., New York, NY 10016

Louisiana State Univ. Press   Baton Rouge,
LA 70893

Macmillan   866 Third Ave., New York,
NY 10022

McClelland & Stewart   481 University
Ave., Suite 900, Toronto, ON M5G 2E9
Canada

Julian Messner   190 Sylvan Ave., Englewood Cliffs, NJ 07632

Middle East Gateway Series   A&M Book
Sales, 15 Prospect St., Rockport, MA
09166

Momiji: Momiji Health Care Society   683
Mount Pleasant, Toronto, ON M4S 2N2
Canada

William Morrow   1350 Ave. of the Americas, New York, NY 10019

Thomas Nelson   Nelson Pl. at Elm Hill
Pike, Nashville, TN 37214

New Mexico Magazine   1100 Saint Francis Dr., Santa Fe, NM 87503

New Readers Press   P.O. Box 131, Syracuse, NY 13210

New Seed Press   P.O. Box 9488, Berkeley, CA 94709

Northland Press   P.O. Box N, Flagstaff,
AZ 86002

Open Hand   600 East Pine, Suite 565,
Seattle, WA 98122

Orchard Books   387 Park Ave. S., New
York, NY 10016

Overlea House   20 Torbay Rd., Mark-
ham, ON L3R 1G6 Canada

Oxford University Press   200 Madison
Ave., New York, NY 10016

Oyate   2702 Matthews St., Berkeley, CA
94702

Pantheon Books   201 E. 50 St., New
York, NY 10022

Paulist Press   997 Macarthur Blvd., Mah-
wah, NJ 07430

Pelican   1101 Monroe St., Gretna, LA
70053

Pemmican Publications   412 McGreggor
St., Winnipeg, MB R2W 4X5 Canada

Penguin Books   375 Hudson St., New
York, NY 10014

Penumbra Press   P.O. Box 248, Kapuskas-
ing, ON P5N 2Y4 Canada

Prentice Hall Press   15 Columbus Circle,
New York, NY 10023

Putnam Berkley Group   200 Madison
Ave., New York, NY 10016

Raintree Publishers   310 Wisconsin Ave.,
Milwaukee, WI 53203

Reader's International   P.O. Box 959, Columbia, LA 71418-0959

Redbird Press   3838 Poplar Ave., P.O.
Box 11441, Memphis, TN 38111

Reidmore Books   012, The Lemarchand
Mansion, 11523-100 Ave., Edmonton,
AB T5K 0J8 Canada

Rizzoli International Publications   300
Park Ave., New York, NY 10010

Scholastic   730 Broadway, New York, NY
10003

Scribner   866 Third Ave., New York, NY
10022

Shapolsky Publishers   136 W. 22 St., New
York, NY 10011

Silver Burdett Press   190 Sylvan Ave., Englewood Cliffs, NJ 07632

Simon & Schuster   1230 Ave. of the
Americas, New York, NY 10020

Smithsonian Institution Press   470
L'Enfant Plaza, Suite 7100, Washington,
DC 20560

Square One Publishers   P.O. Box 4385,
Madison, WI 53711

Steck-Vaughn   P.O. Box 26015, Austin, TX 78755

Gareth Stevens   River Center Bldg., Suite 201, 155 N. River Center Dr., Milwaukee, WI 53212

Stewart, Tabori, and Chang   575 Broadway, New York, NY 10012

Strawberry Hill Press   2594 Fifteenth Ave., San Francisco, CA 94127

Tessera Publishing   9561 Woodridge Circle, Eden Prairie, MN 55347

TexArt   P.O. Box 15440, San Antonio, TX 78212

Texas Christian University Press   P.O. Box 30783, Fort Worth, TX 76129

Thames and Hudson   500 Fifth Ave., New York, NY 10110

Three Continents Press   1901 Pennsylvania Ave., Suite 407, Washington, DC 20006

Three Trees Press   85 King St. East, Toronto, ON M5C 1G3 Canada

Time-Life Books   777 Duke St., Alexandria, VA 22314

Tonatiuh-Quino Sol   P.O. Box 9275, Berkeley, CA 94702

TQS Publications   P.O. Box 9275, Berkeley, CA 94709

Tundra   1434 Ste. Catherine St. West, #303, Montreal, PQ H3G 1R4 Canada

Unicorn Press   P.O. Box 3307, Greensboro, NC 270402

Union of American Hebrew Congregations   838 Fifth Ave., New York, NY 10021

University of Alabama Press   P.O. Box 870380, Tuscaloosa, AL 35487-0380

University of Texas Institute of Texan Cultures at San Antonio   P.O. Box 1226, San Antonio, TX 78294

University of Toronto Press   5201 Dufferin St., Downsview, ON M3H 5T8 Canada

University of Washington Press   P.O. Box 50096, Seattle, WA 98145

USA Today Books   P.O. Box 450, Washington, DC 20044

Walker   720 5th Ave., New York, NY 10019

Ann Walko   287 Hogan Rd., Hamden, CT 06518

Warner-Mattox Production   3817 San Pablo Dam Rd., #336, El Sobrante, CA 94803

Franklin Watts   387 Park Ave. S., New York, NY 10016

Wellington Publishing Company   P.O. Box 14877, Chicago, IL 60614-0877

Western Producer Prairie Books   2310 Millar Ave., P.O. Box 2500, Saskatoon, SK S7K 2C4 Canada

Albert Whitman   5747 W. Howard St., Niles, IL 60648

Women's Press   229 College St., Toronto, ON M5C 1G3 Canada

AUTHOR INDEX

Authors are arranged alphabetically by last name. Authors' and joint authors' names are followed by book titles—also arranged alphabetically—and the text entry number.

TITLE/SERIES INDEX

All titles that are annotated within the text are listed here in italic type. Series titles are also listed and are shown in small capital letters. All numbers refer to entry numbers, not page numbers.

SUBJECT INDEX

Subject headings are to nonfiction works unless designated with the word "Fiction." To make this index easier to use, "Fiction" cross-references can refer to both fiction and nonfiction headings. When a cross-reference does not have the label "Fiction," that cross-reference applies solely to nonfiction works. *Note:* Numerals refer to entry numbers, not page numbers.

Ellis, Sarah. *Next-Door Neighbors*, 337

Fujiwara, Alan. *Baachan! Geechan! Arigato*, 338

Garrigue, Sheila. *The Eternal Spring of Mr. Ito*, 339

Heneghan, Jim. *Promises to Come*, 372

Hewitt, Marsha, and Claire Mackay. *One Proud Summer*, 359

Horne, Constance. *Nykola and Granny*, 341

Houston, James. *The Falcon Bow*, 342

Hudson, Jan. *Sweetgrass*, 373

Hughes, Monica. *My Name Is Paula Popowich*, 360

James, Janet Craig. *My Name Is Louis*, 361

Kaplan, Bess. *The Empty Chair*, 343

Kasper, Vancy. *Street of Three Directions*, 344

Mackay, Claire. *The Minerva Program*, 347

Major, Kevin. *Blood Red Ochre*, 375

Murdock, Patricia. *Deep Thinker and the Stars*, 329

Pearson, Kit. *The Sky Is Falling*, 349

Philip, Marlene Nourbese. *Harriet's Daughter*, 363

Roe, Eliane Corbeil. *Circle of Light*, 364

Sadiq, Nazneen. *Camels Can Make You Homesick and Other Stories*, 350
Heartbreak High, 376

Smucker, Barbara. *Amish Adventure*, 365
Days of Terror, 366
Underground to Canada, 367

Wallace, Ian, and Angela Wood. *The Sandwich*, 332

Weber-Pillwax, Cora. *Billy's World*, 333

Wheeler, Bernelda. *Where Did You Get Your Moccasins?*, 334

Yee, Paul. *The Curses of Third Uncle*, 369
Tales from Gold Mountain, 377

CANADA—Historical fiction

Bellingham, Brenda. *Storm Child*, 353

Greenwood, Barbara. *Spy in the Shadows*, 358

Sutherland, Robert. *Son of the Hounds*, 368

CANADA—Holidays

Parry, Caroline. *Let's Celebrate!*, 348

CANADA—Immigrants

Kurelek, William, and Margaret S. Engelhart. *They Sought a New World*, 362

CANADA—Legends

Cleaver, Elizabeth. *The Enchanted Caribou*, 324

CANADA—Poetry

Downie, Mary Alice, and Barabara Robertson, comps. *The New Wind Has Wings*, 356

CANADA—Travel and description

Harrison, Ted. *Children of the Yukon*, 340

CANADA—War evacuees—Fiction

Pearson, Kit. *The Sky Is Falling*, 349

CANADIANS

SEE African Canadians; Chinese Canadians; French Canadians; Irish Canadians; Italian Canadians; Japanese Canadians; Jewish Canadians; Scots Canadians; South Asian Canadians; Ukrainian Canadians; Vietnamese Canadians

CARIBBEAN AREA

SEE ALSO Cuba; Jamaica

Anthony, Suzanne. *West Indies*, 414

Griffiths, John. *The Caribbean*, 419

CARIBBEAN AREA—Alphabet books

Agard, John. *The Calypso Alphabet*, 379

CARIBBEAN AREA—Art

Lessac, Frane. *Caribbean Canvas*, 407

CARIBBEAN AREA—Biography

White, Timothy. *Catch a Fire*, 438

CARIBBEAN AREA—Fiction

Adoff, Arnold. *Flamboyán*, 378

Berry, James. *A Thief in the Village and Other Stories*, 434

Buffett, Jimmy, and Savannah Jane Buffett. *The Jolly Mon*, 381

Cooper, Susan. *Jethro and the Jumbie*, 383

Hamilton, Virginia. *Junius Over Far*, 421

Kincaid, Jamaica. *Annie John*, 436
At the Bottom of the River, 437

Lessac, Frane. *My Little Island*, 391

Lloyd, Errol. *Nini at Carnival*, 393

Taylor, Theodore. *The Cay*, 430

Moeri, Louise. *The Forty-Third War*, 474

CENTRAL AMERICA—Folklore

Rohmer, Harriet. *Uncle Nacho's Hat*, 446
Rohmer, Harriet, Octavio Chow, and Morris Viduare. *The Invisible Hunters*, 447

CENTRAL AMERICA—Politics and government

Cheney, Glenn Alan. *El Salvador*, 463
Gelman, Rita Golden. *Inside Nicaragua*, 466
Jenkins, Tony. *Nicaragua and the United States*, 471
Randall, Margaret. *Sandino's Daughters*, 487
Sanders, Renfield. *El Salvador*, 479

CENTRAL AMERICANS

Bachelis, Faren. *The Central Americans*, 230

CHATWIN, BRUCE

Chatwin, Bruce. *The Songlines*, 1034

CHÁVEZ, CESAR

Roberts, Naurice. *Cesar Chávez and La Causa*, 222

CHEROKEE INDIANS—Biography

Beale, Alex W. *Only the Names Remain*, 267
Carter, Forrest. *The Education of Little Tree*, 292
Cwiklik, Robert. *Sequoia*, 271

CHEROKEE INDIANS—History

Beale, Alex W. *Only the Names Remain*, 267

CHEYENNE INDIANS—Government relations

Ashabranner, Brent. *Morning Star, Black Sun*, 287

CHEYENNE INDIANS—Legends

Goble, Paul. *The Great Race of the Birds and Animals*, 261
Her Seven Brothers, 262

CHICKASAW INDIANS—Legends

Ata, Te. *Baby Rattlesnake*, 258

CHILD ABUSE—Fiction

Morrison, Toni. *The Bluest Eye*, 119

CHILDREN—Africa—Fiction

Gray, Nigel. *A Country Far Away*, 741

CHILDREN—Australia

Yanagi, Akinobu. *Australia*, 1017

CHILDREN—Bangladesh

Laure, Jason, and Ettagale Laure. *Joi Bangla*, 861

CHILDREN—Biography

Koehn, Ilse. *Mischling, Second Degree*, 562

CHILDREN—Burma

Knowlton, MaryLee, and Mark Sachner, eds. *Burma*, 961

CHILDREN—Canada

Canadian Childhoods, 354

CHILDREN—China

Johnson, Neil. *Step into China*, 905
Pitkanen, Matti A., and Reijo Harkonen. *The Children of China*, 909
Sadler, Catherine Edwards. *Two Chinese Families*, 910
Talan, Sally, and Rhoda Sherwood. *China*, 914

CHILDREN—Fiction

Heide, Florence Parry, and Judith Heide Gilliland. *The Day of Ahmed's Secret*, 672
Say, Allen. *The Feast of Lanterns*, 911
Tran Khan-Thuyet. *The Little Weaver of Thai-yen Village*, 956

CHILDREN—Holocaust survivors

Strom, Yale. *A Tree Still Stands*, 658

CHILDREN—India

Knowlton, MaryLee, and David K. Wright, eds. *India*, 849

CHILDREN—Israel

Meir, Mira. *Alina*, 673

Friedman, Ina R. *How My Parents Learned to Eat*, 133
Wallace, Ian, and Angela Wood. *The Sandwich*, 332

FOOD HABITS—Fiction

Rohmer, Harriet, and Cruz Gómez, adapts. *Mr. Sugar Came to Town*, 205

FOSTER CARE—Fiction

Childress, Alice. *Rainbow Jordan*, 60
Collura, Mary-Ellen Lang. *Winners*, 355
Culleton, Beatrice. *April Raintree*, 371

FRANCE—Fiction

Björk, Christina. *Linnea in Monet's Garden*, 547
Roth-Hano, Renée. *Touch Wood*, 569

FRANCE—History

Harris, Jonathan. *The Land and People of France*, 576

FRANCE—Picture books—Fiction

Bour, Daniele. *The House from Morning to Night*, 539

FRANCE—Social life and customs

Blackwood, Alan, and Brigitte Chosson. *France*, 548
Harris, Jonathan. *The Land and People of France*, 576

FRANCE—Social life and customs—Fiction

Bour, Daniele. *The House from Morning to Night*, 539

FRANCE—Travel and description

Blackwood, Alan, and Brigitte Chosson. *France*, 548
Sullam, Joanna. *Villages of France*, 582

FRANK, ANNE

Gies, Miep, and Alison Leslie Gold. *Anne Frank Remembered*, 575

FREEDOM OF SPEECH—Fiction

Jenkins, Lyll Becerra de. *The Honorable Prison*, 470

FRENCH CANADIANS—Fiction

Hewitt, Marsha, and Claire Mackay. *One Proud Summer*, 359
Roe, Eliane Corbeil. *Circle of Light*, 364

FRENCH LANGUAGE—Bilingual materials

Poulin, Stéphane. *Ah! Belle Cité/A Beautiful City ABC*, 330

FRIENDSHIP—Fiction

Bernatova, Eva. *The Wonder Shoes*, 538
Brooks, Bruce. *The Moves Make the Man*, 56
Ellis, Sarah. *Next-Door Neighbors*, 337
Els, Betty Vander. *Leaving Point*, 921
Forman, James. *My Enemy, My Brother*, 730
Goldreich, Gloria. *Lori*, 706
Gordon, Sheila. *Waiting for the Rain*, 797
Guy, Rosa. *The Friends*, 66
Hamilton, Virginia. *A White Romance*, 110
Hansen, Joyce. *The Gift Giver*, 33
  Yellow Bird and Me, 34
Härtling, Peter. *Crutches*, 550
Horejs, Vit. *Pig and Bear*, 623
Klein, Robin. *Hating Alison Ashley*, 1007
Kline, Suzy. *Horrible Harry's Secret*, 135
Kogawa, Joy. *Naomi's Road*, 345
Lessac, Frane. *My Little Island*, 391
Lloyd, Errol. *Nini at Carnival*, 393
Lowry, Lois. *Number the Stars*, 554
MacMillan, Dianne, and Dorothy Freeman. *My Best Friend Duc Tran*, 152
  My Best Friend, Martha Rodríguez, 216
Miles, Betty. *Sink or Swim*, 40
Moore, Emily. *Whose Side Are You On?*, 41
Myers, Walter Dean. *Scorpions*, 43
Nunes, Lygia Bojunga. *My Friend the Painter*, 455
Ofek, Uriel. *Smoke over Golan*, 688
Phipson, Joan. *A Tide Flowing*, 1011
Rardin, Susan Lowry. *Captives in a Foreign Land*, 720
Sevela, Ephraim. *Why There Is No Heaven on Earth*, 654
Taylor, Theodore. *The Cay*, 430
Trevino, Elizabeth Borton de. *El Guero*, 412
Tsutsui, Yoriko. *Anna's Secret Friend*, 897
Vagin, Vladimir, and Frank Asch. *Here Comes the Cat!*, 628
Woodson, Jacqueline. *The Dear One*, 100

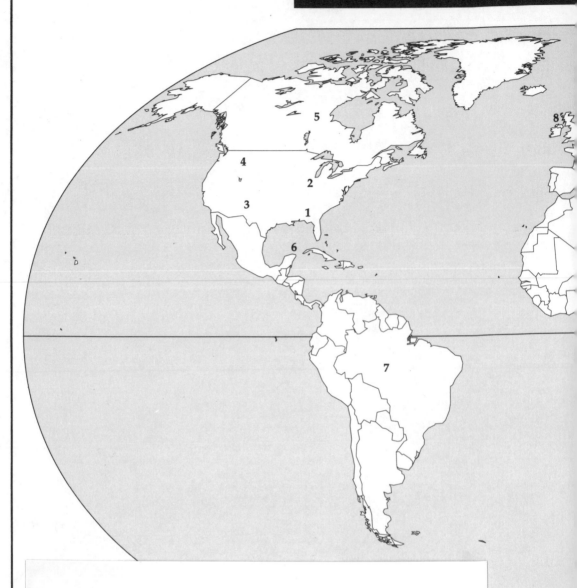

nd South America

itain and Ireland

Europe